AUDIOVISUAL MATERIALS

AUDIOVISUAL

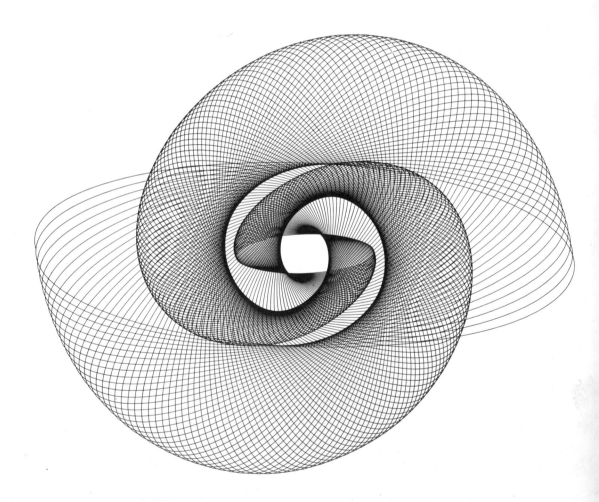

EXPLORATION SERIES IN EDUCATION

UNDER THE ADVISORY EDITORSHIP OF JOHN GUY FOWLKES

MATERIALS

THEIR NATURE AND USE

Fourth Edition

WALTER ARNO WITTICH

Chairman, Department of Educational Communications, University of Hawaii

CHARLES FRANCIS SCHULLER

Director, Instructional Media Center, Michigan State University

HARPER & ROW, PUBLISHER

NEW YORK · EVANSTON · LONDON

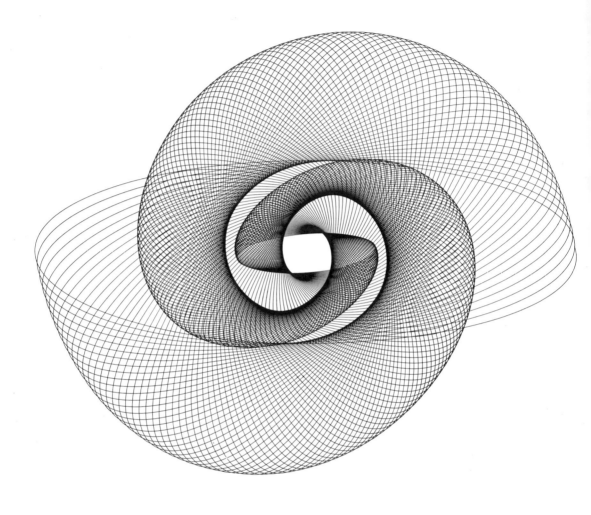

CONTENTS

COLOR PLATES

PLATE 12 / Examine these six study displays carefully; to what extent do they observe good principles of layout, content selection, color use?

PLATE 13 / This display demonstration of the water-cycle and the more complex transpiration-respiration concept illustrates the value of the felt board—when color symbols must be rearranged quickly during classroom discussion. A hook-and-loop board was used to display the heavier components of the hydrogen-helium display.

PLATES 14–20   FACING PAGE **256**

PLATE 14 / A section from a primarily political map for beginners, with few place names and only major relief indicated.

PLATE 15 / This section, also from an elementary map, shows altitude tints for land and water areas.

PLATE 16 / The same region is shown here on a physical-political map, which includes a greater number of place names and other details as compared to the two previous elementary maps.

PLATE 17 / This relief map is shaded in detail to create a three-dimensional effect.

PLATE 18 / Pictures add significant meaning to maps and map symbols. Here, actual photographs of lakes and islands are compared to the map symbols which represent them.

PLATE 19 / Map symbols for cities and roads are particularly abstract, and concrete visual experience in the form of color photographs should accompany early learning of such symbols.

PLATE 20 / Even relief maps cannot show all of the details that are on an accompanying color photograph. Maps, on the other hand, are helpful in showing the broader scope of the physical environment as well as in placing any specific region in its geographical context.

PLATES 21–24   FACING PAGE **432**

PLATE 21 / Change-speed photography can speed up natural processes which are too slow for the naked eye to see—as in the growth of plants and blossoms; or it can slow down processes which are too fast for human perception—as in animal movements. To what other uses might change-speed, motion-picture photography be put?

PLATE 22 / Color motion-picture films are generally available at a considerably higher cost. Examine each of these stills carefully in their black-and-white form. What information is available in the color version that is not contained in the black and white? Which stills contain relationships which depend solely on color for meaning? Are there any other values to the color version of these films? Do your answers justify the additional cost of color films?

PLATE 23 / The extraordinary amount of minute detail involved in Michelangelo's Sistine Chapel becomes lost in black-and-white film presentation; the color version greatly clarifies these details. What additional value does the color version have?

PLATE 24 / The map may be used to provide initial orientation in understanding our fiftieth state. To understand the many meanings of the symbol locating Honolulu (see arrow), the cross-media use of films, filmstrips such as those shown above, pictures, models, etc., is almost mandatory.

EDITOR'S INTRODUCTION

In a real sense, the determining factor in the relative effectiveness of a teacher is the degree and diversity of skill he has in communicating with learners. For long years, this communication was channeled almost entirely through classroom lectures, supplemented by reading assignments in pertinent literature. The child's role in his own learning process was merely to listen attentively to these lectures and to execute diligently all of his assignments.

While chalkboards, chalk, and erasers have long been integral items of equipment in this process, it was not until recent years that teacher-preparation courses offered anything approaching instruction in the use of other teaching materials. The relevance of photographs, films, slides, recordings and other audiovisual (and essentially nonverbal) communication media to classroom teaching was left largely implicit by teacher-training institutions. Yet, since the function—and therefore the focus—of teaching is learning, it is clear that a variety of educational materials must be at the fingertips of teachers who are well equipped, not only to use them effectively in their own teaching efforts, but also to initiate proper pupil utilization of these materials.

In 1953, to provide those who were preparing to become teachers—and those already engaged in teaching—with this needed familiarity with classroom teaching materials, a book entitled *Audio-Visual Materials: Their Nature and Use* was published by Harper & Brothers. The present book represents the fourth edition of this significant work by Wittich and Schuller since that date. The need that this work has filled has been amply demonstrated in its widespread use, not only throughout the United States, but also in nations abroad.

This fourth edition again presents, with unusual expertise, the ways and means of helping people to learn by using creatively a wide range of materials and equipment that involve looking and listening. The rationale, philosophy, and function of the matter at hand are presented in a refreshingly different, broad, and perceptive fashion. Accompanying this foundational treatment of the subject matter is both a wider and more versatile presentation of a vast array of materials and equipment as well as a stimulating discussion of their proper selection and utilization. The book will enable those who teach to stimulate and to help those who learn in a fashion which otherwise would be impossible. It is my belief that the present edition will be even more effective in aiding teachers and learners than were the previous three.

JOHN GUY FOWLKES

December, 1966

PREFACE

As the present authors have prepared this fourth edition of *Audiovisual Materials: Their Nature and Use*, they have tried to reflect five more years of experience in seeking to be of assistance to preservice and in-service teachers who inquire about the classroom use of new media, instructional materials, and methods. As a result of these past five years, we are more committed than ever to several key ideas which support the use of new media in the improvement of instruction:

1. Effective learning begins with *firsthand*, or *concrete*, experiences and proceeds toward more abstract experiences. Thus, pupils who have the advantage of reacting to well-selected and wisely used audiovisual media learn more effectively than do those who are provided with mostly verbal material.
2. The learner profits from instruction when he becomes involved through his *own interest* and *desire*. Well-chosen educational media present concepts in such manner as to create interest and motivation.
3. Pupils who are knowledgeable and whose interest is whetted are better able to *perform* as *creative, inventive* human beings.

While the circumstances for creativity are enhanced by the use of new educational media, it is the teacher, through his example and skill, who encourages pupils toward creative demonstration and use of his new-found information. In this revision are examples of many useful new media and materials, as well as suggestions concerning their effective use.

It will be found that the best and most useful material of previous editions has been retained. However, the last five years have witnessed several refinements in our understanding of various media. For example, educational television at its best is proving more and more to be the result of teamwork in planning, producing, and using ETV in the classroom. There is increasing evidence that effective ETV begins with the classroom teacher as a member of the planning group, and ends with sound classroom-utilization procedures which are teacher inspired. Further, while enthusiasm continues for language-laboratory facilities, recent developments show that the audio-playback advantages used initially for audiolingual instruction apply equally well to instruction in most subjects. On the other hand, additional years of experience with programed instruction has lessened the feeling that this method can improve learning for everyone. Rather, it is now recognized that the tasks one assumes while learning through programed instruction are accomplished better by accelerated learners than by slow learners.

The current book attempts again to anticipate the teacher's desire to improve his instruction, but through accessible, feasible means. The organization of the chapters stresses a beginning review of the role of the teacher as one who guides communication in the classroom. Succeeding chapters describe how it is possible for the interested teacher to begin audiovisual instruction with materials immediately at hand—the chalkboard, pictures, graphics, three-dimensional materials, and learning displays—all of which cost little or no money, but which emphasize creative planning and ways to involve the active participation of pupils. In later chapters, more sophisticated areas are described: films, slides, filmstrips, audiolearning materials, community study, maps, and programed instruction. Here, too, the utilization process begins with the effective communication of information, but learning is not complete until the pupil becomes involved in *using* his knowledge in creative and inventive ways which are the measure of his own potential.

Pertinent research is cited throughout the book in appropriate chapters. Educational media research has contributed much to ushering in the "decade of the Congressional Educational Acts." These include the Magnuson Act of 1962, which has made possible the cooperation of federal and local financing of educational-television facilities; the 1964 revision of the National Defense Education Act which has continued and expanded educational media research and demonstration, and which has funded hundreds of creatively organized and directed educational media institutes for teachers and specialists; the Elementary-Secondary Education Act which has brought about the creation of hundreds of regional and local educational media service centers; and The Higher Education Act of 1965 which has made it possible to carry on workshops for college professors interested in improving their utilization of new media, to remodel and to create new media facilities, and to offer graduate professional fellowships in education to thousands of experienced teachers.

An event which emphasizes the importance of audiovisual or educational media in classroom instruction occurred recently when the National Education Association Research Division conducted an inquiry among a sampling of America's 1,500,000 teachers. In reply to the question: "Do you feel that the various areas of your professional education experiences have been adequate in preparing you to meet the tasks of classroom instruction?" teachers reported that— while, in general, they had—they expressed their great need for *more professional training in how to evaluate and use new educational media in the classroom.*

In this day, when the child who enters the first grade has already become very sophisticated in his reactions to entertainment television, radio, and films, the challenge is very real to teachers who accept such communication-oriented children into their classrooms.

Within this climate of change and challenge, the authors present this fourth edition. The various examples, ideas, and graphics included in the chapters herein have been organized, refined, and tested over a period of the 34 years of the authors' actual classroom teaching experience. Once again, as in the three previous editions, materials which have been gathered and organized in this book reflect the help and suggestions of friends, professional colleagues, and numbers of students of education. To them we express our thanks. Sincere appreciation is also extended to our many colleagues for their helpful reactions, advice, and criticism.

Particular thanks are extended to Dr. John Guy Fowlkes for his friendship and counsel, and to James Prange, Rae Hanson, Virginia MacKay, Marlinda Acuirre, Carol Kingsley, Susan Blake, and Ruth Murphy for their help with source materials and with typing and proofreading manuscript.

Further, since a book about audiovisual materials must rely heavily on pictures, charts, and other visuals, we also express thanks in an acknowledgment section to the various individuals and companies who supplied many of the illustrations. The quoted passages used to amplify our ideas are acknowledged in footnotes.

WALTER A. WITTICH
CHARLES F. SCHULLER

January, 1967

TO THE INSTRUCTOR

We recognize that every professor has his own plans for organizing instruction; nevertheless, some comments on the organization of chapters in this book—and how it may conveniently be altered to fit the specialized needs of individual instructors—are warranted.

As both experienced and novice teachers prepare for a new term, they are usually filled with enthusiasm and ambitious hopes for making their instruction creative and interesting to their pupils. Often, however, there are fewer and less variety of materials available to work with than they would wish. In anticipation of this situation, the present authors have arranged this book's chapters so that, while teachers are waiting for promised learning materials—or perhaps awaiting their turn at scarce media equipment—they may utilize standard and more readily available media and materials effectively. Every room has a chalkboard, for example, and properly used, this familiar medium can provide opportunities for improved and creative teaching. With a little effort on the part of the teacher, flat pictures, graphics, and three-dimensional materials can be obtained or made easily and inexpensively, and these materials can be selected and organized into attractive and informative learning displays which will both motivate and teach pupils. Community-study opportunities are also readily available to the imaginative and resourceful teacher. Maps and globes, too, are generally at hand, and the teacher who uses these wisely and creatively in conjunction with the other media just mentioned should have little difficulty in keeping his pupils actively involved in classwork. Thus, the application of the ideas presented in Chapters III–IX, along the lines of the philosophical approach discussed in Chapters I and II, can pave the way for creative pupil participation and literally fill the classroom with evidence of the pupils' accomplishments.

The more sophisticated and expensive media and materials—the kind that often require special requisitions or administrative action to acquire at all—are therefore discussed in later chapters. However, schools vary widely in the resources they make available to teachers, and thus the instructor may wish to rearrange the material contained in this book to fit local conditions.

He may, for example, be able to secure a good selection of preview films early in the semester. This would justify covering Chapter XIII early in the sequence. Some instructors may wish to follow Chapter II with Chapter XI, "Multimedia Use," both as an interest-arouser and a pace-setter. For those instructors whose needs center around programed learning, Chapter XVI may be covered early in the semester, as well as Chapter X which includes a section on language-laboratory use. In other words, the instructor should find the present organization of chapters flexible and easily adaptable to a wide assortment of needs.

The authors wish to point out that the suggested activities at the end of each chapter are just that—suggestions. The instructor should use those which are, in his opinion, appropriate; modify those which refer to materials not available or irrelevant to his individual needs; and discard altogether those which do not apply, creating his own in terms of his knowledge of the needs of the group with whom he works.

One final remark: Should the instructor have any suggestions, questions, or rebuttals concerning the contents presented herein, he should by all means write to us, and we will be most pleased to reply.

WALTER A. WITTICH
CHARLES F. SCHULLER

ACKNOWLEDGMENTS

The authors wish to express their appreciation to the following companies, individuals, and institutions for their valuable assistance in supplying the fine prints and other visual materials on which the present book so heavily depends.

Academy Films: Fig. 15.10.

Aero Service Corp.: Figs. 9.15 (right) ; 9.20.

Alameda County, California: Figs. 8.5; 11.12.

Abby Aldrich Rockefeller Folk Collection, The, Williamsburg, Virginia: Fig. 4.12 (center).

American International Association: Figs. 4.2; 4.3.

American Iron and Steel Institute: Figs. 4.7 (right) ; 4.8; 5.16.

American Optical Company: Figs. 12.2; 12.22 (top left and right) ; 12.24 (top left).

American Petroleum Institute: Figs. 5.3; 5.4.

American Telephone and Telegraph Company: Fig. 8.9 (right).

Ampex Corp.: Fig. 14.11 (right).

Atkeson, Ray: Fig. 4.18.

Audio Master Corp.: Fig. 10.9 (top left).

Bailey Films, Inc.: Fig. 13.11 (top).

Bausch & Lomb: Fig. 12.11 (left).

Bell & Howell Company: Figs. 11.3; 11.4; 12.19 (right) ; 13.6; 13.32 (left) ; 13.33 (left and second from left).

Bell Telephone and Pacific Telephone: Fig. 13.3 (center).

Bernstein, Lawrence and Hughes, G. W.: Plate 6 (top).

Beseler, Charles, and Company: Figs. 4.13; 12.3 (center and bottom) ; 12.12; 12.22 (bottom) ; 12.24 (bottom left).

Bland, Leslie W.: Fig. 11.7.

Boeing Airplane Company: Fig. 9.1.

Bradley University, Peoria, Ill.: Fig. 14.7.

British Information Services: Fig. 8.18.

Burbank, California Unified School District: Photograph facing page 171.

Chicago Board of Education: Figs. 7.13 (top left) ; 10.14; 10.22; 14.17 (top) ; photograph facing page 331.

Children's Bureau, U.S. Department of Health, Education and Welfare: Fig. 8.1 (bottom).

Consulate General of Japan: Figs. 13.1; 14.10.

Consolidated Vultee Aircraft: Fig. 9.4.

Continental Airlines: Fig. 4.1 (top right).

Coronet Instructional Films: Figs. 13.23; 16.6 (bottom right) ; Plates 22 (bottom right) and 23 (left, second from top).

Creative Educational Society, Inc.: Fig. 4.14.

Crosby, Harold D.: Photograph facing page 195.

Dage Television, Division of Dage-Bell Corp.: Figs. 10.4; 10.18.

Davis Press: Fig. 5.18 (all except far left poster).

Defense Supply Agency: Fig. 1.12.

Denoyer-Geppert Company: Figs. 6.2; 6.9; 9.2; 9.3; 9.9; 9.10 (first three, left and right) ; 9.22 (bottom) ; Plates 14; 15; 16; 17.

Disney, Walt, Productions: Fig. 13.11 (center).

Eastman Kodak Company: Figs. 12.1; 12.5; 12.20 (right) ; 13.28; 13.32 (right) ; 15.2 (right) ; photograph facing page 353.

Educational Developmental Laboratories, Inc., Huntington, New York: Figs. 1.11; 12.21.

Educational Electronics Division, Dage-Dell Corp.: Fig. 10.5.

Edve Equipment and Materials: Figs. 7.15 (bottom) ; 10.8; 10.15 (right) ; photograph facing page 295.

Encyclopaedia Britannica: The following figures are from Encyclopaedia Britannica Films:

The Bill of Rights of The United States: Fig. 13.5. *Classroom Art for Middle Grades Filmstrip Series:* Fig. 12.8 (second row center, right-hand page).

Congress: Fig. 12.8 (second row left, right-hand page).

Eli Whitney: Fig. 2.16.

I'm No Fool With a Bicycle: Fig. 12.8 (second row center, left-hand page).

Inca Lands in Peru: Fig. 12.8 (top row right, left-hand page).

Making Films That Teach: Fig. 13.22 (top and bottom).

Miscroscopic Life: The World of the Invisible: Fig. 13.14 (center and bottom).

The Northeastern States Filmstrip Series: Fig. 12.8 (second row right, right-hand page).

Our Police Department: Fig. 12.8 (top row center, right-hand page).

Peru: People of the Andes (2nd Ed.) : Fig. 13.11 (bottom).

Space Probes: Exploring Our Solar System: Fig. 13.16 (top).

The Sun Filmstrip: Fig. 12.8 (third row right, right-hand page).

The Vanishing Prairie Filmstrip Series: Fig. 12.8 (top row right, right-hand page).

Encyclopaedia Britannica: Figs. 12.1; 13.14 (top); 13.17; 13.20; 13.22 (top and bottom); Plates 21; 22 (bottom, top row, right second from top, and bottom left).

Encyclopaedia Britannica Press: Fig. 16.6 (top right and bottom left).

Encyclopedia Britannica and Bert Ray Studio, Inc.: Fig. 16.2.

Fairchild: Figs. 13.4 (top and center); 13.33 (right and second from right).

Film Associates of California: Fig. 15.11 (right).

First National Bank of Boston: Fig. 4.11 (left).

Fox, Fontaine: Fig. 5.21.

General Dynamics: Fig. 12.17.

General Precision, Inc. (Link Group): Fig. 6.11.

Government of American Samoa: Fig. 14.9 (bottom) by Vernan Bronson.

Graflex, Inc.: Figs. 12.19 (center); 13.32 (second from left).

Grolier Inc.: Figs. 16.1 (right); 16.4, both by Hella Hammid.

Hall Syndicate, The, Inc.: Fig. 5.23.

Harrison, Richard E.: Fig. 9.12 (center).

Honolulu Board of Water Supply: Figs. 8.6; 8.15.

Hubbard, T. N., Scientific Company: Figs. 9.7; 9.11.

Hunter's: Fig. 8.2.

International Harvester Company: Figs. 4.9; 5.12; 6.5; Plate 7 (top left, bottom right).

Instructor, The: Fig. 5.20.

Jacobson, Bob: Fig. 7.3.

Jam Handy Organization, The: Fig. 3.14. *Asiatic Lands and People:* Fig. 12.8 (top row far left); *Introduction to Fractions Filmstrip Series:* Fig. 12.8 (top row second from far left).

Kalart/Victor: Figs. 10.17; 13.32 (third from left).

Keystone View Company: Fig. 12.13.

Lansing State Journal and The Hall Syndicate: Fig. 5.23.

Link Aviation Inc.: Fig. 6.12.

Lockheed Missiles and Space Company: Fig. 15.12 (bottom).

Long Beach Unified School District: Fig. 6.8 (top).

Los Angeles City Schools, Audio-Visual Section: Figs. 6.7; 6.10; 6.14; 6.16; 6.17 (top); 8.7; 8.10 (top); 8.12 (right); 8.17; 9.19; 12.9 (top); 12.11 (right); 15.1; photograph facing page 131.

Lystad, Olav: Fig. 4.17.

McGraw-Hill Text Films: Figs. 4.16 (a CBS News Production); 13.15 (right).

Madison, Wisconsin Capital Times: Fig. 8.3 (top).

Madison (Wisconsin) Public Schools: Figs. 2.4; 8.12 (left).

Manual Arts Press: Fig. 3.2 (right).

Merchant, Robert C.: Figs. 10.12; 10.13 (bottom); 10.16.

Merritt Associates: Fig. 16.6 (top left).

Michigan State University: Figs. 4.10; 5.1; 5.2; 5.10; 5.11; 5.13; 5.19; 6.4; 6.13; 6.17 (bottom);

9.5; 9.16; 9.18; 10.13 (top); 12.6; 12.14; 13.26 (bottom); photograph facing page 255.

Microcard Corp.: Fig. 12.10.

Midwest Program on Airborne Television Instruction: Fig. 14.12 (top and center).

Milwaukee Public Schools: Fig. 10.15 (left).

Minneapolis *Star* and *Tribune:* Fig. 5.24.

Molinare, Vincent: Fig. 7.6.

Monkmeyer Press Photo Service: Figs. 8.1 (top) photo by Hays; 8.3 (bottom) photo by Duryee.

Moody Institute of Science: Fig. 13.13; Plate 22 (second from bottom row).

Mount Wilson and Palomar Observatories: Fig. 4.5.

Museum of Modern Art: Fig. 5.17.

Museum of Science and Industry: Fig. 7.7; Plate 8.

Musgrave, Samuel A.: Fig. 3.2 (left).

National Aeronautics and Space Administration: Figs. 1.13; 4.1 (bottom right); 12.16; 14.2.

National Conference of Christians and Jews: Fig. 4.4.

National Education Association: Figs. 10.2; 10.19; 12.18 by Carl Purcell; 15.5.

National Education Association, Division of Research: Fig. 1.15.

National Educational Television, Atlanta, Ga.: Fig. 14.17 (bottom).

National Life Insurance Company, Montpelier, Vermont: Fig. 4.12 (left).

National Schools: Figs. 14.6; 14.8.

New York State Thruway Authority: Fig. 4.14 (bottom).

North American Aviation, Inc.: Fig. 1.14.

Nystrom, A. J., and Company: Figs. 5.15; 9.6; 9.10 (left first and second from bottom); 9.12 (top and bottom); 9.13; 9.14; 9.15 (left); 9.17; Plate 1; 18; 19; 20.

Oak Ridge (Tennessee) Public Schools: Fig. 2.3.

Orient and Pacific Lines: Fig. 8.16.

Pack Associates: Fig. 8.14 (two photos on right-hand page).

Page, James L.: Fig. 13.10.

Pan American World Airways: Plate 3 (right).

Panoramic Studios: Fig. 9.8.

Parade Magazine: Fig. 2.2.

Pemo Commercial Photography: Fig. 10.6.

Photo Hawaii: Fig. 8.16 (center).

Pickens, Alec L.: Fig. 7.4.

Pictograph Corp.: Figs. 5.5; 5.6; 5.8.

Pittsburgh Plate Glass: Fig. 1.10.

Projection Optics Company: Fig. 12.22 (center row left).

Polynesian Cultural Center, Oahu, Hawaii: Fig. 2.5.

Postlethwait, S. N.: Figs. 15.14; 15.15.

Purdue University: Figs. 15.14; 15.15.

Radio Corporation of America: Fig. 13.32 (second from right).

Realistic Visual Aids: Figs. 6.8 (bottom); 6.15; 13.29; photographs facing pages 39 and 353.

Reinhold Publishing Corporation: Plate 9, reproduced from *The Art of Color (Kunst der Farbe)* by Johannes Itten by permission of Reinhold Publishing Corporation, New York, and Otto Maier Verlag, Ravensburg, Germany. The seven colors used in the original printing have here been reduced to four colors only.

Revell Inc.: Fig. 6.1.

Rheem Califone Corporation: Fig. 10.9 (right); photograph facing page 511.

St. Louis (Missouri) Board of Education: Figs. 4.15; 9.22 (top); 10.21; photograph facing page 93.

San Diego City Schools: Fig. 8.8.

San Diego County, Department of Education: Fig. 12.7.

Santa Fe Railway: Figs. 4.1 (bottom left); 4.7 (left).

Sawyer's, Inc.: Figs. 12.4; 12.20 (left).

Scarsdale: Figs. 15.3; 15.4; 15.6; 15.7.

Scripts Institute of Oceanography: Fig. 15.12 (top and center left).

Shostal, The Agency for Color Photography: Plate 2 (Mr. F. Schneider from Shostal).

Skinner, B. F., from *Science*, Oct. 24, 1958: Fig. 16.3.

Society for Visual Education: Figs. 6.3; 12.15.

Sony: Fig. 14.11 (left).

Spindler and Sauppe Inc.: Fig. 12.20 (center).

Standard School Broadcast: Fig. 7.12.

Stevens College, Columbia, Missouri News Bureau: Fig. 8.9 (left).

Stone and Steccati: Photograph facing page 195.

Tandberg of America: Figs. 10.10 (left); 11.5 (top).

Teaching Film Custodians, Inc.: Figs. 13.12; 13.25.

Technicolor Corp.: Fig. 13.4 (bottom).

Teleprompter Corp.: Fig. 1.16.

3 M Company: Figs. 10.10 (right); 11.1; 11.5 (bottom); 11.10; 11.11; 12.3(top); photograph facing page 543.

TV Viewing: Fig. 14.1.

United Air Lines: Figs. 7.7; 13.3 (bottom).

United Feature Syndicate: Fig. 5.22.

United Nations: Fig. 4.6.

United States Department of Agriculture: Figs. 5.9; 13.2 (right).

United States Department of the Air Force: Plate 6 (bottom right).

United States Navy, Official Photographs: Figs. 4.1 (top left); 13.2 (top); 15.12 (center right).

United States Department of State: Fig. 5.14.

United States Industries, Inc.: Fig. 16.1 (left).

United States Plywood Corporation: Figs. 3.3; 3.5; photograph facing page 73.

United World Films, Inc.: Fig. 13.15 (left).

University of California, Berkeley: Fig. 13.26 (top).

University of Hawaii: Figs. 7.10; 7.11; 11.13; 14.13; photograph facing page 3.

University of Hawaii High School: Figs. 2.14; 2.15.

University of South California: Fig. 13.22 (center).

University of Wisconsin: Figs. 1.17; 4.19; 6.6 (right); 7.14; 11.8; 13.31.

University of Wisconsin at La Cross: Fig. 13.30.

University of Wisconsin and The Racine Journal Times: Fig. 10.20.

Veenendaal, Wilfred: Figs. 4.20; 4.21; 4.22.

Viewlex, Inc.: Figs. 12.9 (bottom); 12.19 (left).

Ward's Natural Science Establishment, Inc.: Fig. 1.9; Plate 6 (bottom left).

Wasten and Hurd, Inc.: Photograph facing page 195.

Wayne University: Fig. 7.15 (top).

Webcor Sales Company: Figs. 10.6; 11:5 (center).

Western Electric Company: Fig. 15.2 (top).

Williams, W. E.: Fig. 8.2.

Wittich, W. A., and Felton: Fig. 3.8.

Wittich and Fowlkes: Fig. 13.27.

Wisconsin Journal of Education: Fig. 9.21.

Young America Films: Fig. 12.15.

Youth Services Section, Los Angeles City Schools: Fig. 8.4; photograph facing page 225.

AUDIOVISUAL MATERIALS

I | THE TEACHER AND COMMUNICATIONS

THE
REVOLUTION

Those responsible for teacher education describe the general goals of the teacher as: (1) knowing the child as a learner and understanding both his nature and needs, (2) mastering subject content as such, and (3) organizing a learning environment which provides, with efficiency, the facilities for pupil experience and understanding. With regard to this last goal, an adequate learning environment has been viewed traditionally as one in which the teacher plays the active role, serving at once as information giver, interpreter, and counselor.

☐ CURRENT IMPEDIMENTS TO EFFECTIVE TEACHING

Today, however—in the midst of social and technological explosions in various fields of knowledge, as well as in the techniques by which this burgeoning knowledge is communicated—the teacher can no longer attempt to be the sole information-giving instrument in the classroom. Indeed, the teacher himself can no longer keep pace with the expanding world of information. Further, the growing school population and its concomitantly larger and more diverse variety of classes make it increasingly more difficult for a single teacher to reach individual pupils with traditional classroom information-giving methods. These methods, what is more, fail to compete with the increasing variety of up-to-date communication techniques to which pupils are exposed outside of school, and even long before they enter school at all. In other words, in our truly remarkable age, the task of effective teaching becomes ever more difficult. Let us examine some of the impediments to efficient teaching and learning which have derived from our modern world.

■ THE CHANGING SCHOOL POPULATION

Never before has our population grown so rapidly by percentage or by sheer numbers. Naturally, the school population, too, increases as the population of

3

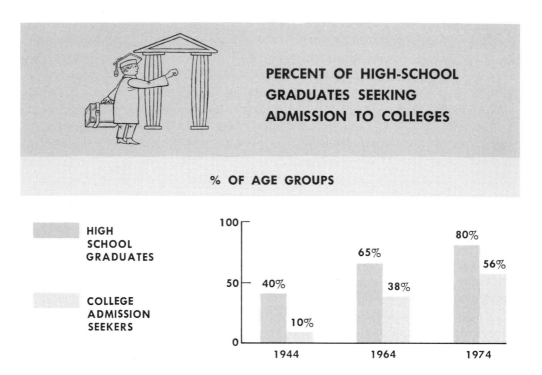

Fig. 1.1. / Today, more children, representing a larger proportion of the school-age population, are achieving higher levels of education than ever before. What are the implications of these facts to teachers? (Educational Policies Commission, 1964.)

the United States leaps ahead. In addition to the national population growth, however, is the fact that more and more of our school-age children are actually attending school. Since 1930, practically all of our children of elementary-school age have been enrolled in school, and there has been an enormous leap in school enrollment at the high-school level. In 1930, only 47 percent of our high-school youth were enrolled in secondary schools, while 1950 saw 83 percent of this age group enrolled in secondary schools; by 1974, it is estimated that this enrollment will approach 100 percent of educable high-school-aged youth. The upsurge in education is also reflected in the increase in the proportion of pupils who actually graduate from high school, and those who seek entrance to college (Fig. 1.1). Never in the history of this country has so large a proportion of our children wanted or been able to continue their education.

The changing numbers of pupils in public elementary and high schools are set forth in Fig. 1.2. During the ten-year period 1955–1965, elementary enrollment rose over five millions from 21.8 to 27.1 millions. During the same period, high-school enrollment nearly doubled from 8.2 to 15.7 millions. These increases in our school population have complicated the problems of instruction. Larger classes present particular burdens to teachers who are less and less able to relate to individual pupils and their needs. Arranging suitable learning experiences and utilizing interesting communications techniques that will chal-

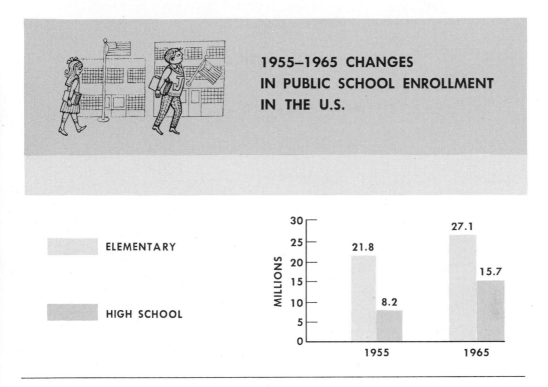

Fig. 1.2. / Increases in the school population also pose challenges to teachers. How can the modern teacher adequately face these challenges? (*NEA Research Bulletin,* February, 1965.)

lenge an ever-widening array of interests, backgrounds, and abilities are formidable tasks. Clearly, to meet these teaching challenges, the best of an increasingly diverse availability of tools must be utilized, particularly those tools by which information is communicated to the learners.

■ THE CHANGING CURRICULA

As the explosion of knowledge continues, teachers are being assigned newer subject-area teaching responsibilities. There is more and more to know, more of social importance, more of scientific and technological importance, and more experience which the learner must be given before he can assume full and desirable social participation in the rapidly expanding world of today and tomorrow. New developments in social studies and science, etc., are far beyond the experience of the teacher who was trained even five years ago. Today, for example, teachers must guide learners toward information about areas of the world never included in the older, Europe-oriented social-studies curriculum. Information advances in vocational arts, home economics, sports, recreation, health, safety, etc. show similar trends.

Consider the developments which have occurred during the past five years in the field of science and yet which appear in few or no textbooks:

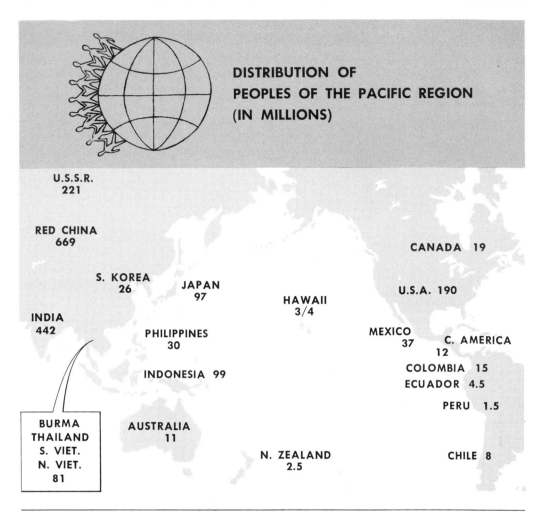

Fig. 1.3. / What is the significance of these figures to the social-studies curricula? (Redrawn from the *Annual Report*, Honolulu Advertiser, March 1, 1965.)

1965 was the year of "the quiet sun." Research during this year uncovered new understandings about the tremendous energy unleashed by the sun, and about the nature of the "solar winds."

The battle to overcome friction has witnessed the development of hovercraft and hydroplane vehicles.

Space developments will permit man to investigate at first hand, through the Apollo project, the dark side of the moon.

Today's teachers are also confronted with keeping abreast of rapid changes occurring in the area of social studies. Consider, for example, the current need for understanding Hong Kong—the international settlement which last year produced more entertainment motion-picture films than the United States—and for understanding the affairs of Communist China, as well as the Nationalist Chinese activities on the island of Formosa. The pupil of today is barely beginning to be aware of the 7000 islands of the Philippines, with its 30 million people who are working industriously to release its immeasurable natural resources. These resources are only now undergoing modern-day industrial development. Australia and New Zealand, too, are no longer distant and little-known "down under" countries; rather, they are emerging as highly indus-trialized complexes which are carrying forward social planning of the most advanced order. The Trust Territories of the South Pacific, long neglected, are now receiving attention from the Congress of the United States, and Amer-ican Samoa is the site of the most modern educational-television installation in the world.

Indeed, the pupil of today is no longer preoccupied with European social-studies backgrounds, but turns his attention more and more to the East. One reason is that this area, which contains the world's greatest concentration of population, is awakening and making tremendous strides in communication and transportation (Fig. 1.3). Japan, home for one-hundred million people is only one example of this new focus on the East. Japan is rushing into the mod-ern American curriculum in new "garb." This island nation has achieved the world's greatest increase in annual gross national product for five years running. Today, that country annually launches more new ocean-vessel tonnage than any other country in the world. Educational television is more universal than in the United States. Japanese winter sports and recreational facilities are burgeoning at a tremendous rate. Yet, how many teachers still retain the im-pression of Japan as a quaint, leisurely, cherry blossom–bedecked island nation of strange people and customs?

At the East-West Center, University of Hawaii, a new teacher interchange program is in progress. Social-studies teachers representing United States' main-land school districts are invited to study side by side with social-studies teachers who represent such Asian countries and territories as Japan, Formosa, Hong Kong, and Thailand, as well as India, Australia, New Zealand, and Mexico. In analyzing the progress of this project, Professor Ronald Anderson reports: "The speed with which Pacific nations are growing in industrialization, popu-lation and communication is almost unbelievable. It is high time that Asian social studies courses are included in mainland U.S. high school curricula."[1]

The situation which Dr. Anderson reports is typical of the dilemma not only in history and social studies, but in every area where the information explosion has been taking place. Today the world is in a state of change and the nature of these changes must be known first to those who teach if it is to be passed on to those who learn.

The knowledge explosion and the changing social world of man are reflected in curriculum changes in our schools. A half century ago, the curriculum was rather rigidly represented by 24 subject units in the fields of grammar, Latin, mathematics, history, and rhetoric. By contrast, in 1962, the United States Office of Education released the results of a survey on *What High School Pupils Study*. A wide sampling of American high-school students reported their enrollment in nearly 1000 distinct and identifiable courses:[2]

1 Ronald Anderson, from a speech delivered at the East-West Media Conference, University of Hawaii, Honolulu, Hawaii, sponsored by the Department of Educational Communications, National Education Association, H.A.V.A., April 28–May 1, 1966.

2 Edith S. Greer and Richard M. Harbeck, *What High School Pupils Study*, Bulletin No. 10, OE 33025, U.S. Office of Education, 1962.

English 137   Music 82
Mathematics 91   Home Economics 73
Foreign Language 44   Business 143
Science 74   Health and Physical Education 87
Social Studies 203   Vocational Education 65
                                     Unclassified 73

In other words, the school today finds itself with more and more subject information to teach. Of necessity, the child spends more time in school. Yet a
dilemma is unfolding. "No longer can one small head [that of the teacher] carry
all that a student must learn. We must do something drastic to better enable
us to handle the staggering build-up of new knowledge."[3] Nor can the chief
instructional medium, the textbook, be relied upon much longer to communicate with efficiency. This does not mean that to understand this new information our old techniques should be eliminated; rather, something must be done
about the means of using new communication techniques—educational media—
to "backstop" the teacher in his task of communicating current, useful, and
accurate information to learners. New instructional materials must be utilized
in sufficient measure to provide pupils with the needed concrete, or quasi-con-
crete, experiences on the basis of which both old and new material may be made
understandable. It is only in the very newest instructional materials—films,
filmstrips, slides, charts, models, and other audiovisual media—that adequate
experience with the modern world may be provided.

■ NEW TOOLS FOR TEACHING AND LEARNING

Ironically, the increasingly difficult task that confronts today's teacher is further complicated by the mushrooming availability of these new and novel educational media. A sizeable portion of these depend on reading skills for interpretation. Table 1.1 outlines graphically the explosion of knowledge as it
has been made available to teachers and pupils in textbook form alone. In
addition to an increasing array of standard textbooks, however, new formats—
including paperback books, cluster systems of series of related booklets, and
programed materials and texts—are being put on the educational market virtually every day. As one teacher exclaimed on his return from the district con-
vention, "I've never seen such a collection of books and reference materials—
I could spend weeks just leafing through what's new in my subject alone!"
The reading load this avalanche of new printed materials represents to the
teacher is made all the more difficult by the teacher's task of interpreting this
material accurately for the pupil.

In addition to the printed materials they put out, however, many publishers
have recently created entirely new subsidiary divisions which are exploring the
dimensions and advantages of educational television, taped teaching, language-
laboratory materials, films and filmstrips, programed instruction, and teaching machines. Manned by staffs of researchers who are called "New Media

3 B. Frank Brown, "Education," *Honolulu Star Bulletin*, February 27, 1965.

Table 1.1

GROWTH IN SALES
OF TEXTBOOKS TO ELEMENTARY
AND SECONDARY SCHOOLS
1940 TO 1970

YEAR	ELEMENTARY AND HIGH SCHOOL SALES
1940	36,600,000
1950	94,300,000
1960	230,000,000
1970/projected	500,000,000

Source: Frank M. Redding, "Revolution in the Textbook Industry." Technical Development Project, National Education Association, 1963.

Experts," these divisions are also actively engaged in establishing publisher-controlled production agencies through which the best audiovisual innovations are being packaged along with textbooks and other educational reading materials. Sets of films and filmstrips are produced to accompany tape-recorded materials, and taped materials are produced to accompany textbooks. Other combinations of interrelated learning materials are also being put together to form educational "packages." Thus, as publisher and teacher continue in the frontal attack on the knowledge explosion, the task of sorting out the best materials for each teaching purpose becomes increasingly more difficult.

■ EXTRASCHOOL INTERFERENCE

As has been said, we are living in an age of revolution in the field of communications. The spectacular manner in which the picture-story magazine, or comic book, has captured the popular fancy has led to a great increase in the number of such publications. Whereas 9,000 magazines were published in 1960, there were 20,000 listed for 1964, and there is a good possibility that 30,000 will be on the newsstands by 1970. The picture-story magazine is ideally suited to the mood of our age—much information is visually presented and can be understood in the shortest possible time.

The phenomenal and continuing growth of radio-set ownership is also symptomatic of the state of communications today. Many 1960 forecasters believed that radio was going to be pushed into a position of secondary importance because of television. However, the greatest impact that television could have made on radio ownership had already occurred by 1960, when 54 million tele-vision receivers were available in slightly fewer household units, indicating that many families had two sets. Radio ownership, however, has added over 30 million sets during the four-year period between 1960–1964, and forecasters now believe that if a similar growth continues, more than 220 million radio sets will be in use by 1970.

At the same time, television continues its rapid growth. In 1950, the United States Bureau of the Census was not at all sure that a nationwide count of tele-vision receivers was worthwhile. The count was made, nevertheless, yielding more than 8 million sets, a figure which surpassed the expectations of many people. In the 10 years that followed, however, television ownership really mushroomed, and has continued to grow at a steady rate. There were 60 mil-lion sets in operation in 1964, and estimates indicate that 72 million sets will be in use by 1970.

In the midst of television's growth, there have been those who thought the motion picture was doomed. This certainly has not been the case in the United States. Even more illuminating is the fact that a recent UNESCO Report states, "Today, the production of the motion picture film is a world wide communica-tions activity. No longer in first place, the United States has given way to more competitive production achievement elsewhere: Japan, India and Hong Kong."[4]

This revolution in communications has had a strong effect on our children. By the time the typical first grader arrives at school, he has become a devotee of television, perhaps owns his own radio, is a consistent reader of picture-story magazines, helps to purchase millions of comic books, and no longer sleeps in the back seat when his parents go to an outdoor theater. Also, most children have begun to read by the time they come to school. Table 1.2 shows how the communications sophistication of our pupils increases year by year.

The influence of these factors on our school children is very real, and has generated forces outside of the classroom which seriously affect the efficiency of classroom communication techniques. The teacher constantly finds himself in the midst of a battle for the attention of the learner. The significance of this battle is made particularly clear when we consider the amount of time the learner spends in school as compared with time he spends out of school under the influence of nonschool-oriented communication devices and messages. The division of the pupil day (figured in a 180-day, six-hour-a-day school attendance schedule) looks like this for the average one-year period:

In-School Living	1080 hours
Out-of-School Living	4395 hours
Sleep (9 hours per day)	3285 hours

Thus, for every hour the pupil is exposed to classroom information and media, he spends more than four under the influence of nonschool communications. For example, an outdoor-theater manager reports, "The number of young children who come in to see the movies!—just tall enough to look over the back

4 Department of Mass Communications, *World Communications* (4th ed.), Annual Report, UNESCO, 1964–1965.

Table 1.2

PERCENTAGE OF CHILDREN WHO HAD BEGUN BY GIVEN AGE TO USE GIVEN MEDIUM

| | | | | | | Books | | Newspapers | |
| | | | | | | READ TO THEM | THEY READ | READ TO THEM | THEY READ |
AGE	TV	RADIO	MAGA-ZINES	COMIC BOOKS	MOVIES				
2	14	11	3	1	1	38	0	0	0
3	37	20	11	6	8	58	0	0	0
4	65	27	20	17	21	72	2	4	0
5	82	40	33	35	39	74	9	9	0
6	91	47	41	50	60	75	40	12	9
7	94	53	53	61	70	75	73	12	44
8	95	62	59	68	76	75	86	12	59
9	96	65	62	70	77	75	89	12	71

Source: *New Teaching Aids in the American Classroom*, Office of Education, U.S. Department of Health, Education and Welfare. OE 34020, 1960.

of the front seat—what impressions they get." And one junior-high-school teacher tells of the invasion of the portable radio:

> Occasionally someone answers my questions in a *very* loud voice. Then I realize—the student grins—and, quickly removes the pocket radio ear plug. He has been listening surreptitiously to the morning news. It was more fascinating than I or the book. "Solid-state" radios are everywhere. I am not always sure who's really listening to me!

Similarly, the testimony of the newsstand operator reveals the power of comics: "The new comic books are selling better than ever—why not? Color, action, excitement—better than most school books. . . ."

The interference with classroom communication that derives from non-school media shows no tendency to diminish (Table 1.3). Rather, the various interference factors grow and reinforce one another to create a demand for attention which seriously challenges the communications techniques employed in the classroom. In light of this, what are we, as teachers, doing for the children of the modern age to help them continue some of their communication expectations once they arrive in our classroom? In too many cases we accept these learners into our schoolrooms and literally shut out the rest of the world and its influences. Too often the classroom teacher finds himself relying on communication methods which cannot effectively compete with methods currently employed in the extraschool environment. Out-of-school communication

Table 1.3

TRENDS IN EXTRASCHOOL COMMUNICATIONS MEDIA IN THE U.S.

MEDIA	1950	1960	1964	1970[f]
Total House Holds[a]	43,000,000	51,000,000	55,189,000	60,000,000
Total Newspaper Circulation[b]	52,000,000	58,000,000	59,000,000	61,000,000
Total Magazine, Weekly, Monthly, etc.[b]	8,000	9,000	20,000	30,000
Radios, Home and Car[c]	62,000,000	151,000,000	183,000,000	220,000,000
Television Receivers[d]	8,000,000	54,000,000	60,000,000	72,000,000
Motion-Picture Theaters[e]				
Roofed	19,000	13,000	12,000	11,000
Drive-in	3,000	5,000	5,000	6,000

Note: All figures rounded to nearest thousand or million.
[a] World Almanac 1950, 1960, 1964
[b] Newspaper and Periodicals, N. W. Ayers, 1950, 1960, 1964
[c] World Communications: Press, Radio, Television, Film, UNESCO, Dept. of Mass Media 1964, p. 165.
[d] World Almanac 1950, 1960
[e] International Motion Picture Almanac
[f] Projections based on 10 year moving averages

media are devised to snare and hold the attention of the individual, whether he be child or adult; yet too often we teachers try our best to satisfy the natural interest and enthusiasm of children by using outworn and outmoded communication tools.

This fact should lead all who teach, supervise, or administer schools to ask themselves these fundamental questions:

1. Is the voice of the school being lost amid the influence of current mass communication techniques?

2. Are today's school communication methods the best that can be employed?
3. Are better educational materials and methods available through which the school may communicate more effectively with learners?

It is time teachers recognized that the school must have effective means of communication if it is to be held responsible for successfully commanding the attention of school children and youth, and for arranging suitable instructional opportunities. The realization of this situation makes imperative a new role for the teacher—one in which he assumes responsibility for providing classroom communications that are adapted to the needs of the pupils and used in ways which will allow learners successfully to reach the recognized goals of instruction. The teacher must decide to put up a defense against, or take active offensive steps to meet, the forces of extraschool communication interference.

□ THE BASIC COMMUNICATION PROCESS

In order to know the world, one should have the opportunity to experience it fully and at first hand. As we seek to lead learners into new fields of inquiry, we run the risks inherent in departing from known backgrounds unless, in the process, we provide new and appropriate, dependable firsthand experiences. But, of course, as the world becomes increasingly more complex, it becomes increasingly impossible to provide children with actual firsthand experience. Obviously, some compromise in the form of a substitute experience must be utilized to enable children to conceptualize their world. This is the essence of teaching communication.

Yet, in order to select appropriate media which will best provide these substitute experiences, one must understand what is involved in the process of communication itself. The basic communications model shown in Fig. 1.4 involves most often an informational or interpretive process. Messages, information, or reactions to information travel between that which initiates and sends them, toward that which receives them. The route along which the messages travel may be thought of as a "communications channel." The message (stimulus) may be the statement made by the pupil or the teacher, or it may be provided in a film, chart, picture, or chalkboard illustration. The receiver of this stimulus reacts in some way; that is, he may listen, see, or examine through touch or taste. These reactions can lead to active responses. A question can lead to an answer or suggestion; examination of a film, specimen or object may lead to a spoken observation or a smile; or the response may be no more than passing the message on to another pupil. A message communicated by the teacher may bring forth interested responses from some pupils—questions, possible answers, or suggestions—or nothing from others. Ideally, the communication channel carries both messages and counter messages; it involves imitation, reception, response, or, as it is sometimes called, "feedback."

This communications channel must be kept wide open so that informational and interpretive messages which have to do with the subject being considered can be revealed and made understandable to the pupil. It is only when the teacher and the pupil are able to communicate clearly and without interference

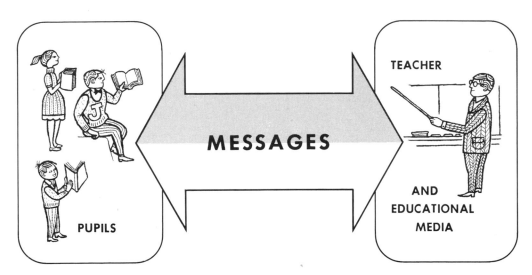

Fig. 1.4. / A basic communication model. To what influences is the channel exposed?

that valid understandings about the social and scientific world can be acquired and recorded correctly in memory for later use.

In an ideal learning environment, either within the classroom *per se* or outside the classroom—as for example, in field-study situations—the communication process goes along a channel clear of any interference. Usually, the more varied and appropriate the sources from which messages originate, the stronger and more valid are the responses and counter messages that occur between teachers and pupil, or among pupils. As we have seen, out-of-school communications media and techniques are often sufficiently varied and appropriate to the pupil —and thus make a greater impact on him—than are school media and techniques (Fig. 1.5). However, not all barriers to effective communication derive from out-of-school interference; some originate during the interactive classroom process.

☐ PSYCHOLOGICAL BARRIERS TO EFFECTIVE TEACHING

The best teaching plans and procedures may fail to materialize because they come up against communication barriers which originate in the classroom. One important group of obstacles to effective teaching derives from our rapidly expanding knowledge of human behavior and learning. Like antiquated and outworn methods of classroom communications, psychological barriers to learning and teaching have certainly always existed; however, as more and more research into human behavior and learning exposes these barriers and points to means of overcoming them, it becomes highly important for the teacher to

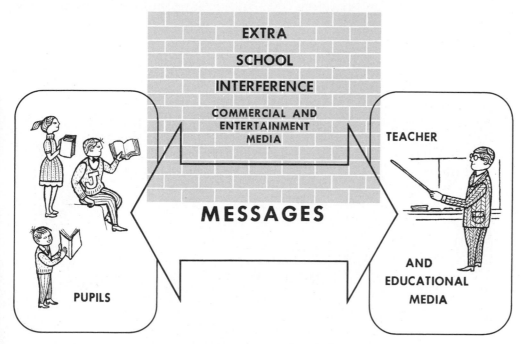

Fig. 1.5. / Extraschool interference serves to obstruct clear classroom communications. Do these factors affect your teaching?

acquaint himself with both the barriers and the techniques by which they may be removed. Thus, although these are of a different nature than the teaching-learning impediments we have previously discussed, they too are subject to the teacher's control.

Success in classroom learning is closely related to the clarity and understandability with which messages are communicated by teachers directly, or by information sources which the teacher has chosen for use. The educational psychologist describes this basic communication process as one which provides for messages that pass between sender and receiver to be clearly recognized and completely understood by both. However, one quickly recognizes that many psychological barriers may lie in the channel area. Some of these arise from exterior, or outside-of-school conditions, such as home life, etc., but others arise from conditions generated within the classroom itself.

The teacher bears the burden of achieving clarity in classroom communications, and he must be ever alert for such "interference." The teacher must not only recognize interference possibilities, but also know the means by which a clear channel of communication may be established and maintained with efficiency, for he is usually the only one who can improve the nature and strength of the messages or remove the barriers to receiving these messages. As long as messages are transmitted with clarity, as long as they are transmitted unchanged or uninterrupted by interfering factors, pupil-teacher communications will proceed efficiently.

Experience indicates, however, that many changes do occur as the messages presented by a teacher—or through the media chosen by him—pass to and are interpreted by the pupils. As a result, the nature of classroom learning experiences are frequently so altered as to lower the general efficiency of instruc-

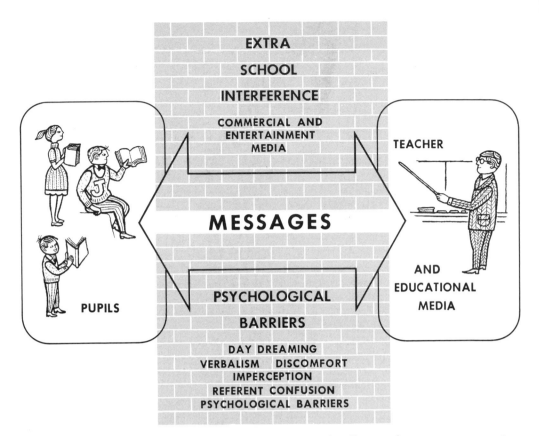

Fig. 1.6. / Psychological barriers also interfere with efficient classroom communications and add to extraschool interference. What are your experiences with the realities of these barriers?

tion. As indicated in Fig. 1.6, the clarity and understandability of the messages transmitted and received in a classroom depend on the avoidance of the following, often overlooked barriers to effective classroom communication: verbalism, referent confusion, daydreaming, imperception, disinterest, and actual physical discomfort.

■ VERBALISM

The human organism is a remarkable thing. It automatically sets up defenses against annoying stimuli. Consider how on one occasion or another we have found ourselves in a noisy committee session or in a gathering at which almost everyone speaks at once and makes continuous demands for our attention. In such situations, we discover how amazingly simple it is to shut out psychologically unwanted noise or unattractive appeals for attention. We concentrate our mental attention on what is interesting and desirable; for example, an interesting private conversation or a point of agreement taken by a fellow committee member. On occasion, one may completely "shut out" unwanted audio stimulation while ruminating pleasanter experiences he has had elsewhere.

Similarly, many learners in the classroom find it very easy literally to "tune us out" when our teaching approach becomes too repetitious, "noisy," uninteresting, or unattractive. Experienced teachers report that continued use of any one kind of device or stimulus results in its decreasing efficiency. Certainly the learning efficiency of words used endlessly actually declines as more and more words pour forth. Just as a muscle tires when overused, so interest and attention lag before a never-ending barrage of words. As one seminar participant reported:

> During the first five or six weeks of school, pupils listen to me. They seem very interested in my descriptions and directions. Then comes a curious change. As week follows week and more words follow more words, interest lags and finally even I realize that it is time for a change, a change in the methods I use to get across the ideas I so urgently seek to teach.

And many a guidance counselor has run into such pupil complaints as the following:

COUNSELOR: You were telling me you can't get interested?
PUPIL: If you were in the classroom you'd know what I mean. It's just talk, talk, talk. Every once in awhile there is a big shout "Listen, listen to me, while I explain again." He's always telling us to listen. I try to listen—but it's always just more words, words, words.

Further, it has been demonstrated repeatedly that unless learning experiences are within the learners' interest and comprehension levels, little or no progress is made toward achieving goals. The teacher knows from experience that he must be aware of the learner's readiness to accept planned learning experiences. Yet many pupils have not been prepared adequately to meet the excessive verbalism with which the school typically communicates information. It has been found that, particularly among the lower socioeconomic strata of our population, a large number of children have received their preschool training from parents and others in the home who themselves have limited verbal ability. Thus, unaccustomed to the barrage of words that pours forth from the teacher and that confronts them in their readers and textbooks, these children do not have the means with which to comprehend the teacher's endless verbal messages.

In short, excessive verbalism can no longer be condoned, particularly in today's world of communication, which offers much more effective alternatives. Excessive verbalism is a limiting psychological barrier which interferes with effective classroom communication.

To alleviate this problem in planning continuing classroom experiences in the language arts, the social studies, science, and mathematics, one may draw from a variety of instructional materials which use the best of the communications techniques to reveal quantities of solid subject content. These include sound motion-picture films, models, specimens, filmstrips, charts, diagrams, tapes, records, transcriptions, television, and many others which will be discussed at length later in this book. Furthermore, allowing students to take part in selecting, using, and interpreting modern instructional materials is a good means of overcoming disinterest that results from a paucity of teaching techniques and materials. The degree to which educational media and equipment is currently in use is set forth in Fig. 1.7.

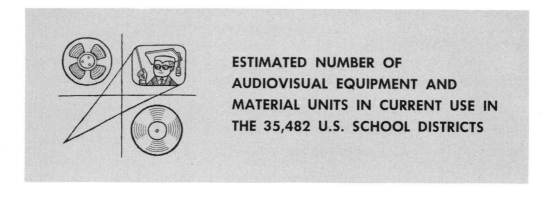

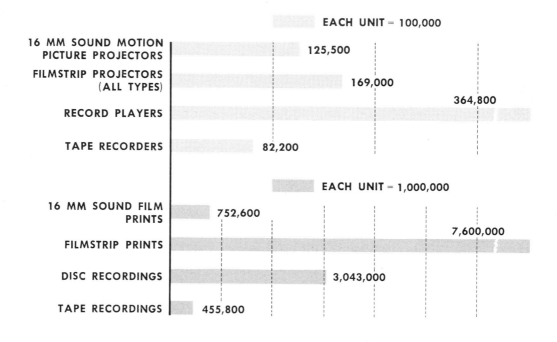

Fig. 1.7. / An increasing variety of audiovisual equipment and materials can help to reduce heavy dependence on verbalistic classroom methods and can provide an interesting and varied array of learning experiences. (Bureau of Social Science Research, U.S. Department of Health, Education and Welfare, 1964.)

■ REFERENT CONFUSION

It is natural for us, in the absence of adequate background experiences, to turn automatically to seemingly related experiences for help in understanding something new, hoping to draw conclusions which may then apply to the new problem. When such reference to previously learned material is successful in aiding our comprehension of the new materials, it is referred to as *transfer* or *positive transfer*. Often, however, this attempt to transfer previously acquired understanding to a new problem results in confusion because such needed

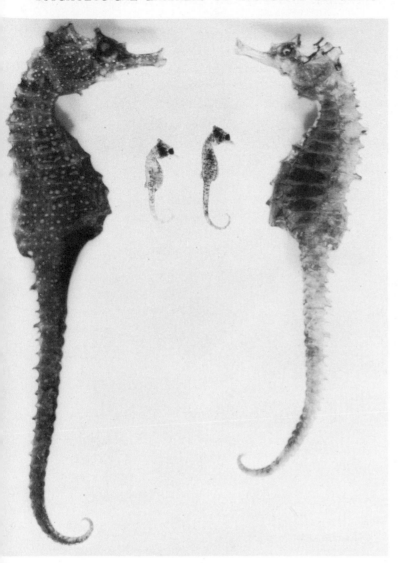

Fig. 1.8. / (Left) Does this visualization of the sea horse above validate your own mental image of this creature?

Fig. 1.9. / (Above) Does this life-sized picture of a tarantula coincide with your own impressions as to size, texture, and structure?

similar understandings seldom are available at the time in the minds of both teacher and pupil. Such an impasse is called *referent confusion*.

Referent confusion can best be illustrated in the following example, in which a teacher was explaining to a group of students in the southwestern United States a unit which had to do with beach and sea animals. "How many of you have seen a sea horse?" inquired the teacher of the class. "What are some of its characteristics—color, size, and texture, for example? From your general information about sea animals, fish, crustaceans, can you make an estimate?"

A pupil volunteered the estimate that a sea horse must be a swift powerful animal capable of predatory raids on other sea creatures. As the teacher continued questioning, it was revealed that the student, not having had any first-hand experience with sea horses, quite naturally drew on past experience with creatures of the nearly similar name—"horses" (Fig. 1.8).

In another classroom, the word *tarantula* was being explored. A pupil had come across it during reading and had raised the question of its structure, size

Fig. 1.10. / Reputation: a quiet, well-mannered child—a good pupil. What (in-school or out-of-school) thoughts might be responsible for her pensive mood?

and deadliness. Other learners, not having had any firsthand experiences with the creature, made estimates of its size—which varied from inches to feet—and invented qualities of size and function which not even this remarkable creature could live up to. The teacher displayed a specimen tarantula (Fig. 1.9). The enthusiasm with which the learners corrected their impressions was delightful.

Referent confusion is common in reading. An author attempts to express his meaning by choosing a series of words which describes experiences he seeks to recreate in the imagination of his readers. Yet, how can he be sure that the reader will have similar, or even nearly similar, background experiences and resulting understanding when he attempts to interpret the words that the author has chosen? In similar fashion, a teacher attempts to describe an experience in appropriate words. However, as these words are heard and interpreted by 25 pupils, is there any reason to assume that the backgrounds of each of these 25 pupils are as uniform and as dependable as that of the teacher who has chosen words based on his own individual experience?

Referent confusion is particularly likely to occur in verbal communication, for differences in frame of reference make it possible for two people to use the same words and yet to arrive at completely different interpretations. In this way, a whole set of communication interference factors is created. Indeed, it is usually the case that the pupils draw upon their own experiences which are related but often much different from those of the teacher, and, consequently, the interpretations the pupils are likely to draw are colored if not altogether confused.

No teacher can ever be entirely sure that the words he chooses to describe an idea or a process will convey adequate meaning to every one of his students. Each pupil's background varies and influences his interpretation and understanding in a unique way. It is logical that the greater the abstractness or remoteness of the subject described, the less similarity there will be between the meaning the teacher intends and the understanding achieved by the pupil. For example, on crossing the state line into Vermont, a geography teacher's son expressed great surprise at seeing forests of trees instead of the never-ending "forests of chimneys" which he had *read* characterized heavily industrialized New England. And a second grader reported that she had ridden up and down on an "alligator" (meaning escalator or elevator) while on a field trip. A high-school student was incensed that his grade in English was lowered because he quoted Poe's famous line as "Quoth the Raven nevertheless." The countless boners made by pupils are, in most cases, due to referent confusion.

■ DAYDREAMING

Another rather common, yet avoidable, block to efficient communication occurs when the learner daydreams; that is, when the pupil turns away from the flow of classroom communication and dwells upon his own private experiences and fantasies. Often these are more interesting, more exciting, and thus, more preoccupying than those which are identified with classroom activities. An introspective "playback" of last Friday's television thriller, a weekend movie, or the reconstruction of scenes from a comic magazine can completely override a pupil's attention to classroom discussion or text assignments. For, in daydreaming, the strongest, the most immediate, or the most completely understood sequence of experiences crowds out the less interesting and the not-so-well understood. Classroom experiences that depend too consistently on verbalism, for example, may be completely rejected, with daydreaming as the inevitable result.

Daydreaming is thus a remarkable defensive device through which the pupil can protect himself against the tedium and boredom of a humdrum classroom environment. Many pupils are remarkably adept at it; some can even smile pleasantly in seeming classroom attention, while actually, they are escaping into their private thoughts. Many a daydreamer is thought of as a "good" pupil, since he causes no disrupting influence, no trouble, and is just as quiet and orderly as can be (Fig. 1.10).

Nevertheless, daydreaming obviously interrupts a pupil's association with the stream of information being communicated in the classroom, and completely thwarts learning from planned classroom activities. The alert teacher will be aware of those students who have a tendency to daydream, and rather than take punitive measures to prevent it, will search for classroom-generated causes for such behavior. Certainly the daydreaming barrier can be lessened or ob-

Fig. 1.11. / These pupils are improving the speed with which they can respond to visual stimuli—in this case, reading. With no loss to comprehension, speed of recognition can be increased. What implication does this have for the teacher?

literated by increasing the understandability and interest level of classroom communication techniques such as those discussed in the following chapters.

■ LIMITED PERCEPTION

The expressions "Do you see?" and "Do you understand?" have become virtually synonymous. Although strictly speaking, of course, the words *see* and *understand* refer to different psychological processes, it is not by accident that the former is often used in place of the latter in everyday conversation. This characteristic of "seeing" what one understands has to do with the cognitive (intellectual) aspects of perception rather than with the physiological acuity of seeing and hearing. Most students have normally functioning sensory mechanisms; however, the psychological aspects of learning and understanding the meaning of perceived data warrant further discussion.

Psychologists have often pointed out that we perceive through our sensorimotor apparatus a great deal more than that of which we are aware. Within our span of vision at any given moment, for example, lie a great many more objects than we consciously perceive. This limitation of conscious perception is connected with the intellectual aspects of perceiving, and has little to do with the mechanical ability to take in sensory data.

It is well known that appropriate training can increase to a surprising extent both visual and auditory learning merely through enlarging the intellectual span of awareness to match more closely the span of physiological perception. It is possible to more than double a pupil's ability to acquire factual information from an experience through just such appropriate training. Reading-improvement programs offer a good example of the principles by which the intellectual field of perception may be widened. Ordinarily the eye span—i.e., how much a person "sees" instantaneously of a word, a group of words, or a line —directly affects the speed and comprehension with which he reads. Most people can train themselves to increase their visual recognition span, and hence their speed of reading, without loss in comprehension.

There are various ways to accomplish this. In one effective method, the pupil progressively limits the time he takes to recognize a printed word or phrase. Or, he increases the length of the word or phrase he can recognize in a fixed interval of time. One means of controlling reading speed for practice and improvement such as this is shown in Fig. 1.11.

Another method of increasing one's skill in seeing is to organize one's visual grasp or perception into units. The airline pilot has trained himself to sweep his eyes across the instruments systematically focussing on every recording instrument in sequence. Next he moves his field of vision across the horizon of the sky, perhaps following a figure-eight line of sight so as to include sky areas above and below the horizon, and from extreme left to right. All of this is carried out systematically and at precalculated time intervals so that the pilot may note immediately any changes in flight conditions, approaching aircraft, radar signals, or warning and all-clear light signals. The bus driver has a similar visual perception routine to follow.

Several techniques have been developed which have improved the "seeing" efficiency of pupils, also. One teacher assembled his pupils outside a hardware-store window and instructed one third of them to observe as many objects as possible as they walked by, and then to record their observations. The pupils in the next third were also instructed to record the objects they noted as they walked by the window, but, in addition, they were told to classify their perceptions according to large and small objects. The last third of them were told to walk by the window, to note the objects, and to classify them, and then to sweep the window area twice according to the lower and upper halves. This last group recorded more than twice the items reported by the first group. In such a way, the span of awareness can be expanded.

When proper listening and viewing techniques are made as much a part of the study situation as is consideration of content, there is a notable increase in the amount of information that pupils can observe and understand.

■ PHYSICAL DISCOMFORT

One's physical environment can produce a favorable or an inhibiting emotional tone. Yet, for decades little or no attention was given to the physical comfort of the student in the classroom. Too often the principal was, "Learning is a painful process, and some discomfort is good for the pupil." By contrast, the economic value of comfortable and efficient working conditions has been made clear to private industry in our new office buildings with their striking interior decor, soundproofing, and lighting systems which can be controlled to

Fig. 1.12. / The multimedia communications auditorium of the headquarters of a defense agenc

supplement the available natural light. Consider the words of one teacher who confided to her colleagues during the lunch break: "I've just transferred my checking account to the new bank. I like to do business there—air conditioning, wonderful acoustics, and the decor of the interior—just beautiful."

The need for comfortable physical surroundings applies to classrooms as well as to business establishments, but only recently has this received attention. In other words, the modern classroom, too, must be thought of as providing a comfortable environment for learning. As Dr. Frank Brum, school administrator and advisor to President Johnson advises:

> Classrooms must be carefully remodeled for comfort and pleasantness. The new concept of a learning laboratory instead of a classroom for reluctant learners has a number of merging characteristics:
>
> 1. It must be air conditioned in order to assure greater physical comfort for tense, frustrated learners.
> 2. The floor should be carpeted for improved acoustical effects.
> 3. Color is important and decor makes a notable difference to apathetic students who have been carelessly educated through indifferent attention to their requirements.[5]

The classroom environment should also be characterized by light control which permits the use of projected materials; by temperature control which encourages mental alertness; and by acoustical treatment which deadens reverberations and permits speaking and listening in comfort. All of these should be automatically controlled.

[5] Atlantic City Education Seminar, Carnegie Corp., *Honolulu Advertiser*, p. B1, February 27, 1965.

Specific planning of the physical facilities best suited to effective classroom communications will be considered in detail in later chapters; however, it is worth noting that, of late, classrooms everywhere are being equipped with the mechanical means of shifting instantaneously from verbal instruction to the use of audiovisual materials and methods. State colleges are constructing entire centers which are devoted to audiovisual learning. Universities are applying the results of research by building lecture rooms which are designed to capitalize on the benefits of using the new communications media. For example, the auditorium shown in Fig. 1.12 incorporates some of these innovations, and permits those who use it to select and to use any needed combination of media: slides, films, projectuals, and tapes.

The task of the teacher to communicate is of prime importance. To do this without taking into account the factors which interfere with streamlined and efficient communication in our classrooms, however, is to court disaster.

□ THE TOLL OF INADEQUATE EDUCATIONAL COMMUNICATIONS

We are living in a remarkable age. We can devise the rig for drilling through the earth's crust into the mantle, as we are doing in "Project Mohole"; we can "program" the means of sending a two-man satellite to the "dark" face of the moon; and we have been able to orbit whole systems of communication satellites in fixed positions 39,000 miles above the earth to provide international, instantaneous television communication (COMSAT) (Fig. 1.13). By contrast, however, we continue to employ outdated and often ineffectual communication methods in our classrooms.

That the traditional avenues for information-getting in our classrooms—reading and listening—are still depended upon is revealed in two reports. In investigating the time spent by children in listening-oriented learning activities, Miriam Wilt reports that approximately two-and-a-half hours per school day—almost half the total school time—are devoted to instructional experiences and exercises which depend upon listening to verbal stimuli.[6] In related studies by William S. Gray, it is made clear that a major share of a learner's skills and information are acquired through the avenue of reading.[7] Beyond all this reading and listening to verbal stimuli, how much time is left during the class day to employ contemporary communication avenues? Is it reasonable to expect that the technology which, in our out-of-school world, has developed to such a high level in the areas of film, television, and other mass media should be so completely forgotten as information-giving channels in our classrooms?

The interest factor involved in efficient learning demands that the teacher include varied methods of communicating. Repetitious use of single stimuli may quickly produce disinterest and boredom. Variety in classroom procedures and in use of teaching materials usually heightens the interest and enthusiasm with which pupils approach their work. Because the communication techniques

[6] Miriam E. Wilt, Study of Teacher Awareness of Listening as a Factor in Elementary Education, *Journal of Educational Research,* 43:626–636.

[7] See William S. Gray, "The Sociology of Reading," in C. W. Harris (Ed.), *Encyclopedia of Educational Research* (3rd ed.), Macmillan, 1960, pp. 1088–1095.

Fig. 1.13. / Can one teacher be expected to "know all" at a time when man's knowledge is exploding through new frontiers with every tick of the clock? What alternatives are there?

Fig. 1.14. / The XB-70A. What referent confusions are you subject to as you attempt to understand the specifications of this machine—altitude: 70,000+ miles; thrust: 30,000+ pounds; fuel: JP-6; weight: 450,000 pounds; speed: 2000 mph—? What are the big "boxes" underneath?

available today are so varied, it is unthinkable for a teacher to delay further the introduction of new and effective techniques.

Words alone no longer suffice as new areas of the world and breathtaking events rush into prominence—the development of the XB-70A (Fig. 1.14), the creation of a new independent nation among the states of the Dutch East Indies, and the development of new industrial complexes in Japan, India, and Australia, for example. As our attention turns to areas of the world in which new explosions in population and industrialization are occurring, to advances in the peacetime uses of atomic energy, and to man's continued exploration of space, etc., experiences with stimuli other than words alone are needed if teaching communication is to be effective. Indeed, as noted previously, the use of words alone may call forth as many interpretations as there are listeners in the classroom.

Our graphic materials, too, tend to be outdated. Consider your own maps when you get back into your classrooms, for example. Do they reveal where the islands of the Trust Territories lie? Do they reveal the locations of the Malaysian Republic? Do they disclose the boundaries of Melanesia, Micronesia, Polynesia? Many of us are still using maps of the South Pacific which represent that region as a vast uncharted stretch of blue water. We need new graphic materials which are up-to-date and understandable. It is the responsibility of the school administration to provide such urgently needed materials.

Teachers more and more sense these dilemmas. Evidence of this appears in estimates made by teachers of the adequacy or inadequacy of the preservice professional education experiences they had as they prepared themselves for the responsibilities of classroom teaching. Figure 1.15 reveals that—while most teachers feel that their professional education preparation was reasonably adequate in the areas of subject knowledge, the psychology of learning, and teaching methods—their preparation in the utilization of audiovisual communication materials and methods in the classroom *was not adequate.*

The result of these circumstances is a communications impasse. Although the role of the school is to educate youth to take its place in society, the breach that

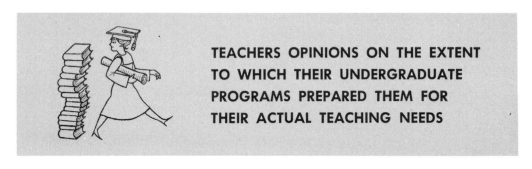

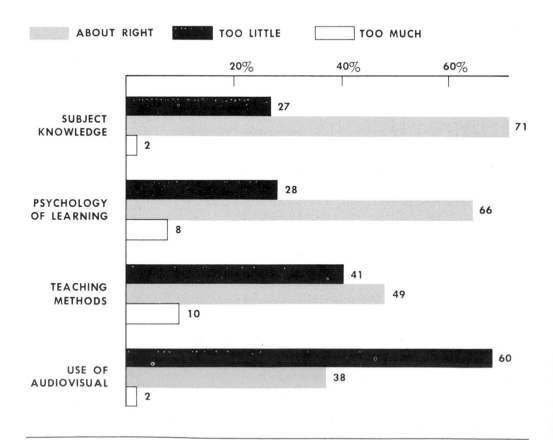

Fig. 1.15. / That teachers are themselves aware of the toll of inadequate educational communications is revealed in these findings. (National Education Association, Research Division, 1964.)

YEAR	Table 1.4 ESTIMATED PUBLIC AND PRIVATE SCHOOL RETENTION RATES FIFTH GRADE THROUGH HIGH SCHOOL		
	FIFTH GRADE	NINTH GRADE	HIGH-SCHOOL GRADUATES
1940–1947	1000	780	480
1950–1957	1000	880	580
1957–1964	1000	930	660

Source: *Digest of Educational Statistics,* U.S. Department of Health, Education, and Welfare, Office of Education, 1964, p. 120.

occurs between extraschool communication techniques and those means traditionally employed to inform learners about their world seems to be ever widening. The teacher who attempts to communicate information in today's classroom sooner or later runs squarely into the effects of this impasse. Boredom, daydreaming, classroom-discipline problems, and other barriers to learning confront the teacher far too frequently, and severely obstruct the educational process. At best, the large portion of "successful" pupils who complete their schooling and graduate into society are less than satisfactorily prepared to meet its demands.

However not all pupils are "successful," and far too many fail to take full advantage of available educational opportunities. The limitations of the school's holding power, and the increasing numbers of dropouts remain continuingly complex and perplexing issues. Table 1.4 shows that, in 1940, 780 out of 1000 fifth-graders remained as members of the freshman high-school group, and, of this group, only 480 graduated. For the group of 1000 fifth-graders in school during 1950–1951, 880 went on to become ninth-graders, and only 580 remained to become high-school graduates. In 1957, 930 out of 1000 fifth-graders survived the freshman year of high school, yet only 660 became high-school graduates in 1964. At the present time, only slightly more than 50 percent of the high-school age group graduates from high school. This high dropout rate has alarming sociological implications. Neither a skilled labor force nor an enlightened electorate can be assured as long as such circumstances persist.

In analyzing the intelligence quotient of 1,040,000 high-school dropouts Ray Warner reports the following:

197,600 dropouts had an I.Q. of 80 and less.
208,000 dropouts had an I.Q. of 80 to 90.
520,000 dropouts had an I.Q. of 90 to 100.
114,000 dropouts had an I.Q. of 100–110.[8]

[8] Raymond Warner, "Scholastic Ability of School Dropouts," *School Life Prerun,* January, 1964.

These figures clearly dispel the popular suspicion that only the dullards and laggards constituted the dropout group. In another investigation, Percy B. Williams discovered that there was no evidence to support the idea that most high-school dropouts are delinquent individuals:[9] Seventy-nine percent of the dropouts he studied were not considered serious behavior problems by either their counsellors or their principals, and 76 percent had never before been suspended from school. Williams corroborated Warner's study by reporting that over 49 percent of the dropouts that he studied had average or better-than-average intelligence.

The actual reasons for high-school dropout, which have been studied on several occasions, are interesting: An early investigation by Edward S. Crooke shows that approximately two-thirds of the withdrawals from high school reflect disinterest in school for one reason or another.[10] Such reasons for leaving as "disliked certain teacher," "disliked certain subjects," and "not interested in school," led Crooke to generalize that lack of interest in school work as such is responsible for about half of the decisions to drop out of high school. Mr. Williams' more recent investigation of school dropouts also indicates that lack of interest and poor success with school work are major reasons given by those who chose to drop out of high school:

    47.5 percent failing in three or more subjects
    35.3 percent reported lack of interest in school work
    17.8 percent reported lack of success[11]

The question is, what opportunity is there for the youth to become enthusiastic about school work which relies on excessive verbalism, instead of the highly keyed extraschool communication environment of modern-day living?

The studies cited point out that the techniques by which information, ideas, and skills are transmitted to school students need careful reevaluation. There is reason to believe that the instructional methods employed today approximate too closely the traditional verbalistic techniques that were considered appropriate two or three decades ago. Clearly, if we are to strengthen the holding power of the school, we must incorporate into our own classroom the attractive, attention-getting communications techniques used outside of the schools.

The problem, then, is three-fold. First, we must acknowledge the existence of much new material in every subject—the explosion of knowledge. Next, we must expand and modernize the school curriculum so it includes this new knowledge. Finally, we must find and select successful and meaningful ways of communicating all of this to the student, for only if we can hold the student's interested attention in class will the newly revised curriculum be meaningful to the individual pupil and thus ultimately beneficial to society.

   9 Percy B. Williams, "Dropouts"; *NEA Journal*, February, 1963, p. 11.
   10 Edward S. Crooke, "An Analysis of Factors Relating to Withdrawal From High School Prior to Graduation," *Journal of Educational Research*, February, 1956.
   11 Percy B. Williams, *op. cit.*

But what, specifically, are the channels and devices of communication through which the information-transmitting goals of teaching can be achieved?

☐ THE RESEARCH BASIS FOR EDUCATIONAL COMMUNICATIONS

During the last 30 years, research has demonstrated the efficiency of individual communication media: the 16 mm. silent film, 16 mm. sound motion-picture film, television teaching materials, still-projected slides, the use of community-resource learning experiences, and many others. The research efforts of such people as Freeman and Wood into the use of silent motion-picture films;[12] Arnspiger and Rulon into 16 mm. sound motion pictures;[13] Gibson, Carson and others in still-projected images;[14] Atyeo into the use of community resources as educational media;[15] and Spaulding into the use of illustrations[16] are a few of many significant studies which support the generalization that new media and learning materials, when properly selected and wisely used, can help students accommodate increased amounts of factual learning and sustain greater retention.

A recent report on the use of *interrelated* media in the improvement of instruction is included in a University of Wisconsin "Report of the Activities of the Multi-Media Telemation Laboratory."[17] The crossmedia-lecture demonstration technique was used by Professors Michael Petrovich, Herbert Klausmeier, Warren Southworth, and others. In the field of Educational Psychology, Professor Klausmeier reported: "This initial short period study showed that the same student group gained substantially more by multi-media instruction than by lectures, and that multi-media material was retained to a greater degree."[18] Professor Petrovich and Professor Southworth reported:

> Analyses which have been carried out primarily in connection with Russian History and Health Education indicates:
>
> a. Strong student preference for multi-media lectures over regular lectures;
> b. Students feel that multi-media lectures present information more rapidly, in more detail, and in a way which is easier to recall; result in clearer concepts, and are better organized than regular lectures;
> c. Students feel that visuals used are appropriately related to each other, are clear and easy to understand, are about right in number and changed at proper intervals.
> d. Visual aids were well chosen, clearly visible, well-timed, and in proper sequence.[19]

12 Frank N. Freeman and Ben D. Wood, *Motion Pictures in the Classroom,* Houghton Mifflin, 1929.

13 Philip J. Rulon, *The Sound Motion Picture in the Teaching Science,* Harvard Univ. Press, 1933, p. 98.

14 David Carson, *The American Way of Life Portrayed in Filmstrips,* Research Publication No. 2, Scottish Educational Film Association, 1947, 34 pp.

15 H. C. Atyeo, *The Excursion as a Teaching Technique,* 1939, 225 pp.

16 Seth Spaulding, "Research on Pictorial Illustrations," *AV Communications Review,* 3:34–45.

17 *Report of the Activities of the Telemation Laboratory,* School of Education, Univ. of Wisconsin, February, 1961–May, 1962, 5 pp.

18 *Ibid.*

19 *Ibid.*

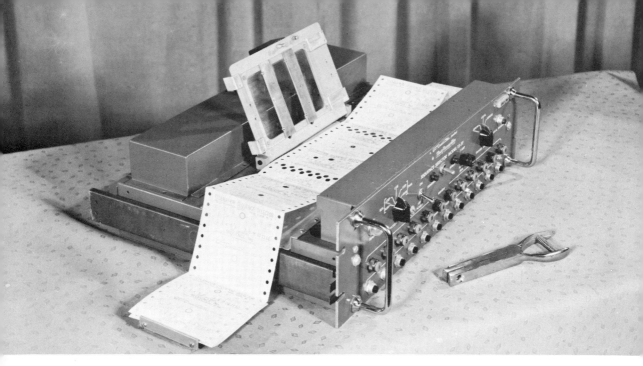

Fig. 1.16. / A Multimedia Preplanned Media Sequencing Device. Through the use of this instrument, a teacher may preplan as a "program" exactly the kinds of interrelated learning materials (films, slides, tapes, projectuals, filmstrips) that are needed to present a completely understandable and varied explanation of a school subject.

Ideally then, learners should be able to witness *combinations* of audiovisual experiences which reinforce one another if we are to provide the most efficient paths possible for the mastery and understanding of concepts. In short, *current development is in the programing or arranging of learning experiences which depend on carefully selected, interrelated combinations of tested media as learning stimuli.*

This kind of planning necessarily requires careful selection and organization of materials so that only the most necessary and useful interrelated materials and content are drawn together for the learner's benefit. This approach—which is currently in use in many school districts—is referred to as "systems learning," "programed, large-group instruction," "multimedia utilization of audiovisual equipment," or as the "crossmedia approach" (Fig. 1.16). In an upper-level American history class, for example, the concept level of the pupils is likely to be quite low and the success with which reading—which involves the handling of symbols—can impart concepts efficiently is likely to be correspondingly low. In this case, the teacher's task is to arrange a sequence of audiovisual experiences which will simultaneously lay the foundations for and enhance the understanding of history concepts. From among the many available materials, the teacher might select two-dimensional study prints or slides: a collection of models, specimens, or realia—or photos of these—which are representative of a certain period in history and which are typical of the utensils and paraphernalia actually used at the time; visualized history schemata or time charts showing the interrelationships of time, place, and movement; and a motion-picture film or videotape recording that enables the class to listen to the way people talked, to see how they dressed, to observe the houses that sheltered them, and to learn of the social issues and the general social background for historical action. When all of these learning experiences are used in conjunction with one another, their interaction permits a maximum of learning reinforcement. In this way, tangible concepts are built which can be successfully related to the more abstract symbols on charts and maps, and to the word symbols that compose history textbooks and resource reading.

As another example of multimedia utilization, a teacher of an elementary-school social-studies unit may seek to provide a similar combination of audio-visual learning experiences for a program on our fiftieth state. Appropriate materials here may include a filmstrip, tape-recorded communication with an actual class of equivalent age in Hawaii, a 16 mm. sound motion-picture film, a collection of handcrafts from Hawaii, and a display of two-dimensional pictures and graphics.

Or consider a science unit which is investigating space and space travel. Since text materials on this subject are usually incomplete, the teacher must gather materials from a wide variety of sources. These materials might include pictures and diagrams from the National Aeronautics and Space Administration; a talk by, or interview with, a member of the community whose experiences in some phase of space-age science would be valuable; chalkboard diagrams; flat pictures; models and specimens; and a student-compiled study display incorporating recent news releases and pictures. Recent current-events filmstrips[20] and, if possible, a motion picture would be useful on this topic, also. The interaction of these various learning materials will yield needed and useful conceptualization of the actual facts and principles involved in the topic.

The need for greater versatility in classroom communication devices has lead to the instituting of a host of new curriculum programs in the schools. For example, in reporting on the interchange program being carried out by the East-West Center at the University of Hawaii, Ronald Anderson says:

> The organization of these new courses is the reason for this interchange program. The teachers who are assembled here learn about the cultures of Asia and gather actual new media learning materials through which to make Asian cultures understandable to high school groups. As they seek to do this the search turns to current communication tools; 16 mm sound films, projectuals and maps of their own making, 2 × 2 slides which they take, develop and, after choosing the best, duplicate so that they all can have sets of materials to take back "home." Much of this work goes on in the summer when they take tours of Asian countries and do their own documentary photography, map-making, etc.[21]

That teachers truly seek more Educational Communications information and skill was evidenced in Fig. 1.15. Educational television, sound motion-picture films, programed-learning devices and charts, maps, bulletin boards, slides, filmstrips, and prerecorded aural materials—all can serve as effective new avenues to learning. Such techniques should not replace tried and tested teach-

20 *Dateline Science*, Filmstrip Series, B&W, Educators Progress Service (Randolph, Wisc.). Issued weekly during the school year.
21 Ronald Anderson, *op. cit.*

Fig. 1.17. / These are some of the old and new tools of communication available to teachers today. Used wisely, they offer the means of

ing materials; rather, they should be used to supplement them (Fig. 1.17). The greatest strength of many audiovisual techniques lies in their ability to provide a solid background of readiness upon which more efficient reading programs of instruction can be based. The result, as we shall see later, is heightened interest, a better vocabulary, and increased reading comprehension.

Yet, in order to supply this needed readiness experience, teachers need to know a great deal more than most of them do about films, slides, maps, and the other educational materials through which necessary concepts may be gained by learners and accurately applied to the verbalized concepts they meet with in their reading. Thus, in the ensuing chapters, we shall make a searching inquiry into the specific instructional procedures, the basic information-giving techniques, the effectiveness of currently used instructional materials, and the role of the teacher in employing these methods and materials within the context of his increasing numbers of children. We shall also examine the roles of audiovisual materials in terms of their ability to interest more completely the average school child today, more effectively to instruct him in the educational goals that

helping the teacher to become a more effective arranger of communications in the classroom.

confront him, and more lastingly to equip him with useful information which he may draw upon when he takes his place in society.

☐ SUMMARY

The teacher who assumes classroom responsibilities in today's society accepts the consequences of a revolution in educational communications. Characteristic of this revolution is a change in the nature of the school population which finds practically all of the children of all of the people in the classrooms of our country. This results in a great spread of interest, intelligence, and enthusiasm for learning. Another characteristic is the explosion of knowledge which has produced a tremendously varied curriculum. No longer can the teacher be expected to know all things, but must, as an alternative, rely more and more on appropriate resource materials and experiences for help.

The teacher today has the opportunity and responsibility to select and use a variety of new tools for teaching heretofore unavailable. These include a 15-fold increase in text and printed resource materials since 1940. Thousands of new sound films, well-organized sequences of language-laboratory audio materials, and related expanding inventories of tapes, filmstrips, slide sets, models, specimen collections, and two-dimensional, projected visual materials have become available to the teacher.

To complicate further the role of the teacher, the students who now enter the classrooms are the product of a world of sophisticated communication experiences: entertainment television, picture-story magazines, entertainment films, commercial radio, and trade and pulp magazines and pocket books. The expectations of students as consumers of education reflect the influence of out-of-school media.

In the face of these changes, the teacher must understand well the basic communication process, the means of communicating efficiently the constantly enlarging world of information to the pupil, and the ways to employ new educational communication tools. Closely related to this need is that the teacher must recognize possible psychological barriers that may lie in the way of effective classroom communications, including verbalism, referent confusion, day-dreaming, limited perception, and physical discomfort. Failure to understand the communication process itself, the existence of barriers to it, and the means by which these barriers may be eliminated usually results in such failures as are evidenced through pupil disinterest, low levels of comprehension, and, in extreme cases, actual school dropout. These can be avoided to a large degree by improving instruction through audiovisual utilization.

Thirty years of educational research supports the generalization that instruction can be significantly improved through the wise selection and utilization of sound motion-picture films, filmstrips, programed-learning materials, educational television, and the interrelated use of appropriate filmstrips, slides, models and specimens, maps and globes, and charts, all of which are closely related to the reading resources we have learned to use so effectively during the past decade. The total teaching task is complicated finally by the teacher's realization that he has not been adequately prepared during his professional training to understand, select, and use new instructional materials with efficiency. It is the purpose of this and succeeding chapters to attempt to remedy this situation.

□ Suggested Activities

1. Arrange to visit a classroom and observe the communications techniques employed. Be alert for communications barriers. In your opinion, how efficient is the communications environment you observed?
2. Interview several "senior" teachers and ask them what social interference and psychological barriers they today encounter which they did not cope with a decade or more ago.

3. Arrange for viewing the films listed in the Bibliography. Provide time for discussion of them.
4. Interview your fellow students and a sampling of high-school students, and ask such questions as:
   a. How many newspapers do you read regularly? What are they?
   b. How much time do you spend each day listening to the radio?
   c. How much time do you spend watching television?
   d. How much time do you spend reading magazines?
   e. How many motion pictures do you see each month?
   What conclusions do you draw from these interviews?
5. Interview a group of elementary-school children and ask them the questions in activity 4, above. What are your conclusions?
6. Interview several teachers in elementary school, high school, or college, and ask them the following questions:
   a. Do you use maps and charts, motion pictures, filmstrips, transcriptions, and recordings?
   b. Do you study community resources which relate to your subject? What are your conclusions?
7. Ask the high-school principal to help you locate the names of students who have dropped out of school during the preceding year. Arrange among yourselves to interview these students to discover:
   a. Reasons for leaving school
   b. Attitude toward school work
   c. The characteristics of best-liked teachers
   d. Least-liked school activities
   e. Things about school that could be improved
Following these interviews, prepare a digest of your findings and report to your class. What are the implications of your findings?

☐ Bibliography

Bereday, Z. F. George and A. Joseph Lauwerys, *Communication Media and the School,* World Book, 1960.

Brown, B. Frank, "Education," *Honolulu Star Bulletin,* February 27, 1965.

Crooke, Edward S., "An Analysis of Factors Relating to Withdrawal from High School Prior to Graduation," *Journal of Educational Research,* 1956.

Greer, Edith S. and Richard M. Harbeck, *What High School Pupils Study,* Bulletin No. 10, OE 33025 U.S. Office of Education, 1962.

Thomas, R. Murray, and Sherwin G. Swartout, *Integrated Teaching Materials,* McKay, 1960.

Warner, Raymond, "Scholastic Ability of School Dropouts," *School Life Prerun,* January, 1964.

Williams, Percy B., "Dropouts," *NEA Journal,* February, 1963, p. 11.

Wilt, Miriam E., "Study of Teacher Awareness of Listening as a Factor in Elementary Education," *Journal of Educational Research,* 43:626–636, 1950.

☐ Films

A Communications Primer, 16 mm., Color, 20 min., Charles & Ray Eames.

Mike Makes His Mark, 16 mm., Color, 29 min., National Education Association.

Problem of Pupil Adjustment: Part 1, *The Drop-Out;* Part 2, *The Stay-In;* 16 mm., B&W, 19 min., McGraw-Hill.

Secure the Blessings, 16 mm., B&W, 30 min., National Education Association.

To Speak with Friends, 16 mm., B&W, 28 min., National Education Association.

II | LEARNING AND

COMMUNICATIONS

We have noted that the broad and varied use of diverse modern communications devices can serve effectively to offset a host of impediments to the teaching-learning process, and that, while each of these various devices can serve a uniquely useful purpose in transmitting information to the pupil, learning is accomplished most efficiently when a careful selection of *several* media is made, each medium serving to reinforce the effects of the others. But this multimedia approach alone cannot truly be effective in its purpose—no matter how well the combination of devices seems to serve from the teacher's point of view—unless the selection of these devices and the subject matter to be communicated take into account the following principles of learning:

1. Learning stems from perceptual—that is, *concrete*—experience.
2. Subject content, and the media used to impart it, must be suitable to the learner.
3. Creativity is the goal of learning.

In applying these three principles, the teacher of any subject is confronted with several tasks: First, the teacher must determine the learners' level of *conceptual attainment* as rooted in their previous experience; second, he must evaluate the *subject matter* to be communicated in terms of this level of pupil conceptual ability; third, he must select the kinds and degrees of concrete learning *experiences* which will best be suited to, or have the best chances of, reaching the pupils at their own levels; fourth, he must select the *media* which will best provide these learning experiences—and in such a manner as to transport the learners higher up the abstraction scale without sacrificing true meaning and understanding in the process; and finally, he must *use* these media and materials in such a way that the pupils' own inventiveness and creativity will be invoked.

In executing these tasks, the teacher must start with the pupils' observable behavior as his prime point of reference. Just as the "proof of the pudding is in the eating," the teacher must constantly observe the students' responses to learning experiences, and attempt to assess realistically the kinds of knowledge, information, and interpretations which have accrued to the pupils; the skills they have acquired; and the beliefs which may underlie their observable behavior. The degree of completeness or accuracy of the conceptualizations the pupils hold will be demonstrated as they write, discuss, and respond in class. This observable behavior provides the *only* reliable measure of the relative efficiency and accuracy with which the subject matter has been assimilated by the learner.

A sixth-grade teacher, for example, must not assume that *his particular* pupils have automatically acquired the experiential basis for, or the conceptual foundations requisite to, so-called "standard" sixth-grade materials. Nor may he assume that a particular combination of audiovisual and printed materials—carefully selected according to the most forward-looking techniques—is automatically going to be suitable to *his particular* pupils, or to evoke from them their interested initiative and creativity. Regardless of how completely plausible the learning materials or experiences the teacher plans may appear to him, it is only after he has analyzed the responses of pupils who were exposed to these planned experiences that the teacher may evaluate the effectiveness of his approach.

That pupils may not be learning all that the teacher feels he is teaching was demonstrated in the case of one midwestern sixth-grade class which the present writer was invited to visit. "We have studied all about Hawaii, but I know the children will love the opportunity to discuss what they have learned, and perhaps to ask you some questions," the teacher explained with confident enthusiasm. The teacher was right: The children were indeed eager to discuss the fiftieth state.

"Did you bring back any Hawaiian money?" one child asked.

"Do children there speak English?" inquired another.

"Does everyone go to school?" asked a third.

Astonished at their lack of basic understanding, the author proceeded to answer the pupils' questions: "There *is* no 'Hawaiian' money in use today; people all over the U.S. use the same money. And most people in Hawaii speak excellent English. In answer to your last question, not only do all children go to school, but they tend to *stay* in school. Hawaii ranks first in the nation in school holding power."

The big question here is: Did the teacher employ adequate learning media? And if so, did he use them wisely? Surely he had not analyzed the responses of his pupils to evaluate the effectiveness of his teaching approach.

Yet, if the results of such teacher evaluation are to be valid and lead ultimately to still more effective teaching approaches, the teacher must understand the learning process itself. Of course, learning is a highly complex process, and volumes have been written about it; to discuss adequately all that is involved in learning—or believed to be involved—in so short a space as provided in these pages, would be to place damaging restrictions upon the teacher's contemplation of the subject. Nevertheless, we may justifiably limit ourselves to those aspects of learning which are most relevant to the careful and efficient planning of learning experiences, and to the proper selection of educational media and materials which are most likely to communicate school subject matter to the pupils. Since firsthand or concrete experience is the universal basis for human understanding of abstract concepts, let us turn to the means by which we obtain this experience—perception.

☐ PERCEPTION: THE FOUNDATION OF LEARNING

Our perceptor sensory mechanisms are our continuing contacts with our world of things and events. The eye, the ear, and the nerve endings in our skin which respond to pressure, to heat and cold, and to odors and tastes are the means through which we come to know our external environment. These sensory mechanisms are the *tools* of perception. However, by themselves, the eyes, ears, etc., do nothing more than feed us data—sensory impressions—and thus, alone, they are not responsible for the coherent "pictures" we see of the objects and events that take place in the outer world. There is also a cognitive mechanism—about which we know relatively little—which receives these various and sundry impressions and organizes them into their meaningful wholes. Together, the cognitive mechanism of our brain and our sensory apparatus provide us with the means of perception. As Kingsley summarized it:

> In perception we apprehend objects or events. When we perceive, we translate impressions made upon our senses by stimuli from our environment into awareness of objects or events. . . . The objects and events of which we become aware are regarded in perception as present and going on. This activity of perceiving is such a universal and intimate feature of our mental life that it is often difficult to realize that objects of the physical world do not merely present themselves and that we do anything more than open our minds to receive them as they really are. It is easy to overlook the fact that we construct our world of things and events out of our sensory processes and that physical objects as we know them through sight, sound, taste, smell, and touch are products of our own perceptions. . . .
> Widely differing qualities of sensory experience depend upon the organs of sense and upon the nervous system. They are the basis of our knowledge of the world about us. Without them, there would be no awareness of anything.[1]

Any given perceptual event is thus a pattern composed of the multiple sensory messages that are sensed by any or all of the learner's perceptor mechanisms which have been stimulated by external occurrences. Further, because perceptual events do not happen in isolation of one another, but rather, are continuously occurring as the result of constant sensory stimulation, there is also a constant shuffling and reshuffling, arranging and rearranging, and selection and reselection of sensory impressions and patterns of these into still larger combinations of patterns. This process leads ultimately to an organized thought pattern that we may call a "concept."

One's concept of "circle," for example, is based initially upon sensory impressions fed to the brain by the eyes; the cognitive process then orders these im-

[1] Howard L. Kingsley, *The Nature and Conditions of Learning*, Prentice-Hall, 1947, p. 262.

pressions into an organized, whole perceptual event, "circle," which is recorded in memory. When the individual comes across another circle and the ensuing sensory data are again organized, the individual thus recognizes the perceptual event. After enough of these repeated experiences, the individual can, on appropriate cue, bring to his mind an image of a circle which generalizes those he has perceived from firsthand experience, without his actually perceiving an objective circle. In this way has the individual acquired a primitive abstract concept.

As one acquires concepts, this learning, in turn, enables him to cognize additional aspects of his objective environment, and to build even larger, more encompassing concepts and, similarly, these abstract concepts provide the experiential background needed by the individual to perceive and to understand increasingly less tangible aspects of his objective world, which lead to ever more abstract concepts, and so forth. This two-way process is schematized in Fig. 2.1. It should be noted, however, that where the *concrete* basis for abstract conceptualization is lacking, acquisition by the individual of the concept involved will be inadequate at the least, and perhaps may not take place at all.

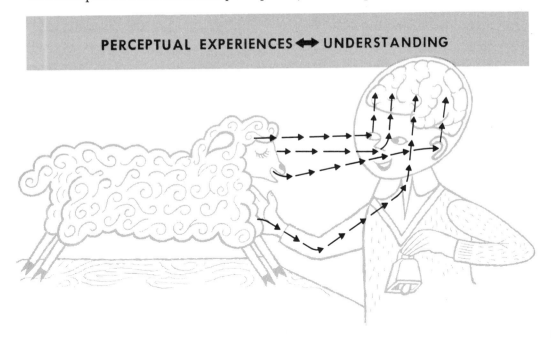

PERCEPTUAL EXPERIENCES ⟷ UNDERSTANDING

Fig. 2.1. / Understandings emerge from perceptual experiences.

Although most primary teachers acknowledge that before the word must come the idea, the teachers of upper grades and high school must also assume the responsibility for being sure that the background experiences which underlie comprehension of the printed word are provided for the student's conscious experience and understanding. This is as true of the second-grade social-studies pupil as it is for the college freshman enrolled in biology, mathematics, or the social history of the United States. For without a sufficient conceptual foundation, not only is the learning process likely to be severely impaired, but also the thinking process itself will be severely limited.

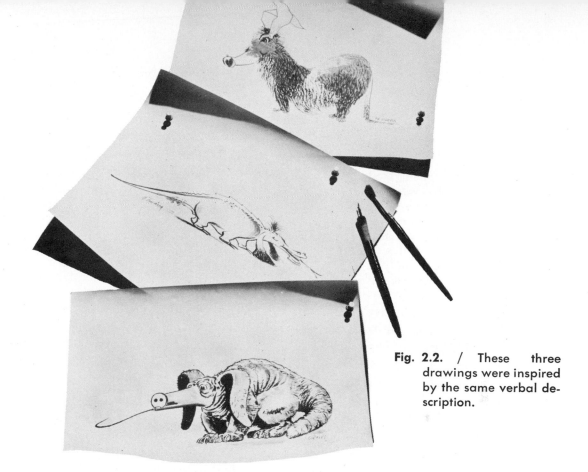

Fig. 2.2. / These three drawings were inspired by the same verbal description.

■ PERCEPTION AND THE THINKING PROCESS

When confronted with a learning problem, the learner becomes involved in the thinking process. If the problem is clearly understood, if it is interesting and challenging to the learner, and if it is not so difficult as to discourage him, the learner will begin to search his mind for and to select appropriate information and concepts which may apply to the solution of the problem. He may be able to recall such background knowledge, or he may have to search beyond his own mind for new information. He may do the latter through reading, discussion, or interviews, or, if his concrete background for the learning task is insufficient, he may seek new perceptual experiences through observation, examination, or experimentation. If the pupil is rewarded in his search, he will blend the newly acquired information into an answer to the learning problem, or, failing to do this, he may give up and leave the task unfinished.

Adults, of course, are generally better thinkers than are children, for they have had broader and deeper experience with both the concrete and the abstract foundations of thought. Teachers are all too quick to forget how limited their pupils are in the number, variety, and scope of perceived experiences in relation to their own. It is unlikely that many, if any, of a teacher's pupils have it within their ability to draw upon as wide a variety of background experiences which can be recalled as easily upon exposure to mere verbal cues as can the teacher. Indeed, it is too often the case that, although the pupils may have learned the *words* used by the teacher or the textbook, they may not have the corresponding firsthand experience necessary to understand the true ideas behind the words (Fig. 2.2).

Consider, for example, the following description of Samoan architecture which was presented to a class during a community-study tour:

> In Samoan architecture no metal is used. Strong central supports of bread-fruit tree trunks are implanted firmly into the earth. A raised platform of rocks and stones of graduated size is built up around the supports. On this a basket-like structure of palm wood is secured to the central supports and sub-supports. All of the members are lashed together with braided sennet—fabricated from the tough fiber of coconut husks. In hurricane winds and rains the inverted basket-like structure may bend or shift but will not give way. The torrential rains drain away through the built-up rock platform which supports the frame and the floor of the house itself. On occasion the structure may be dismantled by sections and moved.[2]

The typical pupil may be familiar with all or most of the words used in this piece, insofar as the words themselves are concerned. But has he ever seen a *real* breadfruit tree or has he experienced for *himself* what palm wood looks and feels like? What picture is likely to come to the student's mind as he reads "braided sennet—fabricated from the tough fiber of coconut husks"? Perhaps he has never directly experienced the dramatic effect of hurricane winds and rains. Clearly, to appreciate the full significance and ingenuity of Samoan architecture from this verbal description—and thus, to appreciate fully the Samoan people and their culture—a learner requires a background which in its entirety most pupils are likely to lack. In fact, if the concrete perceptual background to a learning situation is severely limited, words can be an impediment rather than an implement to further learning.

That words are intrinsically meaningless without an understanding of their referents—the things for which word symbols stand—can be illustrated well in the following situation. Imagine that you are about to learn how to read and that you are making your first acquaintance with the alphabet. Study the following alphabet for no more than a minute or two:

aɪ	(as in aisle)	aɪl	e	(as in data)	deṯə
ɑ	(as in calm)	kɑm	ə	(as in data)	deṯə
aʊ	(as in now)	naʊ	i	(as in unique)	uniǩ
ʊ	(as in put)	pʊt	ɪ	(as in in)	ɪn
u	(as in true)	tru	j	(as in your)	jur
ʌ	(as in cup)	kʌp	ð	(as in these)	ðiz

Presumably you are now prepared to read with comprehension the following primer story:

aur stʌdɪ ʌv wʊl

wi kom ðə wʊl.
wi juz kardz tu kom ðə wʊl.
wi kom ðə wʊl tu mek jarn.
wi mek jarn aut ʌv komd wʊl.

2 Polynesian Cultural Center, Laie, Oahu, Hawaii, 1966.

Fig. 2.3. / Printed words are intended to communicate their author's experience and ideas by cuing the reader's existing store of experience, facts, and concepts. The teacher's responsibility is to provide the experiences which will give readers the ability to understand the author's meaning.

As you read this story, were you able to make sense out of the words? How many times did you have to refer to the alphabet? The chances are that even repeated reference to this alphabet did not help you to understand the words, and few, if any, picture concepts of familiar objects came to your mind. Yet the experience you just underwent was not dissimilar to that which a beginning reader faces as he attempts to gain meaning from verbal abstractions of real things.

These learning difficulties are well known to the first-level reading teacher, and she makes heavy supplemental use of visible objects in the classroom, pictures, and oral reference to objects that the pupils can readily bring to mind at the sound stimulus of each word. However, as the grades progress, too often teachers assume that the children, who are now able to read, have also acquired the equivalent experience with the *referents* for all the words involved in their lessons. Once children have learned to recognize patterns of letters and syllables, they have relatively little trouble learning new words, but often the mental picture or concept behind the word remains vague in their minds. Thus, their vocabulary not infrequently increases at a faster pace than their understanding.

In the case of the above story, a picture (Fig. 2.4) has been provided on the following page. Study this picture. How effective is it in helping you to understand the story?

We are still teaching mainly with a rapidly increasing abundance of reading and verbal materials. In addition to the stacks of books shown in Fig. 2.3, there are also the recent emphasis on programed-learning materials, most of which de-

Fig. 2.4. / Examine the boy's activity. Does this picture aid you in understanding the primer story?

mand reading skills; television instruction in which the televised teacher mostly talks; and a wide variety of workbooks and pupil manuals which are based on the ability to read and write. As a consequence of this heavy reliance on verbal materials, many seemingly successful pupils spend more time learning new word patterns than they do new *idea* patterns. They become adept at recognizing parts of speech and sentence construction and they easily record verbalized facts in their memories; consequently, it is not difficult for these pupils to answer a test question in such a way that it *seems* as if they truly comprehend the idea behind the question. In actuality, however, the real significance of the facts and their relationships may be quite vague in these pupils' minds, in which case the true thinking or problem-solving process is severely limited.

Nevertheless, this problem-solving process will—if permitted and encouraged —quite naturally involve the seeking of needed concrete perceptual experiences. This was demonstrated by one of the pupils who was studying the unit on Samoan culture mentioned earlier. Fortunately in this case, the teacher had not relied solely on such written material as the above, but had also provided a sound motion-picture film on the subject which showed the location, climate, village life, and other features of Samoan culture, including a reference to the unique structural design of the Samoan family house. This architectural reference struck a responsive note of interest in one pupil, who then independently arranged a visit to a museum where he found an actual scale model of the "basket-like structure" he had read about. An accompanying booklet showed diagrams with brief verbal explanations. The combination of the model and the diagrams produced for the student both tactile and visual experiences which could logically be related to the words heard during the field trip as well as to those in the booklet. Now the problem of understanding the Samoan people in terms of their architecture could be "thought through." Appropriate

Fig. 2.5. / A Samoan *fale,* or family house. How and why is it built as it is? What experience need one have to answer this?

combinations of learning material were selected and tested by the pupil and the most relevant complexes of this data were organized into a meaningful understanding (Fig. 2.5). The verbal descriptions which at first had been only vaguely understandable now resulted in a highly articulated comprehension because the pupil had fortified his store of background concepts with new first-hand perceptual experience.

Another illustration of how necessary concrete perceptual experience is to the learning and thinking processes is provided in the case of a typical second-grade unit on the story of wool. The object of the unit is to lead children to understand how wool is grown and made into cloth similar to that from which their own clothing is made.

Few children are likely to approach this study with much more than a super-ficial experience with wool. A child may have touched the woolen fabric of his clothing, and thus have obtained some experience with texture. He may even have observed the fact that the cloth, which at first he had perceived as merely the gross mass of his suit, is actually made up of tiny threads. Perhaps he has pulled one of these threads apart, and noted that the thread is really composed of still more minute but single strands of substance. Perhaps, even, his interest has been aroused. In any case, the average child has probably gained to some extent an immediate understanding of woolen texture and possibly even a super-ficial idea of what is involved in weaving through this or similar firsthand per-ception. It may be that questions have occurred to him, at least implicitly in his mind: What is the relationship of the single fiber to the little bundle of fibers which make up the thread? How do all the threads hold together to make my suit? Where do the threads and fibers come from?

When these or related questions are made explicit for the child in class as the teacher begins the unit on the story of wool, the child has some background of

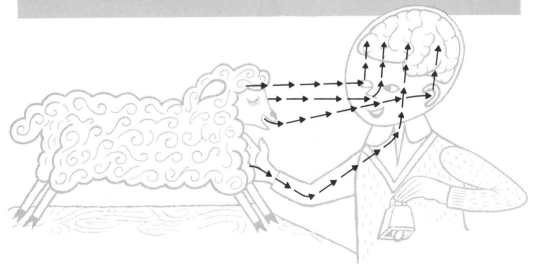

THINKING ↔ REFLECTIVE THOUGHT

PERCEPTUAL EXPERIENCES ↔ UNDERSTANDING

Fig. 2.6. / Understandings become the basis for thinking.

perceived experience, though limited, upon which to draw. To answer the questions posed by the learning problem, the child begins searching through his own past experience with woolen fabrics. If the child's interest has been aroused by the learning problem, he will respond to his own need for further experience to solve it. At this point, the teacher must provide opportunities for additional firsthand perceptual experience. If the only avenue for getting additional information open to the child is through printed materials, his efforts to understand such words as *Australia, sheep ranch, wool exchange, warp, woof, shuttle, shears,* and a host of other unfamiliar word symbols, he may become more bewildered than challenged. Even corresponding pictures are likely to leave much to be desired if the pupil has had little or no direct experience with the objects involved.

On the other hand, a visit to a farm to watch sheep being sheared, or to a factory in which woolen things are fabricated would be valuable. Someone from the community might be invited to the classroom to demonstrate the hand carding, spinning, and weaving of wool—allowing the children to handle and to observe closely the implements, and answering any questions the children ask. A museum visit might be arranged, and other experiences with wool might be provided to help the pupils achieve a variety of relevant concepts about the processes involved in wool and wool production, and to allow them to draw conclusions appropriate to the teaching goal. The child whose curiosity has been aroused will respond enthusiastically to such opportunities for perceptual experience, but if these experiences are lacking, incomplete or half learning will result.

The orderly process of thinking, then, involves the learner's selection of his own background experiences and concepts which apply, and the discarding of those which do not apply, to the solution of a problem. Conceptualization and understanding are the outcomes of perceptual or real experiences with events or things. Clearly, the basis for thinking is a broad background of perceptual experiences (Fig. 2.6).

Usually the difficulties of thinking and problem solving mount as the problem to be solved concerns things that are increasingly remote from opportunities for firsthand experience. The middle-grade child who is presented with the task of gaining an understanding of life in some remote area of the world, for example, is faced with greater barriers than is the child who, say, wants to know more about plant life in the family garden. Nevertheless, in a complex world environment, the learner is often unable to have a wide range of direct perceptual experience and, in many cases, audiovisual materials can be useful in providing desirable and needed substitutes for these direct experiences.

■ PERCEPTION AND ATTITUDE FORMATION

Integrally bound up with the thinking process, and exerting a strong influence on the outcomes of this process, are the attitudes the learner acquires as he proceeds up the ladder from the concrete to the abstract levels of learning and thinking. Although an attitude is not the same thing as a concept, the learner acquires attitudes toward his perceptions at the same time that he acquires concepts of them; and, just as one's store of concepts provides the basis for his further cognition of the world, so his previously acquired attitudes provide the basis for acquiring additional attitudes or changing old ones. These attitudes can even serve to influence what aspects of his perceivable world the learner will select to include in his further perception and learning. Thus, attitudes can strongly color what the learner comes to know, the thinking process by which he comes to know it, and any further learning that is based on his acquired knowledge. Indeed, the attitudes one acquires along with facts and concepts can exercise a strong influence on his orientation to *learning itself*.

But what is an attitude? There are many descriptions of attitudes which might be given, but one which serves our purpose well has been voiced by Gordon W. Allport: "An attitude is a mental and neural state of readiness, organized through experience, exerting a directive or dynamic influence upon the individual's response to all objects and situations with which it is related."[3] To draw on our previous example, if each time an individual perceived a circle he also experienced pain or displeasure, he would acquire a negative attitude toward circles generally. This attitude would then influence all further learning that is related to the concept "circle," and might even prevent the learner from obtaining further experience with these aspects of his environment.

The formation of attitudes can take place in many ways: through the concomitant pleasure or pain which accompanies perception and cognition; as a result of rewards or frustrations which seem to the learner to follow the learned information or its application; through a lack of sufficient facts and concrete experience needed to round out one's conceptual understanding of something; or as a consequence of exposure to the attitudes held by influential people in the learner's social sphere. One illustration of attitude formation is provided in a situation involving a group that was studying Japan. At the beginning of the unit, Japan was to the students a vague, hearsay-inspired place of cherry blos-

3 Gordon Allport, *Attitudes: A Handbook of Social Psychology*, Clark Univ. Press, 1935.

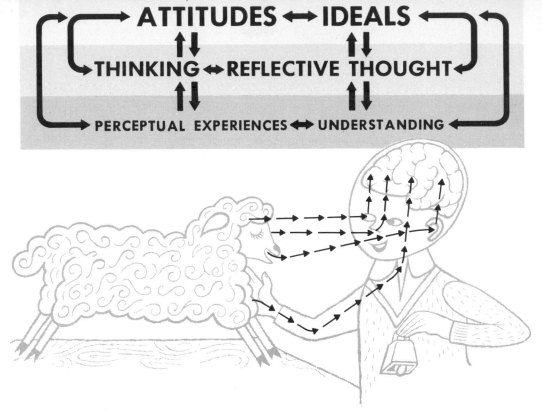

ATTITUDES ↔ IDEALS

THINKING ↔ REFLECTIVE THOUGHT

PERCEPTUAL EXPERIENCES ↔ UNDERSTANDING

Fig. 2.7. / Reflective thinking rather than emotion is a more useful basis for developing realistic attitudes.

soms, bound feet, strange music, customs, and traditions. "Strangeness" and "quaintness" best represented the overall attitudes of the learners toward the country and its people. In all probability, these feelings had been acquired from attitudes which prevailed in the students' homes, from inadequate or half-truths believed by the parents as a result of the parents' own only partially adequate school experiences.

Attitude formation may start during conversations around the dinner table as children listen to parental views. Parent expressions about history, for example, may arouse or deaden the child's desire to investigate American history. Specifically, a child's awareness of the idea of "frontiersmen" or "pioneers" may spring from purely emotional experience gained in home conversations about the subject, or perhaps from television viewing.

Today's schools must acknowledge the attitudes with which pupils enter their classes and provide the means by which erroneous attitudes can be replaced by those which square more accurately with the facts. Simulated realistic experiences can be collected and arranged for pupils by a teacher who has been carefully trained, or, better, one that has participated in many firsthand experiences himself. One advantage that the Japan study group enjoyed was that the teacher had been to Japan and had observed for himself the modern Japanese culture, and thus he was able to provide his class with his own realistic attitudes in addition to the materials he selected for fact learning and concept building. While we can't send all teachers around the world, it is the present-day responsibility of the teacher to investigate current communication materials which are most likely to foster realistic attitudes as well as accurate and complete information.

The diagrammatic representation in Fig. 2.7 shows the multidirectional relationships that exist among concrete experiential backgrounds, recalled perception, attitudes, and thinking. Although the diagram shows three levels of development—*perceptual, thinking,* and *attitudinal*—all are endlessly intermeshed and interrelated. As a learner attacks a learning problem, his thinking may be influenced by an attitude that has been well established in his mind, if only on an emotional basis. As he seeks additional information through discussion, additional concrete experiences, interviews, and reading, he will quite automatically select those aspects of the data that are most in keeping with this attitude, and screen out those which do not fit in the previously established matrix of his accumulated experience. Clearly, such "colored" thinking can be detrimental to the accuracy of the final outcomes of his learning.

In the classroom, the teacher has an opportunity to modify or influence the pupils' attitudinal background and actually to build new attitudes. The alert teacher will be as aware of the faulty or undesirable attitudes held by his pupils as he will be of the inaccuracy of their factual understanding. It should be noted, however, that in too many cases teachers themselves perpetuate and reinforce faulty pupil attitudes because of their own attitudes. Yet, by supplying positive and concrete opportunities for perceptual experience, the teacher can aid children to transcend their inadequate attitudes and to acquire those which are at once socially desirable and realistically oriented to the objective environment.

Inappropriate attitudes toward the "pioneer" idea, for example, can be altered through classroom study situations which provide realistic experiences of pioneer life, thus fostering a clearer conceptual understanding. Concrete experiences provided in school may include exposure to models of pioneer villages and trips to the museum to examine pioneer home construction, costumes, utensils, and other things related to frontier living. A well-planned bulletin board with illustrations can help to visualize pioneer life. A motion-picture film can reveal, in an interesting but not overly romanticized presentation, a reconstructed frontier village complete with people who talk in the pioneer manner. These added experiences and understandings can alter a pupil's original attitude or even replace it with an entirely new one, as attitudes based on imitation or emotion give way to those which the learner himself forms on the basis of his new concrete experiences, thinking, and conceptualization. The facts and ideas the pupil selects from his experience, and the associations he builds in attempting to understand living conditions then and now, will ultimately modify his whole "feel," or attitude, toward the pioneers who opened the West. In this way, the child of today may gradually begin to associate the life of the pioneer with democratic purposes.

In the case of the pupils who were investigating Japan, the fact that the teacher had himself experienced directly modern Japanese culture provided the students with the opportunity of listening to the firsthand accounts and of observing the collection of specimens, artifacts, and souvenirs which the teacher had brought back from his trip. In addition, the pupils were shown up-to-date films, slides, photographs, graphics, and recordings. All these laid a foundation for true understanding which could be applied to the learning problem. Through this process, a basis in fact was laid for the formulation of realistic attitudes about the Japanese and their modern culture, which attitudes then fostered more adequate conceptualization, not only about the Japanese people specifically, but also about people, places, and things generally. It is through just such carefully planned classroom learning opportunities that teachers can more effectively provide students with the bases for discriminating thinking, for dealing realistically with the problems of living, and for responsible behavior both in the present and in the future. This is the high social purpose of education.

☐ SUITABILITY OF LEARNING EXPERIENCES

By "suitability of learning experience" we mean that both the subject matter to be learned and the media and materials by which it is to be learned must be geared to the pupils' interest, abilities, and readiness to become involved in the learning situation. Even the teacher who has put much effort and thought into the planning of concrete perceptual experiences for his pupils may find himself quite discouraged by the lack of pupil responsiveness, merely because the pupils were not ready for these particular experiences. For example, if the unit on Samoan culture previously mentioned were presented to second-graders rather than to older pupils, even a wide and detailed array of models, specimens, and artifacts would not likely aid the children in achieving the desired learning goals. Cultural concepts involve highly complex and abstract facts and ideas, and require a large store of concrete background concepts and understanding—more than second-graders are likely to have acquired. To understand the Samoan culture in terms of its architecture—even to understand the primitive architecture itself—requires an understanding of the geographical and climatological circumstances in which the structural design must exist.

Not only may pupils lack sufficient background information to accomplish specific learning goals, but also they may be far more interested in and curious about some aspects of their environment that are closer to their immediate experience than they are about those aspects which are involved in the learning situation presented by the teacher.

How even carefully thought out and seemingly appropriate classroom learning situations can fail in their objectives if they are not suitable to the needs of the learners was amply demonstrated in the case of one teacher who returned to his midwestern community school duly inspired by the year he had spent in Asian studies.[4] Preparing to teach a new semester course in Asian culture, this man selected for the class's basic reading material three survey texts which included information on Japan, Korea, Formosa, the Philippines, Indonesia, Malaysia, Burma, Cambodia, and Viet Nam. He obtained from the Asian Studies Society some very appropriate sound motion-picture films. From a variety of source books, he patiently prepared a series of hand-drawn maps, historical-event chronology tables, and related tabular charts and graphs. During his tour of

---

[4] The Asian Studies Program carried out by the East-West Center at the University of Hawaii. Students for this program are selected according to the ratio of two Oriental teachers for every U.S. mainlander. The program consists of two semesters of course study climaxed by a tour of the U.S., by the Asian Teachers, or a tour of the Orient for American Teachers.

Japan, he had taken 35 mm. photographic slides, and he organized the best of these into topical sequences for presentation to the class. Finally, he selected and bought a small collection of instrumental and vocal recordings, and recordings of Haiku poetry readings. Thus armed with a wide variety of audiovisual materials to supplement an equally interesting diversity of reading material, the teacher confidently began the new semester with an enthusiastic account of his own personal firsthand experiences of the past year.

The teacher's own enthusiasm was apparently infectious, for at the beginning of the term, the students were equally eager in their responses. As the days wore on, however, the teacher began to notice that these initial sparks were dimming. The students seemed to exhibit more and more preoccupation, and appeared concerned with things other than classwork. Discouraged, the teacher fell back on his traditional approach. He distributed the texts, issued a prescribed reading list, passed out assignments, and set a schedule of exam dates.

What had happened? Now that the class had more or less returned to a "normal" teaching-learning situation, the teacher had time to reflect on some of the causes of his failure. Then he realized that, in his enthusiasm over his own year of experiences—of travelling among the people and places of Asia and obtaining a host of new concrete experiences for himself—he had misjudged the readiness of the class to accept and to profit from his own learning experiences as he had presented them to the class. As soon as this was apparent to the teacher, he began to reorganize his approach. His first step was to arrange for pupil-teacher planning sessions. Through preliminary group discussion and questions, the teacher gained an understanding of the pupils' level of interest and background knowledge of the Orient, what areas of misinformation existed among them, their beliefs, attitudes, and so on. Based on this new understanding of pupil needs, the teacher reorganized his materials and selected those which were more suitable.

It was obvious that neither the teacher's nor the textbooks' descriptions had communicated to the group. Japan's population of 100,000,000, for example, has little meaning to the person who has never been caught in the evening rush hour traffic of Tokyo. The significance of land-use reform, too, has only partial significance to one who has not watched women at work in the rice paddies while nearby, men operate one-man tractors. Those who have not watched the rapt attention of children observing an educational television lesson in the remote Ibaraki School in northern Honshu cannot hope to know the impact of this medium from scanning a table of statistics on the subject. And, reference to aboriginals of the northern islands can invoke in the inexperienced an image of the natives living in Central Australia. The teacher of Asian studies became successful only after he observed these areas of confusion and irrelevance, and adapted his subject matter and the means by which he presented it to the class.

Thus, successful teaching involves the determination of the concept levels already attained by pupils, and the arrangement of new experiences for the pupils—experiences which will provide avenues to additional conceptualization. Only in this way can educational content and material provide the bases for pupils' future thinking and problem-solving. As indicated earlier, it is the

Fig. 2.8. / These pupils are assembling pictures, news clippings, and graphics relating to a new unit. Such activities elicit the active participation of the pupils and help to provide them with a conceptual background. Of what additional values are such activities?

teacher's task to know the pupils well enough to assess their levels of ability, background learning, and interests, rather than the pupils' task to adapt their interests and abilities to the learning situation presented by the teacher. The teacher must understand what subject content is suitable to the pupils' levels of readiness, and how to adapt the subject content for which he is responsible to meet these levels. He must also understand what kinds of communications media and what concrete perceptual experiences are most suitable and appropriate for the pupils' readiness and which will be most likely to arouse the pupils' interest sufficiently to lead them to further search for, and creative use of, new information (Fig. 2.8). To start below the pupils' responsiveness levels usually leads to pupil boredom; to start too far above these levels, often leads to pupil frustration or failure.[5]

Although children learn from simple, concrete experiences which are gained through direct perception, they proceed to relatively more inclusive and abstract

[5] For further study of creativeness concepts see Alice Miel, *et al.*, *Creativity in Teaching: Invitations and Instances*, Wadsworth, 1961.

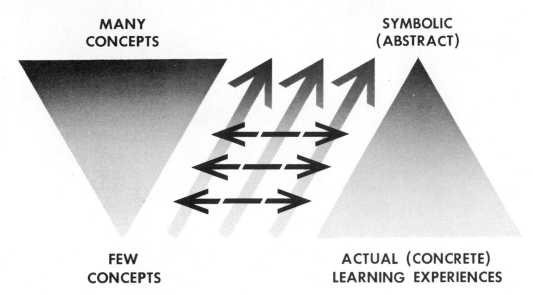

MANY
CONCEPTS

SYMBOLIC
(ABSTRACT)

FEW
CONCEPTS

ACTUAL (CONCRETE)
LEARNING EXPERIENCES

Fig. 2.9. / Concepts and learning experiences.

experiences which are acquired through symbols that stand for objects and relationships. One important goal of education has been reached when individuals have acquired sufficient conceptual understanding of a wide scope to be able to handle reflective thinking and problem solving with respect to a wide range of objective phenomena by means of symbols—words, numerals, and other cues—rather than having to refer continually to the direct experiences for which these symbols stand. But without a sufficiently broad base of direct experiences, this goal cannot be achieved.

Figure 2.9 depicts graphically how this concrete-to-abstract learning takes place. The triangle at the left reveals how the pupil begins with few or no true concepts and gradually builds from primitive concepts—which are narrow in scope and simple in nature—to a larger range of increasingly complex and inclusive concepts. The means by which the pupil acquires this learning proceed in reverse manner (righthand triangle). He must have many and diverse opportunities for concrete and direct experience from which to build concepts in his mind. Only gradually does he become less dependent on these experiences in order to acquire new concepts. Finally he can expand his understanding of his world through indirect experiences derived from symbols.

Ideally, the teacher recognizes that pupils who are relatively low on the concept scale need to have a maximum of new learning opportunities presented in concrete situations. As pupils advance higher on this scale, more abstract experiences provided through more abstract symbolic or verbal experiences may prove to be appropriate. Progress in the concept scale may move in varied directions. Often a student's progress seems to be arrested when in fact the pupil has only temporarily returned to basic, direct experiences in order that he may fill important gaps in his understanding. It is not unlikely, for example, that a musically gifted student might try to improvise his own musical arrangements from

Fig. 2.10. / A graph showing business activity achieved by Japan was the outcome of a pupil project. What learning activities preceded the completion of this project? Where on the two scales of the Concept-Media diagram would you place these pupils? Where do they go from here?

simple aspects of his learnings rather than to proceed directly to more advanced material.

It is worth mentioning at this point that, during recent years, much has been written about "education for excellence," "accelerated study programs," and increasing "challenges." Unfortunately, in many cases, teachers have interpreted this movement as a signal to lengthen assignments, to increase homework, or, in general, to move ahead by increasing the pace so as to invade course content formerly designated for a grade or two beyond. This has taken its toll, as efforts to "get tough" usually do. Often the inevitable result is pupil maladjustment, irate parental reactions, and teacher frustration. Most attempts to meet the demands of modern educational-improvement programs have failed to accommodate the pupils' needs for the sequential steps that lead to this advanced and accelerated learning. Or, if theoretically these steps have been built into the new curriculum "ladder," teachers have not provided sufficient time for the pupils to assimilate the information they are supposed to learn from each step. More than likely the teacher, in her efforts to cram in the required subject matter, has failed to draw upon the pupils' own experience, and has perhaps proceeded too quickly to the abstract levels of information-giving instead of providing the necessary opportunities for concrete experience.

Yet, in most cases, accelerated curriculum programs can be utilized within the suggested period of time with no loss to learning efficiency—in fact, they can result in greater learning efficiency—when the subject matter is presented in terms of the students' existing interests and background knowledge. Indeed, the teacher may find that he can proceed quite rapidly and with great teaching success; but this can only be possible after he has payed due attention to the levels—

or thresholds—of interest, ability, and conceptual development present among the learners.

It is particularly helpful, both to the teacher and to the pupils, if the teacher includes in her evaluation of pupil readiness those extraschool aspects of the pupils' lives that are usually overlooked by school personnel as irrelevant to class activities. The special world of childhood is always of much more interest and relevance to the pupils themselves than is the world adults know; yet, adults, including teachers, typically ignore its intriguing facets as trivial and meaningless. The alert teacher will pay due respect to these more immediately interesting aspects of the pupils' world, noticing the concepts the children have acquired from their experience with their own world, and drawing upon these concepts and experiences to lead the children toward those which are involved in classroom learning goals.

An understanding of the relationship between known concept levels and needs in terms of direct, or, increasingly sophisticated learning experiences enables the teacher to help his class move steadily toward the top of both of the scales depicted in Fig. 2.9. The goal is to employ such classroom plans, materials, and techniques as will permit students to advance upward on the achievement scale starting from their own levels. Significantly, between the base and the apex of the righthand triangle in Fig. 2.9 lies various levels of communication devices which range from the most basic and direct perceptual experience with people, objects, and events; upward through simulated firsthand experience provided through motion-picture films, recordings, slides; still higher through semisymbolic media such as graphs, diagrams, charts; and finally to symbols which have little visible relationship with their referents—numerals, math symbols, and words (Fig. 2.10).

□ PUPIL CREATIVITY

While socially useful concept and attitude formation is a most important purpose of education, the ultimate pupil goal of self-realization is creativity. As one's vivid understanding of his world increases, the individual's store of useful informational and relational concepts automatically lead him to trial-and-error discovery, and this sense of discovery lies at the very heart of the creative process. There are many different levels of creativity, but two among those described by Irving Taylor have particularly important implications for the classroom teacher: (1) creativity through *involvement,* and (2) creativity through *invention.*[6] The first of these is within the grasp of most learners, while the second may be achieved by relatively fewer, depending largely on the imagination and ingenuity of the teacher as well as on the aptitudes of certain particularly alert pupils. The environmental conditions which foster or inhibit pupil creativity are influenced greatly by the teacher; indeed, it is almost axiomatic that, as the teacher leads, so follow the students.

---

6 See Irving Taylor, "The Nature of the Creative Process," in Paul Smith (Ed.), *Creativity: An Examination of the Creative Process,* Hastings House, 1959.

Fig. 2.11. / This is one example of productive creativity through pupil involvement. Does Gemini's meaning come through? Why does this sort of initiative become apparent only in some classrooms?

■ CREATIVITY THROUGH INVOLVEMENT

Although it has been the American ideal to educate everyone, there has recently been an especial emphasis placed on the need to find better means of educating the "slow" learner. The popular belief that poor students simply do not have what it takes to gain from formal education has been exploded as myth, and there is every indication that many of the children we have been accustomed to passing off as "uneducable" are, in fact, merely casualties of faulty teaching methods. However, in the midst of this new search for teaching techniques that will reach these so-called "poor students," we are too likely to overlook the fact that faulty teaching methods also can take a serious, though less obvious, toll of those pupils we acknowledge to be "gifted." The gifted child achieves the learning goals set by the school, and often exceeds the teacher's highest expectations. Nevertheless, often such a child is able to excel by doing relatively little in comparison with the average pupil, and by exerting only a small part of his abilities. The gifted learner usually finds it possible to establish himself in a position of leadership with a good deal less than his best; thus, while such a pupil may seem to be involved in class activities, he is actually releasing only a small fraction of his potential. The alternative is, of course, to challenge the upper limits of the gifted child's potentialities. This, then, is the goal of teaching: to challenge *realistically* the interests and abilities of *all* pupils; that is, to lead all children into creative involvement with the learning content.

Creative pupil involvement is the major result of creative *teaching*. Consider for a moment the cases of two student teachers. The first student teacher complained about having to remind his pupils to get to work. "I ask them to write a report or a story, and they just don't do a thing. They just don't have any work habits!" When the supervisor suggested that perhaps the student teacher was neglecting to provide proper leadership, he responded, "But how can I show the way when I have little or nothing to work with?"

In the second case, the student teacher exclaimed to his supervisor elatedly "This week it was 'all systems go'! Everyone got into it; they came up with ideas better than I'd planned for! Why is it that some weeks everything seems to fall perfectly in place?"

"The students were receptive; they *wanted* to find out," the supervisor observed. "You used just the right materials, those that were appropriate and understandable. . . ."

"And how they responded," the student teacher broke in, "Why they were positively . . ."

"Creative?" suggested the supervisor.

Clearly, the teacher in the first case was not *teaching* creatively, and he thus failed to elicit creative responses from his pupils. How useless it is to enjoin pupils to "pay attention," to "get to work," or to "be creative" unless the teacher himself lays the proper groundwork! One doesn't write unless there are ideas one wants to write about; one doesn't draw a picture, construct a model, or arrange a display unless one has had a variety of meaningfully related experiences from which he has gained a sound conceptual foundation for his activity. As one's own experience is drawn out, his interest is challenged, and from this interest comes a spark of creative curiosity which leads to new understanding, new discovery, and to still higher levels of interest and curiosity. The desire to inquire further leads naturally to a satisfying experience for the normal learner, providing he is presented with the right opportunities for gaining this satisfaction. The result is an increasingly developing curiosity and desire to know, to search, and to restructure one's accumulated knowledge. This is creative involvement.

A further illustration of the rewards a teacher can experience if he himself is creatively involved in classroom activities is provided in the case of a class that was exploring the significance of current events—specifically, the nation's space efforts. It was inspiring just to be in this classroom; a neatly drawn map of Florida was on the chalkboard, under which the caption "Gemini's Home Base—Cape Kennedy" was neatly printed. In the work corner, three pupils were thoroughly engrossed in putting the finishing touches on a model of the space craft, a cardboard mockup of realistic proportions (Fig. 2.11). One wall of the classroom was entirely devoted to a display of the pupil's own artwork, entitled "What Space Explorers May Find."

"We didn't just draw," explained the teacher, "We had to do a great amount of research in books, newspapers, and magazines. We also invited our science teacher in to explain some of the facts of space flight."

Clearly impressed, the supervisor asked, "What would you say was the single most important ingredient which led to this successful classroom situation?"

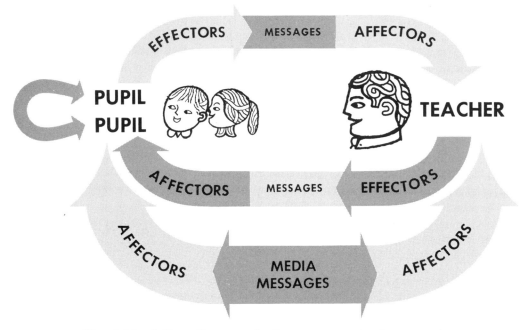

Fig. 2.12. / The affector and effector communication process.

"Effort and imagination," the teacher replied, "there's little or nothing available in ready-made materials. We just plan together, improvise, and find out for ourselves in current sources."

Creative teaching, therefore, must begin with a rich, appropriate, and understandable environment for learning. In the diagrammatical representation of a creative learning environment shown in Fig. 2.12, the term *messages* refers to information transmitted from the teacher, learning medium, or pupil to the teacher or to another member of the class. Regardless of its origin, a message must *affect* the interests and accumulated knowledge of the person to whom it is directed if teaching-learning communication is to take place; for this reason, these messages may be referred to as *Affectors* (A). If the message affects the receiver in such a way as to elicit a *responding* message, this response may be termed an *Effector* (E). It is through the effector messages of the pupils that the teacher may judge the degree of involvement that has occurred as a result of an affector message. Pupil responses usually occur in proportion to the number of useful affector messages which are created within the classroom by the teacher, by educational materials and media, and often by the pupils themselves.

As previously stated, maximum classroom involvement is most likely to result when there are many carefully selected and wisely presented opportunities for firsthand learning experiences, or for simulated but concrete experiences such as those provided through films, filmstrips, models, mockups, and community field trips. Of course, a rich learning environment must also include a well-stocked library of resource materials and many opportunities for pupil-teacher exchange. Indeed, the opportunity for the free interchange of ideas, interpretations, questions, and possible solutions to problems between pupils and teacher and among the pupils themselves is a most important ingredient of an efficient and creative learning environment.

The principles involved in initiating an atmosphere which is conducive to creative involvement are clearly seen in the procedure ultimately followed by the teacher of the course in Asian culture, whose initial discouragement was discussed earlier in the chapter. The pupil-teacher planning sessions that this teacher instituted, once he realized his failure to note the true readiness level of his students, soon revealed that a mixture of knowledge and pure hearsay was prevalent among the pupils. Some pupils had volunteered timidly their ideas of the Japanese culture. References to "cherry blossoms," the "Boxer Rebellion," "warm, soft climate," "bound feet," "queer customs," and "Bonzai movies" illustrate the approximate range of the main notions held by the class. Wisely, the teacher gave his class no indication that some of these notions were ill-informed in contrast to his own knowledge, but instead encouraged the pupils to feel free in telling what they knew and in expressing their interests. Next, the teacher asked the class to bring in pictures and articles on those aspects of the Japanese people in which the pupils were most interested. By encouraging the pupils *own* interests, the teacher made the first move toward eliciting their involvement.

On the basis of the material brought in by the students, the teacher questioned further: Had they learned anything new about Japan? Did they have any new ideas? Having completed the assignment, did the students feel that Japan was more or less an interesting place? Did the students have any further curiosity about Japanese customs? Apparently they did, for the pupils became increasingly more animated during class periods, and seemed to carry out their further assignments with growing enthusiasm.

At an appropriate point in the course, the teacher played some recorded Japanese folk music. At first this new aspect of Japanese culture was regarded by pupils as strange and peculiar: "I don't like it," "It's so different," and "the scale sounds so strange" were the typical comments. But the learners were curious, and soon they began to refine this curiosity into specific quests for knowledge. How many notes are in the Japanese scale, and how does this scale compare with Western music? What are the tone qualities of the various instruments used in Japanese music? A volunteer committee scurried around the school and community to locate the instruments, and several periods of class time were devoted to examination of and experimentation with these instruments (Fig. 2.13). Animated discussions took place over the role of folk music to the Japanese people and to the culture generally.

Thus, the pupils were inspired to creative involvement in their Asian studies through the atmosphere established by the teacher and through their own discovery experiences. Clearly, this is the goal of creative teaching.

A creative learning environment can be provided for any subject content. For example, a science film on the nature of solids, liquids, and gases raises as many questions as it answers. These questions can be explored best when the quest for additional information is encouraged right in the classroom by having students devise their own hypotheses, test these hypotheses—perhaps by improvising their own equipment—and observe their own results. Throughout this process, the teacher merely guides; he does not provide ready-made answers but allows a well placed hint or two to lead the pupils to the thrill of their own discovery (Fig. 2.14).

A creative teacher strives to provide a classroom environment which is complete with understandable and useful learning experiences that will capture the imaginations of students and inspire them to creative involvement. The teacher who has experienced the joys of a room filled with curious and motivated pupils will never return to less rewarding teaching methods.

■ CREATIVITY THROUGH INVENTION

The concept of inventive creativity is much easier to illustrate than to describe; in fact, we know really very little about the cognitive processes that are involved in inventive creativity. This level of creative expression goes beyond ordinary interest and involvement, as important as these are to the learning process. Inventive creativity seems to involve the reshuffling of acquired information patterns into entirely new expressions and accomplishments. For one learner, inventiveness might be expressed in the creation of an original story; for another, it might be expressed through the fashioning of a musical instrument out of tin cans, wires, and wood. For others, invention may be more complex; perhaps the initiating of new organizational plans for the school student body, in which ideas and activities normally limited to the school group are expanded into community participation.

Many pupils, if the learning situations presented to them are conducive, are capable of some degree of creative invention. This was well demonstrated in the Asian-culture study group as they proceeded to explore Japanese culture. As the unit on Japan progressed, several of the pupils evidenced interest in Haiku poetry. Haiku poetry, they learned, is a closely prescribed form of poetic expression. The Haiku poet seeks to express a central idea through the means of a

Fig. 2.13. / Students experiment with a Koto after first hearing its sounds on records. What must a teacher do to elicit this level of pupil interest? What changes are occurring in pupil behavior? What levels of communications are evident?

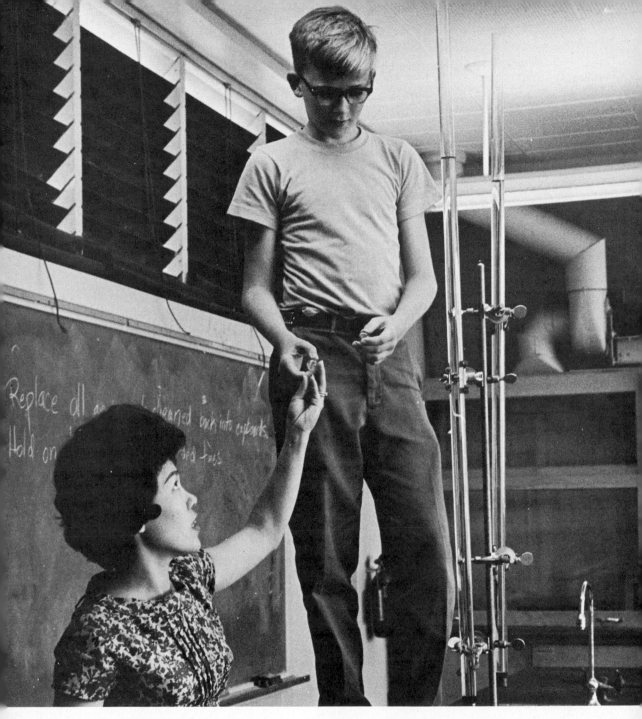

Fig. 2.14. / Why, when, and by whom should this experiment in viscosity be conducted? Whose creativity is being evidenced here?

poetic word picture, which, by aesthetic tradition, is limited to seventeen syllables. It is not impossible to transfer this same task to English. The teacher described the mechanics of Haiku poetry, played some recorded translations, and then encouraged several pupils to experiment on their own (Fig. 2.15).

"It's harder to use fewer words than many, isn't it?" one pupil said.

"Writing a letter to the embassy is nothing compared to getting across one idea in seventeen syllables," a second volunteered.

"I've been at this for two study halls now—but I've got a start!" a third exclaimed happily.

Fig. 2.15. / The gifted learner often produces much less than his best. How may the teacher proceed to tap hidden sources of inventive creativity?

Before the end of the week, several students were able to present to the rest of the group a number of poetic word pictures in the Haiku style. Three were particularly good: "Waves," "Lapping Tide," and the third, "Bird at Dawn" was truly outstanding.

Inventive creativity can be manifested in a variety of ways: through the traditional channels of artistic expression—literature, drama, painting, sculpture, music, dance, and so forth; through mechanical channels, such as carpentry, electrical work, machinery manipulation, and the like; through social channels such as group leadership, helping, understanding, or providing spontaneous entertainment for others; and in the purely ideational realm as exhibited in discussion or writing. Often a pupil's inventive potentialities are revealed in ways not considered desirable by the teacher. For example, the pupil who is constantly disrupting the class with humorous remarks may be exhibiting a real talent for comedy which, if encouraged through more appropriate channels, might prove to be of considerable value both to the class and to the individual's further development. Similarly, the pupil who seems to have a strong but negative leadership influence on his fellow class members may have talents that an alert teacher can develop into those which are actually an aid to his role as teacher. Or, the absent-minded child who seems to be preoccupied with matters other than his classwork may be manipulating profound scientific or mathematical ideas. Even the child who seems to have difficulty expressing himself verbally may actually have an unusually good aptitude for imagery which careful attention and help from the teacher can develop into true literary talent. Many teachers who have worked with culturally deprived pupils have found inherent in their pupils' compositions a great deal of poetic imagination and vision; talent which might easily have been overlooked if the teachers had noticed only the children's limited vocabulary, poor grammar, and slang-ridden expression. Thus, the teacher should be prepared to meet positively even "negative" pupil behavior, on the chance that it might be symptomatic of true inventive creativity.

□ OVERCOMING SOME TEACHING BARRIERS

Ask any teacher whether or not he is truly satisfied with what he is doing and he will probably say, "Yes, reasonably so, but there are many things I know I should be doing, but don't seem able to do for one reason or another." Or he may admit that he does many things he knows he should not do, but, for one reason or another, he is unable to replace these methods with more suitable ones. One important reason that teachers are often unable to apply what are, in theory, good teaching methods is that, unconsciously, they are drawing on the same techniques that were used to teach them when they were school children. In many cases, the concrete perceptual experiences today's teachers had in observing their own teachers' classroom methods made a stronger impression on them than did some of the less concrete and verbal material they were explicitly asked to learn. Thus, they acquired a firm concept of the role of teacher, which now underlies their own teaching roles.

Fig. 2.16. / This reconstruction of Eli Whitney's cotton gin reflects careful and authoritative historical research. How does it compare with your own mental image of the machine you learned to associate verbally with Eli Whitney?

The inefficiency of some of these techniques was amply demonstrated during a teachers' meeting in which classroom methods were being evaluated. In order that the attending teachers themselves might benefit from concrete experience, the chairman utilized the role-playing technique, asking the group members to consider themselves pupils in an upper-grade social-studies class that was about to begin a unit on American inventors.

"Can any of you think of some great American inventors?" the chairman asked of his "class." The teachers came up with Edison, McCormick, Fulton, Bell, and Whitney, the last being the most frequently recalled name.

"Obviously, to most of you, Whitney is an outstanding inventor, so we'll begin our study with him," continued the chairman in his role of teacher. "What do you already know about Eli Whitney?"

The cotton gin was overwhelmingly the largest response; only two of the teachers credited Whitney with having formulated the principles which underlie mass production. The chairman next asked the group members to close their eyes and to indicate with their hands what they remembered to be the approximate size of this famous cotton gin, and to maintain this pose as they reopened their eyes and looked around them. When the teachers compared their own estimate of the cotton gin's size with those of the others in the group, they saw that the smallest estimate was about a foot wide, another was about two feet high, and one so big that the particular member's arms were not long enough to convey his idea of its proportions. The chairman then showed a two-minute film excerpt, in which the actual size of the cotton gin was revealed to be about 15 feet by 4 feet (Fig. 2.16).

"Let's consider the implications of this experiment," continued the chairman. "What are your reactions?"

"Most of us were way off," volunteered one "pupil."

"Yet you all studied Eli Whitney and his cotton gin in grade school, again in high-school courses, and perhaps even later in college courses. Surely you should have a fairly good memory of its size."

The teachers thought about this for a moment and then one volunteered, "But we never had a chance really to visualize it."

"What information sources did you recall just before you indicated the size of the cotton gin?" asked the chairman.

"Well, I remember reading about Eli Whitney, but my idea of the size of his invention was way off," said one teacher.

"I saw a drawing of it," said another, "but apparently I got a wrong impression."

The discussion continued on the efficiency of learning that stems solely from verbal description. The teachers agreed that verbalization is not sufficient to impart a true concept of unfamiliar objects, and that even pictures can leave much to be desired in imparting all the properties of an object. The chairman then led the discussion to one on the merits of similar verbal approaches in teaching such relatively abstract ideas as the social reasons for opening up the West, the events which led to the founding of the United Nations, and the "triggering" of the reaction in a critical mass of fissionable materials. The teachers duly admitted that written and oral media cannot, alone, do a genuine job of teaching these concepts.

"Getting back to Whitney," the chairman continued, "why did only two of you remember him for his major contribution—one of great significance to our country's social and economic progress—the formulation of mass-production principles?"

It is particularly worth noting that, while the teachers had obtained an incomplete understanding of the cotton gin, they had at least retained a firm association of Whitney with that invention—a relatively more concrete aspect of their learning than are the principles behind mass production. Although the latter contribution of Whitney is more important to our nation's history—and, presumably, due emphasis was laid on this aspect at the time the teachers studied it during their own school years—the teachers had remembered almost nothing about this relatively more abstract concept.

Recognizing the desirability of concrete experience in learning, many modern teachers complain that some of the most important aspects of their subject area simply don't lend themselves to concrete, perceptual experience. The social-studies teacher, for example, may say,

> I realize that no pupil can gain a true understanding of the far-away places we study from mere verbalized material, but I can't do much about taking my class to these places. Reading is too often the only medium through which I can provide experience with the peoples and culture of other lands. How can I provide concrete experience for understanding, for example, that the capital of Afghanistan is in the remote part of Asia and for centuries has been largely isolated from the outside world? Unless, of course, I take the whole class right to this city to look up at the high ridges of the Hindu Kush outlined against the horizon, so that the pupils can imagine for themselves the tremendous cultural isolation that these ridges have caused this city. I have a few pictures, but they don't help much. So I just do the best I can.

Or take the teacher who is trying to give his pupils a real conceptual understanding of the growth of plants: "We want to learn just how all this happens, but we can't watch things grow without watching 24 hours around the clock. There are many things in science that we can *only* talk about. We'll just have to do the best we can."

And the home-economics teacher reports:

> Too often I feel that we are just mixing the ingredients: We put in so much of this and so much of that, set the oven at the proper temperature, and presto —out comes the finished product. For a lot of youngsters this much information is satisfying enough, I suppose, but more and more children are becoming curious about *how* the transformation takes place. I do the best I can to explain the leavening process and the action of shortening upon starch granules, but I'm not really sure that what I see in my own mind is really being understood by the children. I guess there isn't too much I can do about it.

It is certainly true that traditional teaching techniques—use of the chalkboard and of pictures to supplement verbalizations—cannot be expected to do an ideal job of communicating to young minds such difficult phenomena as those described above. Even field trips and similar concrete measures do not suffice to impart effectively some kinds of information. But today many innovations have been made in instructional techniques, particularly in the audiovisual field, which can diminish or eliminate these barriers. Motion-picture films are available which, for example, actually show in acceleration the growth of plants. Ingenious animated analogs which illustrate atomic, chemical, and other physical processes are also available on film. Further three-dimensional slides and stereodisks can do a remarkably realistic job of putting the student right into the midst of some far-away locale. Records and tape-recorded transcriptions can bring into the classroom a variety of sounds which are otherwise distant in time and space. Television can bring history right to the pupils at the very time it is being made. In short, the physical environment—whether it is too big, too small, too fast, or too slow for the ordinary senses—can be perceptually demonstrated for today's pupils, and concrete knowledge of the world can be imparted to even the smallest class in the remotest school in the country at the exact moment of need merely by the flick of a switch.

As the science and technology of modern times progress at an increasingly accelerated pace, the world for which we are purporting to prepare our young becomes increasingly varied and complex. If we fail to keep reasonable pace with this exploding knowledge in teaching young minds, we shall surely fail to prepare them for adult life in this world; and if our future adults are ill-prepared, we cannot hope to guarantee the civilization which we are attempting to build today. Yet, unless we provide the necessary concrete conceptual foundations, we cannot hope that these ultimate teaching purposes will be realized. Thus, we turn next to the techniques by which we can provide concrete learning experiences, concept-building experience, and the use of these in creative thought and action.

□ SUMMARY

Volumes have been written on learning psychology, but room permits mention of only a few basic tenets which relate to how learning is effectively communicated in the classroom. Among these are:

1. Learning stems from perceptual—that is concrete—experience.
2. Subject content and the media used to impart it must be suitable to the learner.
3. Creativity is the highest goal of learning.

In applying these principles, the teacher assumes several responsibilities: He must continuingly be aware of the level of conceptual attainment which the learner has acquired; he must choose materials that, while challenging the pupil, will not be in conflict with the pupil's threshold of conceptual ability; he must select the kinds of concrete learning experiences which will be best suited to the needs and levels of the pupil's interests and abilities; and finally, he must select the media which will best provide these learning experiences.

The basis of all understanding, thinking, and attitude formation is found in real experience. In a world which is daily becoming more complex because of the growing interrelationships of man, the school pupil needs to know more and more about his entire environment. Because in this complex world the learner is unable to have a wide range of firsthand or real experience, the problem of the teacher becomes complicated. These difficulties diminish considerably, however, with the proper use of appropriate audiovisual media.

The responsibility for providing firsthand experiences which lead to true understanding affects all areas of the curriculum at all levels of instruction. The goal of learning is to advance up the concrete-to-abstract ladder of conceptualization and understanding as rapidly as is possible through the means of appropriate firsthand, or simulated firsthand, experience. Through these, the pupil will be enabled to rely more heavily on verbal and symbolic means of learning.

The ultimate goal of instruction and learning, however, is to bring students as rapidly and as interestedly as possible toward creativity: creative involvement in the continuing search for information, interrelationships, and solutions to the problems of current and future living; and wherever at all possible, creative inventiveness. Those who seek to teach creatively and to guide students to creative behavior must recognize that before a learner can be asked to express himself through any medium—art, language skills or reading, speaking or writing, he has to have many firsthand or simulated objective experiences through which to gain useful understandings and conceptualizations. The learner who has many of these background concepts and understandings is more likely to succeed in creative expression, because he has the tools with which to work. This goal may be achieved through the careful selection and work-study use of such educational media as will be described in the following chapters.

☐ Suggested Activities

1. Read the following description of an aardvark:

> The body is stout, with arched back; the limbs are short and stout, armed with strong, blunt claws; the ears long; and the tail thick at the base and tapering gradually. The elongated head is set on a short thick neck, and at the extremity of the snout is a disc in which the nostrils open. The mouth is small and tubular, furnished with a long extensile tongue. A large individual measured 6 ft., 8 in. In color it is pale sandy or yellow, the hair being scanty and allowing the skin to show.[7]

Now ask your students to sketch their visualization of this description. Examine the sketches for evidences of differing background experiences. Compare them with those produced by a staff of professional artists (see Fig. 2.2). What generalizations do you arrive at which relate to the universal nature of learning problems?

2. Arrange a role-playing situation similar to that described on page 67. Ask the members of the group to indicate the size of a seahorse or some other object, as they remember it. Use an excerpt from a film comparable to that from Eli Whitney.

3. Examine the learning objectives listed in a typical unit of work in a course of study in a subject area in which you are interested. (As an alternative, analyze some of the study questions at the end of a typical chapter from a textbook.) State the background perceptual experiences a learner must have in order to respond intelligently to the activity in question.

[7] "Aardvark," *Encyclopaedia Britannica*, Vol. I, p. 4.

4. Arrange to view a 16 mm. sound motion-picture teaching film. Select a film you are interested in (see Bibliography: Films). Before seeing the film, list not more than a half dozen impressions or understandings you have about the subject. After you have seen the film, make a list of specific new understandings or changes in attitude that you experienced as a result of viewing it. What generalization can you make about the teacher's responsibility to provide audiovisual readiness experiences not only in film form but through other audiovisual devices?

5. Interview a primary-grade reading teacher, and ask the following questions:
   a. What readiness activities do you help children engage in before attempting beginning reading?
   b. What is the relationship of readiness activity to success in reading?
   c. Are home backgrounds (presence of good books in the home, family travel, family group conversation) reflected in children's reading success? Report your interview to your classmates. What conclusions do you have? Conduct similar interviews with teachers of art, social studies, etc. Formulate similar but appropriate questions for your interviews.

☐ Bibliography

Allport, Gordon W., *Attitudes: A Handbook of Social Psychology,* Clark Univ. Press, 1935.
"Aard-vark," *Encyclopaedia Britannica,* 1962, Vol. I, p. 4.
Kingsley, Howard L., *The Nature and Conditions of Learning,* Prentice-Hall, 1947.
Klausmeier, Herbert J., *Learning and Human Abilities: Educational Psychology,* Harper & Row, 1961.
Klausmeier, Herbert J., and Dresden, Katharine, *Teaching in the Elementary School* (2nd ed.), Harper & Row (in press).
Taylor, Irving, "The Nature of the Creative Process," in Paul Smith (Ed.), *Creativity: An Examination of the Creative Process,* Hastings House, 1959.

☐ Films

Benjamin Franklin, 16 mm., B&W, 18 min., Encyclopaedia Britannica Films.
Desert Nomads, 16 mm., B&W, 22 min., United World Films.
Eli Whitney, 16 mm., B&W, 18 min., Encyclopaedia Britannica Films.
Farmers of India, 16 mm., B&W, 22 min., United World Films.
Republic of the Philippines, 16 mm., Color, 18 min., United World Films.
West Germany—The Southern Uplands, 16 mm., Color, 18 min., United World Films.

III | THE

B = Base

Area of a t

½ Base

CHALKBOARD

The chalkboard—or blackboard as it was long called—is so much a part of classrooms that it has become a symbol for education itself. Even in this modern space age, the chalkboard continues to be a basic means of presenting subject matter. A chalkboard is almost always at hand during a class; yet how many of us are guilty of overlooking its possibilities as a sure, quick, and easily accessible means of demonstrating important ideas—particularly those which arise during discussion and virtually demand visualization for complete understanding?

Teachers can use the chalkboard more effectively as they understand more completely its characteristics, flexibility, and the opportunities it presents for efficient instruction. Although the chalkboard is old, very often it is the best means for presenting concepts which are as new as today's scientific discoveries. Many concepts are so new that about the only means available for presenting them is the chalkboard.

☐ THE ROLE OF THE CHALKBOARD IN INSTRUCTION

Chalkboards have long been used in the primary grades for experience stories which the children themselves dictate and the teacher prints; this use continues, for it is still valuable. In the intermediate grades, the teacher who introduces a new unit of study by writing interesting questions on the chalkboard usually captures the imagination of his pupils and channels their interest toward the new unit. As the lessons continue, the chalkboard is useful for listing the references to be consulted and any further questions posed by the class, and for summarizing work that has been completed.

A combination of chalkboard techniques, including the use of color, is valuable in teaching arithmetic and mathematics at various levels, as, for example, in explaining division of whole numbers in the primary grades, and algebraic division at the secondary level. The magnetic chalkboard enables the teacher to describe quickly the theory behind equations having to do with areas, perimeters, and circumferences, or the plotting of algebraic equations in graphic

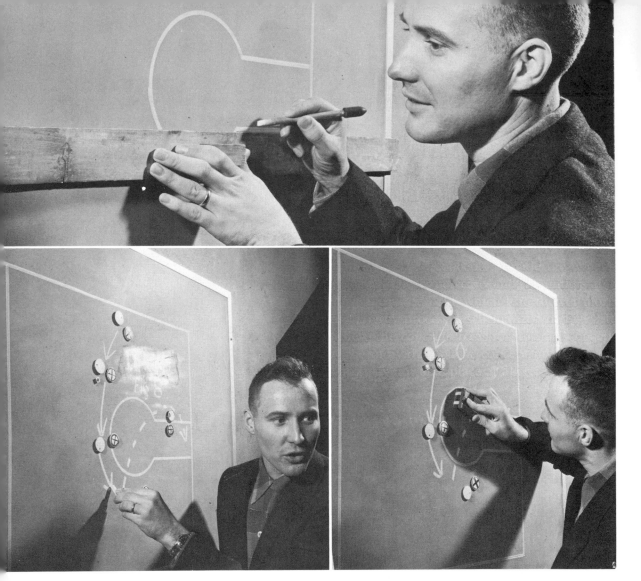

Fig. 3.1. / The steel-porcelain magnetic chalkboard. The "permanent" basketball court is drawn with chalkboard pen and ink, magnet-held player symbols can be slid quickly from place to place, and unwanted chalk marks can be erased easily. The permanent diagram itself can be removed with carbon tetrachloride or other solvent.

form. The hidden-chalkboard technique is valuable in time drills on recognition of arithmetic information and on spelling and vocabulary.

The athletic coach may use a chalkboard and permanent ink to lay out the basic floor plan for a game—for example, basketball as shown in Fig. 3.1. The coach can use one set of symbols to represent the players on a team, another set to show playing strategy. Colored chalk enables him to differentiate between offensive and defensive plays, directions, and action sequences. Perhaps he will use white chalk for key suggestions regarding strategy. By screening part of the chalkboard with an ordinary window shade or a drape, he can test the players' speed of reaction to typical situations that usually arise during a game. A chalk-board enables the coach to help the players realize actual game situations which can be discussed at length later.

An extremely recent development in chalkboards is the white chalkboard. Using soap-base, colored chalk, the teacher has a realistic means of visualizing color effects in art work, interior decoration, and home-economics courses in such fields as costuming and dress design.

As the teacher increases his knowledge of the variety of chalkboard materials and techniques available today, he will wish to experiment with their inter-related use. The uses to which these techniques may be put as a means of illus-trating, supplementing, clarifying, and outlining classroom procedures are as varied as the subject-matter responsibilities and grade levels of the modern school. At one extreme may be the visualization that tells a complete story and may become the core activity around which an entire discussion may revolve. An exploded drawing, for example, which shows the piece-by-piece structure of, say, a modern aircraft, may become the focal point of attention as the junior-high-school teacher explains the structural functions and parts, and relates each to the specific vocabulary the students are to learn from the discussion. At the other extreme, the chalkboard may be used merely for presenting in writing the key words and phrases of the unit under discussion, for the outlined notes of the lesson, or for various diagrams and pictorial representations of the subject matter.

Although many of these uses are familiar to all of us, the teacher should not take too much for granted the standard uses of the chalkboard to which he himself has been exposed since his own earliest school days. Effective use of the chalkboard—even for the simplest of learning experiences—requires thoughtful consideration and creativity. The advertiser who makes use of chalkboard dia-grams to convey his commercial message quickly on television has carefully thought out not only the message itself and its potential value to the viewer, but also how best to present this message so that its value will be efficiently com-municated to the viewer in the shortest possible time. So also may the teacher use chalkboard diagrams. Having described—perhaps unsuccessfully—a concept through verbal means, reference to a quickly sketched or previously prepared chalkboard diagram may clarify the point. The slovenly posture habits of the typing class, for example, may be improved by creative and amusing use of stick-figure diagrams which focus attention on the key lines of the back, arms, and hands to remind students how to sit and how not to sit. The home-economics teacher may use similar figures to show the correct posture for lifting a case of canned goods from the floor to the table top, or the primary teacher may use such sketches to dramatize to her class what can happen if they should stand too close to the swings and other playground equipment in motion. Proper use of playground facilities can effectively be communicated with such diagrams.

Lest teachers and pupils grow weary of endless and tediously similar pupil reports, these reports can be brought alive when students are encouraged to prepare lively chalkboard presentations in advance, in which diagrams and pictorial representations clarify the key ideas. Both teachers and pupils should use the chalkboard when it is the quickest, most effective way to visualize for understanding. For example, chalkboard lines, symbols, and visualizations can be used to clarify the effect of temperature and time on the growth of bacteria; the principle of osmosis when liquids pass through the membrane of an egg; or the evening reversal of land and sea breezes. For more difficult and complex visualizations, the opaque projector may be used to project newspaper or maga-zine diagrams which schematize scientific, social-studies, or mathematical princi-

ples. As we shall see later, projecting such images and tracing their key lines in chalk may be the means of evoking interest and understanding where words alone may fail.

While the teacher should lead the way by using the chalkboard whenever the need arises, he should do so in such ways that his students will be encouraged to do likewise. In other words, the teacher should not monopolize the chalkboard as his own communication medium, but should let it be fully understood that the chalkboard is the joint property of the entire class and its members. In this way, the two-way communication channel described in Chapter I will be maintained; in this way also, pupil care and responsibility for the chalkboard will result.

A teacher who fails to use the chalkboard correctly may frustrate classroom communications. For example, one teacher asked an upper-grade student to work out a rather complex mathematical problem on the chalkboard. The pupil did so—endlessly. Space quickly ran out and the pupil's writing became smaller and more and more cramped. Finally, the answer itself had to be squeezed into a small space remaining at the lower corner of the board.

"Now do you see?" the teacher asked of the rest of the class. Of course they didn't! Only those seated in the front of the room, and who had also had the energy to follow the tedious explanation, "saw." In this case, the teacher should have helped the class and the demonstrating pupil to select out of the scramble the key operations in the example, and had the pupil rewrite these operations clearly and neatly on the board. Here was a good opportunity for class participation and two-way communications which went overlooked.

It should be noted here that, while most teachers make regular use of the chalkboard in their own classrooms, there are some who are reticent about using it. Such explanations as, "I don't use the chalkboard very much because I never

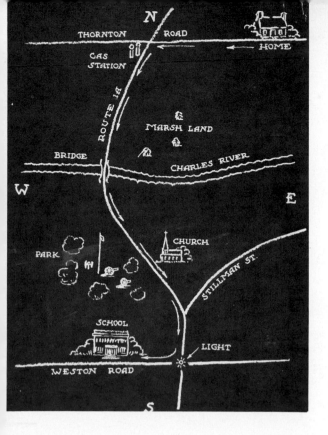

Fig. 3.2. / The chalkboard is used to summarize experiences—when it is used with charts and models, the chalkboard heightens interest, and it is an excellent tool with which to begin map understanding.

could draw a straight line," or, "The chalkboard takes so much time and I don't like to interrupt class discussion to use it," are usually given by these teachers No longer should we tolerate these as valid reasons for neglecting to use the chalkboard. There are available today many tools and drawing aids which enable most individuals to make clear chalkboard presentations, and a well-planned lesson will help to prevent much time-consuming and superfluous material from being included in chalkboard presentations.

On the other hand, teachers should not overuse the chalkboard as a communication medium. As pointed out in an earlier chapter, classroom communications media should be varied to make learning experiences interesting and meaningful. In today's classroom, one must use supplementary chalkboard visualizations when they are needed; one must also dare to interrupt classroom discussions and other presentations which are confusing to the students to clarify with chalkboard demonstrations.

The chalkboard may, and often should be, used in relation to other teaching materials—such as models, experience charts, and flash cards—all of which ultimately create an understanding of the relationships of, and the concepts which underlie, the symbols used in teaching, and of the objects for which these symbols stand (Fig. 3.2). For example, the chalkboard can become an accessible medium for tabulating community geographical features in symbolic form.

Let us summarize some of the advantages of using a chalkboard in the learning process:

1. The chalkboard can become an integral and valuable part of pupil-teacher planning.
2. The chalkboard is useful in recording progress by documenting trial-and-error approaches to subject-matter responsibilities.

78

3. The chalkboard makes possible quick change and rearrangement, both valuable in documenting and developing ideas.

4. The chalkboard may become the medium through which group projects are worked out. Group projects in the social studies, art, arithmetic, nature study, history, and in other subjects can be planned, illustrated, and summarized by means of chalkboard techniques.

☐ TYPES OF MODERN CHALKBOARDS

The chalkboard today has many forms. It varies from the smooth flat surface of quarried slate—still used in many older schools—to the pastel-colored, dull-surface chalkboards which fit beautifully into the general decoration scheme of the modern classroom. Between these extremes, there are dull-finish plastic, moss-surfaced glass, paint-coated plywood or presswood, and vitreous-coated steel chalkboards. These last provide magnetic adhering properties in addition to the traditional properties of chalkboards in general.

In the usual classroom, a minimum of 16 to 20 linear feet of chalkboard space is needed. In classroom situations that call for specialized uses of chalkboard, suitable adjustments in terms of size and position in relationship to viewers may call for special installations. However, in order to take full advantage of the chalkboard as an integral part of classroom teaching you should know the following characteristics of an effective chalkboard:

1. It provides maximum contrast between background and line drawings or printed symbols. In short, the surface "holds" a good chalk image.

2. It eliminates glare. Glare is a common problem with the traditional smooth-ground surface or with surfaces that are poorly maintained.

3. It can easily be erased or cleaned without leaving "ghosts" or smudges. This is true of both white and colored chalk.

4. It is colored to blend with the interior of the room, but at the same time it must be efficient in terms of visual presentation. Effective chalkboards are available in pastel green, or yellow, or in black.

5. It is mounted so as to be within easy arm's reach of the pupils. Its positioning should vary, depending on the age of the students using it.

Any device employed for the communication of information in the classroom should reflect modern trends in classroom architecture and design. As with most classroom media, chalkboard communication requires that the visual lines and symbols be visible to all students. Since visibility depends on contrast, dark-colored chalks on white boards may be used as effectively as the traditional white-chalk-on-black-board arrangement. White boards produce a more pleasing environment than do wall surfaces which are monotonously covered by aging or

Fig. 3.4. / A high-school vocational agriculture teacher provided students with the opportunity to test their knowledge of the skeletal and anatomical arrangements of cattle and dairy animals, by designing this portable chalkboard which is shaped like the animal.

unattractive black chalkboards (Fig. 3.3). Consider also the aesthetic value of pastel-green boards on which contrasting yellow or white chalk produces images of high visibility and recognition. The basic property which must be present in all chalkboard surfaces—white, pastel, or black—is the ability of the surface to hold chalk particles in such a manner as to produce sharply definable images which can be seen clearly by students.

While most chalkboard surfaces are stationary as far as their position in the classroom is concerned, teachers should encourage the use of portable chalk-board surfaces. Chalkboards are available in thin, relatively light-weight panels which can be moved easily about the room. A vocational-agriculture teacher found it desirable to cut his own chalkboard panel in the shape of a cow (Fig. 3.4). On the surface of this portable section, he could describe the animal's anatomy, intake of food, the digestion process, the cut of its meat, and so forth. Similarly, a history teacher fabricated his own portable magnetic board into an outline map of the United States which permitted him to display important

Fig. 3.5. / (Left) The magnetic chalkboard opens up a host of new ideas. Any three-dimensional, lightweight objects can be mounted with adhesive on small magnets for use on steel chalkboards. The interaction of words and symbols and movable type or three-dimensional objects can result in high learning outcomes. How can you apply these ideas to your work?

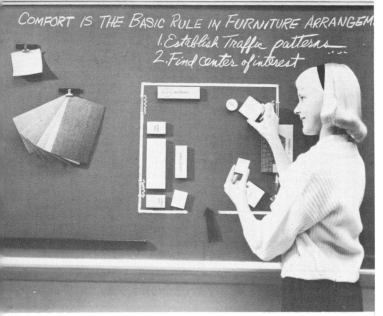

Fig. 3.6. / (Above) The chalk liner serves well to inscribe guidelines quickly. This liner is made from taped-together cardboard.

geographical symbols and names as he explained the westward-expansion period in American History. This board also had the advantage of being readily movable from classroom to classroom.

Ordinarily, the classroom offers good or adequate chalkboard surfaces; but, if—on the basis of the information offered in this chapter—the teacher feels that the quality of classroom work can be improved with better chalkboard surfaces, portable chalkboards, or other chalkboard facilities, the teacher himself must use the initiative in seeking them. The quickest way to proceed is to sketch suggestions as to what is needed and bring them to the attention of the school supervisors or administrators.

■ THE MAGNETIC CHALKBOARD

The magnetic chalkboard is a recent development in classroom equipment which has all the advantages and uses of more traditional types of chalkboard and, at the same time, permits the use of two- and three-dimensional materials which adhere to and can readily be moved on the surface of the chalkboard by means of miniature magnets affixed to the materials (Fig. 3.5).

The surface of a magnetic chalkboard is composed of fine-textured, almost indestructible, permanently colored particles of vitreous material which takes white or colored chalk impressions evenly and visibly. The porcelain-like surface can be washed or gently scoured to remove semipermanent chalkboard ink, colored chalk "ghosts," and adhesive materials. The undersurface of the board is steel, which makes it possible to use magnets attached to two- or three-dimensional materials.

The steel chalkboard, adhesives, magnets, etc., are tools with which imaginative teachers and pupils can create fascinating and highly useful aids to the realization of learning goals. The English teacher can quickly alter the position of word roots, prefixes, suffixes, and stems to indicate the derivation of words. The chemistry teacher can rearrange the symbols of molecular structure, the parts of a chemical equation, or the numerical values ascribed to parts of a formula, all within a matter of seconds. By using magnets attached to objects or cards and moving these about on the surface of a steel or "magnetic" chalkboard, the home-economics teacher can visualize the relationship of floor plans to living efficiency; the primary teacher can introduce high interest—even excitement —among pupils as they manipulate magnetic, mounted word-cards into a "story experience"; and arithmetic pupils can arrange number-set relationships with speed and freedom from the fumbling that often accompanies traditional situations.[1]

□ IMPROVING CHALKBOARD USE

Like the architect who uses accurate lines and correct angles to describe his plans, the classroom teacher must learn to create concise and dependable chalk-

---

[1] Herbert Scuorzo describes some interesting uses of the magnetic chalkboard in "Meet the Magnetic Chalkboard," *The Grade Teacher* (September, 1961), 79:44–45.

board visualizations to illustrate his meaning. A reasonable variety of simple chalkboard devices are available to help him do this: a chalkboard straightedge that is from 4 to 5 feet in length and cut from plywood, masonite, or heavy cardboard; a chalkboard T-square, that is about 4 feet long and large enough to slide easily along the chalkboard molding or railing; and a variety of templates, protractors, and pounce patterns such as will be described later.

■ LETTERING

The primary purpose of the chalkboard is to communicate ideas; hence good lettering techniques are essential. These may include cursive writing, printing, and carefully blocked-out words and phrases.

Like the expert draftsman, the teacher should not proceed until he has laid out a general plan of work. The use of guidelines gives cursive writing and lettering uniform size and insures that they will be easily read. To make sure that the lettering is visible to children even at the rear of the classroom, the letters should be at least 2½ inches in height or, preferably, 3 inches.

Printing usually is more legible than cursive writing. Although one would suppose that cursive writing is much more rapidly accomplished than printing, reasonable practice with simple block letters gives speed in printing. Although the letters may appear unusually large to the person who is writing them, a walk to the rear of the seating area will reveal that they are of comfortable size for reading and understanding.

Depending on the teacher's ability, there are several quick ways of providing guidelines and spaces needed for lettering:

1. Guidelines may be made with a T-square. Rest the base of the T-square against either the left or the right edge of the board and move the instrument up and down, drawing lines where needed.
2. A simple music-staff liner may be used for horizontal lines. Removing the center chalk from the liner provides space for the main body of the letters.
3. A cardboard liner like that shown in Fig. 3.6 can be made quickly and easily by putting a single crease in a stiff piece of cardboard and holding the two edges together with staples or masking tape applied at regularly spaced intervals. The cardboard between the staples or tape is squeezed open, and pieces of chalk are inserted for drawing parallel lines that will accommodate the lettering.

In the primary and intermediate grades, regular amounts of time are spent on penmanship and the correct manner of handling pencils, pen, and ink. Similarly, some time should be spent in learning to handle chalk, for there is a correct way of using it. A few practice strokes will help you to use it effectively.

■ THE PROJECT-ON, CHALK-ON METHOD

The *project-on method* is ideal for presenting needed visualizations in science, social studies, and language arts to the class. Newspaper and magazine pictures

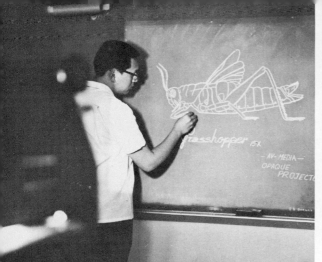

Fig. 3.7. / A diagram can be projected by means of an opaque projector and the key lines are sketched in, or a filmstrip-projected image can be used as a guide for tracing. Under what conditions is the use of a projector to produce a chalkboard image more valuable than the image that is directly projected onto a screen?

and diagrams can quickly be re-created on the chalkboard by cutting them out, placing them on the platform of an opaque projector (see Chapter XII), and moving the projector as necessary to focus an image of the desired size on the chalkboard. The teacher can then chalk on or trace over the key lines in the projected image, thus quickly transferring to the chalkboard the basic idea of the projected material. He may experiment in a darkened classroom to discover how best to place the projector and to sharpen the focus.

A variation of this method is achieved by using specially produced outline maps some of which are available in filmstrip form (Fig. 3.7).[2] A social-studies teacher modified this procedure. He arranged before class to trace on lightly the guidelines to such projected maps; then, during class time, he would chalk over these barely visible lines to produce quickly and surely chalk images that were models of clarity and visual understanding.

■ THE PATTERN METHOD

The *pattern technique*—sometimes called the "punch" or "pounce" system—is well suited for basic visualizations that are needed frequently. The mathematics teacher who is confronted again and again with the problem of explaining line graphs finds this technique of great assistance, as does the music teacher who wants to illustrate note-reading techniques. The pattern technique is also helpful to the geometry teacher who needs to use repeatedly various types of triangles, rectangles, and parallelograms, and to the social-studies teacher who refers constantly to outline maps of county, state, or continent.

Suppose that an intermediate-grade teacher frequently refers to an outline map of her state. Therefore, she wants to devise some means of quickly putting this map on the chalkboard. She is not content with guesswork or with the wobbly map produced by freehand sketching. As the first step, she carefully draws the outline of the state on a piece of heavy tracing paper. Then, with a

2 *Basic U.S. Projecto Maps,* filmstrip series, B&W, Encyclopaedia Britannica Films.

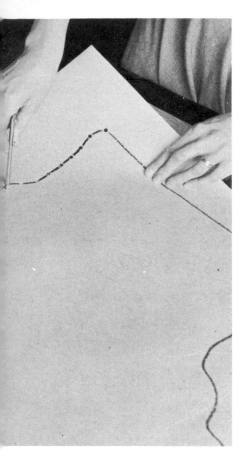

Fig. 3.9. / (1) Punch the holes about an inch apart; (2) hold the pattern firm; (3) check the line before removing the pattern; and (4) connect the dotted outline.

Fig. 3.8. / Making the pattern.

leather-worker's punch $\frac{1}{8}$ or $\frac{3}{16}$ inch in diameter, she perforates the outline at approximately 1-inch intervals, or closer if the detail of the contours is more complex (Fig. 3.8). Experimentation will indicate how close the holes should be. The distance may vary from $\frac{1}{4}$ inch to 1 inch, depending on the nature of the drawing.

When the complete drawing has been punched out, the teacher holds the pattern against the chalkboard and rubs a dusty eraser firmly across the perforated section of the outline.[3] Thus, an outline of chalk dots appears where the perforations in the pattern were. The teacher then connects the dots—by free-hand—with chalk. The entire procedure is shown in Fig. 3.9.

Patterns that are used repeatedly may be mounted on window-shade rollers and filed in an orderly way. They are thus available for use at a moment's notice and they can be suspended easily from hooks along the top of the chalkboard rail.[4]

■ THE TEMPLATE METHOD

The *template* is another device for drawing on those chalkboard diagrams,

---

[3] The eraser should be rubbed back and forth across the perforations, not patted.

[4] Commercial patterns are now available for such subject areas as mathematics and geography. Inquiries may be made of Corbett Blackboard Stencils, 548 Third Ave., North Pelham, N.Y.

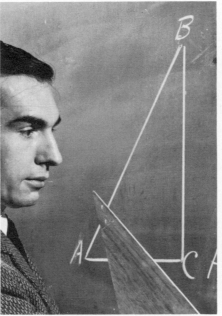
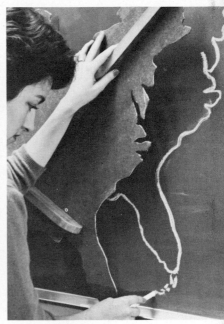

Fig. 3.10. / A clothing pattern is produced accurately by means of a template. In mathematics, templates guarantee accuracy even in quickly sketched figures for theorems, and the social-studies teacher may use templates when accuracy of intricate chalkboard visualizations is needed. In addition to those shown, what ideas for the use of templates do you have?

symbols, and designs which must be accurate and exact, or which need to be drawn repeatedly.

Chalkboard templates may be made of any thin, stiff, lightweight materials—sheet metal, heavy cardboard, plywood, or masonite. The design should be drawn on the materials and then cut out (if possible, cut out a handle, too); the template is then ready for use. The template is held against the board with one hand and is outlined on the board with chalk. Pupils, teachers, and custodians may make templates as the need for them arises. When not in use, they can be hung from hooks attached to the under side of the chalk rails. Templates in use are shown in Fig. 3.10.

■ THE GRID METHOD

The grid technique for chalkboard illustrations is within the grasp of every teacher. The illustration or original drawing may be on any ordinary size of paper, from 3 × 5 inches to 8½ × 11 inches. It is blocked off into squares which may be ½ or ¾ inch, 1 inch, or even larger. Smaller squares are necessary if the original has much detail. The less complex the drawing, the larger the squares may be. The chalkboard is marked off in larger squares which correspond to those on the original. In transferring the drawing to the chalkboard, the teacher

Fig. 3.11. / The grid method can be used to enlarge easily a small diagram.

Fig. 3.12. / The use of the hidden chalkboard allows the teacher to reveal only those portions of the previously prepared complete sequence of illustrations which are most useful to the discussion at the moment. Ordinary wrapping-paper panels may be used to hide given areas of the chalkboard, and these panels are held in place by map rail "pinch clamps."

duplicates the original, one square at a time (Fig. 3.11). Contrary to popular belief, the grid technique is amazingly rapid. A few practice sessions will give the teacher surprising facility in its use.[5]

■ THE HIDDEN-DRAWING METHOD

The *hidden-drawing* technique is a unique way of coordinating demonstration and explanation, by either pupil or teacher, in practically any subject area. By preparing in advance a series of sequential or developmental illustrations, the teacher can describe and expose one illustration at a time. In this way, atten-

[5] The grid method is demonstrated well in the film *Chalkboard Utilization*, 16 mm., B&W, 15 min., Young America Films.

Fig. 3.13. / The cartoon technique applied to pupil-developed safety rules and regulations and to junior-high-school club activities.

tion is focused on the explanation that accompanies the exposed drawing and the sequence can be maintained, since of necessity all eyes are on the chalkboard. Stretching a wire along the top of the chalkboard and hanging inexpensive cloth from it, rolling down a map with reverse side exposed, or punching 30- × 40-inch panels of ordinary wrapping paper into chalkboard rail hangers (see Fig. 3.12) makes the hidden-drawing technique a reality in the classroom.

Using the grid method, one teacher drew a series of air-foil types on the chalkboard. By pulling away the punched-fastened paper panels, each step in the air-foil design was revealed and made the center of visual attention in turn and one at a time as the discussion continued.

In another situation, a teacher planned, drew, and—at the proper time during

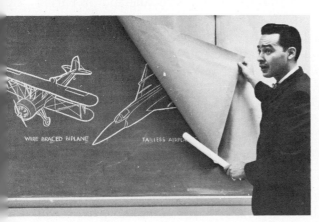
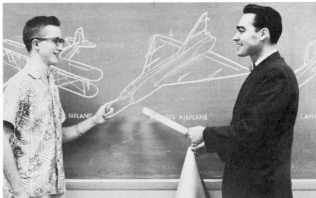

class—revealed the sequential steps in the amoeba's food-getting movements.

In still another class, a physiology teacher discussed the interrelationships of musculature, skeletal structure, and use of protective sports equipment through the hidden-drawing technique.

■ THE COMIC APPROACH

In this day of graphic news and the magazine illustrations, both pupils and teachers are well acquainted with cartoon techniques. Examination of popular cartoons will reveal that not all cartoonists are artists. Many cartoons are rudimentary visualizations in which simple lines are used to outline objects.

The use of this technique applied to the classroom chalkboard is shown in Fig. 3.13. You can draw this well or better; try it. Apply the cartoon approach to

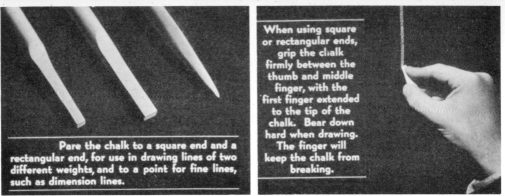

Fig. 3.14. / Proper handling and use of the chalk is important to obtaining clarity and variety in chalkboard presentations. Shaved chalk produces different variations in lines.

some situation you wish to describe to the class—for example, to announce an event or to remind them about the care of their desks, the schoolroom, or their personal belongings. Soon you will develop a visual-cartoon "vocabulary" of simple line drawings which anyone can use to add interest, fun, and clear-cut visualization to chalkboard learning situations.

☐ CARE OF THE CHALKBOARD

An understanding of caring for the chalkboard and of selecting and preparing the chalk is essential to every teacher if he is to maintain his chalkboard in good condition and to acquire reasonable facility in creating chalkboard study opportunities. Although, in most classrooms, the building custodian cleans and cares for the chalkboard, the teacher should know how to keep it at its highest level of efficiency. Further, since a chalkboard's teaching efficiency depends largely on the effective use of chalk, we shall also consider the nature of chalk and some principles for its use.

■ THE SURFACE

A high-visibility chalkboard has a slightly abrasive surface made up of minute "teeth" and "cavities." It is this abrasive surface which holds the particles of chalk and which make the contrasting lines more easily seen.

Before using a chalkboard, remove all excess chalk powder and surface dust with an eraser of felt, sponge rubber, or chamois. A uniform, downward stroke of the eraser is best, for this knocks the chalk dust into the chalk rail; the rail should, of course, be cleaned regularly. If the eraser is felt, wipe the chalkboard again with a soft cloth or dry chamois skin to remove any chalk that may remain. Even a properly cleaned chalkboard has a chalky appearance, but this is not troublesome.

Avoid using oily rags or substance on any chalkboard surface. Chalk consists of a binder and English whiting; hence, chalk dust and oil produce a gluey emulsion which gradually fills up the cavities in the surface so that the chalkboard can no longer carry a well-defined chalk mark.[6]

Some chalkboards may need special care. Instructions accompanying several types of composition boards which are factory-surfaced with green pigment warn

[6] See Dave Smalley, "How Should Chalkboards Be Cleaned?" *American School Board Journal*, 1963, 147:345ff.

against using water or liquid cleaners. However, cleansing agents can be used periodically on the newest types. Some boards can be cleaned with mild abrasives without danger of wearing away the abrasive surface.

■ THE CHALK

As was said above, chalk is manufactured from a mixture of English whiting and a binder. High-quality chalk usually contains a higher percentage of this whiting than the poorer grades; thus, it is poor economy to buy chalk which may cost a few cents less per box, but which contains lesser amounts of whiting. The ingredients in some cheaper grades of chalk are themselves abrasives which slowly wear away the abrasive surface of the chalkboard. In general, a high-quality chalk which is neither crumbly nor extremely hard should be used.

The use of colored chalk should be encouraged for at least two reasons. Color is intrinsically both pleasing and interesting to students. More important, there are many cases in which meaning and understanding can be increased by means of color. Colored chalk is specially made for chalkboard use, and this chalk should not be confused with the colored chalk made for use on plastic-coated surfaces. A good quality of chalkboard chalk produces a vivid visual image and is easily erased; it does not leave unsightly smudges.

Just as pencils are sharpened to broad, sharp, blunt, or rounded ends, so should full-length pieces of chalk be prepared for specific tasks (Fig. 3.14). For harsh outline work, the chalk should first be scraped over coarse sandpaper to produce a blunt-angle surface on its end. For detailed shading or faint guide-lines, the chalk should be sharpened to half its original diameter. For shading, grasp the chalk so as to bring the longest surface against the chalkboard. Discard the last bit of chalk.

When a portion of the chalkboard visualization is to be used repeatedly, a semipermanent chalk may be prepared as follows:

1. Prepare a saturated sugar solution by stirring sufficient sugar into a cupful of cold water so that, after vigorous shaking or stirring, a small amount still remains on the bottom of the container.
2. Prepare a second solution consisting of one part of this sugar solution to three parts of cold water. Soak a few sticks of chalk in this solution. When the chalk no longer gives off bubbles (five to ten minutes), remove it and drain for a short time on paper toweling.
3. The treated chalk can be kept indefinitely by storing it in a tightly covered container, such as a peanut-butter jar.
4. Use the chalk like regular chalk, but it may crumble slightly more easily; hence, care is needed in using it. Lines made with this chalk can be removed from the chalkboard with a damp cloth. (See Source List, page 529, for chalkboard ink.)

□ EVALUATION OF CHALKBOARD USE

Since the orderly use of the chalkboard must at some time be evaluated in terms of the opportunities it affords for improved teaching, the suggestion is made here that after a chalkboard demonstration, explanation, or assignment, pupils and teachers join in discussing the effectiveness of that demonstration.

Basically, chalkboard teaching techniques are either good or ineffectual in terms of whether the use of the chalkboard contributed to higher levels of understanding, interest, and subject-matter accomplishment. For this reason, it is suggested that the following items be used by the teacher as at least one means of evaluating chalkboard use:

CHALKBOARD TECHNIQUES

1. Did our use of the chalkboard illustration help us in the work we are doing? Yes_____ No_____
2. Did the chalkboard information present a learning opportunity which was beyond that available with more accessible, more easily arranged materials? Yes_____ No_____
3. Did the whole class (where possible) help create the chalkboard display, each in terms of his own interest and ability? Yes_____ No_____

MECHANICS

1. Was the chalkboard display free of glare? Yes_____ No_____
2. Was the chalkboard display uncluttered, pleasing in appearance? Yes_____ No_____
3. Was it organized around the focal point of interest? Yes_____ No_____
4. Were titles neat, and headings, captions, and phrases meaningful and as brief as possible? Yes_____ No_____

☐ SUMMARY

The use of the chalkboard and chalkboard aids represents one of the oldest, yet most continuingly useful opportunities through which to clarify and explain visually many ideas which occur in the course of day-to-day teaching, or which become the basis for student explanations, reports, and descriptions. The chalkboard is one of the most accessible means for carrying on visual teaching. Carefully planned utilization of the chalkboard represents a starting point for instruction regardless of what other materials are available.

Many teachers feel that they must have artistic talent to use the chalkboard. This is not true! While the artistic teacher has a natural advantage, any teacher who is aware of basic chalkboard techniques and tools can use this means of instruction effectively.

The chalkboard lends itself to creative planning and ingenuity which is the basis of all creative and imaginative teaching. By being knowledgeable about basic chalkboard techniques, this means of visualizing and clarifying ideas can be used not only by teachers, but more important, by pupils who may employ the chalkboard to express their own creative reports, demonstrations, and explanations.

Among the various suggested chalkboard techniques, tools, and procedures are:

1. Suggestions for creating and/or using chalkboard space
2. Recommendations with reference to size of letters, proper spacing, use of guidelines, and printing to increase legibility
3. Suggestions on how to prepare and use patterns and templates when incor-

porating the use of outline maps, diagrams, scales, and other visualizations into instruction

4. Suggestions as to when and how to use opaque projection in transferring useful but hard to draw diagrams, charts, and pictures to the chalkboard

5. Use of the hidden-drawing techniques to add concreteness, imagination, and interest to chalkboard presentations

6. Procedures for mastering stick figures or cartoon techniques to dramatize and add interest to chalkboard presentations

7. Use of the magnetic chalkboard in creating mobility when explaining floor plans, layouts, mathematics or science relationships, team sports procedures, etc.

With reasonable knowledge of creative techniques, both the teacher and pupil can employ the chalkboard to visualize imaginatively and effectively innumerable learning experiences.

□ Suggested Activities

1. As you prepare lesson plans, sketch in chalkboard teaching ideas. Report on the success of these diagrams, graphs, or other pictorial explanatory devices after you have tried them out in practice teaching situations.

2. Demonstrate how to select and prepare a chalkboard panel for use in the classroom in which you meet to study visual instruction. Demonstrate your ability to handle problems of glare, size of lettering, care of chalkboard surface, erasing, freehand line and circle drawing, etc.

3. Show your ability to heighten interest in chalkboard illustration through your use of stick or cartoon figures.

4. Make a chalkboard ruler, compass, pattern, and template. Show how you will use them in connection with the subject you teach or will probably teach.

5. Using suitable graphic subject material, enlarge and transfer a small drawing or picture to a chalkboard by means of the grid method.

6. Discuss the problem of visibility. Include seating, angle, light sources, printing size, use of chalk, correct width and sharpness of chalk.

7. Discuss the use of color in chalkboard illustrations related to your special subject interest or responsibility.

8. Arrange to view the film, *Chalkboard Utilization* (16 mm., B&W, 16 min., McGraw-Hill). Discuss ways you can adapt to your own teaching use the various techniques and ideas in this film.

9. Prepare some semipermanent chalk. Follow the instructions as given on page 89, and test out your resulting chalk.

□ Bibliography

Grassell, Milton E., "Chalkboards in Action," *Educational Screen and Audiovisual Guide,* August, 1959, pp. 400–401.

Kable, L., "Chalkboard: Number One Visual Aid," *NEA Journal,* May, 1948, p. 306.

Kinder, James S., *Audio-Visual Materials and Techniques,* American Book, 1950.

Kleinschmidt, H. E., *How To Turn Ideas into Pictures,* Publicity Council for Health and Welfare Services, 1950.

Ramshaw, H. G., *Blackboard Work,* Oxford Univ. Press, 1955.

Scuorzo, Herbert, "Meet the Magnetic Chalkboard," *The Grade Teacher,* 79:44–45, September, 1961.

Smalley, Dave, "How Should Chalkboards Be Cleaned?" *American School Board Journal,* 1963, 147:345.

The Care and Cleaning of Chalkboards (pamphlet), Weber Costello Co., 1957, 12 pp.

IV

FLAT PICTURES

Pictures are sometimes referred to as a "universal language." Although this statement does not hold strictly true for people who have had little or no experience with pictures, such as tribesmen in remote areas of the world, it is generally true for our students and most others with whom we wish to communicate. Most people in the world are familiar with pictures and can understand them.

This does not suggest that everyone receives the same impressions or the same information from a picture even when he understands it. The ability to "read" pictures varies widely. Interpretations of pictures are influenced by the viewer's past experience with the picture content and by his own cultural and social backgrounds. Nevertheless, most pictures convey a much more real and concrete impression than do words. Nothing approaches the effectiveness of pictures as a communications medium that can overcome language and cultural barriers around the world.

It is becoming more common, fortunately, for students in the United States to learn another language in addition to English. But there are hundreds of languages in the world, and over 2000 distinct dialects. Hence, we need other means than verbal language to convey the lessons of freedom, health, and technical development to the people who speak these languages and dialects and to learn from them their way of life. In the sense that pictures provide this means, pictures can be considered a universal language. The universality of subject matter which can be portrayed in a photograph, illustration, or painting also makes the picture medium a universal language (Fig. 4.1). Only by learning much more than we now know about other peoples of the world can we help them and ourselves to maintain a free world. Pictures are thus an important medium for international education.

The communicative value of pictures for this purpose is well illustrated by a study made in Venezuela by the American International Association.[1] A wordless pamphlet (Fig. 4.2) consisting of 23 simple line drawings showing proper

[1] *Analysis of the Wordless Pamphlet on Corn Seed Selection,* American International Association, San Jose, Costa Rica, 1957.

Fig. 4.1. / These four pictures represent man's achievements on sea and land, in the sky and in space. What are your judgments about the value of each? Does their juxtaposition strengthen their message?

methods of selecting seed corn was distributed to 921 farmers in seven different zones of Venezuela. These farmers could not read or write and a number of different dialects were spoken in the seven zones. The customary techniques of mass communication were thus impossible. An initial survey was made to determine which methods of selecting corn seed similar to those presented in the pamphlet were already being used by these farmers. The farmers' understanding of each of the drawings in the pamphlet was then appraised before and after explanation by an agricultural agent. The survey showed that 42 percent of the farmers understood the pamphlet without further explanation, but that 90 percent understood it after explanation. Further, analysis by individual pictures indicated that, in six instances, better pictures would have improved the results. In several of these pictures, for example, many of the farmers did not understand the symbols used to represent the sun and rain (Fig. 4.3).

Two points are worthy of note here. The first is that even a simple and imperfect pictorial communications device can be effective in an inherently diffi-

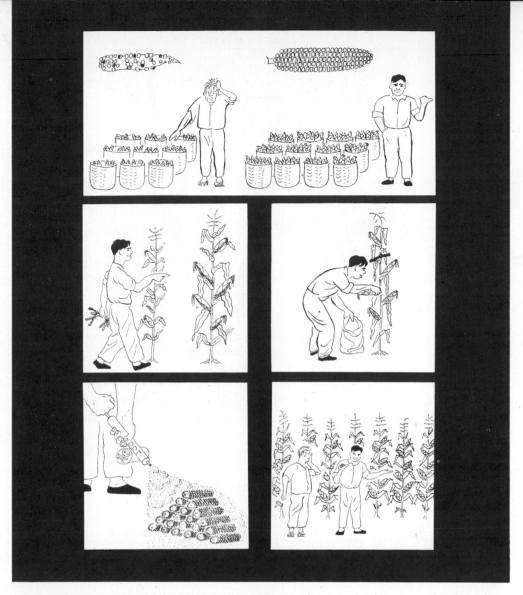

Fig. 4.2. / Five of the 23 scenes in a wordless pamphlet designed to improve seed corn selection by illiterate farmers in Venezuela.

Fig. 4.3. / Portions of the wordless pamphlet—for example, the symbols used for the sun and for rain—failed to communicate. How could they be improved?

Fig. 4.4. / Pictures can communicate visual facts rather readily. What does this picture do in addition?

cult communications setting without verbal interpretation of any kind. The second is that there is more than a 100 percent increase in the effectiveness of picture communication when verbal explanation is added. Seldom do we communicate effectively through a single channel even when conditions are favorable. Thus, words with pictures are usually better than either words or pictures alone. Similarly, combinations of appropriate visual and verbal materials are required for an effective job in many teaching tasks.

☐ THE VERSATILITY OF THE PICTURE MEDIUM

Pictures can do many things for us: they can arouse interest, stimulate discussion, raise questions, supply information and ideas, and otherwise contribute to learning. The picture is a form of communication that has certain attributes of its own. Like other communication media, films, television, slides, stereographs, and flat pictures can overcome time and distance by bringing historical scenes and far places visually into the classroom. The range of subject matter which can be presented through pictures is almost unlimited. For example, a junior-high-school class was discussing what the social-studies teacher calls a "projective" picture, namely, a picture which projects an emotional atmosphere or feeling.[2] The teacher used in this instance a picture showing a judge, a policeman, a boy, and a woman together in a courtroom (Fig. 4.4). After looking at it a minute or so, the students described the scene as one in which the boy is facing some kind of serious charge for a crime he has committed. Here are some of the students' interpretative comments:

"Nobody seemed interested in the boy or understood him. In fact, not many adults understand us."

"The mother isn't angry. Instead she's disappointed . . . disappointed in herself and her boy. She blames herself as much as she does her son."

2 Raymond H. Meussig, "Using Projective Pictures," *Education*, May, 1958, pp. 258–260.

"We have to have certain limits. Even though we call this a 'free country' we are talking about freedom with responsibility."

Thus, the simple scene depicted in the illustration was valuable in communicating a complex situation that might have lost a great deal in purely verbal expression, and presented the students with a challenge to their thinking. The students were able to identify with the characters as they interpreted them and with the various ideas suggested by the scene so that their interest and curiosity were stimulated.

In another classroom, a group of junior-high-school pupils was discussing the subject of advertising. The teacher placed one of a series of colorful soap advertisements in the opaque projector and the students gazed at it intently. "What have you noticed about each of these ads?" asked the teacher.

"They all have a good-looking girl in them," volunteered one student.

"Each calls itself the best or kindest to your skin," added another.

"They're all kind of attractive," another boy said.

"They all use words like 'best,' 'most suds,' 'creamy,' 'soft,' 'fluffy,' 'snowy,' 'pure,'" added a fourth pupil.

"It looks as if everyone tries to find the best picture they can think up so as to attract attention to their ad, and all use the same kind of descriptive words. It makes you wonder how can all be best—are they telling the truth?" another lad summed up.

In this case, pictures were useful to draw the students' attention to an aspect of their everyday environment which most of them had probably come to take for granted, and to stimulate their critical faculty with respect to heavy bombardment of commercial messages.

In still another instance, a primary reading class eagerly followed their teacher's story about birds migrating back from the southland. With the coming of spring, the pupils participated enthusiastically in planning a field trip to a nearby park to see some of the birds they had been reading about. As an additional stimulus, the teacher showed a film about robins and used a number of good pictures brought in by the pupils. As free "reading," she had several sets of colored stereographs showing many birds in their natural surroundings and in striking three-dimensional realism. *Robins, bluebirds, blackbirds, swallows, wrens*—these words came to have vivid meaning as pictures, stereographs, and firsthand experience with the birds gave the words meaning to the children. In short, ideas, leads, questions, suggestions for further activity, high group interest, and creative involvement—all are stimulated by the addition of a few pictures to a learning experience.

There are many forms of pictures. There are still pictures and motion pictures. Some pictures are projected by means of slides or transparencies; others, classified as "flat pictures," appear as opaque representations in books, magazines, and newspapers, in sets of study prints, or as drawings, paintings, or photographic prints. In order to discriminate between several important types of instructional materials involving pictures (films, television, graphics, slides and transparencies, etc.)—each of which has distinctive characteristics and requirements for use in teaching—we define flat pictures as *opaque representations of visual images,* as in a painting, drawing, or photograph.

Fig. 4.5. / A nebula as seen by the 48-in Schmidt telescope on Mount Wilson photographed by the 200-inch "Big Ey on Mount Palomar for detailed stu What other similar applications of flat tures does this suggest to you?

Although many of the characteristics of flat-picture communication apply to other types of pictorial presentation, it will be helpful to begin by considering flat pictures by themselves. Other types of pictorial presentations are discussed in later chapters of this book, where we shall see how some of these characteristics apply also to slides and filmstrips, motion pictures, television, and other visual forms.

In Fig. 4.1 we saw a small sampling of the many types of subjects which flat pictures can represent. Like other visual media, flat pictures can enlarge or reduce scenes that cannot otherwise be seen by the unaided eye. But in addition, they have certain distinct advantages of their own.

☐ ADVANTAGES OF THE FLAT PICTURE

Both practically and psychologically, flat pictures have many advantages for teacher and students alike. Their ready availability in large numbers at little cost, for example, is an advantage. Pictures cover an infinite variety of subjects. Almost anything we can see can be pictured. Good pictures also attract attention, arouse interest, and clarify meanings. In short, pictures communicate. We now examine some of the concepts involved in communication by pictures.

Fig. 4.6. / A shaven-headed priest watches a government worker spray temple walls in a highly effective malaria-control campaign in Thailand. The priest's comment: "Science and religion are one when they work for the good life."

■ LOW-COST AVAILABILITY

Pictures are all around us in books, magazines, and newspapers. The many sources and vast numbers of pictures available at little or no cost is a significant practical advantage to teachers with limited funds for instructional materials. Teachers in poor school districts can and do have excellent picture files of their own. This is a valuable resource for all teachers regardless of the extent to which other materials may be available to them. Furthermore, fine sets of carefully selected study prints can be purchased. These sets are based upon representative curriculum units and include manuals, descriptive information about each picture, and related instructional materials (see Source List, page 530 for both free and commercial sources of flat pictures).

■ FLEXIBILITY

Many of the visual forms we deal with are designed principally for use with groups. Flat pictures, however, are ideal for individual use as well. The student can examine them for as long or as brief a time as he wishes. He can study pictures like those in Fig. 4.5 for detailed information about the moon or get an idea of malaria control requirements in Thailand from a series of photographs, one of which is shown in Fig. 4.6. Picture collections are also a useful resource for student committees working on group projects, reports, or displays.

A unique strength of flat pictures is their particular appropriateness and effectiveness in study displays, which are now widely used at upper- as well as lower-

Fig. 4.7. / These pictures illustrate how a strong impression of depth can be created in a flat picture. What elements in each picture help to do this? What other strengths or weaknesses does each picture have for teaching purposes? In what ways besides subject do these differ from Fig. 4.8?

Fig. 4.8. / The vast Mesabi open-pit mine is difficult to photograph. As you look at this picture, what impression do you receive? Is the picture effective? Does it convey accurate, clear impressions or is there some confusion? Does it please you? Why or why not?

age levels. Although graphics, three-dimensional objects, and other study materials are also used to advantage in study displays, we think of flat pictures as inherent parts of most of them. Displays make good use of the motivational power of pictures which are carefully selected and well presented. (The design and creation of effective study displays are discussed in some detail in Chapter VII.)

☐ LIMITATIONS OF FLAT PICTURES

All teaching materials have advantages for some kinds of teaching tasks and limitations or disadvantages for others. Just as you become skilled at selecting suitable reading materials, so should you become competent in choosing audiovisual materials which will be most effective for each lesson. In part, this choice depends upon the inherent strengths and limitations of the various available materials; in part, on your teaching purposes; and in part, on your method of use. Let us examine some limitations of flat pictures with these factors in mind.

■ SIZE

The vast majority of the pictures in books, magazines, and newspapers are too small to be used effectively in front of a class. Unless enlarged or projected by some means, they simply cannot be seen well enough by everyone in the class to justify using them in this way. Hence, size is an inherent limitation for one type of use. However, this limitation can be overcome if an opaque projector and adequate light-control facilities are available. Moreover, study prints can be obtained that are large enough to be used in front of the classroom provided attention does not need to be focused on small details in the pictures. Size is not necessarily a limitation in study displays, because if the overall effect of the display is good enough, students will go up to examine the display—and the small pictures—at close range.

■ THE TWO-DIMENSIONAL LIMITATION

When accurate perception of depth is essential to learning a particular concept or skill, a model or the object itself may be preferable to a two-dimensional flat picture. Thus, stereo pictures are used in medical schools, along with models and laboratory dissection, to insure accurate understanding of the precise relationships of body tissues. The Army Map Service uses precision instruments in matching flat aerial stereo photographs that provide a basis for accurate contour maps of strategic areas. Technicians' manuals frequently contain complex pictures of the assembly or disassembly of a machine. In these cases where depth perception is of critical importance, flat pictures are used as supplementary rather than as primary sources of information. Other visual forms, plus considerable experience on the part of the viewer, are necessary if the viewer is to read picture depth correctly.

Few classroom situations require accuracy of depth perception to such a degree as these, however. For most purposes, flat pictures provide adequate impressions of depth. Note how the illusion of depth is created in each of the pictures in Fig. 4.7 by such means as converging lines, the reduced size of background objects, highlights and shadows, and decrease in contrast of background colors. Because depth adds realism and lifelike quality to most scenes, artists and photographers strive to achieve a three-dimensional effect. Examine other pictures in this chapter in which depth is important, and note how well and by what means it has been achieved.

For scenes with which the observer has some familiarity—and to which he brings a sufficient degree of experience—these techniques provide the cues that enable him to sense rather accurately the actual depth in the scene that is pictured. When scenes contain few familiar elements, however, the accuracy of one's depth impressions may be considerably reduced. Thus the vastness of the

Fig. 4.9. / One of the great pictures to come out of the dust-bowl era. What is there about this picture that is exceptional? What powers of empathy does it have? How is this achieved?

Mesabi open-pit mine is extremely difficult to grasp from a picture until a person has actually seen the mine (Fig. 4.8). Youngsters who have never seen mountains or skyscrapers have difficulty in sensing their true dimensions from flat pictures.

■ LACK OF MOTION

Flat pictures are sometimes called "still pictures," as indeed they are. One of the more suitable applications is accordingly to communicate ideas by the still scene. Such scenes as landscapes, mountains, forests or trees, buildings, objects, animals, or people in still position (Fig. 4.9) are natural subjects for flat pictures. The general implication for teachers is that flat pictures are well suited to the teaching of concepts in which motion is not essential to understanding.

Here again we sense that this implication is true only in relative terms. For still pictures can depict motion very satisfactorily for some purposes. The question of whether and how they will be used to teach concepts involving motion depends both upon the past experience of the viewer and upon the specific purposes the teacher has in mind. If the class is studying about India, for example, the pupils may have seen one or more good motion pictures showing how people live and work on farms and in cities in India. The class will thus have some concrete ideas about the ebb and flow of life in India, the pace of movement, the meaning of teeming populations in the cities, and life in a village family. At this point, a series of still pictures will serve well to further enrich the pupils' understanding. Still pictures will be helpful even without the films; but their value is increased when the student has seen such things as people and carts in motion, the plodding gait of the water buffalo as it pulls the plow, a woman pounding rice into flour in a stone mortar. Having seen such scenes "live," the pupil can more readily read necessary concepts of motion into still pictures of similar subjects.

Flat pictures of moving subjects also have great value when they are used for study purposes that do not involve motion *per se*. Thus, stop-motion photographs of a hurdler may help students to analyze good points or flaws in his form just as he clears the hurdle (Fig. 4.10). Identification of machine parts is better

Fig. 4.10. / Stop-motion photography enables both coach and athlete to analyze performance in detail.

done with still pictures than with motion pictures; the reverse would usually be true if the purpose is to explain how the machine operates.

☐ WHAT WE KNOW—AND DON'T KNOW

In discussing learning by means of flat pictures, we encounter an interesting paradox. Probably no medium of visual communication is more familiar or more widely used than pictures, nor are there serious questions about the teaching-learning effectiveness of pictures. Much solid research backs up the fact that a superior kind of communication and learning can take place through them. Yet we know relatively little about just *how* or *why* people learn from pictures as well as they do. There is much to be learned about what happens when one looks at a picture. Nevertheless, several good guides to the selection and use of pictures in teaching derive from what we do *not* know about the psychology of learning from pictures.

For example, uncertainty about exactly what concepts can best be taught pictorially in a particular unit leads to the common-sense practice of using several media simultaneously. Further, knowing that marked individual differences are to be expected in ability to read pictures, as with verbal symbols (although we know less regarding the precise nature of these differences in picture-reading ability), leads us to avoid the obvious error of assuming that seeing a picture is enough to insure learning from it.

The need for directed viewing of pictures is supported by Buswell's early study of eye movements of children looking at art subjects. He made the following observations:

> Two general inferences in regard to teaching children may be drawn from study of eye movements. First, the teacher must expect that in studying a new picture the pattern of perception at first will resemble that of a general survey of the picture as a whole. Without some directional teaching, this general survey is likely to be so satisfying to the pupil that he will make no further attempt to study the picture and will be satisfied to say that he has seen that picture. There is little evidence to show that any real taste for art follows this type of superficial looking at pictures.
>
> A second inference to be drawn is that if the child's attention can be centered sufficiently on certain aspects of the picture to induce him to examine those parts in detail, there may result an interest in the picture which will become so compelling that the child will study that picture until he can call it really his own.[3]

More recently, in an analysis of the role of visuals in stimulating desired learning responses, a behavioral psychologist points in another way to the importance of careful selection and use of pictorial representations.[4] While relatively simple visuals probably have cue values for fewer different responses than do their verbal counterparts, other visuals may be more complex and have cue

[3] Guy T. Buswell, "Learning to Look at Pictures," *Progressive Education*, October, 1936, p. 422. See also his *How People Look at Pictures*, Univ. of Chicago, 1935, p. 198.

[4] George L. Grapper, "Why *Is* a Picture Worth a Thousand Words?" *AV Communications Review*, Vol. 11, No. 4, July–August, 1963.

values for *many* responses. Under these circumstances it is entirely possible for visuals to impede learning efficiency. Whether or not such visuals help or hinder learning depends upon the extent to which student attention can be directed and held on pertinent features at the proper times. If attention can be controlled, the complex visual may be significantly better than a verbal description for the purpose. It may also have the added value, when needed, of leading to *other* desired responses: "By controlling student attention to only that feature of the visual which is relevant at a particular time, each response can be cued when needed. Thus, the dense [complex] presentation containing many cues can prove effective or ineffective depending on usage."[5]

There is enough here to suggest the need for directing attention to points of importance in the pictures we use and for ascertaining that they are understood. There is also the broader implication that people have to be taught to read pictures. There are habits and skills to be learned in viewing pictures just as there are in reading the printed page. And there are wide variations in individual ability to read pictures accurately.

Studies in visual perception indicate that the eye can be fooled rather easily by illusory arrangements of lines and objects. For example, you are familiar with the illusion created by parallel lines, such as railroad tracks, that apparently come together in the distance. Further, the viewing of an identical scene by a large number of people rarely fails to provide later a wide range of interpretations of what actually occurred. This is one reason why the credibility of eyewitness accounts is questioned so intensively in the courtroom. More than a few defendants have been the hapless victims of witnesses who hadn't "seen" what they thought they had. This means to us as teachers that we need to be aware of the limitations as well as the strengths of the picture medium, both in terms of what we may expect from it and in the care with which we use it.

As you become better acquainted with the picture medium, perhaps you will realize more clearly that the communication values of flat pictures in instruction depend upon a variety of interrelated factors. Some of these factors are inherent in the nature of the medium. Others equally important—your purposes, intended methods of use, and the viewers' previous experience—are external factors over which you have more control. Both kinds of factors help you decide whether to use flat pictures in a lesson, which ones to use, and how to select them.

☐ GETTING THE MOST FROM PICTURES

From our summary of teacher suggestions over the past few years regarding the selection and use of flat pictures, several general principles emerge. One comment heard often in some form is, "I get the best results with pictures when I know exactly what I want to have 'seen' on each one." Another may be paraphrased this way: "When you get well enough acquainted with what each teaching tool can do and begin to use them as a 'team,' you're getting some place." A third comment says, in effect, "My picture files were getting so jammed that in

---

[5] *Ibid.,* p. 80.

desperation I threw out all but the very best ones. With the few that were left, I soon was getting the best results I'd ever had."

■ USE PICTURES FOR SPECIFIC PURPOSES

Clear-cut purposes are important in using pictures as well as in selecting them. Having chosen a certain picture to illustrate a particular point, you naturally keep that point clearly in mind as you use the picture with a class. A good picture frequently contains much information, perhaps much more than you wish to discuss. Having specific purposes in mind, you can direct the pupils' attention to the most important items in the lesson.

If today's lesson on colonial life in New England is aimed at giving an understanding of the colonists' food, clothing, and shelter, you direct attention specifically to these items in the pictures you use (Fig. 4.11). If the objective is a comparison of living conditions in the northern, middle, and southern colonies, groups of pictures providing these comparisons should be utilized (Fig. 4.12). In one instance, you may point out the comparisons yourself; in another you may let your pupils discover them. In either case you need to know clearly what you wish to accomplish. In other words, the objectives determine both which pictures you use and how you use them.

Williams points to the great variety of teaching purposes for which pictures can be used effectively, ranging from providing initial meanings for words to the stimulation of creative effort.[6] At the creative level, she stresses that guidance should be directed at (1) helping children learn not only to *read* pictures but also to do so at increasingly higher levels and (2) providing numerous opportunities to use pictures and other resources they have made or selected themselves "for achieving their purposes in as independent a fashion as they are able."[7]

Carpenter points to three levels of development in picture reading competence and the importance of developing "picture-scanners into picture readers."[8] The three levels, as illustrated for young children, are simple *enumeration* ("It's Bobby and his dog"); *description* ("Bobby is running. His little black dog is running after him."); and *interpretation* at several levels ("Bobby is crying. He fell down. His dog wants to help."; "Bobby is running home to supper. He's hungry. His dog is hungry too."; and "Bobby played longer than he should. His dog told him it was time to go home. So they are.").[9]

Clearly, such a variety of applications calls for a certain amount of free-wheeling ingenuity on the part of the teacher. The wide range of useful possibilities illustrates both the great potential of flat pictures as teaching tools, and the need to use them wisely.

6 Catherine M. Williams, *Learning from Pictures*, Department of Audiovisual Instruction, National Education Association, 1963, pp. 5–17.
7 *Ibid.*, pp. 4–5.
8 Helen M. Carpenter, "Developing Picture Reading Skills," *The Instructor*, September, 1964, p. 38.
9 *Ibid.*

Fig. 4.11. / Subtle, but important factors can be lost to pupils' historical conceptualizations if they are not pointed out to the pupils as they examine such pictures as these. Many pupils grow up with the impression that these scenes are perfectly representative of Early American culture in its entirety.

Fig. 4.12. / Pictures which contrast the several different cultures that coexisted in Colonial America provide a sound conceptual foundation for understanding the diverse influences upon the historical development of the United States.

Fig. 4.13. / Opaque projection makes small pictures visible to the whole class.

■ USE PICTURES ALONG WITH OTHER MEDIA

A knowledgeable teacher, discussing the cross-media approach to making geography come alive for her pupils, has this to say after describing the great variety of materials she uses:

> When the teacher has skillfully exposed students to these many ways of seeing, hearing, and feeling, and "orchestrates" their impressions through the cross-media approach, communication becomes more effective, and more information is grasped and retained. New ideas are no longer merely scribbled into notebooks, but are planted in minds and hearts as well. Teaching gains enough depth and breadth to meet the tremendous educational challenges presented by today's world.[10]

Effective use of pictures in teaching requires that they be treated as integral parts of the lesson. Generally speaking, if pictures are to be used at all, something definite must be done with them. A purely casual reference to a picture implies to the pupil that it is of minor importance. Brief or limited reference to a bulletin-board display gives a similar impression. For pictures to be of real worth in a lesson they must contribute to the pupils' understanding and be used in such a way as to indicate their importance.

In this way, pictures come to have an integrated place in teaching and learning methods. They are recognized by pupils as teaching and learning methods. They are recognized by pupils as sources of information along with books, films, slides, maps, field trips, and other media, each of which is a valuable member of the team of instructional materials.

■ PICK THE BEST; OMIT THE REST

A third principle in the effective utilization of pictures is that they be used sparingly. A few well-selected pictures usually accomplish far more than twice

[10] Grace Nelson Lacy, "Cross-Media Approach to Geography," *NEA Journal*, January, 1961, pp. 22–24.

as many carelessly chosen pictures do. All too frequently the bulletin board is so filled with materials that nothing stands out. It is unwise to assume that if one picture is good, two will be twice as good. The result may be so many illustrations that pupils are confronted with a mass of interesting but unorganized visual impressions.

The principle here simply involves focusing attention on key ideas. Once these ideas have been well established, additional illustrations may be valuable for enlarging on the initial concepts. A picture of a turret lathe may be excellent for familiarizing the shop student with its important parts and levers. The instructor will then wish to expand these initial concepts by means of a series of pictures showing the step-by-step process of setting up a job. As a good shop teacher he will focus his students' attention by showing one picture in the series at a time. Later he may put the entire series where the students can consult it.

■ PLACE YOUR PICTURES WISELY

Some flat pictures are large enough to present before the class as a whole at the front of the classroom. Large study prints, art prints, simple illustrations, and line drawings can be used to advantage in this way. You can hold them up or use a chalk rail or an easel. Why are the latter better, as a rule, than holding the picture yourself?

Pictures that are too small to be seen well are useless for large groups unless an opaque projector is used. Even very small pictures can be "blown up" to good size on the screen (Fig. 4.13). Brilliance of the image has been increased to the point where a complete blackout is no longer necessary for good results with an opaque projector. Some control of exterior light is necessary, however, if the many benefits the opaque projector can bring to the classroom are to be realized. The 10-inch opening takes most illustrations from magazines and books and they need not be cut out for projecting. It is a good idea to use a piece of Pyrex or other heat-resistant glass to keep unmounted pictures from curling and to flatten the surface of an open book in the projector so that all parts of the page are in focus.

When a series of pictures of similar size is to be shown, a convenient method is to mount each one on a piece of light cardboard such as that used in Manila folders, fasten the pieces together with cellophane tape, and draw them through the projector. This provides a filmstrip arrangement of flat pictures which can be accordion-folded for easy storage when not in use. A picture story drawn by the children on long strips of paper about 10 inches wide can also be run through the projector. (Opaque projectors are discussed more fully in Chapter XII.)

Some of the best communication by pictures can be achieved by study displays. Properly arranged, displayed, and used in conjunction with other media, flat pictures add considerably to most study displays. Refurbished old picture

Fig. 4.14. / Sixty years of highway development, from dirt road to expressway. Could the concepts embodied here be communicated as effectively by words?

frames can be used to advantage around corridors, classrooms, and offices to display student art work and to draw attention to flat-picture displays.[11]

The psychological value of flat pictures lies not only in their lifelike realism, but also in the possibility for individual study at the learner's own rate and interest level. Suppose, for example, that a series of pictures on life in India has been shown in the opaque projector and then arranged in a bulletin board display for an intermediate-grade social-studies class. Once the class has viewed and discussed the pictures, further and more intensive study of these and other pictures by individual pupils may well be made one basis of committee reports and individual projects.

☐ SELECTING PICTURES FOR TEACHING

"Having determined that flat pictures are appropriate to a particular lesson or unit for your class, what guideposts have you found useful in selecting the

11 See Lars H. Souder, "Operation Frameup," *Art Education*, January, 1965, pp. 16–17.

specific pictures to use?" This question, asked of many classes of experienced teachers over a period of years, has elicited numerous helpful suggestions which fall into three principal types. One has to do with the suitability of pictures in terms of teaching *purposes,* another with *age level,* and the other, with the intrinsic properties of the picture itself. This last group includes the content *validity* of the picture, the *interest* factor, the cues the picture contains for proper *interpretation,* and the overall *quality* of the picture.

■ SUITABILITY FOR TEACHING PURPOSES

An intermediate-grade teacher who seemed to have a particular appreciation for good teaching pictures said: "I had used pictures for more years than I care to admit before it dawned on me that my best lessons with pictures were those lessons where I had the clearest idea of what I wanted each picture to do for the class." This is a good summary of a number of similar statements.

Perhaps you recall how your methods and curriculum instructors stressed the importance of objectives in teaching, how these need to be interpreted—not only in long-range but also in day-to-day terms—and how they should help you determine both the materials and the methods necessary to achieve them. *Well-defined and specific objectives* are particularly helpful in selecting pictures for use in teaching (Fig. 4.14).

Suppose, for example, that a teacher is selecting pictures for a lesson on animals. One of her general objectives is to develop an understanding of how to care for pets; another, to build attitudes on conservation with respect to wild-life in general; a third, to bring out how animals are adapted to their environment. For this particular lesson, however, she has a specific objective in mind—the identification of several birds which will soon be coming north. She finds a picture of a cat crouching under a tree; a robin has just alighted on a limb of the tree. The picture has a feeling of tense drama, it is extremely realistic and vivid, the colors are excellent, it is artistically good, and it is sufficiently large for the study of detail—in short, it is a fine picture. The only thing wrong is that the whole emphasis is on something other than identifying a robin. The impact of this picture on the child's mind will be concern with whether the cat is going to get the bird. The teacher wisely passes it by, making a mental note to use it several days later in a lesson on protecting our feathered friends. She chooses, instead, a closeup shot of a robin in a characteristic pose on the lawn after a rain, its head slightly bent as if listening for worms, and its colors highlighted in the afternoon sun. The first picture is undeniably more fascinating and will get the children's attention, but it will not meet the objectives of that particular lesson as well as the less dramatic picture.

Although students at the high-school, college, and adult levels are more sophisticated than are children in their ability to interpret pictures, important general principles of selection still apply. As advertisers are well aware, pictures that are more complex than necessary, or that fail to focus sharply on the precise idea to be conveyed, do not communicate effectively.

For example, in a study of the effectiveness of pamphlet illustrations on learning among newly literate adults in Costa Rica and Mexico, Spaulding

Fig. 4.15. / Younger children learn best from pictures that are not complicated. What, in addition to its simplicity, commends the picture this teacher is using?

found that woodcut-type illustrations which violated perspective and were not clear-cut in terms of items and actions depicted actually interfered with learning. Thus, in the case of eight of eleven booklets tested, people who read booklets with illustrative drawings recalled an average of 66 percent more information than did those who read the same booklets without illustrations. People who read the two booklets with woodcut illustrations, on the other hand, learned 26 percent less than those reading the version without pictures. Spaulding summarizes:

> This led us to believe that illustrative material should be realistic, not violating perspective, and that such material should be carefully planned so that each drawing communicates one or two basic ideas. If the illustrative idea does not communicate a clear-cut idea, it will not help to clarify the accompanying text.[12]

Photographers for *Life* magazine frequently take 50 or more pictures of the same subject to get one that is just right for the purpose. The present authors examined and took many hundreds of illustrations in selecting those to be used in this text. Teachers at *any* level should be satisfied with nothing less than the best pictures they can find. The instructors who are most successful in using pictures are constantly on the lookout for better ones.

■ SUITABILITY TO PICTURE-READING LEVEL

A further consideration in selecting pictures to fit a specific teaching purpose is age level. Although in most cases this is not a difficult problem, it is well to

12 Seth Spaulding, "Communication Potential of Pictorial Illustrations," *AV Communications Review,* Winter, 1956, pp. 31–33.

remember that determining what is to be accomplished in a lesson cannot be separated from the question "For whom?" Picture selection according to age level is not as complex as is the selection of reading materials. In this regard, Mary Bartlett's observation regarding 5-year-old children's ability to interpret flat pictures is worthy of note:

> The child who has arrived at this typical stage of familiarity with pictures has learned to interpret the chief conventions of pictorial representation. He recognizes a two-dimensional black-and-white line drawing as a comprehensible reproduction of three-dimensional colored objects which he has met in daily life. He recognizes as a truck the object which is shown as two inches in height. He knows that an airplane held in a boy's hand is a model plane rather than a real aircraft because of its size in relation to that of the boy. He interprets the portrayal of familiar motion and correctly infers that some of the children are walking while one boy stands still. He understands the effect of perspective— although he does not know the term and could not describe the process—so that he is not confused or misled by the fact that the little girl in the foreground is several times larger than the policeman in the middle distance. Without these and many similar or related techniques, he could not grasp the import of even the simplest picture.[13]

Nevertheless, there must be fewer elements in a picture for young children than in one for older pupils, the pattern must be simpler, the idea less complicated (Fig. 4.15). This is, of course, quite natural because in terms of his experience, the primary child can bring less *to* a picture than can his older brother and sister. To him, a picture of an airplane is usually just an airplane, though he has probably learned to distinguish in his own mind between big planes and little ones. His 10-year-old brother, however, will very likely be able to identify the plane as a jet or a turbo-prop transport and can volunteer information as to its size and the speed and altitude at which it flies.

Evidence showing the importance of selecting pictures suited to age level is reported by French.[14] Using both a complex and a simple, literal version of thirteen pictures, French tested the preferences of 88 elementary-school teachers and 554 pupils in grades 1 through 5. He found that, whereas 89 percent of the teachers preferred the complex versions, 83 percent of the first-graders preferred the simple illustrations. Not until grade 4 did a majority of the children prefer the complex pictures. Thus, French concluded that children show "a logical and consistent basis for their selections" and that they "preferred pictures that were understandable on the basis of their own artistic experience."[15]

Although much remains to be discovered about how we learn from pictures, we know that variations in picture-reading ability are due to a combination of factors of which age is only one. Intelligence, environment, prior experience in reading pictures, and imagination all probably play a significant part. Thus, it is important for a teacher to consider his pupils' abilities, age, and probable experience when choosing pictures for classroom use. In the primary grades,

[13] Mary M. Bartlett, *How to Teach with Pictures,* Informative Classroom Pictures Publishers, 1947, pp. 12–14.
[14] John E. French, "Children's Preferences for Pictures of Varied Complexity of Pictorial Pattern," *Elementary School Journal,* October, 1952, pp. 90–95.
[15] *Ibid.*

Fig. 4.16. / The representative character of this typical driver-education shot is highly important for effective learning transfer to actual driving situations.

he may need to discount his own picture preferences. At any level, he will need to determine when a picture has the necessary concepts for his purpose, plus the right amount of detail, the appropriate degree of abstraction, and the other qualities that make it suited to the abilities and interests of his students.

■ VALIDITY

The effectiveness of a good picture makes it a powerful teaching tool. It is important that the impressions left in a learner's mind be correct and accurate, insofar as the picture can make them so. This means that the photograph, painting, or illustration must provide both a true general impression and accuracy of detail. To accomplish this, the picture in most instances should be typical, like that in Fig. 4.16, rather than unique or startling. The unfortunate fact that the unusual scene frequently lends itself to picture making more readily than does the ordinary run of events should make the teacher pause and think when considering the factor of truthfulness. The dramatic, thrilling, or unusually beautiful scene may have its place in the classroom for decorative or motivation purposes, but you convey accurate impressions more readily by pictures that are representative of the area or subject being studied. Thus, if for language-arts purposes we wish to show the Hollander of another day with quaint wooden shoes and pantaloons, let us keep such illustrations in a story context. But let our social-studies classes see him as he is today on his modern farm or busy city streets, with occupations, interests, and appearance much like those of other western Europeans.

■ INTEREST

It may appear somewhat inconsistent to maintain that a picture should be typical rather than unusual and at the same time that it must be highly interesting. Yet interest among learners tends to be attracted by a vast number of ordinary things with which they are familiar. For instance, consider the great interest usually shown by children in pictures of animals or of other children, or of space capsules, ships, or airplanes. To each of these the child brings some degree of familiarity which helps to arouse his curiosity and to give an outlet to his imagination.

Here again, the purpose for which a picture is used and the intended method of use must be kept constantly in mind. If a picture is to be a focus of attention in a study or advertising display, it must have strong eye appeal or it will be unlikely to be given a second glance. Much of the communications potential of the display will be bypassed before it has a chance to function. Hence, in situations where motivation is a primary consideration, a dramatic or unusual picture may be called for.

Experienced teachers know that motivation can stem from a variety of sources, both internal and external to the learner. Pictures and displays, when pertinent, are one helpful means of arousing or increasing interest among learners. In a display designed for motivation purposes, a large and particularly striking picture may well attract attention. On the other hand, the overall design of the display, the title, the use of color—or some combination of these—may be the primary attention-getting factor (see Chapter VII for further discussion of display techniques).

But once attention has been secured and motivation achieved, interest can be maintained and content objectives attained much better by less dramatic pictures selected because they convey the desired information and ideas more effectively. As a junior-high-school social-studies teacher reported:

> One of my most successful uses of flat pictures has been in letting project committees work with our picture files. They get a lot of information that way which otherwise I feel might have been missed. And when they report on their projects to the class, they often show a good deal of discrimination in the pictures they select to illustrate their points.

In other words, the quality of "interest" in pictures may be increased as viewers come to know more about the subject represented and as they themselves have occasion to use pictures to express ideas to others.

■ INTERPRETATION CUES

Good pictures for teaching normally contain something familiar to the student to give him correct impressions of such information as the size, color, or movement of unfamiliar objects in the pictures. The pyramids or the sphinx frequently are pictured with an automobile, a camel, or a human figure in the foreground. Small objects may be shown on the palm of a hand, or with a small rule or common coin in evidence.

Color codes are commonly used in biology illustrations to differentiate the veins from the arteries or to help identify various organs. Colors and symbols are valuable aids in interpreting mechanical or technical drawings. We use a

Fig. 4.17. / This picture was selected as an example
of good composition. What elements make it so?

colored line to show the path of a film in a projector-threading diagram, and a
series of coded pictures to illustrate the correct handling of simple machines in
industrial arts or the steps involved in creating an effective display. Self-instruc-
tion materials relating to mechanical processes or motor skills typically make
liberal use of photographs or drawings incorporating visual symbols.

Motion is suggested in still pictures by various cues such as a flag unfurled in
the breeze, people in the act of walking, traffic in positions of obvious movement, waves breaking on a seashore, or a football player "shot" in the process
of catching a pass. In such cases, the experience of the viewer supplies the
needed interpretation of motion. The teacher needs simply to decide whether
the experience of the students is sufficient to sense the implied movement in a
picture or at least not to be confused by it.

■ PICTURE QUALITY

Thus far we have been concerned with the more extrinsic factors of selecting pictures—their pertinence to the teacher's specific purposes, their suitability in terms of pupil age level, and their validity and ability to motivate interest. These are fundamental. But we need also to be concerned with the qualitative characteristics of pictures. As one teacher put it:

> I'm a camera fan myself and take a lot of pictures. In the process, I have come to have a great deal of respect for people who can take really *good* pictures. There's a lot of difference between ordinary pictures and good ones and I try hard to find the good ones to use in my biology classes.

What are good pictures in the sense meant by this science teacher? And why are such pictures better than ordinary pictures for teaching purposes? An art teacher had this to say about the second question:

> Well, what we're really talking about is visual communication, isn't it? In my art teaching, I try to instill in my pupils an appreciation for such things as color, line, and composition in good pictures so that they can apply these fundamentals as they make their own sketches and designs. But the same principles apply to any visual material which is intended to communicate. The better a picture is from an art standpoint, the better it is likely to transmit what it has to say to anyone looking at it.

In other words, good art and good visual communication go hand in hand. Let us take a closer look at several of the characteristics found in effective pictures—good composition, effective color, and good contrast and sharpness. In the process, we can equate these three and one other—size—with the teaching functions which flat pictures can fulfill.

▪ Good Composition

The fundamental characteristic of an effective picture is good composition, or good overall organization, such as is shown in Fig. 4.17. Usually an effective picture has a clear-cut center of interest to which the rest of the picture contributes by such means as the balance of the picture as a whole, the position and direction of lines, and the use of light, shadow, and color. The focus of attention is rarely in the center of the picture, a position other than the center being more pleasing to the eye as a rule. The presence or absence of a good center of interest can readily be ascertained by allowing the eye to travel naturally over the picture until it fixes on a point of key interest. Look away from that point, and your eyes tend to go back to it if there is a good center of interest there.

Occasionally pictures of huge crowds, of geometric patterns, or of a large number of similar objects do not have a center of interest in the usual sense. In these pictures, the overall effect is the objective—a general impression rather than specific detail. Thus, 100,000 people in a public square, row upon row of

Fig. 4.18. / The full range of the gray scale is included in this beautiful shot of Mount Hood at sunrise. What advantages can you see for some kinds of study in the many subtle graduations in tone which are possible with black-and-white pictures?

dilapidated houses, or rolling fields of grain extending as far as the eye can see may have a powerful effect on the observer. The center of interest in such pictures is an idea rather than a physical thing. Their effectiveness is determined by how well this idea is communicated. A mass subject is difficult to photograph effectively because it does not have a visible center of interest around which composition can be built. Turn back to Fig. 4.8, the Mesabi mine picture, for an illustration of this problem.

- EFFECTIVE COLOR

The use of harmonious and effective color is a second mark of good art. Colored pictures selected for use with children should generally be true and natural in color. Color values in nature are seldom primary reds, blues, greens, and violets; rather they are composed of infinite and subtle variations of these colors. Hence, where color is important in a teaching situation it should be as true as possible (see Plates 1 and 2, following p. 144).

According to Spaulding's study, referred to earlier, color seems to add to the communication potential of illustrations if it adds to the realism, but it detracts if used unrealistically.[16] Spaulding also suggests that color is valuable in increasing interest. Williams adds a further and significant consideration in observing that, "Color poor in quality offends the sensitive viewer and prevents the development of good taste by the less sensitive."[17] An exception to this must be recognized with respect to art subjects in which color is used as a dominant means of expressing ideas. Thus, children pay little attention to natural colors in expressing themselves in paint or crayons. Trees may be purple splashes, a locomotive a racing giant in flaming red, yet the pictures are highly meaningful to the young artists.

Likewise, in observing such pictures, if they are good pictures children seem to experience little difficulty in grasping the artist's idea. For an art class or any other class in which unique or unusual illustrations bring out a particular point well, "impressionistic" pictures of this type may be entirely suitable. The decision as to whether to use abnormal colors must, of course, be based on the specific purposes of the lesson. Informational concepts are normally conveyed most effectively by accurate color renditions.

Color is a part of our natural environment. Hence, good color in pictures adds realism as well as attractiveness to a pictured scene. Illustrations of particularly effective color use are found in Plates 1 and 2 following page 144. As color film has improved and as color reproduction processes have become more flexible and less expensive, pictures of excellent quality are being used with increasing frequency in text and reference books of all kinds. The better-illustrated magazines, advertising brochures, and trade journals make extensive use of full-range color reproductions.

It should also be noted that black-and-white photography can provide a wide variety of color impressions. Study of the gray scale (a scale of uncolored shades from black to white) suggests the many subtle variations in value that are possible with black-and-white film (see Fig. 4.18). Because of its greater flexibility, many photographers prefer working with black-and-white film whenever color is not an essential element of the picture. For the same reason, it is often well for the teacher to select good black-and-white photographs rather than mediocre colored pictures.

It is important for the teacher to be aware of the fact that poor or inharmonious color frequently evokes a negative response in people who are color sensitive. Students who respond appreciatively to good color tend, consciously or unconsciously, to reject pictures, displays or other uses of color which to them are unpleasant.

When using colored pictures in an opaque projector, the instructor should

16 Seth Spaulding, *op. cit.*, p. 42.
17 Catherine M. Williams, *op. cit.*, p. 20.

Fig. 4.19. / The value of good contrast is shown in these two pictures. Besides being more attractive, what added communicative values has the pictures with the sharper contrasts?

also be aware that fading occurs under extended exposure to heat. Colored printers' inks are fugitive under both heat and strong light. Accordingly, colored flat pictures should be projected for brief rather than extended periods and kept out of direct sunlight, if possible, when used in displays.

■ CONTRAST AND SHARPNESS

Sometimes we say that a picture is "flat." This may mean several things, one of which is that the important parts do not stand out enough from the rest of the picture. In consequence, the picture as a whole lacks luster and vitality. With better lighting, exposure, and developing, the blacks will look blacker, the whites whiter, and the picture as a whole will be more interesting and effective. Notice the difference between the two pictures in Fig. 4.19. Both subject and camera position are identical. The only difference is in contrast.

It is also possible to have too much contrast; this produces a harsh effect. Therefore, the good photographer or artist strives to get just the right amount. And as discriminating selectors, teachers should look for this important quality in the pictures they choose for classroom use.

Clarity and sharpness constitute a related consideration in selecting pictures for school use. Although softness of focus is effective in portrait work and for the portrayal of certain moods, most educational subjects are better illustrated by pictures that are clear and sharp. The sharp picture with strong contrast provides better opportunity for accuracy in detail—a better representation of reality—and thus is preferable when information is the primary objective in using pictures.

☐ ORGANIZING A PICTURE FILE

Experienced teachers know the many learning values of having picture files accessible to their students. But good picture collections are built over the years, and the wise teacher will always be on the lookout for good pictures. As better pictures are found, some of the older, less useful ones should be discarded. This keeps the files from getting filled up with seldom-used pictures, and it keeps the indexing system simple. A good filing and indexing system is like a good budget. It may be a bit difficult at first, but once it is functioning efficiently it works for you.

■ THE FILING SYSTEM

The simplest filing system involves grouping pictures according to the teaching units or topics in which they are used. When rather large numbers of pictures are involved, subheadings are helpful. For example, pictures on Greece may be subdivided as follows: Greece—Mountains, Greece—People, Greece—Farming, etc. Tabbed or color-coded separators should be used, the pictures in each section being listed in pencil on the separator. Other indexing systems include notebook lists, with identification of pictures by numbers or topics for quick location; similar lists in lesson-plan folders; and a simple card file, with related groups of pictures listed on each card. The filing and indexing system should be as simple as possible but still flexible enough to accommodate additional pictures or sections. Further, the system of classification and labeling used needs to be geared to the maturity level of the pupils using it. The same consideration applies to titles and captions. It will also be helpful to place essential information for identification and filing on the upper left corner of the *reverse* side of each picture.

Having selected pictures that are suitable for his teaching purposes and also of good quality artistically, the teacher is faced with the practical question of how to take care of them when they are not in use. Because having pictures in good condition and readily available when needed makes their effective use easier, we next consider mounting and storing flat pictures.

■ MOUNTING PICTURES

The question of whether to mount pictures is a practical one for busy teachers. It boils down to something like this, as stated by an enthusiastic elementary teacher:

Fig. 4.20. / The value of generous margins and of proper margin proportions is illustrated here. Note that the bottom margin is *always* wider than the top or side margins.

I couldn't teach without pictures and have hundreds of them in my files. The big majority of them are not mounted because I simply haven't the time to mount them and besides they take up more filing space that way. But there are some special ones that I *do* mount because I wouldn't want them lost or torn. Still others I use once and throw away because I can easily find as good or better ones the next time the same topic comes up.

We classify flat pictures just as we do magazines, newspapers, and other materials of which we have a plentiful supply—in terms of relative usefulness. Outstanding or unique pictures which are just right and perhaps difficult to replace should be mounted to protect them from damage. Less valuable pictures and those of purely transitory or one-time value may be filed unmounted or on temporary mounts.

Mounting pictures not only improves their appearance but also increases their effectiveness. An appropriate mounting helps to focus the viewer's attention on the picture, and sets that picture apart from others around it. The right mounting of color pictures enhances the color effectiveness. Thus, for a variety of reasons, it is well to mount pictures that are used in teaching.

Some general considerations that should be observed regardless of the type of mounting include the following:

1. *Use generous margins.* Generous margins are not solely a matter of artistic taste, but embody the direct application of the principles of attracting and holding attention. Any object tends to attract more attention when it is by itself than when it is crowded in among a number of other, similar objects. Moreover, an appropriate mounting makes a good teaching picture more attractive, just as an appropriate frame enhances a photographic portrait or a painting. In addition, the mounting protects the picture in handling and makes it easier to file.

Correct proportions for mounting pictures of various shapes are shown in Fig. 4.20. Note the width of the margins used. The width of the top and bottom margins is determined by the shape of the picture, as the illustration shows. Note also that the bottom margin is *always* wider than the top one.

2. *Use colors which direct attention to the picture and not to the mounting.* This means that, as a rule, it is best to select for the mounting a color that appears in the picture in a relatively minor degree. This repetition of color creates a pleasing harmony in the total effect given by the mounting and picture together. It is usually not wise to use a color which predominates in the picture for the mounting because of the resulting loss of desirable contrast. A picture of a field of ripe grain will not appear to the best advantage on a yellow mounting, nor will a picture with a broad expanse of blue sky look well on a light blue mounting. In such cases, the picture loses definition because, from a short distance away, it tends to merge with the mounting itself. When in doubt as to the precise color to use, the teacher will do well to experiment until he gets a satisfying effect.

In general, neutral tones for mountings are more pleasing than primary or brilliant colors, although there are notable exceptions. Bright red or green mountings look well with Christmas pictures, orange mountings with Halloween subjects, and gay pastel mountings with Easter decorations. The idea here is to emphasize a gay and festive spirit; the purpose of these mountings may be primarily decorative, which is entirely appropriate in such cases. As a general rule, however, where informational purposes predominate, the above principles should apply.

Often a narrow border will help to set off the picture from the mounting. Sometimes an inked line around the picture is effective. A similar border effect is obtained by inserting, immediately behind the picture, a sheet of mounting paper slightly larger than the picture and of a different color from that used for the mounting itself. Since this sheet extends slightly beyond the edges of the picture, it provides a border in a contrasting color. White used for a border of this kind is often highly effective because it brings out the color in the picture.

3. *Use mounting materials appropriate to the picture subject.* Teachers fre-

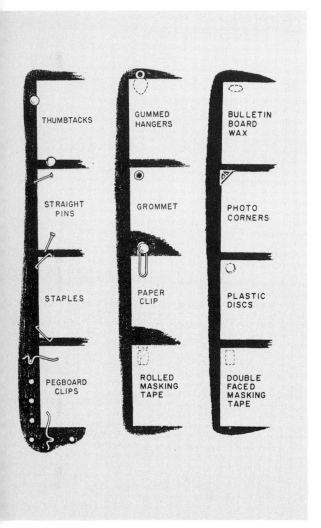

Fig. 4.21. / Examples of satisfactory and effective methods of fastening pictures on various display surfaces.

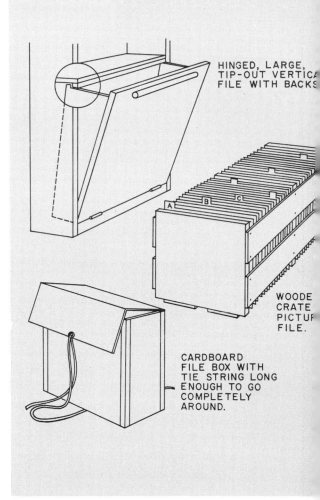

Fig. 4.22. / Here are a few suggestions for solving picture storage problems. Dimensions can be adjusted to suit your needs.

quently find colored drawing paper to be the most readily available material for picture mountings; it is also inexpensive. But once the teacher gets the feel and pleasure of attractive mountings, there is no reason why he should not give his ingenuity free play and experiment with a variety of textures, materials, and colors in obtaining desired effects. A shop teacher, for example, may find a metallic background ideal for a series of metal-working pictures; a background of old maps may be very effective for a series of historical illustrations; fabrics of various kinds or pieces of wallpaper make appropriate and interesting mounting materials for pictures on interior decoration. Dress and suit boxes and even corrugated cardboard make very effective mounts if carefully cut to a uniform size. The possibilities are virtually without limit except as to the time, interest, and ingenuity of the teacher himself (see Source List, page 531, for mounting and display materials for flat pictures).

■ TEMPORARY MOUNTINGS

One of the simplest methods of mounting is to coat the back of a picture with *rubber cement* and lay it on the mounting surface. Rubber cement comes in convenient tubes and jars, is not messy, and has the added virtue of being readily removable. Should some of the cement squeeze out around the edges when a picture is pressed down on the mounting surface, the excess can be rubbed off with the fingers. The cement does not dry completely for a long period of time nor does it tend to soak into the paper surface. This means that a picture can be peeled away from a mounting whenever desired. A more permanent mount is obtained by coating both the picture and the mounting and allowing the two surfaces to "set" for a minute or two before putting them together. This process requires care in fitting the surfaces together because, once in contact, they adhere firmly. It is accordingly advisable to use a piece of wax paper between the surfaces while fitting one edge of the picture accurately on the mounting. Then gradually withdraw the wax paper, pressing the cemented surfaces together as you do so.

Rubber cement can also be applied along the edges of the back of the picture; it will hold very well if the picture is not on heavy stock which will tend to curl. Dabbing on liquid paste or glue at the corners is a well-known method of "pasting" pictures. This can also be done satisfactorily with rubber cement if the picture is on magazine or light-weight paper stock.

In addition to rubber cement, various *gummed tapes* are of some value in mounting flat pictures. The best of these is a double-surface masking tape. Strips of this tape are placed on the back of a picture, which is then pressed on the mounting surface. This tape can also be used for displaying mounted pictures on bulletin boards and other surfaces. It leaves little or no residue when removed. A spray-on adhesive is another convenient means of fastening pictures to mounting surfaces.

A synthetic wax-like adhesive is likewise used for mounting, particularly for displaying mounted pictures on rough or glossy surfaces. Small bits of the wax are sufficient to hold the mounted picture in place for as long as desired.

A bulletin-board display that is studded with shiny-headed thumbtacks is usually less attractive than it should be. A much better effect is obtained by using *straight pins,* as many art teachers do; the pins cannot be noticed more than a few feet away. Pins are particularly useful when time does not permit the use of better methods. Other types of mounting devices are shown in Fig. 4.21.

■ PERMANENT MOUNTINGS

When a picture is to be used repeatedly or handled frequently by students, some type of permanent mounting is demanded. A fairly stiff backing material, such as Bristol board or heavy cardboard, is necessary to provide a firm backing and reduce wear.

In *floating,* the entire back of the picture is coated evenly with a layer of paste, glue, or liquid cement. The picture is then placed on the mounting and carefully smoothed down. Pictures so mounted should be put in a press or under a pile of books until they are dry in order to assure a good bond at every point and to minimize curling. Only enough adhesive should be used to coat the picture very lightly because any excess around the edges is difficult to remove without impairing the appearance.

A good way to eliminate warping or curling in this method of mounting is to cut a piece of paper the same size as the picture, coat this paper with the same adhesive as is used on the picture, and apply the paper to the *back of the mounting.* As both sides dry, the contraction or "pull" is equalized and the mounting stays flat.

Dry mounting requires a special tissue material that is affixed by means of a hot iron. A neat, professional-looking mounting job can be done with a little practice. The dry-mount tissue can be obtained in rolls or sheets from photographic supply stores. Kraft board or some other type of cardboard is very satisfactory for the mounting. The other materials required are plain white paper, clear flat lacquer and thinner, and a sprayer like that used for insecticides or paint. In using the dry-mounting process, a piece of the dry-mount tissue is trimmed to picture size and put on the back of the picture. The picture and the tissue backing are then placed on the mounting material and covered with a piece of plain white paper. An iron heated to about 300 degrees is applied firmly, the picture being literally ironed onto the mounting. The mounted picture is then sprayed with clear flat lacquer to protect it.

Lamination seals the picture in a clear, nonglossy plastic covering that permanently protects it from dirt, moisture, and tearing. The plastic material is flexible, light in weight, and sufficiently strong to prevent damage from continuous handling. The use of a plastic mounting makes feasible the circulation of sets of pictures from school to school within a system. The audiovisual department of the Los Angeles City Schools, for example, uses lamination to preserve certain pictures for long service. Not all pictures need a permanent mounting of this type, but it is well suited for those that are to be circulated or are irreplaceable.

The expense of laminating equipment once restricted its use to larger school systems. Now, however, equipment and plastics can be obtained at a cost which makes the process practical for small school systems. Also available are inexpensive, clear vinyl sheets which can be purchased in many household-supply stores and applied with a hot iron. School- and art-supply houses carry clear plastic sheets specially designed for picture protection. Some are applied with heat and pressure; others are self-adhesive and can be applied by hand. While not as strong or permanent as machine lamination, the above processes are useful substitutes. Large pictures may be readily and inexpensively protected by spraying them with a coat of clear lacquer.[18]

18 See Herbert Scuorzo, "Plastic Picture Protection," *Grade Teacher,* September, 1963, pp. 12 ff. for details on the process.

■ SECTIONAL MOUNTINGS

It is frequently advantageous to use a series of identical mountings for magazine-fold pictures or murals that are too large for a single mounting. When displayed, the series is a unit, for the individual sections are identical in size and coloration and when fitted together look like a panel. They are separated for filing and storage. In another method of sectional mounting, light-weight sections are fastened together with masking tape or cloth tape and accordion-folded when not in use. Either method is a practical solution to handling the ever-increasing number of excellent two- and three-fold materials in such magazines as *Life, Look,* and *Holiday.*

The above methods are those most commonly used for mounting pictures. In determining which method to use, the teacher should select the one that is most practical in terms of time, effort, and utility. Pictures should be mounted if they are to have maximum effectiveness as teaching tools. A few well-selected and well-mounted pictures can provide rich sources of information in an attractive and interesting form.

■ STORING PICTURES

Teachers who go to some trouble to find and use good pictures know that the storing and filing of pictures when not in use is important. The following suggestions from teachers may help you to avoid some of the difficulties and frustrations that result from inadequate storage space or a lack of a filing system.

One way to lessen the storage and filing problem is to use two *standard sizes* of mountings—a small size which will go into a Manila folder or a standard letter file, and a larger size which will fit into a drawer or box file. This plan means varying the width of the margins around pictures, but it is preferable to the alternative of not mounting pictures or of having them misplaced or damaged.

Modern classroom facilities usually include built-in drawers and cabinet space in which various instructional materials and supplies, including flat pictures, can be stored. Standard, letter-size filing cabinets are suitable for small mounted pictures, but legal-size files are better because they accommodate material up to 11 × 14 inches in size. Although many classrooms lack filing cases or other built-in storage facilities, ingenious teachers have devised various ways of storing and filing pictures (Fig. 4.22). Orange crates, heavy cardboard cartons, and boxes built to the desired size can serve the purpose satisfactorily and can be kept in out-of-the-way places when not in use.

Portfolios are also an excellent means of protecting pictures when not in use or while carrying them. Used by art teachers for many years, a portfolio is nothing more than two pieces of heavy cardboard or similar material hinged with a flexible tape on one of its long sides. Pictures or graphic materials are laid flat in the open portfolio, the cover is closed and tied, and it is ready to go. A portfolio can be made up in any size desired; one 34 × 44 inches accommodates most pictures and small charts and still is easy to carry.

☐ SUMMARY

Flat pictures are so readily available that it is easy to underestimate their importance in teaching and learning. The picture medium as a whole has a certain universality and versatility that no other medium of communication shares. But, as is true of all media, there are both intrinsic and extrinsic limitations which must be considered in selecting and using pictures.

In general, it is better for class work to use a few carefully selected, pertinent pictures instead of a larger number, and to combine them with other media to assure maximum learning. The effective use of flat pictures also requires directing the viewer's attention to specific points or impressions to be looked for. The instructor who recognized the importance of the learner's background and prior experience, and of individual differences in ability to interpret pictures, will secure the most satisfactory results from their use.

Effective techniques of using flat pictures with groups include showing those pictures which are large enough in front of the group, projecting those which are small on an opaque projector, and incorporating pictures of various sizes in study displays. Flat pictures also have great value for use with individuals and small groups.

Care in selecting flat pictures is the first essential for effective learning results. The starting point in selection is defining teaching objectives which are clear and explicit. The pictures chosen must be valid and directly pertinent to those objectives. They also must be suited to the maturity level of the students, and they should have good artistic quality. The better the quality, the better the picture is likely to communicate.

Some form of temporary or permanent mounting increases the effectiveness of flat pictures. Also important is a simple system of filing and storing so that the pictures will be protected and can readily be found when needed.

☐ Suggested Activities

1. Ask each student to bring in several examples of good flat pictures in their respective subject-matter fields. Have the class evaluate a selection of these pictures in terms of the principles discussed in this chapter.
2. Have members of the class mount several flat pictures of different sizes, shapes, and colors. Discuss the effectiveness of the mounting used and suggest means of improvement.
3. Assign a committee to prepare a teaching display for the class on the subject "What Is a Good Picture?" Have the committee use the display in presenting the subject to the class.
4. Have a committee prepare an annotated and classified list of good sources of free or inexpensive flat picture materials for duplication and distribution to class members.
5. Ask each pupil to bring in a current issue of *Life, Look,* or a similar publication for use in a class discussion of the qualities of good photographs. Draw up a list of suggestions on how to take good pictures.
6. Instructional pictures that are good from an artistic viewpoint can communicate more effectively than those that are not and can help to improve aesthetic taste. Select a number of pictures from this chapter and other sources which seem to fulfill this requirement; be prepared to justify your selections.

☐ Bibliography

Brown, J. W., R. B. Lewis, and F. F. Harcleroad, *Audio-Visual Instruction* (2nd ed.), McGraw-Hill, 1964, pp. 437–463.

Carpenter, Helen M., "Developing Picture-Reading Skills," *The Instructor*, September, 1964, pp. 37–38 ff.

Dale, Edgar, *Audio-Visual Methods in Teaching* (rev. ed.), Dryden, 1954, pp. 243–258, 269–277.

East, Marjorie, *Display for Learning*, Dryden, 1952, pp. 54–87, 210–237.

Erickson, Carlton W. H., *Fundamentals of Teaching with Audiovisual Technology*, Macmillan, 1965, pp. 70–71, 248–253.

Fleming, Malcolm, "Pictorial Communication: An Essay on Its Plight," *AV Communications Review*, July–August, 1962, pp. 223–237.

Gibson, James J., "A Theory of Pictorial Perception," *AV Communications Review*, Winter, 1954, pp. 3–23.

Hicks, Wilson, *Words and Pictures*, Harper & Row, 1952.

Kinder, James, *Audio-Visual Materials and Techniques* (2nd ed.), American Book, 1959, pp. 50–75, 88–95, 432–450.

Meussig, Raymond H., "Using Projective Pictures," *Social Education*, May, 1958, pp. 250–252.

Ress, Etta Schneider, *The Use of Pictures to Enrich School Resources*, Creative Educational Society, Inc., 1953.

Sites, Raymond S., "Bringing the Nation's Art Treasures to the Classroom," *Audiovisual Instruction*, March 1961, pp. 98–99.

Spaulding, Seth, "Communication Potential of Pictorial Illustrations," *AV Communications Review*, Winter, 1956, pp. 31–46.

University of Illinois, *How Pictures and Graphs Aid Learning from Prints: A Review of the Research Evidence*, Technical Memorandum No. 4, Division of Communications, 1952.

Wetzler, Walter, "Choosing Wisely in Illustrations," *Educational Screen and Audiovisual Guide*, November, 1961, pp. 593–594.

Williams, Catherine M., *Learning from Pictures*, Department of Audiovisual Instruction, National Education Association, 1963, pp. 5–17, 20.

☐ Films and Filmstrips

Dry Mounting Your Teaching Pictures, 16 mm. film, B&W, 10 min., McGraw-Hill, 1958.

Flat Pictures, 16 mm. film, Color, 23 min., Pennsylvania State University, 1959.

Mounting, 8 mm. film cartridges, B&W, Chandler Publishing Company, 1965. Series includes:
    Cloth Mounting (Fold), Part I, 4 min.
    Cloth Mounting (Fold), Part II, 4 min., 10 sec.
    Cloth Mounting (Roll), 4 min., 20 sec.
    Dry Mounting (Press), 3 min., 4 sec.
    Dry Mounting (Hand iron), 3 min., 10 sec.
    Mounting: A Two Page Picture, 4 min., 15 sec.
    Mounting: Overcoming Dry Mounting Problems, 2 min., 55 sec.
    Mounting: Setting Grommets, 2 min., 55 sec.
    Mounting: Using Laminating Film, 4 min., 45 sec.
    Permanent Rubber Cement Mountings, 4 min.

Mounting Still Pictures, 35 mm. filmstrip, Color, 58 frames, University of Texas, 1956.

Passe Partout Framing, 16 mm. film, B&W, 10 min., Indiana University, 1956.

Pictures for Teaching, Series of 36 2 × 2 slides, Color, Chandler Publishing Company, 1965.

Study Pictures and Learning, 35 mm. filmstrip, Color, 63 frames, Ohio State University, 1960.

Teaching with Still Pictures, 35 mm. filmstrip, Color, 53 frames, Basic Skills Filmstrips, 1958.

Wet Mounting Pictorial Material, 16 mm. film, B&W and Color, 11 min., Indiana University, 1952.

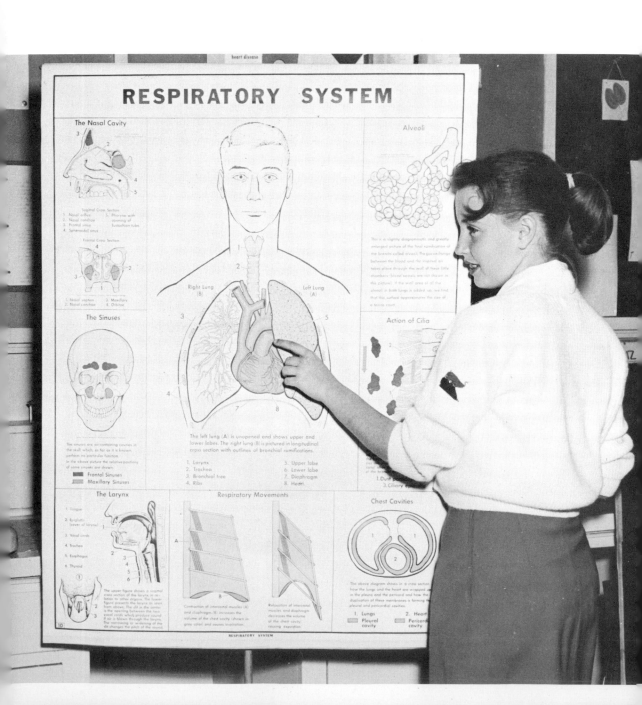

GRAPHICS

The role of graphic materials in visual communication is both unique and significant. Historically, symbols—a basic part of graphics—have made possible the whole range of written languages used in the world today. The science and theory of mathematics are also deeply indebted to symbols. Mathematics remained largely undeveloped until the adoption, less than 300 years ago, of a symbol for zero. You will appreciate the significance of this symbol if you attempt to multiply or divide with Roman numerals such as MCMLIX and MIII. Rudolf Modley used this illustration in discussing symbols before a New York Art Directors Communications Conference:

> Yet, all that was needed to make these operations as simple as they are today was the invention and use of the symbol for "zero"—which made positional numeration possible so that we can write 13, 103, 130, and 1003—all without need for more than 3 different numerals. The Indo-Arabic numerals, including "zero," have become so essential a part of our daily life that we cannot even think where we would be without them.
>
> Algebra, the cornerstone of modern mathematics, too, had to wait for letter symbols to free it from being tied to objects. Only then did the general theory of mathematics become possible.[1]

The dramatic character of graphics in some of man's communications tends to be overlooked in its many familiar applications to daily living (Fig. 5.1). Graphic forms and symbols are essential to highway safety, to reporting myriad economic indices, and to the weather report in the newspaper or on television. Comics, advertisements, billboards, Community-Chest drives and annual reports of countless businesses and community activities employ graphics as an inherent communications tool. We noted in Chapter IV how simple line illustrations unaccompanied by words enabled illiterate Venezuelan farmers to understand an improved method of developing and selecting seed corn. Indeed, drawing in

[1] Rudolph Modley, "The Challenge of Symbology," Paper presented at the 4th Annual Conference of the Art Directors Club of New York, 1960. Reprints distributed by the Department of Audiovisual Instruction, National Education Association.

Fig. 5.1. / Symbols play a key role in our daily lives. What other familiar symbols do these suggest to you?

some form is the most common single characteristic of the various graphic forms. Before going further, however, let us first get a clearer idea of what we mean by the word *graphics*.

☐ DEFINITION OF GRAPHICS

The distinction between graphics and other visual materials is less definite than, for example, that between 16 mm. motion pictures and 35 mm. filmstrips. One reason for this is that the term *graphics* represents a whole group of instructional visuals rather than a single type. It is comparable, in this sense, to such classification terms as *photographic materials* and *three-dimensional materials*.

Webster defines *graphics* as the art or science of drawing—especially mechanical drawing. As applied to visual materials, however, the terms *graphics* or *graphic materials* has a broader meaning than drawing alone. The original Greek *graphikos* included painting as well as drawing, and the verb *graphein* means "to write" as well as "to represent by means of lines." Furthermore, when used as an adjective, *graphic* implies vivid, clear description, effectively presented. Taken together, these definitions combine into a practical concept of graphics as *materials which communicate facts and ideas clearly and succinctly through a combination of drawings, words, and pictures.*

Drawings may take such forms as diagrams, sketches, or graphs. *Words* (and numbers) are used in titles and explanations of graphs, charts, diagrams, and posters, as well as for captions in cartoons and comic strips. *Pictures* include sketches, symbols, and even photographs that are used in graphic materials to give meaning to facts, concepts, and ideas which, by their nature, lend themselves to graphic presentation. Thus, *graphics* includes a variety of visual forms, principal among which is drawing in some form.

The instructional values of graphic materials lie generally in their capacity to

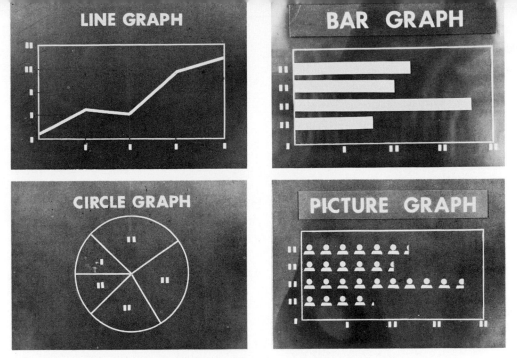

Fig. 5.2. / Would each of these four graph types be equally suitable for the same purpose?

attract attention and to convey certain types of information in condensed, summarized form. A biology chart on cell division, for example, may outline the complete process of mitosis. A diagram of office organization may show quickly the channels of responsibility and departmental function. A graph of automobile production shows at a glance whether more or fewer cars are being produced this year than in preceding years. In each of these cases, the essence of the graphic message is brevity, sharp focus on key information, and—if well executed—a heightened level of viewer interest.

Since symbols and illustrative drawings are usually parts of other graphic forms, we shall discuss them in these contexts. Another type of graphics—maps and globes—has so many distinctive features and uses that these two forms are discussed separately in Chapter IX. The remaining six principal types of graphics include graphs, diagrams, charts, posters, cartoons, and comics.

□ GRAPHS

Graphs may be defined as "visual representations of numerical data." A table of figures may contain a wealth of valuable information, but a graph of the same data presents the gist of that information quickly and effectively. Furthermore, graphs reveal important relationships in the data, such as trends and variations from normal. Finally, and of particular significance for the teacher, graphs are inherently more interesting than numerical tabulations, however well arranged the latter may be.

When a teacher wants to keep interest in library-reading running high among her pupils, she may post a *progress graph* showing the number of books read by each pupil in her class. Progress graphs—which can be purchased from school supply houses—have a number of bright red bars that are revealed by removing small sections of the overlaying paper. The pupils' names are inserted on the chart and one section of the overlay is removed for each completed project.

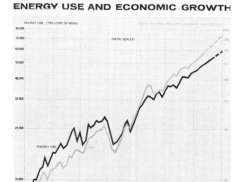

Fig. 5.3. / Note the precision with which information is plotted on this line graph and the accuracy with which trends can be noted.

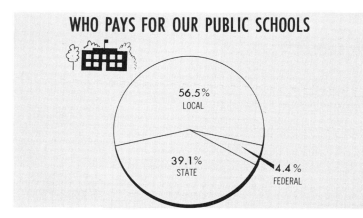

WHO PAYS FOR OUR PUBLIC SCHOOLS

56.5% LOCAL

39.1% STATE

4.4% FEDERAL

Fig. 5.4. / Note the kind of information presented on this bar graph and the means used to make it easily readable. Suggest another graphing method by which the indicated relationship might be shown effectively.

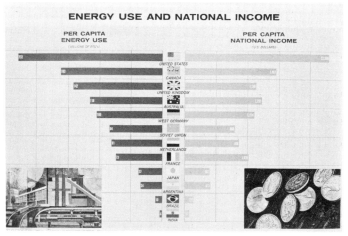

Fig. 5.5. / Is the circle graph well suited for this type of information? Why or why not?

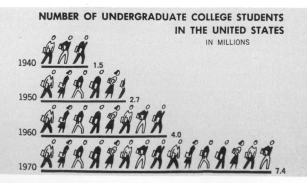

Fig. 5.6. / In what way does pictorial treatment strengthen this graph?

The appeal of graphs is not limited to youngsters. For example, who is not familiar with the large pictorial thermometers used to register progress in fund-raising campaigns for the Community Chest or the new church that is to be built on the corner? The businessman is especially dependent on graphs to show the trends in his sales volume and he refers continually to them for information on business in general.

It is well to remember that the major purpose of graphing is to present comparative quantitative information *quickly* and *simply*. When a graph is intricate and difficult to read, it loses its chief advantage. Complex graphic concepts are more effectively presented, as a rule, in a series of simpler graphs than in a single intricate composite. Even when a composite graph is desirable, it should follow a series of supporting graphs.

■ TYPES AND ADVANTAGES OF GRAPHS

There are many kinds of graphs. Among those most commonly used are the line, bar, circle or "pie," and pictorial graphs (Fig. 5.2). Each type has certain advantages and applications.

■ LINE GRAPHS

The line graph is potentially the most *precise* or accurate of all graphs; it is therefore particularly useful in plotting trends or relationships between two sets of data. A line graph should be used when a considerable number of data are to be plotted or when the data comprise a continuous series which, over a period of time, clearly shows the progress or development taking place. The line graph shown in Fig. 5.3 was plotted from continuous data. There are numerous variations and combinations of the simple line graph used, including shaded-surface graphs of several types and silhouette graphs.

■ BAR GRAPHS

Bar graphs are probably the simplest of all graphs *to read* (Fig. 5.4). They are also easily constructed, as each of the several groups of data to be plotted is represented by either vertical or horizontal bars. The length of the bars is used to express the percentages of the data, while the width of all the bars remains the same. The bar graph is employed to best advantage when the number of values to be compared is small—usually no more than six or eight. Occasionally, a larger number of bars are used but, in such instances, additional elements such as color or pictorial representations are needed to make the graph more readable and interesting. The bar graph provides direct comparison of quantitative data at specified intervals of time.

■ CIRCLE OR PIE GRAPHS

The circle, or pie, graph is divided into sectors, each of which is used to represent a component *part of a whole*. The essence of the circle graph is that its combined parts must always add up to 100 percent. To put it another way, two characteristics are common to all circle graphs: (1) They always present totals or whole amounts and (2) their parts or segments are calculated in percentages or fractional parts of this whole. When the intermediate-grade teacher introduces the subject of fractions, he may begin by cutting an apple into halves and quarters. He may apply a similar technique with the feltboard, fitting segments of a circle together to form the complete circle.

Research indicates that circle graphs are the most accurately read of all common graph forms when used to compare parts of a whole.[2] For example, if a nation produces 10,000,000 tons of coal per year and 7,500,000 tons are bituminous, 2,000,000 anthracite, and 500,000 lignite, this information can be shown on a circle graph by shading 75 percent of the circle to represent bituminous production, 20 percent for anthracite, and the remaining 5 percent for lignite. The resulting "pie" is a natural and easily understood visual device with which to present this data. Such information as the sources of the school dollar, the distribution of expenditures of a municipality, or the proportional sources of the world's petroleum supply can likewise be well represented by pie graphs. A good example is shown in Fig. 5.5.

■ AREA AND SOLID-FIGURE GRAPHS

Area graphs consist of squares, circles, or other outline figures of different sizes, and pictorially represent two or more related totals. These graphs depend upon a comparison of areas to present information and, in consequence, are read less easily than line, bar, or circle graphs. This is because it is visually more difficult to compare areas than to compare lengths of lines or arcs. Area graphs, therefore, sacrifice some of the definitive quality and readability which are characteristics of effective graphing.

One value of the area graph, however, is the fact that it is used infrequently enough to be somewhat unusual; hence, it catches the eye quickly. Another advantage lies in the fact that the components of the area graph take less space than do those of other graph types. For example, you can fit into a fairly small space two squares or two circles of different sizes representing two comparative amounts. The same information presented on a bar or line graph would require a considerably larger area.

The solid-figure graphs contain spheres, cubes, or other figures that give a three-dimensional effect (see Fig. 5.7). Although more striking and interesting in appearance than area graphs with two-dimensional effects, some solid-figure graphs have the particular disadvantage of being less easily read. In fact, many solid-figure graphs are used to show relationships in cubic content, volume, or other concepts which involve three dimensions—rather difficult to do with accuracy.

[2] Lewis V. Peterson and Wilbur Schramm, "How Accurately Are Different Kinds of Graphs Read?" *AV Communications Review*, Summer, 1954, pp. 178–189.

■ PICTORIAL GRAPHS

Much of the eye-catching appeal of figures which give a three-dimensional effect is attained by the flat, simplified, and representational figures that are used in pictorial graphs. Simplified drawings give the graph *realism* and *interest* appeal. This type of graph is actually an adaptation of the bar graph and is usually employed to present the same kinds of data. Used widely in magazines and newspapers, the pictorial graph is easily read and has the added advantage of using realistic representational figures to convey meaning.

Pictorial statistics were first popularized in Vienna by Otto Neurath, a renowned sociologist who sought a means of conveying significant statistical information in a way that would be both interesting and readily understood by peoples around the world.[3] He achieved this by developing simplified, outline figures of such subjects as a man, a woman, child, cow, ship, or sheaf of grain and using them to represent graphic data. Neurath termed his figures "isotypes," and variations of his original figures are now used in most countries of the world. *Pictorial statistics* thus refers to any graphic form employing such figures, as, for example, those shown in Fig. 5.6. Compare these with the other graphs shown on preceding pages, and note the relative degrees of interest and readability of the several types. Which would be most effective for particular purposes with your classes?

MULTIPLE CYLINDER GRAPH

■ RESEARCH EVALUATIONS OF GRAPH TYPES

Peterson and Schramm compared the relative accuracy with which 86 airmen could read eight types of graphs: Unknown to the airmen, each graph embodied the same five proportions totaling 100 percent (Fig. 5.7).[4] The findings of this study indicated that the square-column graph was read as accurately as the ordinary multiple-bar graph. It is worthy of note that the addition of a three-dimensional effect apparently does not of itself make for less accurate reading of a graph. However, there was significantly less accuracy in reading the multiple cylinders than in reading the multiple squares. Least accurately read of any of the eight graph forms were the multiple-area squares. As these researchers point out, the above findings pertain specifically to graphs in which parts are compared to the whole.

CIRCLE GRAPH

DISC GRAPH

Fig. 5.7. / How accurately are different kinds of graphs read? Which of these eight types, do you think are most readable? Do your conclusions agree with the results of the research from which this illustration was taken?

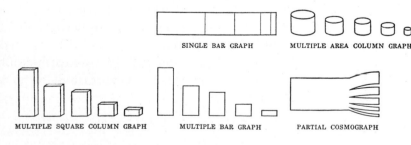

SINGLE BAR GRAPH   MULTIPLE AREA COLUMN GRAPH

MULTIPLE SQUARE COLUMN GRAPH   MULTIPLE BAR GRAPH   PARTIAL COSMOGRAPH

[3] Rudolph Modley, *How to Use Pictorial Statistics*, Harper & Row, 1937, pp. 126–130.
[4] Peterson and Schramm, *op. cit.*, pp. 84–85.

A more recent study tested the relative ease with which 250 high-school students and 100 Farm Short Course students comprehended nine different graph designs.[5] These nine designs were made up into 25 graphs containing 11 graph variables. Each comparison involved two graphs that differed in only one variable. Among the findings of this research were that both horizontal and vertical bar graphs were read more easily than were line graphs; that both symbols and labels were more easily read than were crosshatched keys or legends; and that better comprehension resulted when quantities were written on each bar or element of the graph, as shown in Fig. 5.8, than when grid lines alone were used. However, these investigators used fairly complex graphs for the study and, while they controlled for the variables in terms of their effectiveness in *presenting* information generally, they did not test the suitability of the various graphic presentations according to the *type* of information presented.

Still more recently, a carefully designed study conducted under the auspices of the University of Wisconsin undertook to analyze precisely seven methods of presenting statistical information according to their relative effectiveness in conveying this information to a wide range of people.[6] The seven methods involved various combinations of tables, horizontal bar graphs, and written text, and their effectiveness was measured according to the way 1080 subjects were able to choose the largest of four values, to locate absolute values, to derive totals, and to compare proportions.[7] Significant for teachers as well as for writers and publishers is that the four most effective methods were found to be:

1. Horizontal bar graphs reinforced with text
2. Short, simple tables reinforced with text
3. Graphs without textual reinforcement
4. Short tables without text back up

Further, "Long tables—even if reinforced with text—are less effective with audiences not experienced in reading tabular materials. Casting the figures into a prosaic text was the least effective of all methods tested."[8]

■ EVALUATING GRAPHS

In evaluating a graph, it is important to identify the purpose it is intended to achieve and its suitability to the readers for whom it is designed (Fig. 5.9). If these coincide sufficiently with your own teaching purposes, the graph may be useful. However, its full effectiveness will depend upon other factors, such as the extent to which the design and the other principles of good graphing have been observed in its construction.

The principle of *simplicity,* for example, should be observed in all graphs. Intricate or complex graphs may occasionally be necessary in plotting a variety

5 Hugh M. Culbertson and Richard D. Powers, "A Study of Graph Comprehension Difficulties," *AV Communications Review,* Spring, 1959, pp. 97–110.

6 Gloria D. Feliciano, Richard D. Powers, and Bryant E. Kearl, "The Presentation of Statistical Information," *AV Communications Review,* May–June, 1963, pp. 32–39.

7 Previous studies had established the relative readability of horizontal bar graphs for conveying general quantitative information. Thus the type of graph was not a variable in this study.

8 Feliciano, *et al., op. cit.,* p. 38.

THE MEN TO WOMEN RATIO IN THE U.S.

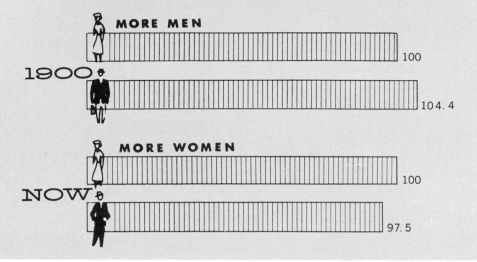

MORE MEN

1900

100

104.4

MORE WOMEN

NOW

100

97.5

Fig. 5.8. / There is substance here for considerable thought and discussion. Our point, however, is to illustrate the inherent readability of the simple bar graph.

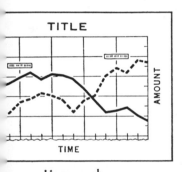

Line graph

Single-surface graph

Combination column and line graph

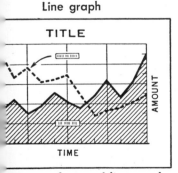

...nation surface and line graph

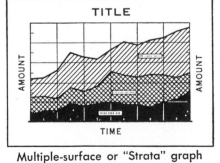

Multiple-surface or "Strata" graph

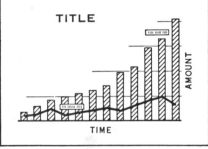
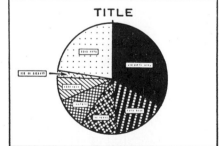

Sector or "Pie" graph

Fig. 5.9. / Can you identify the kind of information which could best be used on each of these types of graphs?

...lumn graph (single-series)

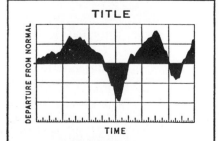

Silhouette graph

of related factors for industrial or economic purposes, but such graphs sacrifice communication effectiveness. The most effective graphs highlight only one or two ideas.

Another principle applicable to all graphs is that *comparisons or relationships must be shown*. For example, wheat production for a single year is not suitable for graphing unless it is compared with wheat production in other years, or with the production of other commodities in the same year. Graphing requires comparative data of some kind. Without comparisons or relationships to make them meaningful, there is little advantage in presenting statistics graphically.

A third principle of good graph construction is that *approximations rather than precise amounts* should be shown. A graph is intended to tell a story at a glance—to present comparisons, trends, and relationships. For these purposes, minute details are not only unnecessary, but also tend to complicate the graph and to detract from its effectiveness. Further, when constructing your own graphs or evaluating them, note that effective graphs have bold lines which contrast well with grid lines, and which are clear and easily read.

There are two principles which apply particularly to pictorial graphs: (1) The pictorial symbols should be self-explanatory, and (2) each quantity is usually indicated by the *number* of symbolic figures used to express it rather than by the *size* of any single symbol. The relationship of one quantity to the others on the graph is more easily comprehended if several symbolic figures of the same size are used—each figure representing a given amount, and the number of figures indicating the number of times by which that amount should be multiplied—rather than a single figure which differs in size from the single symbols used to represent the other amounts. The reason for this is that accurate judgment of the area of an irregularly shaped object is difficult. Thus, pictorial graphs normally use several figures to show each quantity represented, partial figures being used to express fractions of the amount represented by a single symbol. For example, each complete figure in Fig. 5.6 represents 500,000 college students; therefore, the number of college undergraduates for 1940, one and a half million, is expressed by three symbolic figures.

■ USING GRAPHS IN TEACHING

Pictures which are appropriate to a particular topic and its study group tend to convey meaning readily because they normally contain images or representatives of real objects that are already familiar to the student. Graphs, on the other hand, are principally symbolic and abstract in character, and are best used in the body and summary of a lesson after the student has acquired a background of information from other sources.

Children learn formally about how to make and to read simple graphs in middle-grade mathematics. However, they see graphs in newspapers, magazines and some textbooks; consequently, graphic materials need not be regarded as completely foreign to the experience of a child who has not yet formally studied them. The pictorial graph in particular is readily grasped by upper-grade or older pupils.

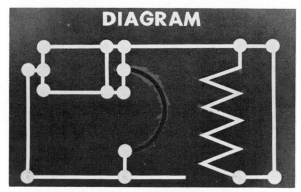

Fig. 5.10. / The diagram reduces a complex theory or process to a few simple symbols. What would the reader of this diagram have to know before he could interpret this one accurately?

But the graph is by nature a summarizing device. It visualizes totals and their relationships to one another, or it expresses certain conclusions about quantities. The well-trained teacher seldom begins a lesson with conclusions; to do so is to apply the principles of deductive rather than inductive reasoning. Educational psychologists find that learning is more efficient and productive when it proceeds from the specific to the abstract and general—from the acquisition of specific information and discrete ideas, to their assimilation as meaningful concepts, and then to the application of these concepts to a sufficient number of situations so that larger generalizations can be drawn. Within this learning process, graphic summaries of quantitative data can probably be used to advantage at several points depending both upon the student's ability in graph reading and the level of knowledge he has already acquired.

At some midpoint during their study of the Scandinavian countries, for example, pupils will profit from the study of graphs which show the trends in such factors as population, exports, and ocean shipping in each country over a period of years. The experience acquired previously in the unit through various learning activities and materials—such as books, pictures, films, and other media—enables the pupils to increase their comprehension of the graph, comprehension which would have been less possible at earlier stages of the learning experience. Later, when comparing and summarizing their learning about the three countries, students will again find graphs a particularly helpful device.

☐ DIAGRAMS

A *diagram* is a "condensed drawing consisting primarily of lines and symbols designed to show interrelationships, general outlines, or key features of a process, object, or area." Although most graphic forms are condensed visual summaries, the diagram is the most condensed of all (Fig. 5.10). The diagram relies heavily on symbols—a form of visual shorthand—to convey information and, because it has also stripped down the full concept to its barest essentials, the diagram tends to be highly abstract. This means that a background of knowledge and experience in the given subject matter is usually necessary before related diagrams can be read intelligently.

For example, have you ever tried to read a blueprint? If you have had the

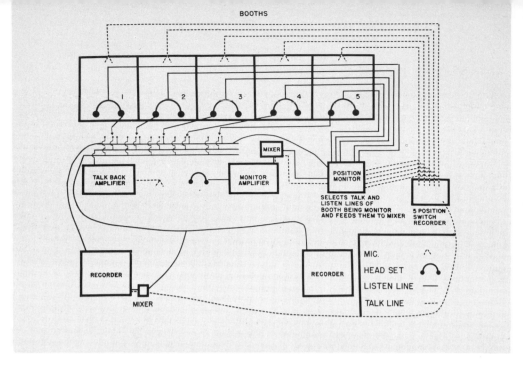

Fig. 5.11. / This diagram describes a simple language laboratory. Can you analyze its arrangement clearly from the information provided?

technicians' training or experience in reading architectural, electrical, or engineering blueprints—and have thus learned the many symbols used for electrical outlets, plumbing lines, kinds of material, and types of joints, etc.—you may be able to read the blueprint rather easily. Without this knowledge, however, it may be confusing and difficult to interpret. Yet this type of diagram is so important that modern construction engineering and manufacturing would be impossible without it.

Diagrams are also useful in our daily activities. A threading diagram is of considerable help in learning to operate a motion-picture projector. With diagrams in dress patterns to follow, many women become proficient in making their own clothes. Diagrams also accompany many of the more complex toys youngsters receive at Christmas time. Thousands of boys (and a good many fathers!) use diagrams to assemble model airplanes, ships, and railroads.

Diagrams are important for learning many concepts in the social studies, sciences, mathematics, and language areas (Fig. 5.11). Do you remember your own early efforts in diagraming sentences to identify the subject, predicate, verb, and modifiers?

Teachers need to be aware that diagrams can *impede* learning if they are not clearly understood. It is often necessary to teach how a particular diagram is to be read before it can serve to implement learning. Yet, the abstract nature of diagraming can also be an advantage in that it permits freedom and flexibility in application. You can ascribe to lines and symbols any meanings desired so long as these meanings are made clear in application. A college teacher of French literature, for example, has found diagrams helpful to her students' understanding of the forms and composition of French novels, drama, and poetry.[9]

Some research has been done on the ability of children to read diagrammatic

[9] Dorothy Wirtz, "Graphic Illustration of Literature," *The French Review*, February, 1965, pp. 508–516.

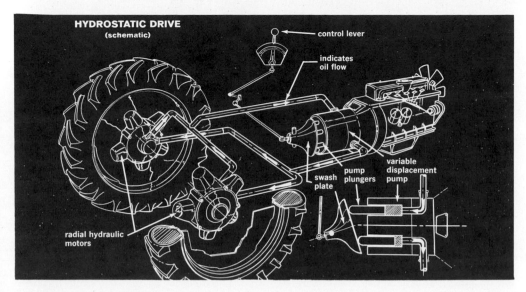

Fig. 5.12. What prior knowledge would be necessary to make this schematic diagram meaningful?

materials. A series of studies conducted among elementary-school pupils revealed, first, that most of the children studied had considerable difficulty in reading cross sections, process diagrams, and conventionalized diagrammatic symbols, such as diagrams of a gasoline engine and lift pump.[10] A follow-up study revealed that the addition of clarifying materials, such as photographs of the actual object, aided the children greatly in reading a cross section, while a third study in the series showed that, when simple directions—such as "Start Here and Follow Arrows"—were added to a process diagram of a flour mill, the children were materially helped in interpreting the diagram correctly. There was also evidence, however, of a need for still further clarifying the diagram.

Malter's studies support the principle that *diagrams and similar materials of an abstract character require careful foundation work before they can be used efficiently with a class of pupils.* It follows that diagrammatic materials usually lend themselves better to summary and review than to introductory use in a lesson. As the teacher realizes, the interpretation of even such relatively concrete media as pictures depends heavily on the experience which the child can bring *to* a picture. A diagram of the steps in flour processing, for example, will have much additional meaning *after* the pupil has had an opportunity of studying more concretely how flour is made—perhaps by going through a flour mill.

A second principle is that *other appropriate audiovisual materials should be used with diagrams to make them more understandable.* Such materials as pictures, slides, filmstrips, and motion-picture films all have as their basic function the clarification of significant concepts (Fig. 5.12). While each audiovisual medium has certain unique advantages in a specific instance, the coordinated use of several types of instructional materials yields the best results in most teaching

[10] The results of these studies are reported in Morton S. Malter, "Children's Ability to Read Diagrammatic Materials," *Elementary School Journal,* October, 1948, pp. 98–102.

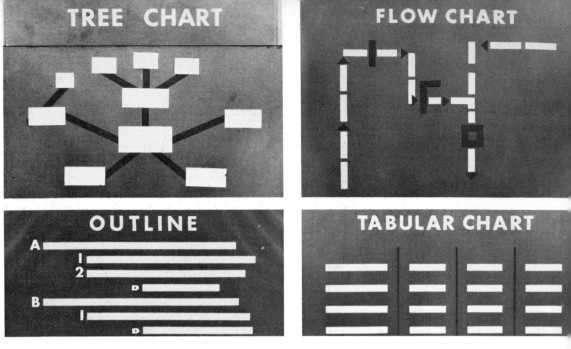

Fig. 5.13. / These charts show only the layout principles involved in the different kinds of charts. What other kinds of graphics and materials are needed to complete these charts? Which could use pictorial symbols? Which would use verbal or numerical symbols?

situations. This is particularly pertinent in the use of diagrammatic materials because of their relatively high level of abstraction.

☐ CHARTS

The term *charts* has a number of meanings. To the navigator, a chart is a particular kind of map. To the businessman, it may be a graph or a tabular treatment of sales data. To the engineer, it may be a diagram. To the teacher, a chart is more likely to be a graphic means of presenting a variety of related materials on large sheets of paper or cardboard at the front of the room. For our purposes, it will be helpful to be more specific, because charts are a distinctive medium of visualization that have certain characteristics of their own.

Charts are combinations of such pictorial, graphic, numerical, or verbal materials which, together, will be most likely to present clear visual summaries of important processes or relationships. The principal steps in the production of steel, the organization of Congress, the parts of a flower, the phases of the moon, the parts of speech, or a historical time-line are typical of the many and varied subjects suitable for treatment on charts. Charts are usually large enough to use with a group or class. Many charts are available commercially in sets, but simple charts can also be developed on the chalkboard or on newsprint pads by teachers or students, during a classroom discussion.

■ TYPES OF CHARTS

There are many types of charts: classification charts, flow charts, relationship charts, tabulation charts, chronology charts, and variations of these, among

RHINELAND, GERMANY

PULPWOOD INDUSTRY, THREE RIVERS, CANADA

Plate 1 / Highly effective study prints of scenes in excellent color and of good size are available in various subject areas. Those shown here are selections from several series of pictures on Europe, North America, and Africa designed to illustrate key concepts in geography. They are laminated, 30 × 21 inches in size, and come in window-type cases which serve for storage of the set or as a frame for individual pictures.

Plate 2 / Besides strong aesthetic appeal, what does color add to this striking
of the Swiss Alps? How does it contribute, for example, to an understandi

e landscape and its vegetation? to comprehension of life and the problems of
ving on a Swiss mountainside?

Plate 3 / Aside fro
excellent design bui
around a creative ide
note how effective poste
are further strengthene
by color.

EUROPE NOW FIVE HOURS CLOSER

ONLY 390 JET MAGIC MINUTES FROM NEW YORK

PAN AM

WORLD'S MOST EXPERIENCED AIRLINE

EUROPE

ONLY 7 JET MAGIC HOURS FROM NEW YORK

PAN AM

WORLD'S MOST EXPERIENCED AIRLINE

SAFETY

SUMMER

SPRING

AUTUMN

WINTER

is a year 'round job

2655-A

WHEREVER YOU ARE
WHATEVER YOU DO

STAY
ALERT
FOR
SAFETY

Plate 4 / Three posters designed for similar purposes. Analyze all three in terms of effectiveness. Which is best? Why?

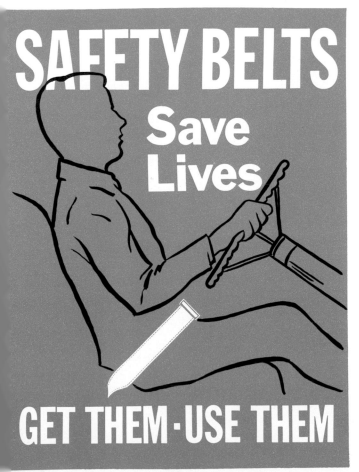

SAFETY BELTS
Save
Lives

GET THEM · USE THEM

© NATIONAL SAFETY COUNCIL   CHICAGO · PRINTED IN U.S.A   T-1967-A

HOW DO YOU SIT?

Plate 5 / Posters, like other visuals, must be designed with the age level and normal interests of the intended viewers in mind. Note how this poster conveys a posture message. Is it well executed for the age group for whom it is designed?

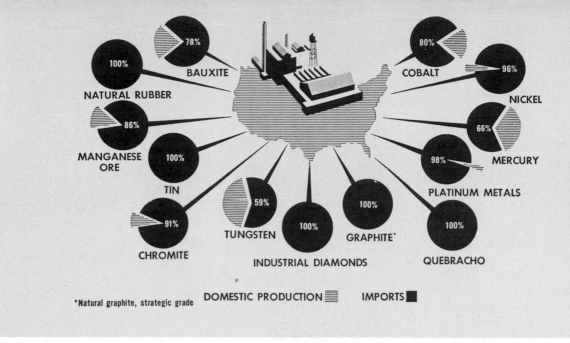

Fig. 5.14. / Is the meaning of this stream chart clear? What elements are used?

others (Fig. 5.13).[11] The charts most commonly used in teaching are tree and stream charts, flow charts, outline charts, and tabular charts.

■ TREE CHARTS

As its name suggests, the *tree* chart is developed from a base composed of several "roots" which lead into a single "trunk." The "branches," in turn, represent developments and relationships. A good example is a genealogy chart in which two individuals are the roots from which a family "tree" grows. The tree chart is useful in showing developments resulting from a combination of major factors. For example, such a chart is suitable for showing the many by-products obtainable from coal. It is likewise effective in showing how iron ore, limestone, coke, and various chemicals may be combined to produce a variety of types of steel.

Sometimes a reverse form of the tree chart is useful in showing how a great variety of elements are combined to form one important product. This type of chart, known as a *stream* chart, can be used to illustrate an industrial nation's dependence on other countries for strategic materials (Fig. 5.14).

■ FLOW CHART

The organization of a student council or a unit of government, the development of a manufacturing process, or the steps whereby a bill becomes a law can be shown to advantage in a *flow* or organization chart (Fig. 5.15). This chart is

---

11 See Willard C. Brinton, *Graphic Presentation*, Brinton Associates, 1939. Chaps. 3–8, and 31 describe types of charts and their uses.

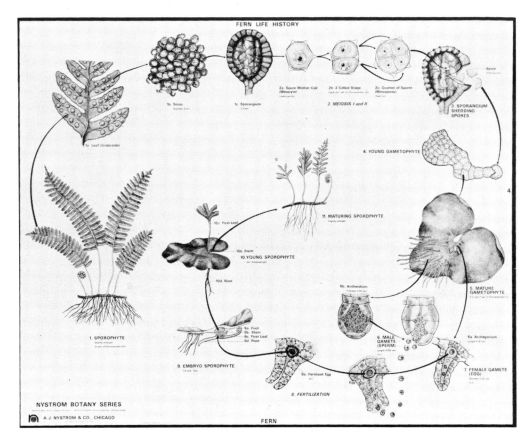

Fig. 5.15. / Pictorial section from one in a series of botany charts. How would you classify this chart as to type? How would you evaluate it? How would you use it?

well suited to showing functional relationships and is used widely in industry and government for that purpose.

▪ OUTLINE CHART

The organization of content into key points and subpoints, which a teacher may do on the chalkboard, is also a useful chart form. Content may range from simple parts of speech or vocabulary classifications to the rationale for a given foreign policy or business investment.

▪ TABULAR CHART

Sequence relationships such as those in a historical time-line or a timetable can be shown on a *tabular* chart. One of the unique values of the tabular chart is its ability to show time relationships. Variations of this form of chart include

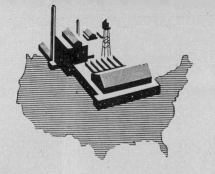

HOT ROLLED PRODUCTS	Ala.	Ariz.	Ark.	Calif.	Colo.	Conn.	Del.	Fla.	Ga.	Hawaii	Ill.	Ind.	Iowa	Ky.	La.	Md.	Mass.	Mich.	Minn.	Miss.	Mo.	N.J.	N.Y.	Ohio	Okla.	Ore.	Pa.	R.I.	Tenn.	Texas	Utah	Va.	Wash.	W. Va.	Wisc.	No. of States
Structural Shapes	X			X	X				X		X	X									X	X	X	X			X		X	X				X	X	15
Piling											X	X											X				X									4
Plates	X			X	X	X					X	X		X		X							X	X			X				X	X		X		14
Sheets	X			X							X	X		X		X	X						X	X			X							X		11
Strip	X			X	X				X		X	X								X		X	X	X			X		X	X						13
Coils for Tin Plate	X			X							X	X				X							X				X			X				X		9
Bars, Reinforcing	X	X		X	X			X	X		X	X		X		X		X	X		X	X	X	X	X		X		X	X		X		X		22
Other Bars & Lt. Shapes	X	X	X	X	X	X	X	X	X		X	X	X	X		X	X	X	X	X	X	X	X	X			X		X	X		X	X	X		28
Wire Rods	X			X	X						X	X		X		X	X				X	X	X	X			X		X	X	X					16
Blanks, Tube Rounds, etc.				X							X	X											X	X			X									6
Blooms & Billets †				X	X						X	X				X							X	X			X		X							9
Rails	X			X							X												X				X							X		6
Splice Bars, etc.	X			X	X						X												X				X					X	X			8
Wheels & Axles											X																X									2
Skelp	X			X							X	X				X								X			X			X				X		9
All Other	X			X							X									X							X			X						6
OTHER FINISHED PRODUCTS (Made from hot rolled items)																																				
Bars (cold finished)				X	X						X	X		X		X	X				X	X	X				X							X	X	13
Pipe and Tubing	X	X		X	X	X	X	X	X		X	X		X	X	X	X	X			X	X	X				X				X	X		X	X	23
Plain Wire	X	X		X	X	X	X				X	X					X	X	X	X	X	X	X	X		X	X				X				X	20
Wire Products	X	X		X	X	X	X				X	X					X	X			X	X	X	X		X	X				X				X	18
Cold Rolled Sheets	X			X							X	X		X		X	X						X	X			X								X	11
Gal. & Long Terne Sheets	X			X							X	X		X		X							X				X								X	9
Cold Rolled Strip				X	X						X	X		X		X			X			X	X	X			X			X					X	13
Galvanized Strip										X	X											X	X	X			X									6
Tin Plate	X			X							X	X				X					X						X								X	8
Track Accessories	X			X	X						X	X									X	X	X	X			X					X	X			12
Products Made in State	19	2	1	20	15	6	2	4	9	1	23	24	1	7	1	15	6	8	6	2	7	10	20	21	1	4	26	4	3	10	6	4	7	11	5	

Fig. 5.16. / What are some of the advantages of the tabular chart? Some of its limitations?

tables of information such as arguments for and against a bond issue, nations participating in the United Nations, etc. (Fig. 5.16).

■ SCHOOL-MADE CHARTS

Any of the types of charts described above are available from commercial sources (see Source List, page 529), but many of them can be made by teachers or pupils. Some elementary teachers in Texas suggest the following possibilities, each named according to its teaching function rather than to type of chart:

1. *Experience charts:*
   A trip to the library, bakery, museum, etc., will be long remembered if some of the salient points are put down on charts.
2. *Achievement charts:*
   Charts setting down principles of spelling, arithmetic, or science that have been conquered by the class.

Fig. 5.17. / What made this famous poster by James Montgomery Flagg highly effective as a recruiting poster?

3. *Charts recording plans and class rules:*
   A field trip plan can be outlined on a chart to give special emphasis in advance to some of the important sights that will be seen.
4. *Instruction charts of wide variety:*

Number charts help bridge this critical step, the gradual realization of numbers as abstract ideas.

Phonetic charts are enormously helpful in establishing familiarity with common syllables and words and introducing the link between writing and speech.

Work charts list series of problems or questions to be answered. They also help develop reading skill and speed.[12]

□ POSTERS

Posters have existed in primitive form almost since the invention of movable-type printing in the fifteenth century. The first posters consisted almost entirely of text and carried notices of royal proclamations, tax assessments, fairs, markets, and newly printed books. Some of them had wood-cut illustrations. But it remained for lithography—developed in the mid-nineteenth century and made possible the first cheap and brilliant color reproduction—to bring the modern concept of posters into being.

The modern poster was born in 1867 in Paris, when Jules Chéret, the first of the great modern poster artists, was commissioned by Sarah Bernhardt to prepare a poster announcing her appearance in the play *La Biche au Bois*. Chéret's use of color, design, and bold lettering was superb, and the poster started a new trend in graphic communication. As the poster idea caught on, many fine artists experimented with it in Europe and the United States. The best of these posters combined simplicity and visual force with emotional impact or wit; many became famous—as did James Montgomery Flagg's recruiting poster shown in Fig. 5.17. During World Wars I and II, the major powers used large-scale poster campaigns to recruit armed forces, to sell war bonds, to maintain morale, and to boost the war effort generally. United States Treasury officials regarded posters as highly significant in the success of the war-loan drives during both world wars. In the meantime, the advertising industry, and particularly the transportation companies, adopted posters on a massive scale.

This is the background of the poster that today has a unique and important function among the visual communication media. Its role is to implant very quickly in the viewer's mind, or to make him recall, a single important idea: "Care," "Support Your Community Chest," "Fly BOAC," "Radio Free Europe," "Stand Tall," etc. Thus, the poster must have strong eye appeal if it is to attract attention and to have enough holding power to put its message across. The poster is therefore defined as a *visual combination of bold design, color, and message which is intended to catch and hold the attention of the passer-by long enough to implant or to reinforce a significant idea in his mind.*

■ CHARACTERISTICS OF POSTERS

Clearly, if they are to achieve their purpose, good posters must have a dynamic, impelling quality. They must be essentially simple, for there is no time to involve the viewer in detailed study. They must also be striking enough to

---

12 See Leona Doss, Ima Sorden, and M. K. Hage, Jr., "Classroom Charts Add the Crowning Touch," *Texas Outlook,* December, 1959, pp. 18–21.

attract attention or their usefulness is lost. We shall examine several of their specific characteristics more closely.

■ DRAMATIC SIMPLICITY

To attract attention, the prominent features of the poster must stand out sharply. These features may be a photograph, a drawing, or a striking design. The World War II poster (Fig. 5.17) showing Uncle Sam pointing his finger directly at the observer is unforgettable. The eye-catcher in that poster is the head of Uncle Sam, shown against a solid-blue background. The piercing eyes and pointing forefinger seem to follow and to hold the observer from any angle. The drawing is vivid and striking enough to reach out and command attention, and the eye travels quickly from the drawing to the printed message below it.

■ SELF-CONTAINED MESSAGE

Having caught the viewer's attention, the message must be transmitted clearly and quickly. This is usually achieved by combining the illustrative picture with a brief text printed in bold type. The meaning must be clear and succinct and able to be grasped at a glance.

■ ATTRACTIVENESS

Effective posters are usually pleasing to the eye. Although the subject itself may not be pleasant—as in the cases of war, traffic safety, fire hazards, and the like—all posters must embody good design, good lettering, and attractive color. Other types of posters—such as those used for school courtesy and housekeeping campaigns—need to be attractive in order to be *appropriate*. The attractive poster is inherently pleasing and interesting, both powerful factors in learning.

■ DESIGN AND COLOR

Good composition, color, and technique are the principal elements in preparing effective posters. These elements are also applicable to flat pictures, charts, billboards, and bulletin boards—in fact, to any visual medium. But just as each medium has certain unique characteristics, so does it have certain unique design and color requirements.

Like a photograph or painting, a good poster requires a center of interest but, in a poster, this center must be particularly strong and commanding. For this reason, subtlety is usually avoided in favor of unmistakable contrast and emphasis. A painting or photograph, on the other hand, frequently contains extensive detail and generally has to be studied to be fully appreciated.

Color provides meaning and expression as well as beauty in a good painting.

It provides force and contrast as well as attractiveness in a good poster (see Plates 3 and 4, following p. 144). Although both are essential, these uses of color are not the same. Again the distinction is based on the quite different purposes for which posters and paintings are created.

This is not to say that poster techniques exclude the characteristics found in other visual forms. Some posters use portraits—with all of their detail—as the center of interest, as in the case of the recruiting poster in Fig. 5.17. Other posters use a complete photographic background for their principal theme, or even a combination of scenes. In such instances the photographic background is normally subdued so that the message carried by the poster will stand out clearly.

■ SUGGESTED USES OF POSTERS

From what has been said about the poster and its purposes, several uses suggest themselves to the classroom teacher.

■ MOTIVATION

The first of these uses may be called "motivational," or "stimulative." A set of good travel posters on Great Britain, for example, can be used effectively in arousing curiosity and interest in a study of modern Britain. A poster on the resort area of Bath will suggest several leads to the teacher. A discussion of what the poster shows may be initiated, or other resorts may be located on a map of England. There is also an opportunity to bring out the fact that the British people enjoy some of the same recreations as we do—swimming, sun bathing, and boating. Here is a possible starting point for cultural understanding—a point of familiarity and common interest.

■ REMINDERS

A poster may also be used as a reminder or to create an awareness of a subject. By the time he reaches the intermediate grades, every child knows that brushing his teeth regularly is important, but, as teachers and parents are well aware, knowledge alone is seldom enough. There is need for frequent and varied methods of "jogging" the learner so that he will put his knowledge into practice until it becomes habitual. One means of doing this is by health and safety posters strategically placed and frequently changed (see Plates 4 and 5 following page 144).

Remember the remarkable ability of the human mind to become accustomed and adapted to its surroundings. Like a bulletin board which is seldom changed, the poster that is seen too often tends to become simply a part of the environment. When it loses its freshness, the poster loses its principal value—the power to attract the eye and to implant an idea.

Fig. 5.18. / Students' ideas flow freely if encouraged. With a bit of guidance, they can produce excellent posters like those shown here.

■ ATMOSPHERE

There is a third type of use, in which the poster may continue to be valuable after its initial impact has passed. This may be called the "atmosphere" or "environmental" use. Teachers of foreign languages frequently find that good posters—as well as pictures, paintings, and exhibits—assist in creating a desirable atmosphere or feeling for the country whose language is being studied. Attractive poster materials enhance this atmosphere, particularly if they are artistic.

■ CREATIVE EXPERIENCE

A fourth helpful use of posters in teaching lies in their creative and participative possibilities. The student who makes his own posters has the opportunity of expressing what he has learned. For this reason, poster-making may be a culminating activity that arises from a unit of work. A few students in a class in English literature, for example, may prepare posters for a Shakespearian display. In studying political campaigns, history students can trace interesting parallels in the political posters used at the turn of the century and those used today. Social-studies committees and student councils analyzing such current school problems as playground safety, lunchroom conditions, recreational programs, and corridor traffic between classes find well-prepared posters an effective means of expressing their conclusions. Preparing these posters is also a valuable activity for the young poster artists.

Closely related to posters which pupils prepare in connection with their class activities is the familiar campaign or advertising poster made in connection with school and community activities. Election campaigns for members of the student council, class plays, athletic contests, cleanup campaigns, music festivals, forensic contests, hobby shows, and the like are "naturals" for the preparation and use of posters. Here is an excellent opportunity for the school to capitalize on the natural drive of pupil interests to accomplish socially important and desirable objectives. If these activities are treated as an important part of the school program rather than as peripheral and extracurricular activities, much valuable educational experience can result. In this experience, the poster can properly be integrated as one of the important media for communicating ideas.

Pupil-made posters generally have much to commend them, from the standpoint of both experience and communication. Psychologically the pupil is primarily interested in his immediate surroundings and the concerns arising from them. This is one basis for the educational principle that we must start instruction where the student *is* and build from there. Effective instruction makes use of natural interests wherever practicable, and develops new experiences on the foundations of the old.

In applying this principle of learning, the social-studies teacher encourages active interest in school political campaigns as one means of developing an understanding of politics in a democratic society. One of the activities implicit in such campaigns is the use of slogans, banners, mottoes, and—of course—posters. School campaign posters, however, cannot be bought; they must be made by the pupils. In the words of one social-studies specialist:

> Pupil-made posters represent the fruition of social concepts and measure the effectiveness of teaching. Their construction and presentation is more apt to result in personal and social growth of students than is the display of posters secured from travel or advertising agencies.[13]

The pupil-made poster, likewise, is well suited to publicity for such school activities as plays and athletic contests. It may well reach its maximum effectiveness in cleanup, safety, courtesy, and similar campaigns, particularly when the campaigns are pupil-initiated. Posters such as those shown in Fig. 5.18 serve as reminders and stimulaters of socially desirable action or as deterrents to undesirable behavior.

Making a good poster is not difficult. The teacher should know the qualities of a good poster and how to make one so he can help his pupils prepare their own. The art teacher is often glad to assist, for poster work provides an excellent opportunity to demonstrate that art is properly a part of daily living rather than just another subject in the curriculum.

☐ CARTOONS

The use of the cartoon to lampoon man and his foibles goes back to the sixteenth century, when Renaissance artists began to caricature one another in

---

[13] Harris Harvill, "The Use of Posters, Charts, Cartoons, and Graphs," in W. H. Hartley (Ed.), *Audiovisual Materials and Methods in the Social Studies,* 18th Yearbook, National Council for the Social Studies, 1947, p. 120.

Fig. 5.19. / Exaggerated caricature of an image or idea is typically employed by the cartoonist in conveying his point. Is it successfully made here?

their studios, as well as passers-by on the street. Archaeologists have uncovered on the walls of ancient buildings many drawings which poke fun at the great and the pretentious. Medieval manuscripts contain similar evidences of refreshing humor directed at persons and groups prominent in contemporary society. One writer has drawn an interesting analogy between the functions of the king's jester in medieval times and those of the modern cartoonist.[14]

Although a pastime at first, the possibilities offered by caricaturing for satire, comedy, and ridicule soon became formally recognized (Fig. 5.19). Caricatures were used initially as a form of protest against people in authority. Later, there developed a visual form of social satire which dealt with groups and their composite characteristics. Eventually the two combined into what we know as the modern political-social cartoon.

The modern political-social cartoon developed in the United States during the nineteenth century.[15] Andrew Jackson and his spoils system were among the first subjects of political caricature. Later, in the 1860s, Thomas Nast conducted his famous cartoon campaign against the notorious Tweed Ring in New York. It was Nast who, during the same period, created the now standard symbols of the Democratic donkey and the Republican elephant. Nast and Joseph Keppler, the latter the originator of the famous cartoon character "Puck," set a pattern of attack against individuals as a way of getting at important issues. This pattern still characterizes most American cartoons on political and social subjects.

The serious cartoon is *a pictorial representation or caricature of a person, idea, or situation that is designed to influence public opinion.* Although an increasing number of excellent cartoons are intended merely to make people chuckle—as is true of those in the *Saturday Evening Post,* for example—it is

[14] Albert J. Nock, "The King's Jester, Modern Style," *Harper's,* March, 1928, pp. 481–488.
[15] *Ibid.,* p. 482.

Fig. 5.20. / For whom is this cartoon designed?

"Now don't start looking at things, or we'll *never* get through."

the cartoon as an instrument of propaganda that has the chief potentialities in teaching and with which the following discussion is concerned.

A good cartoon is built around a single idea. Typically, it may employ caricature, satire, exaggeration, symbolism, and humor of a sort. The humor may, and frequently does, extend to outright ridicule, particularly in cartoons on controversial political subjects in highly partisan newspapers. In some cases, the extensive use of cartoons on political and social subjects has given this medium an abusive characteristic typified by personal attacks on high-placed officials.

The power of the cartoon to influence public opinion lies in its compactness, its simplification of issues, and the considerable interest that can be aroused by sharply drawn illustrations that are laced with humor. The cartoon is a pre-digested source of information with a strong visual impact. Many persons who do not read a newspaper's editorials may follow its cartoons regularly. For this reason, the militant cartoonist on large metropolitan newspapers is regarded as a potent factor in forming public opinion.

■ EVALUATION AND SELECTION OF CARTOONS

An answer to the question "What is a good cartoon?" is somewhat elusive, because a cartoon is so much a product of the creative imagination, skill, and individuality of the cartoonist. Yet there are certain qualities which are typical of effective cartoons, and awareness of these qualities is helpful in selecting cartoons for teaching purposes.

■ APPROPRIATENESS TO EXPERIENCE LEVEL

The first consideration of the appropriateness of a cartoon, of course, is that its meaning be understandable by the class in which it is to be used. A cartoon on foreign aid or the "Great Society," for example, may have little meaning for a sixth-grade pupil who has not studied these topics. Likewise, while many teachers will get a chuckle out of Fig. 5.20, few youngsters will see its humor.

The same pupils, on the other hand, may readily interpret a fairly subtle cartoon on traffic safety or sportsmanship.

Schaffer's study of children's interpretations of social and political cartoons found that, on the average, children begin to interpret such cartoons abstractly at about age 13. The range of greatest increase in percentage of abstract response to symbolic drawings occurs between grades 6 and 8.[16] An analysis of erroneous interpretations, furthermore, showed that the absence of meaningful word elements in cartoon captions—in other words, a lack of background adequate to give correct meaning to words used—was a particular cause of error.[17]

▪ SIMPLICITY

Assuming that the cartoon's meaning is understandable, there are certain desirable physical characteristics common to good cartoons. One of these is simplicity. Generally speaking, the better cartoons contain only essentials; they depend more on key characteristics for recognition than on extensive photographic detail. Uncle Sam's top hat and striped trousers, and Castro's beard are familiar examples. A few sharp lines, some shading, and the necessary background sketched in lightly are the principal mechanical ingredients of a good cartoon. The creative artistry and imagination of the cartoonist are evidenced by the overall effect he can attain with these physical elements and an idea.

Another physical characteristic is brevity of caption. Some cartoons need no caption; the picture itself conveys the idea without verbal assistance. Although the political-social cartoon usually requires a caption, it should be clear, brief, and to the point. Extensive explanation is unnecessary if the cartoon is well conceived and well executed.

▪ CLEAR SYMBOLS

A third quality of effective cartoons is clarity of symbolism used. John Bull, Uncle Sam, the Republican elephant, and the Democratic donkey are standard cartoon symbols whose meanings are well understood by the newspaper-reading public generally. Such characterizations as the burdened taxpayer, the opulent business mogul, the unemployed workman, the laboring man, and the "politician" are also understood without difficulty if the rendition is good. Symbols representing more abstract concepts such as states' rights, humanity, the "common man," tariff walls, "one world," and freedom, on the other hand, are more difficult to devise. Here the cartoonist's ability is challenged to the utmost. Accordingly, teachers must be careful to select cartoons whose symbols are not too abstruse for their pupils.

[16] Lawrence W. Schaffer, *Children's Interpretation of Cartoons,* Teachers College, Columbia Univ., 1930, pp. 51–52.
[17] *Ibid.,* p. 66.

■ SUGGESTED USE OF CARTOONS

■ MOTIVATION

By its nature, an effective cartoon readily attracts attention and arouses interest. This suggests at once that appropriate cartoon materials can be useful motivating devices in the classroom. Cartoons on current topics, if suited to lesson objectives, are effective discussion starters. Such questions as "What does this cartoon mean?" "Does it tell the whole story?" and "What other cartoons have you seen on this subject?" can quickly perpetrate a discussion in a junior- or senior-high-school social-studies class.

The humor in cartoons has a great stimulative benefit, even for students of limited ability. According to a teacher of modern foreign languages in the Benjamin Harrison High School in New York, cartoons selected from French magazines elicited great interest, built vocabulary and confidence in using French, stimulated conversation, and generally increased pupil participation in the French classes. The cartoons without captions were of particular motivational value: These "proved even more interesting because while some of the captional cartoons had sometimes required an explanation by the instructor, in the latter case the explanations came from the students who were eager to give us their own. Consequently, this type was used as a motivating device for short compositions."[18]

Generally speaking, cartoons selected for specific purposes and for appropriate levels of sophistication can, at the very least, provide a refreshing tie-in with life outside the classroom, plus a stimulating variety and change of pace in instructional techniques. At best, and in many subjects, cartoons can open up a whole range of worthwhile learning activities.

■ ILLUSTRATIONS

One teacher reported effective results from using cartoons to illustrate scientific concepts in teaching science.[19] He used some cartoons to raise such questions as whether the situations pictured are scientifically possible or probable, as for example in illustrations which depict insects as having only two legs. Others were used to show the result of disregarding safe practices or the scientific method; this was done by asking the students what is wrong in the situation illustrated. This teacher emphasized the necessity of selecting cartoons carefully so as to avoid purely humorous reactions among pupils on the one hand, and, on the other, pointless attention to details that are unrelated to the cartoonist's purpose.

[18] René Merker, "Cartoons in High School Classes," *Modern Language Journal*, December, 1957, pp. 398–399.

[19] John D. Wollever, "Using Cartoons in the Classroom," *School Science and Mathematics*, April, 1950, pp. 255–258.

Fig. 5.21. / Cartoons may combine humorous appeal with scientific principles.

A college physics teacher reported that for many years he has had his students on the lookout for cartoons which illustrate physical principles. They write an appropriate title and bring the cartoon to class. "Very often," this instructor says, "a good discussion of physics comes out of debating how best to title one. . . . It is all an exciting exercise for my students—and for me—and invites participation irresistibly."[20] One example this teacher cites indicates that cartoon analysis can reach some fairly complex levels:

> A mason is building a brick chimney from the ground up. On each side of the site rests a carpenters horse and across these a plank. On the plank he has put a load of bricks so that the plank is bent in the middle. As he uses the bricks, the plank *unbends,* thus raising the bricks to the level of his work! The artist obviously knew Hooke's law. He may even know that the depression of a beam is given by $d = \dfrac{FL^3}{4} \, Yab^3$. He may even have known the equation of an elastic curve, $EI \, (d^2y/dx^2) = M_x$.[21]

A general science instructor might find in the cartoon shown in Fig. 5.21 a new way to explain the role of friction in relation to movement. Cartoons provide teachers with two valuable assets—good illustrations of significant learning points, and change of pace and variety in presentation of materials to the class.

■ PUPIL ACTIVITY

Another use of cartoons involves the creation of cartoons by the students themselves. Pupils can make cartoons to enliven interest in cleanup campaigns and safety drives. The student council finds cartoons particularly well suited as reminders of courtesy, sportsmanship, and lunchroom-behavior. Such devices, created by the pupils and containing the type of humor suited to their stage of maturity, are psychologically sound. They are likely to be effective even though they may be inexpert in their execution.

Classroom production of pupil cartoons is likewise a useful activity. The social

20 Julius Sumner Miller, "Cartoons and Physics Instruction," *American Journal of Physics,* April, 1960, pp. 406–407.
21 *Ibid.*

studies are a constant source of ideas suitable for cartoons. Literature and grammar also provide opportunities for drawing cartoons as illustrations of the knowledge acquired.[22]

☐ COMICS

Closely related to the cartoon is the comic strip. It is interesting to note that comics received their initial impetus from a newspaper war between William Randolph Hearst and Joseph Pulitzer in the mid-1890s. Colored supplements to the Sunday issues of the New York *Journal* and the New York *World* vied mightily with each other to build circulation.[23] A significant part in this rivalry was played by funny drawings involving a character who came to be known as "The Yellow Kid." This sketch achieved rapid popularity and accordingly increased the circulation of Pulitzer's New York *World*. Within six months, Hearst came out with a new comic section ". . . eight pages of iridescent polychromous effulgences that make the rainbow look like a piece of lead pipe."[24] Headlining his cast of characters was "The Yellow Kid," for Hearst had hired the original comic artist and his creation away from the *World*. Pulitzer promptly bought him back, but was again outbid by Hearst. Thereupon Pulitzer hired another artist and, for a time, both papers attempted to outdo each other with independent versions of the vulgar, raucous "Kid."[25] The yellow color of the strip and the notoriety arising from the contest between the two newspapers gave rise to the term "yellow journalism."

New comics were quickly created. "Buster Brown" and "The Katzenjammer Kids," the longest-lived of all comics, appeared by the close of 1902. With the Katzenjammers, the play-by-play story told in a series of separate pictures with the same characters was introduced; frame lines were added to the boxes and an appealing comic-strip personality in "Little Jimmy" was developed. By 1905, the comics had acquired practically all the physical features which characterize them today—all, that is, except the format of the now familiar comic book.

The comic book came into prominence in the mid-1930s. The lag between universal acceptance of the comic strip and the appearance of comic books on a large scale is curious, for early versions of the comic book had been used successfully as premiums in promotional campaigns as early as 1911. Once the idea caught on, however, comic books developed rapidly into big business.

The significant point of this historical sketch is that the initial purpose of comics was to build newspaper circulation. In the process, comics became firmly embedded in the consciousness of the American public. It is worth noting that their purpose is still primarily commercial—to sell newspapers and comic books. The comics are very much with us. Estimates have placed the readers of comics

---

22 Edith E. Mains, "The Cartoon and the Teaching of Grammar," *English Journal*, April, 1945, pp. 506–507.

23 Coulton Waugh, *The Comics*, Macmillan, 1947, pp. 6 ff.

24 *Ibid.*

25 *Ibid.*

Fig. 5.22. / Comics, like advertising take advantage of people's natural interests. How might you paraphrase this one?

in the United States at nearly 100,000,000. According to Ayer, some 36,500,000 comic books are now published on a weekly, biweekly, or monthly basis in this country and Canada.[26] This represents a reduction since 1961 of 24 percent, perhaps reflecting a shift of popular interest in this medium. Nonetheless, it is still an important factor in the reading habits of millions of young Americans.

Numerous circulation studies have indicated that comic books are read almost universally by children in the intermediate grades, by nearly half of all high-school pupils, and by approximately one-third of our population between the ages of 18 and 30. By their junior or senior year in high school, more than half the pupils stop reading comic books entirely or read them only occasionally. These studies merely substantiate what parents and teachers already know—that comics have become a major influence in the lives of American boys and girls. Thus, comics have certain unique strengths as teaching-learning materials, and, accordingly, deserve the attention of all teachers.

■ DEFINITION AND CHARACTERISTICS OF COMICS

Comics may be defined as *a form of cartooning in which a cast of characters enacts a story in a sequence of closely related drawings designed to entertain the reader.* Whereas the cartoon depends primarily upon a single visual impact, comics consist of continuing story situations in which reading plays an important role. Several other characteristics of comics should be recognized if the force of this medium is to be appreciated (Fig. 5.22). Comics focus on people. The stories are personalized so that the reader can readily identify himself with the

26 William F. McCollister (Ed.), *Directory to Newspapers and Periodicals*, Ayer & Sons, 1965, pp. 1424–1425.

Fig. 5.23. / The appeal of the informal comic book technique transfers to some extent to its use in information fields. Note the dynamic treatment above which appeared in color in a Sunday comic section. How effective would this be for use in schools? How could it be used to best advantage?

feelings and actions of the leading characters. The stories are brief enough to hold attention, they are packed with action, and in the Sunday supplement and the comic book they are made more vivid and appealing through the liberal use of primary colors.

The effect of undesirable types of comic books on children arouses public concern and action from time to time. As a result, several cities have barred such comics from sale at various times. Although a book by Wertham called attention to the possible consequences of unrestricted reading of such comics,[27] Witty and Sizemore's careful survey of all the research in the field concludes that the views both strongly opposing and defending the comic medium are without substantiation.[28] Burton suggests the need for a wholesome attitude toward the constructive use of comics in instruction.[29] He quotes a statement by the faculty of a school in Minneapolis which reflects a sound and constructive viewpoint regarding the teacher's role in this matter:

> Those of us who hope to guide children's tastes and especially their reading interests must certainly take note that the comics are a form of reading each child takes to without coaxing. . . .
> With adult guidance, comics may serve as a bridge to the reading of more lasting books. We must help our children to discover good books that are exciting, too, and teach them to discriminate among comic books; then we may

---

27 Frederick Wertham, *Seduction of the Innocent*, Holt, Rinehart and Winston, 1954.

28 Paul A. Witty and Robert A. Sizemore, "Reading the Comics: A Seminar of Studies and an Evaluation," *Elementary English*, December, 1954, p. 502.

29 Dwight L. Burton, "Comic Books: A Teacher's Analysis," *Elementary School Journal*, October, 1955, pp. 73–75.

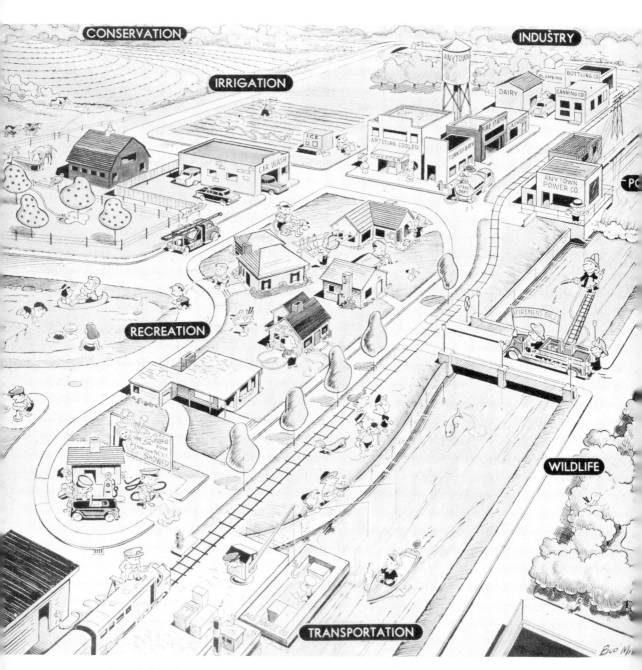

Fig. 5.24. / Because of its wide appeal, the comic technique is often applied to serious explanations. In what classroom situations do you feel that the comic technique, used as in this explanation of water and its importance to us, is justified?

safely accept our children's comic reading for what it is—a stage in their growth —provided we also help them toward wider horizons of interest and appreciation.[30]

■ USE OF COMICS IN INSTRUCTION

The extensive popularity of comics had led many teachers to experiment with this medium in teaching. Much of this experimentation has been done in the language arts at the intermediate and junior-high-school levels, although similar experiments in science, history, the social studies, and even religious education are not uncommon. Figure 5.23 shows comic techniques that have been applied to information in a popular science field.

An analysis of the language of the comics by Thorndike indicated several points of interest.[31] Perhaps the most significant of these is the finding that a child who reads one comic book per month will read approximately twice as many words per year as his reading books contain. Thorndike concluded that both the amount and the character of the vocabulary provided valuable practice in reading for the young reader.

The unique contribution of the comics as compared to that of printed text was investigated by Sones.[32] In an exploratory study with 400 sixth- and ninth-graders he used the comic magazine *Wonder Woman* as one approach to the life and work of Clara Barton. A printed text was used for his control groups. He found that mean scores among the picture groups ran from 10 to 30 percent higher on the first test. When the control groups were given the picture story, their scores on the second test improved significantly more than did the scores of the picture groups who were given the printed text. In summary, Sones says, "In other words, the picture groups seemed to have learned almost as much as they were capable of learning from their first reading while the groups reading the printed texts first had not reached the saturation point, but did so by a second reading in the picture form."[33]

The modern comic book suitable for educational use may be less a comic book in the traditional sense than it is an illustrated story book using comic-book techniques. The instructional comic capitalizes on the familiar and popular comic-book format to transmit useful ideas and information. The teacher who uses comics in any of the curricular areas for which they are available will be aware of the need for applying sound principles of utilization. He will, for example, exploit the motivating potential of comic presentation in getting units off to a good start, but he will not stop there (Fig. 5.24). Once interest has been aroused, the picture story can be supplemented by other reading materials, films, flat pictures, models, experiments, and a variety of creative activities. The principal

[30] *Guide to the Teaching of Reading in the Elementary School*, Division of Elementary Education, Minneapolis Public Schools, 1950, quoted in *ibid.*

[31] Robert L. Thorndike, "Words and the Comics," *Journal of Experimental Education*, December, 1941, pp. 110–113.

[32] W. W. D. Sones, "The Comics and the Instructional Method," *Journal of Educational Sociology*, December, 1944, pp. 238–239.

[33] *Ibid.*

merit of the comic book in instruction may be its capacity to create interest—interest, as teachers well know, that is essential to effective learning. If properly selected and incorporated in teaching methods, the comic can be an effective teaching tool.

□ PUPIL- AND TEACHER-MADE GRAPHICS

Much of what has been said about graphic communications materials relates to the *interpretation* of graphics—that is, graphs, diagrams, charts, posters, comics, and cartoons—by the pupil. In making and designing their own graphics, pupils are provided with a quick, sure, and interesting way of gaining useful information from learning resources. Graphics can be constructed by pupils and teachers to organize and present reports, demonstrations, how-to-do-it explanations, etc. For example, the pupil of English can prepare and use a chart to visualize the story line and action of a short story or novel. The science student may rely on his creative diagram to explain the mechanism and operation of the retrorockets used in space docking. The home-economics student might present charts to show the interrelationship of calories and weight to various methods of meat cookery.

As teachers, we must become more concerned with the creative efficiency with which students express and apply their knowledge. The inventive use of graphics which the pupils themselves produce to meet their own needs is an area of instruction which needs much more emphasis. The alternative is to continue the routine and endless "oral-report" day or hour. To begin in this direction, we should be concerned primarily with the student's understanding of graphics as the means for expressing information and ideas. His decision to use a chart, graph, comic, or poster in the first place should be based on the determination that it will communicate something important and perhaps unique. Accordingly, one circumstance in which it makes sense to *construct* a graphic is where one is needed that is not otherwise available.

Another circumstance in which graphics-construction activities are warranted is when the act of preparing in itself will contribute significantly to the student's understanding of the subject under study. In the preparation of a time-line, for example, the process of locating significant events in juxtaposition on the chart may help the pupil to fix important time relationships in his mind more clearly than were he to study someone else's time-line, read a verbal summary, or get the requisite information from another source, such as class discussion. It becomes a matter of good judgment by the teacher as to when and for whom preparation activity is necessary to bring about desired understandings.

A related and highly important consideration is the fact that one learns a good deal about *interpreting* graphs, diagrams, posters, cartoons, and some chart forms through the experience of *making* them. Development of students' abilities to interpret these graphic forms readily and intelligently is clearly an important function of our schools. Accordingly, to the extent that such experience is needed for improving the interpretive skills of students, construction activities are certainly justified.

In this connection, Carpenter points out the close relationship that exists between the student's ability either to make *or* to interpret graphics and his grasp of related concepts.[34] Thus, the ability to count and some concept of scale are necessary for constructing the simplest bar graphs; percentage and the calculations necessary to convert information to more complex scales are required for most circle or line graphs and for time-lines. In the course of such applications, the pupil both firms up his math and develops insights into the meanings of comparable graphics. Similarly, the often subtle and sophisticated meanings that lie within the symbols used in some political cartoons may be difficult for the pupil to see unless he himself has tried to express his ideas through cartoons and caricatures.

It is also important for the student to learn how graphics can *misrepresent* information by various techniques. In pointing up the contributions which graphics can and should make to critical thinking, Carpenter stresses the importance of students becoming alert to distortions, interrupted scale, and changes in size of symbols as examples of how false impressions can be conveyed on graphs and sequence charts.[35] In constructing the chart or graph for himself, the student often becomes more conscious of these pitfalls than he does through mere exposure to ready-made graphics. Attention to the source of the data (which should always be noted) is another useful factor in critical evaluation which students need to learn in order to deal intelligently with the profusion of graphics used for communication in the world around them.

When students have become reasonably competent in their mathematics and graph-reading abilities, however, graph and chart making as an instructional means toward this end becomes no longer valid.

■ HOW TO MAKE GRAPHICS

Teachers develop their own techniques as they gain experience in preparing charts and other graphic forms. The following principles and suggestions came from a number of teachers and graphic artists over a period of years:

1. Lay out a plan on a small sheet of paper. Make it clear to the pupils that planning lies behind any worthwhile work. Before you complete the chart, sketch in principal lines and lettering lightly on the large chart surface. This is also a good opportunity to introduce simple principles of design to the pupils.
2. Keep the graph, chart, poster, etc., simple. Remember, a good graphic presents *one* principal idea or comparison. When it becomes intricate or complicated, it loses effectiveness.
3. Choose a terse, simple title; allow the pupils to help. Few pupils understand the virtue of economy in words. Use bold but simple letters, for fancy lettering is seldom effective.
4. Make it attractive. Plan for contrast, color, and plenty of space. Employ

34 Helen Carpenter, "Interpreting Graphic Materials," *The Instructor*, December, 1964, pp. 21–22.
35 *Ibid.*, p. 30.

pictures, graphs, or other illustrations as suitable, occasionally using colored construction paper for background outlines and for emphasizing important sections.

5. Avoid crowding or using too many illustrations or other elements. When you use color, keep the colors harmonious. Don't overdo colors or the purpose of the chart may be missed.

6. Make the graphic large enough to be read easily from anywhere in the room. Use an opaque projector to enlarge your planning sketch to the desired size.

■ MATERIALS FOR MAKING GRAPHICS

The following list indicates the various kinds of materials and supplies that are good for making charts:

1. *Paper:* Butcher or other heavy wrapping paper, or plastic-coated papers, which are particularly good; also newsprint. Colored construction papers are fine for color accents, outlines, and silhouettes.

2. *Backing:* Bristol board, poster board, tag board, and similar materials are available in various grades; the price depends on the grade. For large charts (over 30 × 40 inches) bracing is necessary; a light-surfaced building board is good for backing. Corrugated cardboard from cartons is another possibility.

3. *Adhesives:* Rubber cement and glue are always good. For some work, the newer colorless and stainless cements—e.g., model-airplane cement—are particularly useful. Spray adhesives and double-faced masking tape are newer and more convenient adhesives for various purposes.

4. *Letters:* Many forms of lettering are available for use on graphics. Lettering guides of several types and gummed letters on tape or sheets are two examples. Transfer or rub-off letters in various colors and sizes make it possible to do lettering of professional quality with a little practice.

5. *Tapes and Symbols:* Black or colored tapes are recommended for bars and wide lines. Gummed paper tape costs little, as do gummed symbols, such as arrows, circles, stars, etc.

6. *Pens:* Felt pens are handy and easy to use. Speedball pens, Payzant lettering pens (for extended lines), and India or other drawing inks are standard. Don't overlook heavy marking crayons and China marking pencils, particularly for temporary work. Among the better recent developments are India ink fountain pens and a nylon tip felt pen with which fine lines and figures can be drawn.

□ SUMMARY

Graphic materials may be defined as materials which communicate facts and ideas clearly and succinctly through a combination of drawings, words, and pictures. They are particularly well suited to the presentation of information in condensed summary form; the presentation of quantitative information as on graphs; the illustration of relationships as on charts, maps, graphs, and diagrams; and the representation of some kinds of abstractions as in cartoons, diagrams, and charts.

The types of graphic materials commonly employed in teaching include graphs, diagrams, charts, posters, cartoons, and comics. Each type has certain unique instructional applications.

Graphs are visual representations of numerical data. They show quantitative relationships more effectively than any other medium, but like diagrams, they require a background of experience and information to be effective as teaching devices. Typical forms are line graphs, bar graphs, and pictorial graphs.

Diagrams are simplified drawings designed to show interrelationships primarily by means of lines and symbols. Diagrams are highly abstract and have a minimum of detail; hence they require a background of information before they can be used effectively with students.

Charts are combinations of various graphic and pictorial media designed to visualize relationships between key facts or ideas in an orderly and logical manner. Typical forms are the tree chart, the flow chart, and the tabular chart.

Posters are large-scale simplified pictorial illustrations designed to attract attention to key ideas, facts, or events. They are inherently simple and dynamic. Their function is primarily to motivate, arouse interest, remind, or advertise.

The cartoon is a pictorial representation or caricature of a person, idea, or situation designed to influence public opinion. Political cartoons are sources of information with a strong visual impact based upon sharp, compact drawings and humor of some type. There is some evidence that cartoons are chiefly valuable for teaching at the secondary rather than the elementary level partly because most commercial cartoons are prepared for adult readers.

Comics are a form of cartoon in which the same characters enact a story in a sequence of closely related pictures designed to entertain the reader. Although comics have achieved extensive popularity purely as an entertainment medium, certain materials in this category have definite educational values. Their extensive use of colorful illustrations, of a rapidly moving story, and of realistic people as characters appeals to students of all ages. Comic books are being used effectively by teachers to arouse interest, to develop vocabulary and reading skills, and to serve as springboards into broader reading interests.

Most graphic forms can be made rather readily by teachers and pupils. Production of graphics in the school is warranted (1) when suitable graphics are not otherwise available, (2) when preparation will help significantly in understanding of the subject, and (3) when preparation will help the student materially in interpretation or evaluation of graphic forms.

☐ Suggested Activities

1. Analyze a typical unit of work in your teaching field and prepare a list of points at which graphic materials would provide unique teaching values.
2. For a specific unit of work in your teaching field in which graphic materials are applicable, develop a lesson plan incorporating graphics, teach it, and report your results to your audiovisual class.

3. Divide the class into committees and have each committee select and evaluate the best examples it can find of one type of graphic material. Consider such points as
   a. Standards to be observed in selection
   b. Sources of suitable materials
   c. Costs
4. From the members of your class, obtain charts, graphs, diagrams, posters, and cartoons prepared by elementary and high-school pupils. Investigate the learning situation in each case and attempt to assess the educational values derived. Through group discussion formulate a set of principles which will be helpful in determining when and to what extent pupils should prepare graphic materials.
5. Make a committee survey of comic-book materials being sold at key newsstands in your community. Find which comics are best-sellers, which are objectionable (and why), and which are useful from an educational standpoint. Prepare suitable graphic materials for use in presenting your findings.
6. On the basis of the information secured for the preceding survey, draw up a P.T.A. program to consider the comic-book situation in your community. Plan the program so as to include both pros and cons in the discussion.
7. Have a committee of class members investigate sources of free or inexpensive graphic materials, prepare an exhibit of sample materials, and make classified lists of sources for distribution to your class.
8. Request members of the class to bring in and explain their use of graphic materials which they have found particularly helpful in their teaching.

☐ Bibliography

Arkin, Herbert, and Raymond R. Colton, *Graphs, How to Make and Use Them* (rev. ed.), Harper & Row, 1940.

Brackman, Walter, "Cartoons in the English Class," *Clearing House,* January, 1956, pp. 268–270.

Brinton, Willard C., *Graphic Presentation,* Brinton Associates, 1939.

Brown, J. W., R. B. Lewis, and F. F. Harcleroad, *Audiovisual Instruction* (2nd ed.), McGraw-Hill, 1964, pp. 369–386.

Burton, Dwight L., "Comic Books: A Teacher's Analysis," *Elementary School Journal,* October, 1955, pp. 73–75.

Carpenter, Helen, "Interpreting Graphic Materials," *The Instructor,* December, 1964, pp. 21–22 f.

Dale, Edgar, *Audio-Visual Methods in Teaching* (rev. ed.), Dryden, 1954, pp. 319–323.

Entin, J. W., "Using Cartoons in the Classroom," *Social Education,* May, 1958, p. 109.

Erickson, Carlton W. H., *Fundamentals of Teaching with Audiovisual Technology,* Macmillan, 1965, pp. 48–50, 235–237.

Feliciano, Gloria D., Richard D. Powers, and Bryant E. Kearl, "The Presentation of Statistical Information," *AV Communications Review,* May–June, 1963, pp. 32–39.

Harvill, Harris, "The Use of Posters, Charts, Cartoons, and Graphs," in W. H. Hartley (Ed.), *Audiovisual Materials and Methods in the Social Studies,* 18th Yearbook, National Council for the Social Studies, 1947, pp. 109 ff.

Hogben, Lancelot, *From Cave Painting to Comic Strip,* Chanticleer Press, 1949.

Kinder, James, *Audio-Visual Materials and Techniques* (2nd ed.), American Book, 1959, pp. 378–406.

Knisley, William H., "Let's Use Presty-Cartoons More," *Ohio Schools,* December, 1962, p. 23 ff.

Macklin, Ruth, "The Use of Overlay Charts—a Device for Teaching Some Number Concepts," *The Arithmetic Teacher,* December, 1961, pp. 433–435.

Meadows, George C., "Let's Modernize Graph Teaching," *The Arithmetic Teacher,* May, 1963, pp. 286–287.

Modley, Rudolf, *How to Use Pictorial Statistics,* Harper & Row, 1937.

Rose, Charles R., "Safety Posters Ride the Bus," *The Instructor,* September, 1964, p. 123.

Scuorzo, Herbert E., "Chart Construction Made Easy," *Grade Teacher,* March, 1964, pp. 38–39 f.

Sinnema, J. R., "Cartoons in Conversation Classes," *Modern Language Journal,* March, 1957, pp. 124–125.

Smith, Hayden R. and Dean A. Leptich, "Effective Use of Cartoons in the Classroom," *Clearing House,* September, 1963, pp. 38–41.

Waugh, Coulton, *The Comics,* Macmillan, 1947.

Wirtz, Dorothy, "Graphic Illustration of Literature," *The French Review*, February, 1964, pp. 508–516.

☐ Films and Filmstrips

Charts for Creative Learning, 16 mm. film, Color, 10 min., Bailey Films, 1955.

Creating Cartoons, 16 mm. film, B&W, 10 min., Bailey Films, 1955.

Funny Business, 16 mm. film, B&W, 18 min., McGraw-Hill, 1948.

Graphs, 35 mm. filmstrip, B&W, 54 frames, Society of Visual Education, 1948.

Language of Graphs, 16 mm. film, B&W, 13 min., Coronet Films, 1948.

Lettering, 8 mm. film cartridges, B&W, Chandler Publishing Company, 1965. Series includes:
 Lettering: Leroy 500 and Smaller, 3 min., 45 sec.
 Lettering: Leroy 700 and Larger, 3 min., 55 sec.
 Lettering: Prepared Letters, 4 min., 30 sec.
 Lettering: The Felt Pen (Basic Skills), Color, 4 min., 50 sec.
 Lettering: The Felt Pen (Applications), Color, 4 min., 20 sec.
 Lettering: Wricoprint, 2 min., 5 sec.
 Lettering: Wrico Signmaker, 4 min., 20 sec.

Lettering Instructional Materials, 16 mm. film, B&W, 20 min., Indiana University, 1955.

Making a Serigraph, 16 mm. film, Color, 30 min., Harmon Foundation, 1948.

Poster Making: Design and Technique, 16 mm. film, Color, 10 min., Bailey Films, 1953.

Poster Making: Printing by Silk Screen, 16 mm. film, Color, 14 min., Bailey Films, 1953.

Simple Silk Screen Process, 35 mm. filmstrip, B&W, Syracuse University, 1955.

Using Charts and Graphs in Teaching, 35 mm. filmstrip, Color, 51 frames, Basic Skill Filmstrips, 1958.

Wet Mounting Pictorial Material, 16 mm. film, B&W or Color, 11 min., Indiana University, 1952.

VI | THREE
TEACHING

DIMENSIONAL
MATERIALS

Have you ever watched a baby play with his toys? As he sits in his high chair, his chubby little hands grasp whatever he can reach. Somewhat clumsily—but with great concentration—he pushes, pulls, and maneuvers his rattle around until he gets a grip on it. He bangs it on his tray for a while, samples its flavor when he can locate his mouth, and eventually dumps it overboard for the satisfying crash that follows. Pick it up for him and he will repeat the process, with many variations, again and again.

Now let us observe his mother on a shopping tour. At the vegetable counter she picks up and squeezes several heads of lettuce before finding one that will do. She spies some cantaloupes, and again, she goes through the squeezing routine. She thoughtfully smells several which "feel" pretty good—and then walks on without taking any. The watermelons *do* look better today, so she briskly thumps several and finally buys one which produces a satisfactory hollow note.

Meantime, the baby's father stops in to see the new cars at the showroom on his way back to the office from lunch. He isn't really thinking of buying a new car, but like most men, he likes to keep up with new developments in automobiles. So he goes in just to have a look. Subconsciously aware of the danger, he keeps a safe distance and circles casually to look at each car from several sides. Shortly, of course, he finds himself behind the wheel of this or that model, turning it just a little to get the feel and noting appreciatively the comfortable "give" of the seat cushions, the feel of the gear shift, and how smoothly the electric windows slide up and down as he moves the finger-tip controls.

The baby and his parents in these familiar situations are learning and experiencing through their physical senses even as you and I do in various ways each day. As we noted in Chapter II, although we "think" with the brain, the raw material for learning and thinking must come initially through one or more of the physical senses. We can learn nothing without sensory impressions. We know that the more complete, vivid, and accurate our sensory experiences are, the more effective the learning experience will be. Does this mean that we should bring all possible auditory, visual, and other sensory experiences to bear on every learning concept? The answer is no.

Fig. 6.1. / This model of an atomic electric-power plant is precise in every detail excepting the radiation itself. What gains are there for students in model building?

In discussing various audiovisual materials, we have stressed the importance of three principles of selection and use: (1) We select only materials which can make a distinct contribution to the specific learning tasks, (2) we choose the best combination of these and other teaching materials to achieve the desired results, and (3) we use these learning materials in the ways most likely to accomplish our specific learning objectives. To put it another way, we choose teaching materials in terms of the kinds of communication that each type can best perform—we put together a "team" of several types of appropriate materials and we put the team to work in the way dictated by the specific purposes and circumstances of a particular lesson. Clearly, we are talking here about *selective* experience, with materials and methods chosen to provide that experience. When sensory impressions can be utilized to improve learning—as they can in many cases—these, too, must be selectively used. Thus, when sensory experiences are called for, we draw upon those which are most pertinent and use them in whatever available ways seem most likely to attain the desired end. To illustrate, if familiarity with a bakery is important as a part of community study, a field trip to a bakery, a suitable film, and related reading materials might well be used in combination. The film could provide an excellent overview of bakeries in general, the processes involved in baking, and the nature of the industry; while reading materials could provide considerable additional information. However, neither can convey an accurate impression of the heat of the great ovens or the delectable odors which are so much a part of a bakery.

The social-studies teacher, too, is continuously faced with the need for bringing realism into the study of the far places of the earth—mountains, plains, deserts, and jungles; of people and customs of long ago; and of trade, industry, agriculture, and government in the many sections of our own country. He has a great wealth of printed materials to draw upon and he uses them extensively, but he knows that he needs somehow to give added meaning to the words his pupils read. So he uses carefully selected films, maps, models, objects, field trips, and other devices which can help make the learning experience more real and life-like.

On the other hand, we know that many things of a physical character do not lend themselves well even to firsthand experience. One can visit the local water-works and power plant without gaining much understanding of how the great pumps and generators work. One can get a thrill out of watching a giant Diesel locomotive move a heavy train without having any idea of how it operates, and one can observe the moon for a lifetime without acquiring an understanding of its phases. The operation of some things like a pump, a generator, and an engine cannot be seen from the outside, but must be shown from the interior if one is to see how they work, and even then their intricate construction may be baffling. The solar system can be seen to some extent, but it is too vast to be conceptualized from direct observation alone. Teachers need somehow to modify direct experience in such cases if they are to help their pupils learn efficiently. One way of doing this is by using three-dimensional materials.

□ TYPES OF THREE-DIMENSIONAL MATERIALS

We shall consider several types of three-dimensional materials which can provide opportunities for useful learning experiences when direct, firsthand experience is either impractical or impossible. These are models, objects and specimens, mockups, and dioramas.

■ MODELS

Models may be defined as *recognizable three-dimensional representations of real things*. The thing represented may be infinitely large, like the earth, or as small as an atom. It may be an inanimate object such as a building, a monument, or a mine shaft; or it may be a living organism such as a paramecium, an eye, or the human heart. The model may represent something as intricate as a jet engine, a nuclear-powered submarine, or a spacecraft, or as simple as a number of spools on a string. It may be complete in every detail or considerably more simplified than the original.

The satisfaction obtained from models has been translated into a rapidly growing industry—the manufacture of model kits. Model kits for everything from insects to atomic reactors are available, and parents as well as young-sters take to them with enthusiasm. Most are in precise scale and many are accompanied by a manual which contains useful information on the subject. By the time a student completes putting together a model such as the one in Fig. 6.1 he is likely also to have acquired a substantial amount of related interest and knowledge in the process.

In the light of what we know about the importance of sensory experiences in

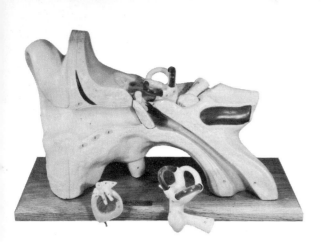

Fig. 6.2. / A detailed model of the human ear which can be disassembled, studied in detail, and reassembled by the student.

Fig. 6.3. / Three dimensions plus greatly expanded size makes this model look like a formidable monster to these youngsters. Does this suggest a precaution that teachers should sometimes observe in using models?

learning, we shall examine several characteristics of effective models for teaching purposes.

■ MODELS ARE THREE-DIMENSIONAL

Most objects around us have a third dimension; that is, they have depth or thickness as well as height and width. Depth is one of the unique characteristics of models and it contributes significantly to their realism. If the third dimension is unimportant to comprehension, a model is probably unnecessary. In that case, a picture or chart may serve as well or better.

The model of the human ear in Fig. 6.2 is an example of how three-dimensional representation can serve instruction. By working with such a model along with an appropriate film, a chart, and related reading, a student can gain an indelible impression of just how the little hammer, anvil, and stirrup bones fit together in the middle ear and how they transmit sound vibrations from the ear drum to the aural nerve and into the brain.

■ MODELS REDUCE OR ENLARGE OBJECTS TO AN OBSERVABLE SIZE

Most of us can see only a very small portion of the earth's surface even from a high-flying jet plane; the astronauts can see much more, but even they can view only a fraction of the earth's surface at a time. With a globe, however, we have a model that enables us to picture the whole earth without difficulty. Conversely, the greatly enlarged model of an anopheles mosquito shown in Fig. 6.3 enables these Indian children better to understand this enemy they must fight in the war against malaria.

Ideally, a model should be large enough to be seen readily by the whole class.

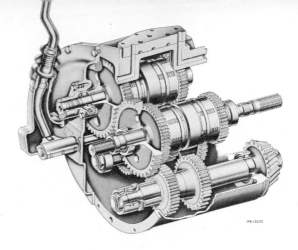

g. 6.4. / A teacher-made model which is useful in identifying and studying the key elements in frame-house construction. What similar cross-sectional models would be useful learning tools?

Fig. 6.5. / Cutaway photo of a Diesel engine transmission showing shift positions and resultant gear-ratio changes. What teaching values would such a photograph have in conjunction with a working model or cutaway transmission?

Frequently, however, the cost of large models and the problem of storage space for them enforce a practical compromise in the form of smaller models than we would like.

- ## MODELS PROVIDE INTERIOR VIEWS OF OBJECTS

A cutaway model of the human tooth reveals the layers of enamel and dentine and the nerve which otherwise would be difficult to visualize. The rapidly spinning parts of a generator, a steam turbine, or an automobile engine are completely enclosed, but a simplified working model with removable or cutaway sides makes it possible to see and to understand how they work. A model like that in Fig. 6.4 will be helpful to an industrial-arts teacher in showing details of frame house construction which are normally invisible.

- ## MODELS ELIMINATE THE NONESSENTIALS OF OBJECTS

As you lift the hood and look at an automobile engine, the impression you receive is likely to be somewhat confusing and complex because of the considerable array of subsidiary parts, wires, tubes, and other paraphernalia that are required for a modern car. But such a look may be more revealing if you have studied a cutaway model of such an engine. The electric motor, the jet engine, and the giant pumps in municipal pumping stations are other examples of complex mechanisms which can readily be explained with the help of simplified models.

The advanced student, however, needs more complete models or the real thing. Students in technical or engineering schools usually have a variety of cutaway engines and models with which to work, such as the Diesel transmission in Fig. 6.5. Agricultural-engineering schools test machinery of many types

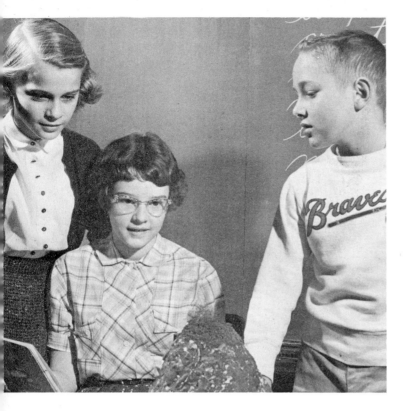

Fig. 6.6. / Everything from a sundial a rocket-ship propulsion device c be made with paper or cardboar and little more is needed to ma your own barometer or a volca that erupts.

and frequently use cutaways and accompanying graphics for instruction. Equipment manufacturers also use this technique for dealer and customer training as well as for advertising.

■ MODELS EMPLOY COLOR AND TEXTURE TO ACCENT IMPORTANT FEATURES

Two related instructional purposes are served by color. The first is identification of important or related parts, as in engine models. The second is increased comprehension of function or operation. In addition, color serves to make models more eyecatching, interesting, and in many cases more attractive. This does not suggest that color should minimize other features of a model. Effectively colored models have a balance in color harmony and intensity which emphasizes the parts and functions that are important to comprehension.

The role of color in models is illustrated in Plates 6 and 8 of the section following page 208. In the algebra model on Plate 6, color serves primarily to enable the student to follow visually what happens when algebraic sums are squared and cubed. In the anatomy model—such as that of the kidney shown on Plate 6, as well as the heart model on Plate 8—color assists understanding mainly because identification is made more easily through its use. This role of color applies to models generally. Important and distinctive parts are colored so that each one stands out clearly. The colors may be natural (this is desirable on some anatomy models), but more often they are made brighter or otherwise changed for better visibility. Parts that are not essential for understanding are often in less conspicuous colors.

Varied surface textures are also used to differentiate among parts of a model. The pistons and other moving parts in a cutaway engine may be chrome plated for better visibility while other areas are left rough or unpolished. Rough and smooth textures on relief-map surfaces have significant and distinctive meanings. Texture is also an important means of conveying accurate impressions from certain anatomy and biology models. Frequently color and texture are used together with good effect as in the kidney model in Plate 6.

▪ MANY MODELS CAN BE DISASSEMBLED AND REASSEMBLED

The value of models in instruction lies not only in their three-dimensional realism, but also in the fact that they can be examined by touch as well as by sight. The model of the ear in Fig. 6.2 can be taken apart so that each part may be examined individually. Fitting each part back in its proper position gives the student a degree of familiarity with the structure of the ear which is difficult to achieve in any other way. Furthermore, the interrelationship of the several parts is made clearer.

▪ MODELS CAN BE CREATED IN CLASS

This section should not leave you with the impression that, to be useful in teaching, models must be complex and expensive. Many can be made rather easily from paper and papier-mâché. The science materials in Fig. 6.6, for example, are largely made from paper cutouts. The papier-mâché volcano erupts convincingly from a can in its cone.

Ammonium dichloride crystals are used as fuel for the volcano. The crystals do not light easily; they burn slowly, spitting sparks no more than a few inches, sending up a bit of smoke, and spreading dark ashes over the top of the cone as the eruption proceeds.

Students can make small weather vanes, anemometers, and similar models which are suitable for their needs and provide greater learning advantages than equivalent purchased models. With new, inexpensive model kits now available, it is also quite practical for pupils to make their own excellent models of molecules, cells, and more complex organisms.[1]

■ OBJECTS AND SPECIMENS

There is little point in using a model if the real object itself can be brought into the classroom and if it is not too complex for easy observation (Fig. 6.7).

[1] See Bibliography; articles by Carboni, Fieser, Hyer and Young, Scurozo, and others for a variety of related suggestions.

Fig. 6.7. / Some firsthand experience with pulleys and weights in one of Los Angeles' Elementary District Science Centers. What learning advantages are there in such experiences as compared with a demonstration in class with typical laboratory pulleys and weights?

You would not, for example, use models of Indian arrowheads, tools, and cooking utensils if you could secure the real objects. You might prepare a model of a wigwam and an Indian village if these were important elements in the social-studies curriculum, but you would probably also have your pupils bring Indian beadwork, arrowheads, tools, utensils, blankets, and other crafts for display. Models and objects supplement each other in providing realism, authenticity, and interest.

Whereas a model is a recognizable three-dimensional likeness or *representation* of the real thing, *an object is the real thing*. However, it should be noted that these objects are removed from their normal setting so that they can be brought together for study and analysis. This means that the object is not seen in its natural surroundings and therefore may appear less "real" than it does in nature. A mounted hawk in a display case filled with other mounted birds loses some of its realism even though it may be a good piece of taxidermy. Obviously, however, this limitation is much less important than the advantages of being able to examine a bird specimen at close range and in whatever detail desired.

Specimens and *objects* are similar though not identical terms. The principal distinction is based on the fact that specimens are typical of a class or group of objects, whereas objects do not have to be typical or representative to be classified as objects. *Specimens,* in other words, *are objects which are representative of a group or class of similar objects.*

There are significant advantages for learning in having objects and specimens available. For one, even though removed from their normal surroundings, they are real things. This fact tends to make the learning situation in which they are used more concrete, more authentic, and more interesting. The firsthand opportunity to observe the hatching of young chicks, for example, can provide an unforgettable experience for the young student (Fig. 6.8).

For another, detailed closeup study can be made of birds, insects, and other specimens which would be next to impossible even if the time and money were available to take classes to where these specimens are accessible in nature. Some are inaccessible in any case—living things in the sea and minerals from deep in the earth, for example.

Finally, even though widely separated in nature, a collection of similar objects and specimens makes possible a comparison and generalization which would be impossible if each example had to be seen separately in its natural habitat. As Dale points out:

> How long would it take you to gather from the world itself the essential information about minerals that is represented in a collection of rocks? It is simple enough to begin to classify, infer, and generalize with the collection before you. The same is true, of course, about any collection of objects and specimens.[2]

Fig. 6.8. / When the real thing is available and feasible for the classroom, it can provide vivid and lasting impressions on the student.

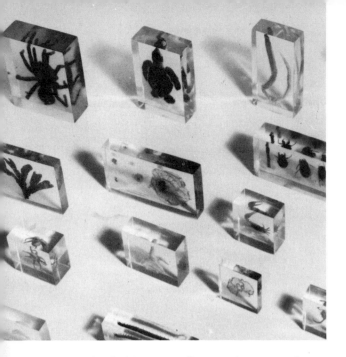
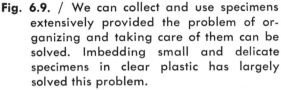

Fig. 6.9. / We can collect and use specimens extensively provided the problem of organizing and taking care of them can be solved. Imbedding small and delicate specimens in clear plastic has largely solved this problem.

Fig. 6.10. / Materials from a kit on Japanese folk art. Such materials add an important dimension to the student's understanding of other cultures than his own. Some 200 kits on various subjects are circulated to Los Angeles schools.

Most children are avid collectors, and teachers can sometimes channel their natural interests into useful learning experience, and, at the same time, into a means of collecting objects and specimens for the classroom. Many objects and specimens can be used to advantage in the classroom or laboratory. The following will provide an indication of the range of subject matter than can be taught by using objects and specimens:

Science: Cocoons; rock collections; plants and flowers; fish, mice, worms, and other small animals (Fig. 6.9); different kinds of coal, oil, and other fuels; samples of ore; seashells; a telegraph key, radio set, doorbell, telephone; dry cells and storage battery.

Social Studies: Locally manufactured products; period costumes; relics and souvenirs (as of political campaigns); coins and stamps; fuels; raw materials such as cotton, wool, flax, ores, and grains; Early-American utensils, toys, tools, furniture, spinning wheels, pictures, and books; and Japanese folk art materials used as in the project shown in Fig. 6.10.

English: Period costumes; clothing and relics; letters and manuscripts; musical instruments; fabrics; stage props; tapestries; speaker's podium and microphone; printing type and layouts.

Mathematics: Slide rule, micrometer, vernier scale, and other measuring instruments; transit; sextant, compass, timepieces, and navigation charts; bottles and other containers for volume measurements; coins; drafting tools such as dividers, T-squares, and triangles; and identical familiar objects for instruction in addition, subtraction, division, and multiplication.

2 Edgar Dale, *Audio-Visual Methods in Teaching* (rev. ed.), Dryden, 1954, p. 121.

Home Economics: Fabrics and sewing equipment; foods and utensils; period costumes to show trends in design; raw fibers such as cotton, wool, flax, and silk; wallpaper sample books; paint and papering tools; table settings.

■ MOCKUPS

A three-dimensional teaching device that has proved particularly useful in industrial- and military-training programs is the mockup. A mockup may be defined as an *operating model, usually in full scale, which has been designed to*

Fig. 6.11. / Driver-trainer simulators of this type have been found to be highly effective for driver-education programs. Students respond to filmed problem sequences and their responses are recorded electronically, including reaction time. At what point or points in the training process would such trainers be valuable?

be worked with directly by the learner for specific training or analysis. The term *mockup* suggests an imitation of a real thing—which in fact it is—but the imitation may or may not involve similarity of appearance which is normally true of a model. In addition, a mockup, some fundamental elements of the real thing are purposely eliminated in order to focus attention upon others. For example, an operable electrical system of an airplane may be laid out on a large panel so that trainees can become familiar with cables and connections that normally are concealed in the fuselage or wings of the plane.

A mockup used in school is the drivers' trainer which secondary teachers use in helping pupils learn how to drive (Fig. 6.11). A simple kind of mockup is frequently used by kindergarten and primary teachers when they have pupils build a grocery store, a flower shop, a Santa's toy shop, or a railroad train out

Fig. 6.12. / One of the better-known applications of mockups is in flight-crew training. This is an exact replica of the cockpit of a 707 jet—the current version of the famous Link Trainer. Closely simulated flight conditions include the sounds and movements of flying. Problems are programed in advance on a computer and crew members' responses are evaluated instantaneously.

of blocks or orange crates. The purpose of these activities is to train the children in cooperative activity, reading readiness, or perhaps elementary number concepts.

A useful mockup for industrial-arts classes is an electrical-wiring and fuse-box installation that includes on one panel all the elements necessary for the lead-in wiring of a home. Placing these various elements on one panel makes it possible to show students the complete installation, parts of which are normally separated by a floor and walls. The student can see quickly just how the installation should be made.

Industries use mockups for streamlined demonstrations of steps in manufacturing processes, for analyzing possible new plant layouts, for orienting new employees regarding the interrelationships of their work with that of others, and for self-testing demonstrations of various types.

Mockups have many applications in training, but none is better known than the device for drivers' training shown in Fig. 6.11 or the Link Trainer for airline pilots shown in Fig. 6.12. Developed initially for fighter pilots, the Trainer is used extensively by commercial airlines not only for training pilots to fly new planes, but also for providing refresher courses for experienced crews. Various flying problems and emergencies can be simulated in the Trainer at no risk to passengers, crews, or planes.

■ DIORAMAS

One of the most fascinating forms of three-dimensional materials is the miniature diorama. Its universal appeal is well known to everyone who has seen dioramas in museums, advertising displays, or classrooms. A diorama is a *three-dimensional scene in depth incorporating a group of modeled objects and figures in a naturalistic foreground which is blended into a painted background.* The scene is usually set up on a miniature stage (Fig. 6.13). The objects in a diorama—such as figures, buildings, and trees—are seldom made to scale. A building is made to look smaller at the far end in order to exaggerate depth. As you look down at the diorama, a street may seem too narrow. This illusion, called "perspective," is fundamental to any representation of depth (see Plate 7 in color section which follows page 208). With small figures and exaggerated perspective, you can give an effect of considerable depth in a relatively small

Fig. 6.13. / In this diorama of a Mayan city, note how the depth effect is increased by the much reduced size of people on the rear temple structure, and how the painted background of plain and mountains blends into the three-dimensional foreground. The extent of miniaturization is shown by the size of the girl looking at the diorama.

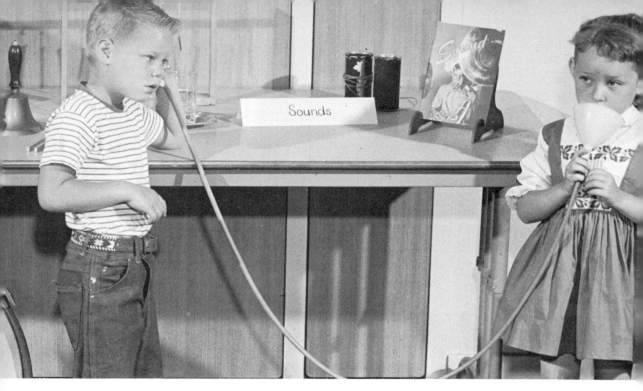

Fig. 6.14. / Models are unnecessary when the real thing is available and suitable. No strangers to sound, these first-graders appear to be getting a new perspective about it.

space. This illusion, well carried out, gives the diorama striking vividness and realism.

Modern museums make extensive use of dioramic exhibits to show scenes involving distant places and historical periods. Teachers in schools in the vicinity of such museums are well aware of the vast educational potential of dioramas. The Milwaukee County Museum, the Los Angeles County Museum, and the well-known Cleveland Youth Museum are among those which are doing outstanding work in coordinating historical and current materials with school programs by means of dioramas. Even though such museums are not available to many schools, the advantages of the diorama need not be lost. Good dioramas can be constructed by the students from easily available and inexpensive materials. Leaves cut from paper and dipped in stained wax are good for some kinds of tropical foliage; fine sawdust stained green will do for grass; the furrows of a plowed field can be imitated by running a comb over a bed of wet clay; and pieces of green rubber sponge do very well for shrub and tree foliage. Detailed and well-illustrated instructions for constructing dioramas are given by Jenkins.[3]

One of the extremely valuable teaching opportunities related to diorama utilization is also explained by Jenkins who points out that the diorama provides the teacher with an interesting opportunity for evaluating pupil learning.[4] When one considers the combination of understandings and skills which pupils must possess before they are able to plan and complete a diorama successfully, it can readily be seen that the completion of such a project is the best

[3] J. W. Jenkins, "Let's Make a Diorama," *See and Hear*, November, 1948, pp. 36–37, and January, 1949, pp. 35 ff.
[4] *Ibid.*

evidence that the pupil really understands the concepts involved. The arrangement of a diorama's background, for example, must be inspired by information known to the learner. The construction of objects in the middle and foreground also reflect the accuracy of the concepts which the pupils have learned. Altogether the diorama becomes a "test" of the facts and conceptualizations that the pupils have achieved, whether it be in social studies, science, or marine biology. Of course, the construction of a diorama also provides the pupils themselves with a concrete learning experience. Facts and concepts that might otherwise remain largely at the abstract level are likely to come alive in the pupils' minds as they embody them in the diorama. Certainly the making of a diorama provides an excellent means of eliciting the pupils' creative involvement in the learning experience.

☐ TEACHING WITH THREE-DIMENSIONAL MATERIALS

A high-school history teacher whose class was visited by one of the present authors on several occasions said:

> I would hardly know how to teach history without using the models and objects we have collected over the years I have taught in this school. They seem to help my pupils actually to live the events and times we are studying. One of the things that pleases me greatly is that many of our former students who have graduated keep coming back to see how our collection is growing.

One had only to watch this teacher at work for a short time to appreciate that her pupils' unusual interest in historical things stemmed in large measure from her own genuine and infectious enthusiasm. She was an excellent teacher. But her classroom also helped to bring history alive. Objects and models pertinent to the lesson were much in evidence. The teacher utilized pictures and old prints liberally, and there seemed to be an interesting story about each one. Objects were discussed in context and examined at close range and all but the most fragile were handled by the students. When questioned about damage and loss of articles, the teacher said that there was virtually none; the students were proud of their collection and treated it accordingly.

■ SELECTING THREE-DIMENSIONAL MATERIALS

By this time, you will have sensed that three-dimensional materials, like other audiovisual materials, should be used when they can make a unique contribution to the lesson. Three-dimensional materials are often more real to the student than pictures because they have depth and substance. They can be seen and handled, and sometimes smelled or tasted, in this way providing a more complete sensory experience. Thus, in learning situations where the third dimension is important, a suitable model, object, specimen, mockup, or the real thing should be used if feasible (Fig. 6.14). There is also the possibility of con-

Fig. 6.15. / Making a model can be busy work or creative learning. What educational goals are probably being sought with these two model-making projects?

structing a simple model or diorama which is worth considering. For example, an English teacher may construct a model of the Globe Theater from cardboard. A mathematics class may be taught more efficiently with a set of cubes, some spools on a string, a nest of tin cans, or a shoestring and a circle of wood for demonstrating the meaning of π. Stockades, Conestoga wagons, and wigwams are practically standard equipment in the social-studies classroom, and most of them can be made by the pupils. With a little help, pupils can easily construct a covered wagon or an oil derrick (Fig. 6.15).

In all such situations, the question to be answered is whether the need is important enough to warrant the time and effort involved in making a model, mockup, or diorama. The same question applies, of course, to collecting specimens and preparing displays. It cannot be answered categorically or in terms of subject-matter learning alone, because, as every experienced teacher knows, the values of such activities to pupils in terms of cooperative experience, individual recognition by the group, and satisfaction in accomplishment may at times far outweigh the value of the information acquired, and the time spent in such activities.

■ PRINCIPLES OF USE

As with all instructional materials, three-dimensional teaching tools will not serve pupil learning effectively—no matter how ideally suitable the materials themselves are *potentially*—unless the teacher presents and utilizes them properly in his teaching strategy. Three-dimensional materials have a natural appeal which suggests some ideas regarding their effective use in instruction.

■ MAKE CERTAIN THAT ALL PUPILS CAN SEE

This principle applies, of course, to all visual materials being used with a group, but has particular reference here because many models and most objects and specimens are too small for detailed use with a class-sized group. Ideally, every model would be large enough to be seen easily by everyone in the class at one time. While this is often impractical because of such factors as space, cost, and storage facilities, such materials should be large enough for all to observe the general features, closer examination being left for small-group and individual study (Fig. 6.16).

- ### USE MODELS WITH OTHER MATERIALS

When you use, for example, a model of a flower to explain pollination to a biology class, you may wish to use a large wall chart for details so that all the class can see it readily. You work back and forth between the two to establish clearly the relationship between parts and functions. At the appropriate point,

Fig. 6.16. / These objects are too small for the class to observe in detail from their seats. How can the teacher plan for adequate learning of the concepts involved in the study unit?

you may also show a sound motion-picture film which uses animation to visualize the fertilization process. Flat pictures would be useful to establish natural surroundings, and closeup shots of blossoms on 2 × 2 slides would be helpful in identifying the principal parts of various flowers. In spring or fall, you would doubtless bring in some real flowers for concrete application of the information required.

In a word, as with other visual and auditory materials, for maximum benefits you use models or objects as part of a *team* of materials. Each part of the team is chosen for the distinctive job it can do as well as for its contribution to the overall effort.

- ### PRESENT MATERIALS EFFECTIVELY BEFORE THE CLASS

While this may appear obvious at first glance, teachers sometimes find themselves stumbling through a presentation because they have not thought each point through carefully or have not practiced sufficiently with the model and related materials. The more complex the material, the more important it is to

Fig. 6.17. / Museum trips are usually received with enthusiasm by pupils. What preplanning is needed to make museum trips worthwhile for a class?

practice the demonstration. The able and experienced teacher is willing to leave little to chance, for he knows that small things can make the difference between a well-planned presentation that "goes over" and one that "just misses."

When using three-dimensional materials in class presentations or demonstrations, the good instructor will bear in mind the following points:

1. The materials should be positioned so that all in the class can see.
2. The specific features to be observed or noted should be clearly indicated.
3. The teacher should have sufficient assurance in his own presentation so that he can be attentive to class reactions.
4. The instructor's movements must not obstruct the pupils' line of vision.
5. The presentation should not proceed too rapidly and should be flexible enough to accommodate review or repetition of points as necessary.

▪ PROVIDE FOR A CORRECT CONCEPT OF SIZE

One of the dangers in using three-dimensional materials is that the pupils may get distorted ideas of actual size unless care is taken to guard against this in teaching. A curator in the Milwaukee County Museum told of a case which illustrates this point. An intermediate class studying some Polynesian exhibits was particularly interested in a small-scale diorama of a native village. Actual coins used by the natives were included in the exhibit. Since the people in the diorama were only a few inches tall, some of the crude coins were nearly as large as the natives themselves. In evident perplexity, a number of pupils asked how the natives managed to carry their money around with them.

One way of emphasizing correct size concepts is by showing the actual object along with the model of the same object. Another is by making comparisons with familiar objects. For example, a picture of a large turbine in a power plant can be helpful when used with a small model if a workman is shown in the picture to indicate the relative size of the giant turbine.

▪ ARRANGE FOR FIRSTHAND EXAMINATION

Since one of the major appeals of objects, specimens, models, and mockups is their three-dimensional realism, this appeal should be used to stimulate curiosity, interest, and imagination (Fig. 6.17). Unlike pictures, such materials appear differently from every angle and hence should be examined from various points. One of the best ways of providing for this is to have students work directly with the materials. Further, since the use of models offers an opportunity of providing well-rounded sensory experiences, there is good reason to let the students handle a model as well as look at it. To do so makes the experience more concrete, tangible, and memorable to the learner. Those models and specimens which are too fragile or too small to permit handling can be mounted in clear plastic (see Fig. 6.8, page 179), thus making detailed examination possible from all angles without risking damage to the specimen.[5]

[5] For directions on simple and effective means of plastic mounting, see Herbert E. Scurozo, "Embedding Realia in Plastic," *Grade Teacher*, January, 1963, pp. 10 ff.

Anyone who has seen intermediate-grade pupils making their own models, or junior- and senior-high-school pupils concentrating on collections of insects will have little question of their ability to handle models and specimens with care. There is little reason for having these valuable tools of instruction if the students are not allowed to handle them.

■ PROVIDE RELEVANT THREE-DIMENSIONAL MATERIALS

Storage problems frequently lead to classrooms that are cluttered with all manner of objects, specimens, and models. At the proper time they are hauled down, dusted off, used, and then put back on the shelf for another semester or year. Too often these collections are in full view of the students at all times, distracting attention and lessening their effectiveness when used for instruction.

Although some materials like aquariums, terrariums, and globes lend themselves well to continuing observation and interest as part of the classroom environment, the great majority of teaching materials are unsuited for this purpose. The enterprising teacher sees to it that they are stowed away out of sight until the psychological moment arrives for using them. He realizes that their interest value is thereby greatly enhanced and that attention can be focused more effectively if unrelated materials are not visible.

Like a good merchandiser, the teacher knows that he must catch and hold his pupils' attention before he can "sell" his ideas effectively. Some teachers cover the glass in their classroom storage cabinets with colored drawing paper, others ask the art department to use this space for simple, appropriate designs which have a decorative effect but are not distracting. When no cabinet or other storage space is available in the classroom, cartons or boxes may be used to store three-dimensional materials between uses.

□ SCHOOL DISPLAYS AND EXHIBITS

Aside from the classroom itself, three-dimensional materials are most widely used in educational displays and exhibits. Although we tend to think of displays and exhibits primarily in connection with retail selling, museums, trade shows, and fairs, they have many useful applications in schools as well. Most schools have Parents' Nights, Hobby Shows, or annual exhibits of some kind. Vocational schools and technical high schools make regular use of displays to show the work done by various departments. Most of the newer elementary- and secondary-school buildings have built-in display cases in the corridors for educational exhibits during the school year. In all of these, three-dimensional materials play a prominent part.

In Chapter VII, we shall discuss the study display in detail. We shall point out here, however, that the effective use of three-dimensional materials in the learning display depends on the proper observation of several important principles, the first of which is to determine the relative importance of the three-dimensional material to the specific purposes of the display. If a model or mockup is to play the featured role in the display, it should have prominence—but not so much as to obscure completely any other two- or three-dimensional materials in the display. If several objects and specimens are to be used as a part of an overall display, they should be chosen for their relevance to the subject of the display and arranged in such a way that they demand only as much attention as their relative importance to the overall display indicates.

Sound principles of design and color use should also be observed when preparing three-dimensional objects for a school study display. It is always wise to consult the art teacher when planning the design of three-dimensional display materials. The principles outlined in Chapter VII should provide some guidance in this regard, however.

Particularly important in displaying objects, specimens, mockups, and models are lighting arrangements. Proper use of lighting can highlight the most important of the objects and can focus attention on the more important features embodied in a model or mockup. Both colored and white lights can help to bring out important distinctions in an attractive way.

Motion, too, can be an effective means of enhancing three-dimensional display materials. A small electric motor can make figures in a diorama or model more realistic and attention-demanding. Changing light patterns are also useful in creating movement, or the illusion of movement, in a mockup, model, or diorama.

Any display or exhibit can profit from heightened viewer interest if provisions are made for the viewer to engage in some activity other than merely looking at photographs, objects, and other display materials, or merely reading headings, captions, news clippings, and the like. Three-dimensional display materials can provide especially good opportunities for the viewer to participate in the exhibit. This was demonstrated by people in two Cleveland suburban communities who cooperated to build a model "safety town" on one of their school playgrounds. They constructed small buildings, laid out streets complete with traffic signs and lights, bought small cars and trucks, and even supplied a policeman to help with safety instruction for their kindergartners. The youngsters alternated between "driving" around the town while the other children were taken around as pedestrians by their teachers. In the process, all learned their safety lessons so well that there was a sharp reduction in the number of traffic accidents involving children.[6]

☐ SUMMARY

Much of the effectiveness of direct concrete experience in learning comes from the fact that such experience involves a well-rounded use of the physical senses. Although firsthand experience is impossible or impractical in many teaching situations, important segments of reality can frequently be brought into the classroom by means of models, objects and specimens, mockups, and dioramas.

These three-dimensional materials can help to make the learning situation more real, lifelike, and interesting to the student. Furthermore, they are frequently an improvement on reality itself. A model of the solar system or of a one-celled animal, for example, reduces the vastness of the former and enlarges the microscopic proportions of the latter to a size which can be seen and studied. Cutaway models provide interior views of objects which ordinarily cannot be

6 "Teach Tots Safety with a Model Town," *School Management*, August, 1962, pp. 42–43.

observed. Among their other useful characteristics, models have the realism of three dimensions, they are usually simplified, important features are made to stand out clearly, and many models have removable parts.

Models are defined as recognizable three-dimensional representations of real things; objects are the actual things. Specimens are objects that are typical of a class or group of objects. A mockup is similar to a model, but is distinguished by rearrangement and condensation of essential elements so that they can be studied more readily. A diorama is a three-dimensional scene made with miniature objects and backgrounds.

In order to use three-dimensional teaching materials effectively, it is of primary importance that they be seen clearly and examined from various angles. Students should accordingly be permitted to handle and work directly with them whenever possible. The instructor must be careful to avoid giving the class distorted size concepts when models are used. As in all effective teaching, he should combine pertinent materials in terms of lesson needs. In general, three-dimensional materials should be stored out of sight when not being used for actual instruction.

Displays and exhibits are other highly effective means of using three-dimensional materials. Although good educational exhibits require careful planning and the application of artistic principles governing arrangement, color, and lighting, they can and should be cooperative projects in which the students participate actively. Here too, as in the construction of dioramas and the use of other three-dimensional materials, valuable concomitant learning can take place in addition to the information gained concerning the particular subject.

☐ Suggested Activities

1. Analyze a course of study in your teaching field and prepare a list of appropriate models, mockups, dioramas, and objects and specimens for use in it.
2. Have a committee prepare a list of sources of three-dimensional materials which are supplied free or on loan to schools. Ask your teachers for suggestions and check such sources as the *Elementary Teacher's Guide to Free Curriculum Materials,* the *Educator's Guide to Free Science Materials,* and local libraries and museums. Organize the list in terms of subject areas and grade level and have it duplicated for distribution to the class.
3. Inspect a number of effective window displays in your community and analyze them in terms of arrangement, use of color, and lighting. Take pictures if possible, and make simple sketches of the layout plans. Show these by means of an opaque projector when reporting to the class.
4. Prepare a report on the display and exhibit facilities of a school building. Include tackboards and exhibit cases in the halls and classrooms. Evaluate your findings and make recommendations for practical improvements.
5. Divide the class into committees and have each committee plan an exhibit for future use in the school. Among the possible subjects are National Education Week, civil defense, conservation, gardening, seasonal sports, hobbies, educational or vocational guidance, and units of school subjects.
6. Storing three-dimensional teaching materials is a constant problem in many schools. Visit several schools in your community and gather information on how this problem is handled. On the basis of your findings, list practical suggestions for solving it.

☐ Bibliography

Brown, J. W., R. B. Lewis, and F. F. Harcleroad, *Audio-Visual Instruction* (rev. ed.), McGraw-Hill, 1964, pp. 413–435.

Carboni, Remo, "Plaster and Burlap—How To Make a Large Landscape Model," *School Arts,* September, 1963, pp. 16–17.

East, Marjorie, *Display for Learning,* Dryden, 1952, pp. 31–53, 255–280.

Erickson, Carlton W. H., *Fundamentals of Teaching with Audiovisual Technology,* Macmillan, 1965, pp. 41–47, 233–235.

Exhibition Techniques, New York Museum of Science and Industry, 1940.

Fieser, Louis F., "Plastic Dreiding Models," *Journal of Chemical Education,* September, 1963, pp. 457–459.

Hyer, James E. and Richard G. Young, "Making a Collection of Preserved Animal Specimens," *Grade Teacher,* March, 1964, pp. 28–29 ff.

Kinder, James, *Audio-Visual Materials and Techniques* (2nd ed.), American Book, 1959, pp. 402–431.

Kniskern, Edna Maki, "An Easily Made Cell Model," *The American Biology Teacher,* March, 1964, pp. 191–192.

Larson, G. Olaf, "Paper Stereomodels," *Journal of Chemical Education,* May, 1965, pp. 274–276.

Ponush, Louis, "The Virus Overcoat," *The American Biology Teacher,* March, 1964, pp. 185–188.

Sanderson, R. T., *Three-Dimensional Teaching of Chemistry,* Van Nostrand, 1964.

Scurozo, Herbert E., "Embedding Realia in Plastic," *Grade Teacher,* January, 1963, pp. 10 ff.

Seehorn, R. W., "Models for Industry," *Educational Screen and Audiovisual Guide,* June, 1958, pp. 286–287.

Sheppard, D., "A Method for Assessing the Value of Exhibitions," *British Journal of Educational Psychology,* December, 1960, pp. 259–265.

Van Fleet, J., "The Diorama Comes to the Classroom," *Educational Screen,* June, 1943, pp. 204–205.

U.S. Department of Agriculture, *Educational Exhibits—How To Prepare and Use Them,* Miscellaneous Publication No. 634, Government Printing Office, 1948.

What Research Shows About Visual Aids, U.S. Department of Agriculture Extension Service, 1949.

Witmeyer, Stanley, "Display Is Visual Communication," *The Instructor,* May, 1960, pp. 47–50.

☐ Films and Filmstrips

Anatomical Models, 16 mm. film, B&W, 15 min., Denoyer-Geppert, 1949.

Atomic Models, Valence and the Periodic Table, 16 mm. Color, 45 min., University of Iowa, 1962.

The Diorama as a Teaching Aid, 35 mm. filmstrip, Color, 58 frames, Ohio State University, 1957.

How To Embed Specimens in Liquid Plastic, 35 mm. filmstrip, B&W, 53 frames, Syracuse University, 1955.

How To Make and Use a Diorama, 16 mm. film, Color, 20 min., McGraw-Hill, 1956.

Make a House Model, 16 mm. film, B&W and Color, 10 min., Bailey Films, 1950.

Model Houses, 16 mm. film, Color, 5½ min., International Film Bureau, 1949.

Museum of Science and Industry, 16 mm. film, B&W, 14 min., United World Films, 1937.

Museums for School Children, 16 mm. film, B&W, 21 min., United World Films, 1950.

New Models of Molecules, Ions and Crystals: Their Construction and General Use in Teaching Chemistry, 16 mm. film, Color, 45 min., University of Iowa, 1962.

Relief Models, 16 mm. film, Color, 10 min., David Lipscomb College, 1955.

Simple Exhibit Technique, 35 mm. filmstrip, Color, 40 frames, Ohio State University, 1958.

A Special Set of Models for Introducing Chemistry, 16 mm. film, Color, 45 min., University of Iowa, 1962.

Teacher as Observer and Guide, 16 mm. film, B&W, 22 min., Columbia University, 1946. (First seven minutes most useful here.)

VII | THE

STUDY DISPLAY

The presence or absence of study displays frequently is a major factor in the general appearance and feeling which a classroom presents to pupils and teachers. How often one has had the experience of walking into a classroom which is characterized by bare walls devoid of any evidences of pupil activity or the excitement of learning! In contrast, one can remember visiting classrooms in which the walls gave dramatic evidence of the nature of pupil and teacher activities. Through the presence of colorful displays—which communicate information and dramatize excitingly the subject content and activities of the day-to-day stream of instruction—learning and progress are evident.

□ DEFINITION OF THE STUDY DISPLAY

The study display is a learning experience, usually arranged on a flat vertical surface, which includes the use of a wide variety of materials. The learning display employs the use of diagrams, photographs, pictures, graphs, news clippings, mobiles, and three-dimensional objects and specimens. Related floor and table-top exhibits may be used to carry three-dimensional objects and specimens. Today's teachers know that "the walls can teach," and they constantly plan for more wall space, tackboard, or other display surfaces.

□ THE FUNCTION OF THE STUDY DISPLAY

While study displays have only recently been used seriously in teaching, their counterparts have been used for decades in merchandising. In business, the "selling display"—which is actually a kind of learning display—is devised to confront the potential customer with some information that will encourage him to buy goods or services. One need but look through the pages of magazines to note that advertisements are in themselves learning displays: Even those which

describe travel services, space hardware, and electronic equipment are devised to teach their audiences something about the service or equipment being offered. The goal of the business display is to command buying attention; analogously, this too is the teacher's goal—to "sell" interest and enthusiasm for the subject matter, and for learning itself. Those who seek to encourage study displays in the classroom might do well to bear in mind the merchant's purpose; namely, does the display present information well enough and dramatically enough to "sell" the idea (Fig. 7.1)?

Too often the bulletin board or tackboard is used for no other purpose than to display announcements of forthcoming events, safety regulations, and other general information. Although this function is necessary, it has little or nothing to do with study displays as such. A true study display also falls short of its purpose unless it involves a maximum number of students in the activities of its initial planning; in the search for and arrangement of useful subject-content materials, such as graphics, pictures and objects; and in creative followup projects.

☐ PROVISIONS FOR DISPLAY SPACE

Well-planned and well-arranged study displays are usually found on bulletin boards or tackboards, but they may also make inventive use of ceilings, walls, floors, table tops or window areas. For example, the ceiling will provide particularly suitable space for the display of such objects as the elements of the solar system, the latest models of aircraft, space platforms and rockets, mobiles of graphics, and various other types of three-dimensional materials depending on the subjects being studied. The classroom floor also can provide space for study situations: the squares of floor tiles and the angles at which chair and table legs meet the floor can be used to teach arithmetic and measurement. Other areas of

the floor can be used to place models, mockups, dioramas, and similar exhibits.

Whole walls can be devoted to project displays, also. As one enters the classrooms at Baylass High School in St. Louis County, for example, one observes tangible evidence of the nature of the work being pursued. In the social-studies classroom, one sees the usual chalkboard, map rail, project cabinets, and work surfaces, but, in addition, large areas of formerly unused walls have become "display walls" where one may find place and event maps 30 × 8 feet in dimension. These may have to do with Asia, the Americas, Africa, or Europe. Such project-display walls provide a continuing record of what the class has accomplished (Fig. 7.2).

Fig. 7.2. / This display wall each semester becomes a growing record of pupil achievement. Such large display areas can be made available by placing bookshelves, cabinets, and shelves below the walls of "vision strip" windows.

Fig. 7.3. / The movable space dividers which form this study alcove also provide additional display surfaces in this classroom.

Displays may be planned for any part of the room where visibility is good. No floor, ceiling, demonstration bench, or wall area should be overlooked in the search for more classroom display space. The form and arrangement which display surfaces may take is limited only by the creativity and imagination of the teacher.

In classrooms where television viewing is scheduled, where team teaching is in progress, or where work areas are separated from study or discussion areas, movable dividers or wall segments can be so constructed that they may be used as combination space dividers and display surfaces (Fig. 7.3). Those who design new buildings should make recommendations which encourage maximum provision for display space on walls in the form of these space dividers or special movable display panels.

Because of the need to keep classroom construction costs low, brick, poured concrete, cement, or concrete blocks are often used for classroom walls. Walls of this nature can economically be prepared for display use by using coverings of coarse, thick fabric, corkboard, plywood, or soft fiberboard, such as canite or Celotex. It is no more expensive to use these coverings than it is to give the porous cement or concrete surfaces enough coats of paint to cover them completely.

Display walls such as those at Baylass School may be repainted a flat buff or white at the end of the school year. The aim of the display wall is to accomplish the acquisition and assimilation of information and present it in graphic and understandable style; once this has been done, the wall is cleared and resurfaced for the next semester's students who will embark on their own quest for information and its graphic presentation.

In older schools, where additional display space is needed, one or more of the following suggestions may be helpful:

1. Unused wall or chalkboard areas can be hung with coarse, loosely woven cloth or strong paper suspended from a light but strong wire that has been stretched along the top of the chalkboard. Cloth provides a surface on which to pin display materials. The heavy paper can be used as the art paper itself, the children drawing directly on it with crayon or pastel chalk. These temporary display surfaces can easily be restored to their original uses.

2. Small areas of up to 4 × 6 feet can be converted for use as display areas by attaching to them composition board or plywood veneer that has been covered with an inexpensive, loosely woven, neutral-colored material. Cloth can be glued to the veneer or, if only a temporary surface is to be provided, the cloth can be stretched over the edges of the veneer and tacked lightly to the back with small tacks or staples.

3. Independently standing display panels of 3 × 4 feet—or 4 × 6 feet, depending on the floor area available—can be constructed in the manner illustrated in Fig. 7.4. In this example, the panels are of lightweight, ½-inch-thick Celotex or similar material. The 1- × 3-inch supporting members are all cut

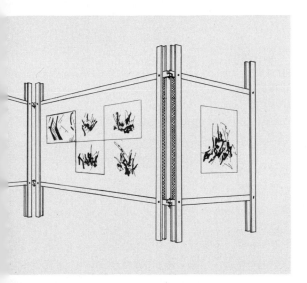 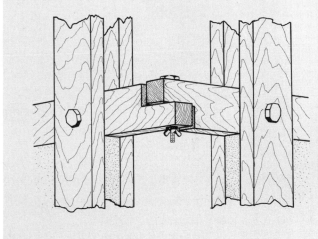

Fig. 7.4. / As many display sections as are needed can quickly be set up or taken down by means of the wing bolts.

into standard interchangeable sizes so that, by removing the wing bolts shown in the closeup view of the joint, the entire display unit may be dismantled, moved elsewhere, or stored. Both sides of such display surfaces may carry materials.[1]

4. Across a little-used corner of the room stretch clothesline from hooks mounted in the edges of the chalkboard frame or cabinets. Stretch clothesline to form a zigzag pattern across this area. On this zigzag clothesline support, attach large sheets of lightweight but strong cardboard cut from old mattress

[1] Plan prepared by Alexander Pickens, Professor of Art Education, University of Hawaii, Honolulu.

cartons, cornflakes boxes, or card table containers. Use these free-form areas as surfaces on which to display objects, specimens, pictures, graphics, or student work.

All four of the above suggestions can be completed by upper-grade or high-school student committees and at moderate expense.

☐ PLANNING AND ARRANGING STUDY DISPLAYS

The characteristics by which a good learning display may be recognized should be understood by the classroom teacher and his pupils before they undertake their planning and creation. One effective technique is for the teacher to arrange, at the beginning of the semester, a "model" study display which has been carefully thought out in terms of its value in presenting information attractively enough to motivate learners to take part in further investigation and planning. After the teacher has demonstrated to the class what a good display is and how it can become an integral part of classroom work, the next step will be to involve students in the planning and creation of additional displays in which they take more and more initiative. As the process "catches on," the students will gradually assume greater responsibility for planning, locating appropriate materials, and arranging them into meaningful displays.

Pupils who have imaginative curiosity can be relied upon to locate the elements of display communication: newspaper items, photographs, graphics, models, specimens, and mobiles. The student who is artistically inclined and who is interested in color, design, and form will become an effective member of the learning-display planning committee. As students progress, they will understand more about the mechanics of mounting pictures, preparing original diagrams, and arranging attractive layouts for the learning elements of a study display. As the teacher comes to know more about the interests and capacities of individual pupils and correlates these with the opportunities presented by study-display work, the group will be more apt to realize the goals of involvement and creative expression.

Although no one wants to follow the same plan, there are certain basic principles for planning and arranging learning displays. Teacher-pupil groups may wish to consider them and apply those which hold promise. While the several steps go on simultaneously, some order must be established through which to explain them; thus, we shall discuss these principles under two general headings:

1. *Learning content.* Materials and devices selected for a study display must communicate understandable and relevant information, and be sufficiently attractive to involve the learner in continuing search and creativity.
2. *Mechanical arrangements.* The materials and devices used should themselves include effective visual layout, headings, captions, and use of color, and they should be so combined in the display that their separate layouts and designs integrate into an overall design which embodies the same principles of attractive and meaningful design.

■ LEARNING-CONTENT ELEMENTS

Unless a learning display contains content elements which are useful and which will motivate the viewer to engage in useful learning, the activity falls short of its goals. Several principles must be observed closely if these goals are to be achieved.

■ ESTABLISH YOUR PURPOSE

As in any other educational endeavor, you must know first what you wish to accomplish and then plan how it is to be done. Bruno Gebhard of the Cleveland Museum of Health gives us sound advice:

> Exhibits are too often made with a minimum of clear thinking and planning. A vague idea is not enough and even a splendid one needs much detailed work. You would not dare to face a microphone without a script, or film a motion picture without a scenario. Treat your exhibit with equal respect. Put down its purpose in writing: describe the basic idea; be specific about the facts and figures to be used; the technique by which they will be shown. Your manuscript should also include complete copy. . . .[2]

The goal may be to arouse interest, to explain a process, to report facts, or to pose a problem, or all of these. In any case, before proceeding further, the primary purpose must be known. It is often helpful to incorporate this purpose in the title of the display itself, or it may be visualized in an attention-demanding graphic diagram or design.

■ GATHER CONTENT MATERIALS

Decide on the nature of the content materials you will want to include. Usually, a good study display results from a wide search for a variety of materials —newspaper and magazine articles, photographs, charts, graphs, diagrams, objects and specimens, and related three-dimensional materials as discussed in Chapter VI. Of these, only the best and the most relevant should be chosen to appear in the final display; that is, only those which are the most *meaningful, graphic,* and *colorful* content elements should be selected for the actual display. Decisions must be made about the best headings to be used, what captions should say, and which pictures or graphics should be mounted.

■ SELECT PROVOCATIVE CONTENT

A good study display will possess much content and information which will lead the learner to study the display in detail and, ideally, to inquire further

---

2 Bruno Gebhard, "How to Make and Use an Exhibit," in *Exhibits: How to Plan and Make Them,* National Publicity Council for Health and Welfare Services, 1946, p. 5.

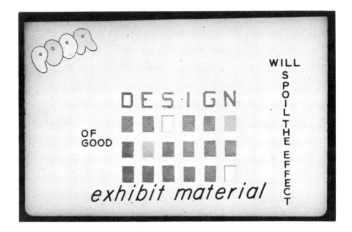

Fig. 7.5. / Note how arrangement, lettering, and contrast can make a difference in a display layout.

on his own. A display that is merely attractive and impressive in its overall effect has not achieved its full purpose; similarly, the exhibit which conveys its message only in part from its larger or more emphasized elements, those which can be viewed from afar or by means of a quick scanning on the part of the viewer, has failed in its ultimate purpose. This is particularly true of advertising or selling displays and of study displays. In the first case, the aim of the display is to arouse sufficient interest on the part of the viewer so that he will buy the product, or at least make the effort to inquire further, while the objective of the *study* display is to stimulate enough curiosity in the pupil so that he will examine the exhibit in its minutest detail. On the other hand, if this close scrutiny leaves the pupil fully satisfied, he will not be motivated to search for further information on his own from other sources.

Thus, the good study display selects for its most outstanding components the most provocative information and presents it in dramatic, attention-getting fashion so that the viewer will be drawn to examine the less prominent constituents of the display. Significantly, these smaller elements should satisfy the learner *just enough to reward him for his closer look*, and no more; rather, they should provoke further questions in the viewer's mind so that he will be prompted to take a still closer look, examining systematically the tiniest elements and reading the "fine print." Similarly, the information contained in these minute details should be sufficiently informative so that the learner will feel rewarded for his efforts, yet left with enough unsatisfied curiosity to be stimulated into investigating libraries, museums, and other information resources on his own initiative.

■ MECHANICAL ARRANGEMENTS

Once the purpose of the display and the type of content that will compose the display have been established, and the variety of classroom relevant materials have been gathered, the layout or design of the display must be planned. *Layout* refers to the overall arrangement of the display elements (Fig. 7.5). Attractive layout will dramatize the display: Through good layout, the eye of the viewer will be led subtly in one direction or the other across the interrelated elements of the display. Here, too, several principles must be observed if the viewer is to be drawn to the display, and to gain a meaningful experience from it.

■ ASSEMBLE NECESSARY DISPLAY SUPPLIES

Your first step in implementing the mechanics of the display is to gather the raw materials with which you will put the elements of the display together. These supplies usually include craft paper; large sheets of heavy paper for backgrounds or for paper sculpture; pastel chalk, wax crayons, and show-card colors; lettering stencils and pens; three-dimensional cardboard, plastic, or ceramic letters with which words and phrases can be formed; and masking tape. Mounting must also be considered, for which wire, tacks, and pins may be used. Light objects and pictures can be mounted with loops of adhesive tape, sticky side out. For heavier objects, a dry adhesive known as Bulletin Board Styx is useful. (See Source List, pages 529–530, for display materials. See also the films listed on page 223.) Supplies for study displays should be made easily available to both teacher and pupils.

■ MAKE A PLAN

Your second step is to carry the plan to the "blueprint" stage. Work it out on paper, showing measurements, design to be followed, color scheme, lettering, and placing of materials. The art teacher can help you here, because effective exhibits and displays always incorporate sound art principles, such as simplicity, design or arrangement, color, lighting, and, on some occasions, movement.

Because a good layout is a matter of imagination and creativity, one should experiment with arrangements. It is usually advisable before settling on a final plan to make copies of the several parts, lay them out on a table top, and try various arrangements until satisfied that you have the best one. Cutout paper forms may be used which can be moved across the desk top or over the surface of a piece of kraft paper which represents, in miniature form, the final display.

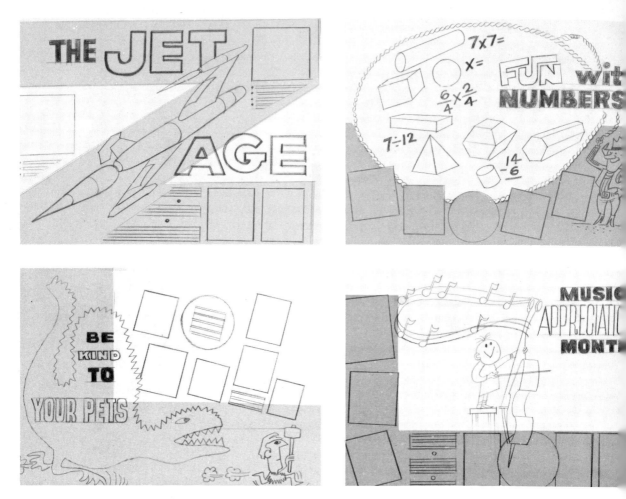

Fig. 7.6. / The dark-toned areas suggest the eye-movement path of the viewer. What layout ideas can you develop which will lead the viewer to examine all the elements included in your display?

Some layout suggestions are illustrated in Fig. 7.6, but these should be used as beginning ideas only. Note how the letter *Z* describes the eye movement of the jet age display. The *O* layout shows the direction of eye movement over the elements of the arithmetic display. An alternative *L* layout describes the eye movement in the "Pets" and "Music" display. The reader is urged to create his own modifications of these ideas.

Plans may have to be modified as students search for and discover exciting and appropriate pictures, graphics, and related three-dimensional materials. For example, verbal information may be made more understandable by converting it to diagrammatic, graphic, chart, or comic-drawing form. As this occurs, the change-and-improvement process goes forward but, as a rule, these changes should be planned out in the "blueprint" before incorporating them into the final display.

In planning the layout of the study display, there are several principles of design which are essential to an attractive, attention-arresting display. These are simplicity, effective use of color, wise choice of headings and captions, clear and artistic lettering, adequate lighting, motion, and provision for the viewer's participation.

■ ADHERE TO SIMPLICITY. McDougall has a suggestion worth remembering: "Poster and display work go hand in hand. A poster must not be loaded with copy. The poster and display must convey one central idea. If you have more to say, put it in another exhibit."[3]

The *design* itself should be simple. Basically designs are merely arrangements of various lines which lead the eye where you want it to go and at the same time produce a pleasing overall effect. Notice the effect of the good and bad arrangements in Fig. 7.5.

A symbol, cutout, or bold and unique design will provide an attention-demanding "device" or center of interest for the display. For example, if the subject is on space exploration, a simplified, abstract representation of a rocket ship might be used as the key symbol. Of course, the pictures, graphs, diagrams, specimens, and the other two- or three-dimensional objects used should all help to bring about specific and concrete understanding of the information displayed. The use of attractive mountings, cartoons, diagrams, charts, and graphics should be employed generously in the overall layout. These materials were explained in Chapters IV and V.

■ USE COLOR WISELY. *Color* is an important factor in any display or exhibit. It can be used for such purposes as attracting attention, emphasizing boundaries, indicating classifications and groups, and providing effective backgrounds for materials and lettering. Along with lighting and good design, color is regarded as fundamental by professional exhibitors such as the New York Museum of Science and Industry: "From our experience here at the Museum we have found that the three-part formula of sound architectural design, proper use of illumination, and good color effects, is the first essential of good exhibition practice."[4]

Use color when color is clearly needed to bring out the essential elements which the study display is to communicate, and when it will attract the learner's attention and interest him in studying the content of the display itself. The use of color in display situations has at least three purposes:

1. *To dramatize or focus attention on key items or relationships.* Study displays involving rules, direction, steps in a process, time-lines, or important dates in history, etc., will profit from the judicious attention-demanding use of colors which help classify or differentiate.

2. *To present visualized information accurately and comprehensively.* Scenes, costumes, persons, and geography and science objects which have color in real life demand the use of color when presented in a study display. Thus, a study display designed to portray wildlife effectively must of necessity be shown in its natural and authentic colors. Similarly, displays involving architecture, costumes, and geographical settings should be shown in natural color if the full truth about them is to be communicated to the learner.

3. *To heighten interest.* Study displays are most likely to attract attention

[3] Kenneth L. McDougall, "Tips for School Exhibitors," *Minnesota Journal of Education*, May, 1950, p. 23.

[4] *Exhibition Techniques*, New York Museum of Science and Industry, 1940, p. 19.

when color is used as part of the design; that is, when pleasing combinations of colors are used in a decorative way for backgrounds, for frames for the graphics in the display, and so forth. Intense colors virtually demand the attention of the viewer, and displays set off against warm complementary colors usually appeal to the learner's aesthetic sense and help interest him in further study of the display.

The selection of color combinations for displays, exhibits, picture mountings, graphics, and models is simplified by using a color wheel (see Plate 9 which appears in the section following page 208). A color wheel is made up of the three primary hues—red, yellow, and blue—and three secondary hues—green, orange, and violet—which are mixtures of adjacent primary colors. Tertiary hues can be created by mixing a secondary color with one of its adjoining primaries; for example, yellow-orange, red-orange, yellow-green, blue-green, and so forth. Many additional colors are possible by changing the value or intensity of primary, secondary, and tertiary colors; this is accomplished by adding black or white, or by mixing the color with its complementary hue.

In choosing combinations of colors for a study display, poster, etc., it is wise to select colors which naturally go well together. These are:

1. Complementary colors—colors which are directly opposite each other on the color wheel
2. Triads—any three colors equidistant from one another on the wheel
3. Split complementaries—any single color plus the two on either side of its complementary
4. Analogous colors—those colors which have the same primary base (red, yellow, or blue). These are usually found next to each other on the color wheel.

Some colors—reds, oranges, and yellows—are cheerful, warm, conspicuous. They are normally associated with fire, danger, excitement. The so-called "cool" colors, on the other hand—green, blue, and purple—are more soothing and restful. These are commonly used to represent grass, water, and sky. Color studies show that blue, green, and red—in that order—are the most *preferred;* orange, red, and blue have the greatest *attention* value; and yellow, green, and orange have the greatest *luminosity* or brightness.

Color wisely used is an important consideration in deciding content and arrangement of effective study displays. Provided that colors which harmonize are used together, the principles illustrated by a simple color wheel may readily be applied to any problem of color selection. However, good judgment and common sense are the teacher's best qualifications for using color intelligently in creating effective color displays.

■ CHOOSE APPROPRIATE HEADINGS AND CAPTIONS.   Every display should have a central heading which states the general purpose and idea of the display. Be dramatic. Ask a question, pose a problem, make a direct claim or statement. Headings and captions are extremely important. The headline, or title, is usually one of the means by which attention is first directed to the display. The captions employed should be as clear, simple, and succinct as possible, and carefully planned to enhance the viewer's interest as he steps closer to examine the display in more detail. Aside from that used for the heading, one letter size for identification of key elements and another smaller one for needed explanation or discussion will normally suffice. The quality of the captions will be determined by the directness and clarity with which they describe information relating to the materials used in the display itself.

■ PROVIDE CLEAR AND ARTISTIC LETTERING.   Lettering for displays and exhibits in schools can be done in several ways. Hand lettering put in by capable students or teachers is distinctive and particularly desirable for large headings. Cutout plywood letters made in the manual-arts shop are excellent. Three-dimensional letters made of cardboard and plaster are highly effective, and can be purchased commercially. Gummed letters in various sizes and colors are also available at low cost. (See Source List, pages 531–532.)

Lettering calls for color "know-how." As Gilbertson says:

> Whether measured in terms of speed of reading or distance that words can be read, the most important factor is the contrast in brightness between color of printed letters and background. The color combinations that can be read most easily at the greatest distance are listed in order as follows: Dark blue on white background, black on yellow, green on white, black on white, green on red, red on yellow, and red on white.[5]

■ LIGHTING SHOULD BE ADEQUATE.   Lighting is a dominant factor in any exhibit or display. It serves not only to focus attention but to bring out the effects that are created with design and color. Artificial light is often better than daylight because the latter varies and is unpredictable; furthermore, strong daylight tends to reduce contrast and thereby weakens the character of a display. A professional exhibitor brings out the point in this way: "The advantages of artificial light are quite simply illustrated by comparing the daylight appearance of a well appointed shop window with the much brighter impression it creates at night. The importance of this concentration of light is very great where the task is to draw and hold attention."[6]

Intricate and expensive lighting arrangements for study displays and other school exhibits are usually impractical and unnecessary. Spotlight and floodlight bulbs which screw into standard light sockets can be obtained in various colors. These can be used with pleasing effect in simple clip-on or self-standing fixtures which are quite inexpensive. For special occasions, such as a public exhibit in the gymnasium, a stage floodlight or two may be desirable for general illumination.

In all cases where a number of fixtures of several types are to be used simultaneously, a sufficient power supply and enough separate circuits should be available to avoid overheating the lines or blowing fuses. Check beforehand with the school electrician or maintenance man on such items.

When exhibit cases are located in corridors, a fluorescent fixture concealed in the case increases the attention-focusing power of the materials displayed. If you want to experiment, you can get pleasing effects by using colored gelatin sheets over the light. Since fluorescent light is "cold" light, no danger of fire is in-

---

5 H. W. Gilbertson, quoted in U.S. Department of Agriculture, *Educational Exhibits: How to Prepare and Use Them,* Miscellaneous Publication No. 634, Government Printing Office, 1948, p. 19.

6 *Exhibition techniques, op. cit.,* p. 68.

volved. Display boards located on inside corridors or in dark corners of class-rooms need lighting to be effective. A shaded fluorescent fixture at the top of such a board is a good way of lighting the display surface evenly. Recessed fixtures in the ceiling over the display area are a decided advantage. Flush-type fixtures are good for general illumination; an adjustable fixture known as a "bullet light" is excellent for baby spots. There should also be standard plug-in outlets in all recessed exhibit cases and adjacent to corridor display surfaces.

Fig. 7.7. / Where participation can be worked into an exhibit, it never fails to increase interest. This little jet plane responds accurately to the pilot controls. While probably impracticable for most school exhibits, this kind of device illustrates a principle which should be applied whenever feasible and appropriate.

■ USE MOTION WHEN FEASIBLE.   Movement can also be important to a display or exhibit both to attract attention and to focus it upon one or more elements within the design. Movement can be actual motion provided by small electric motors, a motion-picture film, or an automatic slide changer; or, it can be simulated by changing light patterns. Changing light patterns can be achieved by such means as Christmas-tree blinker-light fittings, a rotating color wheel in front of a floodlight, or polarized light such as that provided with special accessory equipment on an overhead projector.

Good judgment should be exercised in applying movement to displays or exhibits. Your principal concern must always be to get the message across—to

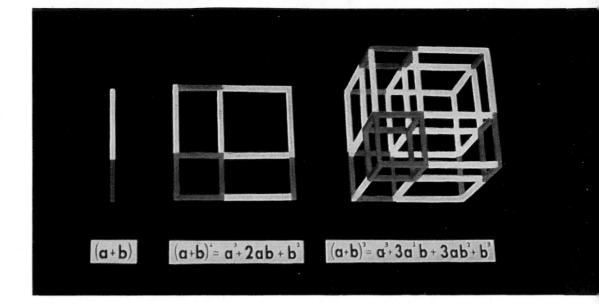

$$(a+b)$$
$$(a+b)^2 = a^2 + 2ab + b^2$$
$$(a+b)^3 = a^3 + 3a^2b + 3ab^2 + b^3$$

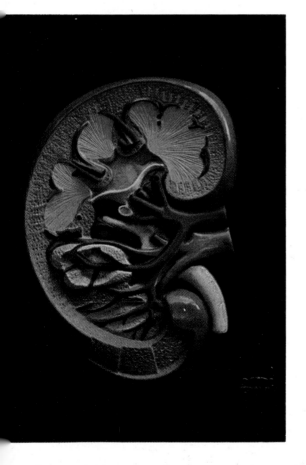

Plate 6 / The type of color used varies with the purpose for which color is employed: For *realism*, use natural colors; to *attract attention*, use bright colors and strong contrasts; the *mood* or *atmosphere* is made gay and cheerful with warm, bright colors, or quiet and restful with cool, soft hues; to *emphasize* and *distinguish* between important parts of models, color contrast should be used.

Plate 7 / Color is particularly important in dioramas which should create the illusion of reality in miniature. The two left dioramas show two representations of a modern farm. The diorama of Costa Rico (top right) was made by prospectiv

...eachers at the University of Costa Rica; the diorama at the lower right shows the ancient cliff dwellers at Mesa Verde.

Plate 8 / Natural colors are important in the study of anatomy, as is clear in this remarkable exhibit of the human heart. People walk right into the model, see the heart valves function, and hear the amplified beat.

Plate 9 / The color wheel is an unlimited palette with which to design your display materials. Use it as a tool in your design laboratory as your visual communications continue to grow in color effectiveness. The primary hues are shown in the central triangle and the three secondary hues—green, orange, and violet—form the hexagon. The wheel itself can be used to mix new colors and to select harmonious color combinations. See pages 205–206 for further discussion.

Plate 10 / The method used to display flat materials, fabrics, leaves, and other small specimens is described in the first Suggested Activity (p. 222). What adaptations of the above display can you think of?

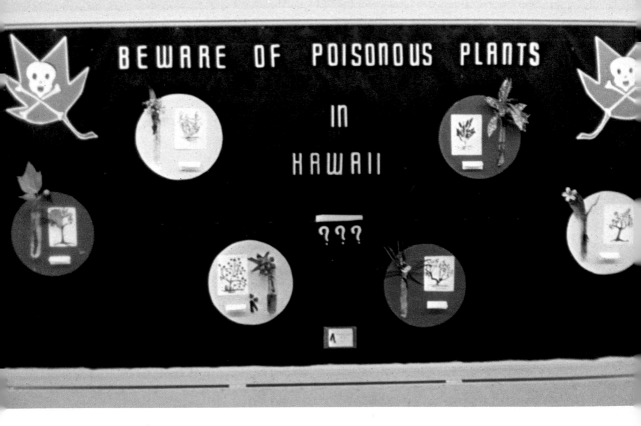

Plate 11 / Three motivational study displays. Do they also accomplish their teaching objectives? How?

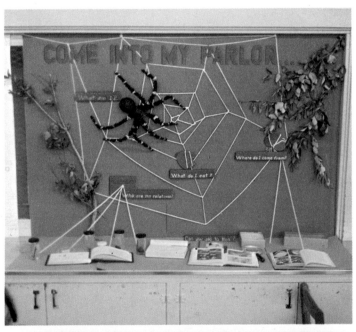

MIRROR, MIRROR ON THE WALL
WHICH ONE AM I ?

MOODY

CHEERFUL

AUTHORITARIAN

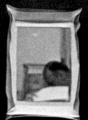

THOUGHTFUL

EXTROVERT

WORRIED

KA WAI WAI O HAWAII
HAWAII'S HEALTH

STOP GUESSING
ASK THE DAISIES
AND BE A LIBRARIAN

WHAT
DO I NEED?

WHERE
CAN I WORK?

WHAT
CAN I DO?

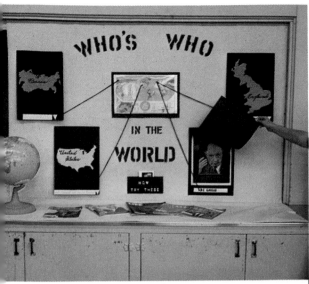

Plate 12 / Examine these six study displays carefully; to what extent do they observe good principles of layout, content selection, and color use?

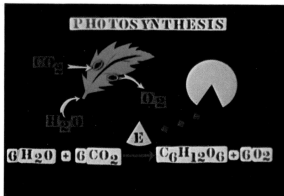

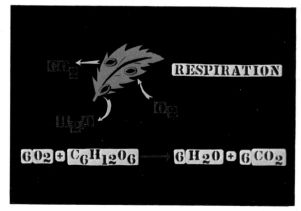

Plate 13 / This display demonstration of the water-cycle and the more complex transpiration-respiration concept illustrates the value of the felt board—when color symbols must be rearranged quickly during classroom discussion. A hook-and-loop board was used to display the heavier components of the hydrogen-helium display.

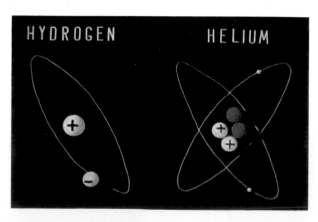

achieve the purpose for which the display or exhibit is designed. Accordingly, you should use those materials and techniques which are most appropriate to that end in any given instance, bearing in mind that over-emphasis of one element, such as movement, may hinder more than it helps. It is possible, in other words, to enliven a presentation to the point where it intrigues but doesn't communicate. It is also possible (and much more common, unfortunately) for displays and exhibits to be unnecessarily pallid, prosaic and, in consequence, to go unnoticed.

■ PLAN TO INVOLVE THE VIEWER.   The most effective exhibits frequently involve the viewer in some type of participation activity. Exhibits in the Chicago or New York Museums of Science and Industry, in which the viewer pushes a button or turns a knob to make something happen, are extremely popular. Anyone who has visited the American Museum of Atomic Energy at Oak Ridge, Tennessee, will not easily forget the part of the tour in which he can have a dime bombarded with neutrons so that it activates a Geiger counter, after which it is returned to him encased in a souvenir plastic disk. Similarly, driver-demonstration devices like the power steering exhibit in Fig. 7.7 are always popular.

Such devices are often costly or unfeasible for some school exhibits and study displays, however. Nevertheless, an attractive, attention-arresting heading and good content elements will lead the learner to become absorbed in the display itself. The reduced size of the print in the captions used to describe highly interesting visuals helps to "pull the learner" closer and closer to the display and further to involve his attention. Captions which ask questions or make suggestions are also useful.

The value of viewer participation in an exhibit is based on familiar principles of learning. Experienced teachers know that pupil activity is closely related to learning and to retention of what is learned.

■ CARRY OUT YOUR PLANS

Planning is the key to a good exhibit or display, and well worth the time it takes. If your "blueprint" has been planned down to the smallest detail, you can proceed to execute these plans in the actual display with assurance and minimum of waste motion. Your students should work with you on the planning from the beginning in most instances, and, with a little help here and there, they can carry much of the load in arranging the display itself. Helping to put on an exhibit offers another good opportunity for valuable learning above and beyond significant gains in factual information. The greatest profit for all, however, is derived from an exhibit which is planned and executed in terms of sound and effective educational principles (see Plates 10–13, in section following page 208).

□ **STUDY DISPLAYS THAT TEACH**

Study designs that teach fall logically into three general categories: those which motivate, the work type, and those which represent the culminative efforts of the class group.

Fig. 7.8. / This display was begun by the teacher and added to as the pupils assumed responsibility for finding and bringing to class appropriate pictures and objects for it. Interest is self-evident.

■ DISPLAYS WHICH MOTIVATE

In creating a motivational display, the teacher often finds it necessary to locate materials, and to plan and to arrange the display himself. This is to be expected, since this type of display serves to stimulate interest in new fields of study and, later, pupil initiative in creating displays. Although motivational displays—like all displays—involve a great amount of work, this should not deter the teacher from using them continuously as learning and motivational tools during the school year.

The teacher may secure display materials from his own files of graphics, charts, and pictures which relate to key subjects, or from the picture-graphics files in the library. If his goal is to present a ready-made or complete display to arouse interest at the beginning of the year, the teacher may reassemble a particularly effective display that was used the year before.

The use of motivational displays is best illustrated in examples of imaginative, creative study displays. As one such example, a science teacher displayed laminated specimens—leaves, seaweed, seed collections and feathers—as a means of encouraging students to collect specimens and objects and arrange them for visualization and study. One such display panel, and the stand which was used to display it, is shown on Plate 10 (see section following page 208). The actual preparation of laminated displays is simple enough so that primary-level students may engage in this activity. Complete suggestions for the preparation of laminated display materials is included in the activities section at the end of this chapter.

Another science teacher arranged, at the beginning of the semester, a display

Fig. 7.9. / A collage. What adaptations can you envision for its use in your classroom?

case in the hall outside the classroom with exciting and interesting pictures, objects, and graphics which represented descriptive and quickly recognizable highpoints of the several units of work to be covered in the course. Each unit of the display could be seen only by looking through peepholes in the paper-covered glass front of the display case (see Plate 11, in section following page 208).

Realizing that her pupils had little opportunity to collect materials of their own, an elementary teacher gathered, over a period of several years, interesting pictures and objects to be used in the first of a series of motivational displays on life in the sea, on the land, and in the air (Fig. 7.8). The teacher began this series of displays with her own collection of pictures and objects, and as soon as she had these arranged, the children became interested in bringing more things from home for the remainder of the series. Significantly, the children also showed interest in the further study of the subject as a result of the ideas conveyed to them by the display.

A collage—a combination of appropriate cutout and fit-together pictures—is of great interest to pupils. "America Is Beautiful," a collage arranged in the pattern of the United States, is shown in Fig. 7.9. It was displayed at the beginning of the semester as an overview of the core ideas in the course—places, activities, and people in the United States. In their free time, groups of pupils studied the details of this collage with great interest and consequent learning benefits. Collages offer opportunities for motivational study in music, language arts, and virtually every subject for which pictures and other graphic materials are available.

At the beginning of the semester, before beginning the study of a unit on

Fig. 7.10. / This motivational display is the result of pupil-teacher planning. The pockets of "real" questions reflect the students' curiosity. What similar plans can you develop?

Fig. 7.11. / This display begins as a motivational device. How does it contribute as a work-progress record of pupil accomplishment? What pupil-evaluation opportunities does the felt surface provide?

insects, a committee of pupils met with the teacher to decide how best to announce the forthcoming unit. Since most pupils had had some experience with bees, a display about these insects was selected as the starting point. A search was conducted for dramatic pictures. As this continued, class discussion was developed around what was known about these insects and, more important, the questions the students had about bees. All of these questions were assembled on cards and arranged with attractively mounted graphics in the motivational display shown in Fig. 7.10. As the work continued, a table had to be moved in to hold some of the first specimens, books, and objects the students collected as they conducted their search for more and more information about bees in the library, in the community, and on the school grounds. Thus, what had started out to be a motivational display developed into a record of progress and accomplishment.

Several days before beginning a junior-high-school unit on the petroleum industry, a teacher put up on the display board several pamphlets and actual sample bottles of petroleum products. He asked the pupils: "Will you be on the alert for more interesting material, pictures, and objects relating to petroleum? If you find anything interesting will you bring it in?" The students were interested—so much so that, even before the unit began, news clippings, additional specimens, and pictures of petroleum products and the petroleum industry were brought in to supplement the initial display.

A high-school mathematics teacher periodically posted a single, but unusual problem in diagram form. These problems never failed to attract a knot of curious students, who would be pondering such a question as: "Which of the one-pound candy boxes would require the shortest length of ribbon to tie it once around each side?" In this case, three beribboned boxes of varying size but of identical volume were attached to the board below the question.

A science teacher encouraged a committee of her pupils to arrange a problem-type motivational display. Among the questions that her display included in its layout were: "Under what circumstances does volcanic activity begin?"; "What is the nature of volcanic materials?"; and, "How can we describe and identify the various zones of activity, temperature, and earth conditions which are hidden deep below the surface of the earth?" In order to attract attention, the student committee hit upon a clever device; namely, the presentation of the problem in terms of a cut-apart puzzle of interrelated parts which, when properly fitted together in correct sequence, would occupy that area of the display covered by a feltboard surface. Participating students were confronted by the scrambled portions of the diagram. The goal was to learn enough about volcanoes and volcanic activity first to enable the student correctly to assemble the scrambled parts of the display, and then to explain correctly just what happened preceding, during, and following volcanic activity (Fig. 7.11).

A final example of how displays can motivate interest in learning was illustrated in the case of a civics teacher who anticipated difficulty in capturing the imagination of her ninth-grade class for a thoroughgoing study of the United Nations. This teacher sought the help of a group of interested students who arranged a display that was studded with questions about the United Nations. Immediately the interest of the class as a whole was captured.

Motivational displays which merely announce coming events and activities are more routine; nevertheless, if this type of display is given the same care as far as planning, arrangement, and content are concerned, its effectiveness will be increased.

■ THE WORK-TYPE DISPLAY

The work-type display is an imaginative, visualized, systematic report of the progress made by the entire class or by committees as they go on to the various stages of study, organizing the key generalizations or conclusions as they reach

Fig. 7.12. / A committee chairman shows a visual plan for a display. Planning, reporting, and cooperative activity provide the basis of creating work-type displays.

them. Usually these can be visualized, either by finding suitable pictures, charts, or objects, or by making drawings and pictures of what they have learned. The work-type display is thus closely allied with general study progress.

This type of display is particularly effective when it is undertaken initially by the pupils and is continued as the product of their own creative and developmental thinking, planning, and doing. This may involve trial and error and the formulation of procedures, questions for study, and techniques for continuing the search for information. The work may be done by individual pupils, or by committees which report their ideas to the class (Fig. 7.12).

The widely known experience chart and mural display continues to reveal the extent to which the day-to-day work-study progress of primary-grade pupils fulfills goals in reading, vocabulary, concept understanding, creative art, and language arts. Work-type study displays can become good evaluation situations. When children are able to create an accurate and understandable mural—for example, about turtles and their habitat—when they write or dictate an experience chart, when they discuss their learning outcomes, the display chart thus produced is a true measure of accomplishment. It is hard to describe the point at which a work-study display becomes a culminative display, nor is the distinction worth much attention. It is important, however, to describe carefully the role both may have in stimulating the processes of useful learning.

At the intermediate level, displays built around nouns and action words offer incentive and pride of achievement to the learner. The work-type display is most effective when it gives evidence of ideas and information which are closely related to, or actually grow out of, the subject being studied.

In classroom situations where there is need for drill—for example, in the language arts, mathematics, the social studies, and history—some work-type displays can be used effectively (Fig. 7.13). Not only is this an attractive way of

Fig. 7.13. / The content of these work-type displays can be changed from day to day. What are your ideas for similar displays in arithmetic, science, mathematics, or foreign languages?

Fig. 7.14. / This display packet of Wisconsin-shaped overlays presents visualized information on the glaciation of the land surface, the history, industry, people, and recreation facilities of the state. Adaptations of this display can be used wherever sequential study and explanation are important, or as a culminating activity.

presenting information that must be memorized, practiced, and applied; but also the words which comprise the drill situation itself may be changed from day to day. Similarly, arithmetic rules, geometry theorems, and other drill materials can be made the subjects of study displays. Initially, such displays must be presented by the teacher, but, as soon as it is possible, interested and able students should assume responsibility for presenting the visual evidence of what rules, theorems, or axioms actually mean.

In a language-arts situation, study materials may include newspapers, magazines, maps, charts, diagrammatic presentations, attention-demanding symbols or graphics, as well as three-dimensional objects or specimens. One junior-high-school class assembled a variety of elements for their foreign-language display as part of their French-language activities. The display thus represented a progress report of their learning achievements, and included evidences of pupil work and accomplishment in this area. When the work-type display is used to record class progress and accomplishment, the group's decision on the main problem to be studied may prominently be displayed on the board. As sub-ordinate problems are developed during classroom discussions, they may be included on supplementary boards or in nearby spaces which have been tem-porarily converted to display use. Display areas can be expanded if necessary by using another wall area temporarily, or by following some of the suggestions that have been made earlier in this chapter. Evidence of the continuing search for information in books, periodicals, audiovisual materials, interviews, com-munity resources, and so forth can be systematically added as a continuing record of progress. The work-study display can be used whenever motivation has been developed in any classroom situation, at any level, or in any subject. This type of display can become an integral, closely associated record of progress of the day-to-day work done in the modern classroom.

■ THE CULMINATIVE STUDY DISPLAY

The culminative display "pulls together" the work accomplished over a period of days or weeks; it summarizes the end products of a unit of work. The degree to which all the pupils participate depends on individual ability; how-ever, unless everyone contributes in some degree, the display activity cannot be carried to its highest level of development. A good classroom study display represents the entire group's thinking, planning, and developing. Because it enables the class as a whole, as well as the individual pupils, to see the end results of what they have done, the culminative display serves as a summarizing, evaluating, or concluding record of a classroom activity.

A group of visiting teachers entered a science classroom where the results of eight weeks of work were exhibited. On a display table that blended into a flat backdrop of blue were replicas of all the parts of a space vehicle. Nearby planets were mounted in three-dimensional perspective—as if suspended at various dis-tances in space—on the backdrop.

"Not only was this fun for all of us," a student commented, "but we had to find out the answers to dozens of questions before we could finish it."

A social-studies teacher described another display which showed the work done by six pupil committees on the geography, history, industry, etc., of the state of Wisconsin: "Each pupil chose the committee on which he wanted to work. After reading resource material and viewing filmstrips and films, each committee reported its key findings in the form of a series of overlying map dis-plays. Each of the overlays recorded the information that its committee con-sidered important." The final cooperative display of the six committees is shown in Fig. 7.14.

Fig. 7.15. / Adhering surfaces may be homemade or commercial. They may be used independently or incorporated into a study display. Either way they encourage pupil participation. What ideas do you have?

□ SPECIALIZED STUDY-DISPLAY DEVICES

Teaching displays may be arranged in a variety of ways on a variety of surfaces. Traditional means for classroom display include tackboards, presswood bulletin boards, panels mounted above the chalkboard—all fixed or built-in areas for display. The teacher may also devise temporary display surfaces (see pages 197–198). There are also, among others, adhering boards—such as the hook-and-loop board; the feltboard; and the magnetic board.

■ THE HOOK-AND-LOOP BOARD

The hook-and-loop board enables relatively heavy three-dimensional objects, as well as pictures and diagrams, to be displayed. The surface of the board consists of a great many small but very strong nylon loops. An adhesive-backed patch, on which thousands of tiny hooks are interwoven per square inch, is affixed to the object to be displayed, and the object is then pressed gently against the hooked surface. The supporting strength of this device is remarkable, as is also the ease of removing the object from the board. The many possibilities of this device soon become apparent to the teacher.

■ THE FELTBOARD

Because hair, wool, and cotton felt or flannel will adhere to like surfaces, the so-called "feltboard" has long been used for arranging study displays. Today, the feltboard—either commercially produced or homemade—affords many opportunities for providing enriching classroom experiences. Cotton-outing flannel or wool felt is usually used for feltboards. This material is stretched and then fastened with glue or thumbtacks to a flat surface—plywood, masonite, or heavy cardboard. The cloth can also be made into a sort of "pillowcase" for covering both sides of the flat surface.

Paper cutouts, diagrams, illustrations from magazines or newspapers, symbols cut from relatively lightweight and somewhat textured kraft paper; and ready-made felt figures all adhere to the surface of the feltboard. The various elements can be moved about easily and quickly during discussion and developing explanations (Fig. 7.15).

The water-cycle display shown in Plate 13 in the section which follows page 208 emphasizes the effectiveness of color. The symbols in this display were cut from construction paper and the foliage was made of heavier paper. Small pieces of lightweight sandpaper were attached to the backs of the various elements to improve adhesiveness. This feltboard display has the advantage of allowing the various elements to be moved around as the discussion proceeds: understanding first the water cycle, then transpiration, respiration, and finally photosynthesis.

Combining cutout figures from an inexpensive children's magazine or book with those made from kraft paper provide the materials for a creative story hour, or for a story demonstration on school playgrounds and street safety. A feltboard is also of value to the chemistry teacher in explaining molecular structure, the meaning of valence, etc. The physical-education teacher will find it helpful for demonstrating marching formations, and language-arts teachers can make use of the feltboard in explanations of relationships between parts of a sentence, vocabulary drill, and other study situations.

Regardless of the age level of the pupils, the feltboard can be the means of visualizing concepts which call for sequential, visual change during discussion, question and answer periods and demonstrations. (See Source List, page 530, for various kinds of display devices.)

What should be done with displays when they are completed? Most should be destroyed, since the learning value of any display stems from the activity in its entirety. In some cases, however, an exceptionally good display may be kept as a challenge to other classes, and should be stored along with display art materials. Suitable storage facilities like those shown in Fig. 7.16 should be provided in the classroom.

Fig. 7.16. / Storage facilities should be part of the classroom furniture.

☐ EVALUATING THE STUDY DISPLAY

Learning displays may best be evaluated by examining the manner in which the display attracts attention through its *initial impact,* through the extent to which it possesses *depth of content* communicated to the learner, and through the way it *involves the learner* in further learning pursuits. More specifically:

1. *Initial impact* refers to the dramatic quality of the display, and the extent to which the study display—like an efficient advertisement or merchandise display—captures the imagination of the viewer and draws his attention to the display and its contents. Initial impact is usually achieved by displays which incorporate good layout, headings, and visual quality—all conditions which cause a display virtually to "reach out" to capture the attention of the learner.

2. *Depth of content* refers to the kind of display content which leads the learner deeper and deeper into the meanings portrayed by the visualized and captioned elements of the display. A superficial learning display communicates its message quickly and broadly rather than in depth. An effective display contains substantial amounts of useful content information that are so cleverly arranged as to hold the attention of the learner until complete communication is accomplished.

3. *Learner involvement* refers to the degree to which the learner is captivated by the display and is led on to further study or activity. For example, does the display content influence him to continue studying the subject presented? A good display provokes further activity; that is, it may lead the pupil to search for additional information about the subject, to plan and produce a model, a picture, a story, or to write a letter of inquiry. In the degree to which the learner is motivated to continue his search—in the school library, in periodicals, in textbook reading, in community-resource investigation, or in other modes of information getting—lies the true measure of the learning display.

No one display will accomplish all of the things suggested above. However, a good display will incorporate as many of the techniques alluded to above as is possible.

☐ SUMMARY

While teachers are awaiting the fulfillment of their requests for film projectors, tape recorders, and educational television, a readily available opportunity to enrich instruction is present through the creation of study or learning displays. A study display is unique as a learning source—it is more than simply pasting up parades of turkeys at Thanksgiving or rabbits at Easter. Rather, the learning display is a collection of related and self-explanatory pictures, graphics, and three-dimensional objects which *together* convey useful information, visual explanations, and actual demonstrations in which the viewer can participate.

When engaging in the creation of effective learning displays, the teacher will do well to follow carefully worked out and proved procedures such as the following:

1. Study displays are learning experiences and should reflect this goal.
2. A good display is the result of a plan which presents informative pictures, graphics, models, and specimens in such an interrelated manner as to communicate meaning to the viewer.
3. Study displays must relate to the subject being studied and the interest and curiosities of the learner. The best study display will involve the learner and will entice him to engage in further search for related information.
4. The best learning displays command attention and study; communicate concepts, facts, and insights; and develop ongoing enthusiasm for the subject being studied.
5. A good learning display reflects good mechanical organization and layout.

Study displays that teach are the carefully planned creative efforts of the teacher and pupils. Such cooperation will involve the pupil in the purposes and spirit of the study display, with the result that the pupils will learn from displays as well as create their own to present information, demonstrations and explanations to their classmates.

☐ Suggested Activities

1. Prepare a lamination display-panel of specimens such as feathers, seeds, leaves, seaweed, or other flat objects or textiles.
   a. Needed supplies include:
      old newspapers
      ordinary waxed paper
      paraffin
      an electric iron (set on "low")
      two-dimensional objects or specimens—dried butterflies or moths, ferns, etc.
   b. Procedure:
      (1) Decide on the size of the finished panel (any size up to 2×6 feet).
      (2) Unroll waxed paper so that one layer of paper (with edges overlapped about 1 inch) represents display area needed.
      (3) On waxed surface arrange two-dimensional specimens or objects.
      (4) Type titles on this tissue or tracing paper.
      (5) Use cheese grater, or scrape with paring knife, fine particles of paraffin onto entire surface.
      (6) Lift objects so that some of the paraffin scrapings are on the under as well as on the top side.
      (7) Unroll more waxed paper to make "sandwich" of the objects between layers of waxed paper.
      (8) Hold paper in place and gently iron over upper surface until heat has melted paraffin to seal upper and lower surfaces together, thus embedding the objects.
      (9) Trim edges of display and mount.
      (10) Place display panel in a window frame so that back lighting will permit illumination of objects.
   An alternative display arrangement is shown in Plate 10.
2. Assemble materials needed to construct additional study-display space. Use any four ideas suggested on page 204 or experiment with one of your own.
3. Arrange to view some of the how-to-do-it films listed in the reference suggestions. Then try out the suggestions you got from the films.

4. Begin to accumulate a file of photographs, diagrams, illustrations, specimens, etc., which will be useful in creating motivational study displays for the subjects you teach or will teach.
5. Plan and arrange a study display of the motivational, work, or cumulative type.

☐ Bibliography

"Bulletin Boards" (a monthly feature), *Grade Teacher,* issues from 1963 to present.

Caldwell, Lee E., "Alcove Workroom Developed in Three Patterns," *Nation's Schools,* September, 1958, pp. 63–65.

East, Marjory, *Display for Learning,* Dryden, 1952.

Exhibition Techniques, New York Museum of Science and Industry, 1940, p. 19.

Ford Foundation, The, *A Living School: Report of the Planning Group for Programming an American International School in New Delhi, India,* 1960.

Gebhard, "How To Make and Use an Exhibit," in *Exhibits: How To Plan and Make Them,* National Publicity Council for Health and Welfare Services, 1946, p. 5.

Lees, M. M., "Bulletin Boards Anyone? Try These Tips." *Business Education World,* September, 1963, pp. 14–15.

McDougall, "Tips for School Exhibitors," *Minnesota Journal of Education,* May, 1950, p. 23.

"Modern Schoolhouse Planning" (Editorial), *Architectural Forum,* February, 1956, p. 140.

Pluss, R., "Sharpen Up Your Bulletin Board!" *Clearing House,* March, 1964, pp. 437–438.

Sheppard, D., "A Method of Assessing the Value of Exhibitions," *British Journal of Educational Psychology,* December, 1960, pp. 259–265.

Visual Instruction Bureau, University of Texas; various pamphlets in the *Bridges for Ideas* series:
    "Bulletin Boards for Teaching" (No. 2)
    "Educational Displays and Exhibits" (No. 9)
    "Feltboards for Teaching" (No. 3)
    "Lettering Techniques" (No. 4)
    "Tearsheets for Teaching" (No. 1)

U.S. Department of Agriculture, *Educational Exhibits: How to Prepare and Use Them,* Miscellaneous Publication No. 634, Government Printing Office, 1948, p. 19.

Witmeyer, Stanley, "Display Is Visual Communication," *The Instructor,* May, 1960, pp. 47–50.

☐ Film and Filmstrips

Better Bulletin Boards, 16 mm. Film, Color, 11 min., Indiana University.

Bulletin Boards: An Effective Teaching Device, 16 mm. Film, Color, 11 min., Bailey Films.

Bulletin Boards for Effective Teaching, 16 mm. Film, Color, 10 min., Iowa State University.

Feltboard in Teaching, The, 16 mm. Film, Color, 10 min., Wayne University.

Flannel Boards and How to Use Them, 16 mm. Film, Color, 15 min., Bailey Films.

Flannelgraph, 16 mm. Film, Color, 27 min., University of Minnesota.

How to Make and Use the Feltboard, 33 mm. Filmstrip, Color, Teaching Aids.

Lettering Instructional Materials, 16 mm. Film, Color, 20 min., Indiana University.

Paper Sculpture, 16 mm. Film, Color, 6 min., International Film Bureau.

Passe Partout Framing, 16 mm. Film, B&W, 10 min., Indiana University.

Techniques of Paper Sculpture, 16 mm. Film, Color, 10 min., Allen-Moore.

Wet Mounting, 16 mm. Film, Color, 10 min., Indiana University.

VIII

COMMUNITY STUDY

As teachers and educators seek to achieve some of the most important objectives of American education, they will do well to consider and explore community-study plans and possibilities. Consider several of the general goals and objectives of education: understanding social life, developing citizenship and civic responsibility, achieving vocational understanding and economic efficiency, and —perhaps most important of all—self-realization of the individual. These objectives were first stated as long ago as 1918 by the U.S. Office of Education; they were restated in 1938 by the Educational Policies Commission; again in 1954 by the National Education Association; and still more recently by educators who have studied the ongoing influence and acceptance of these objectives by the educational profession.[1] Clearly, community study is directly related to each of these objectives. Yet, in spite of the wide recognition of these objectives, community-study experiences are not as integral a part of instruction as one would hope. Too often school districts become enmeshed in the restrictions and traditionalism of rigid class schedules, narrowly prescribed and compartmentalized subject matter, and adherence to outmoded classroom procedures which customarily arrange all formal learning experience within the four walls of the classroom.

While many objectives of education can be achieved through reading, discussion, and simulated experiences (presented by means of films, pictures, filmstrips, etc.), a realistic grasp of the interactions of social and economic existence is best gained from direct experiences with adult life in its societal setting. For example, the pupils in one class on problems of democracy were studying the organization and function of local and state government. The teacher asked, "How many of you have attended a session of the state legislature?" No one had. "How many have attended a meeting of the common council?" Again no response. The teacher continued with questions which sampled pupil awareness of the city's service organizations, such as the water purification plant, the Highway Service Department, the Sanitation Department, and so forth. Although there were a few informed responses, 90 percent of the students had had

1 Harry R. Moore, *Modern Education in America,* Allyn and Bacon, 1962, pp. 119–136.

Fig. 8.1. / These children are learning through their *natural self-interest*, without strong teacher supervision. What kinds of learning outcomes might result from such experiences? How do your teaching methods and your approach compare?

little or no firsthand experience with local governmental agencies or their functions.

During the previous three years, however, this same group of pupils had studied—within the confines of the classroom—the relationships of the earth's atmosphere to space vehicles and space travel; they had traced the story of mankind from the dawn of history to the present; they had textbook knowledge of the regions and countries of the world; and they could relate interesting facts about the Congolese of Central Africa and some of the problems with which the United Nations is confronted. In short, these pupils had spent years studying about the peoples, places, and events of long ago and thousands of miles away, but they were poorly informed about local economic and political functions and the related organizations which affect the daily lives of the pupils and their future welfare.

If we believe that firsthand experience with people and things are primary sources of learning—and research done by educational psychologists assures us that they are—we must arrange to investigate systematically the resources of local communities as part of the organized school curriculum. A program calling for *planned use of the community* enables us, figuratively speaking, to go "through the walls of the classroom" and see for ourselves what people and their activities are like, and perhaps to catch a glimpse of what life may hold for us tomorrow.

In terms of the pupil's own nature, community study is a less remote and highly interesting way of becoming informed about the social, economic, and physical aspects of his environment than are the more conventional means of instruction. Up until his entrance into kindergarten or first grade, the child has spent the bulk of his life probing, examining, questioning, and experimenting in order to gain understanding about his home, back yard, neighborhood, and other aspects of his immediate environment. He has taken walks or trips with his parents, wandered off with his agemates, and pulled apart his toys; he has asked questions endlessly of the grocer, the plumber, or the automobile mechanic. Through this natural self-expression of childhood, he has developed his innate curiosity and satisfied it through firsthand observation.

Yet, when he comes to school, this same child—who has spent so much of his life wiggling, crawling, and exploring—finds himself within the restraining walls of a classroom, confined to a chair, and restricted in his activities to those called for by the teacher!

To expect the 6-year-old to conform to the restricted environment of a classroom for five hours a day, five days a week is to run counter to all we know about his mental, emotional, and physical makeup. But older children, too, have natural needs to explore, to be physically and mentally active, and to express themselves fully through the social channels open to them. Yet too often the school—a social setting deliberately provided for children—has thwarted these needs, demanding that children's natural physical and mental expressions be confined during the long school hours to only those which meet with a narrowly prescribed curriculum. Certainly such an approach to education is one of the anachronisms committed by those who claim to be students of the child, his nature, and his needs.

Arrangements should be made for the pupil to continue his natural exploring behavior in similar but more directed and appropriate community-study activities which permit direct observation, touch, experimentation, and questioning. The child should be allowed to pry into every corner of his environment as he participates in carefully planned, school-controlled community-study experiences. Instead of being confined to the four walls of a classroom, he should be "free" to investigate his "world": the school yard, his friends' homes, the business district, and the open country outside the area he lives in. The "schoolroom" for the child should include the caterpillars in the shrubbery and the small stream with its myriad wonders—water plants, the wriggling insects and pupae, tiny fish, and the sparkling crystalline rocks and stones on the stream bed. The school day should include talks and visits with community helpers—

the mailman, the fireman, the policeman, and the people who are engaged in laundering, dairying, breadmaking, poultry raising, and the other commercial enterprises in the community. Older and more able learners should be permitted to range farther afield: For them, extended stays at school camps, and overnight but study tours, as well as visits to nearby governmental agencies, manufacturing plants, and public-works projects, are means of revealing the facts of and opportunities provided by the society they will enter as participating adult citizens.

The idea of community study is not new. Among the first modern educators ordinarily acknowledged as presenting logical arguments for local study were Pestalozzi, Herbart, and Froebel. These men stated their views about learning again and again; to summarize them: *Learning experiences which are real, life-like, and available to the learner for firsthand scrutiny, questioning, and cog-*

nition are likely to be the most effective avenues through which children become informed about their social and natural environment.

The traditional concept of the classroom is slowly changing, however. Fortunately, there are constructive alternatives to traditional classroom instruction in the form of plans which either can bring useful community-learning experiences and resources right into the classroom, or which will permit the students themselves to go out into the community to observe, to question, and to learn (Fig. 8.2). More and more the classroom is becoming a work-planning base from which learners can look in many directions to gain the needed and useful experiences that exist in the social and physical community at large.

The immediate community often provides extremely dynamic, interesting, real-life opportunities for learning. It is the responsibility of the administrator and teacher alike to investigate the community, particularly the resources which seem to identify themselves with a more clear-cut and fuller understanding of formal school experiences.

☐ COMMUNITY STUDY DEFINED

Community study refers to the various learning situations through which pupils come into firsthand contact with the people, places, and things all around

8.2. / More and more teachers attended relaxed summer workshops and credit courses devoted to community-study planning. What are some of the benefits these teachers will gain from this workshop session?

them. It includes visiting organizations, institutions, and neighborhoods or regions of the community; interviewing public officials and community leaders; participating in community affairs and planning; listening to and observing others plan and operate both public and private enterprises; examining the tools, machines, reports, and various other accouterments involved in the diverse business of the community; and questioning wherever and whenever the pupils' curiosity is evoked. In short, community study provides real-life opportunities to learn by doing and to gain understanding directly from the things, processes, services, and social and political activities that make up the stream of community life.

The terms used to describe the various forms of community study vary widely: *School journeys, excursions, tours, visiting-authority programs* and *hostel trips* are but a few. However, many of these terms include activities which are not specifically designed to inform directly about community life, and many others are not directly useful in realizing the central work-study goals of the curriculum. For example, a community leader might be invited to talk at a school assembly on a subject that has no particular relevance to the specific units being studied by the pupils in their classrooms at that time. Many "visiting-authority" and other programs which involve the community at large are planned and carried

Fig. 8.3. / Civic responsibility is built upon broad and deep knowledge of the community—its nature and organization. When does one begin the development of civic responsibility? How and when are values and attitudes developed in addition to factual knowledge?

Fig. 8.4. / Walking trips are an easy and inexpensive means of providing school children with a wide variety of direct experience with their community as well as with the concrete basis of their abstract learning. What concepts are taking shape in the pupils' minds as they observe the structures of a living plant found in a nearby park?

Fig. 8.5. / A telephone lineman from the community has been invited to demonstrate his work at a site on or near to the school grounds. What responsibilities are here assumed by members of the community? By the school administration? By the teacher? By the pupils?

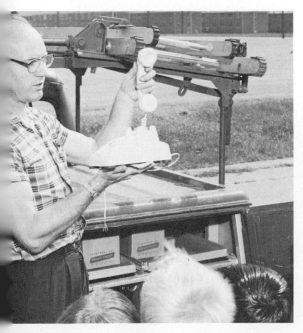

Fig. 8.6. / Seeing at first hand this free-flowing artesian well is an experience which can start an inquiry into water-supply and management questions, from the pumping through purification, storage, and distribution facilities of a large city water-supply organization. Would such an inquiry be related to science, social studies, arithmetic, or government? Or, does it lead to an interrelated study experience?

out in connection with the *total* school, and have little or no articulation with individual courses of study. For this reason, *community study* will be used in this chapter to cover only those excursions, field trips, "visiting-authority" programs, and other community activities that are implemented as *integral parts of specific units of curriculum instruction.* Toward this end, community-study experiences will be presented as that part of the formal school program which *extends the individual classroom into the community,* or which *brings the community into the classroom* in order to give the pupils direct experience with the people, places, and things they are studying about.

☐ THE SCOPE OF COMMUNITY STUDY

Community resources are becoming more and more available as our transportation and communication facilities become more efficient. Community-study opportunities exist through arrangements which either bring resource people or demonstrations into the school itself, or make it possible for students to leave the school grounds to enter the neighborhood. Walking trips, bus excursions, aerial tours, school camping facilities, or extended field trips all offer varied opportunities to learn valuable subject matter (Fig. 8.3).

The use of community study and community resources is a matter for the teacher to think about in terms of his teaching objectives, the age and interest of his pupils, and the climate of the school and community in which he works. As one teacher said: "Our community study opens vistas which demand the investigation of the world itself."

In the upper grades, the learning of various subjects—mathematics, chemistry, physics, and English—may be motivated and made increasingly real for pupils by arranging study situations which involve the community. For example, youthful chemists might be taken to the air-reduction plant and to the petroleum-chemical industries in the nearest industrial center. Young mathematicians, pondering the utility of the formulas and geometric relationships they are studying, need to examine leaf structure, the triangular prismlike form of a conifer needle, the intricate maze of angles in supporting beams, the construction of a railroad trestle, and the form of *setbacks* in architecture and the reasons for their use. The student of English or communications will find substance for his themes in many community-study situations, and he can use this information later in class discussion, in writing advertising copy, or in creating a radio newscast.

Walking trips provide study experiences in the immediate vicinity of the school, such as the parks, fire stations, museums, and stores (Fig. 8.4). Walking trips are a most convenient way of arranging visits to the nearby neighborhood shopping center, to the local park for nature study, or to the nearest fire or police station. Walking trips can also make it possible for pupils to watch simple demonstrations of the typical work activities of various community-service people who travel around the local district. Because these people often pass within the vicinity of the school, a community-service worker—for example, the telephone lineman—might arrange to be near the school at a convenient hour (Fig. 8.5). In the lower grades, the "buddy system"—in which each child is paired off with a dependable fellow pupil—is one effective way of getting the class to places within reasonable walking distance of the school. The teacher learns from experience that the best position for him to take is at the rear of the column. Experience also will reveal which children can be depended upon to head up the column.

Field study usually involves automobile or bus trips to outlying areas—truck farms, dairies, arboretums, museums, television stations, banks, packing plants, or industries—as well as shorter trips to municipal buildings or the town hall where civic affairs are being conducted. For example, although the drinking fountain out in the hall, the water hydrant in the street, and the faucet in the home are used daily to bring life-giving water to everyone, how many of the students really understand the complex processes involved in supplying this water? The intermediate-grade child can read at length about water supply and he can pore over the details of charts which describe one or more forms of water supply—only to discover when discussing the situation in class that the realities of how the local water supply is provided are not entirely clear. As the class study continues, a visit to the local water-supply facility can be a highly individualized discovery experience. While the study of diagrams may show the general principles employed in the location and gathering of water, direct observation is highly desirable if learners are to understand filtering systems, storage reservoirs, pumping mechanisms, and water purification systems. Having witnessed these for himself, the learner gains understandings which may be employed on his return to the classroom in followup discussion, further reading, and the formulation of generalizations (Fig. 8.6).

However, because field trips are often costly, and for several other reasons we shall discuss shortly, they should be made only after carefully planned introductory study has aroused class interest to a point where the pupil curiosity can best be satisfied by the many kinds of concrete experiences made possible by field study. For example, an intermediate-grade class can study at length about mass production in dairying only to find out that, as questions are answered, more and more detailed points of information seem to be needed. As this classroom activity continues, a visit to a dairy is inevitably discovered to be the best solution for gaining a true conceptualization of dairy products. Such a visit can be an exciting means for discovering that dairy cows today are bred to a much larger size as compared to a decade ago, and that they are actually a part of an

Fig. 8.7. / The realities of modern dairying must be seen on location in order to understand how mechanization has changed an old process. What responsibilities does such a visit place on pupils and teachers?

automated mass-production process which begins in the grazing fields and ends with the sealing of the milk in disposable paper containers (Fig. 8.7). The steps involved in achieving maximum learning from planned field study are discussed later in this chapter.

Visits by resource persons are a valuable means of bringing demonstrations and specialized information into the classroom, particularly when field study is not feasible within rigidly defined time schedules such as often exist in junior and senior high schools. Visiting authorities may be recruited from among parents of school pupils, friends of the school and representatives of banking, communications, governmental, transportation, and local industrial groups. Resource persons can usually conduct demonstrations and supply answers that go beyond the teacher's more generalized fund of information. For example, as a group of eighth-grade children continued their study of the state in which they lived, they developed many questions about the nature of the land, and about the manner in which it was utilized within their own community and the area adjacent to it. As their search continued, the pupils learned that the local farm-management director, the high-school geography teacher, and the state aeronautics commission's educational officer were willing to visit the classroom. The men were invited to meet with the pupils, and the ensuing class discussion resulted in a walking trip over the terrain, further library study, and an aerial field trip—all planned by the pupils themselves.

Special learning trips include visits to independent or related educational projects, such as forestry conservation camps, distant school camps maintained by the local school board, and special museums or exhibits. Many school systems —particularly in the Middle West and Pacific Coast regions—maintain school camps. Often pupils in the upper-intermediate grades or in junior high school are given the opportunity to spend a week or two during the regular school year at such a camp. The visit to the school camp is usually scheduled so that systematic firsthand study may be made of conservation, astronomy, wildlife, and plant life; and of marsh, lake, and watershed interrelationships (Fig. 8.8). These studies are usually under the direction of the regular classroom teacher who plans and participates with the resident school-camp instructor.

One of the most frequently employed special learning trips occurs as a term culminating activity, usually at the end of the junior or senior year. As students

Fig. 8.8. / A brisk hike brings these pupils face to face with nature study during a session at a school camp.

complete their work in such subjects as American government, problems of democracy, or United States history, they may plan an extended visit to the state or national capitol. On a recent visit to Washington, D.C. at the end of the spring semester, the present author found his own hotel reservation taken over by eight high-school boys who had converted the room into a temporary dormitory. The city hotels had literally been taken over by thousands of visiting high-school students and their teachers. Available parking areas were jammed with school buses as identified by their banners. Many bore the names of communities as far as 2000 miles away. Other high-school-student groups visit the nation's capital via trains and jet aircraft. Needless to say, such special study

Fig. 8.9. / Two-way communication between pupils and a renowned authority can be arranged as speakerphone interviews (left) or through telelecture availabilities. What learning opportunities are presented through such arrangements that would not otherwise be accessible to classroom learning?

situations are costly and somewhat of a risk to the school. They must be the result of careful planning, selecting only those students who are most likely to benefit from the trip in terms of its instructional objectives.

Research surveys represent a highly valuable kind of community-study activity. Community-survey activities include fact-finding interviews with business, governmental, or community leaders in their normal work setting. This form of community study is usually engaged in by selected groups or by individual students who have given evidence of their ability to handle such opportunities. Gifted pupils, in particular, benefit from the opportunity to ask professionals questions about taxation, law, transportation, communications, art, literature, housing, and job opportunities.

To gain the most from a community survey or professional interview, the students must prepare carefully. They should discuss what they have read, formulate well-thought-out key questions and, with their teacher, list the names of authorities whom they feel could best answer these questions. It is desirable to have the pupils write letters in advance asking these people for a date and hour that would be acceptable, for—when given ample time to schedule the interview—scientists, authors, judicial officials, and administrative department heads are more likely to participate.

Personal interviews with these leaders become more difficult as distance increases, and the cost of transportation usually makes some of these experiences prohibitive. One unique way of solving this problem has been worked out at Stephens College, where long-distance, speaker-phone interviews are carried on. When the teacher and members of the class decide it is profitable to seek information of an expert thousands of miles away, a group-telephone interview may be arranged. Often in speaker-phone interviews the entire 40-minute class period is devoted to the interview. Depending on the distance involved, a series

of interviews of from 30 to 40 minutes ranges from $8.40 to $15.60 each. In view of the fact that these calls make possible authoritative answers to specific questions, the preparation of which may have taken weeks of thoughtful effort, this cost is small (Fig. 8.9).

This kind of research survey can be done entirely by letter, of course, but at the expense of the give-and-take that normally characterizes conversation. A long-distance, speaker-phone interview is much more spontaneous; it is personal rather than impersonal, and results in more information.

The results of speaker-phone interviews which have been conducted are impressive. In one case, students did more outside reading on the topics of the field studied, and there was a 10 percent increase in enrollments in advance courses in the same field. Further, participating students showed increased skill in asking questions and in directing inquiry toward pertinent ends.[2] Research community surveys also often have far-reaching effects. In Wisconsin, for example, a high-school group actually initiated a community housing project. In New York, action begun by a similar group led to a slum-clearance project.

[2] Harold Rubin, "Telephone Network Courses," *Educational Screen and Audio Visual Guide,* March, 1964.

Fig. 8.10. / The cooperation of school and local business officials makes it possible for many of these children to see such live animals for the first time (left). Local citizens can help too; this parent and her daughter, having returned from a visit to Korea, are displaying costumes and realia (right). What contributions do such programs make to the classroom group?

What better way is there of initiating pupils into their future role of responsible citizens?

☐ PLANNING COMMUNITY EXPERIENCE

New ways of arranging for community-study opportunities have recently been investigated. The "world" of the community can be divided into those opportunities which call for the student to observe *outside* the classroom, and those which can just as easily be brought *into* the classroom. Both, needless to say, are important because they complement each other. Is it not logical to expect that communities, which originally authorized the creation of a public-school system to prepare youth for community participation, should welcome the incorporation of firsthand observation of the community as a part of instruction? If this kind of instruction is to be successful, both lay and professional workers should help (Fig. 8.10).

But, because teachers are not sure of the reaction of the administrator, the school board, or the community, they often avoid plans for leaving the classroom for outside study. Thus, the responsibility for making community study a regular part of classroom activities often rests with the community itself, the school board, and the school administrator. For this reason, some school administrators and boards of education have encouraged the planned use of community study with resolutions such as: "The field trip carefully planned, wisely interpreted and skillfully supervised is a useful and vital extension of the classroom program."[3]

The impetus such a statement gives to a community-study program is obvious. Bonded transportation facilities provided by the school bus line or by a local transportation company remove other possible barriers to the execution of such a program. The limits of the environment that can be explored by the children are as broad as the school day itself, which may range from 9:00 A.M. to 4:00 P.M. Good roads, modern transportation, and careful planning can enlarge the school's study and learning environment to the radius of as much as 100 miles, with the school as the center of the circle.

■ LOCATING COMMUNITY-STUDY SITUATIONS

A systematic search for useful community-study opportunities is usually the first step in beginning a program. Such plans may be discussed during faculty meetings, P.T.A. planning sessions, or teacher-principal conferences.

Local study opportunities vary from community to community. The opportunities which the teacher in an open rural area has are only slightly related to those of a teacher in a crowded metropolitan center. However, it is just as desirable for the rural group to have study experience in a metropolitan area

---

[3] *Community Classrooms, a Guide to Educational Field Trips,* Seattle Public Schools, 1956.

Table 8.1

REPRESENTATIVE SAMPLE OF U.S. COMMUNITY-STUDY PROGRAMS

LOCAL STUDY SITUATION	CURRICULUM UNIT	STATE
Intermediate Grades		
Oil Refinery[a]	Science	California
Harbors—Transportation[a]	Social Studies	"
Harbors—Fishing[a]	" "	"
Steam Ship[b]	Science and Social Studies	Hawaii
Water Supply[b]	Science and Social Studies	"
High-School Grades		
Building Trades[c]	Work Experience	Illinois
Farm and Dairy[c]	" "	"
School Camp[c]	Science and Math	"
Aerial Field Study[d]	Science and Social Studies	Wisconsin

[a] "It's Worth a Visit," *Catalogue of School Journeys for Elementary Schools*, Los Angeles City Schools, 1960.

[b] *Field Trips in Hawaii*, Department of Education, State of Hawaii, 1963–1964.

[c] *Instructional Materials*, Community Resources Administration and Supervision Series, Bull. No. 3, State of Illinois Department of Education, 1961.

[d] "Geography Via Aerial Field Trips," *Do It This Way Series*, National Council for Geographic Education, Illinois State University, 1965.

as for the children in crowded city schools to experience being in the open country.

Many schools across the United States have systematically surveyed their communities for useful resources. Table 8.1 presents a cross-section of the kinds of community-study experiences which have been recommended and approved by representative school districts for the upper-intermediate and high-school grades.

In Manhasset, New York, for example, a committee of interested parents and teachers set about to survey Manhasset's resources—*its people and their specific skills and knowledges.* This committee sought to discover the true wealth of the community in terms of the people in it.[4] The committee began by interviewing professional and business people to discover what skills and abilities they had

_____

4 *The World in a Schoolroom*, 16 mm., B&W, 20 min., United World Films.

that would enrich learning situations in the classroom. This information was then catalogued for reference by interested teachers. In this way, the committee discovered, for example, that a very able lawyer could be available when the social-studies class was investigating personal rights and the techniques and procedures of court action. The local nursery man who had developed certain grafting techniques would explain them to general-science students. A local ceramist was willing to explain and demonstrate glazing techniques to the art class. The local music-store proprietor, who happened to be a skilled cello player, was willing to help the members in the cello section of the school orchestra.

There are variations of this Manhasset community-resources program; for example, on school "career" days, local professional men, craftsmen, and tradesmen can come to the school to present to interested pupil groups their own firsthand accounts of their particular role in the community, and to answer the pupils' questions. Other schools have "community" days on which parents attend homeroom sessions and discuss community responsibilities with students.

■ COMMUNITY-STUDY LIABILITY

The community—acting through its school-board representatives—should decide whether community-study opportunities are to be provided. School boards and school administrators have the responsibility of establishing policies concerning community study. Similarly, the teacher has the responsibility of planning for community-study situations with the same care he uses in his day-to-day classroom teaching.

Yet teachers may have questions about their personal liability for accidents or injuries to pupils while participating in community-study situations. Some of these questions may be answered if the classroom teacher first understands which responsibilities fall within his own professional bailiwick. The following are the respective responsibilities which school boards, school administrators, and teachers have in connection with community-study experiences:

1. The school board should acknowledge community study as a desirable enrichment experience and an integral part of the school's regular program.
2. The principal should make the school board's policy known to the teachers.
3. The school board should provide liability insurance for the teaching staff. In Wisconsin, for example, and in many other states, school boards are legally authorized to expend public money for this purpose.
4. The teacher and principal should plan community-resource activities which will help to accomplish goals of existing curriculum plans. Such activities should not be confused with festivals, holiday excursions, and other out-of-school class activities of dubious educational value.
5. The teacher, with the guidance of the principal, should arrange transportation via school bus or other bonded carriers which are required by law to carry liability insurance.
6. Teachers should never assume responsibility for conducting pupils through

Dear ______(Parent's name)______

Because we wish to make your child's experience in ______(Subject or Grade)______ as valuable as possible, we want to give him the opportunity of first-hand acquaintance with things we are studying in the community. We are planning on ______(Date)______ to visit ______(Person or Place)______ as a part of our regular day-to-day study activities.

We encourage only those students to participate in community study activities who prove themselves trustworthy and responsible.

Will you kindly sign below to indicate that you want ______(Pupil's name)______ to participate, and return this letter to me?

Very truly yours,

______(Teacher)______

We wish to have ______(Pupil's name)______ take part in the community study plans described above. We will discuss with him his responsibilities in this connection.

______(Parent signature)______

Fig. 8.11. / Parental consent form for student participation in community-study situations.

a plant or industry themselves, but should arrange to have the management supply a guide. As soon as the tour is ended, the teacher should have the pupils return to school immediately, again by properly insured carrier.

7. The use of the parental permission slip (Fig. 8.11) informs the parent that community-resource experiences that take pupils out of the classroom are an acknowledged part of the school program. This allows parents to restrict their children from this kind of activity, if they wish. But the granting of parental permission does not absolve the teacher who takes his class out into the community from exercising the same reasonable care he is expected to exercise in the classroom.

The teacher and the school who adhere to the above suggestions will proceed with confidence and enthusiasm toward achieving valuable school and community relationships.

■ TEACHER LEADERSHIP IN COMMUNITY STUDY

One may ask, "Shouldn't the teacher be able to do a complete teaching job himself?" The teacher is skilled as a student of child psychology, of classroom method, and of modern techniques for providing educational experience, but he cannot be expected to know the intricacies of community life and activities as well as others do. With the increasing complexity of the modern world of information even the best-informed teacher will be wise to use the supplementing experiences provided by the resources of the community, its people, and their skills (Fig. 8.12).

The teacher should be expected to take the initiative in planning and evaluating the contributions made by resource people, however. In every situation, *the teacher must be the one to decide when a community-resource experience should be incorporated into the classroom program.* He must be the one to invite, to plan with the class in anticipation of the experience, and ultimately to evaluate its success or failure. Under proper teacher initiative and guidance, school and community cooperation offers unlimited enrichment possibilities. Selecting and using resource opportunities in the immediate community can provide learning experiences which the teacher, regardless of his broad training and effective work, is frequently unable to provide.

Following the investigation of community resources and the correlation of local study opportunities with specific units of study, each teacher is confronted with certain responsibilities that must be met during community study. The following are typical:

1. Preliminary preparation
2. Preliminary discussion of study objectives
3. Observation
4. Followup discussion and evaluation
5. Followup projects growing out of community study

Fig. 8.12. / Under the guidance of a well-trained classroom teacher, what are the children in these pictures learning that the teacher himself is unable to reveal to them? What might be the learning outcomes if these children had not the benefits of teacher guidance before and after this community-study experience?

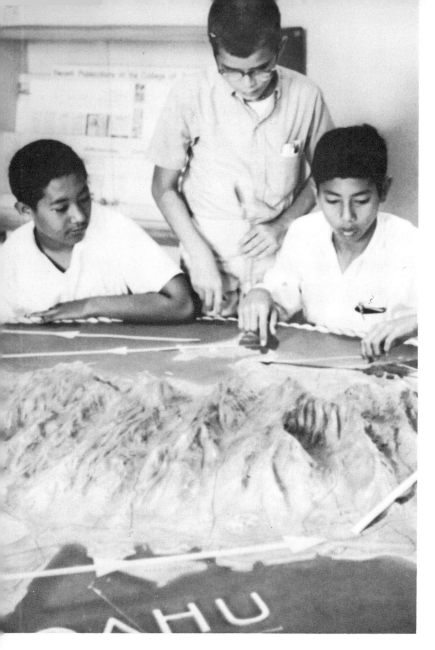

Fig. 8.13. / Preplanning materials—a relief map and an aerial route map—are used in getting ready for the actual field-study situation. Why are such preparations essential?

Fig. 8.14. / The actual aerial trip went by too quickly for adequate assimilation of the information presented. To gain fully from such an experience, long hours of preliminary preparation and learning are essential.

To illustrate these responsibilities, we shall assume that teachers and pupils have selected several field-study situations and have begun preparations. As pupils begin their plans, they and their teachers will want to become as ready for the experience as possible. Carefully chosen preliminary experiences can yield understandings which will make the field-study experience all the more effective.

■ PRELIMINARY PREPARATION

Preparation activities may include a preliminary visit by the teacher or a small student committee to the place which is to be visited by the entire class at a later date. Examination of maps, films, models, or pictures prior to the trip—or to the visit by the resource person—may help the class anticipate what is to be witnessed. A representative of the company, profession, or service that is to be the object of the field trip may be invited to visit the class beforehand to explain some of the basic ideas about the processes or services the pupils will see.

One junior-high-school group, preparing to make an aerial field study of the land around their community, carefully studied a relief map as they planned their flight path (Fig. 8.13). The plan was to fly over as many varied land forms as possible, identify the forms, and observe how they were used in rural and urban situations. Thus, examination of the relief map of the area provided the pupils with a foundation for recognizing what they saw in actual flight (Fig. 8.14).

Similarly, a group of upper-grade pupils examined diagrams of underground water formations to understand better the methods used to gather and pump water to the holding reservoirs they would later visit (Fig. 8.15). And a representative of a steamship line visited the classroom of a senior-high-school

WATER FALLS

HIGH LEVEL TUNNEL AND DISCHARGE LINE

Fig. 8.15. / Diagrams can be useful instructional media in the classroom, but there is no substitute for the real thing. How did the above diagram increase pupil learning from the trip to the reservoirs? In what ways would learning from the actual field trip have been affected if preliminary study of diagrams had not been provided?

group, displaying a "take-apart" model of an ocean liner in preparation for the group's walk-through visit of an actual ocean vessel (Fig. 8.16). Such experiences motivate further planning and background study.

As in beginning any new unit of study, preliminary discussion of a proposed community study will assist pupils in developing definite purposes and will arouse their curiosity and interest in the experiences, understandings, and factual information they will acquire. Such discussion will give them an opportunity to discuss information they already have; it will also reveal inaccurate or purely imaginary concepts and ideas about the local study situation. The aerial field-study group, for example, planned such objectives as:

1. Identifications of land forms: escarpments, erosion remnants, alluvial fans, tidal marshes, coral plains, sea cliffs, and land slides. Preflight vocabulary study of these terms was combined with map and diagram study.
2. Identification of land use: ranches, shopping centers, harbors, piers, quarries, transmission lines, parks, water preserves, bridges, and drainage canals.

Those planning a visit to the water-supply facilities should seek to understand the following information:

Fig. 8.16. / How did preliminary study of the model facilitate learning from the field trip?

1. Alternative methods of collecting and pumping water from artesian wells, gravity-dike complexes, wall shafts, skimming tunnels, and springs
2. The nature of water-storage reservoirs, water purification and filtering systems, and distribution grids

The group preparing to visit the ocean vessel would set up such purposes as:

1. Understanding how an ocean ship supplies food, shelter, recreation, and safe transportation for its passengers
2. Understanding that an ocean vessel is actually a complete city and government afloat

Since every new area of study imposes a certain specific vocabulary responsibility, the teacher will consider in advance new or unusual vocabulary items that might present problems during the visit. The combination of anticipating learning problems and being given a clear-cut, definitive statement of the objectives to be achieved is the best preparation the learner can have in advance of the actual visit. More subtle purposes may have to be suggested by the teacher; for example, challenging pupils to see who can "unearth" the most unusual information, who can be the most courteous, who can be the most responsible for his own good behavior, etc.

Preparation for a field trip or walking tour, etc., will also have to include the mechanical aspects of the trip itself (Fig. 8.17). Both parents and administrator should be notified that the children are leaving the school building. Although the teacher can see to this himself, it is desirable to have the students write letters to their parents and to the principal telling of their plans, the route they will take, the purpose of the trip, etc. This gives the children more opportunity for participation and helps them to acquire a sense of responsibility. If the

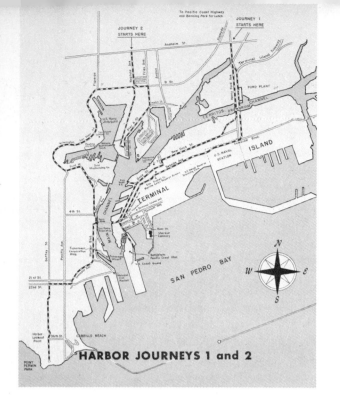

HARBOR JOURNEYS 1 and 2

Fig. 8.17. / (Left) The teacher can acquire such materials as this map in planning the mechanical details of a field trip. What are some of the advantages of involving the pupils in such planning?

Fig. 8.18. / (Right) What outcomes of community study are apparent in this situation? What relationships exist among these activities, community-study experiences, and the achievement of subject skills?

pupils themselves are entrusted—under the teacher's guidance, of course—with these preparation activities, they will be more likely to feel it is *their* trip, and not just another school- or teacher-planned activity of which they are only passive participants. Further, when the students themselves write their parents and the principal, they have an opportunity to articulate—in their own minds as well as for the benefit of school officials and parents—their degree of involvement in the activity. Clearly, such letters also provide a good basis for evaluation by the teacher enabling him to judge the readiness of each student.

The safest route should be chosen. If transportation is needed, the school bus should be used. However, if private passenger cars are used, they should adequately be covered by passenger-liability insurance. Whenever possible, bonded carriers—usually buses—should be engaged. These drivers should be told exactly when to pick up the children at the school and should discharge them in a designated safety zone at the trip site.

■ OBSERVATION

During the actual community-study activity, students must be encouraged to be alert in finding answers to the questions they want answered. Of course, it is impossible to anticipate all the questions the pupils may ask, and some of the advance questions the students had carefully prepared during their preliminary study may go unasked during the trip as new discoveries and areas of curiosity replace them. Further, noise and confusion may interfere with complete understanding, and other mechanical problems—such as space, lighting, or inaudibility—may interfere with full comprehension. Similarly, haste imposed by the necessity of meeting time schedules may make possible only a fleeting glimpse or understanding of an important operation or piece of equipment. For these reasons, it is desirable to take along a camera and photographic

equipment wherever possible, so that the pictures taken on the trip, or the slides made from them, may be examined and discussed in the classroom after the trip. In the case of a speaker-phone interview or a talk given by a visiting authority, a tape recorder is a useful means of recording the proceedings for later reference.

■ FOLLOWUP DISCUSSION AND EVALUATION

After the community experience, the classroom provides the time and place for clarification and discussion of impressions. The pupils who visited the ship experienced an unanticipated demonstration by the engineer of how oil is used to generate the electricity used to turn the ship's propellers. Because there had been no background preparation of these concepts, many of the pupils had questions which, in this case, were answered by other pupils who had been able to understand fully the demonstration of the officer. A chalkboard was used to visualize the concepts.

The aerial-study group discussed the large land area devoted to freeways and parking lots; the variations in the color of soil and crops, and the identification of each; the effects of erosion and the need for land conservation; and the identification of the land forms which, as one pupil said, "are different from the text pictures because from the air one gains a perspective which helps one to grasp the whole situation."[5]

Classroom discussion about the water-supply study tour centered around the diagrammatic chart of the underground structures. The ways in which the various water-collection systems were used to get the most water with the least expenditure was a central topic.

5 Benjamin, F. Richeson Jr., and Carl E. Guell, *Geography Via Aerial Field Trips,* National Council for Geographic Education, Illinois State University, 1965.

Other outcomes of study visits can include making written reports, maps, diagrammatic explanations of newly discovered information, news releases to the school newspaper, letters of appreciation to resource officials, and "logs" which outline highpoint discoveries. Objective tests prepared through pupil-teacher cooperation may also be useful in analyzing outcomes.

■ FOLLOWUP PROJECTS

New experiences and understandings are the first steps toward the development of creative followup projects. One must acquire facts and understandings before one can reassemble or arrange them into projects which can reveal the creative inventiveness and self-expression of the individual. This process is often the most important stage of any learning activity. One of the projects that grew out of the aerial study was the construction of a terrain map similar to that depicted in Fig. 8.18. The selection of the best slides taken by students during a tour and the creation of a set of vividly descriptive paragraphs to accompany the showing of these—perhaps to the class group across the hall—is a possible followup activity after a field trip or walking tour. The construction of models made of reinforced cardboard would also provide a way by which a student group could demonstrate its newfound information.

As the result of other community-study situations, it may be possible for groups actually to participate in projects which benefit the community. One needs only to ride through the reforested sections of the North Central Plains states to see conservation projects that have resulted from student field trips. Along the roadway are signs reading "School Forest"—plantings of young pine trees which are usually the result of school children's study of conservation.

Field trips in the community may create opportunities to participate in civic affairs. Several worthwhile followup projects of this sort are shown in the films *Learning Democracy Through School and Community*[6] and *Our Town Is Our Classroom*.[7] A visit to a meeting of the town council might be followed by the revising of student-government election-campaign regulations. Visits to local industries can lead logically to organizing a school and community vocational-guidance plan, under which professional men and representatives of labor and industry come to the school on scheduled occasions to discuss their work and to advise the pupils about vocational opportunities and choice. Civic cleanup campaigns, the erection of safety signals at danger spots, and the provision of recreation centers, play areas, and hostel circuits are additional community-study projects of the same nature.

Community study may become the basis for many intraschool activities such as discussion panels, mock-radio broadcasts, displays of artwork, and exchange reports with the classroom across the hall. Its most significant outcome, however, is seen when students plan ways in which they, as future citizens, can participate *now* in making their community a better place in which to live.

---

[6] 16 mm., B&W, 20 min., Educational Film Service.
[7] 16 mm., B&W, 18 min., United World Films.

☐ EVALUATING COMMUNITY STUDY

Although community study should be a carefully planned learning experience, the teacher should also evaluate its success, once it has been carried out, in terms of what was experienced by the children who participated. The teacher should ask himself such items as the following as objective measures of the activity's relative success or failure:

1. This visit or interview was arranged because it was closely related to planned curriculum objectives. Yes _____ No _____
2. The experience was worth the time and effort required because it provided useful learning opportunities which could not have been presented by ordinary classroom methods. Yes _____ No _____
3. The students themselves became responsible for:
   a. Knowing the purposes for which they undertook the community study. Yes _____ No _____
   b. Formulating safe-conduct attitudes. Yes _____ No _____
   c. Devising followup discussion and evaluation. Yes _____ No _____
   d. Initiating followup activities. Yes _____ No _____
4. The teacher observed all school regulations concerning community-study visits or interviews by:
   a. Previsiting the place to be studied. Yes _____ No _____
   b. Arranging time of departure, arrival, and return via school bus or other bonded carrier. Yes _____ No _____
   c. Sending study announcements home with children. Yes _____ No _____
5. Followup discussion and activity was arranged which resulted in creative and inventive writing, art, or project accomplishments. Yes _____ No _____

☐ SUMMARY

Community study offers several opportunities to the teacher: It is the means through which pupils may learn at firsthand where, why, and how their society functions; it is within the creative control of the teacher; its planning and preparation may be shared by pupils and teacher alike; and it presents opportunities for living experiences which, for the most part, are available at the time they are needed in terms of the curriculum.

A systematic analysis of the community in which the school is located will reveal many valuable opportunities for learning. Surveying community-study possibilities should be cooperative projects for teachers in locating local industries, distributive agencies, service organizations, etc., which illustrate social processes and provide values important for implementing the school curriculum. Through parent-teacher-administrator planning, the resources of the community should be assayed in terms of valuable firsthand opportunities to discover useful information.

The community-study experience takes two forms. On the one hand, members of the community may come to the classroom; a lawyer, for example, might talk to a social-studies class, a biologist to a natural-science class, an accountant to a commercial class, etc. On the other hand, the whole class or certain members of it may visit nearby plants in order to see industry processes, assembly-line procedures, automatic-business-machine operation, etc.

Because of its realism, community study can become an effective first step in building understanding through real experiences which give additional meaning to subsequent and more abstract learning situations and heighten understanding of them.

The purposes of community study are as follows:

1. To provide opportunity for real experiencing through which to gain valid understandings
2. To arouse and create interest. Few learners fail to be motivated as they contemplate and examine things, processes, and ideas.
3. To create backgrounds of experience which will give meaning to reading and simple research done later in the more formal study situations of the school classroom and library
4. To provide backgrounds of experience which will stimulate students later to participate in class discussion, creative art projects, and written communication (writing letters, themes, stories, poetry, etc.)
5. To encourage and develop keenness of observation, care in observation, and an insatiable curiosity
6. To encourage active participation in community planning. Students can plan the community projects that grow logically out of field trip experiences. Such projects serve as bridges which lead from school experiences to community membership.

These purposes are seldom achieved in the absence of careful teacher guidance. The outcomes of community study are well summarized in the discussion between Mr. Richards, a teacher, and Mr. D., a parent, which occurs in the film *Near Home:*[8]

MR. D.:   Well, I'm greatly impressed by all this, Richards. The youngsters have done a remarkable piece of work.
RICHARDS: They enjoyed it—it's all I can do to keep up with them.
MR. D.:   Now, what do you think your youngsters are going to get out of it? I should say you've given them something very valuable . . . what one might call a real objective view of the town in which they live. . . .
RICHARDS: Yes, I knew that was the side of it that would appeal to you! But don't run away with the idea that they understand all this thoroughly—we don't expect them to. But they've been getting a basis of first-hand information that will still be there when they can make use of it—and they're developing, too, a habit of wanting to know, of finding out for themselves. Instead of learning geography, history, science and so on, all in watertight compartments, they've been finding out how everything fits together . . . and learning a lot of other things, too . . . things that will influence their whole life, and more. . . .

☐ Suggested Activities

1. List as many community study situations as possible which relate to your subject field. List both those which involve bringing representatives of the community to

[8] *Near Home,* 16 mm., B&W, 20 min. British Information Services.

your classroom and those in which you take your pupils out into the community. Since, as you do this, you will need to know more about your community, consider the following suggestions:

a. Consult the Chamber of Commerce.
b. Ask experienced teachers for help.
c. Study the local business directory.
d. Talk with lifetime residents of the community.
e. Interview the county agent and the editor of the local weekly or daily newspaper.

2. Visit some of the community resources which, after careful thought, seem to offer the greatest chance of enriching your subject area through the experience to be gained from seeing them. Take notes while you are there; gather data.
3. Make a list of the people you met during your survey who are willing to come to your classroom to talk to and be questioned by your students.
4. Plan a visit, tour, or field trip into the community. As you plan, keep a record. Devise your own record.
5. Arrange to preview such films as those listed in the Bibliography under "Films and Filmstrips."
6. Arrange to carry on a long-distance speaker-phone interview. Consult your local phone company to arrange for equipment. Follow the suggestions made on page 237.

□ Bibliography

Allegheny County Council for Social Studies Teachers, *Let's Go on a Field Trip,* Allegheny County Schools (Pittsburgh), 1959.
Ames (Iowa) Public Schools, *Conservation Field Day,* 1965.
Becher, Marshall, *Field Trip Handbook,* Department of Audio-Visual Instruction, Michigan Public Schools, 1965.
Chicago Public Schools, *Resources in the Social Studies,* 1959.
Hawaii Department of Education, *Field Trips in Hawaii,* 1963–1964.
Illinois Department of Education, *Instructional Materials,* Community Resources Administration and Supervision Series, Bull. No. 3, 1961.
Illinois State University, "Geography Via Aerial Field Trips," *Do It This Way Series,* National Council for Geographic Education, 1965.
Los Angeles Public Schools, *It's Worth a Visit,* 1961.
Louisville Public Schools, *Our Community Classroom,* 1955.
Milwaukee Public Schools, "Using Your Community Resources," *Curriculum Bulletin,* Vol. 7, No. 1, 1955.
Moore, Harry R., *Modern Education in America,* Allyn and Bacon, 1962.
Rubin, Harold, "Telephone Network Courses," *Educational Screen and Audio-Visual Guide,* March, 1964.
Seattle Public Schools, *Community Classrooms,* 1956.
Texas Education Agency, *How to Plan and Use Field Trips,* 1963.
Western Illinois University, *Knowing Your Community,* 1959.

□ Films

Community Resources in Teaching, 16 mm., B&W, 17 min., Iowa University.
Field Trip, 16 mm., Color, 11 min., Virginia State Department of Public Instruction.
Near Home, 16 mm., B&W, 27 min., British Information Services.
Our Town Is Our Classroom, 16 mm., B&W, 18 min., United World Films.
The World in a Schoolroom, 16 min., B&W, 20 min., United World Films.

IX | MAPS

AND GLOBES

Although we usually think first of maps and globes as part of the study of geography in school, we can quickly recognize how fundamental they are in a whole range of human activities. We use them not only in all forms of travel (Fig. 9.1), but also to interpret tomorrow's weather and today's events in far parts of the world. Maps help us to understand the history of the ages, the world we now live in, and the space age of the future.

As he plans his campaign for a new bond issue, the city superintendent of schools makes extensive use of census plot maps to show population trends in the community, what parts of it have had the most new babies during the past five years, and where needed new school buildings should be located. In tracing the changes in the foreign policy of the United States over the past half century, a lecturer also makes use of a series of map slides, one of which is a world map centered on the north pole. With this, he shows this country's changed position with respect to the rest of the world that modern air transportation has brought about. These are representative of the many daily uses of maps both in and out of school; in fact, map reading has come to be so essential to communication in today's world, that educators might well regard it as an essential element of literacy, along with word reading and a given level of skill in computation.

Today's need to understand the world and its people gives our schools what is perhaps their most vital function. This understanding must be based upon sound knowledge of history and geography. Yet, the very nature of geographical studies has changed. At an earlier stage of man's development, it was considered possible in teaching geography to trace a direct relationship between physical environment and where and how people lived. People settled near rivers, for example, so as to have easy access to transportation; or, in regions of moderate but ample rainfall, so that they could grow crops; or in level rather than mountainous terrain for the greater comfort of living. Such generalizations still have a degree of historical validity. But today, desert areas have been reclaimed by irrigations; modern transportation has eliminated the need to live near rivers; and many mountain areas have become populous as man found satisfaction or wealth in their aesthetic, recreation, or mineral resources. As Preston James points out:

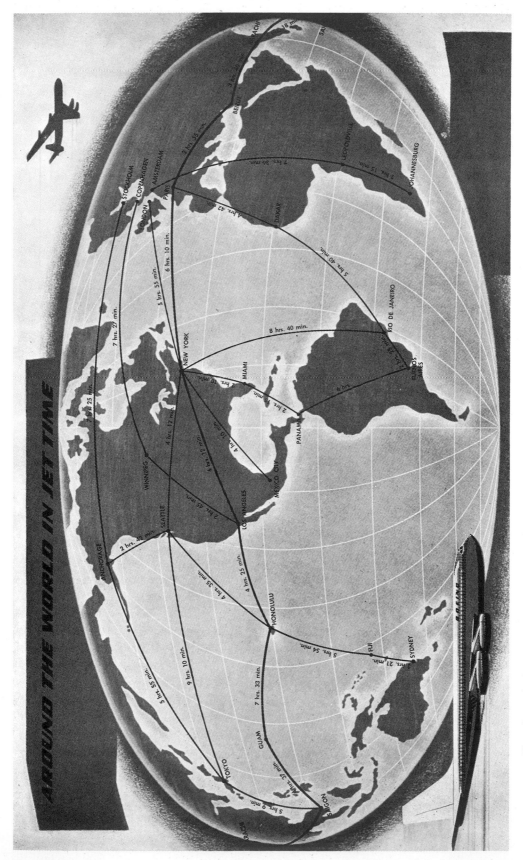

Fig. 9.1. / The jet age and some of its implications are suggested by use of a map. The figures indicate approximate flying time by jet transport over great-circle routes between indicated points.

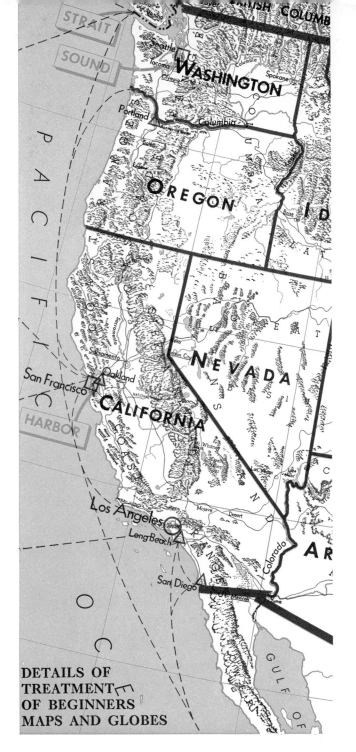

Plate 14 / A section from a primarily political
map for beginners, with few place names
and only major relief indicated.

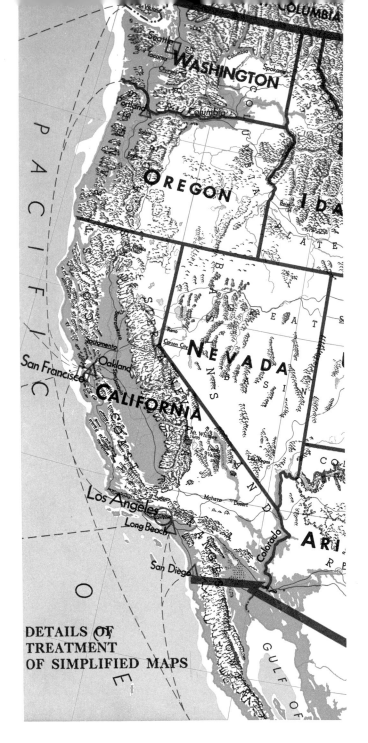

Plate 15 / This section, also from an elementary map, shows altitude tints for land and water areas.

Plate 16 / The same region is shown here on a physical-political map, which includes a greater number of place names and other details as compared to the two previous elementary maps.

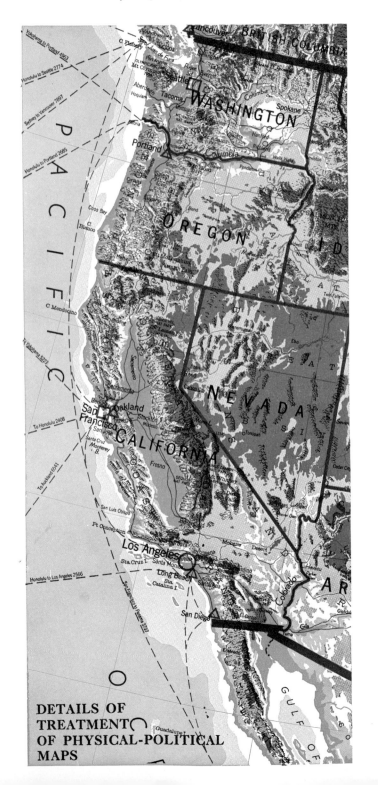

DETAILS OF
TREATMENT
OF PHYSICAL-POLITICAL
MAPS

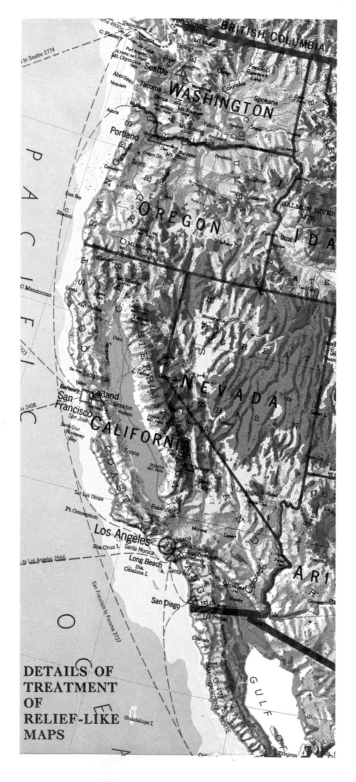

Plate 17 / This relief map is shaded in detail to create a three-dimensional effect.

How an Island is Shown on a Map

How Lakes are Shown on a Map

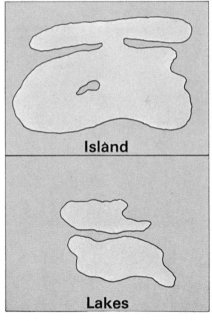

Island

Lakes

Plate 18 / Pictures add significant meaning to maps and map symbols. Here, actual photographs of lakes and islands are compared to the map symbols which represent them.

Small City Map Symbols

Capital City Map Symbols

 <u>Des Moines</u>   (by underlining)

Springfield   (by using a special symbol)

Plate 19 / Map symbols for cities and roads are particularly abstract, and concrete visual ex

How Pipelines are Shown on a Map

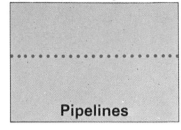

Pipelines

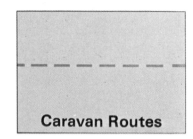

Caravan Routes

How Caravan Routes are Shown on a Map

perience in the form of color photographs should accompany early learning of such symbols.

Rock Outcrop

Monadnock

Plate 20 / Even relief maps cannot show all of the details that are on an accompanying color photograph. Maps, on the other hand, are helpful in showing the broader scope of the physical environment as well as in placing any specific region in its geographical context.

Modern geographers . . . insist on the principle that the significance to man of the features of the physical earth is a function of the attitudes, objectives, and technical abilities of man himself . . . And further, geography examines the relationships not only between man and the physical or biotic aspects of the environment, but also between man and the variety of cultural features resulting from economic, social, and political processes.[1]

Geography, history and related subjects require the abilities both to *read* and to *interpret* maps and globes. The difference between these two levels of map use is much like the difference between reading words as a skill and reading books to explore the secrets of man's knowledge. To help his students learn through maps, the teacher must himself become adept in their interpretation and use.

□ CHARACTERISTICS OF GLOBES AND MAPS

Globes are spherical *models* of the earth, while maps are flat *representations* of the earth's surface. Because the earth itself is a sphere, globes have certain unique values. On the other hand, because most globes are too small for detailed study and cannot readily be carried from place to place, men devised maps long ago to guide them on their voyages.

Two general observations should be made with respect to the nature of globes and maps before we consider them individually. The first has to do with their degree of accuracy; the second with their abstract character.

■ DEGREE OF ACCURACY

A good globe provides inherently correct information regarding *areas, distances, directions,* or *geographical shapes* found on any part of the globe's surface. With these accurate characteristics—or *properties,* as they are known by cartographers—it is possible to plot courses, to determine locations, to measure distances, and to compare areas with assurance. In short, the globe is the most accurate map we have of the earth's surface.

Even the best of flat maps cannot achieve this degree of accuracy. A flat representation of a large portion of any spherical surface involves certain difficulties. This is simply illustrated if you attempt to flatten out half a grapefruit shell or half of an old rubber ball, which can be done only by breaking or compressing the surface. In essence, this is the problem all map-makers face. Although this problem becomes serious only with maps of very large areas, such as hemisphere or the entire world itself, we need to be aware of certain unavoidable inaccuracies when using flat maps.

It is impossible, for example, for a cartographer to make a flat map of the world on which more than one (in rare cases, two) of the four properties of a globe's surface—areas, distances, directions, or shapes—are accurately represented. Of these four, the most important one for general school purposes is

1 Preston E. James, "American Geography at Mid-Century," in *New Viewpoint in Geography,* 29th Yearbook, National Council for the Social Studies, 1959, pp. 15–16.

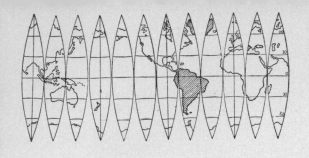

Fig. 9.2. / When gores are removed from a globe and flattened, they look like this.

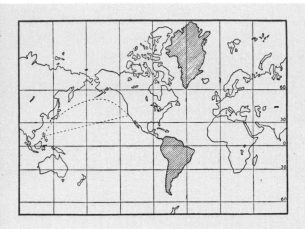

Fig. 9.3. / Here is the Mercator projection of Greenland and South America. To the right, in correct scale, is Greenland. Comment on the accuracy of these representations.

Fig. 9.5. / In what ways are map symbols like new words in reading?

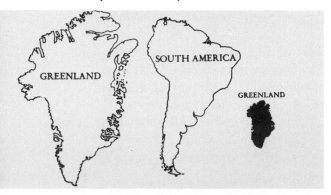

Fig. 9.4. / Note how Greenland compares in size with South America on this Mercator projection. The curved dotted line is the great-circle route, the shortest surface distance from the Philippines to San Francisco.

correct area. When area is badly distorted on a world map, the relative positions, as well as the relative sizes, of countries and continents are thrown off. Let us see how this occurs in the case of one familiar world map.

When the surface of a globe is divided along the meridians, the resulting sections are called "gores" (Fig. 9.2). On most flat maps, the spaces between these gores are filled in or the gores are stretched in some manner so as to avoid gaps in the map surface. This produces *area* distortion.

The farther the distance north or south from the equator on a world map, the greater is the spread between the gores. Hence the farther north or south we go, the greater are the inaccuracies on a flat map which is centered on the equator. Thus, the Mercator projection shown in Fig. 9.3 exaggerates considerably all areas above 50 degrees north latitude.

Because any straight line on the Mercator projection can be used as a compass line, the Mercator projection is very valuable for navigators, for whom it was made. But for school purposes, it is misleading with respect to the actual size of land and water areas. For example, in Figs. 9.3 and 9.4, Greenland appears to be larger than South America, when in reality it is only about ⅛th as large.

We will discuss this problem in more detail in the section on maps. In the meantime, let us note one other important characteristic of maps and globes, namely, their abstract nature.

■ ABSTRACT CHARACTER

By nature, maps and globes are abstract. Their language is one of symbols, lines, colors, names, and space relationships. A dot fixes the location of a city. A line of one type means a highway; another represents a political boundary; still others designate rivers, railroads, trade routes, elevation contours, natural boundaries between water and land, direction, or other features (Fig. 9.5). Usually these map and globe symbols have little visual resemblance to what they represent. Sometimes—as in the case of parallels, meridians, and contour lines—they represent things that cannot actually be seen anywhere on the earth's surface.

The use of color on globes and maps serves two important purposes: The first and more significant purpose is to aid legibility by distinguishing such features as land and water, lowlands and highlands, and political divisions; the second is a matter of aesthetics. This is also important, because pleasing colors can contribute to the favorite reception of a map, atlas, or globe. However, the colors used are different from those in nature. Since it is obviously impossible to show the actual colors of land and water surfaces as they vary with the seasons, vegetation, rainfall, location, and other factors, the cartographer must assign somewhat arbitrary meanings to the colors he uses.

In general, the colors on physical-political globes follow the international color scheme used on the 1:1,000,000 physical map of the world, but aside from this, there is no standard color pattern for either maps or globes. Thus, in order to read maps and globes successfully, we must be able to interpret many symbols and colors. In other words, maps and globes are essentially abstract learning media and the pupil must learn their language in order to interpret them.

Fig. 9.6. / Slated globes have many useful applications such as that indicated here. Globes provide maximum learning potential when used with related maps, pictures, and reading materials.

☐ GLOBES

Because the earth itself is a sphere, the spherical map on a globe is the only *true* map of the earth. The implications of this well-known but little-comprehended reality is expressed by a professor of geography:

> Man has known for centuries that the planet Earth is round. Yet, virtually into our own day, man in his thinking about his planet has never really felt the roundness of Earth. The thought of standing on the surface of a great spinning ball hurtling through space has seemed almost overwhelming. Nevertheless, this overwhelming thought must be a part of our lives as man himself now heads into space to circle Earth and those planets that lie beyond.[2]

Globes are necessary tools with which to convey the concept of Earth's roundness. Significantly, they are also the introductory material necessary for students to learn to interpret flat maps properly:

> Understanding the globe is basic to a development of skills and abilities necessary for reading and interpreting maps. The globe must be understood before much can be done with flat maps. [It is essential] for teaching earth movements, relationships in the solar system, an understanding of rotation . . . of revolution . . . and of such other concepts as time zones, the international date line, and great circle transportation patterns.[3]

Thus, it is essential for the teacher to know something of the nature and types of globes available.

2 Phillip Bacon, "A Way to Teach Children to Use the Globe," *Grade Teacher*, October, 1964, pp. 66–67.
3 Lorrin Kennamer, "Developing a Sense of Place and Space," in *Skill Development in Social Studies*, 33rd Yearbook, National Council for the Social Studies, 1963, p. 152.

■ THE NATURE OF GLOBES

The surfaces on most globes are printed as flat gores like those shown in Fig. 9.2. When they are being mounted on the sphere, these gores are stretched slightly so that they will fit together properly on the spherical surface. Thus, if one "peeled" a globe, he would be unable to flatten out the sections any more successfully than he could in the case of the grapefruit shell.[4]

Actually, only hand-covered globes provide absolute accuracy, for the gores of which they are made are carefully wetted and stretched by hand so as to fit perfectly on the spherical surface. Mounting can be done by machine at considerably lower cost, but with lessened accuracy. In machine mounting, the northern and southern hemispheres are printed separately and joined to make a complete globe. The manufacturer of machine-made globes usually makes no claims for the accuracy with which the gores or hemispheres match, or the durability of the globe, as compared to the accuracy and durability that is possible with hand mounting on steel or plastic balls.

The surface of all globes is treated with a transparent coating to protect it from undue wear. It is important that this coating should not reflect light to the extent of producing a glare and reducing visibility. A semigloss finish provides a smooth surface that can be cleaned easily and creates little glare.

■ TYPES OF GLOBES

Three principal types of globes are valuable for school use: *political globes, physical-political globes,* and *slated-outline globes.* Political globes are designed primarily to show the location and boundaries of countries, principal cities, trade routes, and other features created by man. A simplified political globe with a minimum of details is desirable for use in the primary grades. For some individual uses at both the primary- and middle-grade levels, small, inexpensive, machine-made political globes are quite satisfactory, particularly as political globes tend to become outdated rather frequently through changes in national boundaries or political affiliations. At such times, these globes should, of course, be replaced.

Physical-political globes, as the name implies, show some political features also, but their primary emphasis is on land elevations and ocean depths shown by means of altitude tints. Such globes are very practical for use at the middle-grade levels and above, because they combine essential physical features with sufficient political information to show relationships between the two. A good physical-political globe will be useful for years with reasonable care, serving effectively both for general observation purposes and for detailed, specific reference. Thus, when a physical-political globe is desired, a good quality handmade globe is the best buy.

The slated-outline globe (Fig. 9.6) is of great value at all grade levels. Instruc-

4 This is illustrated in the film *Impossible Map,* 16 mm., Color, 10 min., National Film Board of Canada.

Fig. 9.7. / The transparent celestial globe takes on additional significance in the Space Age. With such a globe it is possible to demonstrate basic relationships between the earth and the stars, planets, and galaxies which make up the universe.

Fig. 9.8. / Plastic globe sections provide another way in which the earth's surface may be studied

Fig. 9.9. / The advantages of a sizable globe and a mounting which permits its removal for improved visibility are illustrated by Dr. Paul Griffin, nationally known geographer and teaching specialist, Monmouth College of Education.

tors and students can write on it with chalk, indicating such features as locations; air, sea, and land routes; and great circles. Psychologically, the unique advantage of this globe is that it permits attention to be focused on one thing at a time. In addition, it is particularly well suited for direct pupil activity and experience. Globes of this type are available with the continents outlined and with grid lines as well as with plain surfaces. Since slated globes are less costly to manufacture than those with printed surfaces, these globes are relatively inexpensive in proportion to their size.

There are various other special globes such as air-age, celestial, physical-relief, and satellite globes. Each has particular advantages for specific purposes. The transparent globe pictured in Fig. 9.7, for example, is used to illustrate the changing locations of stars and planets with reference to the earth's surface.

Also available are useful globe sections of major continental areas (Fig. 9.8). Since these sections approximate areas typically included on flat maps of continents, they can facilitate the transition from globes to flat maps. Constructed of plastic and having raised relief surfaces, these sections are strong, light, and easily handled by students. Their utility for various learning activities is suggested in Fig. 9.8.

■ DESIRABLE CHARACTERISTICS OF GLOBES

In selecting globes for classroom use, there are certain general considerations that should be taken into account regardless of the type of globe that is required. Of course, the globe should be an attractive part of classroom equipment but, in addition, size, complexity of information, and the use of color are particularly important aspects of any globe.

■ SIZE AND VISIBILITY

There are various sizes of globes. Size is usually indicated in terms of diameter, the most common sizes being 8, 12, 16, 20, and 24 inches. The 8-inch globe is suitable only for individual study; the 12-inch and 16-inch globes are most frequently used for group or class purposes. However, the prohibitive cost of hand-covered globes larger than 16 inches, and the amount of space required for a globe large enough for an entire class to see are factors which have prevented the use of larger globes in most schools. Other factors aside, it would be highly desirable, of course, for all globes to be large enough to be seen readily by an entire class. The attention attracted by very large globes, such as the one shown in Fig. 9.9, suggests one value of having 16-inch or larger globes in our classrooms.

The details on most globes are intended primarily for study by individuals and small groups at close range. Such broad features as hemispheres, land-water relationships, and the relative location of continents can be seen by the entire class, however, and for such purposes the globe should be as large as possible.

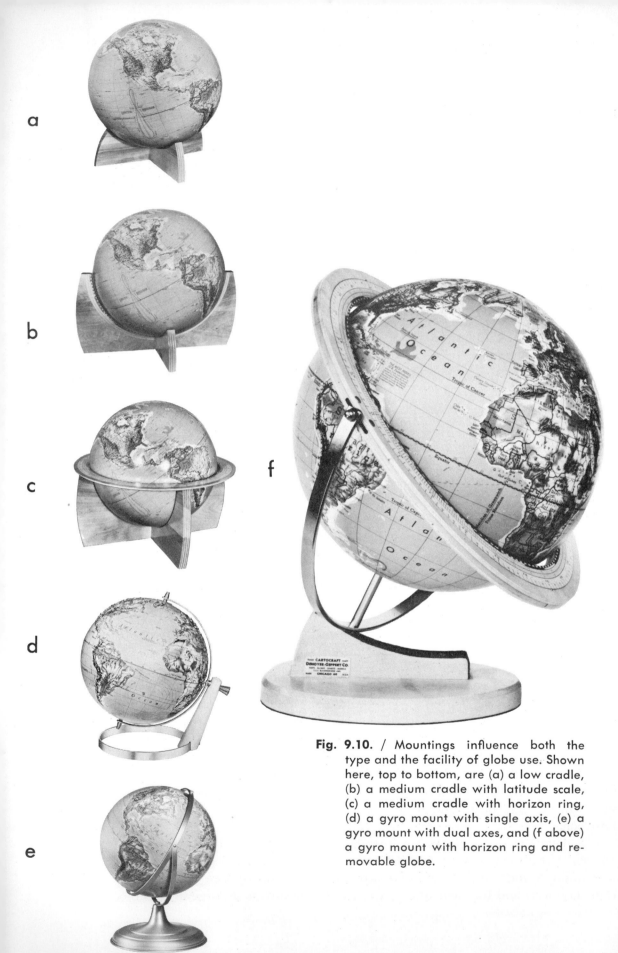

Fig. 9.10. / Mountings influence both the type and the facility of globe use. Shown here, top to bottom, are (a) a low cradle, (b) a medium cradle with latitude scale, (c) a medium cradle with horizon ring, (d) a gyro mount with single axis, (e) a gyro mount with dual axes, and (f above) a gyro mount with horizon ring and removable globe.

In terms of flexibility of use, the type of mounting for the globe becomes important (Fig. 9.10).

Printed data can be presented more clearly on a 16-inch globe than on a 12-inch globe because the surface of the first globe is nearly 78 percent larger. (The surface area of a 12-inch globe is 452 square inches; that of a 16-inch globe is 804 square inches.) Distance, too, can be estimated somewhat more easily on a 16-inch globe because the scale is a convenient 500 miles to 1 inch, whereas the scale on a 12-inch globe is 670 miles to 1 inch.

▪ SIMPLICITY

Closely related to the visibility of a globe is its simplicity. A globe is not an atlas; although much essential information can be presented on it, the inclusion of minute, rarely needed details is unnecessary for its effective use. In recognition of this problem, manufacturers have made political globes and physical-political globes with simplified regional surface features for beginners. For more advanced work, the traditional political and physical-political globes are periodically revised not only to keep them up to date but also to remove unnecessary details.

▪ COLOR

The colors used on globes are a particularly important feature to consider when selecting one for classroom use. The most important aspect of a globe's coloration is its effect on readability. Dark or vivid colors are likely to obscure the words and line symbols printed on the globe. Thus, lighter colors will generally afford greater legibility as well as a more pleasing appearance. On the other hand, there should be sufficient variation in hue and color to provide adequate contrast in the globe's features. On a physical globe, for example, altitude tints should vary enough to allow pupils to distinguish one altitude from another.

Although color correspondence between globes and maps will be discussed in detail later in the chapter, it is worth noting here that classroom globes should be chosen according to the colors that are used on flat map study materials. Because globe mastery must precede map mastery, the transition from globes to flat maps will be easier for the pupil if the color symbols used on the former correspond to those used on the latter.

☐ MAPS

Although some degree of inaccuracy is unavoidable on any flat map, maps are nonetheless highly valuable materials of instruction. A world map, for example, provides the *only* means whereby we can see the whole world at one time. On a

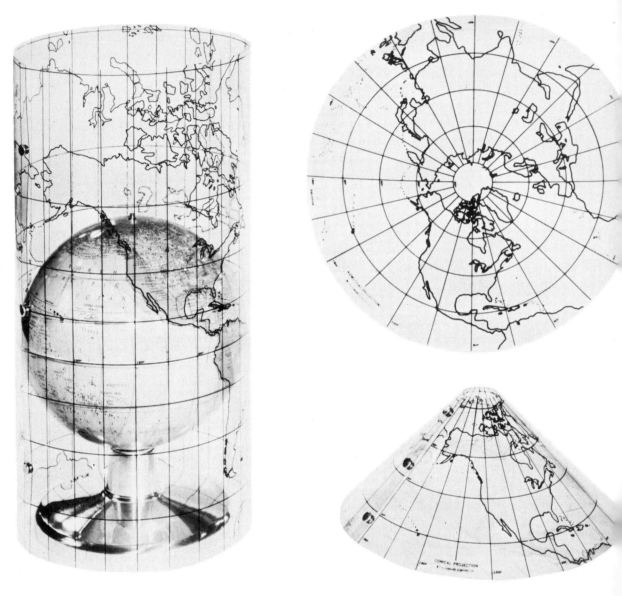

Fig. 9.11. / Three basic types of map projections, cylindrical, conical, and azimuthal can be demonstrated on this inexpensive map-projection model which also explains how a flat map is made from the spherical surface of the globe. The cylindrical and conical sections may be unsnapped to be seen as flat maps.

standard globe, we can see no more than half the world however we spin or tilt the globe. Wall maps are the most convenient means available for enabling all the members of a class to see the same thing on a map at the same time. The great number and variety of maps available to teachers is testimony to their universal acceptance as valuable teaching materials. The flat map is designed to highlight major features of the area it represents. The most effective maps do not contain all of the numerous kinds of information possible on the same map, because too much material makes the map difficult to read and use. Emphasis on one type of information and the avoidance of extraneous details are characteristic of good maps. These characteristics will be discussed in some detail subsequently; in the meantime, we shall discuss map projection, a more important attribute of maps.

■ MAP PROJECTION

The type of map projection chosen for classroom use is a very important consideration, particularly in choosing world maps or maps of a hemisphere. The term *map projection* means the method by which the spherical surface of the earth is flattened out in making a map and, as suggested earlier, this can strongly affect the degree of accuracy presented on a map. There are many different map projections, each designed to achieve somewhat different purposes. Some projections represent *area* reasonably accurately; others are relatively accurate as far as the *shape* of land and water surfaces is concerned; others make it possible to read *distances* accurately from the center of the map; and still others have the property of true *direction*. As was said earlier, the Mercator projection is made for navigators; it is the only projection on which a straight line is a true compass line. Hence, a ship's navigator can draw a straight line between two points on a Mercator map and, with complete confidence, steer the course thus indicated. Unfortunately, no flat map can provide all four of these properties; actually, few can offer more than one. Thus, in order to select the proper map for a particular purpose, it is necessary for a teacher to understand the nature of map projections, and how they compare to the actual properties of the earth's surface.

It is a help in understanding map projections to know something of how they are made. The process is largely mathematical, but the principles can be illustrated rather easily (Fig. 9.11). If you place a translucent cylinder around a transparent globe with a light in it, the grid lines on the globe will be "projected" on the surface of the cylinder. With some modification, this is the Mercator projection referred to earlier. If you place a flat or plane surface against the lighted globe, a different pattern of grid lines is projected. With a cone, still another pattern is projected. And each of these projections, of course, is different from the grid on the globe itself.

The term *grid* refers to the parallels (latitude lines) and meridians (longitude lines) which cartographers universally use as reference lines in plotting their maps. Parallels start at the equator and run parallel to it as east-west lines extending around the earth. Meridians start at Greenwich, England, and extend north and south from pole to pole. Position on maps is measured in terms of the number of degrees east or west longitude and the number of degrees north or south latitude. In essence, therefore, projection is the process of transferring the grid system of a globe onto a flat surface, then drawing in the land areas, point by point, according to the position each has on the globe grid. However, as indicated earlier, it is impossible to transfer the globe grid onto a flat surface without altering it considerably.

Several suitable kinds of classroom map projections are available as *minimum-error projections*. The values of these little-known maps have been described by Robinson.[5] These projections are a compromise in which areas, shapes, direction, and distance properties are balanced so as to present as realistic a map of a

[5] Arthur Robinson, "An Analytical Approach to Map Projections," *Annals of the Association of American Geographers,* December, 1949, p. 287.

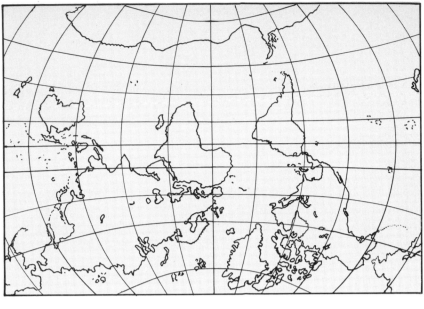

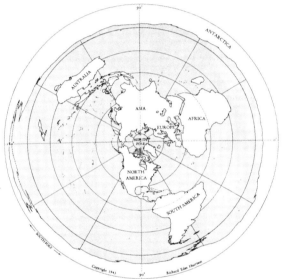

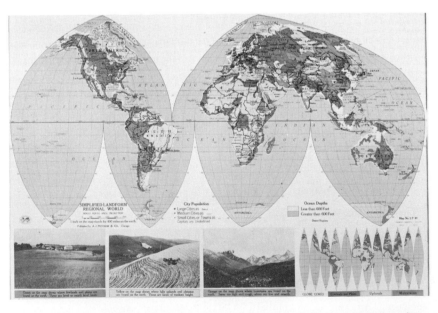

Fig. 9.12. / In terms of the visual test for equal-area properties, how do these three maps measure up?

segment of the earth's surface as is possible. Although no property is completely accurate on a minimum-error projection, the inaccuracies are moderate and inconspicuous even to a skilled observer. For other than technical or scientific purposes, therefore, these projections are quite satisfactory.

The projection on which flat maps which give a correct impression of *area* are based is called an *equal-area projection*. An *equal-area* projection for our purpose means one on which land and water *areas* are essentially correct. The *shapes* of these areas must be sacrificed to some extent to achieve good area properties and, in consequence, *direction* and *distance* properties are likewise distorted. For school purposes, direction, distance, and shapes (so long as they remain recognizable) are of minor importance as compared with good area representation in giving correct impressions of the world or of a hemisphere. On maps of smaller areas, the projection need not concern the teacher.

On maps of regions less than a hemisphere in size, the errors in area are small enough so that, for general school purposes, it makes little difference what projection is used. It *is* important, however, for the teacher to know how to determine whether a map of the world has good area representation. Since the globe grid provides the only completely accurate map there is of the earth's surface, we can do this rather easily by comparing the pattern of the grid lines on a globe with that on the flat map. This is called the *grid comparison method* of evaluating map projections. Visual comparison of the globe grid with a flat-map grid will reveal any significant differences. Although at least ten important characteristics of the globe grid are used for extensive comparison, four of these are sufficient to determine whether a flat map has good area presentation:

1. Parallels are parallel.
2. Parallels are equidistant from equator to poles.
3. Meridians are equally spaced on the parallels and converge toward the poles.
4. The area enclosed by any two parallels and two meridians is the same anywhere between the same two parallels.

Because only a globe grid could have all four of these characteristics, our evaluation must be based on how closely the grid of the map we are examining comes to meeting them. If the above properties are approximated over a major portion of the map's surface, the chances are that the map is based on an equal-area projection.[6]

With a little practice, a teacher can learn to distinguish quite easily which maps have good area characteristics. Try the above tests on the map grids in Fig. 9.12 and then on other world maps in your classroom or media center.

■ TYPES OF MAPS

Maps are available in three principal types: *physical* maps, or maps which show terrain; *political* maps, which show governmental areas; and *special-purpose* maps. There are numerous combinations and variations of these basic

6 See Arthur Robinson, *Elements of Cartography* (rev. ed.), Wiley, 1960, p. 62.

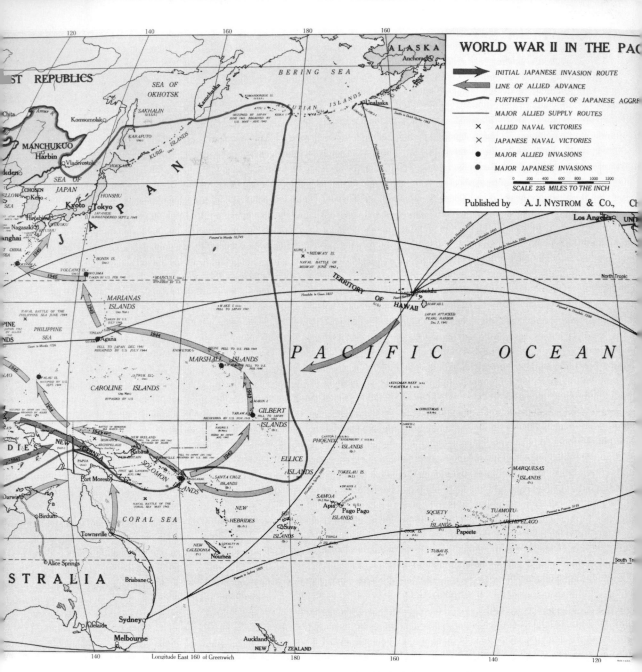

Fig. 9.13. / Special-purpose maps can be helpful in visualizing important time and space relationships in man's history. As an example, what concepts about World War II could be more readily learned with a map such as this?

types, such as physical-political maps, regional maps, and such special-purpose maps as those showing land use, population distribution, rainfall, or historical development (Fig. 9.13).

■ PHYSICAL MAPS

Physical maps emphasize terrain and topographical concepts. These concepts are necessary for understanding such matters as why people live where they do, some aspects of agricultural production, climate, and routes of transportation.

Fig. 9.14. / An understanding of topography is necessary for many social-studies concepts. Some flat maps like this show relief effectively by shading one side of mountains so as to give the appearance of elevation.

The elementary concepts of mountains, valleys, plains, deserts, rivers, rainfall, and temperature all involve an understanding of topography.

Some flat maps visualize relief effectively by shading one side of mountain ranges, thus giving a three-dimensional appearance (Fig. 9.14). Color tints are also used to show elevation. However, because color leaves much to be desired in giving a correct impression of different land surfaces at the same elevation, shaded relief has been used increasingly in recent years, sometimes combined with color. Still more recently, instead of altitude tints, shaded relief has been used on physical maps with a naturalistic color scheme such as one might see from a plane at high altitude. Although the color aspects of a landscape vary,

Fig. 9.15. / Three-dimensional relief maps in durable lightweigh·

a color scheme is chosen which represents landscape colors during good weather in the summer and is keyed to major vegetation differences. For example, grass areas are a lighter green than forest regions, and deserts are buff, brownish yellow, or gray. Texture is sometimes used to represent cultivated areas.[7]

Physical maps which show actual relief and amplify it with color and shading are probably the most effective type of physical map for classroom walls. Although any relief map exaggerates the elevation in relation to horizontal distance, this difference in scale is essential if topographical features are to be

[7] See Edward B. Espenshade, Jr., "Cartographic Developments and New Maps," in *New Viewpoints in Geography, op. cit.*, pp. 93–111.

plastic permit close-up study and "feel" of the terrain.

noticeable, and is standard practice among map-makers. Land-surface concepts are made more concrete by relief than by the use of more abstract hachure and color symbols.

Excellent relief maps in three dimensions are available in sturdy, lightweight, inexpensive plastic. These enable students to feel as well as to see the surface features of a region (Fig. 9.15). Three-dimensional relief maps of local areas can be made by teachers and pupils for any regions for which U.S. Geological Survey topographical maps are available. These maps are not difficult to construct and are of significant value in developing map-reading ability (Fig. 9.16). One method of preparation is to enlarge a small section of a topographical

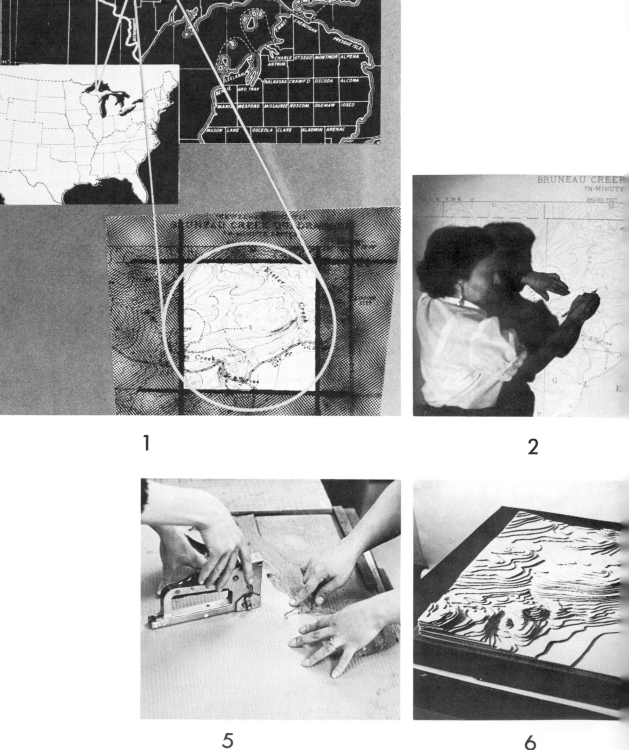

1   **2**

5   **6**

Fig. 9.16. / A good terrain map of a local area can be made by teacher and pupils. These pictures show the principal steps involved in one method.

map and trace the contour lines on corrugated cardboard. The contours are then cut out and mounted on top of one another in the correct relationship. Some exaggeration of the vertical scale results but, as indicated above, this is desirable. The surface is painted with spackling plaster and painted when dry.[8]

3   4

7   8

[8] For a detailed description of this process, see C. F. Schuller, "3D for Better Map Communication," *Audiovisual Instruction*, May, 1956, pp. 76–77.

▪ POLITICAL MAPS

Political maps show phenomena which are principally man-made, such as national, state, and county boundaries; the location of cities, highways, and railroads; and national and state parks. The common road map is a good example of a political map. Another example is a world map showing colonial possessions and the mother country in the same color. A good political map typically presents political boundaries, principal cities, rivers and water areas, important transportation routes, and—depending upon the level and function of the map —perhaps a few other features (see Plates 14–17, in section which follows page 256). Normally, however, such additional information as contour lines, land use, and rainfall or population distribution is not presented on the same map.

Small inset maps are frequently printed on the margins of a map to provide such information as rainfall, vegetation, thermal regions, and population distribution. This information is valuable, of course, and it is useful for small-group close-up study; it may also be helpful in reading the larger map. Sometimes inset maps are used to fill up spaces when the large map is wide and rather squat in shape, as is true of some world maps. It is generally preferable to have the main map larger than to use up space for insets which, at best, can be seen only at close range. An atlas or textbook map is more convenient and more efficient for detailed map study.

Frequently certain terrain and political features are shown on the same map; such a map is known as a *physical-political map* (see Plate 16). These maps are particularly useful in illustrating certain relationships between the terrain and man's settlement of the land. For example, the small number of larger cities in mountainous regions is readily shown on a physical-political map.

▪ SPECIAL-PURPOSE MAPS

An increasing variety and number of maps have become available for specialized teaching purposes. In some cases, these maps are closely related to such basic geographic concepts as climate, rainfall, vegetation, population distribution, and natural resources. In others, they relate to commercial, historical (as in Fig. 9.13), literary, scientific, and foreign-language subjects. The profusion and quality of special-purpose maps reflect the significant role that maps and map reading play in a whole range of important economic, political, and cultural concepts. Maps can be vehicles for the communication of many kinds of information.

Once the basic requirements for globes and for local, state, national and world physical and political maps have been met, the teacher will want to explore the many possibilities to be found in special-purpose maps.

■ WALL vs. DESK MAPS

There is another distinction that should be pointed out in connection with maps for classroom use; that between wall maps—those which are located in a central place in the classroom and can be viewed by the entire class at once—and desk maps, which are principally for use by individual pupils. One writer refers to wall maps as "pointer" devices, explaining that "the wall map is not there to serve every purpose for which teachers and students may require a map, but to make it possible for teacher or students to point out to others in the room some essential features in the distributions which a given map shows."[9] In essence, therefore, wall maps should be accurate, large enough and clear enough to be viewed by the entire class, and clear enough in its colors and symbols to be understood by the class, but they should not be overloaded with detail.

In studying subject-matter units in which special detail is called for, desk maps which bear the same broad features as the wall map should be used. Since desk maps for individual use are subject to several of the same criteria indicated for wall-map selection, we shall devote the rest of our map discussion to wall maps. Suffice it to say here that the larger-size desk maps are only slightly more costly than small ones and, for most purposes, are considerably better for students to read or to work with.

■ DESIRABLE CHARACTERISTICS OF WALL MAPS

Most wall maps are attractive in appearance, and this is certainly to be desired. Less obvious but of much greater importance to the instructor, however, are the other factors—whether the map is large enough to be seen easily in the classroom; how complicated the map is to read; and how effectively color has been used. Let us examine these considerations more closely.

■ SIZE AND VISIBILITY. Wall maps are visualizations devised to present complete or partial global surface information on a single flat surface. Wall maps of the world make it possible to sense key geographical, physical, or political concepts which would be less visible on a globe.

In order to be useful in classroom-study situations, wall maps must be so designed and of such size that students seated normally about the room can see and "read" the important relationships revealed by the map. Important symbols, shapes, names of gross land and water masses, and key terrain phenomena must be presented by means of such effective color and size of print as to be visible and understandable to all viewers. Ordinarily, world maps need to be larger than maps of continents or smaller areas. Because of the area covered by world maps, key relationships, to be visible, must be presented on maps of substantial size. Adequate size is dependent in part on the size of your classroom. World maps 7 feet or more in width are not uncommon; 5 to 6 feet is probably minimum for most classrooms.

The printing on wall maps which relates to important concepts and the names of continents and countries should be in large type and suitably spaced so as to make reading it possible anywhere in the seating area. "In so far as any

9 Edna E. Eisen, "Maps, Globes and Charts," in *American School and University*, American School Publishing, 1947, p. 190.

Fig. 9.17. / Large numbers of maps are available on transparencies for the overhead projector. These range from one-color outline maps to full-color gen-

data on a map cannot be grasped by the eye, and easily read, in just that measure is the map encumbered with useless material, and is a failure."[10]

Precise studies by Luckiesh and Moss have determined the relative visibility of printed type of varying sizes.[11] The relative visibility of that used on wall maps and charts is one important basis of map selection. Other factors than type size—among them background contrast, variations in type design, and crowded elements—also influence legibility.

A study by Robinson shows that 2-inch letters at 30 feet appear the same as letters ⅑-inch high (about the height of the letter *h* on this line) at a normal reading distance of 18 inches.[12] Letters ½-inch in height require above-average vision to be read at 20 feet.

■ SIMPLICITY.   Wall maps are frequently too crowded with information. As a result, they are difficult to read from more than a few feet away and are hard for the average pupil to interpret. It is unnecessary to provide a different map for each geographical concept, but there can and should be a sufficient number of wall maps in the classroom to cover the most significant concepts without overcrowding any one with information. A world map, for example, should not be used in connection with a study of Europe or the United States, for, if it includes much of the information required in either of these units, it is likely to be too crowded and illegible for the pupils to understand readily.

■ COLOR.   Color is important from several standpoints in map selection. The most obvious of these is attractiveness. Closely related and more important is the effect of color on readability. On the whole, a good color contrast that gives optimum legibility and pleasing appearance is the major factor to be considered. Lighter shades are usually more satisfactory than deep primary colors. Recognizing both factors, most map companies now avoid heavy or

10 J. Paul Goode, *Goode's School Atlas*, Rand McNally, 1918.
11 M. Luckiesh and F. K. Moss, "The Quantitative Relationship Between Visibility and Type Size," *Journal of The Franklin Institute*, January, 1939, pp. 87–97.
12 Arthur Robinson, "The Size of Lettering for Maps and Charts," *Surveying and Mapping*, January-March, 1950, pp. 37–44.

eral and special-purpose maps with multiple overlays. What advantages are there for this means of presenting maps?

brilliant coloration which tends to attract attention to itself rather than to the map. However, primary children respond to bright cheerful colors, and for this reason publishers of beginners' maps use somewhat brighter and less subtle colors than are acceptable at higher grade levels.

Color and shading are important, also, in making maps easier to interpret. Historical maps which show colonial possessions or protectorates and the mother country in the same color are an example. Here again, heavy or brilliant colors are apt to make lines and printed data more difficult to read than they should be. In general, colors should implement the teaching effectiveness of the map rather than attract attention to themselves.

■ SUPPLEMENTARY MAP MATERIALS

Because course requirements for map use are so wide and varied, it would be impossible for a classroom to have all of the wall and desk maps necessary to fill all of these requirements. There are several useful supplementary map materials available which combine some of the advantages of both wall and desk maps: They can be viewed by the entire class, and many of them can be marked by the pupils themselves in the course of the study unit—a distinct advantage of most desk maps. These supplementary map materials include projected maps, slated-wall outline maps, and chalkboard stencil maps.

■ PROJECTED MAPS

A map in an atlas or reference book can be projected on a screen by an opaque projector, thus permitting the class to see and discuss it as they do a wall map. Outline maps can be projected on the chalkboard by the same means and used there in various ways (see Chapter III.)

Map transparencies for the overhead projector (Fig. 9.17) are of particular benefit to the teacher who wishes to emphasize certain physical, political, or special-purpose map features and omit others. These overlays enable him to

Fig. 9.18. / Globes and maps are essential for advanced as well as for earlier geographic study. At advanced levels, map- and globe-reading skill is comparable to verbal reading as a primary source of information on political, social, and economic concepts.

Fig. 9.19. / This map of Los Angeles Harbor was made by primary pupils after a field trip. What educational benefits do you see in this kind of map activity?

present detailed map information without extensive room darkening. Similarly, outline maps can be traced on clear acetate with a grease pencil and filled in as the discussion proceeds. Map slides in the small 2×2 or larger $3\frac{1}{4} \times 4$ size are available commercially on a variety of current and historical topics. Handmade slides likewise have useful applications in social-studies classes both for the students who make them and for those who see them.

Projected maps make possible, among their other advantages, a considerable number and variety of maps at low cost, variation in methods needed by both teachers and students from time to time, and enlargement of maps so that details can be seen readily by the entire group.

▪ SLATED-WALL OUTLINE MAPS

Teachers know that pupils learn by doing, that directed pupil activity is necessary for "fixing" concepts in their minds. Teachers also know that complex ideas must be built up step by step, with each step simply and clearly defined. The slated-wall outline map is very helpful in applying both of these teaching principles. The instructor can draw one thing at a time on a slated map without the class being distracted by extraneous details. Teachers know well how group interest is heightened when one member of the class goes to the map and chalks in a name, outlines an area, or traces an important parallel or trade route under the watchful eye of the rest of the class.

Like the modern chalkboard, slated maps have been made attractive by the use of color. A slated world map and a slated globe on the same scale provide an excellent combination for teaching important area and location concepts.

▪ CHALKBOARD STENCIL MAPS

An interesting and practical addition to a school's map materials is a chalkboard stencil map, a wall map that has perforations along state and national boundaries (see Chapter III, Fig. 3.9). Chalkboard stencil maps are used in much the same way as are slated-wall maps. The stencil map is particularly well suited when it is desired to have a number of pupils at the board at the same time, because as many maps can be stenciled on the chalkboard as space permits. They are also convenient when the instructor wishes to present an additional illustration or two without disturbing work already on the slated map. Chalkboard stencil maps can be made rather easily on an inexpensive window shade; a few stencil maps are available commercially. For more details on chalkboard used there in various ways (see Chapter III).

☐ EFFECTIVE TEACHING WITH MAPS AND GLOBES

Because the world is becoming increasingly complex in its political, cultural, and technological relationship, it is more important than ever before that today's pupils fully grasp the concepts involved in map and globe use. As one social scientist says:

An intelligent citizen must use maps. From maps in newspapers and magazines, he obtains information on world and local affairs. Students in school also use maps as a source of information. If student and adult alike are to receive the full value from maps, they must be able to read them easily and accurately.[13]

The U.S. Department of State put it this way: "He who would solve world problems must understand them; he who would understand world problems must visualize them; and he who would visualize world problems should study them on the spherical surface of a globe."[14]

Thus, even if the classroom globe and map materials have been chosen with care and with an eye to both accuracy and suitability to specific learning goals, teachers at all levels need to consider seriously how to use them more effectively in instruction so that their pupils will learn not only to *read* maps properly, but also how to *interpret* them (Fig. 9.18). Clearly, if these goals are to be achieved the globe and map materials should be geared to the age and grade levels of the pupils.

Globes and maps, as we have seen, represent the earth or sections of it by means of lines, colors, and symbols which bear little resemblance to the actual appearance of the earth's surface as a child sees it. Maps have a language all their own which, like any language, must be learned (see Plates 18–20 in the section which follows page 256). No one is born with the ability to read maps and globes. He must learn this just as he must learn how to read words, sentences, and paragraphs. No teacher would think of using an eighth-grade reading text with a second-grade class. Yet often the same maps are used at all grade levels, with little apparent regard for their complexity. There should be distinct levels of complexity in maps designed for primary, intermediate, secondary, and college use. In recognition of this need, map publishers are making available a steadily increasing number of graded maps.

Start where the pupil is. This principle is inherent in good teaching at all levels. It is also a way of expressing another principle: As pointed out in Chapter II, before symbols of any kind are taught, pupils must have *a background of experience which can give these symbols concrete meaning*.

■ MAP-READING READINESS

Where *is* the child so far as globes and maps are concerned? What is he familiar with that the teacher can use as a basis for beginning to teach him globes and maps? In developing map skills in the primary grades. Sabaroff emphasizes the importance of a geographical-readiness program based upon the immediate environment:

> Geographers agree that children should not be faced with a symbol on a map which does not bring to mind an image of the reality for which it stands.

---

[13] Kathryn T. Whittemore, "The Place of Maps in Social Education," *Journal of Geography*, March, 1948, p. 110.

[14] Quoted in Lorrin Kennamer, *op. cit.*

Elementary pupils need carefully graded and appropriately sampled experiences in observing real landscapes in the immediate world around them. They must be given opportunity to think over, discuss and relate what they have seen. They must be allowed to map what they themselves have seen and discussed, and to read simple maps made by others for which they now have adequate images.[15]

The pupil's home and yard, his immediate neighborhood, the way to school, his schoolroom, the school yard, and perhaps other parts of the community where his class has gone on a field trip—all provide sound bases for building an initial conceptual framework for understanding geography generally. Kathryn Whittemore cites how one class of very young children were started out with a sound learning experience of this nature:

Children begin early and without direction to represent places they have seen by representing them with blocks or other materials. After a Buffalo kindergarten class had visited the Peace Bridge, the children built a model of the bridge across the classroom. They were able to tell which end of their bridge represented the Canada end and which represented the end near their school. They pointed out where the river flowed beneath the bridge.[16]

The importance of observation and field trips to nearby areas for young children is universally stressed as a basis for building initial geographical concepts. "No geography worthy of the name is possible," says Scarfe, "without constant reference to a completely understood home region."[17]

By the time they are in the third grade, most children are ready to participate in making pictorial maps of familiar sections. The harbor as they saw it will faithfully be reproduced; and such things as ships, docks, and the lighthouse are likely to be drawn realistically (Fig. 9.19). Perspective and scale may be crude or entirely absent, but nevertheless, such maps show the beginning of a feeling for relative size, location, and distance. Providing experiences which naturally give rise to pictorial murals and maps is a good way to begin formal map work. Before long, symbols can be introduced to represent streets, buildings, important landmarks, and topographical features. These new meanings will be revealed through careful study of standard geographical terms. Fig. 9.20 is a three-dimensional representation of topographical features that aids the student in comprehending such terms as *plateaus, ridges,* and *valleys.*

Pictures also play a vital part in map-reading readiness. They are an interesting supplement to field trips, and open large areas of the earth to observation which would otherwise be impossible to observe. Early concepts of land surfaces and climate can be developed through pictures and films. Charts are available which combine pictures with large-scale maps of small areas to illustrate the

15 Rose Sabaroff, "Firsthand Experiences in Geography for Second-Graders," *Journal of Geography,* September, 1958, p. 306.

16 Kathryn Whittemore, "Maps," in *Geographic Approaches to Social Education,* 19th Yearbook, National Council for the Social Studies, 1948, p. 120.

17 N. F. Scarfe, "Designing a Curriculum to Develop Geographic Concepts," *Journal of Geography,* February, 1956, p. 58.

Fig. 9.20. / The language of maps also involves learning numerous geographical terms, such as those on this three-dimensional representation of topographical features.

meaning of various map symbols. In introducing specific methods of using pictures to teach map concepts, Odell stresses the following point:

> There are an infinite number of ways in which pictures can be of assistance in teaching and lead directly into the use of globes and maps. In the teaching of map understanding and map reading alone, there are many examples of desirable picture use. The use of pictures and maps can be an aid to 'seeing' the relationships.[18]

■ GLOBES AND MAPS IN THE PRIMARY GRADES

Whipple suggests that during the first two years of the social-studies curriculum, and prior to systematic instruction in grade 3, the pupils learn beginning concepts and generalizations about the earth itself, its lands and waters, climate and the seasons, man's use of the land, what maps are, and certain skills preparatory to map reading.[19]

A globe is an essential part of this map-reading readiness program. Not only are all flat maps derived originally from the globe, but it is by all odds the best medium for developing a true idea of the earth's sphericity. The importance of having a globe constantly at hand is clear if the learners are to acquire such concepts as the earth's rotation, the explanation for day and night, the poles and the meaning of direction, and the large proportion of the earth's surface which is covered by water. "If correct concepts of world relationships are to be gained, one must have a globe. The globe is the best representation of the world that we have. . . . Every schoolroom even in the primary grades should have a globe."[20]

For primary rooms, the globe should be a simple one, perhaps showing primarily the land and water areas, the poles, and the equator. It should be easily accessible so the pupils can handle it. The colors used on the globe should be those of basic distinction of the earth's surface only, and should not include the more subtle gradations in sea level, elevation, and so forth. Further, it is wise to choose a globe in which the colors have close correspondence to those used on flat maps to be used later, for this will make transition to flat maps easier.

■ GLOBES AND MAPS IN THE INTERMEDIATE GRADES

In the fourth, fifth, and sixth grades, globe- and map-reading skills are developed at a more advanced level. Systematic instruction includes regular *use* of globes and maps, plus increased skill in reading them. History and geography are brought together in meaningful context, each reinforcing the other and

---

[18] Clarence B. Odell, "The Use of Maps, Globes, and Pictures in the Classroom," in *New Viewpoints in Geography, op. cit.,* p. 207.

[19] Gertrude Whipple, "Geography in the Elementary Social Studies Program," *ibid.,* pp. 118–122.

[20] Zoe A. Thralls, "The Use of the Globe," *Social Education,* April, 1947, p. 165.

Fig. 9.21. / What learning opportunities are possible as these Indian pupils study and work with this relief map of their country? Could you adapt this project to help pupils understand their own locality?

establishing an initial basis for a better understanding of why people live where and how they do today.

It is in these middle grades that *physical-political* globes and maps are introduced. When North and South America and the other lands of the earth are studied in the fifth and sixth grades, the globe should be used regularly to establish and to maintain correct concepts of relative location, size, and climatic influences. Physical-political maps and globes are used at this level and cross reference between them should become habitual. During this period, the student needs to learn the use of legends and color keys in order to interpret maps and globes which do not have similar coloration, since most maps he sees after this time will vary considerably in colors employed.

As more maps are used, the *scale* assumes significance, and its meaning must be taught carefully to avoid extensive misconceptions. The ability to determine locations in terms of latitude or distance from the equator—when combined with the ability to read scales—enables the pupil to compare and to contrast different countries. He may discover such fundamental facts as, for example, that Japan has approximately the same area as California and over six times as many people. Such discoveries stimulate questions and set the stage for further meaningful learning.

Although both subject content and map-reading skills are more complex in the middle grades than they are in the earlier grades, the teacher should not overlook the importance of providing *motivation* and opportunities to *learn by doing*. One fifth-grade teacher utilized both these principles when he asked his class, "Have you made your vacation plans?" A flurry of hands shot up.

"I'm going to camp!" said one pupil.

"We're driving to Yellowstone Park," volunteered another.

"My dad wants to go to the Lake of the Woods and fish, but I think we're going to the Gaspé Peninsula instead," said a third.

Out of the enthusiasm of anticipation, a series of useful writing, reading, and storytelling activities quickly developed. Location of destinations and routes of travel brought into use a map of the state, another of the United States, and a number of road maps as the students reported on their families' vacation plans.

One valuable application of "learning by doing" is to have pupils make maps of their own. This is excellent for developing both map-reading ability and the power to interpret the data on maps. "The preparation of one's own maps," suggests a noted geographer, "through . . . plotting data upon a base map provides not only training in observation, but leads to a fuller understanding of maps as a medium of communication."[21]

It is important here to distinguish between mere copying exercises and creative map construction. While there are certain values in transferring the thirteen colonies from a textbook map to a desk outline map, this should not be confused with actual map construction or the learning values accruing therefrom.

Relief maps of a local area provide an excellent basis for understanding surface features of the area and the physical and elevation symbols used on physical

21 Edward B. Espenshade, Jr., *op. cit.*, p. 95.

Fig. 9.22. / A demonstration by the teacher explains day and night. The students apply this knowledge in exercises, and the class begins to understand time.

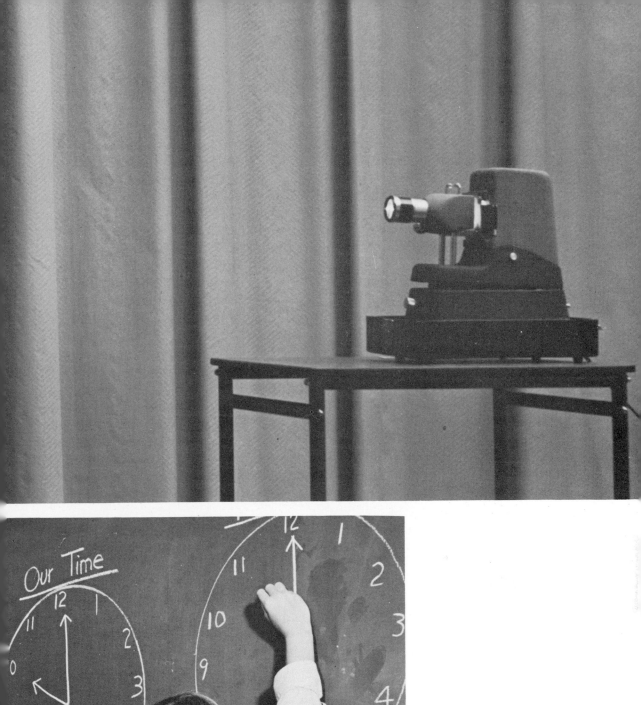

maps. These three-dimensional maps can easily be made by the teacher and pupils (see Fig. 9.16). U.S. Geological Survey topographical maps are available for most local areas and should be used, along with firsthand observation, for accurate construction. Several methods of construction give satisfactory results.[22] The great value of this type of map is that it is considerably more realistic than any flat map and, accordingly, can be very valuable in giving meaning to the physical symbols of flat maps.

Reference should once again be made to the pupils creative and inventive use of maps and globes. Once he understands these instruments, he should be encouraged to use them and even to create needed adaptations of them as he becomes more adept in communicating geographical ideas and concepts to teachers and classmates.

▪ GLOBES AND MAPS IN THE SECONDARY SCHOOL

A wide variety of maps and globes is essential at the secondary level where world concepts are developed on a broad scale. By this time, the student should have learned to interpret maps as well as to "read" them, but this ability cannot be taken for granted (Fig. 9.21). All too frequently he will have missed something along the line, perhaps because the teacher was not well enough trained. As an example, students and teachers alike are frequently unfamiliar with how to read directions on maps having curved meridians or parallels as most maps now do. The relationship between the grid and direction on maps is implied, but "seldom presented clearly in textbooks for any level from elementary to college."[23]

In any case, map reading—like English and spelling—is the responsibility of teachers at all levels. If the secondary-school pupil lacks basic map-reading skills, he must be taught them before he can proceed successfully.

In the junior high school, new concepts must be learned such as the equinoxes and solstices, time zones (Fig. 9.22), the international date line, and great-circle routes. Globes are invaluable for teaching such concepts, and slated globes are particularly helpful for related pupil exercises. At the junior- and senior-high-school levels numerous special-purpose maps containing economic, historical, and literary data are used regularly, in addition to physical-political maps and globes. Before completing senior high school, a student should have become adept at both reading and interpreting a variety of maps and globes. If he is fortunate, his teacher in various subjects will use maps effectively themselves and will recognize the continuing need to help him improve his ability to the point where he is as much at home with maps as he is with books.

As with all other forms of audiovisual materials, the good instructor selects and uses the globes and maps that achieve his purposes better than any other materials available to him. He uses them in combination with such other materials as textbooks, reference books, atlases, flat pictures, slides, films, filmstrips, field trips, bulletin-board displays, and desk outline maps—according to the

22 For details of a simple method of constructing a plastic relief map, see Ralph C. Preston, *Teaching Social Studies in the Elementary School*, Holt, Rinehart & Winston, 1950, pp. 237–243.

23 Joseph A. Hazel, "Most 'Good' Maps Do Not Have a Directional Symbol," *Journal of Geography*, February, 1965, p. 83.

needs of his class. He recognizes that these materials are means rather than ends in themselves—means to gaining a clear and vital understanding of the geographical, social, and cultural concepts that give meaning to the world we live in.

☐ SUMMARY

Globes and maps are a vital part of the school's instructional materials because they are the only means by which large areas of the earth, or the earth itself, can be effectively represented. Although globes are the only true maps of the earth, flat projections are necessary for detailed study, for ease of viewing, and for seeing the whole earth at one time.

Appropriate globes for teaching purposes include simplified political globes for beginners, slated globes, and physical-political globes. Simplicity, size, visibility, and color considerations are important in selecting globes. Several sizes and mountings are available. Although most globes cannot be read from a distance of more than a few feet, there are advantages in using globes 16-inches or larger rather than smaller ones.

Flat maps of the world are unavoidably inaccurate in two or more of the following properties of the globe: correct area, shape, direction, and distance. For most school purposes, good area representation is of primary importance in preventing basic misconceptions. It is necessary, therefore, that the teacher be able to determine whether small-scale maps have good area representation. He can do this visually by comparing the map grid with the grid on a globe in terms of the four characteristics of the globe grid.

Additional factors in evaluating flat maps are simplicity, size, legibility, and color. Maps for beginners should be simplified, larger than is commonly the case, and colored so as to enhance both legibility and attractiveness.

In summary, the primary considerations in the selection of wall maps are:

1. Equal-area projection is important for avoiding gross misconceptions on world maps or maps of a hemisphere; the type of projection is relatively unimportant for maps of smaller areas.
2. Maps should be suited to grade levels in terms of complexity and amounts of information contained.
3. Prefer larger to smaller wall maps in any instance.
4. Coloration should contribute significantly to readability of maps; its use for aesthetics is a secondary consideration.

Valuable supplementary map and globe materials for group and individual instruction include map slides and transparencies, slated wall outline maps, and chalkboard stencil outline maps. Plastic relief maps and pupil-made large-scale relief maps of local areas are of great value in teaching map reading.

Effective use of maps and globes is based on map-reading readiness; this is developed in the primary grades through extensive observation of the local environment. The use of pictures and, later, of motion pictures and other instructional materials give important meaning and visual imagery to maps and globes.

Systematic instruction in geographical concepts and in reading globes and maps begins in the third or fourth grade and continues thereafter. Geography instruction today incorporates history and cultural concepts to the end of promoting better understanding of the peoples of the earth. The ability to interpret maps, above and beyond the essential ability to read them, is vital to the development of this understanding.

☐ Suggested Activities

1. Prepare a simple test on map reading and give it to the class. Include such items as the following:
   a. Alaska is nearly as large as the United States. (True or false?)
   b. Greenland is larger than Mexico. (True or false?)
   c. Name six countries that the 40th parallel runs through.
   d. In what general direction is Moscow from Chicago?
   e. Which of the following is the most direct route from San Francisco to Japan?
      (1) Westward via the Hawaiian Islands
      (2) Westward, but slightly north of the Hawaiian Islands
      (3) Northwestward along the Alaskan coast and the Aleutian Islands
      (4) Northward and nearly over the North Pole
   Have the students check their own papers and discuss the implications of the errors that were made.
2. Using the grid-comparison method, analyze several wall maps of the world and determine which have good area representation.
3. Examine catalogues from several map and globe companies and select specific globes and wall maps for use in one of the following:
   a. A primary room
   b. An intermediate room
   c. A social-studies room in senior high school
   d. An adult class in world affairs
   Be ready to state the reasons for your selections.
4. Send for the following materials to add to your audiovisual library:
   a. *Around the World* and *Teaching and Learning with Maps, Globes, and Pictures,* A. J. Nystrom & Co., 3333 Elston Ave., Chicago 18, Illinois, free.
   b. *Toward Better Understanding and Use of Maps, Globes, and Charts,* Denoyer-Geppert Co., 5235 Ravenswood Ave., Chicago 40, Illinois, free.
   c. *Handbook of Map and Globe Usage,* by Ruby M. Harris, Education Division, Rand McNally & Co., P.O. Box 7600, Chicago 80, Illinois, $1.79.
5. Obtain a road map of your state, a map of the United States, and a map of Europe. Compare the legends on these maps. Note differences in the symbols used for such things as cities, railroads, highways, etc., and also differences in the way these maps indicate rivers, mountains, plains, deserts, etc.
6. Examine your local newspapers, magazines, and even the books you are using to see how widely maps and globes actually are used in our daily lives. Be alert for ideas and materials that you can use in teaching.

☐ Bibliography

Anderzohn, Mamie L., "Globe Centered Classroom," *Grade Teacher,* September, 1962, pp. 72–73 ff.

Bacon, Philip, "A Way to Teach Children to Use the Globe," *Grade Teacher,* October, 1964, pp. 66–67 ff.

Chace, H., "Using Maps in Teaching History," *Journal of Geography,* November, 1960, pp. 380–385.

Goble, James, "Magic Map," *Journal of Geography,* September, 1961, pp. 283–285.

Harris, Ruby, *Handbook for Maps and Globes,* Rand McNally, 1958.

Hazel, Joseph A., "Most 'Good' Maps Do Not Have a Directional Symbol," *Journal of Geography,* February, 1965, pp. 81–83.

Hoffman, H. W., "Map Comes Alive," *Journal of Geography,* February, 1956, pp. 77–80.

James, Preston (Ed.), *New Viewpoints in Geography,* 29th Yearbook, National Council for the Social Studies, 1959.

Joyce, William W., *The Development and Grade Placement of Map and Globe Skills in the Elementary Social Studies Program,* Unpublished Doctoral Dissertation, Northwestern University, August, 1964.

Kennamer, Lorrin, "Developing a Sense of Place and Space," in *Skill Development in the Social Studies,* 33rd Yearbook, National Council for the Social Studies, 1963, pp. 148–169.

Krohn, C. F., "Interpreting Maps and Globes," in *The Teacher of the Social Studies,* 23rd Yearbook, National Council for the Social Studies, 1953, pp. 146–177.

McAuley, J. D., "Maps and Globes in the Elementary School Program," *Journal of Geography,* December, 1960, pp. 431–433.

Manno, A., "Junior Map Makers," *Grade Teacher,* January, 1961, pp. 20 ff., 204.

Robinson, Arthur H., *Elements of Cartography* (2nd ed.), Wiley, 1960, 343 pp.

Rushdoony, Haig A., "Achievement in Map Reading: An Experimental Study," *Elementary School Journal,* November, 1963, pp. 70–75.

Sabaroff, Rose, "Firsthand Experiences in Geography for Second Graders," *Journal of Geography,* September, 1958, pp. 300–307.

Siamis, Winifred and Marian Dekker, "Developing Geographical Concepts in Primary Grades," *Journal of Geography,* February, 1961, pp. 82–88.

☐ **Films and Filmstrips**

Global Concept in Maps, 16 mm. film, B&W and Color, 10 min., Coronet Films, 1948.

Globes, Their Function in the Classroom, 16 mm. film, Color, 16 min., Bailey Films, 1961.

Impossible Maps, 16 mm. film, B&W and Color, 10 min., National Film Board of Canada, 1948.

Introducing the Topographic Map, 35 mm. filmstrip, Color, 58 frames, Stanbow Productions, Inc., 1958.

Introduction to Map Projection, 16 mm. film, 18 min., United World Films, 1950.

Making Geographic Models, 35 mm. filmstrip, Color, 55 frames, Ohio State University, 1957.

Map Symbols, Dots and Lines, 35 mm. filmstrip, Color, 60 frames, Society of Visual Education, 1954.

Maps and How To Use Them, 35 mm. filmstrips, Eye Gate House, 1958. Series includes:
> *Elements of Maps,* 28 frames.
> *Flat Maps of a Round World,* 31 frames.
> *Maps for Air Age,* 39 frames.
> *Maps for Special Purposes,* 36 frames.
> *Maps of Physical Features,* 37 frames.
> *Maps Through the Ages,* 39 frames.
> *The Globe,* 31 frames.
> *Using Common Maps,* 29 frames.
> *Using the Globe,* 36 frames.
> *What a Map Is,* 25 frames.

Relief Models, 16 mm. film, Color, 10 min., David Lipscomb College, 1955.

Using Maps and Globes, 35 mm. filmstrip, Color, 48 frames, Society for Visual Education, 1954.

X

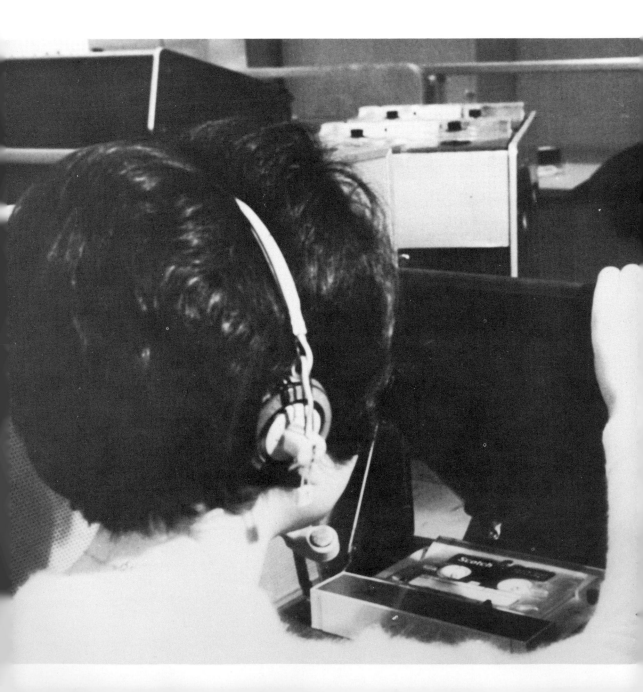

AUDIOLEARNING

As long as there have been teachers and pupils, listening has been a primary means of receiving instructional communication. Research studies have established that nearly 50 percent of a typical class day is spent in listening activities.[1] Further, the higher the grade level, the more class time is spent in listening—at the college level, nearly 90 percent of the students' time is engaged in listening to discussion and lectures.

In terms of the two-way communications channel described in Chapter I, listening involves both a *transmitter* of a message and a *receiver* who hears, interprets, and understands this message. During the last decade, the nature of the listening process and its relation to learning have been the subject of formal investigation and application by educators, particularly in connection with the effectiveness of language laboratories, educational radio, and various instructional records, tapes, and transcriptions as pedagogical tools. This research has been especially concerned with the ways and means by which conditions may be established for improving a pupil's listening—and thus, learning—efficiency. As a result of this research and the applications of its findings, a pupil today may use a variety of newly developed audiolingual approaches in his study of a foreign language, and he may actually improve his *reading* skill merely by sitting quietly in the library *listening!* Some school libraries include recorded readings which are identical to the words in the accompanying books and, as the child listens to the story told by the narrator, he may follow the words printed in the book which he holds in his lap (Fig. 10.1). Further, in a modern science class, pupils may listen to a scientist broadcasting, via radio, instructions on how to assemble the parts of the wind anemometer which lie spread out before them on their laboratory benches. There are a variety of similar audiolearning techniques which are being used in schools with increasing frequency as expedient means of imparting information in an ever-expanding curriculum.

Yet, despite all this focused attention on instructional techniques by which to engage the pupil's auditory processes, little attention has been given to the

[1] Meriam Wilt, "A Study of Teacher Awareness of Listening as a Factor in Elementary Education," *Journal of Educational Research*, April, 1950, pp. 626–636.

Fig. 10.1. / These children are gaining sound practice in reading skills through listening.

equally important area of teaching the pupils themselves *how to listen* more efficiently. Indeed, in no other area of classroom experience is skill development as lacking as in pupil audition. C. Howard Watts, a consultant in management communications, cited research findings which clearly indicated the lack of listening ability among students. In one study conducted among college students, it was found that only a 25-percent listening efficiency resulted when students were exposed to a 10-minute talk. The average person spends about 9 percent of his time writing, 16 percent reading, and 30 percent talking; he spends the bulk of his remaining time listening; yet, of this remainder, only about one fourth of what the person hears makes any sort of impression. Watts attributes this to lack of training in listening skills.

Reading skills are taught and developed regularly from the first grade through the beginning college years. Skills in spelling and writing are taught equally as comprehensively. Listening skills—as they are commonly referred to —receive no such focused attention, however. Certainly, if we are to continue to rely heavily on the pupil's listening faculty in communicating instructional content—and to develop an increasing number and variety of audioinstructional materials—we should devote more teaching time to developing these listening skills.

☐ DEVELOPING AUDIOLEARNING SKILLS

The teacher who wishes to improve audiolearning skills should first understand the nature of the hearing-listening-understanding sequence that is in-

Fig. 10.2. / The listening-learning process. (Adapted from Stanford E. Taylor, *Listening*, Department of Classroom Teachers, American Educational Research Association, National Education Association, 1964.)

volved in audiolearning. Learning from auditory experience is actually more complex than one would think. The mere presentation of audible words and sounds to a pupil is no guarantee that he will achieve the desired learning goals —nor even that he will hear the material presented. Our ears take in much audible information from our environment at every moment, yet we do not "hear" all of these sensory impressions. Indeed, if we were aware of every sound that our ears sense, our world would be an incomprehensible hodgepodge of noise. Thus, those sounds of which we are *aware* at any given moment are the result of auditory discrimination. This is accomplished quite without our knowing it as the result of autonomic response mechanisms in our brains which have been trained in selection of information by our learning to discriminate from among the various sounds taken in from the environment. For example, most people are familiar with the experience of being so concentrated in giving attention to something, that they did not "hear" someone speaking to them. Perhaps an even more familiar experience is that of being annoyed by, and therefore consciously disregarding, an unpleasant or tedious sound which we wish not to hear. Both types of experience are indicative of the complexities involved in audition, a basic factor which affects listening and thus also the efficiency of audiolearning.

■ THE AUDIOLEARNING SEQUENCE

While the scope of audition is too broad and too deep for comprehensive treatment in this chapter, we shall trace in broad strokes the basic sequence through which the learner must pass if he is to achieve audiolearning. First, if the pupil is to hear the instructional message, the message itself must be audible to the normal ear. Also necessary, of course, is that the learner is able to hear the message; that is, his own hearing mechanism must be capable of responding to vibrations that fall within the normal human range of audibility. The sensory impressions taken in through this mechanism must then be transmitted to the pupil's cognitive awareness.

Next, the learner must *listen* to the message. It is possible to hear—that is, to be aware of—a sound without *attending* to that sound. This is particularly true in the case of word sounds which require attention if the subtle syllabic

Fig. 10.3. / Audiometer tests are usually given to school children periodically by the school's speech and hearing specialists.

differences are to be distinguished and the intended message is to be received. Finally, if the communication is to be complete, the learner must be able to *act* as a direct result of the audiolearning; that is, the learned information must create in the learner an ability to demonstrate the learned information (Fig. 10.2).

■ THE LEARNER MUST HEAR

Basically, hearing may be thought of as the physical response of the ear to sound vibrations. In this sense, not all learners hear with normal acuity; it is estimated that 5 percent or more of the school population suffers hearing losses which may interfere with audiolearning. Obviously, those pupils whose auditory mechanism is impaired cannot be expected to profit completely from audioinstructional materials. Thus, the teacher's first responsibility is to determine whether all of his pupils can actually hear sounds which are within the normal ranges of volume and pitch, and which, if any, pupils exhibit difficulty in this area. Auditory sensitivity can be measured objectively by the speech and hearing specialists who are employed in most school systems (Fig. 10.3). If the behavior or performance of a pupil creates doubt that his hearing is physiologically normal, the teacher should refer the child for appropriate therapy or remedial measures.

Even when the physiological aspects of hearing are normal, however, some pupils may seem to exhibit a pathological hearing defect for psychological or psychoneurological reasons. A pupil may have become so accustomed to "tuning out" unwanted noise, for example, that he virtually doesn't hear otherwise audible information. Often this tuning out is so habitual that the pupil himself is unaware of doing it, and though he may want to please by listening and remembering the audioinstructional message, he is unable to control his listening activities. To illustrate by a somewhat extreme, but all too frequent, situation, if a child has been raised in a noisy home—perhaps one in which the parents are prone to raising their voices in anger at him or at each other—he may have adapted at an early age to this environment by shutting out this noise. Of course, a disinterested pupil may deliberately or semideliberately tune out unwanted hearing experiences. This may be a temporary adaptation to tedious or seemingly irrelevant content from the pupil's point of view, or perhaps the result of distraction by some competing sound. As pointed out in Chapter II, a pupil who does not seem to hear may be attending to introspective thoughts or fantasy and thus shuts out the learning message. Rather than view such pupils with negativism, the teacher should give some thought to specific development of their listening skills. Of primary importance to such training is the nature of the subject matter itself—which should be both interesting and relevant to the pupils—as well as to its method of presentation.

In classroom situations where audioinstructional techniques are relied upon excessively, fatigue may interfere with the pupils' hearing. Here again, the pupils may "tune out" the educational communication. Fatigue is apt to occur when teachers rely endlessly on spoken direction, lecturing, prolonged or tedious class discussion, or oral reading of lengthy passages or sequences which could better be left for the students to read individually. Such excessive reliance on the student's hearing faculty will exhaust even the most conscientious student, a factor which should be recognized by teachers to the same extent that it is recognized with respect to excessive *physical* exercise. *The alternative is to arrange a classroom schedule which utilizes various audiovisual techniques and thus permits multisensory learning.*

There are many other factors which can obstruct pupil hearing. Extraneous environmental noises, for example, can strongly interfere with the audibility of the instructional message. Noises which emanate into the classroom from out-of-doors can be disruptive: Drilling and other building-construction sounds, heavy traffic noises, the noise from school playground activities, and so forth often can interfere with audiolearning. Similarly, sounds generated within the classroom itself—perhaps due to poor discipline habits among the class members—can provide highly effective competition to audioinstruction.

Such noises need not be extreme to affect at least some of the pupils' auditory faculties, and the teacher should not ignore extraneous noises of seemingly low volume as potential learning interference merely because he himself is not dis-

Fig. 10.4. / This modern classroom has been equipped especially for audiolearning efficiency. What are some of the features in this example which are conducive to good listening?

turbed by them. It may be that the teacher has become so used to such noises that he has learned automatically to sift them from his awareness, or it may be that his powers of concentration are such as to screen out extraneous sounds. The same may not be true of his pupils.

The degree to which pupils are affected by extraneous noise will vary, not only according to the volume of the noise itself, but also according to the pupils' individual *sensitivity* to the nature and volume levels of the noise, and according to the individual concentration and auditory-discrimination habits of the pupils. Some children may find it easier to shut out the lesson in favor of attending to the interfering noise. Significantly, even annoying or bothersome noises may enable the student to discriminate *against* the audioinstruction.

Another important deterrent to some forms of audiolearning derives from the acoustical situation that exists in the classroom. If the acoustics in the room are such as to create an echo or reverberation of the sounds being communicated, or if the sound is overabsorbed so that it does not reach the student's ear with full impact, audiolearning will be impaired. Thus, even when extraneous noises are not present, audioinstruction will be ineffective in an acoustically inadequate classroom.

To overcome these physical barriers to hearing, the teacher should see to it that the classroom effectively keeps out annoying extraneous noises and, at the same time, provides a good acoustical environment. Excessive reverberating noise within one's own classroom may be overcome by tacking monkscloth or colored display burlap panels neatly across the offending surface; for example, the backwall. This not only traps sounds but offers more pinup display area for student work. With the principal's consent, the janitor and a few competent students can install "do-it-yourself" acoustical tile on the wall surfaces above the chalkboards, an area most frequently the cause of annoying classroom acoustics. In new buildings specified to provide good acoustics, a polite complaint to the principal may secure corrective measures by the contractor. The key idea is to be aware of such problem acoustics and call attention to the fact that instruction can be improved by corrective measures.

■ The Learner Must Listen

Just as it is possible to screen out from one's awareness all of the sounds picked up by his auditory sense, it is possible to *hear* sounds without heeding or responding to them. Teachers are familiar with students who look alert and attentive during class discussion, and who respond when called upon, yet whose quickly adlibbed responses indicate all too clearly that they have not paid attention, or *listened,* to the substance of the discussion itself.

For true audiolearning to be achieved, it is important for the pupil to do more than just follow the thread of the information being communicated, he must become *actively* involved in the information itself—he must think about it, analyze its meaning, organize and reorganize its content elements into his existing frame of reference and, where appropriate, act. If this degree of listening participation in audioinstruction is to be attained, several conditions must coexist: The audioinstructional content must be interesting, provocative, and suitable to the pupils' level of background experience, and the audible messages must be clear and distinct so as to make full impact on the pupil's auditory faculty.

There are many ways by which the teacher can create favorable listening conditions. First, the teacher should arrange the classroom itself so that it is conducive to listening (Fig. 10.4). In addition, if the learning experience is to focus on audioinstruction, any visual materials that are used should be introduced with systematic care or, if the learning experience is to be both visual *and* auditory, illustrations or reading materials should include only those most immedi-

Fig. 10.5. / Recent innovations in audiolearning equipment make it possible for teachers to communicate with individual pupils or with the entire class. How does this factor help the teacher in evaluating audiolearning efficiency?

ately relevant to the specific content under study. Seating should be so arranged as to focus attention on the source of the audioinstruction.

If attentive listening is to be accomplished, the nature of the aural message must be such that the learner will be interested enough to become involved with, and to react to, the material spoken or played. Of primary importance here is that the audioinstructional material be selected in terms of the maturity of the learners and their interests, vocabulary level, and *their need for the audioexperience itself.*[2]

It is futile for the teacher constantly to enjoin pupils to "be alert," "listen carefully," and "pay attention" to listening exercises unless previous teacher-pupil planning has encouraged in them a *desire* to listen and a willingness to investigate audiolearning experiences. The alternative is to arrange experiences which answer questions relating to teacher-pupil planning. When readiness occurs and audiolearning materials are appropriately selected, the chances that pupils will want to listen and to react to listening experiences will be enhanced.

On the other hand, epitomizing the consequences of failing to provide interesting, suitable, and clearly presented material is the illustration cited by Dale, in which one student advises another, "In that lecture room you can't hear Professor X beyond the fifth row. So don't sit any closer than the sixth."[3]

Of considerable value in motivating students to listen is to involve them in activities which are preliminary to the audiolearning experience itself. This may be achieved through pupil-teacher planning carried on before the beginning of the audioinstruction. If possible, the pupils should have a voice in the selection of the materials; this will provide them with the opportunity of realizing their own responsibilities with respect to audiolearning generally, and of understand-

2 See Louis Shores, *Instructional Materials,* Ronald Press, 1960.
3 Edgar Dale, "Why Don't We Listen?" *The Newsletter,* February, 1957.

ing thoroughly the purposes of the specific audiolearning experience. Also helpful are the positive experiences gained from past audiolearning experiences. From such past experiences, students are more likely to know that the dramatic recording or verbal demonstration is apt to be interesting and helpful to them.

■ THE LEARNER MUST ACT

If audiolearning is to be complete, the pupils must not only be able to hear the message and be willing to listen attentively, they must also be capable of demonstrating or applying their newly acquired knowledge (Fig. 10.5). Typically, the avenues by which the pupil is asked to demonstrate this learning is through tests and examinations, pupil reports and essays, classroom discussion "feedback," and similar situations. However, these avenues provide the pupil with little opportunity to exhibit creative involvement with, and expressive use of, his learning and, as stressed earlier, creativity is a most important outcome of any learning. Thus, creative response is the goal of listening-learning activities just as it is of other classroom learning activities. Effective teachers will complete the successful audiolearning situation by encouraging this creativity. A few suggestions from the teacher may stimulate the pupils to carry out one or more of these suggestions or, better, to invent a creative project on their own.

Creative response to audiolearning experience may include the search for further information, the composition of an original mural, the simulation of a radio or television broadcast, or the performance of a dramatized episode in history. The learning achieved through language-laboratory audioinstruction may be demonstrated through such projects as dramatic improvisations—spoken in the language—of humorous situations, a debate carried out in the learned language between two groups from the class, and so forth. It should be noted that there are often many ways in which the pupil can incorporate and express his *personal* interests and experiences within the context of the learned material, and whenever possible, he should be encouraged to do so.

■ IMPROVING LISTENING SKILLS

Listening is a skill which responds well to developmental guidance, and it is possible to provide training by which the pupils may improve their skills in listening for central ideas, details, inferences, following directions, etc. This training can be carried out within the context of many subject areas; for example, in foreign languages, English, literature, and the social studies. The degree to which the teacher can instill among the pupils the motivation to become better listeners is of real importance in improving these skills, but as indicated earlier in the chapter, the physiological hearing ability of each pupil should be known, and mechanical hearing aids provided in extreme cases of hearing pathology. For those with lesser degrees of impaired hearing, and for those whose inability to hear instructional content seems to be due primarily to pyschological adaptation, pupils may be grouped for special instruction. In many cases, conditions may be improved simply by changes in seating.

Fig. 10.6. / In listening-skill development activities, it is important that the student focus his attention on improving his listening processes rather than on learning the subject matter for its own sake. List three factors implied in this situation which are conducive to listening-skill development.

■ Presenting Skill-Training Situations

Skill in listening is usually the result of the pupil's own interest in developing better listening habits, and of their understanding of effective listening methods. The manner in which the teacher may assist in providing the physical setting for better listening has already been discussed, but if the pupil himself is going to take part in listening development, the teacher must begin by awakening the individual's awareness of his own listening process. The pupil's concentration on sounds and his *willingness* to concentrate may be developed and strengthened if the teacher describes the listening habits of such "expert" listeners as the court reporter, the news editor at the city desk, the telephone-order clerks in large department stores, and others. From this foundation of pupil awareness, concentration and willingness, listening skills can be developed through continued classroom practice.

Through pupil-teacher planning sessions, appropriate and interesting recordings should be selected for listening practice. While the subject matter chosen for the listening experience may relate to classroom study units, the teacher should bear in mind that the goal of these practice periods is *listening skill* rather than subject-matter learning, and thus, the materials chosen should be especially geared to pupil interests (Fig. 10.6). In other words, if inefficient learning of regular instructional content is in part due to poor learning skills, it may be wise at first to choose listening-training materials that do not focus on this content. Later, when the pupils have better coordination of the auditory and mental processes, listening practice and content learning may be achieved simultaneously.

In providing listening-skill instruction, the teacher should encourage pupils to record and index—either mentally or in written form—every fact or impression they think is important. It should be made clear to the listeners that they can think much faster than a speaker can talk, and thus, they have ample time to consider what they hear, and to reject, rearrange, or select the information according to what seems meaningful and useful to them. Before the actual listening experience begins, the teacher may demonstrate how to record and index useful points of information, and provide some initial guidance of the kinds of information to be listened for. For example, the home-economics teacher may ask her listeners to organize and to record in number and word

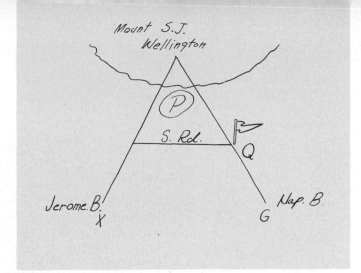

Fig. 10.7. / One way to increase listening efficiency is to visualize key ideas through sketches or "doodles" such as this one. Such "doodling" should therefore be kept simple enough so as not to interfere with listening.

form the important points in her oral description of the nature and quantity of cooking ingredients. The English-literature teacher may instruct pupils to record the names of key characters in a short story or dramatic reading as it is read aloud or presented on tape, and to classify these characters according to their relationships to one another and to the action sequence. The algebra teacher may read several equations or problems aloud, asking his students to record them on paper in symbolic form.

Depending on the subject matter involved, meaningful "doodling"—sketching symbols and diagrams, etc.—can help the pupil to visualize the concepts he hears explained, and the teacher should encourage the pupils to make these sketches as they listen. To illustrate, imagine that the following passage is being recited to you (as you listen use a device of your own choosing to record key information: listing facts, sketching or diagramming):

BATTLE OF WATERLOO

In order to get a clear idea of the Battle of Waterloo, we should imagine in our mind's eye a large capital letter A. The left leg of the A is the road from a town called X. The right leg of the A is the road from a town called G. The crossbar of A is known as the "sunken road." At the top of the A is Mont St. Jean. Wellington is there. General Jerome Bonaparte is located at the lower left leg of the A. The right lower leg is where Napoleon Bonaparte is located. A little below the point where the crossbar of the A cuts the right leg is a town called Q. At this point the final battle word was spoken. Here the lion was placed, the symbol of the supreme heroism of the Imperial Guard.

The triangle formed at the top of the A by the two legs and the crossbar is the Plateau of Mont St. Jean. The struggle for this plateau was the whole of the battle. The wings of the two armies extended to the right and left of the two towns called X and G. Beyond the point of the A, beyond the Plateau of Mont St. Jean, is a large forest. As to the plain itself, we must imagine a vast, rolling country; each rolling hill commands the next; and these hills, rising toward Mont St. Jean, are bounded by a forest.

In order to visualize the various relationships presented in the narrations, and to keep separate in your mind all of the positions mentioned, you had to make a series of notes; perhaps you sketched a diagram. To what extent did your note or diagram compare with that shown in Fig. 10.7? Try this passage out on your friends or pupils, instructing them to make such doodles, and see how closely their sketches match that in Fig. 10.7.

Similarly, the history teacher may narrate a historical episode, asking that the listeners record along a time-line the major events and the principal personalities connected with them as they listen. The science teacher may instruct his pupils to diagram a physical process as he describes it orally. Other examples could be cited in virtually every subject-matter area. Such sketches and diagrams should be kept simple, however, and the act of "doodling" should not be permitted to interfere with listening attention.

■ EVALUATING SKILL-TRAINING SITUATIONS

Listening efficiency should be evaluated immediately after the aural experience. This evaluation may be made by means of a brief quiz composed of short-answer questions such as those that were made up for the passage quoted above:

QUESTIONS

1. What was the Battle of Waterloo a struggle for: (a) Mont St. Jean itself. (b) The forest of Mont St. Jean. (c) The Plateau of Mont St. Jean. (d) The town called Q. (e) The sunken road.
2. Which of the following words will not help your understanding of the battle? (a) Plateau. (b) Plain. (c) Involuntary. (d) Triangle.
3. What is the most direct route between Mont St. Jean and the town called Q? (a) Along the sunken road. (b) Across the plateau. (c) Along the right leg of the A. (d) Along the left leg of the A. (e) None of the preceding.
4. What natural advantage did Wellington hold over Napoleon at the Battle of Waterloo? (a) Superior heroism. (b) Superior concealment. (c) Superior know-how. (d) Superior altitude. (e) Superior initiative.
5. Whom did the author of the passage sympathize with? (a) Wellington. (b) Napoleon Bonaparte. (c) Jerome Bonaparte. (d) The Imperial Guard. (e) None of the above.
6. Which of the following phrases contributes nothing to your understanding of the battlefield of Waterloo? (a) The town called X. (b) The sunken road. (c) The Plateau of Mont St. Jean. (d) Supreme heroism. (e) The town called Q.
7. Where was Jerome Bonaparte? (a) At the point of the A. (b) In the closed triangle of the A. (c) Near the crossbar of the A. (d) At the left lower leg of the A. (e) At the right lower leg of the A.
8. Where is the town called A? (a) At the point of the A. (b) In the closed triangle of the A. (c) Near the crossbar of the A. (d) At the left lower leg of the A. (e) At the right lower leg of the A.
9. Where was the "sunken road"? (a) At the points of the A. (b) In the closed triangle of the A. (c) On the crossbar of the A. (d) At the left lower leg of the A. (e) At the right lower leg of the A.
10. Where is the Plateau of Mont St. Jean? (a) At the point of the A. (b) In the closed triangle of the A. (c) Near the crossbar of the A. (d) At the left lower leg of the A. (e) At the right lower leg of the A.

ANSWERS
1–c; 2–c; 3–c; 4–d; 5–e; 6–d; 7–d; 8–c; 9–c; 10–b

If the pupils were specifically requested to make notes, diagrams, or sketches, the outcomes of the listening experience can be evaluated by having pupils transfer these to the chalkboard and comparing their own notes and "doodles" with those of the other class members. The teacher may use the hidden-chalkboard technique, listing the points in the aural material of which the pupils should become aware during the listening experience, or drawing an appropriate sketch or diagram. When the listening experience is over, the teacher can then reveal the list or diagram, allowing the pupils to compare their own notes with those on the chalkboard. If the listening experience was composed of a set of directions, the pupils' listening skill can be measured by having them carry out these directions at the end of the listening period.

Listening outcomes should be evaluated in terms of both quantity and quality —that is, the sheer *number* of specific points accurately remembered from the listening experience, and the *nature, properties,* and *interrelationships* of these points as they occur in the content that was presented. For example, the child who recorded all or most of the names in a multicharacter story or drama, but who had not properly indexed the roles these characters play in relationship to one another and to the story plot, needs further skill development in the *qualitative* aspects of listening. Conversely, the child who recorded accurately the roles and relationships of only one or two characters needs further development in listening for *quantities* of information.

In providing listening-skill training, it is most important for the teacher to bear in mind that the primary purpose of the audiolearning activity is to improve pupil *listening,* rather than to impart subject matter *per se.* Learning the content of the audiolearning experience is thus secondary to listening skill development. Although both may be achieved at the same time, the child will not devote enough awareness to his listening habits, and to improving his listening ability, if emphasis is placed initially on the subject matter at the expense of the listening activity. Thus, the teacher who begins the class by emphasizing to the children the *listening* aspects of the learning situation, but who terminates the period by testing subject-matter learning only, fails in his purpose and confuses the pupils as well. In addition, the teacher should be sure that listening evaluation occurs immediately following the listening activity, and that its results, especially if obtained by means of written tests or essays, are presented to the pupils before the end of the same period. These results should make explicit to the pupil what *kinds* of information he failed to notice and what kinds of details he should attend to in further aural experiences. The final goal is to improve listening as one means of achieving greater cognition.

□ RECORDED AUDIOLEARNING EXPERIENCES

While there are many ways in which audiolearning experiences can be presented to pupils, much audioinstruction is provided in the form of educational recordings, which present information that has been electronically inscribed in such a way as to capture the original sound and preserve it for later use in classroom learning situations. Wherever appropriate and feasible, aural imagery is utilized, or at least included with the verbal information. Bells, thunder, paper rustling, and other sound effects are incorporated into dramatizations or read-

Fig. 10.8. / The meanings of printed words become very real when they are heard spoken by a professional actor.

ings and wherever else such real-life sounds can illustrate or amplify the meanings in the audiolearning content. Yet, even with verbal materials, the audiolearning experience can convey to the listener the mood embodied in, for example, the words of a poem or the feelings of a literary character as he speaks (Fig. 10.8).

■ TYPE OF RECORDING

■ DISK RECORDINGS

Although recordings made on magnetic tape have largely replaced disk recordings, the latter are still used widely. Long-playing records—or "LPs", as they are commonly called—and transcriptions are particularly well-suited for relatively short pieces of educational content, such as poetry readings; essays and short stories; brief, dramatized historical episodes; songs; and the like. To record such brief pieces on individual tapes would be to use magnetic tape uneconomically, and to record several such items on a single tape poses difficulties in locating individual selections. LPs which rotate at the rate of 45 revolutions per minute (rpm) usually hold anywhere from 5 to 8 minutes of recorded material on a single side, depending on the number of microgrooves engraved on the disk. LPs of 33⅓ rpm contain from 10 to 15 minutes of recorded information per side, depending on the number and spacing of microgrooves. These latter disks are

Fig. 10.9. / Record players such as these are well suited for classroom use; most machines can be played at several speeds.

particularly useful in some situations as several selections can be inscribed on one platter. The location of any one piece can be identified by its "band"—that is, the ring of microgrooves it occupies—in relation to the other bands on the side. Thus, "Side 1, Band 4" would indicate that the particular selection could be played by moving the phonograph needle to the fourth band of microgrooves in from the circumference of the record (Fig. 10.9).

Transcription is the technical term used to refer to professionally recorded disks that are not commercially available to the general consumer. Originally, transcriptions came into use for radio rebroadcasting purposes, before wire and magnetic tape recording processes had been sufficiently developed for these purposes. Transcriptions are generally larger—from 14 to 18 inches in diameter —than the 10- and 12-inch platters available commercially, and are recorded at speeds of 16, 33⅓, and 45 rpms. Transcriptions of 16 rpms are particularly widely used in schools today for "talking books," in which some of the current and classic titles in children's literature are recorded in their entirety.

■ MAGNETIC TAPE

Magnetic tape, however, offers by far the widest and most flexible medium for audiolearning materials, and few schools cannot count at least one tape recorder among its instructional equipment. While records and transcriptions erode or wear with use, and can be damaged permanently if scratched, tape-recorded material can be replayed for an indefinite time with little decrease in efficiency,

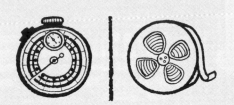

Table 10.1
UNINTERRUPTED RECORDING TIME FOR VARIOUS MAGNETIC TAPE SPEEDS AND TAPE LENGTHS

Reel Size	Tape Length	Tape Speed (inches per second)		
		1⅞	3¾	7½
5″	600′	1 hr.	30 min.	15 min.
5″	900′ᵃ	90 min.	45 min.	22½ min.
5″	1200′ᵃ	2 hr.	1 hr.	30 min.
7″	1200′	2 hr.	1 hr.	30 min.
7″	1800′ᵃ	3 hr.	90 min.	45 min.
7″	2400′ᵃ	4 hr.	2 hr.	90 min.
7″	3600′ᵃ	6 hr.	3 hr.	90 min.

Note: All recording times are computed on basis of single track only. For dual track recording, time is doubled.
ᵃ Special base extra long play.

and it is not easily damaged. If, through improper use, a tape is severed, stretched, or twisted, a simple home-splicing job can remedy the problem with only barely perceptible imperfections in the sound. Further if stored in their original container, tapes will not be affected by dust or atmospheric conditions which take a heavy toll of recorded disks.

Magnetic tape also has the advantage—so important in schools that have storage problems—of occupying a minimum of space. Tape-recorded materials are available in several speeds—1⅞, 3¾, and 7½ inches per second (ips)—and in several reel sizes—3, 5, and 7 inches. Thus, programs of varying length can be recorded on tape, no single reel occupying more than $7 \times 7 \times \frac{1}{2}$ inches of storage space. Examples of speed and time relationships currently available on 5- and 7-inch tapes are shown in Table 10.1, which gives the varying lengths of recorded time that tapes of various thicknesses will hold, depending on the recording speed used. It should be noted, however, that the quality of sound is affected by recording speed—the slower the speed the less fidelity in sound yield. Thus, for recordings which require faithful sound reproduction—as, for example, in musical material and language pronunciation—a faster speed of recording is desirable.

Among the major advantages that magnetic tape has over the recording disk is that a single, relatively inexpensive machine can be used both to record and to play back (Fig. 10.10). Thus, teachers can use professionally produced audiolearning material and can make their own recordings for class use on the same tape recorder. Tapes can be erased and rerecorded with equal ease, another decided advantage of taped audioinstructional materials. However, because magnetic tape can be erased accidentally and so easily, caution and attention are required lest expensive, professionally taped information be lost.

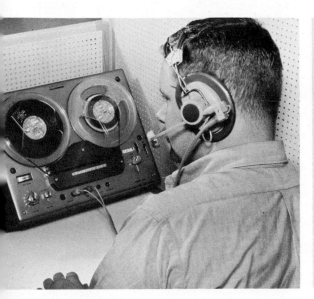 

Fig. 10.10. / Tape recorders are available in a wide variety of models, and can be used for a variety of purposes by both the teacher and the pupil. What are some of the teaching-learning goals that can be achieved by means of the tape recorder?

■ THE SCOPE AND CHARACTER OF EDUCATIONAL RECORDINGS

Most school subjects, particularly in the areas of language arts and social studies, are subjects of professional educational recordings. The social studies lend themselves admirably to recordings of historical reenactment through dramatization: the Landmark Records, the Enrichment Record series,[4] the "You Are There" series by Columbia, and "I Can Hear It Now" (1933 to the present) by Columbia Masterworks,[5] are examples. Because this last example deals with current history, these recordings bear the actual voices of famous personalities, recorded as they were during real-life situations: Roosevelt, MacArthur, Eisenhower, Kennedy, and many others have been immortalized in this way. Imagine the feelings of students in the 1970s who, as they study the causes and events leading to the outbreak of World War II and its aftermath, may hear the "live" voices of famous personalities in history explain important plans and events. The Enrichment Record series which presents dramatized events in American history, includes recordings with such titles as "Voyages of Columbus," "Landing of the Pilgrims," "California Gold Rush," "Riding the Pony Express," "The Louisiana Purchase," "George Washington Carver," "Building the First Continental Railroad," and "The Wright Brothers" (Fig. 10.11). For English-litera-

[4] Enrichment Teaching Materials and Landmark Records, Enrichment Landmark Records, New York, N.Y.
[5] Columbia Records, Educational Services, New York, N.Y.

Fig. 10.11. / Against a background of audio reenactment, these pupils envision the events in history as they come alive in their imagination. What independent study opportunities does this encompass?

Fig. 10.12. / The language laboratory is found increasingly in schools and colleges today. What are some of the advantages of the equipment shown in these classrooms?

ture courses, the creation of recorded readings, interviews with famous authors and poets, and interpretive readings of works whose authors are no longer living has become the accomplishment of the National Council of Teachers of English. Over the years, this agency's collection of recorded readings, interpretations, and dramatizations has grown to include hundreds of useful recordings and transcriptions. The plays of Shakespeare, the prose of American authors, ballads, and verses of the American frontier, all offer excitement and thrilling rewards both for teachers and pupils who incorporate their use into the stream of instruction in literature.[6] Readings by contemporary English-speaking authors and poets virtually bring the author into the classroom to read his own works and to indicate his own interpretations. Through the 16-rpm transcriptions mentioned earlier, complete novels now appear in aural form; "Sound Books" and "Talking Books" are examples (see Source List, pages 539–540). There are many other recordings devoted to the literature of different countries and cultures. For example, a good representation of American ballads is available in the album *America Listens,* put out by Scott-Foresman,[7] and "Haiku"—a recording of recitations made by an English-speaking student of the Haiku—presents an excellent English translation of several selections from this unique literary form.[8] A comparison of these two dramatically different expressions of cultural literature makes an excellent unit in high-school English courses and in social-studies classes as well.

Audioinstruction in foreign language represents a particularly widespread use of recorded materials. As will be discussed subsequently, the audiolingual approach to foreign-language education was developed during World War II. Originally, records and transcriptions were used to record lessons given by a native of the language or by an instructor whose pronunciation in the language was representative of native speakers. Today, while a few disk recordings are still available both in the field of education and commercially, taped materials comprise by far the largest resource for audiolingual instruction. Tape recordings permit a good deal of flexibility, as the same machine can be used to play the master tape, bearing the instructor's prerecorded voice, and to record and playback the student's attempts at imitation. In this way, both drill and self-evaluation are made possible for the student expediently and economically. Tape recordings are available at several levels and in many language areas, not only in the familiar languages of French, Spanish, German, etc., but also in a wide array of Asian and exotic languages ranging from Modern Russian and Greek to Thai, Swahili, and Tagalog. So effective have these audiolingual materials become that whole language laboratories have been built around them (Fig. 10.12). Because the language laboratory as an audioinstructional medium deserves special attention, we shall discuss it in more detail subsequently in this chapter.

Recorded materials comprise a flexible instrument of instruction. Today

---

6 See *Resources for the Teaching of English, 1964–1965,* the National Council of the Teachers of English.

7 *America Listens,* 33 rpm, Scott-Foresman,

8 *Haiku,* 33 rpm, Musical Engineering Association. In most cases, the teacher will do well to seek the assistance of the nearest reputable record dealer.

Fig. 10.13. / The language laboratory permits both teacher and pupil a great deal of flexibility during language courses. Examine the pupil control board and describe some of the activities permitted the pupil with such an arrangement.

teachers of most subjects are confronted with the possibility of varying the nature of instructional experiences by selecting the best of available prerecorded instructional material (see Source List, pages 539–540).

The preparation of educational recordings is now demanding the attention of publishing houses formerly concerned solely with the production of textbook materials as well as of record and tape producers. As a result, there are now available to schools carefully written, professionally produced recordings which can be "previewed" by the schools before purchase.

The present authors well remember when, as beginning teachers, they took it upon themselves to read aloud the poetry and prose included in high-school literature anthologies. Such effects cannot compare with interpretations available in recordings by experts.

□ THE LANGUAGE LABORATORY

The language laboratory is an electronic learning complex which enables the pupil to listen to the way words, phrases, and sentences are pronounced, inflected, and constructed by those whose native tongue a "foreign" language happens to be. The language laboratory is so constructed as to permit the student to imitate these pronunciations and inflections, and to record his attempts so that when he plays them back he can compare the sounds of his own speech with those of the original (Fig. 10.13). Thus, self-improvement through correction and practice proceeds with the learner developing both his hearing and his speech discrimination of the sounds of the language. The student also learns to associate sounds and the grammatical, syntactical, and idiomatic construction of sentences in this foreign language with those in his own tongue. Eventually the student gains the ability not only to say the foreign words well and to know their meanings, but also to *think directly* in the language. This electronic approach to language learning is known as the *audiolingual* method.

Audiolingual materials are developed on the assumption that language is a skill which is best learned through continual correct repetition. As a child, one imitates easily the sounds spoken by his parents, brothers, sisters, and companions. The small child doesn't "study" his native tongue, he imitates it until it has become an integral part of his speech. There are no speaking "lessons" for the young child, no formal discussions—rather, the child's language is a skill which is learned by continual imitation of the speaking models he hears. Significantly, this is true also in bilingual homes, where the child learns easily and automatically to think and speak with fluency in *two* languages.

By contrast, traditional methods in formal language instruction presented the pupil with mostly reading and writing materials: The student was asked to memorize the words and their spellings as given in his text vocabulary and to fill in the blanks and otherwise complete in writing the exercises given at the end of the text lesson. Along with this vocabulary, the student was presented with formal rules of grammar and the other explicit complexities involved in language. Consequently, too often the student who "mastered" the language— that is, who was able to pass the course examination—merely developed a relatively rapid translating ability; he would think in English and then translate these thoughts into the foreign language, or, when reading the foreign language, he would mentally translate the sentences into their English equivalents in order to gain meaning. In short, the product of this teaching approach found himself in the position of the Midwestern French major, who, after graduation and on a tour of France, wrote back the following post card: "Having a wonderful time, but so far haven't been able to locate any natives who speak 'French 205.' "

In the audiolingual system, the formal aspects of language—grammar, syntax, idiomatic expression, and so forth—and reading and writing are placed in a secondary position to the speech aspects of language. The pupil engaged in formal foreign-language learning as presented in the language laboratory goes through a process very much like that through which he learned to speak his native tongue, as the language laboratory presents him with speaking models to whose speech patterns he may accustom his own ear and whose speech patterns he may imitate.

The audiolingual method was developed during World War II, when the U.S. Army was faced with the need to train tens of thousands of personnel to understand and to speak the languages of countries where it set up military bases. Obviously, this training had to be accomplished quickly and effectively. Because traditional methods of language instruction required many years of formal study in order for any degree of language fluency to be achieved, the Army sought the assistance of the American Council of Learned Societies, which, at that time, was at work on developing methods of teaching the languages and dialects of remote and primitive societies which had no written form of expression. Out of this collaboration, the audiolingual approach evolved.

The acceptance of the new audiolingual approach has been gradual but remarkably universal. During the last decade the findings from a number of research studies have invariably established that the audiolingual approach does nothing to interfere with the later learning of reading and writing skills in the language techniques, and that it is highly effective in achieving, in far less time, the mastery and performance of spoken language.[9]

■ AUDIOLINGUAL PROGRAMS

In most school systems that have a language laboratory, a combination of the audiolingual and the traditional approaches to language instruction is used. In the language laboratory itself, tape-recording materials are provided for the pupil's audiolingual learning, while points of grammar, background, and explanatory information are learned during regular class periods. Language-laboratory activities generally comprise about 50 percent of course time or more, although this proportion will vary from school to school.

Preferably the laboratory should adjoin the classroom so that it will be accessi-

9 See Edward M. Stack, "The Keating Report—A Symposium, Laboratories: The Effectiveness Controversy," *The Modern Language Journal*, April, 1964.

Fig. 10.14. / Because many master tapes can be played simultaneously, one student may be studying German while, near by, others are studying French or Spanish.

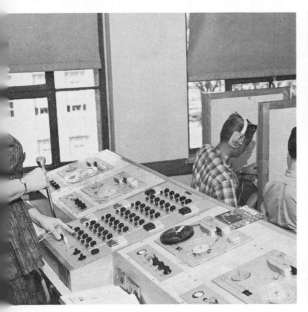

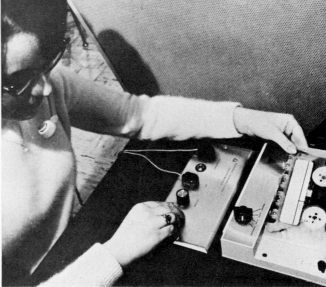

Fig. 10.15. / The control center of the language laboratory permits the teacher to instruct the class as a whole or individual pupils. Individual controls permit the pupil to listen to the master tape, to the classroom teacher's instructions, or to his own voice as he attempts to imitate the correct pronunciation.

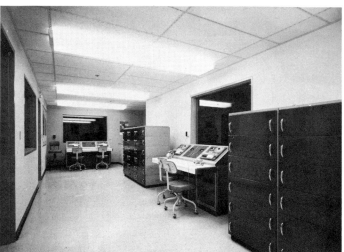

Fig. 10.16. / Hundreds of prerecorded language tapes lie in readiness here, and several may be played simultaneously merely by flicking the appropriate switches at the control board. Additional tapes are stored elsewhere and can easily be substituted for those in this complex of tape machines.

ble to students at the point in their learning when they can profit most from it; this does not mean, however, that part of the classroom itself cannot be used as the laboratory. The study of a language is a social experience; hence, if the classroom does contain the laboratory equipment, another area should be provided for group discussion, for it is essential that teacher and students discuss specific problems that arise in connection with this work.

There are many ways in which a language laboratory can be programmed (Fig. 10.14). *Programming* refers to the kinds of learning materials used, the methods of presenting information, the lesson content and sequence, drilling methods, and so forth. As a general rule, the pupils hear introductory explanations provided on the master tape and then the core of the lesson itself—the language words and phrases. There is then a short pause during which the pupil imitates what he has heard, his own voice being automatically recorded. At this point the teacher, who is at the control center, may have each student listen immediately to the model tape and then to the pupil's own version, thus allowing the pupil to judge his own pronunciation immediately and to correct it (Fig. 10.15). Usually these corrections require the student to repeat the model-imitation-playback-compare procedure several times, and sufficient time should be built into the program for him to do so.

However, while at first pupils in a language laboratory usually work as a group, with all pupils using the same taped lessons, the audiolingual method ideally encourages individual pupils to proceed as rapidly as they can. Since most language-laboratory systems make it possible for the teacher to tune in on an individual pupil, learners who are having special difficulties may be given special attention and drill. Thus, the programming should be flexible enough to accommodate the learning rates of both slow and fast learners. If such flexibility is built into audiolingual programs, the class may soon be strung out into various groups, each of which is proceeding at its own rate of learning, with some slow and fast learners working individually. Indeed, perhaps the greatest advantage of the audiolingual method is that it permits each pupil to proceed at his own pace.

Clearly, such programming requires the simultaneous use of several levels of instruction, and the effectively planned language-laboratory course will provide literally hundreds of prerecorded tapes (Fig. 10.16). Although complete prerecorded language courses are available at several levels of advancement, there are still many needs for which prerecorded materials are not available. For example, the pupils may require emphasized drill and practice in the pronunciation of certain vowels, consonants, diphthongs, or syllables, or in perfecting their inflection of certain phrases. In many of these cases, the teacher will need to plan and record his own materials and exercises. He may pattern these additional tapes on the material in the textbook being used, or record short pronunciation and enunciation drills based on sounds or idioms. For the children who are advancing more rapidly than others, he may tape lessons adapted from more advanced foreign-language source books. If the teacher gives the course another year, he may use most of these tapes again, but others may need to be revised or replaced. Constant improvement of his own prerecorded materials should be the teacher's goal.

The audiolingual program must also provide for class measurement and evaluation, and for supplementary and followup activities. During laboratory sessions, the teacher makes sure that the pupils are making the most of the taped lessons, and he tunes in on any of the pupils to check the progress and quality of the work being done. The teacher also determines, by means of periodic tests, how well the pupils know the meanings of the words, phrases, and sentences they have been listening to. But, interesting followup activities also should take place after the language-laboratory period. These may include conversational situations, games, and cultural drills that enable the students to try out their newly acquired language skills as a group.

There is more to learning a language than being able to speak, read, and write it, however, and understanding the sociocultural backgrounds of the language itself is an important part of language instruction. In providing for this aspect of foreign-language instruction, the role of related audiovisual materials should be considered. Films are available that depict sociocultural scenes in French Canada, Spain, Germany, and other countries. These films have foreign-language sound tracks that give most learners ample time to understand the language as it takes on concrete meaning from the visual presentation itself. Series of photographic slides as well as filmstrips with corresponding taped language narrations are also currently available from commercial sources and are widely used. These tapes carry words and simple dialogues between the characters shown on the filmstrips. This combination of prerecorded tapes and filmstrips offers great promise for efficient foreign-language instruction.

Fig. 10.17. / (Left) Projected visual materials are used to complete audiolingual experience. The visual experience provides for learning language within the context of people and place situations.

Fig. 10.18. / (Below) The language teacher uses the lab as a tool, putting into it either prerecorded or "self-created" tapes. As pupils respond, the teacher listens in to evaluate, explain or encourage as the need arises.

Fig. 10.19. / (Below) With the language laboratory, the teacher is freed from the strains of observing and helping 30 active pupils simultaneously. In what ways does this benefit both teaching and learning efficiency?

An experiment made among East-West Center students at the University of Hawaii revealed the value of coordinating audiolingual materials with specially prepared color slides.[10] The experiment included a group of Asian students who were attempting to improve their spoken English. A basic working vocabulary was incorporated into a tape-recorded narration suggesting how to move about the campus and city, how to use local transportation facilities, how to purchase food, clothing, and school supplies, how to enroll in courses, and how to carry on casual conversations with native fellow students. Visualizations of the settings to which the narration referred were presented through color photography projected on a screen at the front of the English-language laboratory. Participating students reported unanimously their enthusiasm and desire to continue more sophisticated learning experiences with languages in the same manner; namely, the coordination of words with context visualization (Fig. 10.17). Such an outcome is not surprising, as one learns his native language within a visual context.

Many teachers provide a visual environment by using travel posters and pictures of cities, people, and costumes in the country whose language is being studied. Typical folk songs can be brought into the foreign-language laboratory through prerecorded tapes as well as through transcriptions and records. Similar aural materials give students a chance to hear the works of well-known native composers. This use of recorded music makes a learner's interest in good music a powerful motivational device in foreign-language study.

The language laboratory, with its audiolingual and related visual materials, should not be thought of as a replacement for the teacher, but as a powerful tool which allows the pupil to hear language as it is spoken by native speakers and to engage in carefully controlled and recorded drills. When a person is learning to speak a language, he must practice speaking it correctly and, as has already been noted, the language laboratory encourages trial, evaluation by means of self-appraisal, and improvement through practice with a model tape.

Nevertheless, the teacher-pupil relationship of traditional language instruction is changed. In traditional language-class situations, one pupil may recite about once in 30 times, whereas a pupil in a language laboratory is listening about half the time and "reciting" the other half. Instead of 30 children listening to one teacher, the language-laboratory teacher can listen to one or all 30 pupils, each of whom is making individual judgments and responses (Fig. 10.18).

The language laboratory thus imposes exacting demands on pupils, because it places a constant challenge before them: Evaluation and reinforcement are immediate; there is no waiting until the next day while papers are being corrected. For the teacher, the strains of observing 30 pupils simultaneously, and of keeping all of them busy and interested while providing individual attention, are greatly reduced with the aid of a language laboratory (Fig. 10.19). It is through the language laboratory that pupils learn to associate learned skills with later classroom discussion and evaluation which only a qualified teacher can direct. The language laboratory is thus a teaching tool which, like most tools, is employed best by a skilled person—in this case, the teacher.

---

[10] W. A. Wittich, *Coordinated Use of Visualization in Audiolingual Learning*, University of Hawaii, 1963.

Fig. 10.20. / These pupils see and hear a Radio-vision broadcast as they prepare for their own creative art projects. What has this done to change the nature of traditional radio instruction? What other applications of this technique can you suggest?

☐ EDUCATIONAL RADIO

Another effective audiolearning tool is instructional radio. Radio may be thought of as an electronic carrier wave that provides the means of spanning great distances, bringing carefully planned audiolearning experiences into large cities as well as into rural classrooms. Radio is the means of bringing audiolearning experiences into classrooms where often related visual experiences may be coordinated with it.

Educational radio had its beginning in 1919, when, at the University of Wisconsin, state-owned station WHA began broadcasting. Today, vast areas of the United States can tune in on state and regional networks, and 293 educational radio stations provide instructional programming for school use. Typical of this development are the New York State's Empire School Broadcasting Service, the Indiana State School of the Air, the Wisconsin School of the Air, the Minnesota School Broadcast Service, and the Texas School of the Air. City facilities include carefully worked out curriculum-coordinated radio programs in such communities as Cleveland, Cincinnati, Los Angeles, St. Louis, New York City, Detroit, Chicago, Indianapolis, Omaha, Flint (Michigan), and a host of others. Contrary to belief, radio has not been engulfed by the wave of educational television materials and broadcasts, motion-picture materials, and related tools of instruction.

Radio instruction can—through the combined effect of voice, environmental sound, and music—capture the pupil's attention and arouse his imagination. Whereas educational television often provides whole courses, radio is seldom thought of as offering complete instruction, rather, it supplements the carefully planned day-to-day activities.

■ THE SCOPE AND NATURE OF RADIO

Through radio, master teaching—in such diverse fields as science, social studies, art, music, language arts, safety education, etc.—can provide enrichment both for the pupils and for the teacher. In addition to the specialized information—perhaps not otherwise available to the pupils—these master teachers provide the local teacher with effective models which often demonstrate new ideas and approaches to classroom procedures.

Educational radio is a living, changing thing. One recent innovation, for example, is to be found in the University of Wisconsin's newly established *radio-vision* project. Radio-vision is a way of combining the strengths of the expert radio teacher with those of the colored filmstrips that are sent in advance to participating local teachers. Individual filmstrip frames are projected in the local classroom at specified times during the radio program. Instructional examples and how-to-do-it explanations are made both verbally and visually to encourage listeners to proceed with their own creative efforts (Fig. 10.20). A corollary of radio-vision may be worked out by the classroom teacher who arranges in advance of the radio program an appropriate display of pictures

Fig. 10.21. / During or after the broadcast pupils actually try to assemble materials and do the experiments described. What opportunity does this provide for integrating radio into ongoing class instruction? Does this encourage creative followup activity?

which may be secured from periodicals or created by the students themselves.

The comments of teachers who have employed radio-vision reflect great enthusiasm for the combined use of the two media. It is felt that radio-vision coordinates the skill and creative imagination of a master teacher with the local classroom teacher's ability to apply his knowledge of the capacities, interests, and creative potential of the students with whom he works daily.[11]

Another example of how radio broadcast lessons can be coordinated into the local classroom use of related media is demonstrated in St. Louis, Missouri. In this city, radio science lessons are prepared by expert script writers in consultation with teachers and subject experts. As these broadcast programs proceed in the classroom, the teachers assemble the simple science paraphernalia referred to during the broadcasts. The lessons anticipate classroom pupil participation (Fig. 10.21).

This method can be adapted for other subjects with ease. Before a social-studies broadcast on the southwestern states, for example, photographs of the area would be assembled and arranged as a learning display: Specimens, manufactured objects, or agricultural items could be included, and maps of the area would be displayed for reference during the broadcast. Similarly, in anticipation of a broadcast on soil erosion, specimens of sandy loam, clay, or alluvial silt would be gathered and arranged in a tray, so that the students could examine the specimens during or after the broadcast.

Radio broadcasts are also provided for English classes. In addition to dramatic renditions and readings in classic literature, essay and story-writing instruction is provided by many educational radio stations. An example of such a broadcast is the WHA language-arts series, "Let's Write." Week after week, a master teacher, Mauree Applegate, presents examples and illustrations of good written reports which challenge the creative writing efforts of thousands of pupils who work in hundreds of remote classrooms.

■ THE ADVANTAGES OF EDUCATIONAL RADIO

Modern radio broadcasting is a carefully planned audiolearning experience which represents resources beyond those that are usually available in the local classroom. Lessons are usually prepared under the supervision of excellent teachers, radio program specialists, and subject authorities who work directly with a professional radio writer. Radio at its best is the result of mutual planning in terms of both the needs of the classroom and the characteristics of the radio medium:

[11] James Schwalbach, *Let's Draw* (29th ed.), Radio Hall, University of Wisconsin, 1965.

1. *Educational radio broadcasts provide "listening participation" in current history.* "You are there with radio" is more than a slogan. It represents the way in which classroom radio serves to bring special events from the source immediately into the classroom. The launching of the rockets which carried the first space platform into orbit, an interview with a scientist-engineer from the platform of an oil rig, an "on-the-spot" report spoken by an oceanographer who has just emerged from his ocean-floor laboratory—all these represent the unique contribution of classroom radio.

Daily or weekly radio news commentaries (not to be confused with spot newscasts) are designed to interpret the historical or social backgrounds—often omitted in regular news reports—which underlie current events. When a qualified geographer-historian, for example, interprets the causes that underlie an earthquake or a volcanic eruption, the learning which results is often far more significant than the reported news.

2. *School broadcasts are effective means of presenting music for its studied appreciation.* Educational radio broadcasters can arrange for skilled performers to participate in programs that are planned around musical themes which relate to other subjects: the music of other times, other lands, etc. The "Civic Orchestra Concerts"—sponsored by the New York State Empire Network—and "Music Time in Rhythms and Games"—from the Wisconsin School of the Air— are examples of similar music-appreciation broadcasts scheduled in various parts of the country. One such program, "Let's Sing"—in which representatives assemble annually to conduct a song festival—attracts an audience of nearly 100,000 students per year.

3. *School radio broadcasts are actually team-teaching demonstrations.* Because the production of a radio-broadcast series grows out of months of planning and consultation with local classroom teachers and other specialists, the educational radio program represents the combined efforts of the best human resources. Subject supervisors, classroom teachers, and subject-matter experts plan and work together to determine what learning situations can be accomplished through an aural presentation. A qualified radio writer then creates the broadcast script, incorporating the suggested subject content, curriculum validity, and teaching methods that have arisen out of the team planning.

4. *Well-planned radio broadcasts enlist the participation of the local teacher.* Well-planned radio broadcasts are presented in such a way as to engage the active participation of the local teacher and pupils. A radio lesson handbook— which describes the program content, local classroom pupil responsibilities, and the materials that should be on hand when the broadcast is to begin—is usually prepared and distributed to participating teachers long before broadcast time.

Preliminary study and discussion by the class is encouraged. Suggestions for these activities are included in these manuals. Whenever possible, programs include experiments or activities which encourage pupil participation during the broadcast or immediately following it. The class is also encouraged through broadcast suggestions to carry on a followup discussion, projects, or creative activities.

Followup activities may include simple research investigations in the library, reference to related film or filmstrip explanations, or related experimentation.

Fig. 10.22. / Where listening experiences which provide valuable source information in their own right are preceded, accompanied, or followed by related and appropriate sensory experiences—e.g., films, filmstrips, or slides—even more effective learning may result.

5. Radio instructional programs are available on tape. Teachers who work outside of educational broadcast-reception areas now have the opportunity of procuring, in tape-recorded form, "the best of educational radio." Many universities and colleges—Minnesota, Michigan, Illinois, Utah, and Iowa, among others—conduct annual reviews of the current educational program series, and select for tape-recording and subsequent distribution to teachers everywhere, the best in the subjects broadcast. Annotated descriptions of these tape recordings are available in catalogue form (see Source List, pages 542–543).[12] Teachers can rent tapes at a very low cost—usually fifty cents per fifteen minute program—or in many cases, they can send in blank tapes on which the materials they choose are recorded.

☐ SELECTING AND USING AUDIOLEARNING EXPERIENCES

There are several important procedures that should be followed in selecting audiolearning experiences. First, the teacher should, whenever possible, audition the material before using it. Although this is difficult in the case of radio, radio broadcasts are usually announced well in advance and are described in broadcast study manuals or summaries. When they are not sent automatically to the teacher, they are available on request from the broadcasting station.

In general, audio materials should be judged on the basis of educational quality. The audiolearning experience should be presented in an interesting, well-organized manner and the content should be authentic. As with all learning materials, the record, tape, or radio program should be appropriate to the age level of the group that will listen to it. In short, the audiolearning experience should make a real contribution that will be useful and effective in realizing learning goals.

When possible, the teacher should select materials that are accompanied by suggestions for use. In the case of the recording, such suggestions are usually in printed form. In the case of the radio broadcast, study helps are often part of the broadcast itself; however, these may be included in a radio manual. In some cases scripts may be secured in advance so that the teacher can plan more effectively.

If related audiovisual materials are available or suggested for use, the teacher should have available in the classroom, during or after the broadcast or record-

[12] For example, *The National Tape Recording Catalogue*, Department of Audiovisual Instruction, National Education Association, is a master catalogue which lists hundreds of taped radio programs in such fields as science, arithmetic, creative writing, art, and music.

ing, all materials—films, slides, objects, specimens, maps, etc.—which will help children more completely to understand concepts developed during the audiolearning experience (Fig. 10.22).

After he has investigated the program or recording, the teacher should select only those that provide valuable and needed experiences; in other words, a teacher should never feel obliged to use a broadcast just because it is scheduled, or a record or tape just because it is handy. Once a program has been selected, the teacher should assume definite responsibility for its carefully planned use in the classroom.

The appearance of the language laboratory, radio, records, and tape recordings, brings with it the responsibility of selecting suitable equipment. Furthermore, the equipment must be maintained in good condition and must be available to the teachers at the time they need it. Whereas the teacher is most interested in the use aspects of the equipment, the audiovisual supervisor and administrator are interested in its mechanical excellence and cost. Wherever possible the advice and suggestions of local authorized dealers should be sought. It is particularly desirable for teachers, administrators, and dealers to consult one another in this day when the nature of and use potentialities of equipment becomes more and more complicated. The day-by-day use of radio or recordings imposes definite utilization responsibilities on the teacher, which, when met properly, yield positive results in terms of increased interest and efficiency of learning.

☐ EVALUATING AUDIOLEARNING EXPERIENCES

The use of audiolearning materials in teaching is justified only when greater reality, interest, vividness, authenticity, and learning result because of them. Similarly, in each area of school work, aural materials must be evaluated in terms of learning outcomes. In evaluating learning outcomes, however, the teacher should bear in mind the many factors which can affect learning.

For example, the child who is working as a member of a committee to reconstruct the model of the Conestoga wagons used during the days of the westward expansion may need to supplement his listening experiences with the visual study of plans and diagrams which relate to the means of transportation used during this period. Conversely, the pupil who is assigned to write a short story cannot be expected to be very creative unless he first has the opportunity of listening to many short stories from which he can develop a sense of word rhythm, sentence patterns, etc., that will guide his own craftsmanship of word selection, description, and plot development, etc. In short, a child cannot be expected to be creative out of nothing, and the avenues of aural experience should not be overlooked as providing foundations for *creative* response. Thus, it is desirable that—following a broadcast or recorded learning experience— both the teacher and pupil evaluate how effectively these foundations have been acquired through the audiolearning situation:

FOR THE TEACHER

1. Did the audio material provide learning experience which could not have been provided more easily with traditional materials?

2. Am I acquainted with all the sources of audio materials in my subject area?
3. Did I carefully preaudit the material I used?
4. Did I give attention to such factors as acoustics, seating arrangement, location of the speaker, and volume, while the class was listening?
5. Did I adequately prepare students for this listening activity by:
   a. outlining vocabulary problems?
   b. helping them to know what they were to accomplish?
   c. encouraging discussion in which they could show their interest?
6. Did I encourage creative followup activities such as discussion and self-evaluation through testing?
7. Did I encourage creative followup activities such as creative simple research, art expression, dramatic expression, etc.?

For the Pupil

1. Could I hear well enough to understand the material?
2. Did I know what I was to do before I began to listen?
3. Did I contribute any ideas during the discussion?
4. Did I help plan followup activities?
5. Did I initiate original reports, dialogues, dramatizations, or other creative projects that incorporated my new-found information?

□ SUMMARY

While the predominant means of communicating information in the classroom is through verbal and other sounds which are mechanically or orally produced, little or no attention is paid to the development of *listening* skills as such. There are many practical ways through which the teacher can improve listening skills: arranging the classroom as a good listening environment, helping learners gain skill in listening through listening-learning activities which emphasize organization of ideas, recognition of sequential information points, and charting a diagram, to mention only a few. The teacher should continually be alert to the possibility that some pupils may not hear well because of seating, acoustics, extraneous noise, or physiological defects, and should correct such situations.

Many excellent audiolearning materials exist which when selected and used properly will not only provide interesting and useful learning experiences, but will lessen the overuse of verbal communication. Effective audiolearning materials are now available in a variety of forms and for practically all subject areas and grade levels: records, transcriptions, prerecorded tapes, audiolingual tapes, and educational radio broadcasts either live or taped. Audiolearning experiences can enrich instruction particularly when used with related visual materials—films, slides, filmstrips, etc.

Regardless of the type of audiolearning materials used, good listening carries with it certain responsibilities for the teacher. He should select materials on the basis of their real contribution to learning. He must prepare learners for effective listening by helping them to create interest in the material. He should recognize and remove any barriers to successful listening. He should provide the best possible physical conditions for listening (seating arrangement, equipment, etc.) and he should arrange for evaluation and creative followup activities.

As awareness about audiolearning materials increases, and as assurance is gained in using these materials effectively, the capability of these materials to enrich classroom learning environments will be realized.

☐ Suggested Activities

1. Select from the Source List (pp. 539–540) a recording that would be appropriate for listening-skill training. Plan the listening-skill lesson in terms of:
   a. The points contained in the recording which pupils should acquire through good listening
   b. Any sketch or diagram which seems to be appropriate
   c. Instructions given to pupils before the listening experience
   d. Qualitative and quantitative listening evaluation methods
2. Discuss the relative educational advantages and disadvantages of the record or transcription accompanied by teaching and pupil guides (a) printed separately and (b) appearing on the disk itself.
3. Prepare an oral report based on a visit with a local audiovisual equipment dealer to examine the latest audio equipment.
4. Based on an interview with persons engaged in educational radio work, report on one of the following:
   a. The nearest sources of educational broadcast programs
   b. Where in the classroom radio may effectively be used
   c. Descriptions and listings of current classroom broadcasts
   d. Where equipment may be seen in use or on display (describe the equipment)
5. Investigate the means of recording current radio programs for future use in the classroom, and prepare a short oral report of your findings.
6. Plan to use a recorded audiolearning program in a specific teaching situation. Write a paper in which you explain the following:
   a. The characteristics of the recorded audiolearning experience which make it particularly useful as an audiolearning experience
   b. The teacher's responsibilities in using this particular recording effectively in the classroom
   c. The preparation and followup activities the teacher might provide the class in relation to the audiolearning experience
   d. How the listening environment should be arranged
7. Arrange to preview the film *To Speak with Friends,* a very fine explanation of the role of the language laboratory in teaching a foreign language. Since this film is cleared for television use, you may wish to arrange to have your local television station telecast it during Education Week or some other special event.

☐ Bibliography

Dale, Edgar, "Why Don't We Listen?", *The News Letter,* February, 1957.

Department of Audiovisual Instruction, *National Tape Recording Catalog,* National Education Association, 1966.

Hocking, Elton, "Language Laboratories and Language Learning," Monograph No. 2, Department of Audiovisual Instruction, National Education Association, 1964, 210 pp.

The National Council of the Teachers of English, *Resources for the Teaching of English,* 1964–1965.

Schwalback, James, *Let's Draw* (29th ed.), Radio Hall, University of Wisconsin, 1965.

Shores, Louis, *Instructional Materials,* Ronald Press, 1960.

Stack, Edward M., "The Keating Report—A Symposium, Laboratories: The Effectiveness Controversy," *The Modern Language Journal,* April, 1964.

Taylor, Stanford E., *Listening,* Department of Classroom Teachers, American Educational Research Association, National Education Association, Bull. No. 29, 1964.

Wilt, Miriam, "A Study Teacher Awareness of Listening as a Factor in Elementary Education," *Journal of Educational Research,* April, 1950, pp. 626–636.

TAPE RECORDER

The tape recorder is an electronic device which, when used creatively, can produce exciting and rewarding teaching-learning experiences for both teacher and pupil. The tape recorder can be used as a mechanical memory or as a sound mirror to reflect the sounds of pupils' oral efforts for immediate criticism and improvement. It can be an assistant teacher through which directions or instructions can be given to pupils while the human teacher is attending to other teaching tasks, or a visiting authority through which valuable information can be presented to individual pupils, small listening groups, or to a whole room full of learners. As discussed in the previous chapter, the range of subject matter available on prerecorded tape is almost limitless: foreign-language instruction; narrative or dramatized presentations in science, mathematics, literature, social studies, and music appreciation. To accommodate the use of these burgeoning taped materials, increasing numbers of "listening corners" or "alcoves" are becoming evident in classrooms and libraries from kindergarten to college-level school installations. Let us turn now to a sampling of some of the kinds of tape recording machines that are available for expedient use of these taped materials.

☐ TYPES OF CLASSROOM RECORDERS

Several kinds and combinations of audio recording devices are in use. As mentioned in Chapter X, originally, most recording had to be done on disk recorders which converted sound waves that were picked up by a microphone into grooves of various widths and depths; these grooves were then inscribed onto the surface of a plastic-coated disk or blank "record." When wire recorders made their appearance, they soon replaced the disk because of their greater flexibility and use. The wire recorder is a mechanical device that permits the instantaneous magnetic recording of sound on a long strand of fine wire which the machine automatically winds and unwinds on spools. Recording and playback of the material could be accomplished on the same machine and, when desired, the wire could be erased and rerecorded with ease.

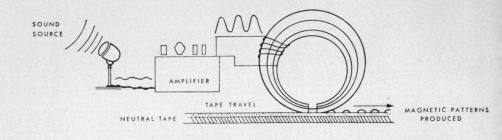

Fig. 11.1. / How your voice is recorded and played back on magnetic tape.

The wire recorder was soon replaced, in turn, by the magnetic tape recorder, which, as described earlier, has the same advantages over disk recorders that wire recorders did, but which eliminated many of the problems unique to wire recorders—for example the tendency for the wire to become tangled. As with wire recordings, tape recordings are made and replayed by magnetic means with the sound patterns magnetically encoded on a plastic, mylar, or paper tape that is coated with an iron oxide. In making a tape recording, sound waves are picked up by a microphone and instantaneously converted into a series of varying electrical impulses. These impulses travel to a small magnet which touches the moving ribbon of the metallic-coated tape. The coating receives and retains magnetic impressions of varying strength which correspond directly to the original impulses set up by the sound waves of voice or music (Fig. 11.1). The tape can be rewound and played back at once. The invisible magnetic impressions excite the magnetic head and create electrical impulses which, after being suitably amplified, activate the loud-speaker diaphragm to produce sound waves identical to those originally set up during recording.

Tape recordings can be used again and again. A reel of mylar tape may be run thousands of times without any visible evidence of wear or any decrease in the fidelity of the sound. If, on the other hand, an error has been made or the recording is no longer needed, the magnetic image can be erased in a matter of seconds. Erasing makes the tape magnetically neutral and the tape is then ready for immediate reuse for other recordings.

There are a deluge of models, types, and adaptations of the reel or cartridge types of tape recorder, which range in price from $15 up to hundreds and even thousands of dollars. The smaller and less expensive machines are likely to have only one or two recording speeds, but there are many speeds at which information can be recorded, the higher speeds being more suitable to faithful reproduction of tone. Some machines record two "tracks" of sound; others—which can be used for stereophonic reproduction—will record four tracks.

■ STEREOPHONIC RECORDING

Stereophonic recording is a process in which two or more microphones and loud-speakers are used so that the quality of the sound recorded and reproduced is close to that of the original. For example, in recording a school orchestra or a language-arts choral speaking group, two microphones may be used, each one recording only one important section of the entire group. Thus, as shown in Fig. 11.2, M1 (microphone 1) will pick up primarily the sound of the string choir and part of the percussion and the brass; M2 will record the sound of the

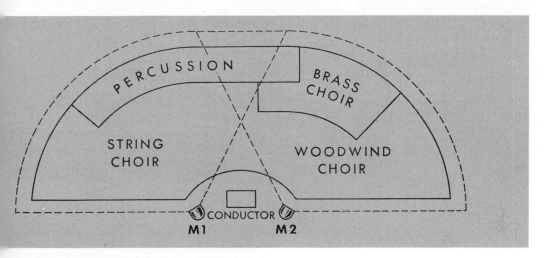

Fig. 11.2. / Stereophonic microphone placement depends on the size and characteristics of the classroom and the sound qualities to be recorded. The teacher should experiment until he finds the placement that produces the best results.

woodwinds, etc. The recording will be played back over a stereophonic tape playback, in which the sounds picked up by M1 are reproduced by one corresponding loudspeaker, and those picked up by M2 are reproduced by a second loud-speaker. In the playback, the relationship and emphasis of the sounds are reproduced so that the actual physical position, quality, and volume in the original performance are closely duplicated.

The listener is usually impressed by stereophonic recording because of the great "presence" or the lifelike quality in the sound reproduction it achieves. He can close his eyes and solely by listening identify sounds as to their type and location—and even change of location, if this has occurred. Listening to stereo recording is not only a remarkably aesthetic experience, but one that enhances audiolearning, particularly in cases where identification of location, emphasis, and relationship of sounds are important factors. Sound reproduction by tape is efficient in that it eliminates both surface noises and the noises due to mechanical sound reproduction techniques. Like tapes generally, stereo tapes are not subject to rapid deterioration and hence can be used over a long period of time.

■ THE LANGUAGE MASTER

With recorders that are used for most purposes, the recording and playback of material is more or less continuous on several hundreds of feet of tape. Separate

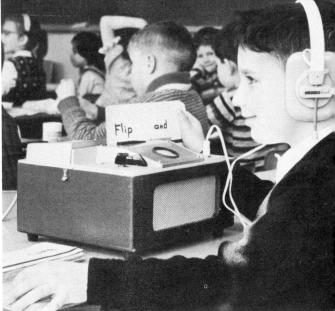

Fig. 11.3. / This machine presents words, pictures or symbols, and audible words or phrases identify them. What applications of this device can you describe for reading, language, etc.?

Fig. 11.4. / A major problem, finding materials which are suited exactly to the learning needs of the pupil, is overcome in this situation. What teaching uses can you think of for this device?

selections that are recorded on a single tape are indicated by pauses, announcements of the selection to come, and "timing tapes"—a nonrecording ribbon that can be spliced into the recording tape to separate two passages.

However, a modification of the continuous tape reel is the *Language Master,* which relies on a 2½- × 15-inch card (Fig. 11.3). Words, sentences, questions, symbols, or pictures may be written or printed on these cards, and to the lower portion of the same card, a short strip of recording tape is attached, providing a "sound track" to describe the printed material on the card. The student inserts a selected card into a slot on top of the recorder and the card automatically moves across a magnetic head. As the card moves slowly from right to left, the user hears his own or the instructor's voice reading or describing the visual material printed or pictured on the face of the card. The learning effect is one which combines the visual with the aural. The recording phase motivates the student to engage in active participation which helps to sustain interest.

To reinforce the "seeing" and "hearing" steps in this learning process, the student turns a "record" switch and repeats the materials which he has just seen and heard. The student's voice may be rerecorded in such manner as will allow him to replay his own response and then that of the "model" for comparison. If the student's performance is faulty, he can erase and record again—as in traditional tape-recording experiences—as many times as he wishes.

Preprinted and precoded card sets are now available in vocabulary building, words and picture, language stimulation, English-grammar development, pro-

Fig. 11.5. / Among widely used tape recorders available for classrooms are (left to right) Wollensak, Webcor, and Tandberg. During a sales demonstration, the teacher will want to ask questions about recording speeds, weight, service, microphone quality, tape duplicating, etc.

nunciation and phonics.[1] Blank cards are also available, making the device readily adaptable to many uses. Applications in teaching the meanings of symbols and vocabulary, modern math, chemistry, spelling, etc., should be explored by imaginative teachers. It is conceivable that the use of this device in the teaching of reading may reveal new pathways to skill mastery and comprehension. A teacher can write, draw, or even paste pictures on a blank card. By inserting the card in the machine, he can then record on the magnetic track the word or phrase describing the image, symbol, or word. His recording can't be erased unless he himself decides to change it. Pupils then play the "sound card" and are free to imitate and learn at their own pace (Fig. 11.4).

As the Language Master and other types of tape recorders continue to capture the imagination and enthusiasm of teacher, pupil, and manufacturer, the teacher may wonder which types of recorder will be the most useful and economical for his teaching purposes. One answer that applies to most electronic equipment is that quality merchandise must command a reasonable price. A current model which is simple to operate, rugged, and attractive should be purchased only after careful classroom try-out is arranged through a reputable audiovisual dealer. The teacher should ask for a demonstration in order to determine which recorder will be best for the type of use that is anticipated. Further, because even the best equipment frequently needs servicing, the availability of service and repair arrangements should be thoroughly explored, before purchase (Fig. 11.5).

[1] Bell and Howell.

Fig. 11.6. / For the teacher who finds his verbal suggestions more and more unheeded, the self-evaluation effects of listening to oneself via tape playback often brings about startling reactions. Why does this occur?

Fig. 11.7. / Once simple operating procedures are learned, the tape recorder becomes an instructional tool to which learners respond. What psychological factors may influence pupils in this kind of learning situation?

☐ USING THE TAPE RECORDER IN INSTRUCTION

In the hands of an imaginative and creative teacher, the tape recorder can be used in a surprising variety of ways to improve classroom learning. As the following case histories indicate, the tape recorder can be a modern day "genie" available at the beck and call of both learner and teacher.

Midway during their study of a unit on Hawaii, one group of fifth-graders wrote to a former exchange teacher who had returned to Oahu asking whether they might initiate a tape-recorded cultural exchange with their Hawaiian agemates. The answering letter promised to send a tape recording made by Hawaiian fifth-graders in response to one prepared by the mainland class. The initial excitement of the mainland pupils was followed by a more controlled planning period. Questions about school, home life, pets, dress, climate, and local customs were quickly formulated and then recorded on tape. The playback of this first effort came as a shock to the pupils.

"We can't send this!" exclaimed one student, "They'll get a bad impression of us!"

"We can do better—if we can't we shouldn't send it," suggested another pupil with disappointment.

The pupils' discouragement was small, however, and soon their enthusiasm mounted again as further discussion involved opinions on how ideas should be more clearly stated. Finally, several groups were formed to put on paper the key ideas they wanted to communicate to the Hawaiian class. These groups agreed that some tape time should be left for extemporaneous comment at the end. Three days elapsed during which writing, recording, and rerecording took place. Finally, when the pupils were satisfied, they mailed the tape reel.

"The students were very critical of their efforts," the teacher reported. "They set standards for themselves which they might not have accepted as reasonable had I suggested them" (Fig. 11.6). Here was an experience in self-criticism and improvement which had taken place through the trial and error made possible by the tape recorder's flexibility.

In another situation, a teacher of music who had tired of continually describing the problems of wavering pitch, finally got his point across to his pupils by recording, playing back, and encouraging self-evaluation by members of the student group. Similarly, a clever dramatic coach who had been unable to effect a change in the voice inflection of the ingénue of the senior play, arranged for her to listen to herself on tape. The student quickly "got the point," and immediately set about correcting the situation (Fig. 11.7).

In a large urban high school, the confusion and noise in the halls were reaching unwarranted levels. The student council decided to act. Quietly but with great effectiveness, they recorded typical hall and stairway noise while classes were changing. The recording was played back at the next meeting of the council and they were asked: "Do we want this in our school?" As a result, the recording was played at the next school assembly and the same question was asked. A month later another recording was made—the reduction in noise was amazing.

These examples are only barely indicative of the almost limitless uses to which

Fig. 11.8. / The classroom tape recorder can be put to many uses and is easily operated and maintained.

tape-recording devices can be put. Most machines are very easily operated and cared for, and under proper guidance, the pupils themselves can implement the principles of proper care and use described later in this chapter (Fig. 11.8). But, it is the teacher's task to provide the context in which the recorder is used and the specific purpose for which it is to be used. Thus, we shall turn to some of the ways the tape recorder can facilitate learning in different subject areas.

■ THE LANGUAGE ARTS

The value of hearing oneself as others do by means of tape recordings has already been suggested. This objective opportunity for self-criticism is valuable during the entire span of school experience. Its value first becomes apparent in the primary grades when the youngsters attempt to read aloud; when they engage in "Monday morning reports" of the weather, week-end activities, and events at home; and also when telephone-answering techniques are recorded and listened to.

In the upper grades, panel discussions, reports of books read, discussions of the news, explanations of processes, and how-to-do-it accounts continue to demonstrate the true importance of *being able to get up on one's feet and express one's ideas verbally in a clear and well-organized manner.*

Children too often become so accustomed to a teacher's admonitions about improving speech or grammar that such remarks are no longer incentives to improvement. But the tape-recorded "voice" played back frequently serves as a fresh new incentive. Errors of grammar and sentence structure and needless repetitions become painfully apparent when the child hears them committed in his own played-back voice.

"Do I sound like that? How can I have a better voice?"

"Do I talk that *fast*," "that *slowly*," or "with all those 'ah's,' 'er's,' and 'and-ah's'?"

When the students have these reactions to themselves and to each other, the teacher no longer needs to wear his own voice and his patience thin trying to drill suggestions for improvement into his pupils. The child is usually his own critic and this role is also played by his classmates.

As discussed at some length in the previous chapter, the tape recorder is also ideally suited to foreign-language instruction. Various specialized equipment has been devised for this usage of tape-recording techniques, including the large complexes of electronic equipment that comprise the language laboratory. Other applications of tape recorders include its use in speech improvement and therapy; listening-skill development as described in Chapter X; in reading improvement; and choral speaking and dramatics. In connection with dramatics, the drama coach should not restrict his use of the tape recorder to individual performance improvement, but should also use it to record entire scenes and acts, showing how each player relates to the whole, the timing of the lines, and so on.

■ SOCIAL STUDIES

A primary goal of the social studies is to provide experiences which are so life-like that they give the learner true understandings of people, places, and things throughout the world. The tape recorder makes possible the experience of listening to others as they express their ideas, and that of exchanging spoken ideas with others. For example, in one civics class, students were assigned to one of several committees, each committee being responsible for gathering information on one aspect of governmental control—public-school and adult education, fire and police protection, traffic control, recreation provisions and maintenance, sanitation and public health, and taxation and finance. In their planning sessions, each committee reviewed and decided upon the offices and personnel they would visit to gather their facts. Some members of the committee decided that by tape recording their interviews—later editing the tape to eliminate secondary information—they could, in effect, bring the government officials right into the classroom. The carrying out of these plans resulted in levels of effort and learning accomplishment seldom experienced through more traditional methods of teaching the same types of units.

The tape recorder also presents a challenge to those who are willing to undertake the research, writing, editing, rehearsal, and final production of "Reports from History." It is one thing to read passively the history-book reports of the Norman Invasion or the Battle of the Coral Sea, or the magazine accounts of our astronauts' first space walk. It is a more exciting project to reconstruct factual occurrences into dramatic, "on the spot" news accounts with background "color" narration of such quality as will hold the attention of the class group. The tape recorder is well suited to such projects, for it enables the students to test themselves and arrange for try-outs before presenting the finished product to the class. Pupil and teacher interest runs high in such projects (Fig. 11.9).

Other uses of the tape recorder in the social studies include historical interviews with local old-timers who remember all manner of interesting things, tape-exchange programs similar to that mentioned earlier, and recording for permanent possession in the school library tapes which other classes or schools have done on appropriate social-studies subjects. Further, group reports and discussions can become objects of self-criticism among the pupils. As class members listen to a taped discussion, the entire group can criticize themselves and one another.

■ MUSIC

In beginning band and orchestra work, the thrill of listening to themselves perform through tape-recording playback can be a great incentive to the pupils to listen, evaluate, and practice—all to the end of better performance. Recordings of individual vocal and instrumental performances, quartet and choral singing all allow the individual or group to listen, learn, and improve. Older pupils can carry on recording and playback activities independently.

Today many school music departments have tape recorders set up on which soloists can record their work, then listen and practice. This procedure places the responsibility on the learner and gives him the opportunity to advance as rapidly as he wishes (Fig. 11.10).

Fig. 11.9. / These photos have captured the pupils' candid reactions to the use of the tape recorder during their own creative efforts to record and playback a short dramatization they wrote. What desirable learning outcomes seem to be present?

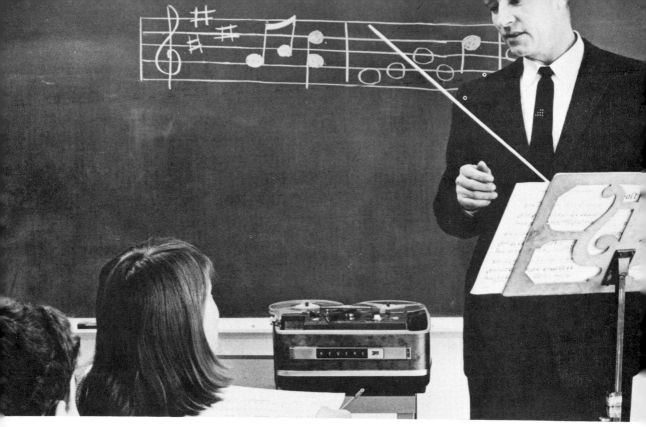

Fig. 11.10. / The tape recorder is the reliable means for testing progress as this chorus practices. Can you envision other comparable work type uses of tape recording, playback and constructive self-criticism?

Fig. 11.11. / How to make tight, noise-free splices.

1/ Cut tape at 60° angle with an overlap so ends will line up. (Cutting tape at 60° angle will eliminate detection of splice on recording.)

2/ Align both ends of tape, uncoated side up (shiny on plastic, gray on paper).

3/ Cover aligned ends with "Scotch" Splicing Tape, evenly and securely.

4/ Trim off excess splicing tape. (Cut into the recording tape backing very slightly as illustrated by dotted lines. This eliminates possibility of a sticky splice.)

Other uses of the tape recorder in music apply advantageously to individualized help for pupils who experience difficulty in note reading and tone accuracy. By presenting prerecorded new songs pupils develop an ear for the tunes and thus learn them more rapidly. The prize-winning effort of a groups' performance at a music festival may serve as a goal and an incentive to those who strove for quality achievement in either instrumental or choral music.

■ GUIDANCE ACTIVITIES

One guidance director reported using tape for anecdotal records which are filed in the student's cumulative record folder. At one-year intervals, the tape-recorded student reports and interviews are spliced end to end (Fig. 11.11) and wound around a flat cardboard "reel." "Teachers," this director says, "are very willing to stop by my office, and as if they were chatting with me, record their comments on tape, knowing that I will add their taped report to the progressively growing information record of a given student. At the time of graduation or on any occasion for listening, the tape record can be played back for parents, teachers, or pupil."

We are only beginning to realize the many important guidance uses that can be devised for the tape recorder. Suppose that when Johnny comes to kindergarten, a simple conversation with him is recorded. As he goes from grade to grade, his oral speech habits, oral reading, and conversations revealing his interests, likes and dislikes, ambitions, and relationships with home, school, and friends could be captured on tape, placed in his record folder, and on graduation be spliced together as an aural document of his school life and progress. Imagine the interest of his parents, and possibly an employer, in such a document.

For students who plan to start working after high school, the tape recorder is also valuable. After the guidance director determines what kind of employment offers the best opportunities for the student, both the student and his instructor may engage in role playing, the instructor taking the part of an employer interviewing the student about a job. The taped interview is then played back for criticism.

Actual employers may be asked to appear before the class and conduct an interview with one of their own employees or a pupil. This also can be taped for later study.

■ BUSINESS EDUCATION

Speed tests and vocabulary and spelling drills all lend themselves admirably to prerecording on tape. In typing and shorthand classes, a tape recording that has been carefully worked out in advance by the teacher can be used repeatedly to measure the speed and accuracy of various classes (Fig. 11.12).

Fig. 11.12. / These girls are taking dictation which reflects a variety of actual business conditions. Tapes were recorded by a dozen businessmen who use many "styles" of pace, articulation, and direction-giving. How does this method expand usual classroom dictation opportunities?

In order to give his pupils experience in doing typing and shorthand in actual business situations, one commercial teacher arranged for each of fifteen local businessmen to dictate on tape three letters of varying length and difficulty selected from his files. The resulting forty-five letters were a challenging and exciting variation from the regular class routine, and gave the class a realistic idea of the requirements expected by business firms. Similar tapes for use in business education have also been commercially recorded.[2]

2 See, for example, *Gregg Shorthand and Dictation Series,* McGraw-Hill.

Other uses of tape recording in business education include taping business telephone conversations, employer interviews at local business firms, and both imaginary and genuine sales talks—the latter recorded by local sales people.

■ DRAMATICS AND SPEECH

Unusual examples of speeches, debates, reporting, or dramatics are frequently heard on radio or television, and these can be useful in teaching speech or dramatics. Most tape recorders are equipped with a radio take-off line, a length of wire with a plug-in device at one end and twin metal clips at the other. By attaching the clips to the "voice coils" of the radio (ask your audiovisual supervisor or physics teacher for help) and then plugging in the tape recorder, the teacher can tape an address by the President of the United States, the audio part of a television drama, a panel discussion, or a well-delivered commercial.

Any of these may become teaching materials at the right time and under the right circumstances. Used as models, such tapes can help pupils make judgments about good speaking, clear enunciation, pleasing phrasing and voice intonation, vocabulary choice, and sentence structure.

When a tape recorder is used during a rehearsal of a play, the members of the cast can gain a vivid idea of their strengths and weaknesses from the playback.

Once the teacher has experienced the unique characteristic of the tape recorder to improve student audiolearning, listening-skill development, and oral criticism, other values and uses of the tape recorder become apparent.

□ PRERECORDED TAPES

Today a new emphasis is being given to prerecorded audiolearning materials, both those which can be secured commercially and those which can be prepared by the teacher or the students. Taped instructions and informative materials offer many advantages. For one thing, the teacher's time may be expanded when prerecorded tapes are used to provide instruction. Further, prerecorded tapes are a highly adaptable medium through which instruction may be further individualized. Groups of gifted children may be identified and helped to move ahead—at their own pace and into their own areas of interest—by presenting them with prerecorded materials. Pupils who need additional drill or memory experience may be assigned appropriate tape listening materials. In such situations, pages of accompanying directions or questions may be included to further individualized instruction, or a work sheet may serve as record of the pupil's response and may be used later by the teacher for evaluation and followup activities. As the teacher prepares prerecorded drill material, he may keep in mind specific needs of pupils and, through the impact of his own voice and personality, make his tape-recorded materials unique. Later, the teacher may work with one group of pupils directly, while prerecorded experiences may be the subject of remedial work carried on by other groups.[3]

3 See A. W. Lalime *et al.*, *Tape Teaching Project*, A Norwalk School Improvement Project Report, 1965.

Fig. 11.13. / Today most school districts are accumulating their own libraries of prerecorded tapes, including those which they make themselves. What opportunities can you envision for doing this in your situation?

Prerecorded tapes are available or may be created for a wide range of subject areas and for varying pupil levels of achievement and interest. The most immediately available of prerecorded materials would be those which result from the teacher's own creative preparation: special drill review, evaluative situations, readings, interpretations, etc. Depending on the nature of the equipment, the teacher may prepare, economically and easily, his recorded lessons during times set aside for lesson planning. Based on classroom use of such materials, the best would be selected and saved for future use. Poor materials should immediately be discarded in the interest of improving instruction and learning efficiency. By retaining only the highest quality and by constantly revising the less adequate materials which hold intrinsic promise, the individual links in the "chain" of excellent recorded teaching materials may continuously be strengthened. The teacher should not overlook the availability of any suitable prerecordings that may have been prepared by his fellow teachers.

One of the most comprehensive sources of prerecorded tapes for use in the elementary- and secondary-school curriculums is the "National Tape Recording Catalog," published periodically by the Department of Audiovisual Instruction of the National Education Association. In this directory are listed tapes which can be purchased outright or which are available for copying or "dubbing" onto school-owned tape. It is a simple matter to set up two tape recorders and to re-record or "dub" onto a blank tape those instructional materials which cannot be purchased outright (Fig. 11.13). Through such provisions, a school library of tape recordings may be built.

High-quality, prerecorded tapes are also provided by many of the Embassy Consulates and cultural services of foreign countries. The Society for French-American Cultural Services and Educational Aid, for example, makes available to schools many prerecorded materials in French music, literature, and special-event programs (see Source List, page 528). Similar tape recordings are available from the Consulate Generals of Japan, New Zealand, Australia, and the Federal Republic of Germany. Usually a letter of inquiry directed to the cultural service or embassy will result in permission to record available taped materials of high quality onto school-owned tapes.[4]

☐ EFFICIENT USE OF RECORDING EQUIPMENT

If both teacher and pupils are to gain the maximum benefit from the tape recorder, several conditions for and principles of its use should be known. For example, the acoustical surroundings in which recordings are made or played can have strong effects on the quality of sound produced on the tape and on that reproduced through the speaker system. Proper control of volume and tone can also make a great deal of difference in sound quality recorded or played back. Similarly, placement of the microphone is another factor which can exert a strong influence on the fidelity of sound reproduction, and on the clarity and audibility of the material recorded.

■ ACOUSTICS

The acoustics of the room or recording area should be studied. Ordinarily, the microphone should be located a good distance away from reverberating surfaces. Corners of the room should be avoided, as should proximity to hard, flat surfaces.

Unfortunately, most teachers have to contend with classrooms which have poor acoustics. You can soon distinguish between what are known as a "live" and a "dead" room: A "live" room is one in which the sound is *underabsorbed*, allowing sound waves to echo and reverberate, while a "dead" room is one in which the sound is *overabsorbed*, preventing the sound waves from carrying far enough. The usual classroom is "live," characterized by hard plaster wall and ceiling surfaces. A "live" room is likely to be filled with reverberated or echoed sound waves which cause confusion as they enter the microphone. Such a classroom can be made less "live" by drawing the shades or, if there are draperies, by spreading these out over as large an area as possible. Wall hangings, cloth-covered screens, and surfaces which can be hung temporarily with sound-absorbing material will also help remarkably.

---

4 *Guide to Free Tapes, Scripts and Transcriptions,* Educator's Progress Service, Randolph, Wisc.

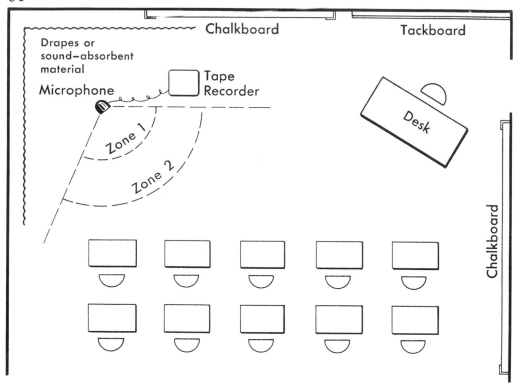

Fig. 11.14. / A schematic plan for classroom tape recording. The pupils leave their seats and take their positions around the face of the microphone. Pupils with weak voices usually stand from 15 to 20 inches away from the recorder (Zone 1); those with stronger voices stand farther away (Zone 2).

In contrast to the "live" room is the "dead" room. Such a room may be crowded with rugs, draperies, overstuffed furniture, or other sound-absorbers, and its ceilings and walls may have good acoustic properties. Here, however, there is an undesirable amount of sound absorption which results in "hollow barrel" recordings. Once simple trial and error has revealed the sound-reflecting surfaces, the hollow recordings can be avoided by placing the microphone properly.

After the acoustic properties of the classroom are known, recommendations may be made concerning the betterment of poor acoustics. If the room is too "live," thick acoustic tile may be installed on the ceiling. Usually this is sufficient, but sometimes additional panels are needed on one or more walls. In rooms which are too dead (the exception) drapery materials or some acoustic tiles may be removed. Those who are planning on remodeling present schools or building new ones should consider the use of acoustic plaster for the ceiling surfaces.

■ RECORDING LEVEL AND TONE

Recording level refers to the volume at which a recording is made. The higher the volume control is set, the greater the pickup range of the microphone. One teacher complained that playground noises outside the building were being recorded along with the songs two children in the classroom were singing. Obviously, the volume control was set at "high" or maximum, with the result that the mechanical ear, the microphone, was reaching out far beyond the walls of the classroom to gather in every sound. To help here, most machines have visual signals which wink or glow when the recording level is correct. But the best procedure is to experiment with volume settings until good results are achieved.

Tone refers to the treble or bass quality of the voice, music, or other sounds picked up by the microphone and recorded. The tone quality can be controlled by adjusting or rotating a tone control on the tape recorder. Short test recordings and a little experimenting—perhaps more or less treble or bass—will reveal when the tone setting is correct.

Recording level and tone are so flexible that the tape recorder has many special uses. The sounds of a busy business district, the whir of machinery in a manufacturing plant, the sounds in a dairy building—even bird calls—may be tape recorded for classroom use.

■ ACHIEVING PRESENCE

In using a recorder in the classroom, the teacher is concerned with whether the playback sounds "real" and "natural." When the recorder is used for evaluation, the recorded sounds must duplicate the original as completely as possible; in other words, the recorder must achieve "presence." The teacher will soon discover that there is more to using a recorder than merely putting a microphone in front of an individual or group. To attain presence, he must know something about microphone placement.

In placing the microphone, the teacher is at first likely to depend on his own hearing. He does not realize that sound heard by two ears is entirely different from that "heard" by a microphone. Our ears and minds possess the ability to concentrate our attention on the one person who is talking to us even though the room is filled with chatting people, and, if we have so trained ourselves, we may disregard extraneous sounds. The microphone, on the other hand, is monaural—one eared—and that one ear can make no discrimination. Every sound that reaches it is picked up.

The microphone should be 4 to 6 feet away from any hard surface that reflects sound. It should be head-high on a small microphone stand or similar support. Visualize the area in front of the open face of the microphone as a "cone of reception," and within this cone experiment with recording and playback to acquire a feeling of the range of pickup and the quality of reproduction characteristic of the microphone. Too low or too high a recording level will actually change the identifying qualities of the voice; a low recording level for a speaker who is only inches from the microphone will eliminate almost all extraneous noises; a gusty voice will be recorded better if the person speaks slightly across the face of the microphone, etc.

Although classrooms vary, the schematic layout shown in Fig. 11.14 embodies general suggestions for tape recording in the classroom. Experiment—that is, record, playback, reposition pupils, etc.—until you discover the location of both microphone and pupils that gives maximum results.

In placing the microphone, move around to various spots and listen with one ear. In this way, you will hear as much as a microphone does and, accordingly, place it to best advantage.

■ DUPLICATING OR "DUBBING"

Frequently a teacher will secure for use a tape recording which is of such value that it will be desirable to make a copy for inclusion in the school tape collection. The procedures involved in duplicating or copying are relatively simple. Ordinarily, two recorders will be used, one to play the recorded tape, the other to duplicate on blank tape this recorded material. Special connecting wires with plugs at one end and "alligator" clips at the other should be employed to pick up the sounds directly from the playing machine. The sound from the recorded tape is transferred to the blank tape by placing the alligator clips on the speaker posts of one tape recorder, and plugging in the other end of the cord to the dubbing or copying recorder. The sounds from the original recording should not be allowed to travel through the air of the room to the microphone as this will lessen the fidelity of the dubbed recording and perhaps add secondary noises to the duplicate.

Since equipment varies greatly it is strongly advised that questions about tape duplication or copying be asked of the dealer from whom the equipment is purchased or made the subject of inquiry with the local building coordinator or audiovisual supervisor.

□ SUMMARY

The tape recorder makes it possible for teacher and pupil to hear themselves as others hear them. Thus, the initial and most impressive use of the tape recorder as a teaching instrument is for self-evaluation. The tape recorder, when used as a self-evaluation and improvement device, is well adapted to use in speech, music, and foreign-language instruction. In these fields, tape-recorded materials serve as models to be listened to, noted, and emulated or improved upon. The tape recorder enables the student of foreign languages, speech, or the dramatic arts to engage in the unique opportunity of immediately hearing his own efforts as others hear him, and seeking the means for further improvement through self-analysis and repeated trial.

Prerecorded tapes have been used with increasing effectiveness as instructional opportunities. Prerecorded tapes are available for gifted students who seek achievements beyond usual class accomplishment levels, and offer source materials which not only factually report information, but also dramatize historical episodes with vividness and a sense of reality. Prerecorded tapes are available commercially; they may be originated by groups or students; or they may be duplicated from existing quality tape-recorded materials which are of value as source information or as models.

In selecting tape-recording equipment, the teacher should consider ease of operation, quality of sound reproduction, and—above all else—the speed with which the recorder can be repaired when anything goes wrong. This is very important. Those who select and use tape-recording equipment should seek the advice and counsel of reputable local dealers or school audiovisual coordinators and supervisors. Since there are so many makes and varieties of tape-recording equipment, as much expert opinion as possible should be secured when selecting modern tape-recording machines and adapting them to local classroom use.

☐ Suggested Activities

1. As a practice teacher or a teacher in service, plan for the actual use of the tape recorder in enriching learning opportunities in your subject area. Include a statement of objectives and a description of the recording activity you will use. Also describe the physical and mechanical arrangements for using the tape recorder.
2. Set up a tape recorder in any normal classroom situation. Later, in private, listen to the playback and ask yourself such questions as these: Is my speech pleasant? Is my enunciation clear and understandable? Is my manner toward children pleasing? Can I learn anything from the children's responses to my questions and leadership?
3. As a teacher, anticipate the problems in language arts, music, or general learning that will arise next week, and make plans for handling them; use the tape recorder.
4. Secure a copy of the National Tape Recording Catalog. Select and order tapes. If they fulfill your expectations proceed to make duplicate copies so that you will have these available for later classroom use.
5. Write letters to the Consulate Generals of France, Germany, England, New Zealand, Australia, and Japan and ask for a list of available prerecorded tapes in social studies, music, and languages. Secure representative recorded materials and dub or duplicate the best of these onto your own tapes for later classroom use (see Source List, page 528).

☐ Bibliography

Department of Audiovisual Instruction, *National Tape Recording Catalog*, Boulder, Colo., National Education Association, 1962–1963.

Dunavan, C. C., "Teachers Make: Slides, Opaques, Tape Recordings," in Emma Fantone, *AV Handbook*, New Jersey State Department of Education, 1961.

Educators Guide to Free 16 mm. Films, Educators Progress Service, 1966.

How to Make Good Tape Recordings, Audio Devices, 1956.

Lalime, Arthur W. *et al.*, *Tape Teaching Project*, A Norwalk School Improvement Project Report, 1965.

Language Master Card Materials and Manuals for Use, Bell and Howell Company, 1965.

Leslie, Louis A., *Tape Recording in Business Education*, Minnesota Mining and Manufacturing Corp., 1956.

Mark, David, *How To Select and Use Your Tape Recorder*, John F. Rider, 1956.

Sloan, R., Jr., *The Tape Recorder*, Visual Instruction Bureau, Division of Extension, University of Texas, 1965.

Society for French American Cultural Services and Education Aid, *Materials for Elementary Schools*, 1966.

Terry, Ruth, *Tape Recordings in the English Classroom*, Michigan Audio-Visual Association, 1956.

XII | STILL

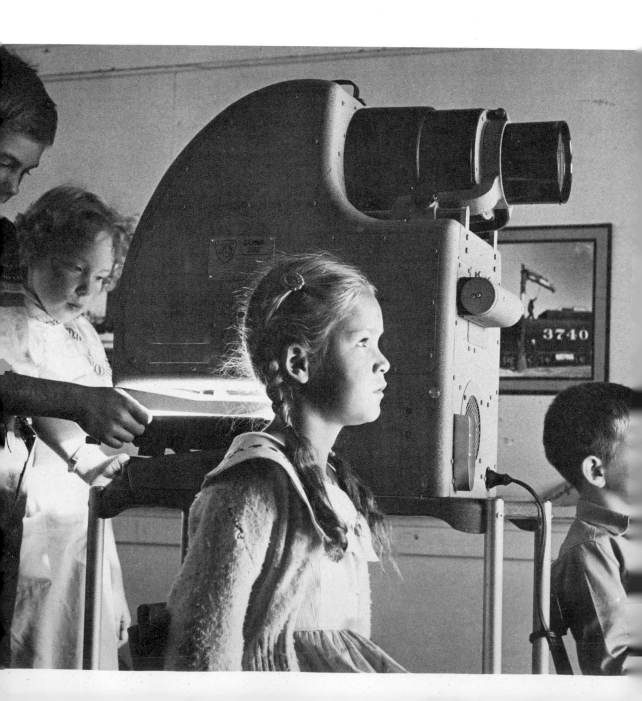

PROJECTION

Through a variety of still-projection techniques, pupils can experience an almost unlimited diversity of learning activities in virtually every subject-matter area. The term *still projection* refers to several methods by which visual materials—photographs, diagrams, posters, cartoons, comics, maps, news clippings, and so forth—can be projected onto a screen or similar surface for group viewing. Projected images generally have a stronger attention-focusing power than do other methods of visual presentation because they center the viewer's attention onto the viewing screen and away from other visual stimuli in the classroom. Thus, still projection provides a convenient and effective means for pupils to examine a great variety of visual materials, in both color and black and white. While many visuals are available on prepared slides, transparencies, and filmstrips, the opaque projector makes possible classroom viewing of nontransparent materials from any book or other printed source, as well as of relatively flat objects and specimens.

Still-projection techniques permit the imaginative teacher great flexibility in arranging interesting and novel learning situations for his pupils. For example, multiscreen projection, by which two or more images are shown simultaneously, makes it possible for students to compare the works of two artists, or to view a close-up of a small map area at the same time the image of the large map area is projected. The microprojector can reduce the need for costly microscopes by projecting the image of any microscope slide. Further, stereoprojection provides three-dimensional realism where the actual three-dimensional materials or experiences are not available. Finally, microfiche and microfilm provide ready means of storage and retrieval of vast amounts of information in a very small space. In short, a variety of still-projection methods and materials is available to the teacher, any one or appropriate combination of which can greatly intensify the learning experience.

☐ TYPES OF STILL-PROJECTION TECHNIQUES

Basically, still-projection materials are of two types, transparencies and opaque material. In its broadest sense, the term *transparency* refers to any surface whose recorded image can be viewed by passing light through it. Thus defined, trans-

Fig. 12.1. / 2 × 2 slides can be projected and stored easily with a drum-type cartridge-load projector, shown above. A sound synchronizer for use with audiotape and a dissolve control unit for fading pictures in and out are available accessories.

parencies include a whole range of materials, such as slides, filmstrips, stereographs, and microfilm. Clearly, we need sharper definitions if we are to discriminate intelligently among the various types of still-projection materials and their many distinctive applications. Accordingly, we distinguish among them as follows:

1. A *slide* is a relatively small piece of film or other transparent material on which a *single* pictorial or graphic image has been placed. Mounted slides range in size from 2 × 2 to 3¼ × 4 inches.
2. A *transparency* (in the context of instructional media) is really a very large slide, usually 10 × 10 inches. While the very large, backlighted pictures used in exhibits and advertising may properly be called transparencies, common usage in education generally restricts the term to those transparencies which can be used on overhead projectors.
3. In a sense, a *filmstrip* is a series of photographic images in fixed sequence on a strip of film, usually 35 mm. in width.
4. *Microfilm* is a special type of filmstrip on which pages of books, newspapers, magazines, and other printed matter have been photographed in miniature form. The film is used in special viewers which enlarge the images to readable size. Variations on microfilm include *microcards,* on which a large number of individual frames have been photographed, and individual slides called *microfiche* which contain hundreds of greatly miniaturized frames.
5. *Microprojection* employs actual microscope slides, such as are prepared normally for examination under a microscope. By use of a microprojector, these slides are projected onto a screen for viewing by a group or a class.

Still-projection materials are not all transparent; the *opaque projector,* using *reflected* light, picks up the image of a magazine illustration, page of a book, a pupil's written work, newsprint, or other opaque material and projects it onto the viewing screen. The opaque projector can also project images of three-dimensional objects for class viewing if these materials are small enough to fit into the projector and flat enough to allow a good focus on important parts of the object.

Although ready-made slides, transparencies, filmstrips, etc. are abundantly available to teachers in every subject-matter area, there are an increasing number of ways by which the resourceful teacher can make his own projection materials by using certain types of plastic sheetings, special copying machines, or by "lifting" materials from the printed page onto a surface prepared for this purpose. All provide the means for teacher-made transparencies. As we shall see, such transparencies are primarily for use with the *overhead* projector.

■ SLIDES AND TRANSPARENCIES

The first slides to achieve wide acceptance in teaching were $3\frac{1}{4} \times 4$ glass-mounted slides. Originally called "lantern slides," these were imprinted with a photographic or handmade image. Early in this century, almost every school owned sets of such slides and could borrow others from a Bureau of Visual Instruction such as the one in the University of Wisconsin Extension Division. In fact, many audiovisual centers got their start through circulating sets of these lantern slides to schools. However, with advances in photographic techniques, the less expensive and more convenient 2×2 slide came into general use and replaced the larger slides for most purposes.

It was not until the 1960s that projectable transparencies in larger sizes— 7×7 and 10×10 inches—came into wide use. While these did not replace the 2×2 slides, the larger sizes made possible important new techniques, including the use of overlays and drawing or writing on the transparency surface while it is being projected. Further, transparency projectors operate from the front of the classroom with the instructor facing the class as he uses it. These projectors are commonly called "overhead projectors," and the materials used on them are referred to as "transparencies."

■ THE 2 × 2 SLIDE

Ever since the development of the 35 mm. camera and color film, photography has become a national pastime, and the 2×2 slide has become a valuable and popular teaching tool. An important advantage of 2×2 slides is the fact that excellent color quality is possible at low cost. Considerations regarding the educational value of color and the selection of colored slides and filmstrips are the same as were discussed in connection with flat pictures (Chapter IV), display boards (Chapter VII), and 16 mm. sound motion pictures (Chapter XV).

Convenience of use, quality, low cost, and ease of procuring are among the principal reasons for the great popularity of 2×2 slides. The convenience of handling and storing small, lightweight slides is self-evident (Fig. 12.1).

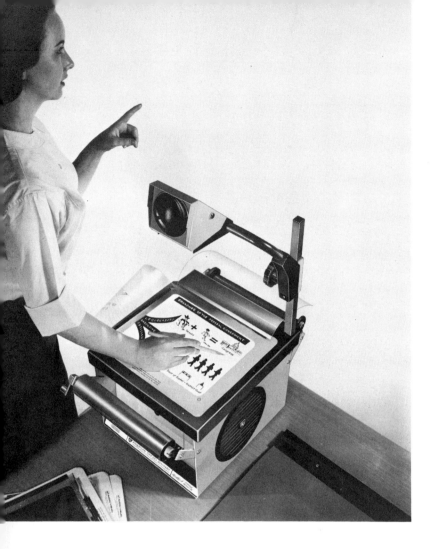

Fig. 12.2. / Once the overhead projector is properly focused and the image aligned on the screen, the teacher can keep his attention on his students.

Furthermore, these slides can frequently be projected in the same machine that is used for filmstrips.

The 2 × 2 photographic slides made commercially are of excellent quality, satisfactory for classroom or auditorium use. Commercially produced slides of this size are available on a great variety of subjects such as art, bird study, foreign and domestic geography, history, literature, health conservation, home economics, meteorology, and zoology (see Source List, pages 541–542).[1] Color slides have little "grain" and hence can be projected in considerable size without loss of satisfactory definition.

The instructor can make his own slides with ease because exposed 35 mm. film normally comes back from the processor in 2 × 2 cardboard slide mounts ready for projection. He can take pictures of field trips, laboratory experiments, class activities, travel scenes, or any subject that lends itself to photographic treatment. Some media centers are providing specialized, illustrated listings of 2 × 2 slide sets available for distribution.[2]

[1] A particularly helpful annual publication on commercial sources of 2 × 2 slides is a booklet by Elsie P. Heyl, *Where to Buy 2" × 2" Slides: A Subject Index,* available from the Enoch Pratt Free Library in Baltimore.

[2] For example, "Italian and Spanish Paintings," *Renaissance and Post-Renaissance Periods,* from Art History Series, Department of Education, San Diego County, April, 1965.

▪ THE 3¼ × 4 SLIDE

Although now largely replaced by the more convenient 2 × 2 slide, the 3¼ × 4 slide still has distinctive applications in instruction. It has an advantage over the smaller size in that its surface is nearly 5½ times as large, and thus, larger and more detailed images can be projected without loss of definition through diffusion.[3] Reproduction of large maps, complicated charts and diagrams, tables, and other materials in which printing and fine detail are important can be presented more effectively on the 3¼ × 4 slides.[4]

The 3¼ × 4 slide is large enough for student or teacher preparation by hand, and photographic slides in this size can be made almost instantaneously with a polaroid camera and a kit of special film and slide mounts.

▪ TRANSPARENCIES

Through common usage—and by reason of the extensive adoption of overhead projectors in education and training—the term *transparency* is now generally accepted as referring to the large transparencies—7- × 7-inch and 10- × 10-inch sizes—that are used in overhead projectors (Fig. 12.2). The 10- × 10-inch size is by far the most popular for this purpose.

Overhead projection with large transparencies is probably the most significant development in still-projection techniques of the last decade. Although initiated during World War II and used thereafter in various military- and industrial-training situations, overhead projection eventually came into general use in schools and colleges. The versatility and convenience of the overhead projector have made it a favorite of teachers who know its many advantages. The fact that the overhead projector is operated from the front of the room enables the teacher to face his class and to maintain direct eye contact with his pupils at all times. From his position beside the projector, the teacher can indicate a point on the transparency or write or draw on it at the same time that he projects the material on the screen. In addition, the teacher can present his material progressively by means of overlays. The overhead projector is the one projection technique on which the overlay method can be used effectively. Successive layers of transparencies, in black and white or in color, can show progressive stages of development, sequences, and sectional views. Lettering, mechanical drawing, the various steps in completing a map or in assembling a machine, and cumulative additions to a chart or graph are typical of the many possible classroom uses of transparent overlays.

The versatility of the overlay technique is utilized in various ways, some of

---

[3] The projected area of a 3¼ × 4 slide is 6.75 square inches; that of a 2 × 2 slide (double-frame) is 1.23 square inches.

[4] See the 16 mm. sound films *Handmade Materials for Projection* and *How To Make Handmade Lantern Slides* (both Indiana University) for details of preparing teaching materials for overhead, slide, and opaque projection.

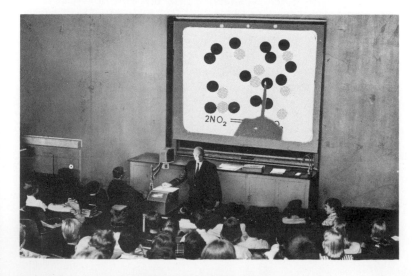

Fig. 12.3. / The 10 × 10 overhead transparency has distinctive advantages for group use. Can you identify three from these illustrations?

which are illustrated in Fig. 12.3. Typically, the several elements of an overlay are hinged on sides of the mounting and flipped on or off the basic transparency as needed. For map projection, the elements may be kept loose for maximum flexibility or grommeted on one corner to swing in or out as desired. One instructor suggests a stacking arrangement of overlays in parallel planes so that separate segments of a problem or concept may be faded in or out of focus as the lens is focused on separate planes.[5]

Transparencies are available in large numbers and in a variety of subject-matter areas from commercial producers; they can also be made up from original materials in media service centers, or, in some cases, from opaque materials in some books and magazines. One way the teacher can make up his own transparencies is by using a grease pencil or felt pen on clear plastic sheeting or cells. This is a convenient and effective technique for making descriptive overlays for commercially prepared transparencies of maps or schematic diagrams, if needed. Of course, most commercial manufacturers of educational transparencies produce related sequences of overlays to go with basic transparent materials. Other types of teacher-made transparencies include carbon film which can be drawn upon or used in a typewriter; thermo-type plastic which reproduces images from an opaque sheet of paper when put through a thermocopying machine; Ozalid and Technifax sensitized sheets which develop copy in color when exposed to ammonia fumes; and gummed plastic sheets designed to "lift" magazine photographs for projection as transparencies.

It should be noted here that the size of the lettering used on transparencies is important if they are to be read easily. Typical book or newsprint type is too small for use with a class. A study by Adams, Rosemier, and Sleeman establishes that smaller-size, typewritten letters (elite and pica) are too small for readability at distances from the screen of more than 20 feet.[6] Recommended for typed lettering is the $\frac{6}{32}$-inch, primer-size typewriter found in many schools. The $\frac{8}{32}$-inch size appears larger than necessary for distances up to 40 feet. For optimum flexibility of use with either small or very large groups (over 100), the $\frac{8}{32}$-inch size is probably best; for purely classroom use, the $\frac{6}{32}$-inch size letter is adequate, but nothing smaller should be used.

It is also possible to "lift" color photographs from most magazines by a process that transfers the ink from the paper to a plastic surface. This is done most conveniently by applying a special acetate sheet to the surface of the picture and inserting both briefly in a hot press.[7] The material is then soaked in water to which a detergent has been added, and left until the paper can be pulled gently from the acetate surface to which the colored ink has now adhered. This surface is then washed carefully and allowed to dry. When dry, it is sprayed with a

[5] Jean A. Wilber, "Multiplane Transparencies," *Educational Screen and Audiovisual Guide,* September, 1964, p. 515.

[6] Sarah Adams, Robert Rosemier, and Philip Sleeman, "Readability Letter Size and Visibility for Overhead Projection Transparencies," *AV Communications Review,* Winter, 1965, pp. 412–417.

[7] The special acetate sheets can be obtained from Seal, Inc., Shelton, Connecticut, and from the Minnesota Mining & Manufacturing Company. See also H. C. Hartsell and Wilfred Veenendaal, *Overhead Projection,* Henry Stewart Co., 1960, for an excellent discussion of specific uses of transparencies and their preparation by the teacher. For demonstrations of their use and techniques of preparation, see *The Overhead Projector,* Sound, B&W, 18 min., State University of Iowa; and *Handmade Materials of Projection,* Sound, Color, 20 min. University of Indiana.

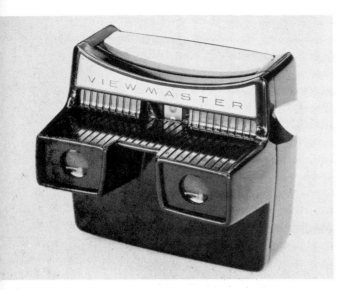
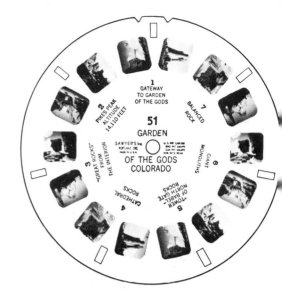

Fig. 12.4. / A popular type of stereoviewer. Beside it is a stereograph consisting of pairs of 16 mm. transparencies on a disk. What are the teaching values of stereoviews?

colorless protective coating, which also brings out the colors more strongly, and the transparency is ready for projection.

Anything that can be traced, drawn, written, typed, lifted or photographed onto a transparent surface can be projected clearly on the screen with the over-head projector, and the teacher can make many of his own transparencies without a darkroom or other special facilities.

A variety of practical day-to-day uses of overhead transparencies has probably occurred to you. The following suggestions from Hartsell and Veenendaal may increase your list:[8]

ELEMENTARY GRADES

1. Number combinations on rotating disks grommeted together to replace a whole stack of flash cards
2. Transparent boxes and buttons for work in number combinations
3. Outline maps for geography, with symbols added or overlays used for names, locations, etc.
4. Words in sentences cut into transparent strips for studying parts of speech or punctuation
5. Photographic "lifts" for reading readiness or experience charts

SECONDARY GRADES

1. Charts and diagrams with overlays to show division of powers in government, legislative procedures, or due process of law
2. Overlays for rapid comparison of geometric figures, for proof of theorems, etc.
3. Solutions of complex problems in mathematics or accounting prepared by means of overlays to save the time of both class and teacher

---

[8] H. C. Hartsell and Wilfred Veenendaal, *op. cit.*, pp. 38–50.

4. Small science charts transferred to transparencies for improved visibility and convenience (these can be marked without damage for purposes of explanation)

5. Comparison of foreign- and English-language sentence structure by means of overlay or uncovering techniques; the same comparison methods for vocabulary tests and drills

6. Letter-writing models, shorthand exercises, and bookkeeping forms for business education classes

7. Plastic models to illustrate gear ratios, jointing, and fitting in industrial arts classes

8. A music staff under the cellophane roll for addition of clef, signature, and notes for simple composition; transfer of a musical score to a transparency for concert audience to follow

9. Scale drawings of playing fields or courts placed under the cellophane roll on which plays can be sketched; silhouette cutouts or transparent plastic pieces representing positions to be manipulated at will

▪ STEREOPROJECTION

Another type of slide which deserves mention is the double-image slide used in stereoprojection. The projection of stereographic views that provides the lifelike realism of three dimensions remained an unattained goal for many years. Even now the process, while used for certain specialized purposes, is not used in schools to any appreciable extent, and certain technical problems must be solved before stereographic projection can be feasible or entirely satisfactory.

Slides for this purpose are prepared in pairs from photographs taken with a stereographic camera, which takes two pictures simultaneously. As the camera lenses are a few inches apart, each picture is taken from a slightly different angle. When both pictures are seen together or in a stereoviewer, a highly realistic and vivid three-dimensional effect is obtained. However, when projected on a screen for group viewing, specially designed eye-glasses are needed for each observer if he is to get anything approximating a three-dimensional image, for without these glasses, both of his eyes see both of the pictures projected on the viewing screen. The result is a confused agglomeration of vaguely defined images. Even when stereographs are viewed through these glasses there is a tendency toward exaggeration of depth in closeup views, and a similar distortion around the edges of a scene. For example, the stem of a tulip near the edge of the picture may seem considerably longer than the stems near the center, although all are approximately the same length. This effect persists even when a special spheroid screen is used. In any case, the special screen and eyeglasses required for group viewing are handicaps to stereoprojection for most instructional purposes. Nevertheless, for certain specialized purposes, such as art, medicine, and engineering, the values of three-dimensional projection are important enough to merit its use.

A modern form of the stereographic slide is the stereodisk. Seven pairs of 16 mm. transparencies taken with a stereographic camera are mounted on flat disks and viewed in a compact and inexpensive viewer (Fig. 12.4). This viewer is

Fig. 12.5. / (Above) A light-box is of great assistance in sorting and selecting 2 × 2 slides. They can be placed in cartridges to assure correct order in projecting them.

Fig. 12.6. / (Right) This picture illustrates two differences between single-frame and double-frame filmstrips. How do they differ in projection requirements?

Fig. 12.7. / (Below) The large number of filmstrips currently used in school systems and their small size necessitate a rapid, convenient system of storage and retrieval. This one is used in San Diego County Audiovisual Center.

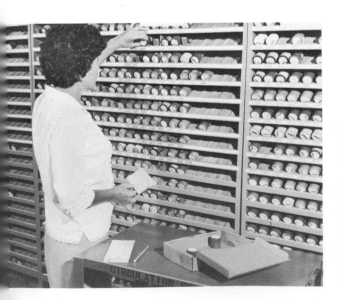

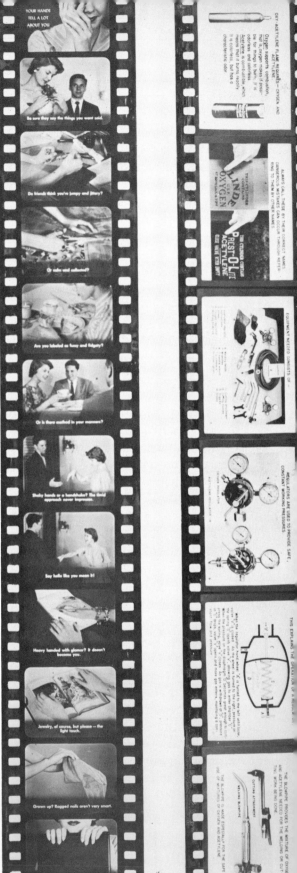

similar to the stereoviewer used for single stereographic slides in that it enables the left eye to see one picture and the right eye to see the other, the brain combining these into one three-dimensional image; but the stereodisk viewer allows the individual to view seven different pictures without changing the slide disk.

Initially these stereodisks, or reels, were devoted largely to popular entertainment and general interest; they were commercially sold and showed such subjects as scenic wonders, world travel, nature, and world events. Children's stories were also presented and sold in this form. The success of the device, however, has led to several more serious applications, especially in the fields of science and technology. For example, stereodisk materials have been prepared on human anatomy, oral surgery, and air contamination. A number of books have been published with illustrations on stereodisks, for which a folding plastic viewer is provided in the book along with the disks.

Slides or transparencies can be used in any desired order and thus permit the teacher a great deal of flexibility of presentation. A convenient method of sorting slides and selecting those needed for a lesson is shown in Fig. 12.5.

It is generally desirable to mount the large transparencies used on overhead projectors, but mounting is essential for 2 × 2 and most 3¼ × 4 slides. There are several types of mounting for slides, the most familiar being the 2 × 2 cardboard mount in which 35 mm. color slides come back from the processor. Better for protection and projection, however, is a glass mounting in which the picture and its mask are held between two thin pieces of glass.

■ FILMSTRIPS

A filmstrip is a related sequence of transparent still pictures or images—in color or in black and white—contained on a strip of 35 mm. film. A filmstrip typically contains from 20 to 50 frames, although it may have more than 50. A large number of filmstrips consist of single-frame pictures of about ¾ × 1 inch in size, each of which is one above another. The individual pictures on double-frame filmstrips are approximately twice as large, and these frames are side by side on the film (Fig. 12.6). Although some filmstrip projectors accommodate only single-frame filmstrips, most projectors can be adjusted for either size.

A complete filmstrip is usually several feet in length, and is easily rolled up to fit into a small plastic or metal container (Fig. 12.7). These containers take up little space and can be stored easily; this factor combined with the low cost of filmstrips (from $3.50 to $8.50 for most) makes it practical to keep sets of filmstrips in each classroom for use when needed.

In addition to their ease of storage and their low cost, filmstrips have many advantages as a still-projection medium, and provide the classroom teacher with a convenient and effective means of communicating instructional content visually. Filmstrips are easy to use and filmstrip projectors are inexpensive, simple to operate, and seldom give trouble. Good pictures can be projected on the screen in spite of limited facilities for room darkening, particularly with black-

and-white filmstrips, and commercially prepared filmstrips are abundantly available in a wide variety of subjects. These advantages help to account for the wide popularity of this still-projection medium, but, in addition, filmstrips have decided teaching advantages.

A major instructional value of the filmstrip is the sequential order of its frames. Subjects are treated in a logical order, and the teacher can develop the learning experience step by step without concern that the pictures might

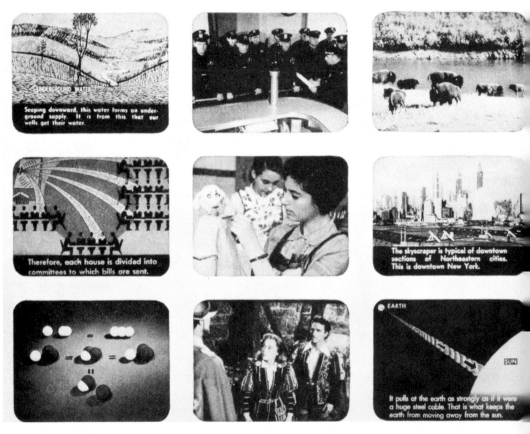

Fig. 12.8. / Selected frames from 18 filmstr made by various producers, that indic something of the variety and number of f

get out of sequence as occasionally happens with slides. Because the order of scenes on a filmstrip is fixed, however, it is not possible to project scattered scenes conveniently; consequently, when flexibility in picture sequence is desired, separate slides or transparencies are preferable. Nevertheless, if the specific purpose for which the filmstrip was prepared corresponds to the teacher's own purpose, the teacher has a ready-made, efficient, and convenient teaching tool.

Another decided advantage of the filmstrip from a teacher's standpoint is that it can be used at any desired pace. For introductory or review purposes, the teacher can run through a filmstrip rather quickly, providing the students with a conceptual overview. Or, if detailed analysis is called for, the teacher can hold each frame on the screen for as long as necessary; he may wish, for example, to use only a few frames during a particular class period.

A third instructional advantage of filmstrips is the range and number of titles available. The popularity of filmstrips and their relatively low production costs have encouraged manufacturers to turn out great numbers of new filmstrips each year on a wide range of subjects. This range of subject matter goes well beyond the elementary-school curriculum into many areas at the secondary-school, college, and adult-education levels. A few examples of this variety of

s available. Aside from flat pictures, no
r form of visual material is so readily
able to the teacher.

filmstrip availabilities are shown in Fig. 12.8, which presents selected frames from 18 different filmstrips. This selection would need to be multiplied hundreds of times to suggest the number of *new* filmstrips currently produced in the United States each year.

The adaptability of the filmstrip medium to diverse subject matter can be illustrated by just a few examples. The filmstrip *Peter and Susan Visit Grandfather's Farm* is designed to provide concrete background experience for a primary reading class, and accompanies a reader of the same title.[9] The scenes in this filmstrip are set up in a sequence which provides an ordered series of

[9] Society for Visual Education.

Fig. 12.9. / Filmstrips lend them
selves also to small-group or indiv
ual use. Prerecorded tapes a
headsets facilitate self-instructi
and avoid disturbance to others.
self-contained, projection-tape u
with cartridge-load tape and re
vision screen is pictured below.

new work concepts about a farm, but at the same time, the filmstrip tells an interesting story that leads the pupils naturally and enjoyably from one part of the farm to another as well as from one set of new word concepts to another. By contrast, the filmstrip *The Micrometer* is designed to show the correct method of using and reading this measuring instrument to older students.[10] This filmstrip moves carefully from the first to the final step in micrometer utilization, and the last frames reinforce the concepts involved by reviewing the salient points. In both cases, the sequence of scenes, the captions, and the treatment are determined by the instructional purpose.[11]

Other distinctive and significant subjects available in filmstrip form include *Life's* pictorial features on the history of man and of the world, and *The New York Times Current Affairs* filmstrips which are published monthly. Several filmstrip services send out information on new releases—on such topics as current events and new developments in science—at regular intervals during the school year (see Source List, pages 541–542).

A fourth characteristic of filmstrips which is favorable to creative and effective instruction is that they lend themselves well to use with other media. For example, filmstrips as a still medium can only imply motion to the viewer who has the necessary background experience, but they are excellent for *detailed* study or review. Thus, motion-picture films—which communicate the motion important to a learning concept—and filmstrips—which permit still analysis of individual components—make excellent instructional companions for many purposes. Concepts in science, engineering, sports, nature study, and many other subjects can be imparted easily and efficiently when these two media are used in conjunction with one another. An interesting development in this context is the extent to which publishers of textbooks are producing filmstrips which are closely correlated with text materials. The filmstrip *Peter and Susan Visit Grandfather's Farm*, mentioned earlier, is but one case in point.

Some filmstrips are accompanied by records and are called "sound filmstrips." The record usually carries narration and may also include appropriate music or sound effects. Combination record players and filmstrip projectors, such as those shown in Fig. 12.9, are convenient and compact; however, separate machines can be used without difficulty. Sound filmstrips are useful in such subjects as music, reading readiness, industrial arts, and guidance. It should be noted, however, that relatively few sound filmstrips are available for school use in comparison to the great number of silent filmstrips produced each year.

When the record and the filmstrip are played together, the pace of the filmstrip is fixed by the record, and this combination is effective for many teaching purposes. However, increased flexibility can be obtained from the sound filmstrip when the record is turned off and the teacher or a student provides the narration at whatever pace is appropriate for the situation. This allows for a more detailed study of the concepts involved, or for a more rapid overview, than that provided by the record.

---

10 United World, Government Films Division.

11 Filmstrips are an efficient medium for communicating ideas in almost any subject. See, for example, Anthony Stampolis and Laurence S. Sewell, Jr., *A Study of Film Strips Communicating Economic Concepts,* School of Public Relations and Communications, Boston University, Boston, 1952.

Fig. 12.10. / Vast accumulation of new and old knowledge necessitate new, condensed methods of information storage and retrieval. Microfilm is one method used widely in libraries. Print-out pages can be made in the same equipment. Shown here are two models of microreaders; the left model uses a card, the right a sheet of film called *microfiche* on which hundreds of pages can be miniaturized. What school uses seem practical for such systems as these?

A fifth advantage of the filmstrip medium is that it is possible for teachers and students to make their own filmstrips. Although single-frame filmstrips require special camera equipment, the individual can make his own double-frame filmstrip with a regular 35 mm. camera. This possibility provides the creative teacher with useful opportunities for involving pupils actively in their own learning, and class projects which include the making as well as the showing of filmstrips can have a sizable effect on favorable learning outcomes.

Like any other teaching material, the filmstrip has its limitations as well as its advantages. The disadvantages, in some cases, of having no motion and of their fixed sequential order have already been alluded to. A physical limitation of filmstrips is that they are rather easily damaged and difficult to repair, and thus need to be handled with more care than do, say, slides and transparencies. The base of a filmstrip is cellulose acetate, a nonflammable substance which is resistant to ordinary wear and tear; however, the sprocket holes will tear easily if the projector is not properly threaded or is out of adjustment. Unfortunately, there is no practical way of repairing damaged sections, and torn filmstrips become useless. Nevertheless, with proper usage of the filmstrip projector (see pages 385–386), filmstrips can be kept in good condition for a considerable period.

■ MICROFILM, MICROCARDS, AND MICROFICHE

Although its purpose as an instructional tool is considerably different from those of the still-projection media just described, the microfilm is also a transparent material useful to education, and deserves mention here. As the volume of human knowledge increases, the physical problems of storing and retrieving recorded information become increasingly difficult. Academic and public libraries are running short of storage space for whole volumes and complete periodicals. To accommodate these pressures, various publications, such as rare books, theses, newspaper files, periodicals, and important documents have been photographed on 35 mm. microfilm, each frame on the film containing a separate page. These small films require very little storage space and can bear a great deal of information. When specific information is called for, the appropriate film is located and projected onto the viewing screen of a microfilm reader, thus enlarging the tiny type recorded on the microfilm for easy reading. A similar system employs microcards or microfiche (pronounced micro-feesh'). Both microcards and microfiche—the same material on film—store images greatly reduced in size even from those on microfilm so that it is possible in some versions to store hundreds of pages on one 2 × 2 slide or on a card of that size. Special readers are necessary, of course, to enlarge these images sufficiently so they can be read (Fig. 12.10).

Although at first limited to large libraries, microfilming is now being used in some secondary schools. Erbes points out many significant advantages of microfilm in its use; for example, in the Reavis High School Library in Oak Lawn, Illinois.[12] A microfilm subscription to all current publications is ordered along with the magazines themselves, and the cost is about the same as it would be for binding a year's accumulation of these magazines. Thus, microfilm solves the magazine storage problem, relieves the librarian from worry about the disappearance of current issues, and practically eliminates the problem of missing pages. Magazines can be cut up for pictures as soon as the microfilm of the issue arrives. Further, while students enjoy using the microfilm readers in the school library, there is no problem of the microfilms themselves being "lost," since no one owns his personal reader and there is no other way by which the microfilmed information can be retrieved. Erbes suggests that "when considering purchases of microfilms, a school librarian consider not only the expense of purchase, but also the long-range saving of money, time, and patience in using this modern, practical way to house back numbers of magazines and periodicals."[13]

Future developments in microfilm storage and retrieval systems promise to be extensive and significant for teachers and students alike. A system of electronic microfilming is being studied with a sizable grant from the Council on Library Resources in Washington, D.C. In this system, a series of central archives over the nation would contain microcards of all publications of a certain type. Each microcard would hold approximately 10,000 pin-head sized pages, and, by means of a code and dialing system, a library—possibly even a private individual—could request any reference. The appropriate source would be transmitted electronically to a small TV screen, and each page would appear as desired by merely pushing a button.[14]

■ MICROPROJECTION

Although the terms can be misleading to the uninitiated, *microprojection* is to be distinguished from *microfilm* and its projection. In *microprojection*, microscope slides rather than film are used and the microprojector is designed to project these microscope slides so that an entire class may see what would be visible to only one pupil at a time if seen under a microscope (Fig. 12.11). Both wet and dry slides may be projected with this instrument.

[12] R. G. Erbes, Jr., "Microfilm in High School Libraries," *Wilson Library Bulletin*, December, 1958, pp. 302–303.

[13] *Ibid.*

[14] Hyman M. Boodish, "Automation in Education: Electronic Microfilm Archive," *Social Studies*, December, 1959, pp. 264–265.

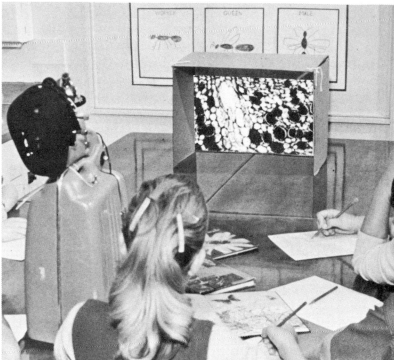

Fig. 12.11. / A microscope slide is projected into a shadowbox screen. A micropro-jector can be used effectively for an entire class in a darkened room. Three levels of magnification are normally available. For what purposes is a microprojector superior to individual microscopes?

The microprojector thus not only minimizes the need for expensive micro-scopes for each pupil, but it also assures the instructor that his students are seeing precisely what he wants them to see. The proper and effective use of microscopes is often a difficult skill to learn in its own right, and training in this area often retards instruction in the subject under study. Furthermore, even when instruction in the use of the microscope has been given, the instructor cannot be sure that each of the pupils has properly adjusted the microscope lenses to view the specimen clearly, or that he is seeing precisely what the in-structor wishes him to see. With the microprojector, however, microslides can be projected on the screen so that the proper view is provided for all and atten-tion can be directed as desired.

Numerous phenomena suited for presentation on microscope slides can be shown with marked effectiveness on a microprojector. Sargent lists such uses as the following:

1. Illustration of stresses and strains on fibers, filaments, and surfaces
2. Physical examination of wood, cotton, silk, rayon, linen, and other textile fibers

3. Gross projection of prepared slides showing fingerprints or other semitransparent print materials such as blood smears

4. Visualization of interference patterns of light, and optical principles of refracted light

5. Gross examination of properties of crystals and other common compounds such as minerals, food, rubber, and petroleum by means of white and polarized light

6. Projection of crystal growth in various solutions; further, since removal of the projector cooling cell causes melting, replacement of this cell results in crystallization which can be shown without changing the field of projection

7. Projection of one-celled animals and plants on wet slides, cell division, plant and animal tissues, bacteria, mold spores, and the like[15]

Virtually all prepared microscope slides now available can be projected with the microprojector. However, the light beam must be cooled sufficiently to prevent damaging the material on the slide.

■ OPAQUE PROJECTION

Potentially one of the most useful types of still projection for instructional purposes is opaque projection. This technique permits nontransparent materials—such as flat pictures, book illustrations, tables, drawings, photographs, pupils' work, and even certain specimens and objects—to be shown on a screen for group observation.

The instructor with access to an opaque projector has available an almost unlimited amount of illustrative material at little or no cost. Furthermore, much of this material can be used just as it is, for a minimum of mounting or other preparation is required. A theme, a mathematics paper, a sheet of typing, a page or diagram in a book, a picture in a magazine, a culture dish, a watch, coins, stamps or leaves—in fact, nearly anything that is within $8\frac{1}{2} \times 11$ inches in size—can be projected by an opaque projector.

The principal and unique advantage of opaque projection in instruction is the great mass of readily available and cost-free materials which can be projected. Much valuable material such as pupils' written work and useful illustrations, diagrams, and tables from magazines and reference books can be projected as it is. Some three-dimensional materials can also be projected to advantage (Fig. 12.12).

Another unique value of opaque projection is the convenience with which illustrative material can be enlarged and transferred to a chalkboard or chart. A small news map, for example, can be projected on a chalkboard in any desired size and quickly traced for a current events discussion (see Chapter III). In addition, opaque projection has the attention-focusing advantage of any projected image. Even when other methods of presentation such as charts or bulletin boards are used, the projected image provides for effective enlargement and focuses attention.

---

15 See Theodore Sargent, "Using the Microprojector in Physics and Chemistry," in Harry C. Mc-Kown and Alvin B. Roberts, *Audio Visual Aids to Instruction* (rev. ed.), McGraw-Hill, 1949, pp. 512–513.

Fig. 12.12. / Specimens as well as flat materials can be shown readily in the opaque projector.

The flexibility and convenience of opaque projection for a great variety of uses have been effectively illustrated by Denno as follows:

ELEMENTARY GRADES

1. Language arts—story sharing, animated word games
2. Arithmetic drill—pull strips that reveal numbers of objects
3. Science—the enlarging of pictures to show size; the showing of collections of shells
4. Social studies—maps locating school and homes
5. Enlarging figures for bulletin boards
6. Science specimens; weather-map symbols
7. Test reviews
8. Book illustrations
9. Music—sharing a song
10. Mathematics—diagrams, problems, exercises

SECONDARY GRADES

1. Social studies—map projection
2. English—creative writing, correction of grammar on written work: letter forms

3. Civics—current maps and pictures
4. Art—drawing techniques, illustrations
5. Science—specimens
6. History—reference pictures, artifacts

COLLEGE

1. Business education—business and accounting forms
2. Journalism—creative writing, advertising layouts
3. Home economics—textiles
4. Fine Arts—photos, graphs, charts, instruments, drawings; illustrations for various subject areas[16]

☐ EFFECTIVE SELECTION AND USE OF STILL-PROJECTION MEDIA

The value of still-projection techniques in teaching a variety of subjects at levels ranging from the primary grades to the college and adult levels has been studied both here and abroad for many years.[17] While most of them have dealt with the effectiveness of filmstrips and slides as teaching tools, the main findings of this research also summarize the values of such materials generally; namely:

1. Still projection is an effective means of communicating factual information and certain skills.
2. A combination of still-projection media is a more efficient instructional approach than is the usage of any single type. Similarly, combining still-projection media with other types of teaching materials as appropriate—aural media, motion-pictures, three-dimensional objects and specimens, community study, and the like—is likely to produce the most efficient learning outcomes.
3. The extent to which still-projection methods embody unique pictorial or graphic content of good quality has a direct bearing on their effectiveness in teaching.

As is true of other teaching materials, however, still-projection materials must be selected and used effectively if they are to provide the maximum benefits.

■ SELECTION OF STILL-PROJECTION MATERIALS

The first step in efficient selection of materials involves a consideration of whether the particular projection method and the material to be used can serve the teaching purpose better than another learning device or medium. This must be decided partly in terms of what the projection material itself can and cannot

---

16 See Ray Denno, *Using the Opaque Projector*, Squibb-Taylor, 1958, pp. 12–25.

17 An excellent summary of the research done on the effectiveness of filmstrips and slides will be found in William H. Allen's article on audiovisual materials in Monroe's *Encyclopedia of Educational Research*, Macmillan, 1960, pp. 120–121.

do; that is, what are its inherent characteristics. Some questions the teacher might well ask himself are:

1. *Is the purpose for which I would use this material one in which motion is essential for pupil understanding?* If it is, the still-projection device will not be the best learning medium. At best, still projection can only imply motion and should not be used to teach concepts of motion. On the other hand, projected diagrams, schemata, and the like can be effective means of analyzing in detail the component *parts* of motion if the motion itself is visualized before or after the still-projection presentation by a motion-picture film or a working model, etc.

2. *Are suitable materials available for the particular teaching job I have in mind?* This is a question of practical import to most teachers, because keeping track of the large number of slide sets, filmstrips, transparencies, and other educational materials put out each year in a given field is a considerable task. Professional journals frequently contain sections that review new educational materials, and several publications are specifically devoted to the task of providing periodic evaluations of such materials.[18]

3. *Does my teaching purpose involve a series of step-by-step developments according to a fixed logical progression?* If so, the teacher must assess whether a filmstrip will best provide this sequence or whether the job would best be accommodated through a series of transparent overlays projected by means of an overhead projector. The latter would be particularly appropriate if the teacher himself is to provide sequential analytic markings on plastic sheeting during the class discussion. If the overlay technique is not called for, a filmstrip may present the material most effectively. Cartridge-type slide projectors permit the same control over fixed sequence as do filmstrips, but it must be remembered that slides can become disordered. Slides are most suited to learning situations which demand no particular sequence or when it is desirable to change the sequence to show different aspects of the content under study.

4. *Does my teaching purpose require materials which tell their story primarily through pictures rather than words?* Because still projection is essentially a visual medium, it should be relied upon to communicate visual ideas—pictures, graphs, diagrams, and the like. Projection materials should emphasize that which is visual; verbal materials, while useful and even necessary for complete understanding of visual media, should not dominate the usage of still projection. An exception is in remedial reading and arithmetic where visual images of word and number symbols are often used heavily. It should also be borne in mind that many visual materials for which still projection is an excellent teaching tool are also symbolic: Graphics, diagrams and schemata, maps, and so forth are also largely symbolic rather than pictorial. Thus, the teacher should decide on the kind of material—pictorial, diagrammatic, etc.—which will be the most

---

[18] *The Educational Media Index*, McGraw-Hill, 1964, provides basic information on films, filmstrips, kinescopes, videotapes, sets of slides, transparencies and flat pictures, disk and tape recordings, and maps and globes. *The Educators Progress Service*, Randolph, Wisconsin, compiles annually revised listings of free films, filmstrips and their instructional materials in both general and special subject areas. Film evaluation services are available from the Educational Film Library Association, 250 W. 57th St., New York, N.Y. 10019, and from the Landers Film Review, P.O. Box 697601, Los Angeles, California 90069.

useful means of presenting the concept. A particularly good picture in a recent magazine might best be projected by means of the opaque projector, a series of highly intricate map or diagrammatic overlays projected on the overhead projector may be more appropriate, or a combination of several different media and materials may be the best answer.

Vandermeer stresses that the pictures on a filmstrip must contribute something unique if the filmstrip is to be any more effective than words in the learning situation. He compared results, in terms of immediate factual learning and recall of information over a three-week period, from using a particular American history filmstrip with one group and only the reading material from that filmstrip with another group. He found no significant superiority for either group. In assessing his findings Vandermeer came to the conclusion that ". . . when the pictorial element of the filmstrip is deficient in detail, definition, or clarity, it not only fails to contribute to the students' knowledge but may actually serve to inhibit learning."[19]

5. *Are speed or other aspects of timing an important consideration to my teaching purpose?* Although all still-projection devices permit detailed analysis of each image by holding it on the viewing screen for as long as necessary, it may occasionally be desirable to show several images in rapid succession to provide an overview or review. Further, such subjects as remedial reading and arithmetic can employ flash views of single images to advantage. If speed or presentation is desirable for the instructor's purpose, a filmstrip may provide the wisest choice, providing that it fulfills the other criteria demanded by the learning situation. Also, some overhead projectors are equipped with a *tachisto-scope* (Fig. 12.13) which enables the teacher to flash images onto the screen at speeds up to $\frac{1}{100}$ of a second. Certain 2×2 slide projectors are designed for tachistoscopic use, as are some filmstrip projectors.

The tachistoscope technique was used extensively during World War II for aircraft recognition training; it replaced the earlier WEFT system in which wings, engine, fuselage, and tail were analyzed separately in identification. The new system, developed by psychologist Samuel Renshaw of Ohio State University, was based on *total perception* of visual elements rather than on *step-by-step perception*. Thus, the aircraft is seen as a whole rather than in terms of wings, an engine, a fuselage, and a tail. In other words, the whole is something more than the sum of its parts and is seen as such. This is a basic concept of such Gestalt psychologists as Wertheimer, Kohler, and Koffka.[20]

The Renshaw system employed thousands of photographs of airplanes on 2×2 slides. The planes were pictured in as many different positions, angles, distances, and conditions of visibility as could be secured. The slides were projected slowly at first, and then for progressively smaller fractions of a second. Pilots, gunners, and other military personnel became adept at recognizing aircraft almost instantaneously after sufficient practice with the tachistoscope technique for flash recognition to become habitual. The latter point

19 A. W. Vandermeer, "Relative Contributions to Factual Learning of the Pictorial and Verbal Elements of a Filmstrip," *School Review*, February, 1950, pp. 84–89.

20 For an interesting summary of the principles of Gestalt psychology in relation to perception and insight, see James B. Stroud, *Psychology in Education*, Longmans, Green, 1956, pp. 359–369.

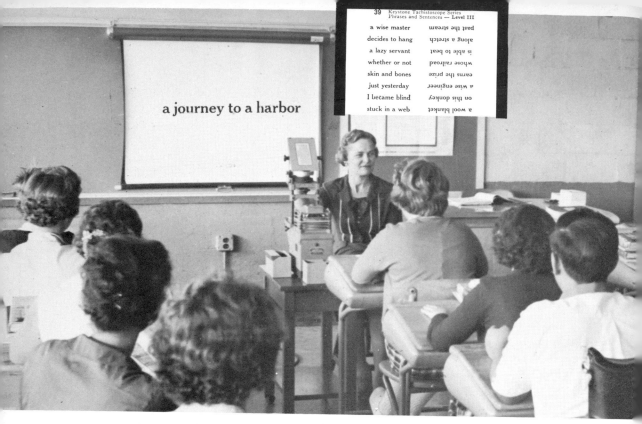

Fig. 12.13. / Group use of tachistoscopic techniques with a 3¼ × 4 overhead slide projector. A portion of a representative slide is shown in the inset.

appears to be crucial in increasing reading speed and perceptual span with a tachistoscope or other accelerating devices such as the Iowa Reading Training Films and the Harvard Films for the Improvement of Reading.[21]

To summarize, the teacher must first evaluate the specific purposes for which the learning materials are to be used, and then judge which types of material and means of projection will be most efficiently geared to accomplishing these purposes. Finally, the visuals he chooses must be of such a nature and quality as to contribute something at once significant and unique to the learning situation. Preview of the materials is clearly indicated if the teacher is to make good judgments on these points (Fig. 12.14). Not only is he guided in his final selection, but preview also serves to prepare him for the specific teaching situation. The teacher must know the content rather precisely if he is to plan and to execute the learning situation efficiently—what points to emphasize, what points will need additional clarification, and, unless he is using a filmstrip, the order and sequence in which the slides, transparencies, or opaque materials are to be presented.

■ UTILIZATION OF STILL-PROJECTION MATERIALS

Once the teacher has determined the projection and other materials he will use with his class he must know how to present them in such a way as to impart

21 Bureau of Audio-Visual Instruction, State University of Iowa; and Harvard Films Service, Biological Laboratories, Harvard University.

their content effectively to the pupils. In planning and executing the teaching situation, the teacher should bear in mind that the pupils should not only learn the information and concepts involved, but should also be able *to apply them accurately and creatively as a result of the experience*. If use of the still-projection materials is to achieve these goals, the teacher must consider not only the presentation or the actual showing itself, but also preparation for the experience and followup activities as well.

■ PREPARATION

As suggested previously, the first step in preparation is that in which the instructor himself becomes fully acquainted with the points to be highlighted or clarified in the learning situation. In previewing the filmstrips, sets of slides, or transparencies, the teacher should outline the salient features in order and note any comments or questions he may wish to raise in classroom discussion.

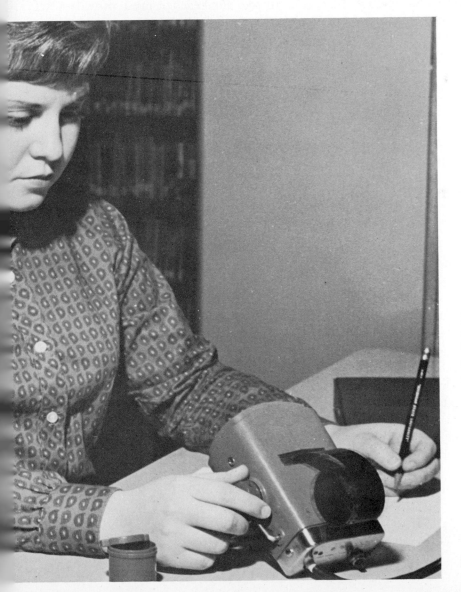

Fig. 12.14. / Evaluating a filmstrip means assessing its quality in terms of general curriculum requirements. Selecting one for a particular lesson is a much more specific task requiring examination of the individual frames.

It may be desirable to record his presentation or his comments on sound tape in the form of a narration. Such a prerecorded narration not only establishes beforehand the ideas to be covered and the pace at which they will be presented, but also prevents the ideas from getting lost by pupil questions or spontaneous digressions. The tape—like the projection—can be stopped at any point for discussion, and can later be replayed for review so that the pupils are presented with the ideas in a consistent fashion.

Having planned the overall presentation, the instructor must prepare the class to see it. Just how he goes about this will depend on the pupils' readiness and initial interest, but the important point to bear in mind is that the students should *want* to see it for reasons of their own. Thus, if the instructor feels that an introductory explanation made by himself of why the pupils are being shown this particular material at this particular time, the purpose of the experience, etc., he should be sure not to overlook pupil motivation. As stressed repeatedly throughout this book, preparation activities which involve active pupil participation should be incorporated wherever it is feasible to include them.

In preparing the class for what it is to see, the teacher must provide ways by which the pupils will understand clearly what to look for. How an instructor uses a filmstrip or any other kind of teaching material naturally depends on *why* he is using it—in other words, on his specific objectives. Should his purpose be to provide a general overview and to arouse interest, he may indicate general rather than specific points to be looked for. On the other hand, if he wishes to clarify certain definite concepts, he will wish his students to be alert for the answers to specific questions. For example, in using the filmstrip *The Slide Rule —Multiplication and Division,*[22] the mathematics instructor might well ask in advance such questions as the following:

1. What two scales on the slide rule are used for multiplication and division?
2. How should the scales be lined up to multiply? To divide?
3. How and where is the result found?

The teacher should also anticipate new or difficult words, phrases, and symbols. For example, one teacher of a primary reading class which was using the filmstrip *Peter and Susan Visit Grandfather's Farm* asked her children—before she wrote new words on the chalkboard—"Now, children, what did we see with Peter and Susan yesterday on their grandfather's farm?"

"We saw their grandfather," said one child; "a cow," offered another; and "a sheep and some pigs" said a third. "There were little pigs and big pigs," volunteered still another child. "What were we about to see with Peter and Susan when our reading period ended yesterday?" asked the teacher. Again there was a flurry of hands, and one little girl blurted out, "The barn. We were going to see the barn."

The teacher went to the chalkboard and wrote the words *barn, red, big, hay, cows, horse,* and a few others as they came up in the children's discussion. "Now shall we see if we can find all these things with Susan and Peter when they go to their grandfather's barn? And maybe we'll find some other things too. Let's watch closely."

[22] U.S. Office of Education; available from United World Films.

Thus, the stage is set by one primary teacher for an exciting filmstrip adventure which will give pleasure to her pupils and help develop several new concepts with them.

Unless the primary purpose of using a filmstrip is to teach new word concepts, as in this reading lesson, it is essential to remove in advance such barriers to learning as new words and symbols. This can be done through discussion, use of the dictionary, and illustrations. The new concepts will then be applied promptly when the filmstrip is shown, and they are likely to be well learned as a result. Of greater importance, however, is the pupil's improved comprehension of content made possible by the removal of vocabulary barriers.

Mechanical as well as instructional preparation must be taken into account in the effective use of filmstrips and slides. Most teachers quickly sense the convenience, as well as the great effectiveness, of having all their teaching materials ready for use at the beginning of the period. The filmstrip or slide projector can be set up and tested in a few minutes, so that at the proper moment a flick of the switch will bring the first picture to the screen without delay and confusion. More important is the fact that when everything is in readiness, lesson interruptions are held to a minimum. The filmstrip, slide, or other projected medium fits smoothly and naturally into the learning experience. It assumes its proper role in helping to put across certain ideas without attracting undue attention to the operator or to the projector.

▪ PRESENTATION

The particular mode of presentation of projected materials—for example, the pace at which they are presented, the kind of narration or accompanying sound effects used, the way captions are handled, and whether or not other learning media are used in conjunction with the still projection—are contingent on the specific objectives the teacher hopes to achieve in the particular learning situation (Fig. 12.15). For example, if the initial showing of the material is to provide an introductory overview of a new unit of study, the instructor may wish to show a complete filmstrip in one showing and save class questions, comments, and detailed analysis of any one frame or idea for later when detailed study of individual frames may be appropriate. For such an overview, a filmstrip may be run through at a fairly rapid pace to emphasize only the highlights to be assimilated by the pupils. In this case, the captions on the filmstrip might be read aloud by the instructor as the filmstrip proceeds in order to save time, to keep things moving, and to assure that everyone is following the basic story as it unfolds on the screen.

When still-projection materials are to be used as a basis for class discussion—perhaps in a detailed study of materials they have already seen—there is no reason to hurry, and flexibility in timing and discussion should be built into the presentation. It may be that the entire class period is to be devoted to the showing of just a few frames of a filmstrip or to a few individual slides. In this case, captions on the filmstrip or transparency need not be read aloud, as the concepts verbalized in these captions undoubtedly will be covered in the class discussion. Similarly, a prepared explanation or narration would be pointless when individual frames are held on the screen for full discussion, questioning, and classification.

Still projection can also be used spontaneously, to clarify or to communicate ideas that have arisen unexpectedly in a class discussion or unit of study. This is particularly true in the case of the overhead or opaque projectors. For example, as one social-studies class assembled, there was a buzz of excitement over the remarkable rendezvous of the Gemini VI and VII spacecraft the day before. Many students had watched the recovery of the space capsule on one of the school's television sets, and were particularly eager to discuss the space flights. The teacher had naturally anticipated this opportunity, and produced a spectacular news photo from the morning paper (Fig. 12.16). As he projected the photo by means of the opaque projector, he commented, "Some of you may have seen this this morning, but no one in the world before today has ever seen two spacecraft rendezvous 160 miles above the earth, and I thought you would like to look at it again."

The discussion which ensued resulted in a planned investigation of the national space program in which the pupils, arranging themselves in committees, read, and reported on the moon shot program and other space projects planned for the future. One committee located and planned to demonstrate with a filmstrip showing photographs of satellites and missile launchings (Fig. 12.17).

There is also the possibility that the filmstrip, slide series, or transparencies projection is to be used for a quick review to "clinch" ideas which have been developed in detail previously. Here, too, the pace of the showing may be fairly rapid, and it might be a good idea to read the titles or captions again. The teacher is the best judge as to whether or not the ideas contained in the captions should be read aloud for reinforcement learning of these ideas. But if so, why not let some of the students do the reading? The teacher can tell something about how well the pupils understand the subject by the way they read the captions, and this provides an opportunity for pupil participation.

A further consideration is that a group of students may be using the projection materials by themselves. Learning from still projection occurs in this way (Fig. 12.18). In this case, the students can help one another read the captions and titles as necessary.

A fundamental principle in educational-media usage is that wherever feasible and appropriate, we should employ a variety of media, each of which is selected on the basis of how it can best implement learning of the subject matter involved. In this connection, several still-projection techniques and materials can be used together in multiscreen presentations. For example, in geography, a map of a large area may be projected onto one screen by use of the overhead projector, with a small section on this map projected in enlarged form next to it by use of another projector. Perhaps a small mountainous area that is represented symbolically on the map can be visualized concretely by use of slides of the same area. Climatic or cultural effects of geography might also be shown by slides, transparencies, or filmstrips which show schematic diagrams of airflows, rainfall, etc., or cultural scenes depicting clothing worn by inhabitants of the area, the dwelling structures, and so forth.

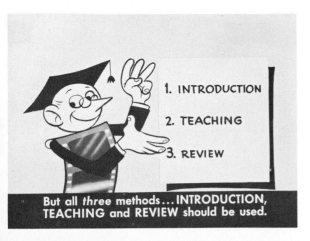

1. INTRODUCTION
2. TEACHING
3. REVIEW

But all *three* methods...INTRODUCTION, TEACHING and REVIEW should be used.

Fig. 12.15. / (Left) This frame from the filmstrip *Teaching with the Filmstrip* suggests several ways in which filmstrips can be used.

Fig. 12.16. / (Below) This photograph of the National Aeronautics and Space Administration's Gemini VII spacecraft was taken through the hatch of Gemini VI at an altitude of approximately 160 miles during the first successful rendezvous of two spacecraft achieved by man on December 15, 1965.

Fig. 12.17. / A missile launching at Cape Kennedy.

Similarly, in mathematics, a problem projected on one screen can be retained while the solution is worked out on another through a series of transparent overlays, or by writing on the surface of the continuous plastic roll on a second overhead projector.

By the same token, the learning situation may call for several different media to be used in a single lesson. A few slides, a short film, a section of sound tape and perhaps a summary of points on the overhead might be an appropriate combination to use within a class period. Should it be—and the answer must lie in the specific learning needs of the particular lesson—a second screen will frequently facilitate the operation and placement of equipment.

In a study of multimedia usage, Johnson found that a combination of three motion-picture films and three filmstrips definitely improved retention and ability to apply geometric principles and facts regarding circles.[23] Neither films nor filmstrips alone produced comparable results. The initial learning of facts and problem-solving skills in geometry was not increased by the use of films and filmstrips, but Johnson suggests that this may have been due to the fact that the materials themselves were similar in nature to those commonly found in textbooks or drawn on the chalkboard by the teacher.

If multimedia use appears farfetched to the teacher who is still having difficulty getting a single projector when needed, let two things be noted: One is that multimedia applications are already common in industrial- and military-training programs where they have effectively demonstrated their value, and they are also found in increasing numbers of colleges and universities where serious and often highly imaginative efforts are being made to improve the quality of undergraduate instruction; the second factor is that Federal support programs for education are making it increasingly practicable for schools and higher institutions of learning to have the instructional equipment and materials they need to strengthen their instructional programs. In light of the essential importance of education to national progress, there is little doubt that Federal support to all levels of education will increase in the

[23] Donovan A. Johnson, "Are Films and Filmstrips Effective in Teaching Geometry?" *School Science and Mathematics*, October, 1950, pp. 570–574.

Fig. 12.18. / Another type of viewer well-suited to individual student use or teacher preview.

future. The key questions now are the extent to which teachers and administrators will avail themselves of these opportunities and then translate them intelligently into educational programs which are significantly better than those we now have. Clearly, media have an important role to play in instructional developments of the future. But just as clearly, the quality of new educational planning which educators can bring to bear on the problems of learning, teaching, and curriculum will provide the real measure of whether or not we are equal to the task.

■ FOLLOWUP ACTIVITIES

As stressed repeatedly throughout this book, no learning situation is complete without ample provision and planning for followup activities which will permit the pupils to reinforce their learning through self-evaluation, demonstration of the concepts learned, and application of the learning in new situations. Such followup activities, of course, permit the teacher to evaluate pupil learning, and also the relative effectiveness of the learning media used.

Thus, after the filmstrip, slides, or other still-projection presentation has been given in full, the teacher may wish to give a brief written or oral test on the material covered. Wherever possible, however, the instructor should call for a practical demonstration of the concepts learned. Suppose that a filmstrip was shown on how to read a micrometer. The real test in this case of pupil learning is how well each pupil can handle and read a real micrometer. From these evaluative activities, the teacher may judge the pupils' weak areas and those points which need to be reviewed or taught again, individual pupil difficulties, and, significantly, pupil interest in further learning. The teacher may also judge from the results of the evaluation whether the particular still-projection medium, or the teacher's presentation of it, has efficiently accomplished its purpose. If the class generally seems to exhibit less understanding than hoped for—if a fairly sizable number of pupils seem to be having some difficulty—the teacher should review in his own mind the adequacy of the

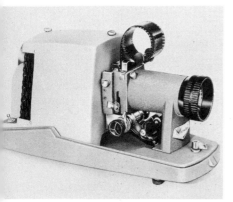  

Fig. 12.19. / Three of the many good filmstrip projectors available to the teacher. (Left to right: Viewlex, Graflex, and Bell & Howell.) Note what considerations are important in selecting such equipment.

materials he chose and the methods he used in presenting them. It may be that the teacher failed to prepare the pupils sufficiently for the learning experience, or failed to elicit their interest in the experience.

Aside from evaluation, the followup period serves to provide the students with avenues for applying their new learning and which make it their own in areas and in ways which interest them.

The learner normally proceeds from concrete observation to abstract retention of ideas, to application of these ideas in real and concrete situations, to generalizations drawn from a number of such applications, and finally to assimilation of these generalizations as a part of the learner's permanent understanding. Thus, the viewing or reading of materials is only a small part of this process. A variety of further activities should develop from the new learning gained. Class discussions can lead to the initiating of projects which truly interest the pupils and which will enable them to acquire greater depth of understanding. Some pupils may wish to work together in small groups on projects; others may prefer to carry out projects individually on some aspect of particular interest.

As the children report on the progress or completion of their respective projects, they have an opportunity to make comparisons with similar experiences they have had. Out of such comparisons, some generalized conclusions may come. When these generalizations provide the basis for all further learning, we say that the learner has *assimilated* his knowledge.

□ THE NATURE AND USE OF PROJECTORS

Certain mechanical considerations of the equipment used in still projection is essential knowledge for the teacher. In most cases, instructions on how to use and care for the projector accompanies the school projector; however, certain points may be noted here, especially to provide a comparative view of what is involved in the mechanics of the different still-projection techniques.

■ FILMSTRIP AND 2 × 2 SLIDE PROJECTORS

A filmstrip projector is essentially a simple mechanism (Fig. 12.19). It consists primarily of a lamp, a reflector, a series of lenses, and a smooth channel for the film. Near the base of this channel is a knob which is turned by hand to pull the filmstrip through the projector. The knob turns a sprocket wheel whose teeth fit into sprocket holes on the filmstrip. The projector is easy to operate and is inexpensive and light in weight—all points of practical importance.

A slide projector is also a simple mechanism, incorporating essentially the same principles utilized in filmstrip projectors, except that it has a slide carrier into which the slides are placed one at a time and changed by shifting the carriage from one side to another. Some models of slide projectors are equipped with "cartridges" into which a complete selection of slides can be loaded in advance (Fig. 12.20). Some models of filmstrip and slide projectors can be operated by remote control as well as manually, enabling the teacher to face his class as he manipulates the projector located at the rear of the room.

A number of reading-rate accelerators of various types are available for slide or filmstrip projectors. The system shown in Fig. 12.21 controls the reading rate (0 to 1000 words per minute) by means of a slot and a left-to-right scanning mechanism.

Although some projectors are made only for filmstrips and others only for 2 × 2 slides, filmstrip projectors frequently have attachments which can be inserted to project 2 × 2 slides. These vary somewhat from one make to another as to threading, ease of interchanging the slide carriage and filmstrip mechanism, brilliance of the projected image, projection lenses, and quality of the cooling system. Each of these factors should be considered in selecting a projector.

■ THREADING

Most filmstrip projectors are threaded by inserting the film into the film channel from above and pushing it down to engage the sprocket teeth. This method has the advantage of insuring correct alignment in the film channel and proper engagement with the sprocket teeth. Since the sprocket holes on

Fig. 12.20. / Three cartridge-type 2 × 2 slide projectors—again representative of the many available. (Top: Sawyer's; bottom: Spindler Sauppe, and Kodak.) Most filmstrip projectors are adaptable for 2 × 2 slides.

filmstrips are easily damaged, ease of threading the projector is an important consideration. Since sprocket-hole damage ordinarily occurs on the leader strip while the projector is being threaded, it can usually be detected before the picture section itself is damaged. Rubberized pressure rollers or other substitutes for sprockets may sometime provide a solution to the problem of sprocket-hole damage. Meantime, reasonable care in using the projector will hold such damage to a minimum. As new models of filmstrip projectors are introduced, the threading operation is being made easier and more foolproof.

▪ Light Intensity

The intensity of light determines the brilliance of the projected picture on the screen and hence the degree of darkness necessary for effective projection. Light intensity is determined primarily by the power of the projection lamp and the quality of the lens system. Although projectors with lower power are still found in use occasionally, nothing less than a 500-watt capacity should be considered in a projector for classroom use. This amount of power is necessary to project a picture that is of sufficient size, brilliance, and color quality.

With larger groups, as when several classes are combined, a 750- or 1000-watt projector is needed for best results. For very large groups, as in a large auditorium, a 1000- or 1200-watt lamp is the minimum necessary and, in this case, professional-type arc-lighted equipment may be required.

■ PROJECTION LENSES

The quality of the lenses and reflectors is almost as important as the power of the projection lamp in obtaining a brilliant image on the screen. Manufacturers agree that brilliance over the entire picture area is important for effective projection of filmstrips and slides. Accordingly, the most satisfactory way to compare several projectors is to line them up side by side and project the same color picture simultaneously on each projector under conditions of normal use. By aligning the screen images from several projectors, first side by side and then overlapping them slightly, a good comparison of their relative quality can be made.

The focal length of the lens, the size of the aperture, and the distance from

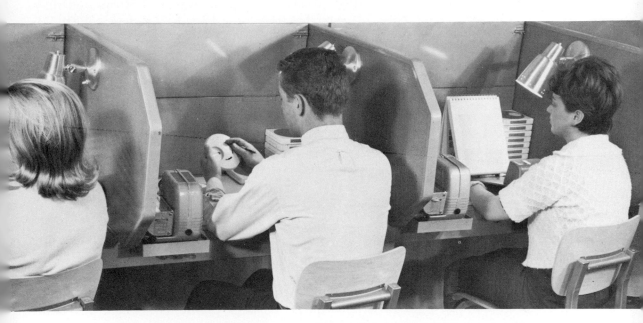

Fig. 12.21. / Individual drill with a tachistoscope using a filmstrip and a specially designed projector.

projector to screen determine the size of picture seen. It is normally desirable to project from the rear of the classroom to avoid distracting pupils or blocking the view of those who are seated behind the projector. For these reasons, the length and size of the projection should be considered when purchasing a projector.

Most filmstrip projectors are equipped with a 5-inch projection lens which produces a single-frame image about 4 or 5 feet wide from a distance of 30 feet. Although the 5-inch lens is suitable for most classrooms, a 7-inch lens is preferable for larger classrooms and assembly rooms. With this lens, a projector 50 feet from the screen provides a picture 58 × 77 inches.[24] At this distance, the

24 The figures given are for the usual single-frame filmstrip. Double-frame filmstrips and 2 × 2 slides provide pictures which are 4.5 × 6.5 feet from a distance of 25 feet; 5.4 × 7.8 feet from a distance of 30 feet, and 9.0 × 13.0 feet from 50 feet away.

picture projected by a 5-inch lens would be too large for the average portable screen. Hence, if the same projector is to be used in both large and small rooms, it is desirable to have more than one lens. Another advantage of the 7-inch lens is that it projects a 2×2 slide picture which is approximately the same size as a 16 mm. motion picture projected from the same distance with a standard 2-inch lens. If a teacher wishes to use both slides and motion pictures in a lesson, the two projectors can be placed side by side.

■ COOLING SYSTEMS

Heat is the enemy of all film, and projector manufacturers have been working for years to refine cooling systems to the point where filmstrips and slides can be left on the screen for extended periods without risk of damage. All filmstrips or slide projectors suitable for school use are cooled by an electric fan or blower system. Good engineering has steadily reduced the noise of these forced-air systems to a minimum, but both the adequacy of cooling and the noise level of projectors should be checked when making a selection. For the most part, on newer projector models, heat is no longer a problem.

An additional item to note is the ease and simplicity of operation of the framing device on filmstrip projectors. Although mechanically a minor item, the framer can be a nuisance if not readily accessible and operable.

■ THE OVERHEAD PROJECTOR

The overhead transparency projector transmits a strong beam of light through a transparency and onto a screen behind the instructor, who is at the front of the room facing his class (see Fig. 12.2 on page 356). In most overhead projectors, the light is reflected through a large plastic lens, which directs the light through the transparency into a second reflector above, and on out to the screen (Fig. 12.22). One lightweight model of the overhead projector provides the light source in the head, directs it downward to a reflector in the base and then back through the transparency to a reflector in the head and onto the screen (Fig. 12.23). The principle is the same as that described above though the mechanics are different. The light is sufficiently brilliant so that little room darkening is required.

The operation of the overhead projector is very simple; little more is involved than placing the transparency on the projector stage. The material is focused by raising or lowering the upper reflector unit by turning a knob. The projection area is commonly 10×10 inches in the numerous models available. Most overhead projectors contain a 100 foot strip of clear plastic which passes over the projector stage between two rollers located inside the projector. The instructor can write on the clear plastic as he would on the chalkboard or he can prepare panels ahead of time and roll them into position by turning a small crank. Diagrams, lesson assignments, tests, and similar material can effectively be presented in this way with a minimum of time and effort.

A unique accessory for the overhead projector provides for the use of polarized light to create an effect of animation on projected transparencies. This involves a motor-driven polarized disk beneath the projector head, and polarized strips on the transparency itself. The disk revolves, causing the light and color patterns to change rapidly, giving the effect of animation. This device is useful for providing animated diagrams, graphs, lettering, or other display material.

Another device which can be attached to some overhead projectors, and to some 2 $\times$ 2 slide projectors, is the tachistoscope. This attachment enables the instructor to flash scenes onto the viewing screen at speeds up to 1/100 of a second. A refinement is provided by a device which holds a constant reference point on the screen for the student and keeps the image lighted but out of focus except for the split-second exposure desired. This technique is reported as eliminating retinal afterimages. Aside from the motivational effect of these devices, their proper use appears to result in a significant improvement in speed of reading and number recognition.

Expert use on the part of the instructor is called for, including short, follow-up practice sessions for the student, and a high level of motivation to maintain increased speeds. For, as Stroud points out in discussing the film programs:

> . . . If the student tires, as he must in longer periods, he will have a tendency to revert to a slower and more comfortable rate. After the faster rate becomes habitual, it is no more tiring than a slower rate. Effort requires motivation. Here the attempt is made to arrange conditions so the student will practice reading in a different way. Mere practice, reading in the accustomed way, will only maintain the status quo. One learns by practice what he practices.[25]

■ THE OPAQUE PROJECTOR

Opaque materials are projected by means of *reflected* light. A strong light from the projector lamp is thrown onto a book page or other opaque material and is reflected by a tilted mirror through a lens onto a screen (Fig. 12.24). Although the screen image is normally less brilliant than in the case of a slide or transparency, where the light passes directly through the material, highly satisfactory images can be obtained if the room is reasonably well darkened. Further, the lighting efficiency of the newer projectors has been improved to the point where effective projection is possible even in moderately darkened rooms. These improved projectors have a 1000-watt lamp, an opening large enough to accommodate 8½- $\times$ 11-inch materials, and an efficient, motor-driven cooling system. Down-draft ventilation holds loose or unmounted material in place without fluttering or loss of focus. A loose postage stamp, for example, can be projected without difficulty with this type of projector. When

25 James B. Stroud, *op. cit.*, p. 153.

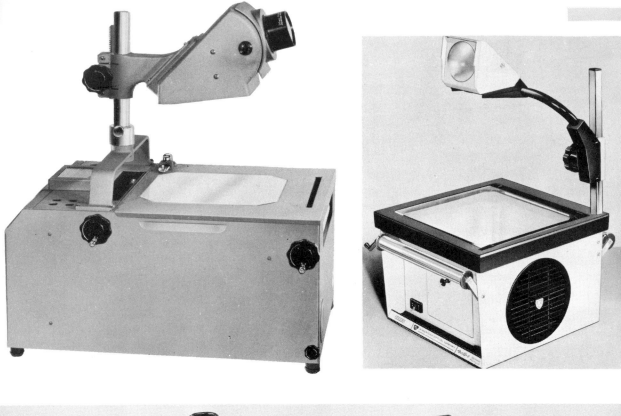
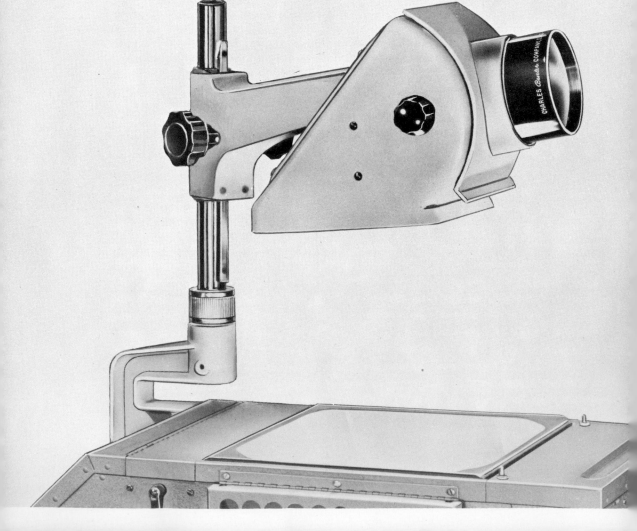

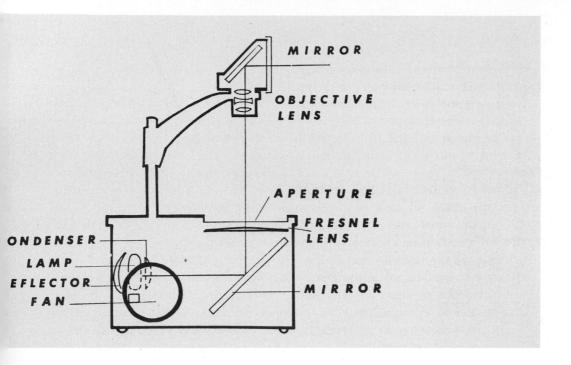

MIRROR

OBJECTIVE
LENS

APERTURE

FRESNEL
LENS

ONDENSER

LAMP

EFLECTOR

FAN

MIRROR

Fig. 12.22. / Three representative overhead projectors. (Left to right, top) Transpaque (Projection Optics); American Optical Co.; (bottom left) Vu-Graph (Charles Beseler Co.).

Fig. 12.23. / This useful, lightweight model of an overhead projector contains the light source in the head.

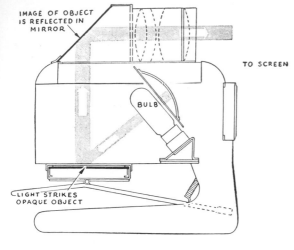

IMAGE OF OBJECT
IS REFLECTED IN
MIRROR

TO SCREEN

BULB

LIGHT STRIKES
OPAQUE OBJECT

Fig. 12.24. / From this diagram can you explain how the opaque projector (left) works? Also shown is one of the several good 1000-watt opaque projectors available.

projecting a page in a book, a piece of heat-resistant glass will hold the page flat so that all parts of it can be focused sharply.

☐ SUMMARY

Still projection makes possible group examination of individual pictures and illustrative materials for as long as the teaching purpose requires. It also has the attention-focusing power of all projected images. Together, these advantages make for a powerful and effective teaching medium when motion is not essential to comprehension.

There are various forms of still projection such as filmstrips, 2×2 and $3\frac{1}{4} \times 4$ slides, opaque projection, overhead transparency projection, micro-projection, and stereoprojection. In addition—and primarily for individual use —there are stereodisks and microfilms. Each of the above forms has unique advantages and uses in instruction.

As with other audiovisual materials, the effectiveness of still-projection media depends to a large extent on how they are used. In general, the familiar principles of all good teaching apply: preview and selection of the most appropriate materials; class preparation, including motivating pupils and directing them as to what to look for; good projection conditions; and followup activities, including testing, application, and reteaching as needed. Good procedure is flexible rather than rigid; it adapts itself to the requirements of the individual learning situation.

Familiarity with the various still-projection media and materials will enable the teacher to apply each of those available to him so as to achieve maximum learning among his pupils.

☐ Suggested Activities

1. As a committee or individual project, have units of work in a given subject and grade area analyzed as to
   a. Where still-projection materials could make significant contributions to learning
   b. What specific materials could do the job
2. Survey the still-projection equipment and facilities of your school and prepare a report for your principal or superintendent that includes:
   a. Present status
   b. Recommended additions and changes for next year
   c. Recommended changes and additions for the next five years. Draw up supporting statements for your recommendations
3. As a building director of audiovisual instruction, you have been concerned for several years about the tendency of most of your teachers to use motion-picture films rather than available still-projection materials, regardless of the latter's superiority in many teaching situations. You get permission from your principal to call a faculty meeting for the purpose of "educating" your teachers regarding the potentialities of one or two types of still-projection. Prepare a demonstration for your audiovisual class showing how you might do this.
4. Divide the class into committees and have each one prepare a demonstration showing interesting applications of one of the following:
   a. The opaque projector
   b. Handmade slides
   c. The filmstrip projector
   d. 2×2 slides
   e. $3\frac{3}{4} \times 4$ slides
   f. The microprojector
   g. The overhead transparency projector
   h. A stereoviewer
5. In order to give class members information about various types of still-projection equipment, ask an interested group to write for literature in sufficient quantities so that each member will have individual copies. If feasible, arrange with your local dealer to demonstrate several makes of equipment during a laboratory period or outside of class. Report to the class your reactions concerning new ideas and the strong and weak points of the equipment demonstrated.

☐ Bibliography

Bastion, J. W., "Slides and Tape in Language Teaching," *Educational Screen,* October, 1953, p. 347.

Booher, Edward H., "Textbook Publishing—An Art Extended," *Audiovisual Instruction,* January, 1961, pp. 15–18.

Brown, J. W., R. B. Lewis, and F. F. Harcleroad, *Audiovisual Instruction* (rev. ed.), McGraw-Hill, 1964, pp. 142–161, 464–476, 535–545.

Clark, Jay, "Making Sound Filmstrips from 2″ x 2″ Slides," *Audiovisual Instruction,* May, 1965, p. 402.

Dale, Edgar, *Audio-Visual Methods in Teaching* (rev. ed.), Dryden, 1954, pp. 258–268.

Dennis, Donald A., "Preproduction Planning: Key to Successful Slide Shows," *Audiovisual Instruction,* May, 1965, p. 401.

Greeshaber, Emil W., "Overhead Projection—How to Make the Most of It," *Audiovisual Instruction,* April, 1962, pp. 236–237. (Entire issue devoted to overhead projection. Note also articles by Arthur Lalime, Neville Pearson, and Emma Starstream.)

Hartsell, H. C., and Wilfred Veenendaal, *Overhead Projection,* Henry Stewart, Inc., 1960.

Jenkins, Orville, "Filmstrips for Home Use," *Educational Screen and Audiovisual Guide,* September, 1963, p. 514.

Keystone Tachistoscope: Advanced Teaching Techniques, Keystone View Company, 1956.

Kinder, James, *Audio-Visual Materials and Techniques* (2nd ed.), 1959, pp. 99–154.

Nelson, G. K., "Unconventional—But it Works" [Slide projector at front of room], *Audiovisual Instruction,* May, 1963, p. 335.

Robinson, M. M., "Using the Opaque Projector in Teaching Composition," *English Journal,* October, 1946, pp. 442–445.

Sands, Lester B., "Films and Filmstrips for Arithmetic," *Grade Teacher,* February, 1960, pp. 25 ff.

Sands, Lester B., "The Overhead Projector—A Fresh Approach to Slide Projection," *Grade Teacher,* November, 1957, pp. 52 ff.

Scuorzo, Herbert E., "The Overhead Projector Comes of Age," *Grade Teacher,* April, 1963, pp. 15 ff.

Siergiej, E. J., "Using the Opaque Projector in Tool Subjects," *Instructor,* June, 1953, pp. 92–93.

Shampo, Marc A., "Homemade Filmstrips for Science," *The Science Teacher,* May, 1962, pp. 43–45.

Thomas, R. Murray, and Sherwin G. Swartout, *Integrated Teaching Materials,* McKay, 1960, pp. 160–184, 234–238.

Thompson, J. H., "Colored Slide Collection for Geography Teachers," *Journal of Geography,* March, 1954, pp. 117–123.

Van Vlack, Milt, "Captions Were the Key" [Preparation of captioned transparencies], *Educational Screen and Audiovisual Guide,* November, 1965, pp. 28–29.

Visual Instruction Bureau, "The Opaque Projector," *Bridges for Ideas* Series, No. 10, University of Texas.

Warner, M. E., "Overhead Projection for Teaching Drafting," *Industrial Arts and Vocational Education,* December, 1953, pp. 350–353.

Washcoe, W. C., "The Versatile Overhead Projector," *Educational Screen and Audiovisual Guide,* May, 1959, pp. 242–244.

Wilber, Jean A., "Multiplane Transparencies,'" *Educational Screen and Audiovisual Guide,* September, 1964, p. 515.

Wimmer, M., "Microscopic Projection and Micro-Photographic Slide Making," *Educational Screen,* January, 1939, pp. 8–9.

☐ **Films and Filmstrips**

Children Learn from Filmstrips, 16 mm. film, B&W and Color, 16 min., McGraw-Hill, 1963.

Enriching the Curriculum with Filmstrips, 35 mm. filmstrip, B&W, 60 frames, Society for Visual Education, Inc., 1952.

Handmade Lantern Slides, 35 mm. filmstrip, Color, 50 frames, Ohio State University, 1954.

Handmade Materials for Projection, 16 mm. film, Color, 20 min., Indiana University, 1956.

High Contrast Photography, 16 mm. film, Color, 21 min., Indiana University, 1955.

How to Make Handmade Lantern Slides, 16 mm. film, Color, 22 min., Indiana University, 1947.

Introducing Filmstrips, 35 mm. filmstrip, B&W, 29 frames, National Film Board of Canada, 1947.

Lettering Instructional Material, 16 mm. film, B&W, 20 min., Indiana University, 1955.

Magazine to Transparencies, 16 mm. film, Color, 12 min., Florida State University, 1959.

The Opaque Projector, 35 mm. filmstrip, Color, 42 frames, Ohio State University, 1958.

The Opaque Projector—Its Purposes and Use, 16 mm. film, B&W, 6 min., State University of Iowa, 1957.

Overhead Projector, 16 mm. film, B&W, 16 min., State University of Iowa, 1953.

Photographic Slides for Instruction, 16 mm. film, B&W and Color, 10 min., Indiana University, 1956.

Simplified Filmstrip Production, 35 mm. filmstrip, B&W, 40 frames, Ohio State University, 1952.

Slidefilm in Teaching, 35 mm. filmstrip, B&W, 46 frames, Young American Films, 1946.

Still Projectors, 8 mm. film cartridges, Chandler Publishing Company, 1965. Series includes:
  2 x 2 inch Slide Projectors, 3 min., 33 sec.
  35 mm. Filmstrip Projector, 3 min., 10 sec.
  Opaque Projector, 2 min., 55 sec.
  Overhead Projector, 3 min., 33 sec.

Teachers Consider Filmstrips, 35 mm. filmstrip, Color, 27 frames, Eye Gate House, 1950.

Teaching with a Filmstrip, 35 mm. filmstrip, B&W, 50 frames, Society for Visual Education, Inc., 1953.

Transparency—Making, 8 mm. film cartridges, Color, Chandler Publishing Company, 1965. Series includes:
  Transparencies: *Adding Color,* 3 min., 45 sec.
  Transparencies: *Diazo Process,* 3 min., 45 sec.
  Transparencies: *Handmade Method,* 3 min., 5 sec.
  Transparencies: *Heat Process,* 2 min., 15 sec.
  Transparencies: *Making Overlays,* 3 min., 45 sec.
  Transparencies: *Mounting and Masking,* 3 min., 15 sec.
  Transparencies: *Picture Transfer 1,* 3 min., 10 sec.
  Transparencies: *Picture Transfer 2,* 3 min., 30 sec.
  Transparencies: *Principle of Diazo Process,* 4 min., 40 sec.
  Transparencies: *Spirit Duplicator,* 3 min.

XIII

THE
MOTION-PICTURE
FILM

Man has searched since the time of Babel for the universal language. He has found it—and every government in our world "speaks" this language repeatedly and with clarity of communication. The new universal language is the motion-picture film.

For example, when a Midwestern university completed a descriptive 16 mm. sound motion-picture film about its state-school system, the picture message— which was clearly told—was in demand not only in the United States, but also abroad. Foreign governments purchased copies of the film, requesting that a special sound track be arranged for each country in its native language. Thus, while the picture story speaks its universal visual language, the sound track is changed according to the idiomatic local dialect of each country. Prints of the film are used in India, Norway, Israel, and South America.

Today, every recognized governmental embassy in the world prepares sound motion-picture films which explain its people, culture, and national achievements (Fig. 13.1). Such films are used both at home and abroad. As they are sent out to fringe areas, each of the picture stories is accompanied by a specially prepared sound track in the appropriate language. Almost every agency of our own federal government employs the film medium to report its activities and to carry on programs in adult education (Fig. 13.2). In the cases of the United States Department of Agriculture, the Department of Forestry, the Surgeon General, and the Department of Justice, annual film-production expenditures each year are increased in order that millions of adults and school children may witness the clear-cut reports of the U.S. government agencies.

Service and manufacturing industries also use the film as a prime medium of communication as they describe their achievements and methods, and report their progress (Fig. 13.3). The 1966 edition of an annually edited publication that describes films produced by industry includes nearly 8000 titles.[1] It is estimated that each title costs from $35,000 to $45,000 to produce. The hundreds of millions of dollars that are represented in such film productions are justified in terms of the communication, clarity, and interest value of the films.

Most of the major colleges and universities of America also have established

---

[1] *Educators Guide to Free 16 mm. Films,* Educators Progress Service, 1966.

Fig. 13.1. / Machines come to the rice paddies. These stills are from the film *Agriculture in Japan,* distributed by the Consulate General of Japan.

Fig. 13.2. / These stills are representative of the wide variety of subject matter covered in the many films planned and produced under the auspices of most of our Federal agencies. What are some uses to which teachers can put the U.S. Department of Agriculture film (right) and the U.S. Navy film (left)?

Fig. 13.3 / U.S. private industry spends hundreds of millions of dollars in producing films such as these sponsored (left) by Bell Telephone Company with Pacific Telephone and (right) by United Airlines.

film-production departments. The film medium is used by these institutions to document and to explain their research; to report to citizens new techniques in education, business, and agriculture; and to explain higher education itself. The teacher and the school administrator have sensed the power of the motion-picture film as a communication tool for educational purposes. Teachers have been quick to sense the great potential of the motion-picture film as a means for realistically and interestingly bringing the entire world of meaning into the classroom at the time it is needed. The teacher understands that, in order to learn well, one needs to see and hear things as they exist. Sooner or later, the pupil needs to see and to hear everything and everywhere; to look into the past and to examine the future; and, on occasion, to acquire a kind of "super-sight" which permits him to observe natural phenomena in slow motion or in acceleration, or in magnified or diminished representation.

Today, much of this kind of experience can become part of classroom learning through the motion-picture film. This need has encouraged the establishment of many film-production organizations to create filmed learning materials which are useful in all areas of the curriculum (see Source List, pages 528, 533). Following the leadership of successful pioneers in educational motion-picture production—Encyclopaedia Britannica, Coronet, McGraw-Hill Films Division, United World, Academy, International Film Bureau, and a host of others— almost every "old line" textbook publication today produces films for the classroom.

Sound motion-picture films enable teachers to fulfill better their demanding roles. The social-studies teacher must help his pupils learn about the farthest reaches of the earth and space. The science teacher must help his students understand all manner of natural phenomena. The history teacher must help his class understand the events of the past and the present. The language teacher must help his pupils understand the people and the cultural patterns which have produced the language. The film medium is an excellent and economical way of achieving these teaching goals.

During the brief span of its existence, the educational motion-picture appeared first as the silent 35 mm. motion-picture film and next in the form of the silent 16 mm. motion-picture film. After 1930, sound was introduced, and today, while a few silent films remain in use, the 16 mm. sound film occupies the center of the instructional "stage." But, vigorous new developments in 8 mm. silent and sound film already share the spotlight. Altogether, these instructional motion pictures offer exciting and understandable teaching-learning experiences to teachers and pupils.

☐ THE HISTORY OF EDUCATIONAL FILMS

Little did Thomas Edison realize, when, in 1908, he perfected the motion-picture film, that he was creating one of the most significant communication tools for use in American education. With great foresight, two of Edison's first 35 mm. silent films—*The House Fly* and *The Frog*—quickly caught the imagination and attention of schoolteachers. Even though these films were only of short duration and had no sound, a few teachers and administrators incorporated them as "experimental materials" in their teaching.

It was not until 1922, however, that significant attention was given to teaching films as possibly an important classroom teaching medium. During this year, and shortly after the invention of the Eastman 16 mm. silent motion-picture projector, Yale University produced a series of fifteen motion-picture films in American history entitled "The Chronicles of American Photoplays."[2] A board of editors which included historians and teachers supervised every step in the writing of the script and the production of each film. Great care was taken to recreate costumes and properties, and historic sites were actually rebuilt. Everything was done that would realistically and correctly recapture the essence of the 15 historical episodes presented by this series.

The completion of these films led to the undertaking of the first carefully controlled research in this field which attempted to answer the question, "Was the motion-picture film a serious and worthwhile means of contributing to classroom learning experiences?" The results of this research established that the use of the "Chronicles of America Photoplays" series increased pupils' knowledge of places, personages, and events from 19 to 35 percent. More important, it stimulated 40 percent more free reading by pupils who had seen and studied the silent film materials.

Shortly after the completion of this study, the National Education Association and the Eastman Kodak Company cooperatively produced the materials for a second research experiment.[3] Several 16 mm. silent films in science and the social studies were tried out in classroom situations, with the result that over 60 percent of the pupils who saw and studied the films achieved a level of proficiency obtained by only 50 percent of the pupils who did not see the films. Once again it was established that there was greater interest in voluntary reading among the film-using group of pupils.

These early experiments heightened the interest of educators everywhere. The addition of sound to the motion-picture film during 1929 and 1930 brought in the era of the educational sound motion-picture film. Since that time the production of educational sound films has advanced steadily in both quality and quantity. Today, the newest innovation which has claimed importance and the attention of teachers is the 8 mm. film, often called the "continuous loop film," "8 mm. silent films," "8 mm. cartridge films," etc. These are available usually in silent form but, with increasing frequency, also in sound.

The 8 mm. motion-picture film is related to the 16 mm. film in approximately the way eight compares to sixteen when describing the width of the projected individual frames of the films. Usually the 8 mm. film is projected onto a smaller screen, or onto a rear-view screen to produce a highly visual and well-defined image. A process described as "super 8" is a method of photography and projection which yields an advantage through using proportionately more of the available film stock to carry each picture image.

2 Yale University Press Film Service, 1922.
3 Ben D. Wood and Frank N. Freeman, *Motion Picture in the Classroom,* Houghton Mifflin, 1929.

Most 8 mm. silent films are available in from three to five minutes in length and are mounted in continuous-loop cartridges which may be pushed into the projector, shown, and removed for reuse or storage with great simplicity. Sound 8 mm. films are becoming increasingly available in lengths of from 10 to 20 minutes and are available either in standard reels for manual threading, or in larger continuous-loop cartridges. In the latter case, the sound is carried by a thin strip of magnetic material which lies on the surface of the film. This slightly raised strip acts as a relatively frictionless transport surface, making possible longer continuous-loop cartridges which eliminate manual threading (Fig. 13.4).

The production record of 8 mm. silent and sound teaching films is the clearest indication of its status. More than sixty film producers throughout the world, most of them long experienced in the production of 16 mm. silent and sound motion-picture films, are now engaged in producing silent 8 mm. film

Fig. 13.4. / 8 mm. film equipment is becoming in increasingly widespread use today. Represented here are Fairchild's film cartridge and Mark IV projection system (top), and Technicolor Corp.'s version of similar equipment (bottom).

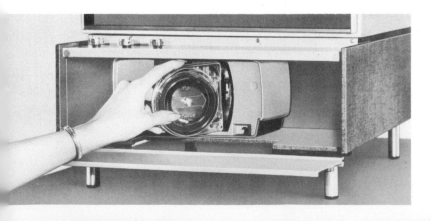

cartridges on various subjects, most of which are three to four minutes in length. A composite listing of available 8 mm. films includes over 3000 titles.[4]

The subjects of 8 mm. films parallel closely those available in 16 mm. film. Silent film cartridges, or single-concept films, are available in physical education, oceanography, vocational arts, social studies, and other subjects. Entire series of 8 mm. *sound* films are available for teaching foreign languages. However, since most 8 mm. film subjects are silent, eliminating the need for costly dubbing of sound-track translations, there is a free interchange of these films throughout the world. Consequently, the 8 mm. silent film is a dramatic force in bringing large amounts of American "know-how" to the rest of the schools of the world. International developments in the audiovisual field are being pushed forward rapidly for these reasons. Also, foreign producers in Europe, Africa, South America, Asia, and even Iceland, are now producing 8 mm. cartridge films for their own and export use.

The development of 8 mm. motion-picture techniques has led to the availability of 8 mm. cameras which are inexpensive, simple, and easy to operate, and the application of 8 mm. films to school activities promises to be useful in a variety of ways. For example, the project on educational communications conducted by the Teachers College at Columbia University reveals one such application of this medium.[5] By recording on 8 mm. film simple documentaries of young children in preschool programs and later showing these to other preschool children, it was discovered that the 8 mm. picture record can contribute effectively to the successful entry of young children into school programs. Another advantage of making 8 mm. documentary film records of school achievements and activities lies in their parent-education value when they are shown to parents during PTA meetings or Education Week gatherings.

□ THE VALUE OF SOUND MOTION-PICTURE FILMS

Of the many manifestations of twentieth-century genius, the sound film is perhaps the greatest. The motion-picture camera records what it sees, the sound track carries a record of what is heard. Thus, two of man's primary senses—seeing and hearing—can be stimulated simultaneously. The sound motion-picture film is an almost living document of our social world and the world of nature (Fig. 13.5).

Beginning in September, 1965, *Project Discovery*—a searching examination of the impact of maximum, or "saturation," availability of films and related materials in a learning environment—was undertaken among several thousand students in widely separated independent school districts.[6] Teachers in Shaker Heights, Ohio; Daley City, California; Washington, D.C.; and Terrell, Texas were given easy access to from 600 to 1000 motion-picture films, up to 2000 re-

4 Technicolor Corporation of America, *Source Directory* (2nd ed.), 1965.

5 Horace Mann—Lincoln Institute, *Newsletter of 8 mm. Film in Education,* Teachers College, Columbia Univ., June, 1965.

6 *Project Discovery: An Adventure with Teaching and Learning with Film; Progress Report,* Encyclopaedia Britannica Films, 1966.

Fig. 13.5. / Would you find use in your classroom for the actual film record of this situation? Unfortunately, the motion picture was invented too late. However, historians working with actors and film producers can re-create important historical episodes. This is a scene from *The Bill of Rights of the United States* (16 mm., color, 20 min., Encyclopaedia Britannica Films).

lated filmstrips, and a variety of other related educational materials. Participating teachers and their pupils were encouraged to use materials freely and without restraint, and in whatever way they wished. In this atmosphere, teachers evaluated, selected, and used various combinations of the films and other materials according to how they deemed the materials were appropriate to the actual units of study that they undertook in their day-to-day teaching (Fig. 13.6).

Although Project Discovery continues as an experiment, progress reports reaffirm existing research findings about the advantages of film use, and are rich with evidence that film use stimulates creative response by pupils: creative writing, research reading, map study, vocabulary searches, interpretative reading, pupil team-project construction, etc. Beyond this, however, the important generalization is that *availability* of films fosters their utilization:

> Students discover that maximum availability of films and filmstrips provides a front seat to learning, attracts attention to the wonders of the past and present, and supplies a wealth of information. "People come alive," students say. "It's like taking a trip. You see things you've never seen before."
> Films and filmstrips stimulate visionary thoughts of the future, make it possible to see those things which cannot be seen because they are too small, too large, or move too fast or too slow. "They motivate learning," a fifth grade girl claims. "You don't have time to sit back, you're too interested." They broaden reading interests, improve self-images, and encourage involvement—all students strive to be projectionists at all grade levels.[7]

7 Alice S. Van Deusen and Florence S. Witten, "Availability Fosters Usability," *Educational Leadership*, March, 1966, pp. 499–505.

Fig. 13.6. / Creative use of the sound motion-picture film as a *basic* instructional tool lies at the heart of Project Discovery. To what uses would you put the motion-picture film in your classroom?

Films can affect the whole climate of instruction. Careful selection and use of teaching films can result in positive changes in students' interest, learning efficiency, retention of learning, and reading performance. Films offer a natural path to learning and creative expression.

■ INCREASED PUPIL INTEREST

Various independently undertaken investigations have confirmed the increased pupil interest in subject matter when motion-picture films have been woven into the curriculum. A research study by Wittich and Fowlkes, for example, reports reactions of school children to the use of films.[8] Members of the intermediate grades were allowed to see carefully selected teaching films in science and the social studies. At first some of the children did not display much interest in the use of films in work-study situations but, by the end of the school year, changes in interest and attitude were evident, as the following sampling of verbatim comments reveal:

> Sound movies made it easier for me to understand about things. They don't use such big words as the geography book does.
> Seeing the films gave me new and different ideas.
> I learned from the films how countries really look, how people look. I got a better idea of what part of the world the country was at.

[8] Walter Arno Wittich and John Guy Fowlkes, *Audio-Visual Paths to Learning*, Harper, 1946, p. 29.

I never knew how some of the people lived when I read in books and I didn't know what kind of clothes they wore or how they looked.

It's fun and interesting because it tells what books don't tell. It makes it more plain to me. I can really see things.[9]

In response to the question, "Do you like this way of learning?" such statements as the following were made by these students. Note the individual differences in IQ and reading score among the respondents.

CASE 1 (IQ 135; reading score 9.6):
I liked the sound films because they are a new way of learning, and a movie gives more information than just reading. . . .

CASE 12 (IQ 114; reading score 7.6):
I like the sound films because I get more out of what I can really see. . . .

CASE 18 (IQ 105; reading score 8.2):
This way of learning shows the ways things are done. It's easier to understand the subject. . . .

CASE 28 (IQ 95; reading score 5.9):
I like this way of learning because I get information that I would not be able to find in books. . . .

CASE 30 (IQ 85; reading score 5.7):
I like this way of learning because I can see all the details. . . . In books there are only words and I can't see much of a background. In films I can hear the people.[10]

The fact that these pupils so consistently mentioned the clarity and understandability of films as learning devices leads to the observation that pupil interest is enhanced because the sound film is a realistic way of learning, like that used in out-of-school situations. We are conscious of our everyday environment because we observe it through sight, sound, and mind. A good teaching film is interesting because it presents information in a realistic manner. It is natural to learn by seeing and hearing.

■ INCREASED FACTUAL LEARNING

Research has also demonstrated that pupils actually learn more when motion-picture films are integrated into classroom work. Early studies by Wood and Freeman,[11] Wise,[12] and Knowlton and Tilton[13] uniformly gave evidence to the effect that when carefully selected silent films were used with regular classroom study materials, advantages in learning resulted that were far beyond what was possible with more traditional instruction materials. These studies reflected the presound film period in the school use of films.

After the sound film was brought into the classroom in the 1930s research

9 *Ibid.*
10 *Ibid.*
11 Ben D. Wood and Frank N. Freeman, *op. cit.*
12 Harry A. Wise, *Motion Pictures as an Aid in Teaching American History,* Yale Univ. Press, 1939.
13 Daniel C. Knowlton and J. Warren Tilton, *Motion Pictures in History Teaching,* Yale Univ. Press, 1929.

was undertaken to discover if it was as successful as the silent film. The chart in Fig. 13.7 answers this question in the affirmative. One of these investigations by Rulon describes the results obtained from using several selected sound films with ninth-grade general-science students: "In terms of immediate student achievement, our results indicated that the teaching technique employing the motion-picture film was 20.5 percent more effective from the instructional standpoint than was the usual unaided presentation."[14]

Arnspiger, measuring the effects of using sound films with almost 2400 fifth- and seventh-graders in five eastern cities, found that their use made distinct contributions to learning: "The per cents of superiority ranged from 22 to 30 in the natural science units and from 18 to 34 in the music unit."[15] Other researches conducted during these same years by Consitt, McClusky, and Weber, among others, showed similar results.[16]

Meierhenry, and others in Nebraska, measured the results of using 16 mm. sound motion-picture film with high-school students in 28 Nebraska communities.[17] The findings indicated superior gains among students who used films,

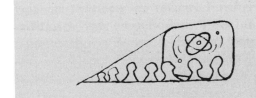

ADVANTAGES IN LEARNING THROUGH FILM USE

RESEARCHER		
ROULON - 1933	20.5%	JUNIOR HIGH SCIENCE
ARNSPIGER - 1933	22 TO 30%	5TH GRADE NATURAL SCIENCE
ARNSPIGER - 1933	18 TO 34%	7TH GRADE MUSIC

Fig. 13.7. / Advantages in learning resulting from using 16 mm. sound motion-picture films as compared to using traditional materials. (Compiled from P. J. Rulon, *The Sound Motion Picture in Science Teaching*, Harvard Univ. Press, 1933 and V. C. Arnspiger, *Measuring the Effectiveness of Sound Pictures as Teaching Aids*, Teachers College, Columbia Univ., 1933.)

14 Philip J. Rulon, *The Sound Motion Picture in Science Teaching*, Harvard Univ. Press, 1933, p. 98.

15 Varney C. Arnspiger, *Measuring the Effectiveness of Sound Pictures as Teaching Aids*, Teachers College, Columbia Univ., 1933, p. 83.

16 Francis Consitt, *The Value of Films in History Teaching*, G. Bell Sons, 1931; Frederick K. McClusky, *An Experimental Comparison of Different Methods of Visual Instruction*, doctoral dissertation, Univ. of Chicago, 1922; J. J. Weber, "Comparative Effectiveness of Some Visual Aids in Seventh-Grade Instruction," *Educational Screen*, 1922.

17 Wesley C. Meierhenry, *Enriching the Curriculum Through Motion Pictures*, Univ. Nebraska Press, 1962.

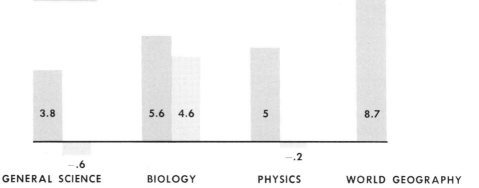

STANDARD TEST

FILM TEST

| 3.8 | 5.6 | 4.6 | 5 | 8.7 |

—.6

—.2

GENERAL SCIENCE   BIOLOGY   PHYSICS   WORLD GEOGRAPHY

Fig. 13.8. / High-school gains in learning through the use of motion pictures. (Note: no control test was made in measuring learning from films in world geography. Adapted from W. C. Meierhenry, *Enriching the Curriculum Through Motion Pictures,* Univ. of Nebraska Press, 1962.)

RESEARCHER

ROULON - 1933   38.57%   JUNIOR HIGH SCIENCE

ARNSPIGER - 1933   9 TO 18%   5TH GRADE NATURAL SCIENCE

ARNSPIGER - 1933   14 TO 32%   7TH GRADE MUSIC

Fig. 13.9. / Advantages in retention of learned information resulting from using the 16 mm. sound motion-picture film as compared to using traditional materials. (Compiled from P. J. Rulon, *The Sound Motion Picture in Science Teaching,* Harvard Univ. Press, 1933 and V. C. Arnspiger, *Measuring the Effectiveness of Sound Pictures as Teaching Aids,* Teachers College, Columbia Univ., 1933.)

particularly in general science, biology, physics, and world geography (Fig. 13.8).

Thus, research supports the fact that *using carefully selected teaching films* results in the more effective learning of factual information.

■ RETENTION OF LEARNING

Research studies which measure, by delayed or duplicate-form tests, the retention of information learned from films consistently show that films are superior to verbal materials. Knowlton and Tilton administered delayed tests at intervals of from three to seven months after the film lessons were completed. They found that films influenced retention as follows: About 12 percent more information was retained from film than from verbal learning; the increase was 14 percent in the case of historical geography.[18] The relationship between retention and sound films is shown in Fig. 13.9.

■ INCREASED READING INTEREST

The relationship of films to reading interest and skills has been one of the points most argued by both those who favor and those who oppose the use of films in the classroom. Some people believe firmly in the inviolability of reading as a source of information and, thus, maintain that the use of films in instruction adversely affects interest and skill in reading. This concern is unwarranted. Wood and Freeman, who asked 93 teachers their opinion on the effect of silent films on interest in reading, report:

> Three fourths of the teachers believe that the films increase the quantity and quality of the children's reading. This opinion is confirmed by the report of the school librarians. In several cities, administrative officers of the schools said that school librarians have reported that library facilities were not adequate to care for the increased library demands of the children involved in this experiment.[19]

The teachers' own responses further confirm this reaction:

> The quality of reading has been improved because the child has an intense desire to find out a definite thing. The study guide was an aid in organizing and judging the information found on the topic. The many contacts the picture gave increased the quantity of reading.[20]

According to Knowlton and Tilton, seeing silent films caused children to "read voluntarily more supplementary history material under controlled classroom conditions."[21]

---

18 Daniel C. Knowlton and J. Warren Tilton, *op. cit.*, p. 91.
19 Ben D. Wood and Frank N. Freeman, *op. cit.*, pp. 153–154.
20 *Ibid.*, pp. 153–154.
21 Daniel C. Knowlton and J. Warren Tilton, *op. cit.*, p. 91.

In a later attempt to check such information, the school librarian was asked to devise a means of checking the reading done voluntarily by the intermediate-grade pupils of a large urban elementary school, and, in 1946, a system of recording book withdrawals was instituted which enabled study of the reading habits of over 300 children. The children who regularly saw sound films in their classes did over 50 percent more voluntary reading, as evidenced by book withdrawals, than the group with whom no films were used.[22]

The usefulness of the sound motion-picture films in improving reading was measured in 1952–1953 by Paul Witty, James Fitzwater, and Harriet Gorman. Their study, which tested the influence of eight selected sound films on the reading ability of second-grade children, showed that 95 percent of the children improved in reading, 95 percent showed vocabulary improvement, 70 percent expressed more and better ideas during class discussion, and 99 percent wanted to continue the work with films. Teachers participating in the study confirmed these findings.[23]

Clearly this research evidence establishes the fact that the regular use of teaching films produces in pupils the desire, interest, and readiness not just for more reading, but for more *comprehensive* reading.

□ THE SCOPE OF THE INSTRUCTIONAL MOTION-PICTURE FILM

Because the instructional motion-picture film is a means of presenting the actual social and natural environments of man, or of closely simulating these environments in a realistic way, the effective teaching film allows the learner a maximum of personal identification with the situation recorded in sound and motion. The experience it re-creates may be only slightly removed from actual firsthand observation or participation.

In what we shall call "direct photography," scenes are shot and recorded as they actually happen, or, in some cases—for example, history and literature—they are simulated or dramatized and photographed. But the motion-picture camera is not limited to scenes which can be observed only by the naked eye. Various processes that occur in nature and that cannot be seen naturally are made observable with camera techniques. The growth of plants, for example, can be recorded photographically, making still frames at different stages of growth, and then projecting these at a much faster rate (see Plate 21 in section which follows page 432). Conversely, processes which naturally occur at too rapid a pace can be photographed with a fast-action camera and the frames projected in "slow-motion." With photomicrography, phenomena too small to be observed naturally can be filmed. Other phenomena—for example, atomic or molecular structures—can be visually demonstrated on film by animated mock-ups and theoretical models. Indeed, motion-picture technology has enabled us

22 Walter Arno Wittich, *Effects of Film Use in Reading Habits,* unpublished study, Univ. of Wisconsin, 1946.

23 Paul A. Witty and James P. Fitzwater, "An Experiment with Films, Film-Readers, and the Magnetic Sound Track Projector," *Elementary English,* April, 1953, pp. 231–232.

to perceive and to conceive a host of phenomena otherwise unavailable to us in concrete form (Fig. 13.10).

■ DIRECT PHOTOGRAPHY

Many motion-picture films which are useful in teaching social studies, science, and the language arts are direct photo-sound records. Such motion-picture teaching films open up major avenues of information in areas where for generations the means of gaining information has been the textbook, the spoken word, the diagram, and the still picture.

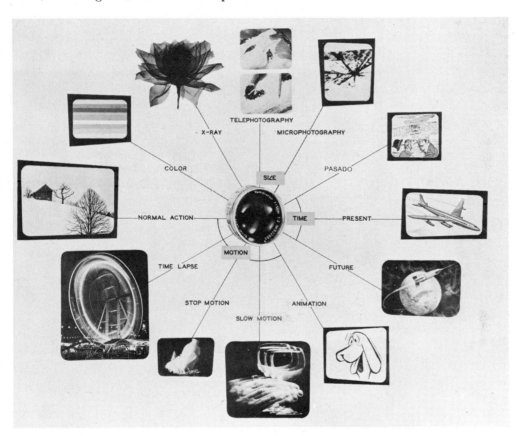

Fig. 13.10. / 16 mm. sound motion-picture photography can provide needed learning experiences that are life-like and understandable. Which of the motion-picture innovations shown here will help you to improve the efficiency of classroom instruction?

For example, the teacher and pupil who have long been residents of a limited geographical locale—their home town, their home state, or nation—now have the opportunity of seeing the world and its people through motion-picture film records (Fig. 13.11). Three comprehensive geography film series by Coronet, United World, and Encyclopaedia Britannica offer the teacher a wide selection of carefully produced and authentic documentary records of life in the major countries of the European continent. For those who seek to witness the expand-

Fig. 13.11. / How does direct photography and environmental sound recording effect the learner who seeks to understand Mississippi River commerce, wildlife in the Arctic, or the culture of the Peruvian Andes?

ing developments of the Pacific, these and other film producers have color series depicting the Philippines, India, Australia, and Japan.

The value of direct photographic motion-picture films is dramatically revealed in the field of history. Thirty years ago, students of American history examined wall charts containing crosses, dotted lines, and other symbols, and they read about battles, treks, and hardships. Their textbook had portraits of historic figures, black-and-white steel engravings of Old World architecture, and a woodcut or two of sailing vessels. The pupils listened to descriptions of historical events given by their teacher, who had learned about these incidents largely through the same medium—books. Neither teacher nor pupil had ever "witnessed" any of these episodes.

The motion-picture film makes it possible to reconstruct the circumstances of history. Homes, castles, farms can be rebuilt; museums can supply costumes, utensils, and other authentic paraphernalia. Through research, the patterns of speech and pronunciation can be reconstructed. Finally, the carefully planned reenactment of historical events that have present-day social significance can be photographed by skillful cameramen.

Through the historical film *Westward Movement—The Gold Rush,* we can observe and listen to episodes which resulted in the development of the California gold fields.[24] We can almost be "one of the crowd" at Sutter's Mill when on January 24, 1848 gold was discovered and crudely constructed "cradles" were used to separate the gold particles from the gravel of the stream bed. Through a companion film, *San Francisco—Story of a City,* we can observe the effects of the gold rush on the development of that city.[25] Other historical films offer the opportunity to observe the lives and accomplishments of such great men of history as John Marshall, Horace Mann, Daniel Webster, Louis Pasteur, and others (Fig. 13.12).

Direct photography also provides high-fidelity visual opportunity to witness natural phenomena which ordinarily are inaccessible. The camera and the sound track can record the life development of a family of polar bears as in *White Wilderness* (see Fig. 13.11),[26] and *The Life Cycle of the Northern Seal Elephant.*[27] Life in the heart of the swamps is documented in such films as *World in a Marsh,*[28] or *Singing Frogs and Toads.*[29] Direct photographic records are also available which can bring the entire physical environment of these remote areas right into the classroom to be witnessed and understood.

■ CHANGE-SPEED PHOTOGRAPHY

Many times things we attempt to observe occur too quickly or too slowly to be readily observed and understood. In such cases, the motion-picture camera

[24] 16 mm., B&W, 23 min., Encyclopaedia Britannica Films.
[25] 16 mm., Color, 21 min., Hoefler Productions.
[26] 16 mm., Color, 20 min., Walt Disney.
[27] 16 mm., Color, 20 min., University of California.
[28] 16 mm., Color, 22 min., McGraw-Hill.
[29] 16 mm., Color, 11 min., International Film Bureau.

Fig. 13.12. / *The Story of Louis Pasteur* as presented by Warner Bros. (distributed by Teaching Film Custodians). What advantages does such a film have compared to a textbook description of the same subject?

Fig. 13.13. / A bee with a load of pollen on its hind legs. Bees collect pollen and bring it to the hive as their source of protein. How does this shot from *Biography of a Bee*, produced by the Moody Institute of Science, help you to visualize this concept?

may be slowed down or speeded up, the resulting film being projected at "normal" speed. Through such photographic means we can see beyond the limitations of human vision. High-speed cameras exist which take as many as 4000 individual pictures per second. One camera photographing at the rate of 2400 frames per second has been used to capture the action of the human vocal folds as the sounds of the human voice are produced.[30] When these pictures are projected at the usual rate—24 frames per second—the action which originally took place in one second will last one hundred seconds as the 2400 frames are projected on the screen. Now the eye has time to observe and the brain to comprehend how the miracle of the human voice is actually produced.

The reverse of this occurs when a camera records movement that is so slow that we cannot observe the movement with the naked eye. In the film *Climbing Plants*, single still pictures of climbing plants were taken at intervals of several minutes.[31] In this manner the growth and development over hours and days, of such plants as aerial rooted ivy, tendril climbing peas, and thorned

[30] *Your Voice*, 16 mm., B&W, 11 min., Encyclopaedia Britannica Films.
[31] 16 mm., B&W, 11 min., United World.

climbers may be recorded by slow-speed photography which, when projected at the normal rate of 24 frames per second, reveals the progress of months of plant growth condensed into ten minutes of viewing time.

Science teachers, particularly, welcome change-speed motion-picture films. The development of plants extends over too much time, some chemical changes occur too rapidly, and the process of crystallization is too slow for practical classroom observation. Yet, in each of these cases, needed learning experiences never before witnessed can be brought into the classroom through such films.

A decade ago one could cite only occasional films which capitalized on change-speed photography. Today, interested teachers have available whole series of science films. The Basic Life Science Program produced by Encyclopaedia Britannica Films employs change-speed photography in explaining *The World of Animals, The World of Plants,* and *The Stream of Life.* Coronet Films completely revised and reissued a series on life science; United World puts out a series on earth sciences—botany and space science; and Moody Science Institute Films also puts out motion pictures on a variety of subjects in which change-speed photography is employed.

■ PHOTOMICROGRAPHY

In order to witness and to understand much of the phenomena of our natural environment, one often seeks to see beyond the limits of human vision. One way to observe things which are too small for the human eye to see is to use the enlarging microscope lens of the camera, or to combine the use of the motion-picture camera and microscope to record microcosmic phenomena (Fig. 13.14). This process is usually called "photomicrography" or "microphotography."

The science teacher who wishes to arrange for his pupils to see how the honey bee actually gathers pollen and meticulously taps pollen granules into the pollen baskets on its legs has discovered that motion-picture films provide such never-before-possible experiences, as, for example, is done in the film *Biography of a Bee* (Fig. 13.13).[32]

Film producers who attempt to reveal the body mechanics, digestive system, and bacteria-carrying capacity of small or one-celled animals, invariably use photomicrography. Outstanding examples of such films include: *The Housefly,*[33] *How Green Plants Make Food,*[34] *Microlife,*[35] *What Is a Cell?,*[36] *The World of Little Things,*[37] and *Roots of Plants.*[38]

Through photomicrography, motion-picture images 3 feet high or larger can be shown of actual, living microscopic plants and animals (see Fig. 13.14).

[32] 16 mm., Color, 15 min., Moody Institute of Science.
[33] 16 mm., Color, 15 min., Encyclopaedia Britannica Films.
[34] 16 mm., Color, 13½ min., United World.
[35] 16 mm., Color, 13½ min., United World.
[36] 16 mm., Color, 27 min., McGraw-Hill.
[37] 16 mm., Color, 14 min., Moody Institute of Science.
[38] 16 mm., B&W, 11 min., Encyclopaedia Britannica Films.

Fig. 13.14. / By photographing what the microscope sees, photomicrography is created (top). (Below) Examine the photomicrographs shown and estimate the learning value of the details you can see (middle: cyclops with eggs; bottom: colony of volvox). What specific learning advantages are offered by such films as *Microscopic Life, The World of the Invisible?*

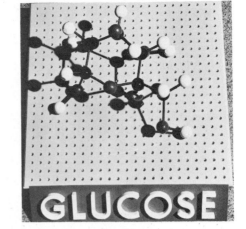

Fig. 13.15. / Animated analogies such as these from the *Force of Magnetism* (below) and *Chemical Organization of the Cell* (right; 16 mm., color, 28 min., McGraw-Hill) are used to portray phenomena which men cannot perceive in their actual forms.

■ ANIMATION

The teacher often encounters learning problems that demand explanations which are beyond what can be observed in real life. If motion and sound are effective in explaining tangible, observable things, visualization should be even more effective in explaining theories, ideas, and hypotheses. Animated photography serves this area of learning.

Animation is the process by which a concept is visually demonstrated, and usually it is used to illustrate an abstract concept. Abstract ideas can often be explained through visual analogies which embody the same principles and essential properties of the actual concept (Fig. 13.15). For example, to demonstrate molecular structures and processes, mockups of molecules are constructed, usually employing spheres to represent each atom. Rods separate the atoms to signify the position of the atom in relation to the other atoms in the molecule. In a chemical exchange, the molecular structure is altered, and through a variety of photographic techniques this reaction is visualized as are the resulting structures.

Today the need for animation is increasing as the new and very complex science concepts become part of the rapidly changing science curriculum. An example of motion-picture film animation of science concepts is found in *Celestial Mechanics and the Lunar Problem*.[39] In this film, animation is used to explain how scientists guide a space vehicle to the moon, calculate the path of the moon's orbit around the earth, allow for the 18½-year deflection of the

39 16 mm., B&W, 10 min., National Aeronautics and Space Administration.

Fig. 13.16. / Visualized speculations, such as this from *Space Probes: Exploring Our Solar System,* are drawn based on the most accurate scientific data available. What new conceptualizations of the design and purpose of space probes do you get from this still?

moon's plane of orbit in relation to the earth—and the interaction of these. In this film, carefully drawn models are used as the visualizations, and these actually interact as they are explained on the screen.

Splendid examples of film animation are also to be found in such films as *Science & Technology,*[40] *Way Stations in Space,*[41] *Biography of the Unborn,*[42] and *Space Probes—Exploring Our Solar System*[43] (Fig. 13.16).

A particularly good example of how complex processes can be simply demonstrated lies in the case of the almost incomprehensible DNA (deoxyribonucleic acid) molecule and its function in heredity. In the film entitled *Gene Action,* the theoretic description of DNA molecular structure and action—how DNA structures divide and how the DNA code determines the structure of cell proteins—is visually explained with the help of animated diagrams.[44] So clearly presented are the concepts in this film, that one teacher who has just completed her graduate degree admitted that she never thoroughly understood the chemical structure of DNA, until she had witnessed this film.

Thus, through skillfully prepared animation, complicated meanings are reduced to simple visual explanations which increase greatly the teaching power

[40] 16 mm., Color, 20 min., Moody Institute of Science.
[41] 16 mm., Color, 13½ min., United World.
[42] 16 mm., B&W, 20 min., Encyclopaedia Britannica Films.
[43] 16 mm., Color, 20 min., Encyclopaedia Britannica Films.
[44] 16 mm., Color, 16 min., Encyclopaedia Britannica Films.

of the film. The animated film can explain virtually anything which exists in man's mind. In short, through the many techniques available to motion-picture photography, there are few areas of human thought and experience which cannot be well and efficiently taught with the motion-picture film. Many of the physiological limitations of man's ability to observe can be overcome by means of the motion-picture film:

1. Things which exist in understandable but inaccessible form can be photographed from life by means of *direct photography.*
2. Things which are too small to be seen can be made visible by *photomicrography.*
3. Things which happen too rapidly for normal observation can be *slowed or accelerated* to comprehensible speed.
4. Things which are too abstract, too large, too hidden, or too theoretical for effective comprehension by the average learner can be visualized by *animation* and portrayed on film.

The motion-picture film can bring the entire world into classrooms anywhere and at any time. No idea or phenomenon is too remote, inaccessible, or abstract for graphic and understandable explanation through this medium of communication.

□ THE NATURE OF THE SOUND MOTION-PICTURE FILM

Any physical description of a sound motion picture must be divided into two parts: (1) the photography and (2) the sound electronics of a device that in reality is many inventions. A motion picture is a series of still pictures taken in rapid succession, developed, and finally projected again as a series of still pictures, but under such conditions as to give the viewer an *illusion* of motion. The addition of a coordinated sound signal or track results in a sound motion-picture film.

The first step in film production is the writing of the script itself, and, after this has been done, it is usually reviewed and checked by one or more subject-matter experts. Next the action called for in the script is rehearsed. Studio light experts arrange the lights so as to focus attention on the action.

■ THE PICTURE TRACK

The motion picture camera, actually a device for recording a series of still pictures at 24 exposures per second, is then set into operation. Figure 13.17 shows the result of this photography in the making of *Daniel Boone*.[45] Note how only slight changes in Boone's position appear from one still picture, or motion-picture "frame," to the next. This happens because the motion-picture camera rapidly "snaps" 24 still pictures or frames per second (16 frames for silent mo-

45 16 mm., B&W, 16 min., Encyclopaedia Britannica Films.

Fig. 13.17. / It took Boone half a second to drop to a kneeling position as this sequence was photographed. How can you tell? For this sequence, the camera recorded 12 still pictures of the action at the rate of 24 exposures per second. As these "stills" are projected on the screen, note Boone's changing position frame by frame. Why does this happen?

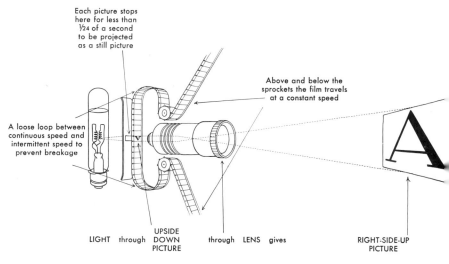

Each picture stops here for less than ¹⁄₂₄ of a second to be projected as a still picture

Above and below the sprockets the film travels at a constant speed

A loose loop between continuous speed and intermittent speed to prevent breakage

LIGHT through UPSIDE DOWN PICTURE through LENS gives RIGHT-SIDE-UP PICTURE

Fig. 13.18. / How the impression of motion is created by the projector.

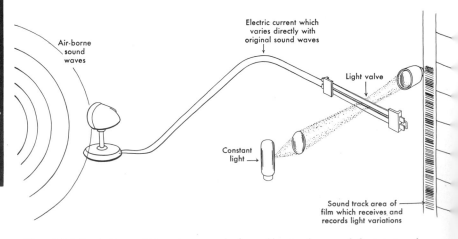

Electric current which varies directly with original sound waves

Air-borne sound waves

Light valve

Constant light

Sound track area of film which receives and records light variations

Fig. 13.19. / Sound that is recorded on film is changed first into electric impulses and then into variations in light that are recorded on the sound track. To understand how sound is reproduced later, see Fig. 13.21.

tion pictures). When these "still frames" are projected or flashed in sequence on a screen, the impression of life and motion is apparent to the viewer.

After the film has been developed, it is run through a motion-picture projector. This projector controls the direction of light so that light is projected through the series of frames onto a screen. The projector diagram in Fig. 13.18 shows how 24 separately projected still pictures are flashed onto a screen each second. Each frame has a slightly different picture than the preceding one. A revolving shutter excludes the light during the time required for one frame to move out of the light beam and the next frame to move into it. Thus, the screen is devoid of light for brief periods between projected still pictures.

The human eye is so organized that the image it sees persists in the mind for a brief time after the source of the impression, the actual stimulus, has disappeared. Because the normal eye is not constructed to detect these brief lightless intervals of less than 1/50 of a second, but is rather influenced by the persistence of the image, the mind gains the impression that the screen is continuously lighted. Since the eye cannot detect when one picture is replaced by the next, a visual-mental impression of motion is received in the brain. Thus, *the illusion of motion arises from what in reality is a rapidly changing sequence of still pictures.*

The ability of the eye and brain to carry a delayed impression of a visual image for a very small fraction of a second is called "persistence of retinal impression." This characteristic is present in varying degrees in people. It is this quality which has made possible today's motion-picture industry, for both entertainment and instruction.

■ THE SOUND TRACK

The discovery of the photoelectric cell made sound recording on film possible. The first sound pictures represented a combination of sound recorded on phonograph disks that were later synchronized with the film. In 1928, the recording and reproduction of sound on film became a reality.[46] Sound is photographed on photographic film. The two photographic negatives, picture and sound, are then printed on one positive by ordinary photographic processes. The resulting film, when run through a modern sound projector, gives rise to the audiovisual impression that we call a "sound motion picture."

When the sound for a motion-picture film is photographed, the sound waves are picked up by a microphone which converts the varying sound waves into similarly varying patterns of electric current (Fig. 13.19). These current variations control a light valve which, in most sound recordings, is composed of two metallic ribbons that move apart or together in response to the variations in current. A constant beam of light is focused on this valve. The opening and closing of the valve allows similar light variations to be recorded as light and dark areas on photographic film. The sound-image film moves at a speed of 24

[46] See *Sound Recording and Reproduction*, 16 mm., B&W, 10 min., Encyclopaedia Britannica Films.

frames per second, the same speed at which the photographic film moves. The sound motion-picture sequence, *rifle action* for the film *Daniel Boone,* is shown in Fig. 13.20.

The means by which sound is reproduced from a sound motion-picture film is practically the reverse of the way it is recorded (Fig. 13.21). As the film moves through the sound motion-picture projector, a light of constant intensity is directed through the sound track on the film. The light passes through the track in lesser or greater amounts depending on the light variations in the sound track. This residual variable light is directed toward a photoelectric cell which converts the variable intensities into similarly varying electric currents. These in turn set up corresponding movements in the loud-speaker diaphragm. Thus, the original sounds recorded when the sound track of the film was made are once again reproduced.

□ CHARACTERISTICS OF EFFECTIVE TEACHING FILMS

Today, teaching films are being produced in virtually all curriculum areas. Collections of educational films are available in all state universities, in most public and private colleges—particularly those with courses leading to teaching certificates—and in audiovisual centers in hundreds of city schools. Because of the nature of this market, the producer of a teaching film is usually a student of school curricula. He is well aware of the values of a film in relation to instructional problems. He believes that when a subject demands visualization, motion, and natural or environmental sounds in order to be understood by the learner, the motion picture can make a contribution to both teacher and learner (Fig. 13.22).

Thus, a good teaching film may be described in terms of several of its most inherent and valuable characteristics: visualization, motion, sound, organization, use of color, content, suitability, and accuracy.

■ VISUALIZATION

Much of the material studied in school demands to be examined, manipulated, and seen in order to be understood. The effective teaching film completely and understandably visualizes its subject through good photography. It visualizes also through charts, diagrams, and animation if these techniques are needed for clear, understandable explanations.

Instructional films must be photographed as vividly and carefully as possible. The film must be well lighted rather than too dark. The viewer must be able to see a well-defined projected image. The camera must be in focus so that the image on the screen is sharp and distinct. The photography may vary with the type of material; in other words, a subject must remain on the screen longer when time is needed to understand it, but for a shorter time when only an impression is required. A film that is merely a series of architectural views is

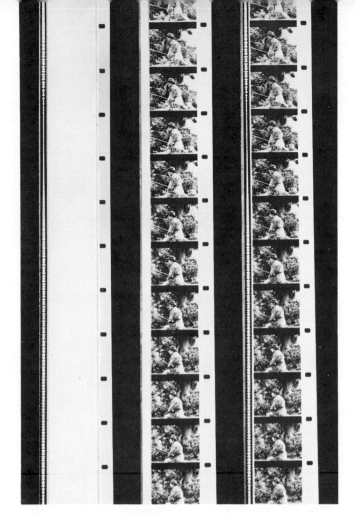

Fig. 13.20. / The sound record is first printed on one film (left) and later the sound and picture records are printed together on one film to produce the sound motion-picture film.

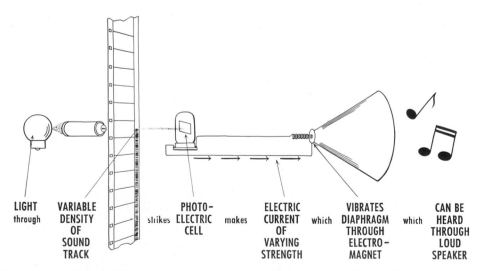

| LIGHT
through | VARIABLE
DENSITY
OF
SOUND
TRACK | strikes | PHOTO-
ELECTRIC
CELL | makes | ELECTRIC
CURRENT
OF
VARYING
STRENGTH | which | VIBRATES
DIAPHRAGM
THROUGH
ELECTRO-
MAGNET | which | CAN BE
HEARD
THROUGH
LOUD
SPEAKER |

Fig. 13.21. / How the sound projector reproduces sound. Note that this reverses the process shown in Fig. 13.19.

Fig. 13.22. / An effective teaching film is the result of creative teamwork. Hours of research work (top) are followed by planning and photography (middle), and this in turn by accurate editing of pictures and sound (bottom).

not truly a motion-picture film. Such views are better presented on still pictures or slides.

■ MOTION

Things that move or in which action is an identifying characteristic make effective motion-picture subjects. A motion picture which explains the action of a jet engine will show the parts of the engine in action if it is an effective film.

A "motion picture" made of still views of charts, graphs, and diagrams, and whose motion may be restricted to that of a demonstrator who is explaining these still media, is not an effective motion picture. Brief scenes of this sort inserted to recapitulate mobile aspects of a filmed concept may be helpful, however. For example, if the motion-picture camera has filmed the actual action of a jet engine, and this is followed by a brief diagrammatic explanation when the moving aspects are isolated in still form for analysis, a pupil may learn more from the film experience. On the other hand, these still-action sequences should only be supplementary to the actual motion involved in the subject and should not occupy large portions of the film.

■ SOUND

A good teaching film does not have to have sound to be effective. As mentioned earlier, there are many good teaching films—particularly in the 8 mm. size—which are silent. However, when sounds help to identify an object or process, a clear lifelike sound track is essential. Thus, the effective film records action and also documents as much of the original environment as possible. Such sounds as the whir of machinery, the lapping of water, the characteristic noises of a railroad yard, the lowing of cattle, etc., add great realism to motion-picture communication.

Often, helpful explanatory narration accompanying motion photography is useful in directing the learner's attention and establishing his understanding of visualized relationships. Such narration is inherently related to the visual content; it is not merely a "lecture" that accompanies a photographic story.

Learning advantages are greatest when the viewer can see and hear what he is investigating. The film whose sound track has muffled or entirely inaudible low notes, or distorted, thin high notes, does not impress the viewer as being realistic. Today clear, natural, and easily heard sound films can be produced. The listener can hear a good teaching film so distinctly that he becomes engrossed in the visual experience and pays no attention to the quality of the sound itself.

■ ORGANIZATION AND COORDINATION

By *organization* is meant the smooth flowing together of the photographed scenes and the accompanying sound. The viewer is not conscious of this in a well-organized film because the narration of explanation moves along from scene to scene with scarcely noticeable shifts. Such a film is punctuated and given meaning by the skillful use of mechanical devices such as *fades* (the slow disappearance of one scene before the next one appears), *quick cuts* (abrupt shifts from one scene to another), and *dissolves* (the merging of the end of one scene into the beginning of the next). A film which is jerky, meanders, or has confusing sequences interferes with the audiovisual experience it attempts to create.

■ COLOR

When should a colored, sound or silent motion-picture film be used in the classroom? Although often asked by teachers, this question is even more frequently asked by the people who are responsible for buying films and who are thoroughly aware of the wide differential in the price of a film that is released both in color and in black and white.

The effective teaching film records what actually exists. If color will assist in imparting understanding, comprehension, and aesthetic appreciation, then color is obviously desirable. Colored motion-picture films should be used when the color enables the viewer to gain a more accurate, realistic, and vivid understanding of what is being shown. Many subjects—such as animals, mechanisms, objects in nature—are identified through color (see Plates 22 and 23 in section which follows page 432), and thus, films on these subjects will provide far more valuable learning experiences if they are in color.

Although this sounds like a simple rule of thumb, it is difficult to remove from consideration the interest and enthusiasm in color *per se*. Such slogans as Hollywood's old "In gorgeous Technicolor" are not easily dismissed from the minds of movie-conditioned teachers and young people. However, in assessing the role of color in the selection and use of classroom teaching films, the single most important consideration should be whether it *contributes to learning*.

In the realm of nature, color and meaning are virtually synonymous. In nature, color has the function of attracting and, in other cases, of camouflaging or distracting. Hence, to understand how color helps camouflage desert animals, such films must be shown in color, not in black and white. Colored films are equally important in describing the coloration of plants, birds, and animals. For aesthetic appreciation and accurate understanding of architecture and of the costumes of other social groups, particularly those that are remote in time or distance, color films, not black-and-white films, are necessary.

When color is used it should be as close to the real color as possible. Color photography which is heavily overcast with bluish or greenish hues is not desirable because it does not portray the true natural colors. Poor color is often worse than no color at all.

Although it is said that the average learner can "read" color into black-and-white pictures, this is not usually the case. When situations are too far removed for his firsthand experiencing of color, he probably will not have the opportunity for enough color experiencing to enable him to impose his own sense of color on the black-and-white pictures.

You can investigate the role and value of color by means of Plates 22 and 23. Plate 19 shows several black-and-white frames from current sound motion-picture teaching films. Examine these frames carefully and at length, and list mentally or in writing what you see in each one.

Now look at these same frames in color; it was from these that the black-and-white frames were made. Examine the color frames carefully. Check your notes on each black-and-white picture. What additional information and, as important, aesthetic impression did you gain from the color frame? Then answer these questions:

1. What specific additional information was supplied through the color alone?
2. What relationship depended solely on color for meaning? (This is brought out particularly well in the frame showing the nymph and the mature grasshopper.)
3. What aesthetic feelings did you have after viewing the color frames which the black-and-white frames did not give you?

You are now as well prepared as anyone to assay the role of color in the sound motion-picture teaching film.

With the communication of facts as important as it is in the learning situation, the use of color as means of centering attention, inciting interest, and creating sheer aesthetic appreciation should not be overlooked. Many educational film producers are convinced that if the economics of film production permitted the production of low-cost colored films, teachers would use only color films.

■ CONTENT

There are several criteria by which the content of a motion-picture film should be judged as an effective learning medium. These are suitability to the curriculum, and to the age of the pupils, and accuracy and factuality of the content itself.

■ CURRICULUM SUITABILITY

The teaching film is definitely related to the content and subject matter of the school curriculum. The film was made because it can provide understandable explanations by means of visualization and sound and thus make unique contributions to classroom learning.

The good teaching film serves the curriculum areas where it is most effective as a teaching and communication device. There are exceptions; a film which compares two forms of government with the obvious purpose of "proving" the superiority of one over the other may not be suitable for a Problems of Democracy class, but it might be valuable in studying propaganda methods. A film on social behavior records the dialogue used when making introductions, but practically the same dialogue will be found in any modern English textbook in use in a junior high school. If the textbook version accomplishes as much as the film version, the film makes no outstanding contribution.

In contrast, there are films which bring remote people and places into the social-studies classroom. Others show demonstrations involving equipment seldom found in classrooms. Still others present interesting, graphic, and authentic records of events that occur once in a lifetime. Because films of this type present experiences which cannot be presented by any other medium, they are extremely valuable in enabling a given learning problem to be understood completely. The question is no longer, "Is the film interesting?" but rather, "Does it help in what the school is attempting to accomplish today?"

■ AGE SUITABILITY

Many well-produced films present information on the same general subject, but it is presented in such a way as to be interesting and completely understandable to a specific age group, such as primary or junior-high-school children, or adults (Fig. 13.23).

One film about polar bears describes their antics and habits in terms understandable by small children. Another film on the same subject painstakingly describes the genus *Thalarctus maritimus* (polar bears). The latter film will be most interesting and understandable to college zoology students.

The teacher must search for the film that will challenge the age group it will be used with. The speed with which the film moves from scene to scene, the pace of the dialogue or narration, the age level of the content—all must be evaluated in terms of the learners who will use the film.

Fig. 13.23. / For what age groups do you think this film, *The Grasshopper: a Typical Insect,* will make its greatest contribution?

■ SUBJECT ACCURACY

In the past it was not at all uncommon to find gross errors in films for class-room use. Now, however, their production includes painstaking study and authentication of content. Today, most teaching films carry the name of a well-known and respected authority on the subject of the particular film. The name on the title page of a textbook bears much the same relationship to the content of the book as does the name of a collaborator to the content of a film.

In summary, an effective teaching film has been described as follows:

> The "educational sound film" implies the following points . . . (1) The sound film should include environmental and interpretive sounds appropriate to the action so as to make the content of the film more realistic. (2) The visual concepts included should be those which ordinarily cannot be interpreted to the student in the classroom. (3) The sound film should interpret, by a blending of the foregoing two factors, such audiovisual concepts as will stimulate the learner's eye and ear and make it possible for him to become aware of the whole situation, portrayed just as if he were actually there at the scene of action observing a segment of life in all its completeness.[47]

□ EFFECTIVE SELECTION AND USE OF TEACHING FILMS

Just as the teacher who is selecting a textbook or supplementary reader considers size of type, quality of paper, binding, illustrations, and general attractiveness, so the teacher in selecting films must consider similar characteristics—quality of photography, quality of the sound, general organization of content, and accuracy of subject matter.

The teacher of almost any subject and grade has available numerous sound motion-picture films. Today three of the leading producers of teaching films (Encyclopaedia Britannica Films, Coronet, and Young America) release new films at the rate of one or more each week. From this large supply, the teacher must select the few that will improve the learning opportunities of the class.

In addition to the general characteristics which make for an effective film, the teacher who chooses films for specific purposes must have on record a variety of additional information, such as film sources and costs, the particular purpose and content inherent in the film, the particular purpose for which he will use the film, and the age level and interests of his pupils.

Thus, effective teaching with motion-picture films begins with proper film selection. However, even the best and potentially most suitable film will not achieve its purpose if the teacher does not adequately prepare his class for the film experience, provide the necessary relevant learning materials, or follow up the film with suitable activities which will reinforce the film message and encourage creative response among the students.

[47] Walter Arno Wittich and John Guy Fowlkes, *op. cit.*, p. 29.

GAINS IN VOCABULARY FROM USING SELECTED SOUND MOTION PICTURES & FLAT PICTURES

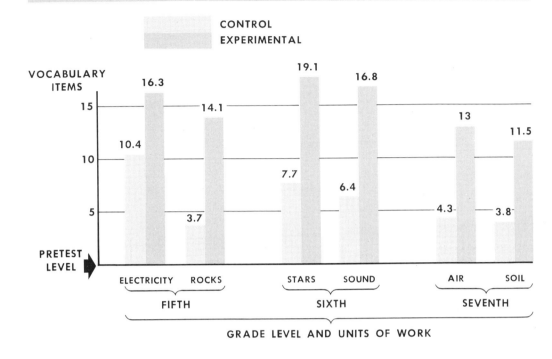

Fig. 13.24. / Pupils in the fifth through seventh grades made substantial gains in science vocabulary when film use is incorporated into classroom instruction.

■ SELECTION OF FILMS

The producer of a teaching film usually studies carefully the sales possibilities of a proposed film; he may also consider the teaching problems. If he believes the film can improve the learning situation, he will invest the time, effort, and money required for its production. This in itself is one important phase of film selection for, in the past, many poor films were produced, with consequent bankruptcy for their producers.

The responsibility for selecting films for classroom viewing rests entirely with the teacher, however. Most distributors of teaching films ask teachers to try the film out in their classrooms before they are purchased. This provides valuable information about the effectiveness of the films. In some cases, teachers' comments are included in film catalogues.

Before selecting a film, the teacher should have definite reasons for using one. If his students are to learn about the culture of people in North Africa, he assembles suitable learning materials, including such traditional materials as books, maps, a globe, bulletin-board pictures, models, and specimens (Fig. 13.24). His knowledge of what a film can contribute may lead him to search for a film, but he must consider the pupils' interests, maturity level, and reading ability in selecting *the* film which can make a real contribution to his class.

Under some circumstances, films may be previewed in class so that the reactions of the students may be noted. However, sound film equipment should be accessible to every teacher so that he may preview whenever films are available. *There is no substitute for preview.* In previewing, the teacher should keep in mind the characteristics just discussed.

Unlike books, which can be quickly skimmed over if there is no time for more leisurely examination, a teaching film must be seen—if not in its entirety, at least as long as is required for the teacher to decide whether it is of such potential value that he should see all of it. A sound film takes 10 minutes for each 400-foot reel, and there is no satisfactory way of speeding it up.

Methodical previewing leads naturally to record keeping. Preview records kept over a long period of time enable the teacher to be informed about useful films in his subject area. The following record form is suggested:

FILM SELECTION GUIDE

Title of film _____ Previewed by _____
    Rental source and charge _____
    Purchase source and charge _____
    Produced by _____
Use data:
1. Is the film authentic? _____ Comment: _____
2. Useful in grades _____
3. Are experiences contributed which are beyond what can be accomplished with traditional materials now used? _____
    List outstanding contributions _____
4. Curriculum or unit of study use suggestion: _____
5. Color is not used _____ is used _____ to give meaning to such things as _____
Format
1. Photography: excellent _____ good _____ poor _____
    Comment _____
2. Sound: excellent _____ good _____ poor _____
    Comment _____
3. Organization of content: excellent _____ good _____ poor _____
    Comment _____
4. Accompanying study materials _____
5. Color: superfluous _____ desirable _____ demanded for complete meaning _____
    Comment _____
Brief description of film content _____
General film rating: excellent _____ good _____ poor _____
Recommend for future use: Yes _____ No _____ Reason _____

Frequently teachers report difficulty in securing films for use in their classrooms. While waiting receipt of pre scheduled school-owned films, or films already ordered by the school administration, other sources do exist and should be investigated and used. Hundreds of usable film subjects are currently available, largely free of charge, if the teacher is willing to put forth the effort to order, preview, and select those which are of use in the accomplishment of teaching responsibilities.

As already indicated, useful films are available from industrial, manufacturing, and other commercial sponsors; from foreign governments and federal and state governments; and from the authorized agency of the Motion Picture Association of America, TFC.[48]

■ COMMERCIALLY SPONSORED FILMS

American manufacturers, distributors, and merchandisers have successfully employed the 16 mm. sound motion-picture film as an efficient means of communication. The number of titles produced by business sponsors and judged to be of use to classroom teachers has grown from 2121 in 1951 to 4071 in 1965.[49] No group is as continually concerned with analyzing the nature of services or accomplishments than are industrial sponsors who are interested in reporting to the public and to the schools. Years ago, there were many film sponsors who mistook "sales pitches" for straightforward documentary film reporting. Recently, however, four national conferences of sponsored-film producers have been devoted to the subject of how best to report objectively methods, services, and procedures so as to produce film materials which might be suitable for school use. Increasing numbers of sponsored films are now available which are useful in helping meet educational objectives. The teacher must, of course, assume the responsibility for preview and selection in order to determine which films or sections of films will actually make contributions as useful classroom learning experiences. However, the qualified teacher is well able to single out commercially sponsored films which do not contribute to the accomplishment of learning goals.

As was described in Chapter VIII, there is a growing insistence on the part of curriculum workers, parents, and teachers that students become more and more aware of the community, its strengths, its weaknesses, and its opportunities for future vocational involvement. One effective way to discover the resources of the community is by using sponsored films. Who is in a better position to describe techniques and opportunities in space research than the companies which design and manufacture space hardware? Who is better qualified to describe land, air, or sea transportation facilities than are the commercial companies whose livelihood depends on efficiently meeting the public's needs for such services? Today, sponsored films are available in increasing numbers, telling their stories with simplicity and effectiveness (see Source List, pages 528 and 533).

■ ENTERTAINMENT FILMS

In 1937, the motion-picture producers and distributors of America invited a group of educators to form an advisory committee on the use of motion pictures

---

[48] TFC refers to Teaching Film Custodians which make films available on a low cost annual lease basis.
[49] *Educators Guide to Free Films*, Educators Progress Service, 1966, p. vii.

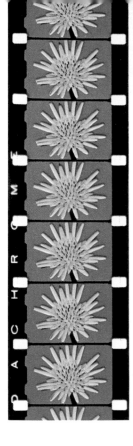

Plate 21 / Change-speed photography can speed up natural processes which are too slow for the naked eye to see—as in the growth of plants and blossoms; or it can slow down processes which are too fast for human perception—as in animal movements. To what other uses might change-speed motion-picture photography be put?

Plate 22 / Color motion-picture films are generally available at a considerably higher cost. Examine each of these stills carefully in their black-and-white form. What information is available in the color version that is not contained in the black and white? Which stills contain relationships which depend solely on color for meaning? Are there any other values to the color version of these films? Do your answers justify the additional cost of color films?

Plate 23 / The extraordinary amount of minute detail involved in Michelangelo's Sistine Chapel becomes lost in black and white film presentation; the color version greatly clarifies these details. What additional value does the color version have?

 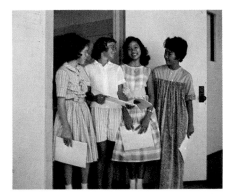

Plate 24 / The map may be used to provide initial orientation in understanding our fiftieth state. To understand the many meanings of the symbol locating Honolulu (see arrow), the cross-media use of films, filmstrips such as those shown above, pictures, models, etc., is almost mandatory.

Fig. 13.25. / Through what means do the best excerpts of entertainment films become available for classroom use? Two examples: *Shaw's Pygmalion* (16 mm., B&W, 18 min., Teaching Film Custodians), and *The Trial of Billy Budd, Sailor* (16 mm., B&W, 20 min., Teaching Film Custodians).

in education. This committee set up plans through which usable excerpts from existing entertainment motion pictures might be made more available to teachers. This Board of Directors of Teaching Film Custodians, as the group is now called, includes many of the great men and women of the professional education community.[50] Cooperating subcommittees are now at work and include teachers already participating in the National Education Association Departments of Health, Physical Education and Recreation; Home Economics; Vocational Education; English; Human Relations; Linguistics; Social Studies; Mathematics; Science; and Music. The teacher members meet periodically to give hours of professional service in reviewing, advising, and discussing how useful motion-picture excerpts can be selected and made available to teachers for effective use in classroom instruction (Fig. 13.25).

■ WORLD GOVERNMENT FILMS

At one time, communication through motion-picture films was largely an American prerogative. This is no longer true; most of the governments of the world use the film to report economic and cultural progress with reality, interest, and clarity. One cannot deny that the Japanese are best able to describe in film the people, geography, agriculture, business, etc., of Japan; the Hindus, best able to report on film the people, places, and culture of India; or the citizens of Middle Africa most adroit in presenting filmed information about

[50] See *TFC Films for Classroom Use*, Teaching Film Custodians, Inc., 1966.

themselves which expresses their point of view to the outlying world. There is an upsurge in interest in person-and-place world geography. How can the teacher better bring experiences from abroad into the classroom than through carefully selected motion-picture films produced by professional agencies and sponsored by the governments of the world?

It is not suggested that the carefully produced social-studies works of American film-producing companies be disregarded; rather, it is urged that the teacher search among films which have been produced by professional film writers, producers, and technicians at work for the governmental agencies of the world: The Consulate Generals of Canada, Japan and India; the Embassies of Finland, Malaysia, Australia, New Zealand, and Viet Nam; all of whose governments are active in the production and distribution of sound motion-picture film reports to the world (see Source List, pages 528 and 533).

▪ LOCAL GOVERNMENT FILMS

The various agencies of our own federal and state governments also rely greatly on the motion-picture film for reports or instruction to the American public. The teacher is advised to investigate film lists available through the Bureaus of Mines, Public Roads, Reclamation, Fisheries and Wildlife, Land Management; the United States Departments of the Air Force, Army, and Navy; the United States Atomic Energy Commission, Bureau of the Census, Civil Service Commission, Coast Guard, Geological Survey and the Weather Bureau (see Source List, pages 528 and 533). Almost every state in the union maintains a visitor's bureau, a Chamber of Commerce, or a tourist-information section from which film lists are also available.

▪ EDUCATION-SPONSORED FILMS

Most state universities and larger colleges now maintain film units in connection with the documentation of the increasing numbers of research-and-development projects going on. Films produced under such auspices usually reflect great care with respect to content authenticity. The teacher is encouraged to write for lists of films produced at any of the large American universities and colleges (Fig. 13.26).

▪ COMPLETE MOTION-PICTURE STUDY COURSES

The ever widening use of individual 16 mm., and now 8 mm., sound motion-picture film titles has evolved into the use of *sequences* of closely related titles, as in the case of social studies, science, and literature. More recently, this trend has culminated in the complete film course. A film course is a set of films varying from 18 to over 100 separate sound films—each of 20 to 30 minutes

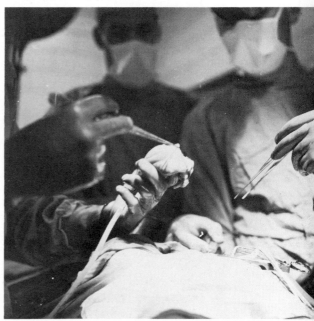

Fig. 13.26. / What advantages do university and college film producers enjoy in producing such films as *Totem Pole* (16 mm., color, 27 min., University of California at Berkeley); *Excision and Replacement of the Heart* (16 mm., color, 15 min., University of Michigan).

in length—prepared in such manner as to provide a significant and, in some cases, a major portion of the classroom learning experiences of a semester or full-year course. Such courses are usually prepared for the upper-elementary or high-school levels.

That complete motion-picture film courses—like film instruction generally—are effective educational media has been demonstrated in research evidence. In 1957–1958, 60 high-school districts in Wisconsin investigated using the White physics films as supplements to the daily classroom instruction. Careful objective measurement of pupil progress revealed that there was no significant difference in the scores on standard or traditional physics tests made by the pupils who used films and those who did not. However, there were significant differences in the scores of the film-using groups on achievement tests which measured mastery of information in modern physics. It was also established that correspondence-school students who studied physics on film made fewer errors, completed the course in less time, and achieved a higher level of mastery than correspondence-school students who did not use the film course.[51]

[51] *The Wisconsin Physics Film Evaluation Project*, Report, Regents of the University of Wisconsin, 1961.

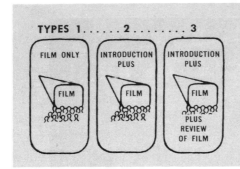

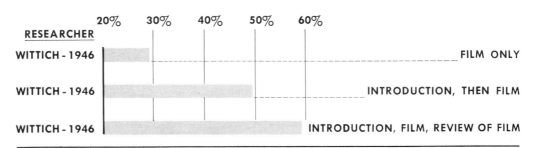

Fig. 13.27. / The importance of preliminary and followup activities are clearly seen in this graph. (W. A. Wittich and John Fowlkes, *Audio-Visual Paths to Learning*, Harper & Row, 1946.)

Film courses are now available in chemistry[52] and in biology.[53] The foreign-language area is also well served by several film courses in both 8 mm. and 16 mm. For example, *Learning French the Modern Way, Learning Spanish the Modern Way,*[54] *Beginning French,* and *Beginning Spanish,*[55] and Encyclopaedia Britannica Films' 120-film series with accompanying audio tapes for language-laboratory experiences are currently in wide use. Interested teachers will want to be on the alert for a wide variety of additional subjects currently in production on 8 mm. sound films.

■ CLASSROOM TEACHING WITH FILMS

The proper study of films is similar to studying from books and other traditional resource materials—reference periodicals, source books, or encyclopedias. The key idea is to *study* seriously the messages which are skillfully arranged into a film learning experience. Of the many ways to present a film to pupils, perhaps the most superficial is for the teacher to say simply, "We now shall see a film. Be alert and you'll learn many things."

One's experience with teaching films leads to the conclusion that unless carefully directed film-study plans are made in advance, only a part of the film's message—from one-fourth to one-third—will actually be perceived and understood by learners. Further, it has been demonstrated that learning through motion-picture films is considerably more efficient if both preparatory and viewing activities are followed by followup learning activities and review (Fig.

52 *Chemistry: An Introduction Course,* 16 mm., Color, 160: 30 min., Encyclopaedia Britannica Films.
53 *Modern Biology,* 16 mm., Color, 120: 28 min., McGraw-Hill.
54 16 mm., B&W, McGraw-Hill.
55 16 mm., Color, Film Associates.

13.27). The upper bar in Fig. 13.27 indicates the level of achievement gained when pupils in the fourth, fifth, and sixth grades viewed a film without any organized preparation. The class had been prepared for seeing films only in the course of casual classroom work. After seeing the film, the pupils answered test questions. The middle bar indicates the level of achievement when these pupils viewed films after being definitely prepared. The class was asked, prior to seeing the film:

1. To read a brief storylike description that conveyed a general impression or mood
2. To study difficult words and phrases in the sound track
3. To anticipate the content of the film by studying questions leading toward large areas of information presented in the film
4. To view the film after the above three steps were completed
5. To take a test immediately after seeing the film

The third bar indicates the level of achievement when these pupils viewed a film after definite preparation and were given followup activities. In addition to the above five steps, the class was asked to do the following things twenty-four hours later:

1. To answer a prearranged series of discussion questions
2. To see the film a second time
3. Immediately afterward, to take the test a second time

The figure shows that careful planning can nearly double the effectiveness of a teaching film in terms of the information acquired by the pupils who see it.

The teaching film is a powerful and useful instructional tool. Its ultimate effectiveness, however, is largely determined by the teacher and the way he uses it. In too many cases, the film is considered a "package" of information. Because it tells a rather complete story or gives a well-developed explanation of a process or phenomenon, many teachers use it in a way that assumes it to be both "book" and "teacher." Yet, if the teaching film is used as a supplementary teaching material, a great deal of its potential effectiveness depends on the way it is introduced into the classroom.

Several teaching responsibilities apply as surely to the effective use of films as to the intelligent use of books, maps, models, charts, and field trips. These responsibilities include motivating interest, anticipating vocabulary problems, planning, establishing good classroom conditions, evaluating pupils, and implementing followup activities.

■ PUPIL-TEACHER PLANNING

Purposeful activity usually depends in following well-understood and accepted plans. Plans which are the result of *pupil and teacher* activity will usually be accepted by students and pursued with interest. Even the best teachers cannot *make* learners be interested; interest is something the learner develops within himself. The teacher can, however, guide classroom learning experiences which are appropriate and enticing to the extent that curiosity and interest will be created within the learner—in this case, about film experiences. Usually this is an outgrowth of pupil-teacher planning (Fig. 13.28).

For example, the following situation developed as a high-school group anticipated viewing the film *Medieval Manor:* [56]

TEACHER: What do you recall? What impressions do you have about medieval life and society—the organization of the manorial states?
PUPIL: I remember the strongholds, the castle-forts, moats, and drawbridges.
PUPIL: The life was hard. All work for almost everyone. I can't imagine why people would work all year at growing beans, wheat, and grain and then be willing to "pay" most of it to the lord of the manor.
PUPIL: They didn't give it—the lord took it.
TEACHER: Was that the way it was?
PUPIL: That's right—they couldn't get by with that today—we're too smart.
PUPIL: Oh? How about taxes?
PUPIL: That's different—we pay taxes to a government, not to a lord!
PUPIL: It's almost the same. They paid homage. We pay taxes.
TEACHER: Who sees similarities between the people of the manor and the people of today?
PUPIL: They raised crops and gave away part for protection!
PUPIL: Why didn't they have any army like we do?
PUPIL: The Romans were after them.
PUPIL: No they weren't, they left.
PUPIL: The poor people stayed close to the castle.
PUPIL: They couldn't travel—they had no cars or roads. . . .
PUPIL: Nor telephones. . . .
PUPIL: Nor air travel. . . .
PUPIL: It wasn't much fun then!
PUPIL: I'd *like* to have lived then—horses, squires, castles—
TEACHER: Living as we do today, we can't be sure we really understand these feudal people. Can we agree on some of the things you would like to find out about— about which we have questions?
PUPIL: Is there any difference between taxes and paying a lord?
PUPIL: What happened to the Romans?
PUPIL: I want to know about the castles and what it was like to live in them.
PUPIL: Did boys and girls our age go to school?
PUPIL: Did they have chores to do? What about games and sports?
PUPIL: Who elected the "lords"? Did they have laws?

Discussion continued as the teacher placed key questions on the chalkboard and then added two of his own:

1. Did the serfs have any way to make suggestions to the lord of the manor?
2. Why did the manorial system develop in Europe?

By encouraging discussion with a suggestion and a question, and by helping to keep the discussion organized in relation to the lesson being considered, the teacher and pupils anticipated seeing, listening to, and studying the approaching film. The desired result is achieved when teacher and pupils engage in mutual planning—pupil-teaching planning. Through such planning well-motivated pupil purposes can be developed.

---

[56] 16 mm., Color, 20 min., Encyclopaedia Britannica Films.

Fig. 13.28 / To what extent can pupils enter into the film-selection process? What film-selection responsibilities can the teacher profitably assign to more mature or reliable pupils?

Related preparation and planning may reveal possible barriers to film study; for example, vocabulary or concept difficulties may be encountered and should be anticipated. It is too late once the film showing has begun to do anything about inadequate preparation.

On occasion the teacher, because of his familiarity with the learning concepts and vocabulary of the film subject being studied, overlooks the fact that the pupils are not as well informed as he may be. In the case of the *Medieval Manor* film, the teacher chose to continue and to discuss in advance of the film showing vocabulary items which he thought were apt to cause trouble: *Montbref Castle, seneschal, homage, feudalism,* etc.

It is not always possible to anticipate vocabulary problems or concept barriers before a film showing is begun. An observant teacher will wish, under certain circumstances, to interrupt the film showing. For example, following a brief teacher-pupil planning and vocabulary discussion, one teacher began the film showing of *Looking at Reptiles*.[57] The pictures moved across the screen and the accompanying narration went as follows:

> Today there are only a few survivors of the primitive reptiles. The *tuatara,* which can be found only on a few small islands off the cost of New Zealand, are the sole living members of a group of reptiles that lived long before the *dinosaurs.*
> The four other kinds of living reptiles are the *crocodilians,* the turtles, the snakes, and the *lizards.* Although they do not all look alike, reptiles resemble each other in five important ways. Like *amphibians,* they have backbones and are *cold-blooded.* Unlike *amphibians,* however, their bodies are covered with dry scales. They breathe air with well-developed lungs. And, except for a few *lizards* and snakes, they lay shelled eggs on land. . . .

As the showing proceeded, the teacher noticed increasing shuffling and inat-

[57] 16 mm., Color, 11 min., Encyclopaedia Britannica Films.

tention among the pupils. He thought it wise to shut off the projector and inquire.

"I don't understand," said one pupil. "It goes too fast—it's all those words."

"What should we do about it?" asked the teacher.

There was a pause, then suggestions began to pour forth from the class.

"When we read, we have a chance to study 'tough' words."

"Yes, look them up!"

"But with a film you can't."

"Not while it's going. . . ."

"That's why I stopped the film," the teacher continued, and before returning to it, the students engaged in a search for the meanings of such words as *tuatara, dinosaurs,* and *crocodilians.* Almost as naturally, the group turned to the clarification of such concepts as: the evolution and disappearance of primitive reptiles; the difference between cold-blooded and warm-blooded animals; and the similarities of snakes and lizards.

Teachers realize that no group of students approach a new subject area with complete vocabulary knowledge or concept understanding. Rather, it is generally assumed that because of the nature of special subject areas, each has its own new vocabulary and concept responsibilities. A film does have the unique advantage of explaining much of its own vocabulary, because of the simultaneous presentation of the visualization and the word concepts used to describe it. Nevertheless, words of unusual difficulty should be studied beforehand, as a film often proceeds at a pace which does not permit the pupil to think about the meanings of the specific words and their relationship to given scenes. Thus, every teacher should accommodate potential vocabulary difficulties.

The need for pupil-teacher determination of study purposes, as well as the need for specific vocabulary study, is apparent in almost every area of film utilization. Many pupils lose much of the advantages films offer because they are not given the opportunity for preliminary planning experiences which inevitably can lead to greater interest in studying films.

In addition to classroom discussion, there are many alternatives for preparation activities. Key concepts of the reptile film could have been presented for preliminary study through a chalkboard time-line on which dates and names show the appearance and disappearance of reptiles. To understand better the feudal system, chalkboard diagrams could have been drawn to show the physical arrangements of the castle, moats, fields, and their positions among the neighboring manors. A beginning display of pictures or fossils might be the focal point of questions and clarifying discussion preparatory to the showing of the reptile films. Another appropriate alternative is a selected filmstrip which could be used in a similar manner.

Any number and variety of pupil-planning activities can be arranged by the teacher and students before viewing. Once this becomes a continuing part of film-utilization activities, additional learning outcomes can be achieved. A good study plan is largely an expression of the pupil's own search for answers and information. It is not teacher-imposed; rather, it is an outgrowth of *pupil-teacher* planning.

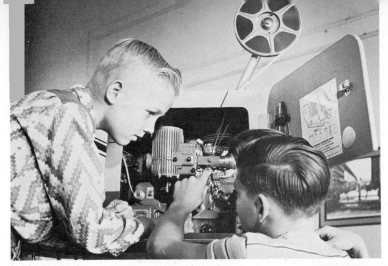

Fig. 13.29. / Under what circumstances can pupils help to create a good classroom viewing situation?

Fig. 13.30. / With few exceptions, teacher-education institutions now offer comprehensive credit courses to acquaint pre- and in-service teachers with projection equipment and classroom film use. Students get practice in the preview and selection of films for classroom showing, and in planning the study units for which they will be used.

■ CREATE GOOD VIEWING CONDITIONS

Because pupils work on day-to-day school projects in their own classroom, it is here that teaching films should be viewed and studied. Classrooms should be so arranged and equipped as to allow every pupil to see a well-defined image on the screen, and to hear the sound track without distortion or strain (Fig. 13.29).

Before a film is shown, the projection equipment should be set up and placed properly in relation to the screen. The film should be threaded into the machine and the projector tested for focus and sound so that it can be switched on the moment the class is ready to see the film (Fig. 13.30).[58] The screen should be of such size and so placed that all can see it perfectly. By walking from pupil to pupil, the teacher can quickly judge the viewing and hearing conditions for each child in the room.

Room ventilation should duplicate the general air-change and circulation specifications recommended by school building authorities for regular classroom use, namely, 15 cubic feet per person per minute.[59] The acoustics should allow every pupil to hear lifelike, completely understandable tones from the sound track.

[58] *Facts About Projection* (2nd ed.), 16 mm., Color, 16½ min., International Film Bureau; and *Facts About Film* (2nd ed.), 16 mm., Color, 16½ min., International Film Bureau.
[59] National Council on Schoolhouse Construction, *Guide for Planning School Plants*, 1949.

Control of the light in the room is essential. The distance from the camera to the screen and the power of the light source in the projector determine whether more or less light should be kept out of the room in which a film is being shown. Shades, drapes, louvers, or blinds should be standard equipment in every classroom in which day-to-day teaching incorporates the use of projected instructional materials.

■ ARRANGE CREATIVE FOLLOWUP ACTIVITIES

One of the most widely practiced activities following film learning experiences is to arrange for pupils to measure how much factual information they have learned. This may be accomplished through class discussion, provided the teacher is aware of how many of the pupils actually contribute responses. A more reliable method may be to use paper-and-pencil procedures, either essay or objective questions. The following—used to test information gained after the film *Our Changing World*[60] had been viewed—provides an example:

1. Along the time-line, enter in their proper order, the following geologic ages:

   a. Age of hard-shelled sea animals
   b. Age of seed plants
   c. Age of forests
   d. Age of dinosaurs
   e. Age of fish
   f. Appearance of man
   g. Age of coal forests
   h. Age of ice

/   /   /   /   /   /

500M   400M   300M   200M   100M   Present
                                                                                    Age

2. Write in the correct words: Scientists are able to determine the shorelines of land masses as they existed hundreds of millions of years ago by locating and identifying

   _____ _____.
   (shore)   (fossils)

3. The skeletal remains of fish which lived 100 million years ago reveal that these creatures possessed (underline the correct words or phrases): dry scales, gills, lungs, fins, claw-fins, spines, were egg layers.

Evaluation of information learned from film viewing is an essential activity. It must not, however, be thought of as an end in itself. Modern learning psychologists believe that the acquisition of factual information, as such, is a necessary *beginning* activity. Teachers today estimate that the acquiring of facts is only the first step in learning—*the first step only*. Once facts are learned, reflective thinking, problem solving, and creative activity—the higher goals of learning—can be undertaken.

[60] 16 mm., Color, 14 min., Film Association of California..

Once facts have been learned, progress toward the highest goals of learning—reflective thinking, problem solving, creative activity, and creative repatterning of information into inventive application—has only begun. Thus, followup activities must not only facilitate reinforcement of the information gained from the film experience, it must also provide the context in which pupils may learn to express themselves creatively.

For example, a senior English class viewed the *Great Americans* series which includes *Franklin, Longfellow, Alcott, Cooper, Jefferson* and others.[61] This led to a class-planned essay assignment, to "If They Were Alive Today," simulated radio interviews, to reports on the independent reading of works not in textbook anthologies, and to original simulation of television dramatizations of interesting episodes in the lives of these men. Thus, while learning of information is the initial step, learning applications which demonstrate the creativity of the individual learner are the goal. This may be applied to film learning as well as to all other resource learning experiences.

Another high-school group involved in United States history had concluded their study of the film "John Quincy Adams," in the *Profiles in Courage* series.[62] As they had witnessed the film, they had learned of Adams' decision to support President Jefferson's embargo of the New England states to force England and France to stop abusing American shipping on the high seas, even though Adams' Federalist policy was opposed to Jefferson, and the embargo would ruin Adams' native New England. The effect of this decision on Adams' political life is a matter of history. His decision, however, is one of the courageous acts of a great American.

Following the showing of the film, a lively discussion developed among the students on what might have been the consequences of John Quincy Adams' alternate decision—failure to support President Jefferson's embargo. One group of students set about logically assembling their statements of such consequences —a true invention based on information gained through witnessing the film. Another group studied additional source materials concerned with the period. Their reported findings gave rise to a debate on the issue of that period—the pros and cons of Jefferson's embargo. A third group searched the same political period to discover other political figures of importance. As more and more such information was acquired they set about judging the character of these men as revealed through their political and social performance.

Films which show how-to-do-it procedures invariably are followed by the formation of groups headed toward creative efforts. Following the showing of a film explaining the preservation of milk in cheese form, intermediate-graders interviewed store managers, dairymen, and druggists until they had the additional information they needed. They tested their information and made cheese themselves.

After their study of housing, a junior-high-school group located films on brickmaking and concrete construction, and then assembled the materials they needed to make crude but durable bricks.

61 16 mm., B&W, 16 min., Encyclopaedia Britannica Films.
62 16 mm., B&W, 30 min., Encyclopaedia Britannica Films.

The strength of the teaching film lies in its graphic portrayals. Film-inspired pupil activities are a natural outgrowth of viewing films. Unless provision is made for creative followup activities that are intelligently planned by teacher and pupils, one of the greatest values of using educational sound films—or, for that matter, learning itself—will be lost.

■ SUPPLEMENT FILM LEARNING WITH RELATED MATERIALS

Teaching films are usually accompanied by teaching aids such as study manuals or suggestions concerning the effective use of the film, but recently, companion media have been produced as study materials which may be used to supplement effectively the film learning experience itself. Tape recordings in foreign languages, filmstrips in social studies, or collections of realia for examination and clarification are now being produced with films in packages. More will be said about the interrelated use of films and accompanying media in Chapter XV, but it is important to notice at this point that teachers who use such supplementary audiovisual materials where films are the focus medium of the study unit will achieve far more efficiently the learning outcomes desired.

In 1955, Louis Romano investigated the effect, among fifth-, sixth-, and seventh-grade pupils in the Shorewood, Wisconsin, Public Schools, of the 16 mm. motion-picture film and related still pictures (both projected and nonprojected) on mastery of specific science vocabulary taken from reading materials.[63] His study is unique in that he chose as his subjects children who were already accustomed to a learning environment that their teachers considered unusually enriched.

Greater vocabulary gains were made by the film-using groups (see Fig. 13.24). The fifth-grade pupils learned up to 300 percent more science vocabulary, the sixth-grade groups twice the vocabulary, and the seventh-grade groups 200 percent more than the control groups learned.

Four years later, Nicholas Georgiady studied the effect of the 16 mm. sound motion-picture film and the use of related projected still pictures on vocabulary development and growth among pupils of the upper intermediate grades.[64] This study closely paralleled Romano's investigation, and the results almost matched those of the earlier study. Thus, two careful investigations of using films with related audiovisual materials substantiate the value of cross-media utilization.

Further, as mentioned previously in this chapter, *Project Discovery* was instituted to encourage the use of study films and related materials in day-to-day classroom learning.[65] Progress reports on this project reaffirm evidence to the

[63] Louis Romano, *The Role of 16 mm. Motion Pictures and Projected Still Pictures in Science Unit Vocabulary Learnings at Grades 5, 6, and 7,* unpublished Ph.D. thesis, Univ. of Wisconsin, 1955.

[64] Nicholas Georgiady, *The Role of 16 mm. Motion Pictures and Related Projected Still Pictures in Social Studies Unit Vocabulary Learning, Grades 6 to 8,* unpublished Ph.D. thesis, Univ. of Wisconsin, 1959.

[65] *Project Discovery, op. cit.*

effect that both factual learning and the higher educational goals of problem solving and creativity, etc., are outcomes of the cross-media instructional approach.

☐ THE SOUND MOTION-PICTURE PROJECTOR

The mechanism used to project sound motion-picture films is called a "sound motion-picture projector." Although several types and makes of sound motion-picture projectors are available for school use, there have been developed during recent years several projectors with characteristics that specifically adapt them for classroom use. Such projectors are, first of all, light in weight for easy carrying, or they may be mounted on rolling projection stands so that they can be moved easily from classroom to classroom. Good sound systems and light sources in projectors allow motion pictures to be projected effectively in any classroom in which the light can be controlled by blinds, shades, or drapes.

Basically, *all* sound motion-picture projectors are a combination of three mechanical devices, each of which performs one of the functions which together constitute the modern projector:

1. A mechanism for passing light through a series of rapidly changed still photographs recorded on film. To do this, the projector must move the film in front of a strong light source, and it must mechanically start and stop this film 24 times per second in front of this light.
2. A mechanism for moving the sound-track portion of the film between a constant light source and a photoelectric cell in order to reproduce sound. The film must move at a constant speed so as to produce lifelike sound.
3. An amplification unit much like a small radio set which will amplify a tiny sound impulse to a degree of loudness that allows the listener to hear lifelike voices and sounds.

A *composite projector,* a stylized version of any or all of the projectors currently in use, is shown in Fig. 13.31.

The several manufacturers of sound projectors emphasize various characteristics and elements of design. Differences in price exist because of such factors as quality of workmanship, sound output, amount of light that falls on the screen, quality of the lens system, sturdiness, and design of the carrying case. Several of the current models of 16 mm. sound motion-picture projectors for classroom use are shown in Fig. 13.32.

Learning how to operate the 16 mm. projector may be accomplished by practicing with 15- to 20-foot lengths of expendable film. Most sound motion-picture film projectors are produced with the expectation that primary children will be able to operate them, and the film paths are clearly marked by raised metal or painted guides. Teachers should study these marked film paths and printed directions, practice threading the projector, and then test their work by setting the projector in motion. Sound motion-picture film producers have now developed automatic film-threading attachments which are either built into or attached to the standard classroom projector. By contacting the local audiovisual supervisor or distributor, needed information and instruction can be secured on an up-to-the-moment basis.

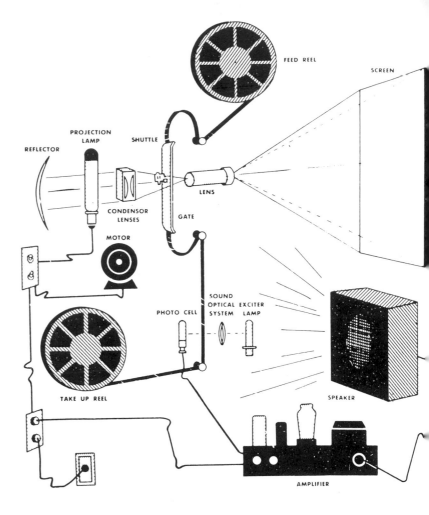

Fig. 13.31. / This stylized diagram shows the three basic mechanical devices present in any of the several 16 mm. sound motion-picture projectors now used.

FEED REEL

SCREEN

REFLECTOR

PROJECTION LAMP

SHUTTLE

CONDENSOR LENSES

GATE

LENS

MOTOR

SOUND OPTICAL EXCITER SYSTEM LAMP

PHOTO CELL

TAKE UP REEL

SPEAKER

AMPLIFIER

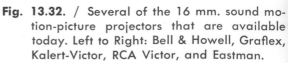

Fig. 13.32. / Several of the 16 mm. sound motion-picture projectors that are available today. Left to Right: Bell & Howell, Graflex, Kalert-Victor, RCA Victor, and Eastman.

A number of quality, silent continuous-loop, 8 mm. film projectors are available which sell for less than $100, although 8 mm. sound projectors cost considerably more. The availability of a wide variety of inexpensive 8 mm. projection equipment from such manufacturers as Eastman, Anscovision, Argus, Bell & Howell, Bolex, Dejur, Keystone, Fairchild, Technicolor, and others warrants the attention of school personnel who are interested in improving classroom instruction through motion picture materials and techniques. Those who are interested in 8 mm. silent or sound film production techniques and equipment would do well to investigate newly announced large film capacity 8 mm. cameras (Fig. 13.33).

Teachers and administrators who are selecting a projector should ask reputable dealers to demonstrate the various models in the same kind of conditions that apply in the classroom. Although demonstrations are desirable, perhaps even more important is the dealer's reputation and the performance and service guarantee given with the equipment. Service is particularly important, for unless equipment is kept in the proper condition, it may not be functioning when needed.

Though they differ in price, design, and efficiency, most modern motion-picture projectors are basically similar in operation. Although 8 mm. film cartridges do not require threading (Fig. 13.34), anyone who understands that the reel film must be threaded in the machine so that the stop-start action of the film can take place and a visual image can be produced, and where sound is included, that the film will move smoothly and continuously between the lamp and the photoelectric cell—thus enabling clearly audible sound to be reproduced—should be able, regardless of inexperience, to use any modern projector.[66]

By studying operation manuals, by using practice film, and by taking assurance from the fact that most women operate complicated household equipment, teachers—particularly women—should have little trouble in learning how to use this supplement to good teaching.

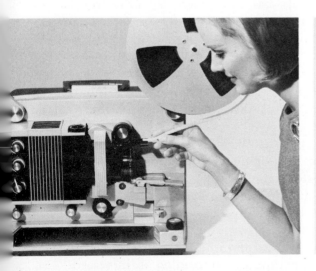 

[66] For diagrammatic instructions in 16 mm. sound projection, see Phillip Mannino, *ABC's of Visual Aids and Projectionist's Manual* (rev. ed.), Pennsylvania State College, 1965.

Fig. 13.33. / Two of the many 8 mm. motion-picture photography systems available are shown here. Left: Bell & Howell's new Super 8; right: Fairchild. What are your interests in such facilities? What creative activities can you envision?

☐ SUMMARY

One of the most carefully evaluated and widely used new learning media is the basic teaching film. The basic teaching film has been produced directly as the result of curriculum analysis and the application of important film-communication characteristics. Films produced for other purposes, however, may also be very useful in instructional situations. This is becoming more and more true as the makers of supplementary films—which include business and industry and domestic and foreign governments—become more and more skilled at producing materials which contribute to classroom curriculum objectives.

The 16 mm. sound motion-picture film made its debut in 1930. Since that time it has continued to be a major learning resource for pupils and teachers interested in the improvement of instruction through audiovisual techniques. The appearance of newer and additional communication techniques—language laboratories, educational television, the overhead projector, the filmstrip, and related projected materials—has not interfered with the values attached to the use of well-selected and wisely used 16 mm. sound motion-picture films. Now an adaptation has been developed—the 8 mm. films for classroom learning situations.

Not only has classroom film utilization steadily climbed, but accompanying research evidence continues to prove its value to ever-increasing numbers of teachers who employ increased numbers of sound motion-picture film titles in instruction.

The sound motion-picture film offers many opportunities for the improvement of instruction. Through basic motion-picture techniques such as direct and change-speed photography, photomicrography, and animation, great areas of greatly needed but heretofore inaccessible instructional experiences and visualized explanations can now be brought into any classroom.

Classroom use of the teaching film has many values. For example, as pupil interest is heightened, more learning is accomplished, the retention of learning materials is more permanent, and interest in reading is increased. The foregoing conclusions are well established by research.

READY

REMOVE CARTRIDGE FROM CONTAINER. THE FILM IS PRE-WOUND INSIDE IN A CONTINUOUS LOOP.

SET

JUST SNAP THE CARTRIDGE IN PLACE-- THE FILM IS READY TO PLAY AND REPLAY.

SHOW

THE FILM IS A CONTINUOUS LOOP. NO NEED TO REWIND. START, STOP, OR REPEAT.

Fig. 13.34. / 8 mm. projection systems are easy to use, as this four-step demonstration illustrates.

STORE

FILM CARTRIDGES AND PROJECTOR STORE EASILY, AND ARE READILY ACCESSIBLE.

The teacher who uses films in the classroom must accept new and increased responsibility if films are to be used with the greatest efficiency. The teacher must choose those few films from ever increasing large numbers which, on the basis of systematic judgments, are estimated to make the greatest contribution to classroom learning situations. Selection should be made by estimating the extent to which the film includes such characteristics as authenticity, grade-level suitability, curriculum purpose, quality photography and sound, and good organization. Film study guides should be available. The teacher who uses the films approaches its use as another study resource material. The film should not be considered to be a mechanical substitute for good teaching or an automatic means of communicating information apart from the teacher's influence; rather, a good teaching film is a tool which will yield maximum results when its use has been carefully planned and is supervised by a skillful teacher. Films should be used within the context of the work-study atmosphere of the on-going classroom routine. Research evidence establishes that the teacher in using films with efficiency should arrange for preliminary planning through pupil-teacher purposing; an audiovisual learning environment in which all can see and hear with comfort; and finally, teacher-pupil planned and executed followup activities which emphasize creative, inventive, and individualized use of film-learned materials in such projects as creative dramatics, creative writing, creative art, learning displays, model and exhibit arrangements, rather than the recall of facts per se.

Whereas motion-picture films were previously thought of as piece-meal additions to the course of study, today complete courses of films are available as a major supplementary learning experience pursued over the course of a semester or a full year. For example, foreign-language film courses are available, and often employ accompanying prerecorded tapes for reinforcement purposes.

A new development is the 8 mm. silent or sound film. While still in its developmental stages, the 8 mm. film is experiencing ever-widening acceptance by the classroom teacher because of its ease of operation, ease of use by students who wish to work in small groups or individualized study situations, and great availability and accessibility.

In the hands of an intelligent, well-trained and understanding teacher, the teaching film—both 16 mm. and 8 mm.—can become a vivid, interesting, dynamic, and socially useful instrument of instruction.

□ Suggested Activities

1. Secure through the help of your instructor the film entitled *Fidelity of Report*. Without any preparation ask your fellow students to view the film. Immediately following, give a written test on 15 to 18 of the 100 questions which accompany the film. What is the average score of the students? What are your generalizations about these scores with respect to the teacher's responsibilities when using the film?

2. Arrange to use selected 8 mm., continuous-loop films in social studies, science, or the language arts. Encourage some fellow students to select a film, to view it, and to study it, and then to attempt to write a narration which will explain in detail the visualizations included in the film. What are the outcomes? What do you conclude about the results?

3. Refer to the diagrams in this chapter on the motion-picture projector, sound recording, and reproduction. Use them to help you learn to operate as many kinds of 16 mm. sound motion-picture projectors as are available for classroom use.

4. View one or more of the films listed at the end of the Bibliography which explain the use of films in instruction.

5. Preview many sound motion pictures (see Source List, pages 528, 533) . On the basis of the characteristics discussed in this chapter, select the best for your immediate use.

6. In terms of your own subject-matter interest, select a film and plan for its use in a teaching situation. Note the responsibilities the teacher accepts when using a film in the classroom, and keep them in mind as you make your plan.

7. Arrange to put your plan into use. Either as a teacher in your own classroom, or as a student teacher in a "practice classroom," introduce, through pupil-teacher planning, the project, its evaluation, and creative followup activities appropriate for the film.

8. Keep a diary of the pupils' reactions, questions, and outcomes you note during the film lesson. At the completion of the lesson, consult this diary and evaluate your success or oversights in terms of the above responsibilities.

9. Following this self-evaluation, select another film and plan to use it in the classroom. Afterwards, record results and again evaluate your effectiveness in teaching with films.

☐ Bibliography

Arnspiger, Varney C., *Measuring the Effectiveness of Sound Pictures as Teaching Aids,* Teachers College, Columbia Univ., 1933.

Dale, Edgar, *Audio Visual Methods in Teaching* (2nd ed.), Dryden, 1965.

Educators Guide to Free 16 mm. Films, Educators Progress Service, 1966.

Films For Classroom Use, New York Teaching Film Custodians, January, 1965.

Instructional Materials for Teaching Audio Visual Courses, Syracuse University Audio-Visual Center in cooperation with the U.S. Department of Health, Education and Welfare, Department of Education, March 1, 1965.

Liston, James M., "Project Discovery: An Adventure in Teaching and Learning With Film," *Grade Teacher,* May–June, 1965.

Mannino, Phillip, *ABC's of Visual Aids and Projectionist's Manual* (rev. ed.), Pennsylvania State College, 1965.

Newsletter of 8 mm. Film in Education, The Horace Mann–Lincoln Institute, Teachers College, Columbia Univ., June, 1965.

Rulon, Philip J., *The Sound Motion Picture in Science Teaching,* Harvard Univ. Press, 1933.

Sheridan, Marion C. and Harold H. Owen, Jr., *The Motion Picture and the Teaching of English,* Appleton-Century-Crofts, 1965.

Source Directory, Educational Single Concept Films (2nd ed.), Technicolor Corporation, February, 1965.

Teacher Education and Media 1964: A Selective, Annotated Bibliography, The American Association of Colleges for Teacher Education, 1965.

☐ Films

Facts About Film (2nd ed.), 16 mm., Color, 16½ min., International Film Bureau.

Facts About Projection (2nd ed.), 16 mm., Color, 16½ min., International Film Bureau.

Film Research and Learning, 16 mm., B&W, 15 min., Michigan State University.

How To Splice Film, 16 mm., B&W, 10 min., Encyclopaedia Britannica Films, Inc.

Making Films That Teach, 16 mm., B&W, 20 min., Encyclopaedia Britannica Films.

Projectionist's Job, 16 mm., B&W, 6 min., Iowa State University.

Sound Recording and Reproduction, 16 mm., B&W, 11 min., Encyclopaedia Britannica Films.

The 16 mm. Film Projector, 16 mm., Color, 10 min., National Film Board of Canada.

XIV

EDUCATIONAL TELEVISION

Few areas of education have had the effect on pupils, teachers, and the public as has ETV—educational television. As one teacher put it, "I was highly skeptical at first, but now that I have a 'say so' in the planning of programs we use—well, ETV has become necessary. It represents another teacher on my team. It brings experiences into my classroom I ordinarily can't get my hands on." From a high-school pupil's point of view, "TV brings more ideas right into our classroom. When you add ETV to what we have now—it's really what they say—more to learn and find out about." And a parent reported, "I'm glad it's finally being used in the classroom. Why, when I think of our living room just before dinner time—the youngsters sit 'glued' to the TV screen! That kind of interest should be incorporated into our classrooms."

In the short space of time during which serious attention has been given to ETV, no one area of education has been more intensively researched, had more dollars spent per pupil, or had so many faculty meetings and in-service programs arranged around it than has this new and burgeoning way of instruction (Fig. 14.1).

From the start, educational television has been a rapidly changing, highly fluid program. It has received added impetus during recent years as the federal government has appropriated hundreds of millions of dollars to assist local school districts in developing expanded ETV programs for use in classroom learning situations. Between 1959 and the present, at least four separate federal bills—the National Defense Education Act, the Magnusen Act, the Elementary-Secondary Education Act, and the Higher Education Act—have allocated large sums of money for (1) the purchase and installation of television equipment, (2) carrying on research in ETV production and classroom use, (3) holding institutes and workshops devoted to educating workers and teachers in ETV production and classroom use, and (4) encouraging college and university faculties to investigate the role of television in the improvement of learning. Educational television has had an impact on education from the kindergarten to the adult levels, and thus represents one of the most thrilling and exciting communication breakthroughs ever to appear in American education.

Why is television so fascinating? Why has it captured the attention and interest of children, teachers, and adults? How does it work? How is the best

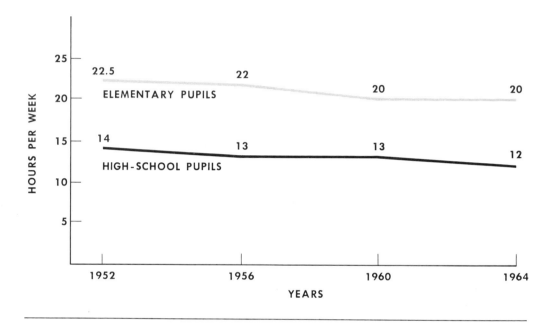

AVERAGE WEEKLY HOURS
TELEVIEWING BY
1500 TO 2000 PUPILS
IN CHICAGO
AND LAKE SHORE AREA

Fig. 14.1. / Average hours spent each week in televiewing by a sampling of elementary and secondary pupils in the Chicago area.

ETV programing produced? How may it serve as an effective part of day-to-day classroom instruction? Where is television used with greatest success?

This chapter will answer some of these questions by describing local, state, and regional programs of educational television, both closed and open-circuit broadcasts.

☐ TELEVISION—AN AUDIOVISUAL SYNTHESIS

For years, teachers have been much more knowledgeable about the nature of needed classroom learning experiences than about how to overcome the barriers which too often have prevented access to the remarkable new audiovisual tools for teaching. Films, models, slides, projectuals, charts, demonstration equipment—all these abound, yet ironically are often very hard to acquire for classroom use. Educational television, at its best, has overcome much of this inaccessibility problem by serving as a tremendous carrier for needed learning experiences which have long been associated with the audiovisual field. On any

Fig. 14.2. / History as it occurs may be a classroom television experience—in this case, the occurrence of the first space walk.

one well-planned and well-presented school television program, we may find lessons which are communicated through the interrelated use of film clips—i.e., selected short, but useful segments of 16 mm. films—chalkboard illustrations, slides, models, specimens, and short segments of tape recordings, all of which are explained by television guests or cooperating teachers who are able to support such use with clear-cut explanations or demonstrations. In short, educational television is capable of making available many needed and heretofore inaccessible learning experiences which most teachers are quick to recognize as lending efficiency to classroom instruction.

Educational television brings about the continuing cooperative planning by teachers, supervisors, learning materials experts, and skillful ETV production teams. Educational television at its best results from the outgrowth of curriculum planning, of study content analysis, and of the selection and interrelated use of the most appropriate instructional media. Under these circumstances, one may anticipate the production of high-quality ETV programs for classroom use. These programs are usually subjected to classroom use and evaluation. Scores of teachers participate in integrating the television program into the stream of classroom instruction. Other groups of teachers evaluate the quality of the content, its appropriateness to the age group of the learners, and the efficiency with which the channel—closed-circuit or broadcast—communicates the instructional message. On the basis of such evaluations, teachers, subject experts, and ETV producers work toward the end of further improving some of these programs. Throughout this cycle of production, classroom utilization, and evaluation, the weaker "links" in the television series are gradually replaced by more effective teaching demonstrations until finally the best educational-television instruction is realized.

Many additional advantages may be attributed to educational television. For example, for the first time in history we can be eye witnesses to events that occur now, anywhere within the range of the television camera: the launching of the great space vehicles, a video account by the captain of an ocean vessel advancing westward through the St. Lawrence waterways, an action account by the space crew describing another successful rendezvous in space to establish an orbiting platform, and virtually any other modern event that will make history (Fig. 14.2). Master teachers can televise expert science demonstrations, visualized explanations of grammar or arithmetic, handcraft techniques, and descriptions of foreign cultures and people. Television is a means of bringing enriching experiences into the classroom.

As teachers, we should understand the great hold television has on our young people and realize its potential strengths. We should also realize the inherent danger of its reducing viewers to a passive, dream-like identification with what too often is provided as television *entertainment*. To understand the role of television in the contemporary social scene it is well to begin by gaining at least a rudimentary understanding of it as an electronic device.

□ HOW TELEVISION WORKS

Technologically, television is a means of converting a scene into an electronic image. This image is sent through space, picked up on an antenna, and translated into a duplicate of the original scene on the surface of a picture tube or, to use the correct name, *kinescope*.

The television process is remarkably similar to the visual process of the human eye. Light waves, reflected from an object, strike the lens of the eyeball which focuses these waves onto the retina as an image of the object seen (Fig. 14.3). So it is with the television camera or "eye"—it too moves and focuses. And, as the retina contains myriad nerve endings which are sensitive

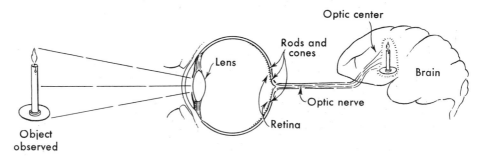

Fig. 14.3. / How the eye functions.

to light and which "record" each tiny portion of the image that falls on the retina, there are similarly thousands of tiny light-sensitive "nerve endings" on the television camera "retina" or plate. These react to the strong and weak light areas in the image received. In the human eye, the optic nerve carries the light signals from the thousands of retinal nerve endings to the brain, where the "picture" of the object being viewed is perceived. In the television camera, minute electric currents are "swept" off the surface of the light-sensitive "retina" by a scanning beam and carried in sequence over a signal beam which is telecast to the "mind" or picture tube. These signals are re-created on the end surface of the picture tube as the original scene "observed" by the television camera.

Scientifically, television cannot be described except electronically. It is a mechanical-electrical means of converting light patterns into electric impulses

and then into light patterns. These changes must occur so rapidly and continuously that the human eye continues to see after all of them have taken
place. As in the motion-picture film, so in television: A scene appears, disap-
pears, and is replaced by another still scene many times each second. Thirty
complete images appear on the camera plate—and therefore on the kinescope
tube—every second; this is rapid enough to give the viewer a mental *impression*
of motion.

How pictures are televised is shown in the schematic drawing in Fig. 14.4
which shows a television camera, amplifier, transmitter tower, antenna, and
picture tube or kinescope. Sound and pictures are sent over the air simultaneously by means of radio. A camera tube records light patterns and changes them
into electrical impulses by means of a plate (*P*) which, covered with hundreds
of tiny chemical eyes, is very sensitive to light. The lens of the camera focuses
the picture to be televised onto the surface of the plate. Since all the picture
images are combinations of lighter and darker areas, the plate changes the light

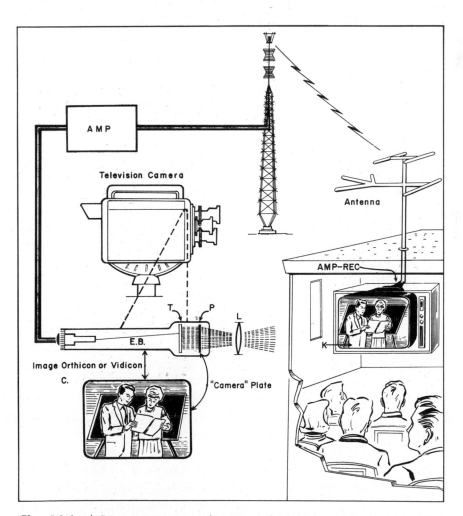

Fig. 14.4. / Diagrammatic explanation of television; the sequence of action begins at the lower left.

striking its surface into corresponding electrical charges, which are then sent to the target (T).

The charges are swept off the target in single file by a scanning or "sweeping" beam (EB); hence the whole picture is not sent out or telecast at once. Rather, the beam sweeps back and forth across the target and travels in an interrupted descending path from top to bottom of it, creating a continuous signal or message. The scanning beam sweeps the signals at the rate of 4,000,000 per second, fast enough for 30 complete images to be swept from the camera target every second. This signal is then strengthened or amplified (AMP) and transmitted into space.

The reverse process occurs in the picture tube or kinescope (K). When the signals are intercepted by the receiving antenna they are led to a receiver (REC), where they are selected or tuned, amplified (AMP), and then led to the small end of the kinescope. In the same order in which these charges were swept off the camera target, they are instantaneously scanned or sprayed onto the inside surface of the large flat end of the kinescope. This end of the tube is coated with a chemical like that used in fluorescent lights, which is sensitive to electrical charges. As the electrical energy variations are "sprayed" against the kinescope, they are transformed into light that varies in proportion to the strength of the corresponding charges. Since these electrical charges strike the kinescope screen in the same order as that in which they were swept off the camera target, an identical picture image is reproduced. This process occurs at the same rate—4,000,000 impulses and 30 complete pictures per second.

□ THE HISTORY AND SCOPE OF EDUCATIONAL TELEVISION

The beginning of American educational television is marked as the Federal Communication Commission's "Order of 1952," which reserved approximately 12 percent of all of the available television channels for education. In 1953, the first educational television station came on the air at Houston, Texas; in 1954, the National Educational Television (NET)—an organization devoted to the production and recording of quality educational television—began to provide the first of thousands of recorded programs for use by instructional television stations. Shortly thereafter, there appeared A. J. Stoddard's report entitled *The School for Tomorrow*.[1] This report contained an account of actual techniques for television utilization designed to improve existing standards of classroom education.

Educational television has been propagated through two main avenues, closed and open circuit. *Closed-circuit* television refers to a network of coaxial cables through which television signals may be distributed from a broadcasting source to the reception points, the classrooms. *Open-circuit* television, on the other hand, broadcasts its signals into the atmosphere to be retrieved by antennas at the reception point from which the signals are led into the classroom.

Attention should be called to the diversity of educational television installa-

---

[1] A. J. Stoddard, *The School for Tomorrow*, The Ford Foundation.

tions now working in schools. Television is no respecter of traditions. Across the nation, one may find that some of the nation's oldest school systems have been among the first to establish educational television installations. In the public schools, colleges, and universities of the United States, there are more than 900 closed-circuit television systems in operation. These systems serve a student population of more than 10 million.

As of January 1, 1966, 111 open-circuit educational television stations were on the air, and another 42 were in the process of being constructed. As can be seen by examining the map in Fig. 14.5 these stations serve most of the nation's most populated areas including Hawaii and Puerto Rico.

One of many well-established closed-circuit systems is at Hagerstown, Maryland, where under the leadership of Superintendent William Brish, and the be-

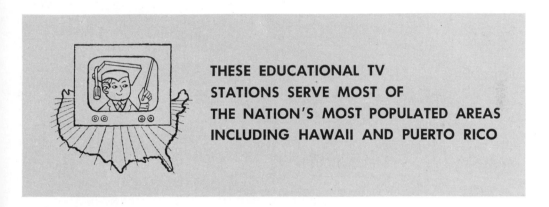

THESE EDUCATIONAL TV STATIONS SERVE MOST OF THE NATION'S MOST POPULATED AREAS INCLUDING HAWAII AND PUERTO RICO

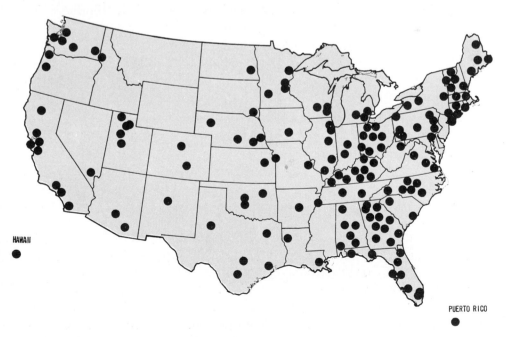

HAWAII

PUERTO RICO

Fig. 14.5. / Over 110 parent and satellite stations are now telecasting regularly scheduled programs over channels set aside for educational television.

ginning financing of a coalition of foundations and industry, a comprehensive closed-circuit educational television net was placed into operation in 1956. At Hagerstown one may witness high-quality educational television programs in widespread use. As shown in Table 14.1, the success of educational television at Hagerstown is verified by research studies carried on in that school district:

> This table shows an improvement between 1958 and 1961 which is statistically significant even after adjustments for differences in mental ability. Both groups gained least during 1959–1960, a period when the television course was being revised. Achievement reached a peak under the revamped course in 1960–1961. During the first four years, the television lessons occupied half of each period and classroom work the other half. In 1960–1961, the schedule was changed to provide three full periods of television and two of classroom work each week. News events broadcasts over regular commercial television channels were utilized during the course.[2]

A closed-circuit installation operated in conjunction with three open-broadcast stations is carried on in South Carolina (Fig. 14.6). The legislature of that state authorized $1,000,000 for educational television in 1960. The educational closed-circuit network in South Carolina ties together more than 100 schools in the Charleston and Columbia areas, and 67 junior and senior high schools in most of the state's counties.

Microwave broadcasting at 2500 megacycles serves well to bring educational television to limited areas. A school, college, or university may apply to the Federal Communication Commission for several channels in a given location. Such an installation may broadcast over a radius of from five to 20 miles. An example is found at Bradley University, Northern Illinois where, in 1966, 300 classrooms in 22 public and nine private schools within a 15-mile radius received television lessons in both black and white and color through a two-channel television system (Fig. 14.7). Bradley's installation transmits from two channels on a 2500-megacycle, microwave system, convertible to color.

On the basis of successful pioneering use of educational television, many state and regional networks have now been established. Through open-broadcast, closed-circuit, and microwave means, the advantages of cooperatively planned and accomplished educational television of proven worth are now being carried to large numbers of students. Such state-wide and regional educational television networks are now in operation in many states (Fig. 14.8).

Educational television is not limited to the United States, however. Many countries around the world—especially those which are more primitive in their technological development—are relying more and more on ETV to help train their people quickly and efficiently. On the remote island of American Samoa, 2300 miles southwest of Hawaii, for example, an open-broadcast facility and studios have been constructed at a cost of nearly $2,000,000. Samoa's three-channel system represents a unique educational-television system, for it provides an entire core of educational experience rather than a supplement to the local education effort. It is designed to produce a much desired immediate improvement in the educational system of a long neglected territory. At the present time,

---

[2] *Washington County Closed Circuit Television Report,* Board of Education of Washington County, Maryland, 1964.

Table 14.1
INFLUENCE OF CLASSROOM TV INSTRUCTION ON ACHIEVEMENTS IN ENGLISH AND SOCIAL STUDIES BY EIGHTH-GRADERS IN MARYLAND

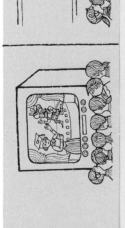

GRADE 8	Hagerstown Schools						Rural Schools					
	Sept., 1957		May, 1958		May, 1961		Sept., 1957		May, 1958		May, 1961	
	Grade Equivalent	Percentile	Grade Equivalent	Percentile	Grade Equivalent	Percentile	Grade Equivalent	Percentile	Grade Equivalent	Percentile	Grade Equivalent	Percentile
Vocabulary	7.59	(23)	8.13	(23)	8.44	(35)	7.06	(10)	7.30	(8)	7.89	(16)
Reading Comprehension	7.69	(19)	8.26	(18)	8.46	(24)	7.29	(10)	7.63	(8)	8.08	(14)
Spelling	7.56	(15)	8.18	(22)	8.61	(33)	7.17	(10)	8.05	(15)	8.14	(20)
Capitalization	8.10	(48)	8.65	(50)	9.18	(72)	7.37	(16)	7.94	(19)	8.38	(37)
Punctuation	7.44	(21)	7.98	(29)	8.60	(55)	6.93	(10)	7.63	(19)	7.82	(24)
Usage	7.37	(17)	7.89	(17)	8.27	(29)	6.67	(7)	7.47	(10)	7.65	(13)
Map Reading	7.95	(31)	8.52	(24)	8.86	(44)	7.65	(17)	7.99	(8)	8.49	(23)
Reading Graphs and Tables	7.79	(28)	8.52	(27)	8.76	(29)	7.51	(16)	7.93	(16)	8.20	(22)
Knowledge and Use of Reference Material	7.97	(39)	8.66	(43)	8.93	(57)	7.55	(18)	8.09	(16)	8.47	(31)

Source: Washington County Closed Circuit Television Report, Board of Education of Washington County, Maryland, 1964.

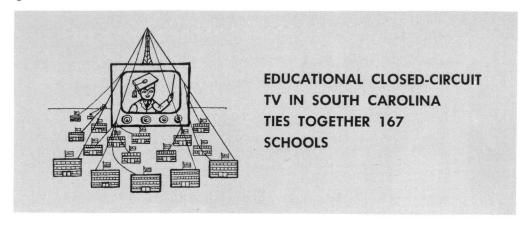

EDUCATIONAL CLOSED-CIRCUIT
TV IN SOUTH CAROLINA
TIES TOGETHER 167
SCHOOLS

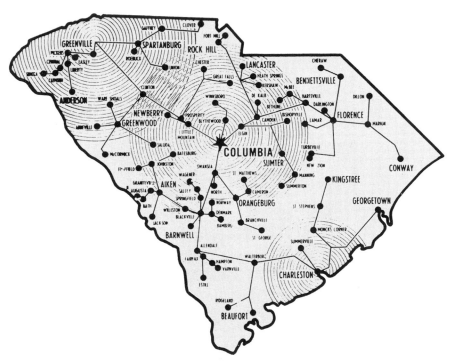

Fig. 14.6. / In South Carolina, ETV reaches over 100,000 students through a complex closed- and open-circuit system.

three hours per day of television teaching is scheduled in Samoa. All educational television instruction is developed at the broadcast center by U.S. mainland teachers who work closely with Samoan teachers. The completed broadcasts are sent into every classroom on the island where mainland-trained and Samoan teachers cooperate to adapt theory and practice to Samoan cultural needs. Together they advise classroom teachers how to prepare for the telecast, what to watch for, and how to follow up after the television portion of the class is over (Fig. 14.9).

Educational television is also provided in Japan. As is the case in Great Britain, Japanese television is governmentally controlled, and educational tele-

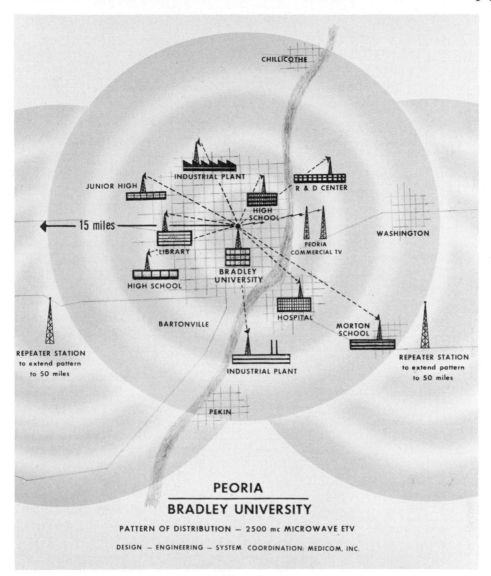

Fig. 14.7. / This inexpensive 25,000 megacycle, microwave, educational-television transmission system represents a cost of $1.00 per pupil or less. It will be as valuable as the teachers employing it will make it.

vision is a part of the national television system (NHK). Japanese national television has one great advantage—a monthly tax of about one dollar is collected on approximately 20 million receivers, and the proceeds are used to finance the network. Thus subsidized by a state tax on every receiver in use, the project has tremendous educational and social impact. NHK devotes most of its schedule to educational programing—approximately 70 percent may be classified as formal or informal education. At the present time, 94 separate relay stations interconnect with key open-broadcast circuits to provide the most complete educational television coverage in the world. Ninety percent of all primary schools, 81 percent of all intermediate schools, and 72 percent of all high schools participate in a broadcast schedule of 10½ hours per day (Fig. 14.10).

STATE-WIDE AND REGIONAL EDUCATIONAL TELEVISION NETWORKS WITH MICROWAVE RELAY INTERCONNECTION

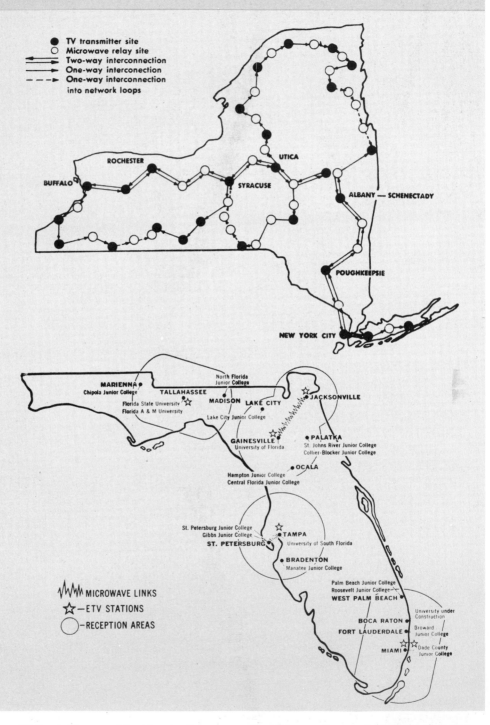

Fig. 14.8. / The combined use of microwave cables and open-broadcast television foresees the future when the entire nation will be thus served by educational television. The diagrams shown above describe developments in Florida and New York.

Fig. 14.9. / Educational television in American Samoa is a team-teaching effort to upgrade quickly the level of education in a primitive society. Educational television in Samoa is described as "total teaching." What are your reactions? Note location of the television receivers.

Fig. 14.10. / In Japan, as in the U.S., the reading load of the school child is on the increase. Can educational television be employed to enhance reading readiness? Why are the publishing and electronic-communications industries progressing at about the same rate?

In addition to the broadcast and closed-circuit distinctions, educational television programs may be classified according to those which are recorded and those which are broadcast as they happen, or "live." Just as an aural experience which is worth saving for later use is recorded on magnetic tape, educational television programs—both sound and visual, or video, impressions—may be recorded electronically on magnetic tape. Today this may be done on either high-fidelity, 2-inch recorders, on 1-inch, or even on ¼-inch *videotape* recording machinery. In Florida for example, tape-recorded educational television is mailed with great economy from station to station in the state's network. The use of ¼-inch, low-cost equipment makes it possible for a school either to record broadcast educational television for use at a later, more desirable time, or to record materials for inclusion in the school library (Fig. 14.11).

Kinescope recording is another means of "saving" educational television programs. This process involves making a motion-picture film record of the program, either while it is being produced, or by transferring the videotape recording to 16 mm. sound motion-picture film. The result is a "kinescope"—actually a 16 mm. sound motion-picture film—which can later be rebroadcast or used in a classroom as a standard 16 mm. sound film.

In the Los Angeles Public Schools, these two processes have been so skillfully implemented that, within minutes after the completion of an educational-television studio lesson, both a 2-inch videotape recording and a completed 16 mm. sound film are available.[3]

The continuing progress of the Midwest Program of Airborne Television Instruction should be noted. MPATI was begun in 1959 and financed by a grant of over $8,000,000 by the Ford Foundation and private industry. The

---

[3] Those in the area may visit the Audio Visual Section of the Los Angeles City Board of Education, Los Angeles, California, to see this equipment in operation.

Fig. 14.11. / Ten years of educational television have produced a whole history of recording invention—V.T.R. (Video Tape Recording (left), and a new solid-state (transistorized) 2-inch videotape. What do these developments mean to you as a classroom teacher?

MPATI program made it possible to assemble a staff of quality technical personnel to work closely with teachers and supervisors in the production of educational television lessons. Lessons are produced and recorded on videotape and later broadcast by videotape playback equipment carried aboard a "flying antenna" (Fig. 14.12). It is estimated that these are used by 6,000,000 pupils and 250,000 teachers who work in the seven-state area adjacent to Purdue.

Since 1960, the MPATI project has become more and more self-sufficient. Over 2000 member schools participate in the program by paying enrollment fees of $2.00 per student per year. MPATI now leases its taped courses to educational television stations and state networks throughout the United States. At the present, between 55 and 65 educational television outlets are using these courses as an integral part of their television broadcast services.

The development of the ¼-inch videotape recorder provides an interesting new avenue to student self-evaluation. Like audio recording tape, videotape can be utilized as an instantaneous "mirror." The students can both see *and* hear themselves perform! For example, students enrolled in speech, instrumental or choral music, and classes in any performing situation can be recorded with relative ease and small expense by using a videcon camera and ¼-inch videotape recorders. Immediate playbacks of this tape through classroom television monitors will confront the performer with an audiovisual image of himself for evaluation. This technique is becoming a growing reality in many school districts, and its applications are limited only by one's imagination. The use of small, inexpensive videcon cameras that are equipped with enlarging-lens systems are currently in use in classrooms where subject content deals with small objects or specimens which must be visualized to be understood. Images are displayed on monitors or on large screens in one or many interconnected classrooms or auditoria. Every student may see the display as if he were standing next to the teacher (Fig. 14.13).

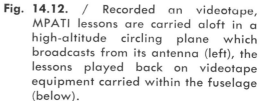

Fig. 14.12. / Recorded on videotape, MPATI lessons are carried aloft in a high-altitude circling plane which broadcasts from its antenna (left), the lessons played back on videotape equipment carried within the fuselage (below).

Fig. 14.13. / The enlarging lens of the recording television camera picks up the 1-inch object and displays it on monitors in the same classroom and many others interconnected into the closed-circuit system. What advantages does this yield? What demands does it place on the teacher?

Now prerecorded television can be used to provide a "total television program," such as that found at Chicago City Junior College. Those who are enrolled in this school may receive all instruction via television. The method of preparing the lessons which the students observe is similar to that described earlier; however, no classroom teacher participates. Related activities include assigned reading and the preparation of written assignments, yet even here there is no classroom teacher.

The Chicago television-college record is impressive. Over 34,000 students have enrolled in over 53,000 course registrations for credit. An unseen audience regularly watches television college programs; this audience has grown from 10,000 viewers in the fall of 1956 to over 200,000 viewers per telecourse in 1964. The 900 students who have graduated with the Associate in Arts Degree took, on the average, one full semester of their two years of work by television. The Chicago City Junior College was examined recently by a panel of distinguished educators who pronounced the enterprise an unqualified success.

Today the electronic aspects of educational television transmission are being solved rapidly and with efficiency. From the largest state or district to the very limited use of closed-circuit television with a single school building, the advantages of educational television are a present day part of learning improvement programs.

□ TELEVISION AS AN EFFECTIVE INSTRUCTIONAL MEDIUM

During the few years that educational television has existed, more than 1700 investigations have been made as to how television can be best employed in learning situations. During the 1953–1959 period, many educational television programs were arranged—often too hastily and without careful preparation. Teachers and television producers often relied excessively on verbal communication techniques. Examination of early efforts in televised teaching reveals that often it was little more than verbal teaching. It is remarkable to note that research studies which probed such programs revealed levels of learning efficiency which were not better, although invariably no worse, than were traditional instructional forms. Reports of "no significant difference" characterized scores of such investigations.

It was soon recognized that there is no magic in television! It is now widely recognized that the effectiveness of educational television depends on excellence of planning, production, use of audiovisual media, and systematic classroom utilization. An example of this kind of television production is to be found in the program, "Pacific Oceania" (Fig. 14.14). Each of the lesson demonstrations of this series is the product of team efforts contributed to by audiovisual-media personnel, a team of television producers, directors and assistants, knowledgeable teachers, and participating resource persons; and the use of appropriate objects, specimens, film clips, flat pictures, graphics, charts, etc.

The classroom teacher welcomes this kind of television production as a means of bringing understandable, needed experiences into the classroom. Following their use, the classroom teacher continues as the one responsible for

Fig. 14.14. / This planning session, devoted to one lesson on Pacific Oceania, is aimed at achieving maximum "in-put"; that is, the lesson includes recorded music, environmental sounds, motion-picture film sequences, slides, models, specimens, charts, and diagrams, in addition to an impressive list of participating resource experts—authors, museum curators, linguists, and a geophysicist. How does this array of learning materials compare with what is ordinarily available to the classroom teacher?

guiding and inspiring the inventive creativity of those pupils who can respond in such ways. As such programs are produced, used, and evaluated, it is to be expected that research results support such generalizations as these:

1. Current evaluation of educational television use reveals statistically significant advantages in the acquisition of factual information and retention.
2. At first students tended to dislike educational television because of the lack of "personal contact." However, pupils like lessons which are followed immediately by classroom activities which encourage the participation of the classroom teacher and pupils.
3. Classroom teachers are overcoming "anxieties about educational television." The classroom teacher who participates as planner, user, and evaluator of quality television becomes a working partner.
4. Quality educational television programing relies heavily on the use of interrelated and appropriate audiovisual media.
5. Quality television programs encourage followup use of audiovisual materials. Television programs often serve as entrees to the use of specific classroom films, filmstrips, etc.
6. Optimum physical surroundings assure maximum seeing and listening, enhance the learning values of educational television.
7. Quality educational television programs encourage most pupils to do simple followup resource investigation—reading particularly.
8. Gifted pupils benefit uniquely. They are quick to respond to suggestions and challenges made by curiosity-arousing educational television programs.

All of this is the result of slightly more than one decade of television production and classroom utilization. In the words of a Midwestern educational television director:

> Never have so many educators worked so hard during such a short period to master new educational techniques. Slightly more than a decade ago there were no educational television experts—just teachers, audio visual personnel, educational radio personnel, professional educators eager and willing to work at and learn about the educational television medium.[4]

■ THE STUDIO-CLASSROOM TEACHING TEAM

A new kind of teaching team has been brought into existence. This team includes the studio teacher and the classroom teacher. These two professional educators are closely bound together as they plan, produce, and use classroom television. Most studio teachers have classroom teaching experience backgrounds. How else can a television teacher anticipate pupil needs and the nature of learning activities needed in the classroom? Working closely with him is the classroom teacher. An analysis of programing and production in the public schools in Milwaukee, Miami, Tampa, South Carolina, New York, Los Angeles, and Hawaii reveals the circumstances by which these two teaching partners are involved with production.

The initial step in television production in these communities involves decision by the classroom and the television teachers regarding the grade levels and subject areas to which television can make its best contributions. In other words, in what situations can educational television offer learning experiences beyond those possible within the routine day-in and day-out classroom teaching situation.

It is recognized that the classroom teacher has known strengths that stem from face-to-face classroom teaching. The television teacher has unique strengths that stem from his having the time to arrange needed, highly complex demonstrations which often call for hours of planning and for the use of learning materials usually not available to the classroom teacher. When both classroom and television teacher bring their unique skills to the pupils, learning goals are achieved more completely (Fig. 14.15).

At the time of the educational-television broadcast, it is the classroom teacher alone who can provide the continual interpretation of the television lessons and lead students to go beyond the basic fact assimilation stage. It is essential to provide classroom opportunities for inventiveness and creative use of factual information in traditional learning situations; this is true also in the case of educational television. Unless the classroom teacher is willing and able to integrate smoothly the television content lessons into the stream of day-to-day classroom instruction, little benefit can be gained from all the careful, cooperative planning that has proceeded. It is almost axiomatic to say that educational-television utilization is no better than the ingenuity and creativity supplied by the classroom teacher, the most important link in the cooperative television planning-production-utilization cycle (Fig. 14.16).

The audiovisual media expert, the professional educational-television director, producer, and technical crew members find in their hands the tremendous

4 Robert M. Reed, speech presented before The Educational Media Institute, Department of Educational Communications, Univ. of Hawaii, 1966.

Fig. 14.15. / A great amount of time and effort go into preparing a single 20- or 30-minute TV lesson. At Hagerstown, each TV teacher has a private office in which he plans and creates demonstrations. He also spends hours in rehearsal to make sure each sequence is logical and the demonstrations are correct and understandable. To what evaluation is the television teacher continuously subject?

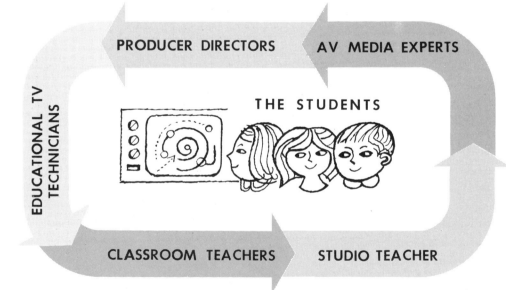

Fig. 14.16. / The educational-television cycle. The members of the educational-television, production-utilization team are responsible one to another. Where in this cycle would you feel that you would enjoy membership? Why?

task of producing a highly visual, clearly heard and seen, educational television lesson or program. Needless to say, this trio is headed usually by an education-oriented producer-director. In the hands of this trio lies the responsibility for finally molding all of the planned "in-put" information—the contributions of classroom and television teacher—into one highly understandable and interesting learning experience.

☐ SELECTION AND USE OF EDUCATIONAL TELEVISION PROGRAMS

Educational television instructional experiences are created in the classroom through a variety of electronic and optical systems. Once this is accomplished, the important consideration is that pupils see, hear, and use these experiences in a work-study-learning situation. The actual utilization procedures closely parallel those already described for the sound motion picture, filmstrips, community resources and other audiovisual experiences. In the case of educational television, there are other factors which influence classroom utilization which should be known to the teacher.

Because the teacher may seldom, if ever, preview educational television materials, judgments often must be based on experience with educational-television programs. Just as in the case of a book or film, the reputation of the educational television producer, the caliber of the teachers who participate, the reputation of the guest or demonstrators who appear on a program, the care taken in organizing the content of the telecast—all help the classroom teacher estimate the probable usefulness of current telecasts and those which are to be produced in the future.

In addition, judgments should be made about content and suitability for the grade level, just as they are made about other audiovisual materials: (1) Is the general level of the program keyed to the age of the group that will see it? (2) Is the content of the telecast of such nature that it will make for better understanding of the subject? (3) Does the television learning experience contribute learning experiences which are needed, and, which are beyond the usual resources available to the classroom teacher through traditional means?

The quality of the telecast itself must also be evaluated. For example, is the program of high quality? Does it communicate clearly and concisely the meanings which are needed?

The classroom teacher is solely responsible for planning and guiding the use of television experiences in the classroom. The television teacher rarely has opportunity to communicate face-to-face with the classroom group or to hear their explanations or statements of further need. The classroom teacher alone reads the planning manuals, carries on preliminary pupil planning and then following the television experience, arranges and guides the use of appropriate additional learning experiences through the use of filmstrips, sound motion-picture films, transcriptions, models and specimens, etc. Finally, the classroom teacher encourages pupils to become involved in inventive or creative utilization of their new-found information.

Ordinarily, the television series will be announced in advance. Manuals of instruction distributed in advance usually include diagrams, explanations of details, and suggestions about concepts which should be clarified before the broadcast begins. The classroom teacher usually will encourage preliminary discussion through which the purposes of the learning experience will be identified by the classroom group. On many occasions, particularly in the fields of science and the social studies, the program manual will suggest supplementary materials which should be on hand for use during or directly after the educational-television lesson (Fig. 14.17).

Fig. 14.17. / As teachers and pupils broadcast a lesson (above), thousands of pupils at work in hundreds of classrooms may find themselves closely identified (below). The educational-television manual describes what paraphernalia is to be in readiness for use in the classroom.

The television-learning experience serves mainly to communicate useful information. The classroom teacher understands that, while the facts may be learned with efficiency through participation in educational television, his responsibility is to lead members of the class group into followup experiences which will rearrange and use this newfound information in an inventive or creative manner. For example, one group of pupils who were studying American government witnessed a television program on Central Europe during the years 1935–1940. The program had carried a sequence of documentary film clips depicting events prior to the involvement of the United States in World War II. These were interspersed with photographs showing meetings of the Nuremberg Party Congress, photos of the men and equipment of the Panzer Divisions, and action photos of the "Drang nach Osten" into Poland. Finally, a documentary visual report of the use of these excerpts in the takeover of the Sudetenland was shown. When the lesson was over, the members of the class had many questions: Why was it that the people who were the victims of this kind of activity were "paralyzed" into inactivity? How can such bitter treatment be tolerated in today's society? Considerable discussion took place, then two of the students suggested going to the library to search for possible answers. News articles which had been written during this period were examined. Short stories about incidents which had occurred during this period were also analyzed, as were novels that had been written during the same time. A few days later, the students' oral reports showed real and new understandings. A mock "freedom broadcast" included "eye-witness" reports and appeals for assistance. A dramatization was created about one of the underground-resistance activities of the time. Throughout all of these activities, the class was enthusiastic.

In an intermediate-grade class, similar creative response and participation was elicited through followup action. Following a broadcast given by a team of science teachers who had used feltboard demonstrations of sedimentary rock formation, chart explanations of subsequent changes in the ocean's surface, and demonstrations with fossilized remains and rock specimens; the pupils were encouraged to conduct their own search for further information. The manual gave suggestions about followup films, filmstrips, and reference reading, but the pupils decided to conduct their own search for rock specimens available in their locality. They were able to locate only quartz and granite specimens, which they soon discovered had little relationship to the story of sedimentary deposits. They then decided to conduct a search among resource people in the community. A mineralogist from the local college was invited to visit with the class to display and to discuss his collections of sedimentary rocks; a geologist from a nearby oil company came to answer questions and to explain how sedimentary deposits hold oil-bearing strata and how these are tapped. Both men left lists of the names of additional men and companies who could be contacted for further information. The pupils wrote to these contacts requesting specific information and assistance. A week later, the teacher had to ask that the group bring the unit to a close—a situation much in contrast to the usual labored pursuit of knowledge.

More usual followup responsibilities associated with the use of television include planning demonstrations, creating arithmetic problems, planning and arranging learning displays, creating dialogues and short stories, and the creation of historical models or dioramas which reflect objective knowledge of costumes, utensils, and "period" paraphernalia. Good followup activities invariably lead to utilizing factual information as the building stones to be arranged in inventive and creative patterns. Such activities reveal the individual's capacity for problem solving, creativity, and inventiveness. Only when such behavior is evident may the teacher feel that he has fulfilled his responsibility.

In the midst of all this tremendous world-wide progress in educational-television techniques and skills, the teacher must not lose sight of his continuing central role in guiding the nature of instruction and the instructional techniques within his own classroom learning situation.

□ SUMMARY

Television has experienced remarkable growth. From a small number of experimental sets owned in 1946, the year 1966 witnessed 62 million receivers installed in the homes and schools of the United States. At the present time, most of the school population is served by educational television—either closed- or open-circuit.

Today, 110 educational-television stations are producing classroom programs and distributing them for use. No longer does television distribution depend on any one channel: open-broadcast, closed-circuit, 2500 megacycle, videotape recordings, or kinescope films all help to make ETV of widespread use. Most television facilities use these techniques in combination in order to obtain maximum distribution of educational-television teaching opportunities. The use of educational television in various parts of the world should be noted: American Samoa for example, and in Japan.

The ¼-inch videotape recorder is an extremely important innovation in educational-television use. This relatively low-cost recording device when used with inexpensive videon cameras permits teaching and pupil self-evaluation. The videotape recorder may be used in a way comparable to that in which the ¼-inch tape recorder is used: to record performance, to witness performance through immediate playback, and to accomplish self-evaluation of what is seen and heard.

Educational-television production is the key consideration in achieving excellence in the use of this new medium. Television production at its best depends on efficient planning, the cooperation of a team of classroom teachers, studio teachers, television technicians, media specialists, and television producers —all working towards the same end: the accomplishment of maximum learning "input." Educational television should be thought of as a channel over which the result of maximum planning may be carried to the classroom teacher who uses educational television as an important supplementary learning experience along with other available resources.

The classroom teacher is the key to efficient educational-television utilization toward the end of improved instruction. The classroom teacher is the only person who can advise, interpret, coordinate, utilize, counsel pupils and arrange for the creative use of educational-television communications in the stream of day-to-day classroom instruction.

In using educational television in the classroom the teacher accepts the responsibilities that are very similar to those assumed in any work-study situation. In addition, he becomes increasingly important as he guides the followup or creativity aspects of television programing after the actual reception of the materials has been completed. Television is an efficient channel for the communication of needed information. It remains for the classroom teacher, however, to help students apply television learned information to new patterns which reflect inventiveness and creativity.

As is the case with all communication media, the school has great responsibility in preparing, selecting, and using television programing; and in providing the necessary equipment so that television programs can become an inherent part of classroom instruction.

☐ Suggested Activities

1. Visit the nearest school television studios. Investigate such factors as:
   a. Techniques and procedures employed in planning and deciding upon the nature of educational television lessons
   b. Procedures followed in producing classroom educational television utilization manuals
   c. The nature of educational television classroom-utilization studies which examine the efficiencies of educational television
   d. The findings of such research studies
2. Arrange to visit classrooms in which television is being utilized. Observe the teacher at work before, during, and following the television programs. Discuss with the teacher the nature of his involvement in the planning and classroom utilization of television programing. Observe the receiving equipment used and ask for an evaluation by the teacher.
3. Plan and conduct a survey based on the question: "To what extent do you feel that classroom learning efficiency can be improved through the use of educational television?"
4. Arrange for the viewing of several of the films which report educational television planning and progress (see Bibliography: Films).

☐ Bibliography

Brown, James W. and James W. Thornton (Eds.), *New Media in Higher Education,* Association for Higher Education and the Division of Audiovisual Instruction, National Educational Association, 1963.

Educational Facilities Laboratories, *Planning for Schools with Television,* Dave Chapman, Inc., 1960.

Lewis, Philip, *Educational Television Guidebook,* McGraw-Hill, 1961.

Midwest Program on Airborne Television Instruction, Purdue University, 1965.

Schramm, Wilber (Ed.), *Educational Television: The Next Ten Years,* The Institute for Communication Research, 1962.

Washington County Closed Circuit Television Report, Board of Education of Washington County, Maryland, 1964.

☐ Films

Dawn Over the Mountains: Educational Television in Japan, 16 mm., B&W, National Educational Television Center.

Knowledge and Ideas, 16 mm., B&W, National Educational Television Center.

Television in Education, 16 mm., Color, Bell Telephone Co.

The Second Classroom, 16 mm., Color, National Educational Association.

XV

MULTIMEDIA USE

Since the early 1960s, the increasing student population, together with a shortage of qualified teachers and an "explosion" of new knowledge in virtually all fields, has forced numerous educational institutions to explore new means of instruction. The preceding chapters have described, item by item, the instructional media and materials that can implement these new means. The reader has been informed that a film, for example, may provide an effective learning experience in itself, or a field trip may provide valuable and unique information for the participating learner. A map can provide the means for becoming acquainted with the world, and books have untold values.

It does not necessarily follow, however, that such educational media will be used individually as isolated learning experiences in typical classroom situations. On the contrary, it has been indicated throughout the book that the classroom teacher may, and usually will, select and plan to use combinations of media which fit together as parts of a kind of learning "mosaic." The imaginative teacher soon comes to recognize that when films, field trips, maps, objects and specimens, books, etc., are carefully coordinated for classroom use, the learning that results can be much more than the sum of the individual parts.

The idea of multimedia utilization is increasingly being applied in various educational areas, from preschool programs to adult education and industrial and military training. For example, a recently published foreign-language system, *La Familia Fernandez,* is available as a multimedia learning program which reinforces understanding through the interaction which results from the use of 54 sound motion-picture films, 54 language-model drill tapes, a set of filmstrips, and verbal materials in printed form.[1] The Los Angeles City Schools encourage the interrelated use of audiovisual materials by making "media sets" available to teachers (Fig. 15.1). These sets are compiled by teachers and media experts who work together, and represent a wide range of interrelated materials that the classroom teacher may employ to "get the message across."

The multimedia approach to classroom instruction places great responsibility

[1] *Spanish, La Familia Fernandez: An Audio-Visual Lingual Program for Learning Spanish,* Encyclopaedia Britannica Films.

Fig. 15.1. / This multimedia set on Central America includes artifacts from the area as well as the various communication tools available to teachers at work in the Los Angeles City Schools. What preplanning does this represent? What classroom management plans would you need to make to get the most out of such materials?

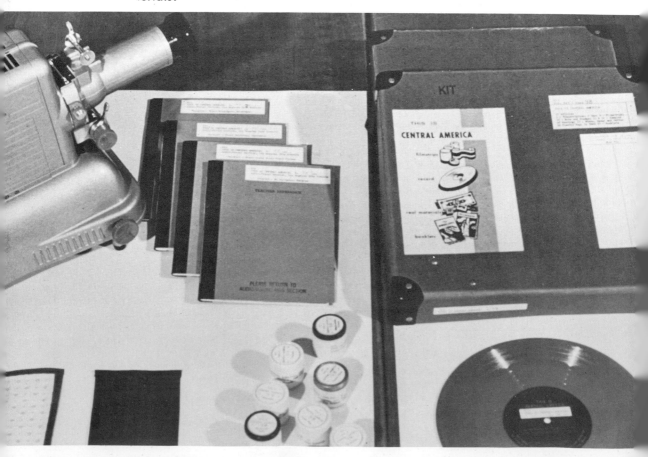

on the teacher to analyze the learning goals of pupils, to know sources of audio-visual materials from which he can select those which will help satisfy these learning goals, and to know how to use this array of materials so as to achieve the full measure of the pupils' learning potential.

□ IDENTIFYING LEARNING GOALS

Learning problems in the classroom are as broad as the curriculum offered by the school. The primary teacher's goals may be to develop number readiness, greater language facility, or increased interest in reading and attainment of reading comprehension. The middle-grade teacher may have the tasks of building and strengthening pupils' concepts of number and mathematical relationships, of developing pupil interest in and understanding of the general nature of the earth's surface characteristics, or of imparting the information about the cultural patterns and social relationships of other peoples of the world, and—more important—establishing favorable pupil attitudes toward them. The secondary-school teacher may aim to bring his pupils to a true understanding of current local, national, or international affairs and the historical forces which shaped them. Whatever the broad teaching goals established by the curriculum, however, the teacher must translate each curriculum study unit into specific learning goals which, in step-by-step sequence, will result in the efficient learning of the major goals of the unit. Moreover, he must define these learning goals in terms of the needs and relevance to his *particular* pupils.

One of the factors which has contributed to teachers' continual dependence on outdated and essentially verbal classroom methods has been their failure to translate the general objectives outlined in the curriculum into finer and more specific *learning* goals which will be meaningful to the pupils and relevant to their existing frames of reference. In history units, for example, learning objectives include understanding historical events, knowing the people and situations which caused and were affected by these events, and conceptualizing these events in their chronological contexts. Too frequently, teachers have equated these objectives with the *memorization* of historical names, places, dates, and events, and thus have lectured to their classes, assigned reading, and given tests with these in mind as the desired learning goals. The result has too often been little or no conceptualization of the placement of dates on the time continuum; little or no understanding of the drama, excitement, and human emotions involved in the historical events; and little or no interest in the significance of the ideas which led to and resulted from these events.

The definitive assessment of curriculum objectives in terms of the pupils' particular deficiencies or proficiencies, and the translating of these into specific learning goals, must precede the selection of appropriate means by which to attain these goals and the instructional tools used to implement these means. The alternate to this step is likely to result in an extensive expenditure of time, energy, and money, with only limited opportunities for truly satisfactory results.

Table 15.1 CONTRIBUTIONS OF AUDIOVISUAL INSTRUCTIONAL MATERIALS TO LEARNING

	16 mm. Sound Motion-Picture Films	8 mm. Silent or Sound Motion-Picture Films	Filmstrips	Slides	Flat Pictures and Learning Displays	Posters and Charts	Maps	Chalkboard	Community Study	Radio	Recordings and Transcriptions	Language Labs and Tape Recorders	Models and Specimens	Educational Television	Programed-Learning Materials[b]
VISUAL															
Visually re-creates situations involving motion which occur anywhere	X	X							X				X	X	X
Visually re-creates the past	X	X	X	X	X	X		X					X	X	X
Visualizes theoretical ideas and microscopic life	X	X	X	X	X	X		X	X				X	X	X
Visualizes with natural color	X	X	X	X	X	X							X	X	X
Visualizes natural dimensions (three-dimensional)	X	X	X	X	X			X	X				X	X	
AUDIO															
Re-creates characteristic or environmental sounds	X	X	X[a]						X	X	X	X		X	X
Re-creates events through dramatization	X	X	X[a]							X	X	X		X	X
UTILIZATION															
Sequence fixed	X	X	X											X	
Flexible organization permits rearrangement				X	X	X	X	X	X		X	X	X		X
Permits restudy	X	X	X	X	X	X	X	X	X		X	X	X	X	X
Permits leisurely examination, discussion, etc.			X	X	X	X	X	X	X		X	X	X		X
Control of time and place of use	X	X	X	X	X	X	X	X	X		X	X	X	X	X
Can usually be produced locally		X		X	X	X	X	X	X		X	X	X	X	X

☐ SELECTING SUITABLE TEACHING MATERIALS

After the goals of instruction have been defined, the teacher will need to arrange for learning experiences which will be useful in helping his pupils to attain these goals. The means by which teaching goals may be achieved are varied and complex. In some cases, a learning outcome may be obtained satisfactorily merely by having pupils read pertinent literature (providing, of course, that the prerequisite concepts and understanding have been attained); in other cases, effective learning may result from having pupils participate in real-life situations that occur at places and circumstances far removed from the four walls of the classroom—for example, living for a period of time in a different cultural setting as is arranged by various student-exchange programs. Between these two extremes are the diverse and flexible array of audiovisual instructional materials available to the teacher. Properly selected and employed, these tools can bring within the reach of the classroom tangible, real-life information about abstract concepts and remote peoples, places, and things.

These teaching-learning materials—the chalkboard, pictures, charts and diagrams, models and specimens, maps and globes, field trips, transcriptions and sound tapes, filmstrips and slides, films, television, etc., as well as books and other verbal materials—all have their own unique characteristics. Thus, the selection of suitable materials to be used singly or in combination should be based on how well they can be expected to help pupils reach the specific learning goals desired. The various characteristics of the audiovisual materials that were discussed in earlier chapters are summarized in Table 15.1, which includes also the characteristics of programed learning (to be discussed in Chapter XVI). In selecting these materials for use in a particular study unit, however, the teacher must also bear in mind the following general characteristics:

1. Suitability for the grade level in terms of vocabulary, pace, and general understandability
2. Accuracy and authenticity of the information
3. Mechanical excellence of sound, vocabulary, color, and other general "see and hear" factors

In analyzing the role of media in learning and the basis on which they should be selected, Gagne points out that planning for media and planning for optimal learning are essentially parts of the same process.

> The various modes of instruction are employed for the purpose of getting the greatest instructional usefulness from media and combinations of media. Thus the choice of modes is also a matter of aiming for optimal functioning in generating the proper conditions for learning . . . *it is these conditions that provide the immediate instructional purposes on the basis of which correct decisions can be made about media and modes of instruction.*[2]

Instructional development along the lines of the Gagne approach was demonstrated at the Department of Physiology at Michigan State University where it was

---

2 Robert M. Gagne, *The Conditions of Learning*, Holt, Rinehart and Winston, 1965, pp. 28–29. Italics added.

discovered that basic laboratory instruction in physiology courses was failing to achieve adequate learning results. With the assistance of professional consultants, the staff undertook an extensive analysis of the entire course of study, including laboratory work. During the first several months of the investigation, course objectives were overhauled and refined into new and sharper goals, and changes in the course and laboratory content were changed accordingly. While tryout of the revised content revealed some improvement in student learning, there were still serious deficiencies in laboratory performance. Further analysis suggested strongly that much laboratory time was being wasted because students were deficient in the basic skills and information necessary to carry out the exercises. It was then hypothesized that if a student could be familiarized with the necessary lab equipment, background information, and experimental procedures in advance of performing a given experiment, the student could not only perform the experiment itself more successfully, but also he would be able to devote more time to the broader implications of the experiment and the principles involved. A plan was accordingly devised for a program that would achieve three goals:

1. Acquaintance with the equipment, instruments, animals, and procedures to be used in the regular laboratory
2. Detailed grasp of the operation of pertinent equipment and of the procedures to be employed in the regular laboratory
3. An introduction to and overview of the actual experiment to be performed

In implementing the attainment of these goals, it was necessary to accommodate the varied scientific backgrounds of the students; thus, laboratory-preparation study was individualized, permitting each student to go through the work at his own pace. At the moment of this writing, two units of a series of program alternatives—all geared to meeting the three goals outlined above, as well as those indicated by the specific needs of each student—have been completed along with the corresponding media and learning materials for the programs. While it is too early for critical assessment of results, faculty and student enthusiasm for the revised approach are most promising.

A combination of media selected for use in a particular unit should be based not only according to how suitable each of the media is to its particular purpose in the unit, but also according to how well and in what ways each supplements the others in providing information, and how each reinforces the learning effect of the others. While the spread of the school-level continuum, the range of subject matter involved, the diversity of curriculum and specific classroom objectives, and so forth obviates the presentation of a single set of multimedia selection criteria, two general guidelines should be observed: (1) Other factors being equal, the teacher should select media combinations that will provide a variety of appropriate sensory experiences, and (2) media, materials, and methods should be selected or designed as much as possible in terms of specified outcomes desired. In the absence of scientifically established rules of selection and application of media and methods to specified learning goals, the assistance of learning and media experts is probably essential. The alternative is apt to result in something less than an adequate solution to an instructional problem.

☐ USING INSTRUCTIONAL MEDIA COMBINATIONS EFFECTIVELY

The teaching-learning tasks to which various combinations of instructional materials can be put are virtually limitless. The teacher himself may present a sequence of learning situations through a planned combination of these media, or he may use them to substitute for him as information giver while he attends to other professional matters. He may provide extra tutoring for those pupils who need it by planning individualized instructional programs which employ combinations of media, or encourage gifted pupils to learn on their own through similarly planned programs.

For whatever purpose the combination of instructional media is to be used, however, the learning situation comprised of a sequence of media experiences must be planned and prepared carefully by the teacher, and include provision for evaluative and creative followup activities. It should be noted also that the media should comprise essential rather than peripheral ingredients of the teaching-learning process, and, that media selection and use is determined on the basis of clearly defined pupil learning needs. These principles apply equally well for any subject or grade level; however, we shall discuss some of the uses of media combinations in the contexts of three subject areas: Foreign languages, the social studies, and science.

■ IN FOREIGN-LANGUAGE INSTRUCTION

Foreign-language instruction has been receiving greatly increased emphasis in our schools—both elementary and secondary—during the 1960s than was formerly the case. One reason is the focus on modern foreign languages (along with science and mathematics) in the National Defense Education Act of 1958. Another and more basic reason is our widespread realization of the need for foreign languages as a means of better understanding the peoples and cultures of the rapidly shrinking world in which we live.

Almost universally, courses of study in modern foreign languages cite two primary objectives. The first is competence in the four language skills—aural understanding, speaking, reading, and writing. The second is a steadily increasing understanding of the foreign culture of which the language is an element.

As pointed out in Chapter X, there is little satisfaction with the results of traditional methods of language instruction which have emphasized tedious memorization of vocabulary and rules of grammar, and which have relied primarily on reading and writing exercises as means of language learning. This process—quite alien to the way people learn to speak and understand their native tongue—has not only required long years of study for the attainment of any significant degree of mastery, but also in the end too frequently lead to little more than a rapid translation ability rather than an ability to think directly in

Fig. 15.2. / The individualized character and effectiveness of language instruction can be materially increased by appropriate use of the language laboratory. Language laboratories can range from the more simplified, as shown above, to elaborate electronic complexes such as that shown at right. In the example above, all tables are wired so headsets can be plugged in every few feet along the back side of the table.

the foreign language. Further, accurate pronunciation resulting from such a reading-writing approach has left much to be desired, as opportunities for speaking and hearing the actual sounds are limited in such an approach. One important means devised to answer the need for more speaking-hearing opportunities in foreign-language instruction is the language laboratory (see Fig. 15.2) which was discussed at some length in Chapter X. As was said there, the language laboratory can greatly increase both the quantity and the quality of the student's aural-oral experiences; it reduces outside distractions and hence increases concentration; it enables him to work at his own pace both in and outside the class, the latter by means of master tapes. Furthermore, the instructor can listen in on any pupil at any time and provide assistance as necessary.

The language laboratory enables pupils to practice individually and at their own pace, and permits class time to be devoted to study of the culture of the people who speak natively the studied language, their literature, art, and customs, etc., and for learning formal rules of grammar and syntax. Full advantage of its potential is, of course, lost when the language laboratory is used merely for the repetition of work done previously in class or for the practice of formal grammar exercises; in such cases a simple tape recorder can serve as well and a learning laboratory is probably unjustified.

Ready access of tapes for language students' individual study is recognized as important for optimum progress and is provided in various ways. At Purdue University, for example, lesson or practice tapes may be checked out and used in listening rooms in the Audiovisual Center. The University of Texas Library provides a similar service. At the University of Michigan, a random access dialing system has been developed which permits both listening access and recording over telephone lines at low cost. With this system, it is possible to extend learning laboratory facilities to dormitories, classrooms throughout the campus, and even to distant resource centers. The system has since been put to use on various college campuses and some secondary schools.[3]

A portable, wireless, language-laboratory system is used in the Scarsdale, New York, Junior High School and other school systems. This system includes a teacher's control unit; battery-powered headsets, each with a small receiver-amplifier; and an "audio notebook" which is a lightweight self-contained recorder-reproducer. The audio notebook has a capacity of $5\frac{1}{2}$ hours of material in 15-minute segments, either prerecorded or received via the headsets (Fig. 15.3). In effect, the system provides at low cost a number of the functions of a full-scale laboratory plus portability.[4]

Material the teacher wishes to transmit to the class either for immediate use or for recording for later study can be fed from a tape recorder, record player, or her own microphone into the control unit and is then broadcast to the students who receive it through their headsets (Fig. 15.4). As the tape is played, the instructor can plug in on the headset of any student, listen to his progress, and give assistance as needed. The student can record and play back his own responses in the audio-notebook unit. Since it has several channels, the unit can also accommodate prerecorded material for study at home or in school.

With language-laboratory equipment available and its use scheduled into the course work, classroom periods can be used to make the language come alive to the pupils. A variety of audiovisual materials—films, slides, flat pictures, three-dimensional objects and specimens, maps and globes, study displays, field trips, and recordings of folk music or literary readings all make useful implements toward this end (Fig. 15.5). Dr. George Borglum, former head of the Department of French at Wayne State University, and now director of a pilot program of audiovisual language teaching at that university, makes extensive use of specially photographed slides and films in his French classes. His coordinated approach combines the visual and audio components of language learning in a manner calculated to secure the optimum benefits of both:

> Most language laboratories make possible the repetition of audio experience but do not supply the original visual experience. At Wayne State University, the student not only can become quite glib with sentences like *"Certains touristes ont des caravanes,"* pronouncing the sentence rapidly and perfectly, but also comes to understand what *caravane* means by seeing the actual object on a screen.

[3] David Jaslow, quoted in Elton Hocking, *Language Laboratory and Language Learning*, Department of Audiovisual Instruction, National Education Association, 1964, p. 58.
[4] The equipment described is available from Electronic Futures, Inc., 301 State Street, North Haven, Conn.

Fig. 15.3. / The audio notebook is a portable electronic storage and retrieval system for the individual student. What other subject uses might there be for such equipment?

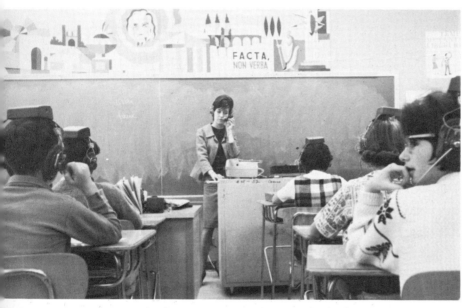

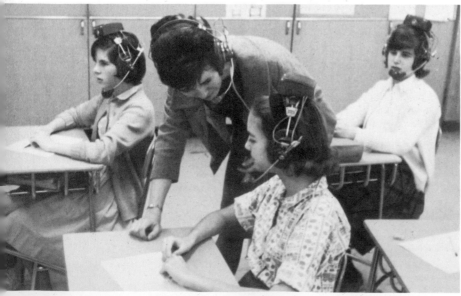

Fig. 15.4. / What are some practical advantages of the portable language laboratory? Above: The instructor listens with the students as a pre-recorded tape is transmitted through the control unit. Below: She is listening in to a student's receiver to note his responses and to assist if needed.

And this visual link is necessary because a modern French trailer no more resembles an American trailer than a Renault Dauphine resembles a Cadillac. In other words, if the purpose of teaching French is to talk about things that are French, both seeing and hearing are necessary parts of the learning process.

The integration of the video and audio senses—made possible by films, colored slides, synchronized tape recordings, and the live voice of the instructor—places the learner of a new language in situations similar to those in which he learned his native language.[5]

Slow-scan television which can be transmitted over telephone lines appears a practicable means for adding the visual element to the random access dialing system of extending the language-laboratory facilities mentioned earlier. When the visual element becomes as readily accessible as the audio, we may anticipate far-reaching applications of language-laboratory techniques to numerous sub-

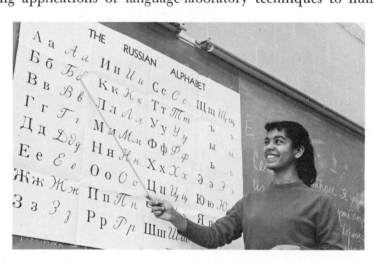

Fig. 15.5. / Traditional visuals like this chart, when used in proper context, are by no means outmoded in modern language instruction.

ject fields. The day is close at hand when students of all ages will be receiving substantial amounts of instruction over telephone lines and other electronic means. The technical capacity is already available; the capacity to adapt technological developments and put them into effective use in schools will take longer.

In addition to listening to a master tape of the language laboratory and attempting to duplicate the accurate pronunciation, pupils can benefit strongly from the opportunity to employ their learning in actual conversations with a native of the tongue. One of the authors of *La Familia Fernandez,* Professor Gonzales Arauze of the University of the Americas in Mexico City, observes that it is necessary for a student to identify with situations and people in other lands before he can get really to "know" their language. "The proper procedure, then," he adds, "is to immerse the student in the world in which this language is used, a world inhabited by people he knows and cares about. This

5 George Borglum, "AV-Active French," *NEA Journal,* November, 1958, pp. 566–568.

sharing of everyday experiences with people of a foreign tongue creates the necessary climate of sympathy and establishes the *sine qua non* for the learning of language—the desire to communicate with the people of that language."[6]

One teacher of a first-year French class in high school arranged to have a French chef from a local hotel visit the class one day. Although the teacher had to help a little as the chef was no more fluent in English than her pupils were in French, she reported the pupils' amazement and delight when they discovered that they could actually converse in French with a real live French-man. Such experiences can have immeasurable value in adding zest and purpose to the learning of a foreign language, and serve as effective motivating agents. For, as in any other subject, interest and true learning go hand in hand in a modern language class, and stimulate creative pupil involvement.

Pupils are most likely to become motivated to learn when the subject matter appears relevant and related to the facts and understandings that have already become an integral part of their frame of reference—particularly those which are a personal part of their daily lives. Realizing this, one teacher of a French class in a Wisconsin school starts the first semester by calling attention to the many American cities with French names, such as Detroit, St. Louis, Joliet, and Racine.[7] As the students compile a substantial list of similar names from maps and atlases, questions are typically raised as to the origins of some of the cities, especially of those in the students' home state of Wisconsin. This preliminary unit leads naturally into the lesson on "Les Français en Amerique," and the reading, in French, describes such early French explorers as Cartier, Champlain, Marquette, Joliet, and LaSalle. In this way, the pupils gain drill in pronunciation and grammar in the language as they attempt to find answers to their own questions about the origins of American cities with French names. Significantly, they learn important facts and concepts in geography and history at the same time.

In this connection, effective learning in one subject matter area can contribute to effective learning in another, as information learned in one course can provide the conceptual and motivational foundations for learning the similar or related material in a different subject. This *cognitive transfer,* as educators call it, is a highly desired learning outcome in its own right, yet when classwork is presented by essentially verbal methods and materials, this cognitive transfer is likely to remain limited and, at best, restricted to material covered within the same formal subject area. In part, this is because the terminology used to impart similar subject matter often differs in each curriculum area, but also because heavy reliance on verbal instructional media and materials fails to provide pupils with the necessary concrete experience of the words' referents. Thus, pupils who "learn" by traditional reading-and-writing methods the vocabulary, grammar, and syntax of a foreign language, as well as some aspects of the foreign culture involved, are likely to have to "learn" much of the same information all over again in a pertinent social-studies unit, or vice versa.

6 Quoted in Elton Hocking, *op. cit.,* p. 146.
7 See Laura B. Johnson, "Mechanical Aids for Learning Languages," *French Review,* October, 1949, pp. 37–39.

The learning sequence worked out by the French language teacher in Wisconsin leads into a unit on French Canada, and both pupils and teacher gather illustrative material for a bulletin-board display. Postcards and magazine pictures of French Canada, dolls and rugs made by peasants in the Gaspé area, and photographs taken by several pupils' families who have toured the region are included in the display. During this phase of the work, recordings of French Canadian folk songs are played also. Much of this audiovisual material is used as a frame of reference for vocabulary drills and oral practice. Further, as the lesson proceeds, a film on French Canada, with a narration in French, is shown. Before showing the film of course, the teacher reads the narration to the class, noting new words and phrases on the chalkboard as she does so, and, after the showing, questions and points of clarification are discussed and provide the basis for learning simultaneously French vocabulary and grammar, and cultural, geographical, and historical points about French Canada. The teacher then shows the film once again to reinforce pupil learning. As a culminating activity on the French Canada unit, a native French Canadian woman is invited to the classroom to talk with the pupils and to answer the questions they have prepared in advance. This interview is conducted in French, and the students' pleasure at being understood by the French Canadian visitor, and at being able to understand her, is testimony to the effective learning outcomes derived from this program. Followup letters written by the students—to say nothing of the successful examination results—provide further substantiation of the learning achieved.

Clearly, the quality of planning and of the stimulating guidance of an expert teacher involved in such a program is well rewarded. In commenting on this type of language instruction, Hocking notes that "genuinely integrated courses—complete with visuals, pre-recorded drills on tapes, student's workbook and text, and a teacher's manual, plus tests and keys for scoring—are so recent (since 1960) that high school teachers do not generally understand or even know them."[8]

Yet, the above illustration is taken from the experience of an inspired high-school foreign-language teacher who was using an integrated-materials approach nearly two decades ago!

Due to the work of such men as Hocking and Borglum and the position taken by the Modern Language Association regarding language instruction, many new materials are available to the teacher. *Je Parle Francais* is an integrated film-text-tape method for introductory and intermediate French consisting of 120 color films and related tapes plus student texts, teachers' manuals and supplementary drill tapes.[9] The first level of *El Espanol Por El Mundo,* entitled "La Familia Fernandez" is a comparable visual-audiolingual package for learning Spanish; it has 54 filmed lessons, 54 filmstrips, 54 laboratory tapes, 54 test tapes, textbooks, manuals and a special visually cued text containing the key visuals presented in the films and filmstrips.[10] These and similar visual-

8 Elton Hocking, *op. cit.,* p. 58.
9 Encyclopaedia Britannica Films, 1961, 1963.
10 *Ibid.*

Fig. 15.6. / Mme. Anne Slack, the TV teacher, converses with one of the puppets created for "Parlons Français" by Bill and Cora Baird.

Fig. 15.7. / With televised teaching as with other media, the classroom teacher's role continues to be central. After the telecast, a St. Louis elementary-school class does a followup lesson.

audiolingual programs[11] provide complete teaching programs with sufficient variation and flexibility to accommodate individual needs and interests of both students and instructors. All are undertaken to combine language study with study of the people who speak the language and their culture.

Related to language and cultural studies is an international tape exchange program initiated by Ruth Terry, a Muskegon, Michigan high-school English teacher. Originated initially as a unique means of communication among students in the United States, the idea spread to teachers and students in nearly 30 percent of the other countries of the world. While most of these were countries in which English is a second language, the possibilities for exchange of current foreign language tapes for enrichment of language instruction are apparent.[12]

---

11 For example, Webster Division, McGraw-Hill Book Co., has *Learning French, Learning Spanish* and *Beginning German with Films*. The French and Spanish programs include specially designed films, filmstrips, texts, tapes, tests, manuals, and practice records. The German program combines texts, motion pictures, and tape recordings.

12 Ruth Y. Terry, "A Study of Educational Tape Exchange," unpublished study, University of Michigan, August, 1965, p. 107. (For further information, address Mrs. Ruth Terry, International Tape Exchange, 834 Ruddiman Avenue, North Muskegon, Mich.)

A development of major proportions during the past decade has been FLES —Foreign Language in the Elementary School. While there are some unresolved questions about the value of FLES, there is no question about the wide interest attracted by this program. Because few elementary teachers have sufficient background in foreign language to teach it, FLES moved early into broadcast television. In 1964, there were an estimated 3,000,000 children in FLES and perhaps 100 TV programs. By far the most popular and widely used of these is "Parlons Français," carried by some 50 stations to an enrollment of about 2,000,000. The program is also available on film with supplementary disks and picture books for the children and comparable appropriate materials for the teacher.

The evident popularity of the "Parlons Français" program is probably due in considerable measure to the personable and highly effective TV teacher and to imaginative programing, including the use of the famous Baird marionettes (Fig. 15.6). Following each program, the local teacher needs to conduct practice sessions on the material covered and it is here that the program thrives or fails. As in the application of programed instruction, team teaching or other innovations in educational materials and methods, the attitude and ability of the teacher are of paramount importance. Where the attitude is positive, enthusiastic and intelligent, results tend to be uniformly good (Fig. 15.7).

■ IN THE SOCIAL STUDIES

Related to the study of language and of the cultures in which languages exist are the social studies—history, geography, government, and so forth. The rather dry exposition of facts provided in most textbooks in this area can be made to come alive for pupils by an imaginative teacher who utilizes a combination of creatively chosen audiovisual media. As in other subjects, the teacher must first secure his pupils' interest and motivation if he is to achieve his teaching goals. This is done best by appealing to the pupils' existing conceptual framework; however, it should be noted that prerequisite subject matter formally achieved by the class in earlier grades may not have provided the concepts prescribed by the *curriculum* as necessary to forthcoming work. This is particularly likely to be true where earlier learning has been based primarily on listening to the teacher lecture, reading textbooks, and writing assignments and reports. The children may have achieved the ability to recognize and to learn the words involved in passing the work without having learned the *concepts behind* the words.

Thus, rather than assume that earlier studies have become a part of his pupils' frame of reference, the teacher must first establish where his pupils *really are* in readiness for current social-studies units. This can be done in many ways: a period devoted to posing interesting questions may be conducive to assessing pupil understanding, or the teacher may devise a creative class project—such as constructing a study display or making a recorded tape to be sent to children in the area to be studied, etc.—which will at once involve the pupils in active participation and reveal how much or little they know about the forthcoming study unit. Or the teacher may read a fictional story based on historical or cultural facts which, because of its drama and plot, will elicit the pupils' interest as well as their curiosity about points they do not understand. These preliminary activities can serve not only to stimulate creative pupil involvement and provide the teacher with a means of evaluating pupil readiness, but can also provide the basis for leading naturally into learning the subject matter at hand.

Once the pupils have become interested and involved in the curriculum material, the teacher should continue his efforts to motivate pupils by drawing upon a wide array of relevant teaching materials—films and filmstrips, sound-recorded, dramatic reenactments of historical events and similarly recorded storytelling, objects and specimens such as cultural artifacts, and so forth. Some teachers carefully plan out the first week or so of grade work in a creative and imaginative sequence of learning situations and then, perhaps because of time pressures and other factors, gradually slip into relying upon basic text materials and class discussion periods. Clearly, to achieve the desired learning results throughout the school term or year, the teacher must have on hand early in the year—perhaps before the term starts—an extensive list of relevant materials and where they can be obtained. Further, the teacher should make a complete outline of lesson sequences before the term starts—anticipating the use of specific films, recordings, and other materials and alternates—which relate to each unit and subunit of study. This outline should also anticipate possibilities in creative class learning projects and followup activities. The course outline should be flexible enough, however, to accommodate the special learning needs of the pupils in the class.

In order to plan efficiently so that the lesson sequences and the materials used to implement them may achieve maximum learning results, the instructor must first translate curriculum objectives into clearly defined and specific classroom study goals. This was done by a group of teachers in a Honolulu school for a fifth-grade unit on the home state of Hawaii. Curriculum objectives called for pupils to learn the geological origin of the islands, and their composition, geographical facts such as land area, population, indigenous plant and animal life, climate, and the history of its people, and its cultural status today. Because the history, geography, and culture of the 50th state differs widely from those of the other United States, it was decided that the unit on Hawaii be undertaken after the children had studied a number of other lands, rather than in connection with U.S. studies. These objectives were translated by the teaching committee into the following subunits:

    I. Origin
       A. Volcanic activity—causes and effects
       B. Size and nature of islands
   II. Plant and Animal Life
       A. Climate circumstances and their causes
       B. Plant and animal life
  III. History
       A. Polynesian and European "discovery"
       B. Polynesian culture

    C. European cultural influences

    D. Americanization and statehood

IV. Current Status

    A. The people—their ethnic backgrounds and influences on the culture

    B. Agriculture and industry (related to subunit II)

    C. Culture and historical influences (related to III: B, C, and D)

    D. Government and education

With these basic learning goals in mind, the committee of teachers next began to consider the materials they would use to help build conceptual understanding among the learners. With the aid of the school's educational television staff, specialists from the University of Hawaii, and personnel from a nearby museum, a series of educational television lessons was produced and manuals distributed to teachers throughout the school district. Additional materials to be used between and in connection with these programs were compiled: maps, films, diagrams, slides, sound tapes, and reading literature.

Typical of the application of learning sequences devised is the way one classroom proceeded through the unit. As the class had just completed several units on different countries and cultures, the teacher used a quick review of these units to lead into the unit on Hawaii. "Can anyone summarize quickly what we have studied so far this term?" she asked the class.

"We have covered Cuba and South America . . . and Central Africa . . . oh, yes, and China, too," offered one pupil.

"And what kinds of things did we learn about these places?" continued the teacher.

"About kinds of schools they had," said one girl.

"The history of the countries," volunteered another.

"What people do for a living," said a boy.

"What the people wore, and what they make," chimed in another girl.

The teacher noted the pupils' answers on the board, and called for some quick descriptions of historical and cultural comparisons among the countries studied, leading from this discussion into the geographical and climatological reasons for some of the pupils' answers.

"What do we know about the geography of our own land, Hawaii?" asked the teacher.

"It's a group of islands," said a boy.

"Yes, but were these islands always here?"

"No, a long time ago, there was nothing but ocean," stated a Japanese boy.

"Then volcanic eruptions started and made mountains. We're living on top of these," volunteered another child.

"How did this happen?" questioned the teacher further.

"There was great pressure deep in the earth, and one day the eruptions began. . . ."

A girl was waving her hand, and the teacher called on her. "If it happened in the ocean, why didn't the water put it out?" she asked.

The teacher paused and waited for more ideas, but at this point most of the children had more questions. These were written on the chalkboard, and then summarized into two basic areas which needed clarification:

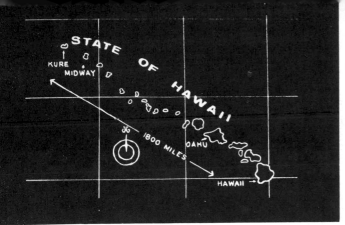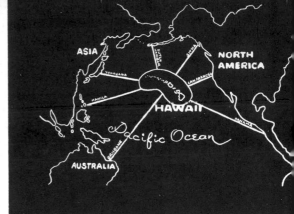

Fig. 15.8. / Two chalkboard illustrations prepared by students: the orientation of the 50th state, and a description of the arrangement of the island chain along a rift in the earth's surface. Both were produced by the grid-enlargement method.

1. Why and how did the Hawaiian volcanic activity occur where it did?
2. How are volcanic mountains, craters, and valleys formed?

The teacher divided the class into two groups, each of which was to do some research into one of the above topics. Then she recorded on the board a number of words the pupils would be likely to come across in their assignment: *fault, fissure, atoll, volcanic cones, lava banks, pumice, fumerals,* and so forth.

The next few days were spent on informal presentation of the information the pupils had gathered, and clarification of ideas. The pupils were encouraged to draw diagrams on the chalkboard as they described the processes which formed the islands, and to answer and raise questions whenever they seemed relevant (Fig. 15.8). Some pupils brought in samples of lava, pumice, and other geological specimens. The teacher refrained from lecturing or providing answers to questions that could be answered by further pupil research, and restricted her role to guiding the discussion and explaining where pupils had some difficulty.

A few days later, the first of the series of scheduled television broadcasts was tuned in on the television monitor. The pupils' initial research and discussion had prepared them for understanding the information presented by a world-famous geologist on the program. Referring to diagrams, film clips, models and maps, this geologist explained how millions of years ago, along an 1800-mile fault three miles beneath the ocean's surface, volcanic outpourings began along the floor of the Pacific. Animated drawings showed how the domes of volcanic materials pushed finally above the ocean's surface, became eroded, formed atolls, and how continued activity caused the development, over millions of years, of the lofty, craggy islands of the present chain. When the broadcast concluded, the children had more questions about the circumstances which caused magma to flow, whether further volcanic activity was still going on and where, and how today's soil cover was formed.

The teacher encouraged the same two groups to investigate further. With the teacher's help, one of the groups arranged to climax their report with the film *1955 Kilauea Eruption,* while the other group constructed and presented, among other things, a model of a volcano which simulated eruption and a three-dimensional map of the major Hawaiian islands. These latter materials, along with the geological specimens collected earlier, were made into a study display

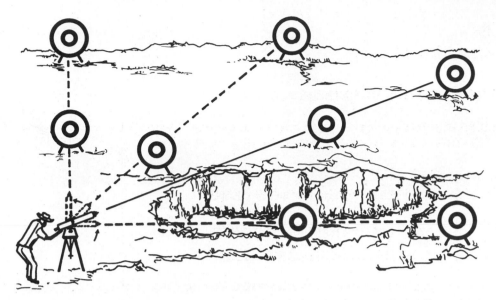

Fig. 15.9. / This pupil-made diagram was used to explain how volcanologists detect and measure shifts in the earth's crust by sighting through "targets" mounted solidly in the earth near the rim of an active volcano.

by the whole class. Various pupils were given responsibility of devising captions, clipping articles, and finding pictures and diagrams for use in the display (Fig. 15.9).

This study of the geological origin and composition of the Hawaiian islands led naturally into a study of their geography and climate. Overhead-projector transparencies and a marking pencil enabled the teacher to trace the trade-wind adiabatic change phenomenon which provides the islands' remarkable climate and ample water supply, and which maintains the year-round, 71–82 degree temperatures. The vegetation that flourishes in such a climate was investigated and discussed by the pupils, many of whom brought in specimens of pandanus and palm leaves, sugar cane, and so forth—all of which would provide the concrete basis for understanding later studies of the native culture as well as the modern industry in Hawaii. These specimens were incorporated into the developing study display, as were flat pictures of animal life found on the islands. The teacher presented slides of the birds which inhabit the islands, as well as of the parasites which plague the flora and fauna.

A few days later, a student committee that had been formed to answer some remaining questions on plant and animal life showed a filmstrip which helped to answer these questions and also to show how man found his way to the islands and how the native culture developed. Thus, the next topic of study—the historical background of the islands—evolved naturally. From this filmstrip showing, discussion proceeded and questions were asked about ocean-going catamarans, hurricane-proof thatched housing, King Kamehameha, and tribal customs (see Plate 24 in section which follows page 000). The teacher guided these questions into a series of student research projects, and as findings were reported by the pupils, the pupils became more and more interested and curious. On his own initiative, one pupil compiled a report on the dramatic life of James Cook, the first European to find the islands, while a group of girls reported

Fig. 15.10. / These two frames from the motion-picture film *Hawaii, The Land and Its Uses* illustrate little known but highly realistic facts about Hawaiian land use—ranching and coffee culture.

on the historical development of island costumes, including the introduction of the Mother Hubbard dress by the missionaries and the evolvement of this dress into the now fashionable muumuu that is currently worn by the girls and women who reside in the state (see Plate 24).

Coinciding with these activities were the television programs in the scheduled series, and soon the pupils found themselves immersed in a study of Hawaii today, its population size and composition, its agriculture and industry, its land conservation, and the people. Earlier study of China, for example, enabled the class to get additional meaning from the Chinese immigration waves that began in the mid-nineteenth century for sugar-cane production, and which led to the Chinese becoming an important and influential segment of Hawaiian citizenry. The multifarious composition of the state's residential population and its implications to world relations was discussed with animation by the pupils. The importance of sugar-cane production and pineapple raising came clear to the pupils as they studied modern agriculture and industry, for much of this learning had been shaped naturally by their earlier geographical studies. The teacher showed a recent film report on *Hawaii, the Land and Its Uses* which both recapitulated earlier concepts of the origins and climate of the islands and described modern land use and industry (Fig. 15.10).[13]

As a culminating activity, the pupils arranged to take an aerial field-study tour of the islands, which provided an opportunity to see at first hand just how man has used and conserved the priceless land resources of the islands. The pupils themselves, under the direction of the teacher, planned the tour, made contacts with the airport personnel, and recorded information on film and in writing during the actual flight. In preparation for this aerial study, the pupils drew heavily on the material they had accumulated in the study display, using the three-dimensional map they had constructed earlier to plan the flight and to prepare for what they would see.

With such creative teacher planning as occurred in this case, creative behavior is automatically the result. However, no teacher should expect to enjoy his

[13] 16 mm., Color, 18 min., Academy Films.

pupils' creative efforts unless first a rich background of well-understood conceptualizations have been achieved by the pupils. To enjoin pupils to "be creative" is hopeless and futile; there must be the desire to create as well as the conceptual framework out of which creation evolves. The carefully conceived use of related audiovisual media can provide this conceptual framework, and can also provide the focal point of creative projects. 35 mm. slides taken by the pupils themselves, for example, offer opportunities for a creative project and for further conceptual learning. Similarly, mockups, models, objects, and specimens can be made or brought in by the class members, and the compiling of these and other materials into a study display offers creative learning opportunities for a wide range of social-studies topics. The showing of a film on the cultural aspects of a nation or a historical period can lead to the devising of a dramatized story which can be performed by some pupils "live" before the rest of the class or in recorded form on sound or videotape. To achieve these many and varied opportunities for pupil creativity the social-studies teacher need only to translate curriculum requirements into a preplanned sequence of interesting and lively study situations which involve the well-guided use of appropriate audiovisual instructional media.

■ IN SCIENCE

Many science teachers complain that while the social studies and other subjects which relate to people and places can be made colorful and interesting to pupils, science subjects do not lend themselves to such treatment. "My basic chemistry course requires the understanding of a great deal of chemical-reaction formulae, and the students only seem to see the course as mostly mathematics," reported one high-school science teacher. And a physics teacher sadly admitted, "Even when I use three-dimensional materials to illustrate a principle, the pupils seem bored or to have difficulty understanding." Teachers who have problems such as these may be relying too heavily on lecture demonstrations of the principles involved, or they may be failing to elicit the pupils' motivation at the outset. Or perhaps they are misusing their instructional tools. Providing pupil interest has been evoked, the conceptual framework for chemical-reaction computation, for example, can be amplified both efficiently and stimulatingly with animated films of the processes involved, in which all of the atoms in the initial substances are visually accounted for after the reaction has taken place. With proper understanding of the concepts involved, the mathematical computations themselves become basic mechanics. The difficulty is that many science teachers stress the mechanical aspects of the mathematical operations rather than the conceptual relationships involved. "What makes things tick" is the objective of *natural* human exploration from early childhood into adulthood, and when learning sequences are planned properly to accommodate this natural human curiosity, science subjects are usually received enthusiastically by students.

It is not enough merely to employ seemingly relevant teaching materials, the information they are to convey must have some relationship to the students' existing frame of reference. In the early grades, science principles may be introduced within the context of children's everyday activities, for example, the physical principles involved in the successful baseball hit, or the construction of a doll carriage. Further, since "making things" is a favorite childhood activity, pupil participation is to be encouraged at all costs. As pupils work on such a project as, for example, the making of a model volcano, a simple chemical reaction, or a model house or airplane, questions naturally occur to them: *Why* does the volcano erupt? *Why* does the airplane fly? Such questions can provide a solid foundation for introducing curriculum science concepts.

Similarly, in the middle and upper grades, there is a large store of background understanding among the pupils which the science teacher can draw upon to launch his curriculum unit. The initiation of a learning situation should be based on the pupil's own interests and curiosity, however, rather than on what the curriculum supposes pupils to have gained from earlier courses. The teacher of one high-school science course drew upon the particular interests of two students to launch the class into a unit on oceanography. Because these two students were themselves interested in the subject, they were asked to prepare a preliminary report, which included the following information:

> TOM: I've been reading in the library. Oceanography is a very new field. People have been so busy doing things on land and in the air, that they haven't had much time to explore the ocean or what's under it. I've discovered that Government agencies are interested in ocean research. One of these, the Interagency Committee on Oceanography, has published an excellent report. You should read it. Here are a few examples of what you'll find.
> Eighty percent of the world's minerals are actually dissolved in the oceans. In addition, about four-fifths of the world's plant and animal life is in the oceans. Almost everything we have today has been found in or on the surface areas of the earth. Just imagine what the future holds when we discover how to find and use the wealth of the oceans!
> Maxine, who was working with me, has some other interesting information . . .

> MAXINE: I have a quotation that I think describes the idea. This is from the late President Kennedy:

> "Our goal is to investigate the world ocean, its boundaries, its properties, its processes. To a surprising extent, the sea has remained a mystery. Ten thousand fleets still sweep over it in vain. We know less of the oceans at our feet, where we came from, than we do of the sky above our heads. It is time to change this, to use to the full our powerful new instruments of oceanic exploration, to drive back the frontiers of the unknown in the waters which encircle our globe. I can imagine no more important field among all those which are so exciting today than this great effort which our country and others will carry on in years to come."

> You can see that he believed that the future depends on knowing more and more about the sea and its resources.

When Tom and Maxine had completed giving their reports, discussion was opened to the class. The technological implications of the sea's potential resources to the future of mankind were discussed and questions emerged which the teacher recorded on the chalkboard. With land supplies of minerals running short, how can the ocean's mineral resources be tapped? As human civilization consumes and pollutes greater and greater portions of the earth's fresh-water supply, how can ocean brine be converted into usable water? As the earth's population continues to explode, can underwater cities be built for practical living? With a large proportion of the peoples of the world existing on starvation diets, can the food resources in the terrestrial seas be utilized efficiently?

Many pupils also expressed curiosity in how scientists go about exploring and mapping the ocean, the possibilities of finding new information on the evolution of life forms and of the paleontological potentials of ocean exploration, the life and habits of various animal life forms, and so forth. The teacher let the discussion and questions take their course unguided until ten minutes before the end of the period, at which time she helped the class toward summary of the discussion. The chalkboard was completely covered with interesting questions which covered an enormous range of topics!

The unit on oceanography promised to be an unmanageable area of study unless measures were taken to control it, so a committee was appointed to establish the main learning goals, based on personal interviews with the class members. Another committee was formed to compile a list of available information sources pertinent to the subunits defined by the Goals Committee. A third committee was established to preview and select materials for actual classroom use from the list compiled by the Resources Committee, and a fourth, Projects Committee was appointed to suggest interesting and challenging ways for class groups to report their findings as the study got underway, and, more important, to put to creative use the information the students learned from their class work.

The following day the chairman of the Goals Committee ruefully admitted that the class wanted to know more, in more areas, than the class time allotted to the unit would permit. Nevertheless, the Goals Committee had selected the following for the class to study:

1. To know about the geography of the sea floor, its mountains, sea plains, valleys and deeps
2. To find how and where the natural resources of the ocean exist—mineral deposits, plant life, fish, crustaceans, and animals
3. To understand the fishing industry and the methods and equipment used by the nations of the world to carry on this industry
4. To find out about and, if possible, demonstrate aqualungs and scuba-diving equipment
5. To find out what vocational opportunities exist for high school students, what colleges and universities are best, what degrees are offered, and whether or not scholarships exist

After the chairman had made his report and recorded the list on the chalkboard, the class refined these goals and minor alterations were made in the basic list. Although the Resources Committee was still to submit its list to the Preview Committee, the rest of the class elected to form small groups and to

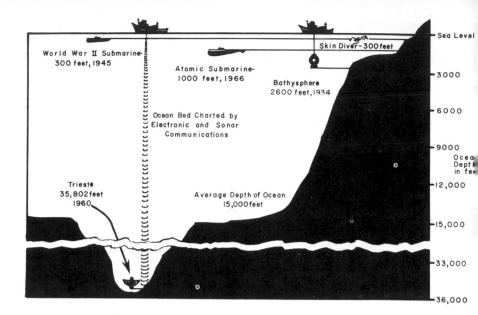

begin research on the topics on the board. The next several days were devoted to preliminary reports and refining areas of investigation, and at the end of this period, one group of pupils presented a chart which showed the status of ocean exploration efforts, and another group produced a topographical map of the floors of the earth's oceans (Fig. 15.11). Still another group submitted a chart which represented many hours of research and which drew together in one large cardboard panel the existing information about the Pacific Ocean floor. These materials were displayed on a prominent wall which then provided a continuous reference point.

The following day the Resources Committee made a brief report of its findings and turned the discussion over to the Preview Committee which had outlined the specific media it had selected and the sequence it recommended for using these materials. These materials included several introductory films on the nature of the ocean beds and undersea life, a number of filmstrips on various types of minerals found in solution or in deposits in the ocean bed, a series of slides on plant and fish life found in terrestrial waters, several pictorial magazine articles on the fishing industry carried on throughout the world, and many other related materials. The committee also reported on the possibility of going to visit a nearby fish hatchery and an aquarium, and of inviting a local sportsman to demonstrate his scuba-diving equipment. A few days later, following further study and the use of many learning resources, the Projects Committee made its report. Reference was made to display panels and table-top exhibits. On one display surface, an imaginative model of an underwater "farm" was beginning to develop, while in another display area, a group of pupils was working on a diagrammatic plan of a commercial fishing corral. A third group was hard at work assembling a three-dimensional model of an underwater living apartment which might shelter undersea farmers and equipment of the future. A diverse array of objects, specimens, pictures, and news clippings was also gathered. One group of pupils had organized their own search for specific information through written requests to governmental and other agencies involved in oceanographic research: The United States Coast Guard, U.S. Coast and Geodetic Survey, Smithsonian Institution, National Geo-

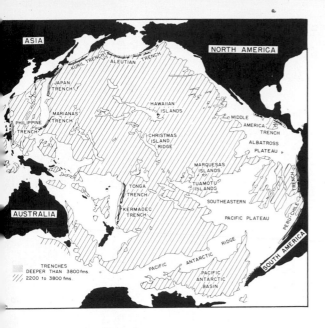

Fig. 15.11. / Two charts were used to present key background information on the status of oceanographic study. What learning opportunities are represented in such chart presentations?

graphic Society, National Science Foundation, Bureau of the Navy, U.S. Army Corps of Engineers, and the Scripps Institute of Oceanography. Exciting charts, photographs, and reports were received from these agencies, and as they came in, the best were arranged as an accumulating display. Here were incorporated photographs of some of the strange ocean research vessels including *Flip* and *Trieste,* special atomic deep-diving submarines, and photographs of young men and women at work in undersea research (Fig. 15.12).

In a subject as little known to the average high-school student as oceanography, the need for interrelated audiovisual experiences is great. Through such means the imaginations and interests of young people can be captured (Fig. 15.13).

Properly selected and interrelated, combinations of audiovisual media can also serve as an effective and efficient means by which the science student may study independently. An excellent example is a freshman botany course plan developed by Dr. S. N. Postlethwait and his associates at Purdue University over a period of several years of experimentation. This audiotutorial system devised has proved highly successful in college work and has implications for a number of high-school subjects as well, particularly where block-of-time scheduling has been put into effect.[14]

Postlethwait began with the scientist's approach of clearly defining the problem and adapting the materials and methods currently available to its solution. Early in the process, he determined that effective student learning of specified subject content would require a different approach than the traditional "lecture, recitation and laboratory" with required attendance typical of much college science instruction:

14 Other notable examples of organized efforts in instructional development at the higher-education level are the Educational Development Program (EDP) at Michigan State University; the Articulated Instructional Media (AIM) program at the University of Wisconsin; the Office of Instructional Resources at the University of Illinois; the Instructional Media Research Unit at Purdue University; the Center for Research on Learning and Teaching at the University of Michigan; the Instructional Resources Center at the Pennsylvania State University, and the Instructional Materials and Development Center of the newly established Department of Educational Communications Center at the University of Hawaii.

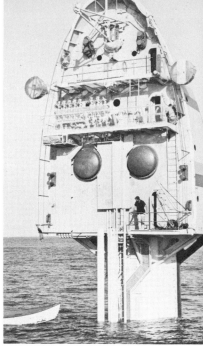

Fig. 15.12. / Man's quest for knowledge of the ocean is carried on at many levels, near the surface by *Flip,* shown in both horizontal and vertical positions (upper left and right); by the deep-diving bathyscaph, *Trieste II* (lower left); and the very new, *Deep Quest* (lower right). Why are related experiences, such as those shown in films, needed to help learners understand these vessels and their function?

> Whether we like it or not, the time has come when the "luxury of teaching" must give way to programs designed primarily to facilitate student learning. Let us proceed in our teaching activities with the same open-minded attitude and vision we apply to our own research.[15]

In this open-minded spirit, Postlethwait and his colleagues completely restructured the botany course along lines of independent individual study exercises, including laboratory experience which the student could gain at his own pace and repeat as necessary to achieve the necessary learning results. In addition to this independent study, one hour a week was set up for a general-assembly session and one hour a week for small-group sessions where assignments could be turned in, new ones picked up, and points of general concern could be discussed by the group with an instructor. In the general-assembly session, opportunity would be provided for students to meet the senior instructor, to hear special lectures by research professors, to view long films, to gain enrichment in the subject matter covered during independent study, and to set an intellectual tone for the course.

A comparison of the old and new botany course schedule indicates a substantial saving of time for the average or above-average students:

Old		New	
Lecture	—2 hrs.	General Assembly	—1 hr.
Recitation	—1 hr.	Small Assembly	—1 hr.
Laboratory	—3 hrs.	Independent Laboratory Study	—2½ hrs. (ave.)

The specially designed laboratory contains 28 to 30 study booths (Fig. 15.14). Each booth is equipped with a tape player, tapes pertinent to the lesson, an 8 mm. film-loop projector, a microscope, specimens, and other necessary materials for the week's work. The student may go to the laboratory any time at his convenience between 7:30 A.M. and 10:00 P.M. He signs in and goes to a study station where materials for the week's lesson are ready for him. Materials too bulky to be included in the booths are placed on a demonstration table and the student is directed by his tape when and where to locate them (Fig. 15.15). He receives his directions and basic information from a sound tape prepared in advance by the senior instructor as part of a series of taped learning situations. The lessons "may include listening to the senior instructor introduce the week's work, reading specified materials, comparing specimens with diagrams, examining specimens, doing experiments, collecting data, and any other activity which may be useful to the student in the learning process."[16] An instructor on duty in the laboratory is available for assistance whenever needed.

As one example, in a taped lesson on twigs, the instructor introduces the subject; the student is then directed to take a twig from location *A* in the booth

15 S. N. Postlethwait, *op. cit.*, p. 187.

16 S. N. Postlethwait, "Course Organization for Individualized Instruction," Burgess Publishing Co., *Newsletter*, June, 1965.

Fig. 15.13. / The future belongs to young people who wish to carry on oceanographic activities. These pupils are selecting materials for their culminating display in oceanography.

and examine its specific structures which are identified by pointers and labels attached to the twig.[17] The tape discusses these in some detail as the student observes the specimen. Should the student fail to understand some point, he can run that section of the tape over again or ask the lab assistant for help.

The student is then requested to pick up a diagram of the twig from location *B* in the booth and to label parts which correspond to the specimen just observed. Following this, he is directed to turn off the tape and to read certain paragraphs in his text, after which he again listens to a taped discussion—this time of key points covered in the reading material. Additional twigs—exhibiting variations from the first twig and without labels—are located at points *C, D,* and *E* in the booth, and the student is asked to identify their parts. As a final step in the study of twigs, the student performs a series of exercises specified in the laboratory manual.

This lesson on twig structures is representative of the types of study to which the taped lessons direct the student. The tapes call for:

1. Listen to brief lectures or discussions
2. Examination of a demonstration or exhibit at some location in the booth or elsewhere in the laboratory
3. Study charts, diagrams, models, etc.
4. Performance of an experiment using these or other related materials
5. Collection and analysis of data from these experiments
6. Study of microscope slides, labelled photos of which guide the student to the pertinent structures seen under the microscope
7. Identification and labelling of parts and features of other, unidentified samples
8. Do exercise from the laboratory manual

17 S. N. Postlethwait, "A Systems Approach to Botany," *Audiovisual Instruction*, April, 1963, p. 244.

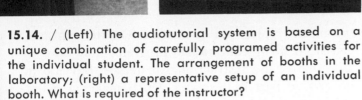

Fig. 15.14. / (Left) The audiotutorial system is based on a unique combination of carefully programed activities for the individual student. The arrangement of booths in the laboratory; (right) a representative setup of an individual booth. What is required of the instructor?

Fig. 15.15. / What roles does the demonstration table play in the audiotutorial learning system? Note the several "aids" to learning that are illustrated here.

More extensive research projects—three of which are required during the semester—are explained in mimeographed materials. Full directions are given on the first problem and progressively more is left up to the student on succeeding problems. The student must report his work in the form of a research paper and read research reports in the process.

Dr. Postlethwait notes several significant values accruing to the student and the purposes of the course. One is that more student contact with instructors is possible and instruction is better tailored to the individual needs of the student than under the old system. The student is free to repeat any part of the study he wishes or omit anything he feels he knows well enough. He has full control of his own rate of study and is able to take tests whenever he feels ready for them. He can get help immediately when needed and can converse with the instructor or his fellow students in the learning center to ascertain whether or not he is giving emphasis to the right ideas. He has ready access in optimum combination to whatever teaching materials and media are pertinent to a given topic. Finally, since specimens are associated at once with visual and taped information provided in the booth, the student has a chance to apply newly acquired information and to test it until he is satisfied that he understands it.

Students learn more in less time under the audiotutorial system, achieve better grades than formerly, and retain the information learned. It is not surprising that the students themselves uniformly prefer the new system to the old, despite the fact that the course contains 50 percent more information than under the old system. Grades have risen significantly at all levels, and the same sized staff previously required to handle 300 students with two laboratories is now doing a better job with 500 students and one laboratory.[18]

The uniqueness of the audiotutorial system of instruction lies in the fact that it both individualizes instruction and accommodates large numbers of stu-

18 S. N. Postlethwait, "Audio-Tutoring, A Practical Solution for Independent Study," *Medical and Biological Illustration*, London, July, 1965, p. 187.

dents. Like programed instruction, it requires that emphasis be placed on clearly defined *learning* behaviors rather than on *teaching* objectives as commonly interpreted by subject-oriented instructors. But unlike early forms of programed instruction, the system makes use of a variety of instructional media, each according to its appropriateness to specific learning requirements. Systematic analysis is required both to specify the needs and to determine the best means for meeting them.

☐ SUMMARY

New study programs by no means replace the instructor. On the contrary, teachers will always be essential in good educational programs—not only to create ideas for putting to imaginative use instructional materials, but also to do the human, creative, and artistic part of teaching which makes a major difference both in how well students learn and, more important, in how well they develop as individuals and as responsible members of the society.

Various technical advances of potential significance to teaching and learning occur more rapidly than they can be comprehended and used by educators. Many advances are being made with such developments as portable language laboratories, programed-instruction devices, 8 mm. motion-picture film, and broadcast television. Many such developments are of particular significance to teachers of foreign language who should weigh them in terms of how they can benefit the student and the educational program as a whole. For many teachers and educators, efficient use and coordination of audiovisual media will involve complete rethinking and restructuring of the traditional course of teaching. Probably the most difficult part of any important innovation, such as a major change in the way one teaches, lies in the natural reluctance we all have to exchange the comfortable and familiar for an unknown alternative. Yet it would be difficult and probably impractical to attempt to teach one part of a course in the manner herein described while the balance was handled in the conventional pattern. Thus a start must be made if significant changes in instructional models are ever to occur, and the creation of much needed new teaching approaches, one unit at a time, is a practical way to begin. The principles described in this chapter could apply with equal validity to the teaching of most subject areas and grade levels of instruction.

☐ Suggested Activity

1. Create a plan through which you use interrelated audiovisual media. Following this, put the plan to use in your own classroom. Observe the following steps:
   a. Set up the learning goals to be achieved.
   b. Preview (if possible) and select the learning materials to be used.
   c. Plan and describe pupil motivational activities which will incite interest in the subject.
   d. Describe the pupil-planning activities which will help pupils to understand the nature of the purposes to be achieved.

e. If possible, secure the learning materials and actually use them with learners.

f. Plan the evaluation methods you will employ.

g. Plan for the possible kinds of creative or inventive pupil activities that you hope will be the means through which pupils will use or rearrange their new-found information and/or skills.

h. Evaluate objectively the nature of the behavioral changes that you observed in the pupils who participate, particularly in (g), above.

☐ Bibliography

Alden, Douglas W. (Ed.), *Materials List for Use by Teachers of Modern Foreign Languages,* Modern Language Association, Foreign Language Research Center, 1959.

Alexander, Theodor W., "Functional German at Texas Technological College: Audio-Visual Approach," *German Quarterly,* May, 1955, pp. 175–179.

Borglum, George, "AV-Active French," *NEA Journal,* November, 1958.

Brooks, Nelson, *Language and Language Learning; Theory and Practice,* Harcourt, Brace, and World, 1960.

Cornfield, Ruth R., "Not by Sound Alone," *Audiovisual Instruction,* December, 1960, pp. 338–339.

Forsdale, Louis (Ed.), *8 mm. Sound Film in Education,* Teachers College, Columbia University, 1962, 166 pp.

Gagne, Robert M., *The Conditions of Learning,* Holt, Rinehart and Winston, 1965.

Garrabrant, Frederick, and Pillet, Roger, "French with Slides and Tapes," *Elementary School Journal,* May, 1962, pp. 417–421.

Hocking, Elton (Ed.), *Language Laboratory and Language Learning,* Monograph 2, Department of Audiovisual Instruction, NEA, 1964, 210 pp.

Hocking, Elton, "Methods and Techniques in Transition," *French Review,* February, 1962, pp. 396–401.

Johnson, Laura B., "Films in Foreign Language Teaching," *French Review,* April, 1956, pp. 414–417.

Kale, S. V., and J. H. Grosslight, *Exploration Studies in the Use of Pictures and Sound for Teaching Foreign Language Vocabulary,* Technical Report SDC 269-7-53, Instructional Film Research Program, Pennsylvania State University, August, 1955.

Kone, Elliott (Ed.), *Language Laboratories: Modern Techniques in Teaching Foreign Languages,* Bulletin 19, Connecticut Audio-Visual Association, 1960.

Lado, Robert, *Linguistics Across Cultures: Applied Linguistics for Language Teachers,* Univ. of Michigan Press, 1957.

Mueller, T., "Audio-Visual Approach to Modern Language Teaching," *Modern Language Journal,* May, 1955, pp. 237–239.

O'Connor, Patricia, *Modern Foreign Languages in High School: Prereading Instruction,* U.S. Office of Education Bulletin 1960, No. 9.

Ollman, Mary J. (Ed.), *MLA Selective List of Materials for Use by Teachers of Modern Foreign Languages in Elementary and Secondary Schools,* Modern Language Association of America, New York, 1962, 162 pp. (Order from MLA Foreign Language Research Center, 4 Washington Place, New York 3, New York.)

Parker, Edna, "Materials Make a Difference," *Audiovisual Instruction,* January, 1960, pp. 6–7.

Parker, William R., *The National Interest and Foreign Languages* (3rd ed.), U.S. Government Printing Office, 1962.

Pond, Karl, "A Language Teaching Tool: The Overhead Projector," *Modern Language Journal,* January, 1963, pp. 30–33.

☐ Films and Filmstrips

Language Teaching in Context, 16 mm. film, Color, 28 min., Wayne State University, 1961.
Pattern for Improvement, 35 mm. filmstrip, B&W, Visual Education Consultants, Inc., n.d.
Teaching Science, sound filmstrip series, Color, 33⅓ rpm, Bailey Films, Inc., 1959.

XVI

PROGRAMED INSTRUCTION

Programed instruction, teaching machines, programed learning—these are terms which do not fail to trigger spirited discussion of their definitions, advantages, and limitations as teachers and parents contemplate the possibility that here may lie the solution to many educational problems. Those who support the idea hope for release from the time-consuming tasks of fact giving by assigning these responsibilities to mechanical instruction. Those who oppose the idea believe that, as yet, there is no research evidence to show that programed instruction can accomplish better learning outcomes. Nevertheless, programed instructional materials are in increasingly wide use.

The interest in programed instruction is not confined to the United States. Over 1000 programed learning sequences are in use in Japan; and England, France, Germany, Nigeria, and the Union of South Africa are among those countries where experimentation is being now pursued.

☐ PROGRAMED INSTRUCTION DEFINED

Programed instruction is the means by which information is provided for the pupil in bit-by-bit, step-by-step sequences, each segment of which contains a highly specific idea, asks a question directly related to this idea, calls for the student to reply to this question before proceeding to the next segment, and then supplies the correct answer to this question which the student can compare with his own response. Each segment, or "frame," leads logically to the information contained in the next.

Of course, the concept of programed instruction involves the basic assumption that the information contained in a unit or course can be arranged into such clearly defined, specific segments; unfortunately, the larger part of man's knowledge does not lend itself to this programing. For example, name-and-place geography, spelling, basic number operations, rules of grammar, interpretation of electrical diagrams—all lend themselves well to segmentation of

Fig. 16.1. / Many programed-instruction materials are manipulated in machines which expose each item in the sequence. (Above) A device which projects materials; (right) one which exposes one item at a time from a reservoir of printed sheets. The teacher should consider the content and nature of the program as well as ease of manipulation and cost.

ideas. However, land-use and conservation science, style of writing, political and sociological understanding, and the like are fields which call for value judgments and interpretive analysis. While these, too, might conceivably be programed, such segmentation of their concepts would be difficult; at best, the learning outcomes may be expected to leave much to be desired in terms of the learner's creative thinking ability.

Programed instruction is presented to the pupil in a variety of forms using a variety of materials (Fig. 16.1). The several types of programs include step-by-step, branching, and cross-media programs. In the step-by-step programs, the subject content is usually broken down into the most logical sequence of developmental steps. This learning process may be compared to climbing a long stairway on a series of uniformly spaced steps; some learners will climb faster and farther than others. This kind of organization of programed instruction is also called "straight line" programing.

Branching programs resemble step programs, but the intervals may be larger. Some pupils find themselves unable to proceed at a certain point in a step program because they need intermediate or smaller steps to provide them with background information. In branching programs, they are led to "bypaths" which fulfill this need by means of supplementary sheets of materials that can be studied and learned. Other pupils who do not need to take a bypath can

Fig. 16.2. / Today the bulk of programed materials appear in low-cost folders. Many programs produced in this format are easily handled and readily available for use.

skip it and proceed to the next major step. Branching thus is designed to accommodate individual differences in pupil learning behavior.

The programed sequences may be presented on long paper rolls, on sheafs of paper, on cards, on accordion-folded paper, in folders, or in textbook or workbook format (Fig. 16.2). Charts, diagrams, pictures, and other visuals—including filmed sequences and filmstrips—can also become part of the program, as can tape-recorded materials. In many cases, programed learning is presented to the pupils through a complex of mechanical equipment, such as teaching machines. Several machines, now in the experimental stage, call for slides, filmstrips, audio tapes, and sound motion-picture films. As such teaching machines are developed further, it is possible to envision the highly individualized use of many of the audiovisual materials described earlier in this book.

In all forms of programed learning, the following principles obtain:

1. The learner is given a specific item of information and asked for a response which relates directly to the item.
2. The learner is given immediate feedback about his response which, in the case of a correct response, provides reinforcement of the learned idea or, in the case of an incorrect response, allows him to go back and repeat the sequence until his response matches that provided in the programed material.
3. The learner thus proceeds at his own pace and is freed from the restrictions placed upon him by the pace established in group learning.
4. Information is presented in logical sequences which lead the learner from simple to increasingly advanced work.
5. Programed learning activity requires the learner's sustained participation.
6. Because the learner cannot proceed without providing correct responses each step of the way, successful learning outcomes of a programed unit or course is ensured, providing that the learner perseveres and completes correctly the required sequence of responses.

In the usual classroom situation much of the recitation time is taken up by one pupil as he recites to the teacher, who cannot be sure that the other pupils are following the recitation, or supervise their ongoing processes. It would be impractical to have each pupil in the class repeat the same recitation during the period, and thus it becomes impossible to assess the detailed learning processes of those who are not actively participating.

When a student is using an autoinstructional device, however, all interaction takes place between him and the subject program. In other words, there is intense individual participation over a short period of time rather than the sporadic participation provided him in group activity over a longer period. It is entirely feasible for a classroom to have several different programed instructional materials available to individual learners. By staggering the students' work—for example, on arithmetic and on spelling, and vice versa—the materials could be kept in use profitably. Or, the pupils in an entire class might take turns using the various sets of programs available and pace themselves in terms of their abilities and interests.

□ THE DEVELOPMENT OF PROGRAMED INSTRUCTION

Programed learning was being investigated as early as the 1920s, when Dr. Sidney Pressey designed a pioneer form of teaching machine. This device provided the student with questions and multiple-choice answers. After selecting his answer, the student recorded it by pressing a numbered button which corresponded to the number of the answer. The machine immediately indicated whether this response was correct or not. Thus learning took place, evaluation was immediate, and progress was encouraged.

This early research work has been repeated and improvements made by many investigators, of whom the best known is B. F. Skinner. The learning programs devised by Skinner incorporated improvements which not only measured the information learned, but also provided the pupil with a logically developed sequence of ideas. In Skinner's System, the instructional material is presented to the student, one "frame" at a time, in a small window on the face of the machine. The student writes his response on a section of paper in a slot near this window. He then moves a lever which exposes the correct response, and the student compares this with his written response. If his answer is correct, he brings the next frame into view and repeats the process. If the response is incorrect, the question is automatically "marked"; it may reappear later to give the learner a chance to correct himself and to learn the accurate information. Skinner describes the characteristic of his machine program as follows:

1. There is a constant interchange between the programmed materials and the student. Unlike lectures, textbooks and the usual audio-visual aids, the machine induces sustained activity. The student is always alert and busy.
2. Like a good tutor, the machine insists that a given point be thoroughly understood, either frame by frame or step by step, before the student moves on. Lectures, textbooks and their mechanized equivalents, on the other hand, proceed without making sure that the student understands and easily leave him behind.
3. Like a good tutor, the machine presents just that material for which the student is ready. It asks him to take only that step which he is at the moment best equipped and most likely to take.
4. Like a skillful tutor, the machine helps the student to come up with the right answer. It does this in part through the orderly construction of the

1. MANUFACTURE means to make or build. *Chair factories manufacture chairs.* Copy the word here.
   — — — — — — — — — —

2. Part of the word is like part of the word *factory.* Both parts come from an old word meaning *make* or *build.*
   MANU __ __ __ __ URE

3. Part of the word is like part of the word *manual.* Both parts come from an old word meaning *hand.* Many things used to be made by hand.
   __ __ __ __ FACTURE

4. The same letter goes in both spaces.
   M __ NUF __ CTURE

5. The same letter goes in both spaces.
   MAN __ FACT __ RE

6. Chair factories __ __ __ __ __ __ __ __ __ chairs.

Fig. 16.3. / The step-by-step learning sequence that forms the basis for all programed instruction is illustrated here. Note the several repetitions of information presented in earlier steps. What is the purpose of the repetition?

programmed information and in part with technics of hinting, prompting, suggesting and so on, derived from an analysis of verbal behavior.

5. The machine, like a private tutor, reinforces the student for every correct response, using this immediate feedback not only to shape his behavior most efficiently but to maintain it in strength in a manner which the layman would describe as "holding the student's interest."[1]

The material Skinner uses to teach the spelling of the word *manufacture,* for example, is based on the difficulties involved in mastering this word. It is not enough to memorize; the pupil is expected to understand its meaning from analyzing the root of the word, the choice of letters, the repetitious use of letters, and so forth. The technique is shown in Fig. 16.3. The pupil's first task is to copy the word. He must next identify the root *fact,* and then the root *manu.* In the fourth and fifth frames, he is asked to insert letters. Finally, he is tested on his ability to grasp the entire word.

Arithmetic provides another illustration. Too often arithmetic has been taught by drilling for memorization. However, it can be taught as a matter of understanding number relationships logically. In the multiplication table for 9, for example, the machine cards present not only the table for 9, but some of the basic principles involved in understanding the behavior of this number. For example, 9 times a number is the same as 10 times that number minus the number; i.e., 9 times 3 is 27; 10 times 3 is 30 minus 3 is 27. So also, the digits in a multiple of 9 add up to 9; thus, 18 is 1 plus 8; 36 is 3 plus 6; 81 is 8 plus 1. The cards also point out that, in composing successive multiples of nine, one counts backward: *nine, eight*een, twenty-*seven,* thirty-*six,* forty-*five,* fifty-*four,* sixty-

[1] B. F. Skinner, "Teaching Machines," *Science,* October 24, 1958.

Table 16.1

HIGH-SCHOOL STUDENTS' OPINIONS OF PROGRAMED INSTRUCTION[a]

	Strongly Agree	Agree	Uncertain	Disagree	Strongly Disagree
Students Agree that:					
1. Automated learning helps a student to learn.	15.3%	68.1%	9.7%	7.0%	0
2. Automated teaching is the best method of learning for good students because they are not held back by the class.	11.1	50.0	22.2	15.3	1.4%
3. Automated teaching offers a challenge to the student because it makes him think.	8.3	47.2	17.9	23.6	2.8
4. Automated teaching is an excellent method of learning because the student always finds out immediately whether he was right or not.	8.3	47.2	18.1	22.2	4.2
Students Disagree that:					
5. Automated teaching is the only efficient way to learn.	2.8	0	5.6	51.4	40.3
6. There is no thinking involved in learning with automated teaching.	2.8	4.2	9.1	57.0	27.8
7. Automated teaching is a boring method of learning. It offers no challenge.	7.0	19.4	11.1	44.4	18.1
8. Automated teaching will ruin the educational system.	1.4	4.2	19.4	50.0	25.0

three, and so forth. Thus, as the subject card outlines these relationships and calls upon the student to fill in the blanks correctly. The student's ability to understand the logic of a multiplication sequence and to multiply accurately are tested simultaneously.

Today, the principles advanced by Pressey, Skinner, and others are being applied in a variety of ways—using a variety of assorted materials—in many subject areas.

☐ PROGRAMED INSTRUCTION AND RESEARCH

Since 1955, more than 300 research investigations have been made probing the question of whether programed instructional materials could communicate information as well as the teacher. The results of most of these have shown no significant differences between traditional teaching methods and programed instruction. This is regarded by some people as an indication that the present forms of programing are inadequately conceived and used; that is, they interpret these findings as a natural consequence of early attempts to cope with the great problems involved in organizing and writing programs. Certainly it is conceivable that the progress in programed instruction over the last ten years has actually resulted in little more than enabling those who make and use programed instructional materials to begin to understand its tremendous potential. The danger of accepting and being satisfied with current progress in programed instruction is expressed in a recent publication:

> The potential of programed learning is, so far, largely unrealized. Although the research gives us little reason to be satisfied with the theories and the standards of today's programing, and every reason to believe that it will be possible someday to make programs vastly more effective than today's, nevertheless, programed instruction shows signs of hardening, partly under commercial pressure, into a fixed and mechanical technology, with theories and procedures taken for granted.[2]

However, a research project of special note is occasionally reported. An experiment at Roanoke, Virginia, for example, has shown that eighth-grade pupils accomplished a full year's course in algebra in one semester—half the time required by their ninth-grade friends who took the traditional course; 45 percent of the eighth-grade group attained the level of performance attained by 50 percent of the ninth-grade group.[3] Still other research on the use of programed instruction indicates that substantial areas of subject content can be learned with efficiency through their use.

What does the "consumer" think of programed instruction? One good way to do this is to ask students who have worked with it. One survey of pupil opinion is presented in Table 16.1.

The sum of the research findings can be generalized as follows:

1. Gifted children who have self-motivating qualities can progress at a pace limited only by their interest.

2 Jack V. Edling, *et al., Programed Instruction: Four Case Studies,* The Fund for the Advancement of Education, June, 1964.

3 E. W. Rushton, "Teaching Machines, A Research Report," *Nation's Schools,* February, 1961.

Fig. 16.4. / Assuming that much of the "information-giving" role of the teacher can now be assigned to automated learning programs, the teacher is freer to do things which only a teacher can do—encourage, help with special problems, and challenge the talents of pupils who seek ways to put factual information to creative use. What are your reactions to programed learning?

2. The use of programed materials will free teachers to give additional time to counseling, individualized instruction, and the teaching of difficult areas of subject content not readily adaptable to programed presentation.

3. The use of programed materials can increase the speed of accomplishment for those pupils who can and will use these new materials to move ahead at an accelerated pace.

4. Teaching machines will be developed which incorporate audio and visual experiences, thus invading subject content areas more complicated than those which rely on the written word alone.

5. Programed instruction permits the pupil to correct or to evaluate his work immediately, permitting him to move rapidly from step to step in learning a sequence—an obvious advantage over the use of workbooks and assignments where hours or days may elapse before the pupil knows whether his work is correct. While the pupils await the return of their graded tests and papers, they are usually working on their next assignment; yet the students should know the results of their previous efforts before going on to a more advanced task.

The continuing research in this field will explore the effect of the intelligence of the learners. Related questions are also likely to be investigated, particularly those which concern the effect of programed instruction on the creativity of students and the relationship between this means of instruction and maturity level and the possibility of boredom.

Even if we assume that no difference does exist between the efficiency of the teacher and that of programed instructional methods there are advantages to communicating some kinds of information through the programed approach. For, if the latter does at least as good a job as the classroom teacher, it is not logical to assign instruction of the programable information to teaching machines and similar materials and thus free the teacher for other more creative tasks (Fig. 16.4)?

☐ THE CURRENT STATUS OF PROGRAMED INSTRUCTION

Carefully constructed and field-tested programs currently enjoy wide use. For example, *English 2600, A Program Course in Grammar and Usage* put out by Harcourt, Brace & World; *TEMAC—First Year Algebra* published by Encyclopaedia Britannica Inc.; *Vocabulary Development* by Science Research Associates; and dozens of related series published by Grolier, Coronet, Harper

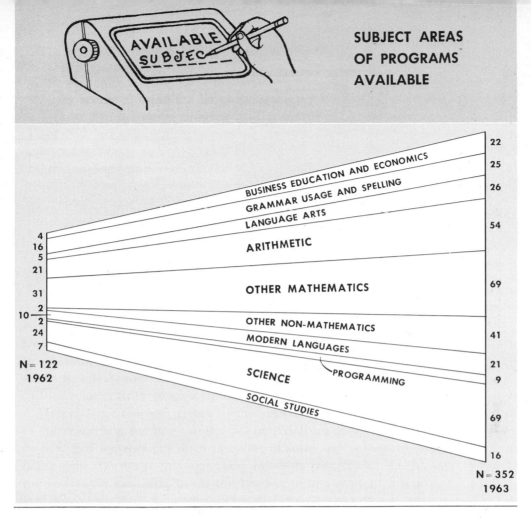

BUSINESS EDUCATION AND ECONOMICS — 22
GRAMMAR USAGE AND SPELLING — 25
LANGUAGE ARTS — 26
ARITHMETIC — 54
OTHER MATHEMATICS — 69
OTHER NON-MATHEMATICS — 41
MODERN LANGUAGES — 21
SCIENCE — PROGRAMMING — 9
SOCIAL STUDIES — 69
16

4
16
5
21
31
10 — 2
2
24
7
N = 122
1962

N = 352
1963

Fig. 16.5. / While there are considerably more instructional programs available in some subjects than in others, availabilities have mushroomed in all areas. (Adapted from Center for Programmed Instruction, *A Guide to Programmed Instructional Materials,* U.S. Office of Education, 1963.)

& Row, and others are being used at a rate of hundreds of thousands of units per year.

The first flurry of enthusiasm for programed instruction witnessed the invention of dozens of mechanical devices for exposing program materials to learners. At one time, there were more machines than programs. Those who inquired about this were often told that all the teacher needed was "a machine," and then he could write all the programs he needed. Teachers who have undertaken to write programs usually discover that the time and skill necessary to produce a precision program is far beyond that available. It is comparable to saying, "Here is a five-hundred-page blank notebook; now, write your own textbook." Thus, it follows that the task of writing instructional programs has been accomplished more and more by textbook publishers and by newly formed groups which specialize in the preparation of programed instruction as such.

The usual procedure followed by these groups is to produce program learning materials through the cooperative efforts of a learning psychologist, a subject expert, and an educator. Such teams have produced programs which are widely accepted.

The number of programs available for school use has been growing rapidly—

This lesson will help you learn how to use correctly two more of our "demon" friends.

<u>May</u> and <u>can</u> give some of us a lot of trouble. But you should have no trouble after finishing this lesson.

Let's see what there is to help us keep these two straight.

<u>Can</u> means "to be able"

<u>May</u> means "permit" or "allow" or "has permission"

In other words, if you were talking about your mother giving you permission to go to the show, you might say this: My mother said I __?__ go to the show.

| 2-6 | can |
| 10-7 | may |

If you meant you were able to do something, you might say something like this: I __?__ run fast.

| 8-24 | can |
| 9-20 | may |

VERBAL PROBLEMS

A PREVIEW ■ In Chapter Eleven, we discussed verbal problems which can be solved by finding the solution of one equation containing one variable. Now, we are able to find the simultaneous solution of two linear equations containing two variables. Our ability to solve systems of equations of this type enables us to solve a much wider variety of verbal problems than those we have already discussed.

However, the basic principles discussed in Chapter Eleven apply here as well. The idea of translating, the use of formulas, and the general principle we introduced there are all important for our work in this chapter. You may wish to review Chapter Eleven before continuing with this chapter.

16 1   CONDITIONS AND RELATIONS

1070.   Suppose x represents any rational number. If we are told that the sum of x and 3 is 5, we can translate this into the equation $x + 3 =$ ___.   5

1071.   The equation $x + 3 = 5$ contains one variable. The solution of this equation is the number ___.   2

1072.   The sentence, "The sum of x and 3 is 5," states a condition which is satisfied only by the value ___ of the variable x.   2

1073.   Thus: "Find a number whose sum with 3 is 5" can be translated into the equation $x + 3 = 5$, containing one variable. The solution of this equation is the number ___, which we are asked to find.   2

198

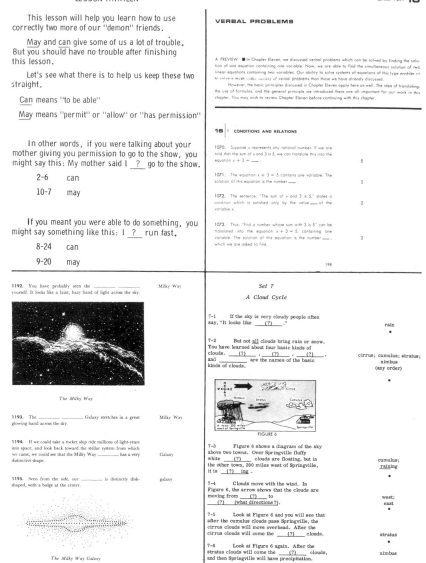

1192. You have probably seen the _____ _____ yourself. It looks like a faint, hazy band of light across the sky.   Milky Way

The Milky Way

1193. The _____ _____ Galaxy stretches in a great glowing band across the sky.   Milky Way

1194. If we could take a rocket ship ride millions of light-years into space, and look back toward the stellar system from which we came, we could see that the Milky Way _____ has a very distinctive shape.   Galaxy

1195. Seen from the side, our _____ is distinctly disk-shaped, with a bulge at the center.   galaxy

The Milky Way Galaxy

Set 7
A Cloud Cycle

7-1   If the sky is very cloudy people often say, "It looks like ___(?)___ ."   rain

7-2   But not <u>all</u> clouds bring rain or snow. You have learned about four basic kinds of clouds. ___(?)___ , ___(?)___ , ___(?)___ , and _____ are the names of the basic kinds of clouds.   cirrus; cumulus; stratus; nimbus (any order)

FIGURE 6

7-3   Figure 6 shows a diagram of the sky above two towns. Over Springville fluffy white ___(?)___ clouds are floating, but in the other town, 200 miles west of Springville, it is ___(?)___ ing .   cumulus; <u>raining</u>

7-4   Clouds move with the wind. In Figure 6, the arrow shows that the clouds are moving from ___(?)___ to ___(?)___ (what directions?).   west; east

7-5   Look at Figure 6 and you will see that after the cumulus clouds pass Springville, the cirrus clouds will move overhead. After the cirrus clouds will come the ___(?)___ clouds.   stratus

7-6   Look at Figure 6 again. After the stratus clouds will come the ___(?)___ clouds, and then Springville will have precipitation.   nimbus

Fig. 16.6. / Four specimen pages from programs currently available: *English Usage* (Merritt Associates, San Francisco); *Modern Algebra* (Encyclopaedia Britannica Films); *General Science: Astronomy* (Encyclopaedia Britannica Films); and *Weather* (Coronet). What judgments do you make about grade level, content validity, appropriateness to learner's abilities?

122 in 1962, 352 in 1963, and an estimated 1000 or more programs at the time of the publication of this book. Sales of programed materials, mostly in "textbook" form, have zoomed from 2 percent of the national school-book sales in 1961, to 12 percent in 1966.

Despite the advantages of programed instruction, and its enthusiastic reception by educators, however, there are some limiting factors which need to be considered:

1. Materials are available primarily for mathematics, science, the social studies, and the language arts, and are lacking for many other subjects such as art, music, home economics, and various interpretive studies (Fig. 16.5).
2. Because of their verbal quality, programed instructional materials greatly increase the reading task. Reading ability may greatly influence the progress which students make.
3. Programed instructional materials rely on the principle of reinforcement of learning. The result is likely to be oversimplification and narrowness of concept building in programs where reinforcement involves a single-track approach consisting of rather narrowly interpreted series of steps through

which the pupil is expected to gain an understanding of broad aspects of the subject.

These limitations are not unsurmountable, however, and if anticipated by an imaginative teacher who selects and uses programed learning materials wisely, programed instruction can be an effective learning device for pupils and an efficient time-saver for the teacher.

□ THE SELECTION OF PROGRAMED INSTRUCTIONAL MATERIALS

One of the first things a teacher needs to understand is that programed instruction is not available in all areas of school subject and teaching responsibilities. For this reason, the teacher is urged to secure the survey entitled "Programs, '63: A Guide to Programmed Instructional Materials," compiled and produced by the Center for Programmed Instruction, Inc. in cooperation with the U.S. Department of Health, Education and Welfare. In this the teacher will be able to examine actual specimen pages which represent several hundred programs. No better impression of the magnitude and coverage of existing programs can be gained than from examination of this publication.

In selecting materials, the teacher must apply most of the same criteria as have already been stated for films, tapes, filmstrips, or related instructional materials: suitability to subject content, validity, appropriateness to age level of pupils, etc. However, in the case of programed materials, the degree to which the program effectively fulfills the information-giving responsibility of the teacher must also be considered. A good program not only communicates factual content information at a rate that participating pupils choose for themselves, but also may take many of the students much farther into the subject than would be possible were they limited to the pace of the rest of the pupils in the class. The teacher must also carefully identify and supervise the pupils for whom branching experiences should be provided.

It is suggested that the reader examine the panel of specimen programs which are included in Fig. 16.6; the four specimens are representative of the programs in each of their subjects. It is suggested that, as he examines the content and the way it is presented, the reader keep in mind:

1. For what grade level is the program described?
2. Is grade level now the criteria, or is it the actual accomplishment potential of individual students that must be considered?
3. Under what use conditions can one program selection be made which will meet the needs of pupils in the class group of thirty-five or forty?
4. How does one actually schedule program use in the classroom?

In addition, a good part of the programed materials available rely on verbal stimuli and responses, and the teacher should take into account the degree of verbalism used in the materials. Where a good concrete experiential background to the concepts verbally presented has accrued to the pupils, as well as a high level of verbal skill, verbal program-learning materials may be quite suitable. However, many pupils do not have the verbal skills adequate to such programed experiences, and may lack sufficient conceptual background as well. Thus, when selecting his materials, the teacher must consider the abilities of his *particular* pupils, and where possible, plan to supplement programed instruction with related audiovisual media that will fill conceptual gaps with concrete experience.

☐ USING PROGRAMED INSTRUCTION EFFECTIVELY

Programed instruction can take the place of the teacher as information giver *per se,* yet the teacher who accepts and makes programed instruction work discovers that it is a device which can actually help to accomplish what once took a large part of the teaching day—communicating factual information and explaining. One need only to recall how often teachers need to repeat and repeat explanations to realize how valuable programed instruction can be. Thus relieved, the teacher has more time to carry on planning, guidance, and creative functions which no mechanical device can now fulfill. Indeed, the rewards of programing are great enough to warrant its planning and management. There is no reason why the core activity of a classroom cannot continue, especially if this activity puts to creative use that which is learned through programing.

Before using the materials that have been selected, it is helpful to review with pupils the responsibilities which need to be accepted. Learning from programs is quite different from the usual socialized activity of the classroom. Instead of group activity and interaction, reactions to programs are highly individualized. Thus, pupils should know that comparison, discussion, or group consensus of opinion are things quite apart from their activities with programed materials. Rather, each pupil must accept program-learning responsibilities as a personal challenge. The reasons for using the materials should be made known, and the way in which program books are manipulated—not necessarily page by page, but item by item in terms of the concise directions to be followed—should be made quite clear to the pupils.

It should be pointed out that "peeking ahead" at answers will result in half-learning and will actually penalize the student. The individualized nature of pupil responsibility—reading, concentration, and self-honesty—should be stressed. If machines are used to present the learning stimuli or sequences of stimuli—stalemates, questions, or problems—instructions as to their use must be clearly understood so that this factor will not frustrate learning from the program itself. The pupil should also understand that he may proceed at his own pace. However, since few, if any, programs are so automatic that they anticipate all unforeseen questions or problems which students will encounter, the teacher must be accessible to pupils to help those who encounter difficulties.

When a learner is using a program, he is directly and continuously involved for the entire period. There is no delay. He moves from step to step just as rapidly as he can—just as if there were only one learner and one teacher. This kind of learning is likely to be much more demanding and more strenuous than traditional classroom instruction, and the pupil may experience fatigue more quickly. There is much yet to be learned about the relation between pupil interest and attention span and programed instructional materials. The best plan for the teacher who uses programed materials to follow is to keep program-learning activities relatively brief, integrating into the study day a variety of other activities such as discussions, creative planning sessions, pupil followup activities, and so forth.

The creative teacher will also supplement program learning materials with audiovisual media. While it seems reasonable to assume that, as experimentation with programed learning continues, the degree of verbalism will be decreased, and a wider variety of learning experiences will be included in available programed materials, the teacher need not rely solely on commercially prepared programs that include such audiovisual materials. A greater variety of learning stimuli and a more interesting program can be devised by the teacher herself by showing an appropriate film, planning a suitable tape or transcription, or arranging a field-study trip at a profitable time in the program. The program itself may well call for the use of audiovisual materials to create resource learning opportunities. In such subjects as nature study, language arts, and science, the student can make effective use of sound films, prerecorded tapes, filmstrips, slides, and models and mockups of laboratory apparatus. His work with these audiovisual materials can provide him with the more subtle kinds of information that cannot easily be made available in programs, that is, resource information. Properly integrated into the learning program, such resource information will not only foster more interest in the subject context of the learning program, but may also serve to stimulate pupil initiative to search independently.

The teacher may rely on the program provisions for accomplishing the evaluation stages of learning, but imaginative followup activities must be stimulated by the teacher. Realizing that active pupil participation and creative involvement are the keys to true learning, the good teacher will encourage pupils to plan their own avenues of expression, which will both demonstrate the learning outcomes and reinforce the learned information. Ideas for such followup activities may be suggested and guided by the teacher, but it is the pupils' *self*-expression which is of major importance here, and thus it is desirable that the teacher does not prescribe specific projects.

Thus emerges the possibility of a differentiated kind of educational opportunity that envisions a new climate of instructional materials, a new array of programs and teaching machinery, and a new kind of teaching—all organized to challenge the student. There are many who believe that programed instruction is another factor which will hasten the day of ungraded school organization, more effective team teaching, and closer coordination between library, learning resource centers, and the classroom. However, programed instructional materials—because of their number and bulk—will *increase* the classroom management tasks of the teacher. The teacher should seek the assistance of the school librarian with respect to insuring accessibility to the materials, and students should be assured easy access both to materials and to the records which indicate the status of their progress. It should be possible for students to turn to programed tasks at any time that interest and time permits. For, perhaps the greatest change which the use of programed materials will create for pupils is the feeling of personal responsibility to accept the challenges presented by this communication channel.

The management of the classroom and its organization for programed instructional use presents other challenges. It is inevitable that with heavy reliance on programed materials, the comfortable "togetherness" or homogeneity of the group will be threatened, as fast learners widen the gap between their levels of achievement and those of the slower pupils. It is almost inevitable that successful use of programs will identify those who can concentrate and also possess good attention span, read well, have high intelligence and who move steadily ahead at their own pace. Not all pupils will respond in a positive manner. Those who do not possess these qualities seldom "stay with it." Rather, they fall behind and sometimes give up entirely.

Ultimately, however, increased heterogeneity may be the desired outcome of programed instruction used wisely. For as those who thrive on the thrill of setting their own goals and of reaching out at a pace limited only by their initiative and abilities are identified and grouped, more and better programs can be devised to accelerate these pupils even further. Similarly, those who fall behind can be grouped for special attention and reevaluation, perhaps resulting in the devising of new programed approaches that better meet the levels of interests and abilities present among so-called "slow" pupils.

Such a possibility is quite in contrast to traditional instruction, where pupils from widely diverse backgrounds and of widely differing interests and aptitudes are somewhat arbitrarily grouped according to age-grade levels. The pace at which these heterogeneous pupils learn is geared to the usual recitation situation in which, at best, a pupil may be directly involved for only the few minutes he is responding directly to the teacher's questions or suggestions.

☐ SUMMARY-

During the ten short years of the existence of programed instructional research and experimentation, unusual progress has been achieved. At first *programed learning* was synonymous with the term *teaching machines*. During this time, an unfortunate emphasis was put on elaborate mechanical hardware. Dealers and audiovisual experts who have noted the decline in school people's interest in teaching machines have equated this with a similar decline in interest in programed instruction as such. This does not seem to be the case. Interest in programed instruction seems to be increasing continually, but most of the learning programs now developed are "packaged" in textbook-like formats, or as a part of simple folios or folders that can be used easily by students.

There is every evidence that programed instruction properly used can take over a large fraction of the time-consuming responsibilities of the teacher which are now spent with information giving per se. As this use of programed instruction is accomplished, the teacher is set free to engage in creative activities which only the human teacher can accomplish. This development would yield great dividends not only to teachers, but to pupils who respond to creative planning and opportunities for personal achievement.

The use of the programed instruction presents new responsibilities for most pupils and teachers. These are quite apart from those accepted in the usual socialized atmosphere of classroom instruction. Teachers should be alert to new information about the development of programed instruction and to the research evidence which indicates more and more that here is a profitable means of better accomplishing the persisting tasks of instruction and teaching.

☐ Suggested Activities

1. Arrange to view the filmstrip *An Example of a Teaching Machine,* edited by Dean M. Luxton and Robert E. Corrigan, Basic Skill Films, with a group of your fellow students who agree to play the roles of electrician apprentices. At the end of the showing discuss such questions as:
   a. To what extent does this kind of material relieve an instructor of his information-giving responsibilities?
   b. In what manner does this kind of learning influence the homogeneity of the group?
2. Secure a copy of a programed book, for example, *The Analysis of Behavior,* James G. Holland and B. F. Skinner, McGraw-Hill Book Co., Inc., 1961.
   a. Study several sets and note your own reactions to this kind of learning.
   b. Analyze the kinds of competence one must possess in order to carry on this kind of learning experience.
3. Most college book stores now carry many examples of programed instruction. Discuss the buying trends of students in selecting and using programed instruction with the manager of the store. Examine copies of the best sellers. Report your findings to the group.
4. Consult the section on Programed Instructional Materials in the Source List appended to this text. Using post cards, request that your name be placed on the mailing list for samples of currently published programed instructional materials.
5. Secure a copy of Programs '63 (see Bibliography). Select programs of use to you and ask the publishers for literature and, if possible, examination copies. Discuss these materials with your colleagues.
6. After your pupils have had some experience with programed instruction, ask them questions similar to those in Table 16.1. Compare the responses. What are your conclusions?

☐ Bibliography

Belton, John R., "Programmed Learning—20 Questions," *The Bulletin of the National Association of Secondary School Principals,* December, 1962.

Brethower, Dale M., *Programed Instruction: A Manual of Programing Techniques,* Educational Methods, Inc., 1963.

Edling, Jack V. *et al., Programed Instruction: Four Case Studies,* Fund for the Advancement of Education, June, 1964.

Green, Edward J., *The Learning Process and Programmed Instruction,* Holt, Rinehart and Winston, 1962.

Hilgard, Ernest R. (Ed.), *Individualized Instruction,* NSSE, Chicago, 1964.

Lumdaine, A. A., and Robert Glaser (Eds.), *Teaching Machines and Programed Learning,* National Education Association, 1960.

Lysaught, Jerome D. and Clarence M. Williams, *A Guide to Programmed Instruction,* Wiley, 1963.

Skinner, B. F., "Teaching Machines," *Science,* October 24, 1960.

U.S. Office of Education, Center for Programmed Instruction, Inc., *Programs '63,* U.S. Government Printing Office, 1963.

APPENDIX

SOURCE LIST

To accomplish his teaching purpose effectively, today's classroom teacher must, on the one hand, offset the competing influence of a wide variety of extra-school communication media and, on the other, provide his pupils with concrete experiential backgrounds for their subject-matter learning through multi-sensory stimulation. The wise and creative use of an increasing abundance of audiovisual teaching materials is essential to meeting these instructional needs, and the teacher who carefully plans his lessons with this in mind will have little difficulty in reaching his teaching goals.

The first step in this planning, however, is to become acquainted with the sources from which the teacher can obtain readily and easily those media which are most suited to his pupils' specific learning needs. Toward this end, the following directory has been compiled. Although the list is not exhaustive of the organizations which make available useful instructional materials, the companies and agencies presented here are representative; they are intended to provide the teacher with solid foundation for compiling a source file of his own, and for initiating a storehouse of useful teaching media, as well.

The entries in this Source List have been grouped according to type of materials provided and, wherever it seemed necessary, cross references among headings have been made.

☐ AUDIO EQUIPMENT AND MATERIALS

See RADIO RECEIVERS; RECORD AND TRANSCRIPTION PLAYERS; RECORDINGS AND TRAN-SCRIPTIONS; TAPE MATERIALS AND EQUIPMENT

☐ CATALOGUES OF FREE AND INEXPENSIVE MATERIALS

Catalog of Free Teaching Materials, 236 pp., Gordon Salisbury, P.O. Box 1975, Ventura, Calif., $1.85, revised regularly.

Educators Guide to Free Films, Educators Progress Service, Randolph, Wis., 1966, revised annually.

Educators Guide to Free Social Studies Materials, Educators Progress Service, Randolph, Wis., 1966, revised annually.

Educators Guide to Free Tapes (11th annual ed.), Educators Service, Randolph, Wis., 1966, Scripts and Transcriptions.

Elementary Teachers' Guide to Free Curriculum Materials, Educators Progress Service, Randolph, Wis., 1966, revised annually.

Free and Inexpensive Learning Materials (12th ed.), Division of Surveys and Field Services, George Peabody College for Teachers, Nashville, Tenn. 37203, 1964, revised biennially in the even numbered years.

☐ CHALKBOARDS AND CHALKBOARD SUPPLIES

■ CHALKBOARDS

Beckley-Cardy Co., 1900 N. Narragansett St., Chicago 39, Ill., SlatoSteel chalkboard: porcelain or vitreous surface, steel, magnetic.

Benjamin Electric Manufacturing Co., Crysteel Division, Des Plaines, Ill., Porcenell chalkboard: vitreous surface, steel base, magnetic; and Visionell chalkboards.

Brunswick Corporation, 2605 East Kilgore Road, Kalamazoo, Mich., chalkboard school equipment.

Neal, W. E., Slate Co., 1121 Dartmouth Ave. S.E., Minneapolis 14, Minn., slate chalkboard.

■ CHALKBOARD SUPPLIES

Corbett Blackboard Stencils, 548 Third Avenue, North Pelham, N.Y., chalkboard stencils: ready-made, perforated patterns of maps, graph outlines, etc.

Eyrich, Ronald, 12720 Robin Lane, Brookfield, Wis., magnets: approximately $3/4'' \times 1/4''$, strong enough to hold lightweight objects to steel chalkboards or metal display surfaces; $.05 each and up, 40 magnets for $2 postpaid in the U.S.

Ideal School Supply Co., 8312 Birkhoff Ave., Chicago, Ill. 60620.

Time-Saving Specialties, 2816 Dupont Ave. S., Minneapolis 8, Minn., blackboard marking set: includes $1/4''$ pen, semipermanent chalkboard ink, solvent for cleaning chalkboard, chalkboard marking pens.

☐ CHARTS AND GRAPHS

Aero Service Corporation, 210 E. Courtland St., Philadelphia 20, Pa.
Allied Chemical and Dye Corporation, Barrett Division, 75 West St., New York 6, N.Y.
American Chart Service, Inc., 101 Dover St., Somerville 44, Mass.
American Forest Products Industries, 1816 N St., N.W., Washington 6, D.C.
American Museum–Hayden Planetarium, 81st St. and Central Park West, New York, N.Y. 10024.
American Optical Co., Instrument Division, Buffalo 15, N.Y.
American Petroleum Institute, 50 W. 50th St., New York 20, N.Y.
Clay-Adams Co., Inc., 141 E. 25th St., New York 10, N.Y.
Coca-Cola Co., Inc. (inquire of local bottler).
General Motors Co., Department of Public Relations, General Motors Bldg., 3044 W. Grand Blvd., Detroit, Mich. 48202.
National Forum, Inc., 407 S. Dearborn St., Chicago 5, Ill.
National Industrial Conference Board, Inc., 460 Park Ave., New York 22, N.Y.
State Teachers' Magazines, 307 N. Michigan Ave., Chicago 1, Ill.
U.S. Forest Service, Education Section, Washington, D.C.
Ward's Natural Science Establishment, 3000 E. Ridge Road, Rochester, N.Y.

☐ COMICS

Educational Comics, Inc., 225 Lafayette St., New York, N.Y.
General Electric Co., Educational Service Division, Department 6-235-A, Schenectady, N.Y.
Gilbertson Co., Inc., 826 Broadway, New York 3, N.Y.
Swift and Co., Educational Services, Union Stock Yards, Chicago, Ill.

☐ DISPLAY MATERIALS

■ BULLETIN-BOARD MATERIALS

Acme Bulletin Board and Directory Co., 37 E. 12th St., New York, N.Y. 10003.
Advance Products Co., 2300 E. Douglas Ave., Wichita, Kans., easels.
Bangor Cork Company, Williams and D Sts., Pen Argyl, Pa. 18072.
Beckley-Cardy Co., 1900 N. Narragansett Ave., Chicago 16, Ill.
Brooks Manufacturing Co., 1051 Meredith Dr., Cincinnati, Ohio 45231, Plasti-tak reusable adhesive.
Brunswick Corporation, 2605 E. Kilgore Rd., Kalamazoo, Mich.
Bulletin Board Styx, Lea Audio-Visual Service, Sun Prairie, Wis.
Bulletin Boards and Directory Products, Inc., 724 Broadway, New York 3, N.Y.
Judy Co., 310 N. 2nd St., Minneapolis 1, Minn.
Lea Audio-Visual Service, Sun Prairie, Wis.
Magnet Sales Co., 3657 S. Vermont, Los Angeles, Calif. 90037.
Masonite Corp., 111 W. Washington St., Chicago 2, Ill.

■ DISPLAY SURFACES AND FLANNEL-BOARD MATERIALS

Adhere-O-Learning Aids, Inc., Box 32, Wilmette, Ill.
American Felt Co., 121 Wacker Dr., Chicago 6, Ill.
American Felt Co., Glenville, Conn.
Florez, Inc., 815 Bates St., Detroit, Mich. 48226.
Holt, Rinehart and Winston, Inc., 383 Madison Ave., New York, N.Y. 10017.
Jacronda Manufacturing Co., 5449 Hunter St., Philadelphia 31, Pa.
Judy Co., 310 N. 2nd St., Minneapolis 1, Minn.
Follett Publishing Co., 1010 W. Washington Blvd., Chicago, Ill. 60607.
Mayer, Charles, Studios, Inc., 776 Commins St., Akron 7, Ohio.
Ohio Flock-Cote Company, Inc., 5713 Euclid Ave., Cleveland, Ohio 44103.
Oravisual Company, Inc., Box 11150, St. Petersburg, Fla. 33733.
Program Aids Co., Inc., 550 Garden Ave., Mt. Vernon, N.Y.
Self-Teaching Aids, 6435 Crenshaw Blvd., Los Angeles 43, Calif.
Visual Crafts Supply Co., 640 N. Willow St., Kent, Ohio.
Visual Specialties Co., 203 N. Saginaw St., Byron, Mich.

□ FILMS

See MOTION PICTURE FILMS

□ FILMSTRIPS

See STILL-PROJECTION MATERIALS

□ FILMSTRIP PROJECTORS

See PROJECTORS: Filmstrip and Slide

□ FLAT PICTURES

Air Age Education Research, 80 E. 42nd St., New York 17, N.Y.
American Museum of Natural History, Central Park West at 79th St., New York 24, N.Y.
Artist Prints, Inc., Strawberry Hill Ave., Norwalk, Conn.
Audio Visual Enterprises, Box 8686, Los Angeles 8, Calif.
British Information Services, 45 Rockefeller Plaza, New York 20, N.Y.
Colonial Art Co., 1336–8 N.W. 1st St., Oklahoma City 4, Okla.
Creative Education Society, Mankato, Minn.
Friendship Press, 475 Riverside Dr., New York 27, N.Y.
Hi Worth Pictures, P.O. Box 6, Altadena, Calif.
Informative Classroom Pictures Publishers, 31 Ottawa Ave. N.W., Grand Rapids, Mich.
International Communications Foundation, 870 Monterey Pass Rd., Monterey Park, Calif., kits of pictures, sound filmstrips, graphics, and 3-D materials from various countries.

Motion Pictures Association of America, Inc., 1600 Eye St. N.W., Washington, D.C.
National Geographic Society, 16th and M Sts., Washington, D.C.
Owen, F. A., Publishing Co., Dansville, N.Y.
Perry Pictures Co., Box 4, 42 Dartmouth St., Malden, Mass.
Realistic Visual Aids, Highland, Calif.
State Teachers Magazine, Inc., Dept. E, 307 N. Michigan Ave., Chicago, Ill., travel
    pictures.

■ MOUNTING MATERIALS

Grant, Henry H., P.O. Box 366, Redondo Beach, Calif., Chartex.
Seal, Inc., Brook St., Shelton, Conn.

□ FREE AND INEXPENSIVE MATERIALS

See CATALOGUES OF FREE AND INEXPENSIVE MATERIALS

□ GRAPHICS

See CHARTS AND GRAPHS; POSTERS; LETTERING

□ LANGUAGE-LABORATORY EQUIPMENT

Audio Teaching Center, 137 Hamilton St., New Haven, Conn.
Audiotronics Corp., 7428 Bellaire Ave., P.O. Box 151, N. Hollywood, Calif. 91603.
Brunswick Corp., 2605 E. Kilgore Rd., Kalamazoo, Mich.
DuKane Corporation, St. Charles, Ill.
Merchant, Robert C., Co., P.O. Box 594, W. Lafayette, Ind., language laboratory
    systems.
RCA Educational Electronics, Camden, N.J.
Science Electronics, Division of General Electronic Laboratories, Inc., Simon and
    Ledge Sts., Nashua, N.H.
Tandberg of America, Inc., 8 Third Ave., Pelham, N.Y.
Webcor Sales Co., 5610 W. Bloomingdale Ave., Chicago 39, Ill.
Wible Language Institute, Allentown, Pa.

□ LETTERING

■ LETTERING EQUIPMENT

Carter's Inc Co., Cambridge, Mass., lettering equipment and felt markers.
Cushman and Dennison Mfg. Co., 730 Garden, Carlstadt, N.J., Flo-master pen for
    speed lettering; nibs from $1/4''$ to $3/8''$ wide.
Dietzgen, E., Co., 2455 N. Sheffield Ave., Chicago, Ill.
Dietzgen, Eugene, Co., 850 Mitten Rd., Burlingame, Calif.

Dri-Flo Pen Co., 716 Junction Ave., Detroit 9, Mich.
Esterbrook Pen Co., P.O. Box 230, Cherry Hill, N.J.
Esterbrook Pen Co., Delaware Ave. and Cooper St., Camden, N.J.
Grace Letter Co., 5 E. 47th St., New York 17, N.Y.
Hernard Mfg. Co., 21 Saw Mill River Rd., Yonkers, N.Y.
Hunt, C. Howard, Pen Co., 7th & State St., Camden, N.J.
Keuffel and Esser Co., 300 Adams St., Hoboken, N.J.
Keuffel and Esser Co., 520 S. Dearborn St., Chicago, Ill.
Letterguide, P.O. Box 4863, State House Station, Lincoln, Nebr.
Lockwood Co., 336 Boston Post Rd., Milford, Conn., Dri-Rite Pen.
Mark-Tex Corp., 453 W. 17th St., New York 11, N.Y., Tech-pen for inking glass,
    metal, porcelain, paper, plastic, cloth, etc., in colors; Action Marker.
Marsh Co., Bellville, Ill., Marsh 77, Mark-n-draw, M-3, Marsh 99 markers, Squeeze-
    o-Marker.
Speedry Products, Inc., Richmond Hill 18, N.Y., Magic Marker.
Time-Saving Specialties, 2816 Dupont Ave. S., Minneapolis 8, Minn., felt marking
    pens.
Varigraph Co., 841 W. Lakeside, Madison, Wis.
Wood-Regan Instrument Co., Nutley, N.J., Wrico.

■ LETTERS

Artype, Inc., 127 S. Northwest Highway, Barrington, Ill.
Cello-Tak Lettering Corp., 131 W. 45th St., New York 36, N.Y.
Grace Letter Co., 5 E. 47th St., New York 17, N.Y.
Hernard Mfg. Co., 21 Saw Mill River Rd., Yonkers, N.Y., plaster letters.
Manhattan Wood Letter Co., 151 W. 18th St., New York, N.Y., wood letters.
Mich, Harry, Co., 1627 S. Michigan Ave., Chicago, Ill.
Mitten's Display Letter Co., Fifth Ave., Redland, Calif.
Mutual Education Aids, 1946 Hillhurst Ave., Los Angeles, Calif.
New York Wood Letter Co., 18 Green St., New York, N.Y., wood letters.
Redikut Letter Co., 12617 S. Prairie Ave., Hawthorne, Calif. 90250, cardboard let-
    ters and Plasti-Tak adhesive for mounting on changeable backgrounds.
Stik-a-Letter Co., Rt. 2, Box 1400, Escondido, Calif.
Tablet and Ticket Co., 1021 W. Adams St., Chicago, Ill. 60607, gummed paper
    letters.

□ LIGHT-CONTROL EQUIPMENT[1]

Draper Shade and Screen Co., P.O. Box 505, Spiceland, Ind., shade equipment in
    light-proof black, both roller shade and "Pakfold."
Duracote Corp., Ravenna, Ohio, Dura-Decor-coated Fiberglas audiovisual darkening
    drapes, permanently fire-resistant, color-fast, shrink-and-stretch-proof; available in
    four weights and a variety of colors.
Flexalum Division, Alcan Aluminum Corp., 111 West 50th St., New York, N.Y.
    10020.
Force Mfg. Co., 2347 Sullivan Ave., St. Louis 7, Mo., heavy-duty canvas draperies,
    tan, gray, or black; opaque or light-proof.
Levolor Lorentzen, Inc., 391 W. Broadway, New York 12, N.Y., audiovisual Venetian
    blinds, aluminum; light control; decorator colors and textures.

---

[1] In each case, brochure and samples are available on request.

Luxout Plastic Products, Inc., 1822 E. Franklin St., Richmond, Va., room-darkening and light-control draperies.
Mackin Venetian Blind Co., 300 W. 6 St., Momence, Ill., Venetian blind type.

☐ MAPS AND GLOBES

Aero Service Corp., 210 Courtland St., Philadelphia 20, Pa., plastic relief maps.
Cram, George F., Co., 730 E. Washington St., Indianapolis 6, Ind.
Denoyer-Geppert Co., 5235 Ravenswood Ave., Chicago 40, Ill.
Dick, A. B., Co., 5700 W. Touhy, Niles, Ill., map stencils.
Farquhar Transparent Globes, 3727 Irving St., Philadelphia 4, Pa.
Geo-Physical Maps, Inc., School Division, 101 Park Ave., New York 17, N.Y.
Hammond, C. S., & Co., 809 N. 19th St., Philadelphia, Pa., maps.
McKinley Publishing Co., 112 S. New Broadway, Brooklawn, N.J. 08030, desk and wall outline maps.
National Geographic Society, 16th and M Sts., Washington, D.C., maps.
Nystrom, A. J., & Co., 3333 Elston Ave., Chicago 18, Ill.
Rand McNally & Co., 8255 Central Park Ave., Skokie, Ill.
Replogle Globes, 315 N. Hoyne Ave., Chicago 12, Ill.
Weber-Costello Co., 1212 McKinley, Chicago Heights, Ill.

☐ MICROFILMS AND MICROCARDS

See STILL-PROJECTION MATERIALS: Microfilm and Microcards

☐ MODELS

See THREE-DIMENSIONAL MATERIALS

☐ MOTION-PICTURE FILMS

■ 16 MM. SOURCES

Academy Films, 800 N. Seward St., Hollywood, Calif.
Air Force Film Library Center, 8900 S. Broadway, St. Louis, Mo.
Association Films Inc., 12435 Euclid Ave., Cleveland, Ohio 44106.
Bailey Films, Inc,, 6509 De Longpre Ave., Hollywood 28, Calif.
Barr, Arthur, Productions, Inc., 1029 N. Allen Ave., Pasadena, Calif.
Brigham Young University, Provo, Utah.
Carousel Films, Inc., 1501 Broadway, New York 36, N.Y.
Cenco Educational Films, 1800 Foster Ave., Chicago, Ill. 60640.
Chandler Publishing Co., 124 Spear St., San Francisco, Calif. 94105.
Churchill Films, 6671 Sunset Blvd., Los Angeles, Calif. 90028.
Classroom Film Distributors, Inc., 5620 Hollywood Blvd., Hollywood 28, Calif.
Colburn, John, Associates, Inc., 1122 Central Ave., Wilmette, Ill.
Columbia University Press, Center for Mass Communication, 1125 Amsterdam Ave., New York, N.Y. 10025.
Continental 16, Inc., 241 E. 34th St., New York, N.Y. 10016.

Coronet Films, 65 E. South Water St., Chicago, Ill. 60601.

Disney, Walt, Productions, 16 mm. Film Division, 350 S. Buena Vista St., Burbank, Calif.

Du Art Film Laboratories, Inc., 245 W. 55th St., New York, N.Y. 10019.

Encyclopaedia Britannica Films, Inc., 425 N. Michigan Ave., Chicago, Ill. 60611.

Films of the Nations, Inc., 305 E. 86th St., New York, N.Y. 10028.

Frith Films, 1816 N. Highland Ave., Hollywood, Calif.

Heidenkamp Nature Pictures, 538 Glen Arden Dr., Pittsburgh, Pa. 15208.

Hoefler, Paul, Productions, P.O. Box 1313, La Jolla, Calif.

Ideal Pictures, Inc., 15924 Grand River Ave., Detroit, Mich. 48227.

Indiana University, Audio Visual Center, Bloomington, Ind.

International Film Bureau, Inc., 332 S. Michigan Ave., Chicago, Ill. 60604.

International Film Foundation, Inc., 475 Fifth Ave., New York, N.Y. 10017.

Johnson–Hunt Productions, Film Center, La Canada, Calif.

Key Productions, Inc., 527 Madison Ave., New York, N.Y. 10022.

Mahnke, Carl F., Productions, 215 East 3rd St., Des Moines, Ia.

McGraw-Hill Text-Films, 330 W. 42nd St., New York, N.Y. 10036.

Michigan State University, Instructional Media Center, East Lansing, Mich.

Modern Learning Aids, 3 E. 54th St., New York, N.Y. 10022.

Moody Institute of Science, 11428 Santa Monica Blvd., Los Angeles, Calif. 90025.

National Educational Television and Radio Center, 10 Columbus Circle, New York, N.Y. 10019.

National Film Board of Canada, 680 Fifth Ave., New York, N.Y. 10019.

New York University Film Library, Distribution Department, Washington Place, New York, N.Y. 10003.

Pan American World Airways System (films booked by Ideal Pictures, Inc.; see listing above).

Pennsylvania State University, Audio-Visual Services, Pattee Library, University Park, Pa. 16802 (also Psychological Cinema Register).

Purdue University, Audio-Visual Center, Lafayette, Ind.

State University of Iowa, Bureau of Audio-Visual Instruction, Extension Division, Iowa City, Ia.

Sterling Educational Films, Inc., 241 E. 34th St., New York, N.Y. 10016.

Syracuse University, Center for Instructional Communications, Bldg. D–7, Colvin Lane, Syracuse, N.Y. 13210.

Teaching Film Custodians, Inc., 25 W. 43rd St., New York, N.Y.

Thorne Films Inc., 1229 University Ave., Boulder, Colo.

U.S. Department of Agriculture, Motion Picture Service, Office of Information, Washington, D.C. 20250.

U.S. Department of Interior, Bureau of Sport Fisheries and Wildlife, 1006 W. Lake St., Minneapolis, Minn. 55408.

U.S. Department of Interior, Bureau of Commercial Fisheries, Washington, D.C.

U.S. Department of Justice, Federal Bureau of Investigation, Washington, D.C.

U.S. Forest Service, A–V Branch, Washington, D.C.

United World Films, 221 Park Ave. S., New York, N.Y. 10003.

University of California, Extension Media Center, Film Distribution, 2223 Fulton St., Berkeley, Calif. 94720.

University of Michigan, Audio-Visual Education Center, Frieze Bldg., Ann Arbor, Mich.

University of Minnesota, Audio-Visual Education Service, Wesbrook Hall, Minneapolis, Minn. 55455.

University of Nebraska, Bureau of Audio-Visual Instruction, University Extension Division, Lincoln 8, Nebr.

University of Oklahoma, Audio-Visual Education, Norman, Okla. 73069.

University of Southern California, Department of Cinema, Filmstrip Distribution Unit, University Park, Los Angeles, Calif. 90007.

University of Wisconsin, Bureau of Audio-Visual Instruction, University Extension, 1312 W. Johnson St., Madison, Wis. 53701.

Virginia State Department of Education, Film Production Service, Richmond, Va. 23216.

Wayne University, Audio-Visual Materials Bureau, Detroit 1, Mich.

Wexler Film Productions, 801 N. Seward St., Los Angeles, Calif. 90038.

■ 8 MM. FILMS AND FILM LOOPS

Athletic Institute, The, 805 Merchandise Mart, Chicago, Ill. 60654, physical education films.

Avis Films, Inc., P.O. Box 643, Burbank, Calif. 91503, hygiene and handwriting films.

Colburn, John, Associates, Inc., 1122 Central Ave., Wilmette, Ill., physical education films.

Ealing Corp., 2225 Massachusetts Ave., Cambridge, Mass., science films.

Encyclopaedia Britannica Films, Inc., 425 N. Michigan Ave., Chicago, Ill. 60611, physics and biology.

International Communications Foundation, 870 Pass Rd., Monterey Park, Calif., social studies, foreign lands, art, science, and vocational.

McGraw-Hill Book Co., Text Film Department, 330 West 42nd St., New York 36, N.Y., science.

National Film Board of Canada, P.O. Box 6100, Montreal 3, Canada; Suite 819, 680 Fifth Ave., New York 19, N.Y.; or Suite 2320, 230 N. Michigan Ave., Chicago 1, Ill.

Sigma Educational Films, 11717 Ventura Blvd., Studio City, Calif. 91604.

Society for Visual Education, Inc., 1345 Diversey Parkway, Chicago, Ill. 60614.

Sutherland Educational Films, 201 N. Occidental Blvd., Los Angeles 26, Calif., elementary and secondary science.

Technicolor Corp., 1985 Placientia, Costa Mesa, Calif.

Thorne Films, Inc., 1229 University Ave., Boulder, Colo. 80302.

Wasp Filmstrips, Palmer Lane West, Pleasantville, N.Y., elementary science and physical education.

Wexler Film Productions, Inc., 801 N. Seward St., Hollywood 38, Calif., hygiene.

□ MOUNTING MATERIALS

See FLAT PICTURES: Mounting Materials

□ OBJECTS

See THREE-DIMENSIONAL MATERIAL

□ POSTERS

American Dental Association, 222 E. Superior St., Chicago, Ill. 60611.

American Humane Education Society, 180 Longwood Ave., Boston, Mass.

Atchison, Topeka, and Sante Fe Railway System, 80 E. Jackson Blvd., Chicago, Ill.

Cunard Line, 25 Broadway, New York, N.Y.

French Line, Publicity Department, 17 Battery Place, New York, N.Y.

Hamburg American Line, c/o U.S. Navigation Company, General Agents, 17 Battery Place, New York, N.Y.

National Safety Council, 425 N. Michigan Ave., Chicago, Ill.

Pan American World Airways System, 28-19 Bridge Plaza North, Long Island City, N.Y.

Wild Flower Preservation Society, Inc., 3740 Oliver St. N.W., Washington, D.C.

☐ PROGRAM LEARNING MATERIALS

Adler Educational Systems, 1 Fevre Lane, New Rochelle, N.Y.

American Systems, Inc., 1625 East 126th St., Hawthorne, Calif.

Appleton-Century-Crofts, Lyons & Carnahan, 34 West 33rd St., New York, N.Y.

Applied Communications Systems, Division of Litton System, 18107 Sherman Way, Reseda, Calif.

Audiotronics Corp., 11057 Weddington St., North Hollywood, Calif.

Behavioral Research Laboratory, Ladera Professional Center, P.O. Box 557, Palo Alto, Calif.

Center for Programed Instruction, 365 West End Ave., New York 25, N.Y.

Central Scientific Co., 1700 Irving Park Rd., Chicago 13, Ill.

Coronet Instructional Films, 65 E. S. Water St., Chicago 1, Ill.

Corrigan Communications, Inc., 8701 Adah St., Garden Grove, Calif.

Cosmic Voice Inc., Box 11, Jackson, Mich.

Doubleday & Co., 277 Park Ave., New York, N.Y. 10017.

DuKane Triumph & Monitor Language Laboratories, 103 North 11th Ave., St. Charles, Ill. 60174.

Dyna Slide Co., 600 S. Michigan Ave., Chicago 5, Ill.

E-Z Sort Systems, Ltd., 45 2nd St., Cambridge, Mass.

Education Engineering, Inc., 381 West 7th St., San Pedro, Calif.

Educational Developmental Laboratories, Inc., 284 Pulaski Rd., Huntington, N.Y.

Electronic Teaching Laboratories, 5034 Wisconsin Ave. N.W., Washington 16, D.C.

Encyclopaedia Britannica Press, 425 N. Michigan Ave., Chicago 11, Ill.

Field Enterprises Educational Corp., Merchandise Mart, Chicago, Ill.

Foringer & Co., Inc., 535-A Southlawn Lane, Rockville, Md.

Fridel Manufacturing Co., Baytown, Tex.

General Atronics Corp., 1 Bala Ave., Bala-Cynwood, Pa.

General Programmed Teaching Corp., 960 N. San Antonio Rd., Los Altos, Calif.

Ginn & Co., 72 Fifth Ave., New York, N.Y. 10011.

Graflex, Inc., 3750 Monroe Ave., Rochester 3, N.Y.

Grolier Society, Inc., Americana Corp., Teaching Materials Corp., 575 Lexington Ave., New York 22, N.Y.

Hamilton Research Associates, Inc., Rt. 5A, New Hartford, N.Y.; Cambridge, Mass.; Philadelphia, Pa.

Harcourt, Brace & World Inc., Department of Programed Instruction, 575 Third Ave., New York, N.Y. 10017.

Holt, Rinehart and Winston, 383 Madison Ave., New York 11, N.Y.

Honor Products Co., 20 Moulton St., Cambridge, Mass.

Hughes Aircraft Co., Videosonic Systems Division, Box 3310, Fullerton, Calif. 92634.

INRAD—Institute of International Research and Development, Inc., Box 4456, Lubbock, Tex.

Kalart/Victor, Plainville, Conn.

Koncept-O-Graph Corp., 179 Berkeley St., Rochester 7, N.Y.

Learning, Inc., 131 E. 6th Ave. at Wells Fargo Dr., Scottsdale, Ariz. 85251.

Macmillan Co., The, 60 Fifth Ave., New York 11, N.Y.

McGraw-Hill Book Co., 330 West 42nd St., New York, N.Y. 10036.

National Bank Book Co., Holyoke, Mass.
National Foreman's Institute, Waterford, Conn.
Parker Publishing Co., Nyack, N.Y.
Perceptual Development Laboratories, 6767 Southwest Ave., St. Louis, Mo. 63143.
Prentice-Hall, Inc., Business and Professional Book Div., Nyack, N.Y.
Programed Teaching Aids, Inc., 3810 S. Four Mile Run Dr., Arlington 6, Va.
Psychotechnics, Inc., 105 W. Adams St., Chicago, Ill.
Rheem Califone Corp., 1020 N. LaBrea Ave., Los Angeles 16, Calif.
Teaching Machines, Inc., 575 Lexington Ave., New York 22, N.Y.
U.S. Industries, 250 Park Ave., New York, N.Y.
U.S. Industries, Educational Science Division, 12345 New Columbia Pike, Silver
    Springs, Md.
Universal Teaching Machine Institute, 510 Hudson St., Hackensack, N.J.
Viewlex, Inc., 4 Broadway, Holbrook, Long Island, N.Y.

□ PROJECTORS

■ FILMSTRIP AND SLIDE PROJECTORS

American Optical Co., Eggert & Sugar Rds., Buffalo, N.Y.
Audio-Master Corp., 17 E. 45th St., New York 17, N.Y.
Automatic Projection Corp., 545 Fifth Ave., New York 1, N.Y.
Bausch & Lomb Optical Co., 626 St. Paul St., Rochester 2, N.Y.
Bell & Howell Co., 7100 McCormick Rd., Chicago 45, Ill.
Beseler, Charles, Co., 219 S. 18th St., East Orange, N.J.
Brumberger Sales Corp., 68 34th St., Brooklyn 32, N.Y.
DuKane Corp., 103 North 11th St., St. Charles, Ill.
Eastman Kodak Co., 343 State St., Rochester 4, N.Y.
Heitz, Karl, Inc., 480 Lexington Ave., New York 17, N.Y.
Keystone View Co., Hamilton & Crandall Sts., Meadville, Pa.
Leitz, E., Inc., 468 Park Ave. S., New York 16, N.Y.
Minnesota Mining and Mfg. Co. (3-M Co.), Photo Equipment and Optical Depart-
    ment, 2501 Hudson Rd., St. Paul, Minn. 55119.
Naren Industry, Inc., 2104–06 N. Orchard St., Chicago 14, Ill.
Standard Projector & Equipment Co., 7433 N. Harlem Ave., Chicago 48, Ill.
Viewlex, Inc., 4 Broadway, Holbrook, Long Island, N.Y.

■ AUTOMATIC CONTINUOUS SLIDE AND FILMSTRIP PROJECTORS

Graflex, Inc., 3750 Monroe Ave., Rochester 3, N.Y.
Spindler & Sauppe, 1329 Grand Central Ave., Glendale, Calif. 91201.
Viewlex, Inc., 4 Broadway, Holbrook, Long Island, N.Y.

■ SOUND FILMSTRIP PROJECTORS

Audio-Master Corp., 17 E. 45th St., New York 17, N.Y.
DuKane Corp., 103 N. 11th St., St. Charles, Ill.
Electronic Teaching Laboratories, 5034 Wisconsin Ave. N.W., Washington 6, D.C.
Kalart, Victor, Animatograph Corp., Division of Kalart A-V Products, Plainville,
    Conn. 06062.

McClure Projectors, Inc., 1122 Central Ave., Chicago, Ill.
Olesen Co., 1535 Ivar, Hollywood, Calif. 90028.
Viewlex, Inc., 4 Broadway, Holbrook, Long Island, N.Y.

■ THREE-DIMENSIONAL SLIDE PROJECTORS

Bell & Howell Co., 7100 McCormick Rd., Department 8523, Chicago, Ill. 60645.
Compco Corp., 1800 N. Spaulding Ave., Chicago, Ill. 60647, Attn: S. J. Zagel, Pres.
Sawyer's Inc., 8585 S.W. Highway 217, Portland 7, Ore.
Spindler & Sauppe, 1329 Grand Central Ave., Glendale, Calif. 91201.

■ 3¼ BY 4 SLIDE PROJECTORS

American Optical Co., Eggert & Sugar Rds., Buffalo, N.Y.
Bausch & Lomb Optical Co., 626 St. Paul St., Rochester 2, N.Y.
Beseler, Charles, Co., 219 S. 18th St., East Orange, N.J.
Keystone View Co., Hamilton & Crandall Sts., Meadville, Pa.

■ MICROPROJECTORS

American Optical Co., Instrument Division, 155 E. 44th St., New York 17, N.Y.
Bausch & Lomb Optical Co., 626 St. Paul St., Rochester 2, N.Y.
Bioscope Mfg. Co., Box 1492, Tulsa, Okla.
Heitz, Karl, Inc., 480 Lexington Ave., New York 17, N.Y.

■ MOTION-PICTURE PROJECTORS[2]

■ 16 MM.

Bell & Howell Co., 7100 McCormick Rd., Chicago 45, Ill.[3]
Busch Film & Equipment Co., 214 S. Hamilton St., Saginaw, Mich.
Eastman Kodak Co., 343 State St., Rochester 4, N.Y.[3]
Graflex, Inc., 3750 Monroe Ave., Rochester 3, N.Y.
Harwold Co., 1245 Chicago Ave., Evanston, Ill.
Kalart Co., Inc., Hultenius St., Plainville, Conn. 06062.[3]
Movie Mite Corp., Executive and Sales, 8811 Puritan Ave., Detroit 38, Mich.
Paillard, Inc., 1900 Lower Rd., Linden, N.J.
Radio Corp. of America, Audio-Visual Products, Bldg. 15–6, Camden, N.J.[3]
RCA Educational Electronics, Camden, N.J.
Technicolor Corp., Commercial and Educational Branch, 1985 Placentia Ave., Costa
    Mesa, Calif. 92627

■ 8 MM.

Avis Films Inc., P.O. Box 643, Burbank, Calif. 91503.
Electronic Audio-Visual Devices, Inc., 8022 N. Monticello Ave., Skokie, Ill.
Fairchild Industrial Products, 221 Fairchild Ave., Plainview, N.Y.

[2] All provide for sound.
[3] Makes standard types of sound reproduction as well as magnetic sound type.

■ OPAQUE PROJECTORS

American Optical Co., Eggert & Sugar Rds., Buffalo, N.Y.
Bausch & Lomb Optical Co., 626 St. Paul St., Rochester 2, N.Y.
Beseler, Charles, Co., 219 S. 18th St., East Orange, N.J.
Heitz, Karl, Inc., 480 Lexington Ave., New York 17, N.Y.
Keystone View Co., Hamilton & Crandall Sts., Meadville, Pa.
Lacey-Luci Products, Inc., 31 Central Ave., Newark, N.J. 07102.
Projection Optics Co., Inc., 271 11th Ave., East Orange, N.J.
Squibb Taylor, Inc., 10804 Harry Hines Blvd., Dallas, Texas

■ OVERHEAD TRANSPARENCY PROJECTORS

American Optical Co., Eggert & Sugar Rds., Buffalo, N.Y.
Beseler, Charles, Co., 219 S. 18th St., East Orange, N.J.
Minnesota Mining and Mfg., Co. (3-M Co.), 2501 Hudson Rd., St. Paul, Minn.

□ RADIO RECEIVERS

Audiotronics Corp., 7428 Bellaire Ave., N., Hollywood, Calif.
Newcomb-Audio, 6824 Lexington Ave., Hollywood, Calif. 90038.
Zenith Sales Corp., 1900 N. Austin, Chicago, Ill. 60639.

□ RECORD AND TRANSCRIPTION PLAYERS

Audio-Master Corp., 17 E. 45th St., New York 17, N.Y.
Audiotronics Corp., 7428 Bellaire Ave., P.O. Box 151, N. Hollywood, Calif.
DuKane Corp., 103 N. 11th St., St. Charles, Ill. 60174.
Newcomb Audio Products, 6824 Lexington Ave., Hollywood 38, Calif.
Radio-Matic of America, Inc., 760 Ramsey Ave., Hillside, N.J.
Rheem Califone Corp., 5922 Bowcroft St., Los Angeles, Calif. 90016.
U.S. Recording Co., 1347 S. Capital St., Washington, D.C.
V-M Corp., P.O. Box 659, Benton Harbor, Mich. 49023.
Webcor Sales Co., 5610 W. Bloomingdale Ave., Chicago 39, Ill.

□ RECORDINGS AND TRANSCRIPTIONS

American Library Association, 50 E. Huron St., Chicago 11, Ill.
Audio-Education, Inc., 55 Fifth Ave., New York 3, N.Y.
Book-Records, Inc., 222 E. 46th St., New York 17, N.Y.
Bowmar Records, 10515 Burbank Blvd., N. Hollywood, Calif. 91601.
Caedmon Records, Inc., 461 Eighth Ave., New York, N.Y. 10001.
Cadence Records, 40 E. 49 St., New York 17, N.Y.
Capitol Records Distributing Corp., 1750 N. Vine, Hollywood, Calif. 90028.
Chandler, Gloria, Recordings, 277 W. 12 St., New York 14, N.Y.
Children's Music Center, 2858 W. Pico Blvd., Los Angeles 19, Calif.
Children's Reading Service, 1078 St. John's Pl., Brooklyn 13, N.Y.

Children's Record Guild, 27 Thompson St., New York 13, N.Y.
Coffey, Jack C., Co., Inc., 710 17th St., N. Chicago, Ill.
Columbia Records, Educational Services, 799 Seventh Ave., New York, N.Y. 10019.
Decca Distributing Corp., 321 E. Chicago St., Milwaukee, Wis.
Disneyland Records, 800 Sonoria Ave., Glendale, Calif.
EMC Recordings Corp., 180 E. 6th St., St. Paul, Minn. 55101.
Enrichment Records, 246 Fifth Ave., New York 1, N.Y.
Epic Records, 51 West 52nd, New York 19, N.Y.
Folkways Records, 121 W. 47th St., New York, N.Y.
Ginn and Co., 72 Fifth Ave., New York, N.Y. 10011.
Goodman, Harry S., Radio Productions, 19 E. 53 St., New York, N.Y.
Harcourt, Brace & World, Inc., 757 Third Ave., New York 17, N.Y.
International Communications Foundation, 870 Monterey Pass Rd., Monterey Park, Calif.
Kaydan Records, 12240 Ventura Blvd., Studio City, Calif.
Kimbo–U.S.A. Records, Box 55, Deal, N.J.
Landmark Records, 246 Fifth Ave., New York, N.Y. 10001.
Linguaphone Institute, 30 Rockefeller Plaza, New York, N.Y.
London Records, 539 W. 25th St., New York 1, N.Y.
Materials for Learning, Inc., 1376 Coney Island Ave., Brooklyn, N.Y.
Poetry Records, 475 Fifth Ave., New York 17, N.Y.
RCA Victor Record Division, Radio Corp. of America, Educational Department, 155 E. 24th St., New York, N.Y.
Scholastic Magazines, Inc., 50 W. 44th St., New York, N.Y. 10036.

☐ RUBBER STAMPS

Beckley-Cardy Co., 7632 Indiana Ave., Chicago 16, Ill.
Krengel Mfg. Co., 227 Fulton St., New York, N.Y.

☐ SLIDES

See STILL-PROJECTION MATERIALS: Filmstrips, Slides, Transparencies

☐ SPECIMENS

See THREE-DIMENSIONAL MATERIALS

☐ STENCILS

Brown, Arthur, and Brothers, Inc., 2 W. 46th St., New York 36, N.Y.
Graphic Arts Center, 1534 W. 7th St., Los Angeles, Calif.
Stenso Lettering Co., 1101 E. 25th St., Baltimore, Md.

☐ STEREOPROJECTORS

See PROJECTORS: Filmstrip and Slide, three-dimensional slide projectors

☐ STILL-PROJECTION MATERIALS

■ FILMSTRIPS, SLIDES, TRANSPARENCIES

Amco, Inc., P.O. Box 218, Port Richey, Fla.

American Museum of Natural History, Central Park West at 79th St., New York 24, N.Y.

Anti-Defamation League of B'nai B'rith, 515 Madison Ave., New York, N.Y.

Art Color Slides, Inc., 235 E. 50th St., New York 22, N.Y.

Audio-Visual Materials Bureau, Wayne University, Detroit 1, Mich.

Bailey Films, Inc., 6509 De Longpre Ave., Hollywood 28, Calif.

Block Color Productions, 1309 N. Genessee Ave., Hollywood 46, Calif.

Bowmar, Stanley, Co., Inc., 12 Cleveland St., Valhalla, N.Y.

British Information Services, 45 Rockefeller Plaza, New York 20, N.Y.

Budek, Herbert E., Co., Inc., 324 Union St., Hackensack, N.J., geography and art history.

Chandler Publishing Co., 124 Spear St., San Francisco, Calif. 94105.

Church-Craft Pictures, Inc., 4222 Utah St., St. Louis, Mo. 63116.

Clay-Adams Co., Inc., 141 E. 25th St., New York 10, N.Y.

Colorslides Enterprises, Box 150, Oxford, Ohio.

Coronet Films, Inc., 65 E. South Water St., Chicago 1, Ill.

Creative Arts Studio, Inc., 814 H St., N.W., Washington, D.C.

Current Affairs Films, 527 Madison Ave., New York, N.Y. 10022, filmstrips only.

DuKane Corp., 103 N. 11th St., St. Charles, Ill.

Educational Screen & Audiovisual Guide, 434 South Wabash Ave., Chicago, Ill. 60605.

Encyclopaedia Britannica Films, Inc., 458 S. Michigan Ave., Chicago, Ill. 60611.

Eulo Co., Box 178, Denver 1, Colo.

Filmfax Productions, 80 W. 40th St., New York, N.Y.

Filmstrip House, 347 Madison Ave., New York, N.Y.

Informative Classroom Picture Publishers, 31 Ottawa Ave. N.W., Grand Rapids, Mich.

International Film Bureau, Inc., 332 S. Michigan Ave., Chicago 4, Ill.

Jam Handy Organization, The, 2821 E. Grand Blvd., Detroit 11, Mich.

Key Productions, Inc., 527 Madison Ave., New York, N.Y. 10022, motion pictures and filmstrips only.

Keystone View Co., Hamilton & Crandall Sts., Meadville, Pa.

Knowledge Builders, Visual Education Center, Floral Park, N.Y. 11001.

Life Magazine, Inc., Filmstrip Division, Time & Life Bldg., New York, N.Y.

Long Filmslide Service, 7505 Fairmount Ave., El Cerrito, Calif. 94532.

McGraw-Hill Book Co., Text-Film Department, 330 W. 42nd St., New York 36, N.Y.

Meston's Travels, Inc., 3801 N. Piedras, El Paso, Tex.

Metropolitan Museum of Art, Fifth Ave. and 82 St., New York 38, N.Y.

Moody Institute of Science, Educational Film Division, 11428 Santa Monica Blvd., W. Los Angeles 25, Calif.

National Audubon Society, Photo and Film Department, 1130 Fifth Ave., New York 38, N.Y.

National Film Board of Canada, 680 Fifth Ave., New York, N.Y. 10019.

New York Times, The, Office of Educational Activities, 229 W. 43rd St., New York, N.Y. 10036.

Nu-Art Films, Inc., P.O. Box 23, Elmhurst, N.Y.

Photo & Sound Co., 116 Natoma St., San Francisco, Calif. 94105.

Pictorial Events, 220 Central Park S., New York, N.Y.
Popular Science Publishing Co., Audio Visual Division, 355 Lexington Ave., New
    York, N.Y.
Sawyer's Inc., Portland, Ore. 97207.
Society for French-American Cultural Services and Educational Aid, 972 Fifth Ave.,
    New York 21, N.Y.
Society for Visual Education, Inc., 1345 Diversey Parkway, Chicago 14, Ill.
United Nations, Films and Visual Information Division, New York, N.Y.
United World Films, Inc., 1445 Park Ave., New York 29, N.Y.
VEC, Inc., 2066 Helena St., Madison 4, Wis.
Vocafilm Corp., 424 Madison Ave., New York 17, N.Y.

■ MICROFILMS AND MICROCARDS

Eastman Kodak Co., 343 State St., Rochester 4, N.Y., Recordak microfilm viewers;
    Microprint readers.
Microcard Corp., West Salem, Wis.
Microlex Corp., 1 Graves St., Rochester 14, N.Y., microcards.
Microtext Publishing Corp., 112 Liberty St., New York 6, N.Y., microcards.
Readex Microprint Corp., 100 Fifth Ave., New York 11, N.Y.
University Microfilms, 313 N. 1st St., Ann Arbor, Mich.
University of Rochester Press, Micropublication Service, Rochester, N.Y., microcards.

■ TRANSPARENCY-MAKING MATERIALS

Ansco, Binghamton, N.Y.
Beseler, Charles, Co., 219 S. 18th St., East Orange, N.J., general supplies and sensi-
    tized plastic sheets.
Brown, Arthur, and Brothers, Inc., 2 W. 46th St., New York 36, N.Y., "Frisket," a
    plastic material for lifting materials from the printed page.
Eastman Kodak Co., 343 State St., Rochester 4, N.Y.
Ozalid Division, General Aniline and Film Corp., Johnson City, N.Y., sensitized
    plastic sheets.
Technifax Corp., 195 Appleton St., Holyoke, Mass.
Seal, Inc., Shelton, Conn., Transpara magazine page lift materials.
Victorlite Industries, Inc., 4117 W. Jefferson Blvd., Los Angeles 16, Calif., general
    supplies and prepared materials.

□ TAPE MATERIALS AND EQUIPMENT

■ TAPE RECORDERS AND PLAYBACK MACHINES

Audio-Sell, Inc., 311 E. Liberty, Ann Arbor, Mich.
Audiotronics Corp., 7428 Bellaire Ave., N. Hollywood, Calif.
Bell & Howell Co., 7100 McCormick Rd., Chicago, Ill. 60645.
Curtin, Frank M., Co., 15925 E. Whittier Blvd., Whittier, Calif.
Edex Teaching Systems, 3940 Fabian Way, Palo Alto, Calif.
E. I. Du Pont de Nemours & Co., Inc., Film Department, 1007 Market St., Wilming-
    ton, Del.
Newcomb Audio Products, 6824 Lexington Ave., Hollywood 38, Calif.

RCA Educational Electronics, Camden, N.J.
Sony Corp. of America, 580 Fifth Ave., New York, N.Y. 10012.
Tandberg of America, Inc., 8 Third Ave., Pelham, N.Y.
3 M Company, Revere Div., 2501 Hudson Rd., St. Paul, Minn. 55119.
Webcor Sales Co., 700 N. Kingsbury St., Chicago, Ill. 60610.
Webster Electric Co., 1900 Clark St., Racine, Wis.

■ TAPE SERVICES AND LIBRARIES

Audiovisual Communications, Division of Instructional Services, State Department of Education, 600 Mt. Pleasant Ave., Providence, R.I. Rhode Island service only.
National Tape Repository, Bureau of Audiovisual Instruction, Stadium Bldg., Rm. 348, University of Colorado, Boulder, Colo.
Oklahoma State University, Audio-Visual Center, Stillwater, Okla.
Tapes for Teaching, Education Department, Centennial Bldg., St. Paul 1, Minn. Available only to public and tax supported institutions of Minnesota.
University of Connecticut, Audio-Visual Center, Storrs, Conn. Connecticut service only.
University of Illinois, Visual Aids Service, 704 S. 6th St., Champaign, Ill. 61822.
University of Iowa, Bureau of Audio-Visual Instruction, Iowa City, Ia.
University of Michigan, Audio-Visual Education Center, Ann Arbor, Mich.
University of Nebraska, Bureau of Audio-Visual Instruction, Lincoln, Nebr.
University of New Hampshire, Audio-Visual Center, Durham, N.H.
University of Oklahoma, Educational Materials Services, Norman, Okla.

■ TAPES AND TAPE RECORDINGS

Ampex Corp., 401 Broadway, Redwood City, Calif.
Capitol Records Distributing Corp., 1750 N. Vine St., Hollywood, Calif. 90028.
EMC Corp., Educational Materials Div., 180 6th St., St. Paul, Minn. 55101.
International Film Bureau, Inc., 332 S. Michigan Ave., Chicago, Ill. 60604.

□ TELEVISION

Adler Educational Systems Division, Litton Systems, Inc., 72 E. Main St., New Rochelle, N.Y.
Ampex Corp., 401 Broadway, Redwood City, Calif.
Dage-Bell Corp., 455 Sheridan Ave., Michigan City, Ind.
Diamond Electronics, P.O. Box 415, Lancaster, Ohio.
Educational Broadcasting Corp., 304 W. 58th St., New York, N.Y. 10019.
GPL Division, Aerospace Group, General Precision, Inc., 63 Bedford Rd., Pleasantville, N.Y. 10570.
Great Plains Regional Instruction Television Library, University of Nebraska, Lincoln, Nebr.
Jerrold Electronics Corp., 15th and Lehigh Ave., Philadelphia, Pa. 19132.
Memorex Corp., 1180 Shulman Ave., Santa Clara, Calif.
Microwave System, Micro-Link Division of Varian Associates, Akron St., Copiague, N.Y.
RCA Educational Electronics, Camden, N.J.
Riker Industries, Inc., Norden Lane, Huntington Station, Long Island, N.Y.
Sony Corp. of America, 580 Fifth Ave., New York, N.Y. 10012.
Sylvania Commercial Electronics Division, 730 Third Ave., New York, N.Y. 10017.

☐ THREE-DIMENSIONAL MATERIALS

Audio-Visual Enterprises, P.O. Box 8686, Los Angeles, Calif. 90008.

Bicknell Macalaster Co., 253 Norfolk St., Cambridge 39, Mass., apparatus kits.

Bradley, Milton, Co., 74 Park Ave., Springfield 2, Mass.

Brunner, Robert, Division Cadan Corp., 635 Madison Ave., New York, N.Y. 10022, Weber: cut-out model of the human brain.

Central Scientific Co., 1700 Irving Park Blvd., Chicago, Ill., models.

Clay-Adams Co., Inc., 141 E. 25th St., New York 10, N.Y., cutaways, models, anatomical wall charts, 2″ × 2″ color projection slides.

Creative Playthings, Inc., Box 110, Princeton, N.J., manipulatives for instructional materials centers and classrooms—kindergarten through grade 8.

Denoyer-Geppert Co., 5235 Ravenswood Ave., Chicago 40, Ill., models.

General Biological Supply House, Inc., 8200 S. Hoyne, Chicago, Ill., 60620, models, manikins, charts, Kodachrome slides, biological colored movies, and plastic-embedded specimens.

Goodrich, B. F., Co., Koroseal Division, Oak Grove, Marietta, Ohio, Koroseal flexible magnetic strip.

Imitation Food Display Co., 197 Waverly Ave., Brooklyn, N.Y., models of food.

Instructional Productions Co., 2527 Honolulu Ave., Montrose, Calif., transportation kits.

Jonas, Louis Paul, Sculptor, R.D. #2, Hudson, N.Y., miniature animals.

Judy Co., 310 N. 2nd St., Minneapolis 1, Minn., instructional toys, models.

Models of Industry, 2100 Fifth St., Berkeley, Calif., instructional materials and teaching aids.

New York Scientific Supply Co., 28 W. 30th St., New York 1, N.Y., models.

Nystrom, A. J., & Co., 3333 Elston Ave., Chicago 18, Ill., models, raised relief maps.

Science Materials Center, 59 Fourth Ave., New York, N.Y.

Viking Importers, 113 S. Edgemont St., Los Angeles, Calif., models.

Ward's Natural Science Establishment, 3000 E. Ridge Rd., Rochester, N.Y., models, Bio-Plastic.

Weber-Costello Co., 1212 McKinley, Chicago Heights, Ill., models.

☐ TRANSPARENCIES

See STILL-PROJECTION MATERIALS: Filmstrips, Slides, Transparencies; and Transparency-Making Materials

INDEX

INDEX

Format by Carl Weiss
Set in Baskerville
Composed by The American Book–Stratford Press
Printed by The Murray Printing Company
Bound by The American Book–Stratford Press
HARPER & ROW, PUBLISHERS, INCORPORATED